VISUAL C++ 4 HOW-TO

Scott Stanfield
with **Ralph Arveson**

Waite Group Press™
A Division of Sams Publishing
Corte Madera, CA

Publisher: *Mitchell Waite*
Associate Publisher: *Charles Drucker*

Acquisitions Manager: *Jill Pisoni*

Editorial Director: *John Crudo*
Project Editor: *Laura E. Brown*
Copy Editor: *Michelle Goodman*
Technical Reviewer: *Jeff Bankston*

Production Director: *Julianne Ososke*
Production Manager: *Cecile Kaufman*
Production Editor: *Mark Nigara*
Cover Design: *Sestina Quarequio*
Production: *Deborah Anker*
Design: *Sestina Quarequio*
Illustrations: *Pat Rogondino*

© 1996 by The Waite Group, Inc.®
Published by Waite Group Press™, 200 Tamal Plaza, Corte Madera, CA 94925.

Waite Group Press is a division of Sams Publishing.

All rights reserved. No part of this manual shall be reproduced, stored in a retrieval system, or transmitted by any means, electronic, mechanical, photocopying, desktop publishing, recording, or otherwise, without permission from the publisher. No patent liability is assumed with respect to the use of the information contained herein. While every precaution has been taken in the preparation of this book, the publisher and author assume no responsibility for errors or omissions. Neither is any liability assumed for damages resulting from the use of the information contained herein.

All terms mentioned in this book that are known to be registered trademarks, trademarks, or service marks are listed below. In addition, terms suspected of being trademarks, registered trademarks, or service marks have been appropriately capitalized. Waite Group Press cannot attest to the accuracy of this information. Use of a term in this book should not be regarded as affecting the validity of any registered trademark, trademark, or service mark.

The Waite Group is a registered trademark of The Waite Group, Inc.
Waite Group Press and The Waite Group logo are trademarks of The Waite Group, Inc.
Visual C++ is a trademark of Microsoft Corporation.
Windows is a registered trademark of Microsoft Corporation.
All other product names are trademarks, registered trademarks, or service marks of their respective owners.

Printed in the United States of America
96 97 98 99 • 10 9 8 7 6 5 4 3 2 1

Library of Congress Cataloging-in-Publication Data
   Stanfield, Scott.
      Visual C++ 4 how-to/ Scott Stanfield, Ralph Arvesen.
        p. cm.
      Includes index.
      ISBN 1-57169-069-7
        1. C++ (Computer program language) 2. Microsoft Visual C++.
   I. Arvesen, Ralph. II. Title.
   QA76.73.C153S714 1996
   005.26'2--dc20   96-2079
                                                         CIP

DEDICATION

For Judi and Stan,
my biggest fans and parents

Message from the Publisher

WELCOME TO OUR NERVOUS SYSTEM

Some people say that the World Wide Web is a graphical extension of the information superhighway, just a network of humans and machines sending each other long lists of the equivalent of digital junk mail.

I think it is much more than that. To me, the Web is nothing less than the nervous system of the entire planet—not just a collection of computer brains connected together, but more like a billion silicon neurons entangled and recirculating electro-chemical signals of information and data, each contributing to the birth of another CPU and another Web site.

Think of each person's hard disk connected at once to every other hard disk on earth, driven by human navigators searching like Columbus for the New World. Seen this way the Web is more of a super entity, a growing, living thing, controlled by the universal human will to expand, to be more. Yet, unlike a purposeful business plan with rigid rules, the Web expands in a nonlinear, unpredictable, creative way that echoes natural evolution.

We created our Web site not just to extend the reach of our computer book products but to be part of this synaptic neural network, to experience, like a nerve in the body, the flow of ideas and then to pass those ideas up the food chain of the mind. Your mind. Even more, we wanted to pump some of our own creative juices into this rich wine of technology.

TASTE OUR DIGITAL WINE

And so we ask you to taste our wine by visiting the body of our business. Begin by understanding the metaphor we have created for our Web site—a universal learning center, situated in outer space in the form of a space station. A place where you can journey to study any topic from the convenience of your own screen. Right now we are focusing on computer topics, but the stars are the limit on the Web.

If you are interested in discussing this Web site or finding out more about the Waite Group, please send me e-mail with your comments, and I will be happy to respond. Being a programmer myself, I love to talk about technology and find out what our readers are looking for.

Sincerely,

Mitchell Waite

Mitchell Waite, C.E.O. and Publisher

200 Tamal Plaza
Corte Madera, CA 94925
415-924-2575
415-924-2576 fax

Website:
http://www.waite.com/waite

CREATING THE HIGHEST QUALITY COMPUTER BOOKS IN THE INDUSTRY

Waite Group Press
Waite Group New Media

Come Visit
WAITE.COM
Waite Group Press World Wide Web Site

Now find all the latest information on Waite Group books at our new Web site, http://www.waite.com/waite. You'll find an online catalog where you can examine and order any title, review upcoming books, and send e-mail to our authors and editors. Our FTP site has all you need to update your book: the latest program listings, errata sheets, most recent versions of Fractint, POV Ray, Polyray, DMorph, and all the programs featured in our books. So download, talk to us, ask questions, on http://www.waite.com/waite.

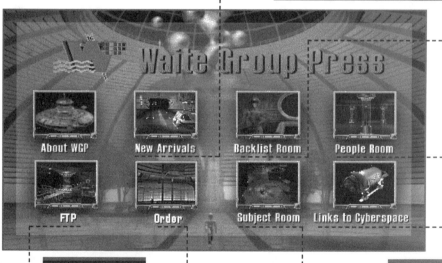

The New Arrivals Room has all our new books listed by month. Just click for a description, Index, Table of Contents, and links to authors.

The Backlist Room has all our books listed alphabetically.

The People Room is where you'll interact with Waite Group employees.

Links to Cyberspace get you in touch with other computer book publishers and other interesting Web sites.

The FTP site contains all program listings, errata sheets, etc.

The Order Room is where you can order any of our books online.

The Subject Room contains typical book pages, which show description, Index, Table of Contents, and links to authors.

World Wide Web:

http://www.waite.com/waite
Gopher: gopher.waite.com
FTP: ftp.waite.com

COME SURF OUR TURF—THE WAITE GROUP WEB

ABOUT THE AUTHORS

Scott Stanfield's first adventure into programming was tweaking Atari 800 games written in BASIC to achieve higher game scores. In college he managed to graduate with a BS in Computer Science from Cal Poly in San Luis Obispo without taking a single course in COBOL or FORTRAN. He soon found himself at Pixar developing a really cool Windows graphics program called Typestry. Presently, he's the director of software development at Finnegan O'Malley in San Francisco, hard at work on Windows applications (using Visual C++, of course). He lives in the Bay Area with his wife Cyndi and two cats.

Ralph Arvesen is a software engineer who has been developing Windows applications for seven years. He began his quest in the Bay Area at a small startup company and later moved to Austin, TX. He currently works at Tivoli Systems, Inc. and is responsible for designing and implementing a distributed user-interface server-supporting object-based (OMG/CORBA) application running on Windows 3.1, Windows 95, and Windows NT. Ralph is also using OLE to design a new application interface to Tivoli's core technology. He is a consultant to the HCI (Human Computer Interface) group on style guidelines and issues and company evangelist for Win32, OLE/COM, and Microsoft technology. In addition to this book, he writes various articles for the COBB Group's Inside Microsoft Visual C++ journal. Ralph lives in the country near Marble Falls, TX with his wife Cathy and numerous animals.

TABLE OF CONTENTS

INTRODUCTION xii

CHAPTER 1
DOCUMENT AND VIEW 1

CHAPTER 2
STATUS BARS AND TOOLBARS 57

CHAPTER 3
CONTROLS 121

CHAPTER 4
MULTIMEDIA 195

CHAPTER 5
BITMAPS AND ICONS 261

CHAPTER 6
DIALOGS 311

CHAPTER 7
OLE AND DDE 353

CHAPTER 8
SYSTEM 437

CHAPTER 9
WINDOWS 95 SHELL 511

APPENDIX
COMMON QUESTIONS, ANSWERS, AND TIPS 603

INDEX 651

CONTENTS

INTRODUCTION xii

CHAPTER 1
DOCUMENT AND VIEW 1

1.1   Remember the state and position of my application 5
1.2   Control the size of my CFormViews and CScrollViews 10
1.3   Associate multiple file extensions with one document 16
1.4   Automatically scroll a view during mouse drags 22
1.5   Open more than one document at a time 28
1.6   Show different views of a single document 35
1.7   Lock a splitter window containing different views 44

CHAPTER 2
STATUS BARS AND TOOLBARS 57

2.1   Maximize the first pane while displaying menu help 61
2.2   Put the current time in the status bar 65
2.3   Change the status bar font and style 78
2.4   Add a status bar to my views 81
2.5   Display a progress meter in the status bar 86
2.6   Put bitmaps in the status bar using an image list 91
2.7   Put line and column indicators on the status bar 97
2.8   Customize a toolbar for display in a dialog 103
2.9   Create a custom CControlBar to display static text? 111

CHAPTER 3
CONTROLS 121

3.1   Change the cursor when it passes over a control 125
3.2   Associate data with a list box item 131
3.3   Limit an edit control to allow only floating-point numbers ..136
3.4   Color items in a list box 141
3.5   Create a dynamic shortcut menu 148
3.6   Create a progress meter custom control 154
3.7   Create an auto-sizing multicolumn list box 161
3.8   Write a custom button to display a menu 174
3.9   Draw bitmaps in a list box 182

CHAPTER 4
MULTIMEDIA **195**

4.1 Preview an AVI file using the common file dialog 199
4.2 Display bitmaps using the DrawDib functions 202
4.3 Play AVI files in a CView 211
4.4 Play large WAV files 216
4.5 Play tracks from an audio CD 227
4.6 Create 3D animation using OpenGL and MFC 250

CHAPTER 5
BITMAPS AND ICONS **261**

5.1 Paint a bitmap in my MDI application's background 264
5.2 Animate my application's icon 270
5.3 Draw text on top of a bitmap 276
5.4 Draw a bitmap with transparency 281
5.5 Smoothly drag bitmaps with the mouse 290

CHAPTER 6
DIALOGS **311**

6.1 Display help for dialog controls on the status bar 314
6.2 Open multiple files with the FileOpen common dialog 319
6.3 Customize the common file dialog 325
6.4 Expand and contract dialog boxes 331
6.5 Display a dialog as either modal or modeless 336
6.6 Write customized DDX/DDV routines 344

CHAPTER 7
OLE AND DDE **353**

7.1 Create a simple OLE object and automation server 357
7.2 Use OLE's drag-and-drop features 370
7.3 Use structured storage 380
7.4 Create a DDE object to talk to other applications 397
7.5 Write an OLE spin control 403
7.6 Create a color cell OLE control 426

CHAPTER 8
SYSTEM **437**

8.1 Prevent multiple instances of a running application 441
8.2 Localize MFC applications using resource DLLs 447
8.3 Use the Win32 registry database 458
8.4 Make multiple inheritance work in MFC 466
8.5 Detect when launched applications terminate under Win32 473
8.6 Use system hooks under Win32 486
8.7 Share data between 32-bit MFC applications 501

CHAPTER 9
WINDOWS 95 SHELL 511

9.1 Write a tray application to play CDs 515
9.2 Create a property sheet handler for a file or folder 540
9.3 Create an appbar to display the system palette 572
9.4 Extend the context menu for certain files 591

APPENDIX
COMMON QUESTIONS, ANSWERS, AND TIPS 603

INDEX 651

ACKNOWLEDGMENTS

My first thanks go to Laura Brown, my managing editor, whose contributions to the bookbuilding process made this possible. Thanks also to everyone at Waite Group Press for all their hard work.

Ralph Arvesen, my friend and co-author, provided the System chapter (the toughest one) and the Appendix. He was always eager to provide technical advice and, more importantly, rewrites. Karin Hanson, James Plamondon, Darby Williams, and Stawsh Murawski of the Microsoft Developer Relations Group provided more support than I ever expected or deserved.

The second edition spanned two jobs. My colleagues and friends at The Digital Foundry and Finnegan O'Malley have both endured their fair share of comments like, "Really, I'm almost finished."

Thanks to David and Rosalie, for encouragement not only on the second edition, but the second addition to our house. Also thanks to my good friends James Burgess and Lori Bartlett, the other half of the Idaho Special. And thanks finally to my wife and partner, Cyndi Sunderman, who was always there with loving support for the past two books. She still hasn't collected all the sushi I owe her for help on the prior edition.

—Scott Stanfield

I would like to thank my wife Cathy for always being there, my parents, and Don Hsi, Dave Baker, and Jim Seaborg.

—Ralph Arvesen

INTRODUCTION

What This Book Is About

With Visual C++ it takes just a few mouse clicks to generate code that includes all the bells and whistles of a top-rate Windows program. Yet even with all the time saving features of MFC, AppWizard, and ClassWizard, unless you're content with "Hello World," you're still going to have to write some serious code. That's where things get tough. Even the most experienced Windows programmers hit a wall when they attempt to go beyond the simplicity of the sample programs and tutorials included with Visual C++. That's where *Visual C++ 4 How-To* comes in—this book is designed to help you navigate the uncharted areas of MFC, and discover solutions to real-world programming problems.

Our aim is to give you easy access to useful MFC techniques that are not immediately apparent. By following a few simple steps, you can take advantage of solutions discovered by experienced MFC programmers. The bottom line is that *Visual C++ 4 How-To* is packed with hundreds of useful tricks and tips that you can start using right away.

Question and Answer Format

Visual C++ 4 How-To, like all books in The Waite Group's popular How-To series, emphasizes a step-by-step, problem solving approach using Visual C++ and MFC. Each How-To follows a consistent format that guides you through the technique and steps used to solve an authentic problem. A "How it Works" section thoroughly details each solution. Most of the How-To's come with stand-alone classes that you can use to extend the capabilities of MFC. Simply drop the code into your program and start it right away. To demonstrate the techniques and custom classes developed for the How-To's, we have provided all of the Visual C++ projects for you on CD-ROM.

INTRODUCTION

Who This Book Is Written For

If you want to get the most out of this book, make sure you have a few prerequisites out of the way. A background in Windows programming is a must. It's also important to have written some programs in Visual C++ so you're familiar with the environment and the philosophy behind MFC. If you've only done the Scribble tutorial included with the documentation, that's fine—just stick with the easier How-To's at first. There are many beginning books that teach the fundamentals of Visual C++ and MFC; this is not one of them. You won't learn the basics of MFC here—you'll learn how to use MFC better.

We designed this book for all levels of expertise. To accomplish this, we've given each question and its solution a heading that indicates it's level of complexity. If you're just starting out with Visual C++ you can use the easy How-To's. These almost exclusively use techniques that are well documented and can be solved with a few lines of MFC code. If you're comfortable with the traditional Windows SDK, the intermediate level How-To's will be just your speed. Most of these How-To's rely on features not wrapped by the MFC and are only available through SDK function calls. If you are experienced in Visual C++, check out the advanced How-To's. These tend to solve problems that stretch the boundaries of the MFC classes by incorporating solutions from the C/SDK realm or by diving into the internals of MFC itself.

The topics in *Visual C++ 4 How-To* derive from real programming situations that we ran into while writing various MFC applications. Some ideas came after we went through some old programs, line-by-line, saying, "Yeah, I remember this tricky problem." Others were taken from the subject lines of common questions posted to various Visual C++ programming forums on CompuServe and the Internet. We knew the book was on the right track when we started pulling code out of the chapters to use in our programs at work.

What You Need to Use This Book

Of course you'll need a computer capable of running some flavor of Windows and Visual C++. If you have the bucks (or someone else is buying your machine), you won't be disappointed with slow compile times on a speedy Pentium box equipped with at least 32 MB of RAM. And unless you're a fast typist, a CD-ROM drive will come in handy when you want to play with the projects and executables that accompany each solution.

All of the How-To's were written specifically for Windows 95 or Windows NT 3.5.1. I can't guarantee the solutions will work under future versions like Windows NT 4.0 or the "Nashville" addition of Windows 95, but they probably will. Microsoft is pretty good at backwards compatibility.

All projects were developed under Visual C++ 4.0 (also known as Microsoft Developer Studio 4.0). With the advent of the subscription service, new releases of MFC appear quarterly, much faster than I can revise this book. Most, if not all, How-To's will work under future releases of Visual C++ and MFC (unless they specifically say they use undocumented features).

Changes From the First Edition

The first edition of this book, *Visual C++ How-To,* was released to coincide with Visual C++ 2.0, back around January 1995. A lot has changed since then. The release of Windows 95 coupled with the sweeping changes in Visual C++ 4.0 prompted me to update the first edition. At first I thought it would be adequate simply to recompile the projects and redo the screen shots. As I got further into the project I realized that some techniques were either no longer valid, or a simpler method existed. The end result was a similar looking table of contents, but a radically different approach to solving the problems.

For example, new Win32 SDK calls let me do transparent blitting with just one line of code, not the 100 lines from the first edition. New controls like the slider, let me replace the klunky scroll bar. The spin control added some flair to otherwise boring edit fields. Custom AppWizards allowed me to write truly reusable How-To's. Also, the integration of the Control Development Kit into Developer Studio made it much easier to write and use OLE Controls.

Another big change from the first edition is that 16-bit compatibility was dropped. To take advantage of the new features in Windows 95 but retain backwards compatibility to Windows 3.x was simply too tough. The differences between Visual C++ 1.53 and 4.x were simply too great to get around with #ifdefs. If you really want your code to run on Windows 3.x, Win32s 1.30.x will allow most of these 32-bit solutions to run unchanged in the 16-bit world.

Periodically throughout the book you'll see a ⇒ symbol at the end of a line of code. This indicates that the code has wrapped. It should be assumed that the code line is one continuous line.

Finally I've added several new Custom AppWizards, custom components, and stand-alone OLE Controls you can start using right away. Refer to the "About the CD" section for installation instructions.

What You'll Learn

Before you start using the techniques offered in this book, it's a good idea to get an overview of the variety of topics covered in each How-To. The book is divided into nine chapters as follows:

Chapter 1, *Document and View,* deals with the classes that make up the cornerstone of MFC. You'll learn how to do tricks with *CDocument* and *CView* that go way beyond the topics covered in the *Class Users Guide.* You'll probably want to include the techniques in this chapter to make your application remember it's state and position when restarted. One How-To demonstrates how to gain full control over the size and scrolling of *CScrollViews.* One of my favorites, the auto-scrolling view, lets you pan around the view by dragging the mouse. Opening more than one document at once is easy when you apply the technique shown in another How-To. Everything you ever wanted to know about splitter windows is covered in another How-To in this chapter.

INTRODUCTION

Chapter 2, *StatusBars and Tool Bars*, introduces many techniques to extend the usefulness of *CToolBar* and *CStatusBar*. Besides putting the current time into a status bar pane, you'll learn how to put a progress meter in a status bar pane. Did you know you can change the status bar's font and even drop them into an MDI view? Another How-To creates a new class derived directly from *CControlBar* to display titles in an MDI child.

Chapter 3, *Controls*, uncovers little-known secrets of Windows controls by using several powerful MFC classes and C++ techniques. You'll learn how to combine classes like *CMenu* and *CButton* to come up with a completely new control; add a useful progress gauge to dialogs; and how to easily change the color of items in a list box. There's a How-To that creates a new edit control that only accepts valid floating point numbers and another that customizes a list box to display bitmaps.

Chapter 4, *Multimedia*, explores the exciting realm of audio and video. How-To's included in this chapter teach you how to build a CD player utility and how to play WAV files that are too large to be handled by *sndPlaySound*. New features of Video for Windows like the MCIWnd class and the *DrawDIB* functions are explored in two other How-To's. Graphic programmers will find 3-D graphics programming much easier after mastering the How-To that deals with OpenGL, the real-time rendering engine on Windows NT. Finally, palettes and the Windows palette messages are handled in another How-To.

Chapter 5, *Bitmaps and Icons*, shows you techniques necessary to annotate bitmaps with text and to draw bitmaps with transparency. Another How-To shows you how easy it is to put a bitmap like your company logo in the background of an MDI application. The last How-To is a fun one: it uses the playing cards from the CARDS.DLL file to illustrate how to drag bitmaps around the screen.

Chapter 6, *Dialogs*, uncovers tricks and techniques to extend the usefulness of the *CDialog* class. You'll learn how to turn a normal dialog into a modeless one, expand a dialog into a larger one when a button is pressed, and customize the look of the common dialogs by extending the *CFileDialog* class.

Chapter 7, *OLE and DDE*, is designed to provide a taste of what is involved in using OLE and DDE in your MFC applications. You'll discover the techniques necessary to use DDE communication and see just how easy it is to create an OLE server with full automation. Two How-To's take you through the steps to write a special spin-button and color well OLE Control.

Chapter 8, *System*, demonstrates the advanced features of both Visual C++ and the Win32 operating system. First you'll learn how to generate a source browser library for MFC. Another How-To demonstrates how to use multiple inheritance in an MFC app. There's a whole bunch of advanced operation system features How-To's: manipulating the registry database, system hooks, multi-threaded apps, memory-mapped files.

Chapter 9, *Windows 95 Shell*, features techniques to integrate your application with the Windows 95 Shell. One How-To adds a Register option for DLLs and OLE controls using the context menu interface. Another adds a second property page to the Properties dialog for Folders. You'll see how to create an AppBar that displays the current system palette. Yet another CD player utility is created to illustrate tray applications in the final How-To.

Appendix, *Common Questions, Answers, and Tips,* presents a large list of Visual C++ Frequently Asked Questions: they're quick solutions to some of the most common problems encountered in Visual C++. Most of the solutions are one-liners, but they're very powerful.

Note: If you work directly off the CD-ROM, you will receive the following error when opening a Project Workspace file: "Cannot recognize the current ClassView information file. Would you like to overwrite the file?" Just click No, and then click OK when prompted. You will be able to read the files, but won't be able to write or to compile them. To avoid this error message, please follow the CD-ROM installation instructions.

CHAPTER 1
DOCUMENT AND VIEW

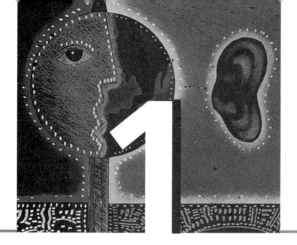

DOCUMENT AND VIEW

How do I...

1.1 Remember the state and position of my application?

1.2 Control the size of my CFormViews and CScrollViews?

1.3 Associate multiple file extensions with one document?

1.4 Automatically scroll a view during mouse drags?

1.5 Open more than one document at a time?

1.6 Show different views of a single document?

1.7 Lock a splitter window containing different views?

Although it's the cornerstone of MFC, the document/view paradigm is probably one of MFC's least understood features. Since it's more conceptual than hard-core SDK functions, it takes a little practice and a few programs to get the hang of using it. Simple tasks quickly become difficult because the MFC documentation and tutorials are geared toward a narrow usage of the class library. The How-Tos presented in this chapter should flatten the learning curve and provide some useful tricks to add to your MFC knowledge base.

CHAPTER 1
DOCUMENT AND VIEW

We'll explore the intricate details that connect the *CDocument* and *CView* classes. We'll also discuss *CDocTemplate* and *CFrameWnd*, two other classes that play an important part in connecting the document/view framework to a real application.

You'll learn how to teach your application to remember its state and position, open multiple documents at once, and associate multiple file extensions with a single document type. There's a custom component that adds code to scroll your views automatically when the mouse drags outside the client area. You'll also learn how to control the way Windows sizes your views and discover how to show different views of a single document. A final trick demonstrates a lockable splitter bar showing two different views of the same document.

A lot of the How-Tos in this chapter use a special Picture AppWizard that generates a simple MDI program capable of viewing 256-color bitmap files. It's a generic multiple-document application with two classes called *CPictureDoc* and *CPictureView* that take care of loading and painting the bitmaps.

1.1 Remember the State and Position of My Application

Give your application the memory of an elephant. When this sample application quits, it saves its position and state information in the registry. Then, next time it's run, it uses that data to restore itself to the same place on the screen. You can use the Persistent Window Position component in all your MDI and SDI applications.

Additional Topics: GetWindowPlacement, ActivateFrame

1.2 Control the Size of My CFormViews and CScrollViews

You may have noticed that when converted and displayed as a *CFormView*, your carefully crafted dialog has no upper limit on its size. In other words, a user can extend your dialog beyond the right and bottom boundaries that you set up when you designed it in App Studio. This How-To introduces an MDI child class that restricts the total size of any *CFormView* or *CScrollView* to the correct size.

Additional Topics: GetMinMaxInfo, ResizeParentToFit

1.3 Associate Multiple File Extensions with One Document

Sometimes you'll have documents of the same type with more than one extension. Some examples of this are the device-independent bitmaps that use both *.BMP and *.DIB file extensions. This How-To modifies the code generated by Picture AppWizard to support multiple file extensions.

Additional Topics: document template string segments

1.4 Automatically Scroll a View During Mouse Drags

You may have seen drawing programs that let you select an object and then move it to some off-screen location by dragging the mouse cursor beyond the window. Mysteriously, the window scrolls in the direction of the mouse cursor and even accelerates as the mouse moves farther away. These secrets are revealed when you insert the *AutoScroll* component in your *CScrollViews*.

Additional Topics: ScrollToPos, elliptical regions, local message processing

1.5 Open More than One Document at a Time

The standard file selection dialog class, *CFileDialog*, provides a mechanism for allowing the selection of multiple files. However, it's not obvious how to use this feature in a Document/View application. This example demonstrates a component that creates a class called *CMultiFileDlg* that you can use in your applications to let users open more than one document at a time.

Additional Topics: OnFileOpen, OFN_ALLOWMULTISELECT flag

1.6 Show Different Views of a Single Document

Learn how to select and show different views attached to the same document. You can use this trick to show a "Debug" view on a normal document. Also, you'll see how to customize the automatic text captions.

Additional Topics: switching views, OnUpdateFrameTitle, CDC::PolyLine

1.7 Lock a Splitter Window Containing Different Views

Splitter windows can provide a very effective user interface. This How-To creates an application with two views separated by a static splitter window. You'll learn how to lock the splitter bar in place so the user can't move, or even select, the splitter bar. Plus, you'll learn a simple trick that draws a cool looking 3D sphere.

Additional Topics: OnSetCursor, static splitters, drawing a sphere

---

COMPLEXITY
BEGINNING

1.1 How do I... Remember the state and position of my application?

Problem

I've used applications that remember their last size and position on the screen. I'd like my programs to reappear at their last location. While we're at it, the visibility and position of the toolbar and status bar should be remembered as well.

CHAPTER 1
DOCUMENT AND VIEW

Technique

Sometimes the default placement that Windows chooses for your programs just isn't good enough. By using the component demonstrated below, you'll give users total control over the size and placement of your application each time it's launched. Plus, all the state information for any toolbar or status bar will be remembered. Like all good Win32 applications, the pertinent information is stored in the registry instead of an INI file.

In the Component Gallery, under the "Visual C++ How-To" tab, you'll find a control called "Persistent Window Position". When you insert it into an MDI or SDI application, it displays a dialog listing all the descendants of *CFrameWnd* in your app. Here you'll choose which class gets the new persistence functionality (it's usually the *CMainFrame* class).

The component adds two helper methods, *LoadWindowPlacement* and *SaveWindowPlacement,* called from *OnCreate* and *OnClose,* respectively. When the main window is closed or destroyed, *OnClose* uses *SaveWindowPlacement* to store the size, position, and visibility state of the toolbar and status bar in the registry. Conversely, when the application is launched, *OnCreate* calls *LoadWindowPlacement* to retrieve the coordinates saved in the registry. It uses some of these numbers to prepare the WINDOWPLACEMENT structure for *SetWindowPlacement*—a handy MFC method that sets the placement and state of a window. *CFrameWnd::LoadBarState* and its partner *SaveBarState* save the visibility and position information for the toolbar and status bar.

Steps

1. **Create a new project called Remember using the Picture AppWizard.** You can't set any options with this custom AppWizard; it simply creates an MDI application capable of viewing bitmaps.

2. **Insert the Persistent Window Position component.** Use the Component Gallery to insert the Persistent Window Position component. Unless you've moved it, it should be under the "Visual C++ How-To" tab. Select the *CMainFrame* class in the list box and press the Apply button (see Figure 1-1). Close the Component Gallery when you're ready to continue.

3. **Edit CRememberApp::OnInitInstance().** Add the following line of code near the top of this method. If you don't call *SetRegistryKey, WriteProfileString* saves data in the application's INI file instead of the system registry (yuck!). Unless you work at Waite Group Press, feel free to change the string passed to *SetRegistryKey* to your company's name.

```
BOOL CRememberApp::InitInstance()
{
    AfxEnableControlContainer();

    // Standard initialization
```

1.1
REMEMBER THE STATE AND POSITION OF MY APPLICATION

```
    // If you are not using these features and wish to reduce the size
    // of your final executable, you should remove from the following
    // the specific initialization routines you do not need.
#ifdef _AFXDLL
    Enable3dControls();         // Call this when using MFC in a shared DLL
#else
    Enable3dControlsStatic();   // Call this when linking to MFC statically
#endif

    SetRegistryKey("WaiteGroupPress");
    LoadStdProfileSettings();   // Load standard INI file options (including MRU)
```

4. Build and run the app at least twice. To test the new "persistence" feature, turn off the status bar and resize the application so it's really small. Then quit and restart. Notice that the size, position, and status bar state have been remembered. The program will even remember if the application was minimized or maximized when it was closed. The new code also restores the toolbar's position if it was floating or docked anywhere on the frame.

How It Works

The key to this whole How-To is the WINDOWPLACEMENT struct shown below:

```
typedef struct tagWINDOWPLACEMENT {
    UINT    length;
    UINT    flags;
    UINT    showCmd;
    POINT   ptMinPosition;
    POINT   ptMaxPosition;
    RECT    rcNormalPosition;
} WINDOWPLACEMENT;
```

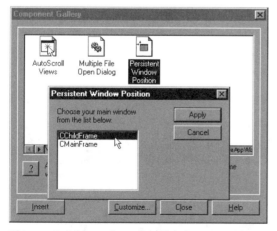

Figure 1-1 Inserting the Persistent Window Position component

CHAPTER 1
DOCUMENT AND VIEW

GetWindowPlacement and *SetWindowPlacement* use this structure to load the visibility state and the normal, minimized, and maximized positions of any window. For our example, let's use this structure to store the position of the main window. But when do we save the coordinates and how do we retrieve them? That's what the component is for.

The component added three new methods (*OnClose*, *SaveWindowPlacement*, and *LoadWindowPlacement*) and modified another (*OnCreate*). Let's walk through the code and see what these modifications do.

The two helper methods, *SaveWindowPlacement* and *LoadWindowPlacement* are pretty simple. The first one converts the WINDOWPLACEMENT struct (explained below) into a string and saves it using *WriteProfileString*. Because we called *SetRegistryKey* earlier in *OnInitInstance*, the data is saved in the registry. *LoadWindowPlacement* implements the reverse: It retrieves the string and creates a WINDOWPLACEMENT struct out of it. Here's the code from MainFrm.cpp:

```
BOOL CMainFrame::LoadWindowPlacement(LPWINDOWPLACEMENT pwp)
{
    CString strBuffer = AfxGetApp ()->GetProfileString ("Settings", ⇒
        "WindowPos");

    if (strBuffer.IsEmpty ())
        return FALSE;

    int cRead = _stscanf (strBuffer, "%i:%i:%i:%i:%i:%i:%i:%i:%i:%i",
            &pwp->flags, &pwp->showCmd,
            &pwp->ptMinPosition.x, &pwp->ptMinPosition.y,
            &pwp->ptMaxPosition.x, &pwp->ptMaxPosition.y,
            &pwp->rcNormalPosition.left, &pwp->rcNormalPosition.top,
            &pwp->rcNormalPosition.right, &pwp->rcNormalPosition.bottom);

    if (cRead != 10)
        return FALSE;

    return TRUE;

}

void CMainFrame::SaveWindowPlacement(LPWINDOWPLACEMENT pwp)
{
    CString strBuffer;
    strBuffer.Format ("%i:%i:%i:%i:%i:%i:%i:%i:%i:%i",
        pwp->flags, pwp->showCmd,
        pwp->ptMinPosition.x, pwp->ptMinPosition.y,
        pwp->ptMaxPosition.x, pwp->ptMaxPosition.y,
        pwp->rcNormalPosition.left, pwp->rcNormalPosition.top,
        pwp->rcNormalPosition.right, pwp->rcNormalPosition.bottom);

    AfxGetApp ()->WriteProfileString ("Settings", "WindowPos", strBuffer);
}
```

It would be nice if WINDOWPLACEMENT had a method to make this a little easier, but it doesn't. As a side note, if you ever want to save other complicated classes

1.1
REMEMBER THE STATE AND POSITION OF MY APPLICATION

in the registry, consider adding an *AsString* and *FromString* method to the class to facilitate this approach. It will hide your private data from the user (remember, encapsulation is good for you!) and make code like this a lot easier to write.

When the application quits, a WM_CLOSE message is sent to *CMainFrame* which handles it in *OnClose* with the following code (don't type this in):

```
void CMainFrame::OnClose()
{
    {
        WINDOWPLACEMENT wp;
        if (GetWindowPlacement (&wp))
        {
            if (IsZoomed ())
                wp.flags |= WPF_RESTORETOMAXIMIZED;

            SaveWindowPlacement (&wp);
        }

        SaveBarState("ControlBars\\State");
    }
    CMDIFrameWnd::OnClose ();
}
```

CWnd::GetWindowPlacement happily retrieves the current size and position of the main window. Next, the coordinates are saved to the registry by calling *SaveWindowPlacement*. *CFrameWnd::SaveBarState* enumerates all the control bars in the application, saving each one to a spot in the registry specified by its only argument "*ControlBars\\State*". You should step inside this code some time and be thankful you didn't have to write it. Figure 1-2 shows all the stuff in the registry necessary for restoring the state and position of your app.

Comments

If you insert this component into a class that already has *OnClose*, it won't replace it. Instead, it sticks the necessary code at the top of the method. The same holds true for *OnCreate*. If the method doesn't exist, it's created; otherwise it's added.

Figure 1-2 The registry entries for the Remember application

This component doesn't work with dialog-based applications, although the technique can easily be extended to support dialogs. Instead of using *LoadWindowPlacement* in *OnClose,* the dialog would call it from *OnInitDialog.*

If you're feeling adventurous, you could modify the source code directly for *CFrameWnd* and rebuild the MFC class library. That way, every application you write will automatically gain this feature.

**COMPLEXITY
BEGINNING**

1.2 How do I ... Control the size of my CFormViews and CScrollViews?

Problem

There's no built-in way to limit the size of a *CScrollView.* In other words, the user can grab the lower right corner of the MDI child and drag the window out as large as she wants (see Figure 1-3). The extra area to the right and bottom is filled with the current background color.

Under some circumstances, this isn't a problem. But if I'm writing a bitmap viewer or displaying a carefully designed *CFormView,* I don't want the user to make the window any larger than the maximum defined size. Will the technique extend to support views with splitter bars?

Figure 1-3 A CScrollView with no size restrictions

1.2
CONTROL THE SIZE OF MY CFORMVIEWS AND CSCROLLVIEWS

Figure 1-4 CChildFrame size restricted to size of bitmap

Technique

The heart of the solution lies with the seldom used Windows message WM_GETMINMAXINFO. Your MDI child can intercept this message, which is normally ignored by MFC, and set the maximum tracking size. The maximum tracking size of the window is the largest window size you can get by using the borders to size the window. So, as you can see, we need to handle this problem in the MDI child frame, not in the view.

Since we're processing these messages inside a child window, we can figure out what view we're displaying using *GetActiveView*. Then, assuming the view returned is a *CScrollView*, the maximum size can be retrieved through *GetTotalSize*. We then take these numbers, fill in the correct fields, and return from *OnGetMinMaxInfo*.

Figure 1-4 shows a user trying to resize a modified *CChildFrame* that limits the maximum size or tracking rectangle. Since the view was initially shown at its maximum size when it was created, you can't make it any bigger. If the standard *CMDIChildWnd* had been used instead, you'd be able to size it larger (see Figure 1-4).

It's easy to figure out how big to make the client area. What's hard is figuring out how big to make the whole window. Since *OnGetMinMaxInfo* wants the width and height for the whole window, we'll have to account for borders and scroll bars.

We're going to start with the Picture AppWizard and modify its *CChildFrame* to support the size restrictions. A later step will add splitter bars and show you how to change *OnGetMinMaxInfo* to support them properly.

Steps

1. **Create a new project called SizeView using the Picture AppWizard.**
You can't set any options with this custom AppWizard; it simply creates an MDI application capable of viewing bitmaps.

2. **Use the WizardBar to add CChildFrame::OnGetMinMaxInfo.** Add the following code:

```
void CChildFrame::OnGetMinMaxInfo(MINMAXINFO FAR* lpMMI)
{
        // The following technique works only with CScrollView derived views
        // with or without splitter panes
        CScrollView* pView = (CScrollView *) GetActiveView();

        // we might not have a view attached yet
        if (pView)
        {
                ASSERT(pView->IsKindOf(RUNTIME_CLASS(CScrollView)));
                DWORD dwExStyle = pView->GetExStyle();

                CRect rect (CPoint(0, 0), pView->GetTotalSize());
                CalcWindowRect (rect);

                CSize size;
                size.cx = rect.Width();
                size.cy = rect.Height();

                if (dwExStyle & WS_EX_CLIENTEDGE)
                {
                    size.cx += 4;
                    size.cy += 4;
                }

                if (GetExStyle() & WS_EX_CLIENTEDGE)
                {
                    size.cx += 4;
                    size.cy += 4;
                }

                lpMMI->ptMaxTrackSize.x = size.cx;
                lpMMI->ptMaxTrackSize.y = size.cy;
        }
}
```

3. **Modify CChildFrame::PreCreateWindow.** Locate the *PreCreateWindow* method in *CChildFrame* (if your class doesn't have this method, you can easily add it through the WizardBar). Modify the code to look like this:

```
BOOL CChildFrame::PreCreateWindow(CREATESTRUCT& cs)
{
        cs.style &= ~WS_MAXIMIZEBOX;
        return CMDIChildWnd::PreCreateWindow(cs);
}
```

We don't want the child window showing a maximize button because the maximum size is now dictated by the view instead of the mainframe's client area.

4. **Edit CSizeViewApp::InitInstance.** AppWizard-generated programs usually display an empty document when the app first starts (if there's nothing passed

1.2
CONTROL THE SIZE OF MY CFORMVIEWS AND CSCROLLVIEWS

on the command line to initiate OLE linking or embedding). For our test application, however, an empty picture document will look funny, especially since the *OnGetMinMaxInfo* will make the child window tiny. In earlier versions of MFC, all you had to do was comment out the *OnFileNew* line. Now, we need to comment out a different set of code:

```
BOOL CSizeViewApp::InitInstance()
{
        AfxEnableControlContainer();

        // Standard initialization
        // If you are not using these features and wish to reduce the size
        //   of your final executable, you should remove from the following
        //   the specific initialization routines you do not need.

#ifdef _AFXDLL
        Enable3dControls();          // Call this when using MFC in a shared DLL
#else
        Enable3dControlsStatic();    // Call this when linking to MFC statically
#endif

        LoadStdProfileSettings();    // Load standard INI file options (including MRU)

        // Register the application's document templates.  Document templates
        //  serve as the connection between documents, frame windows, and views.

        CMultiDocTemplate* pNewDocTemplate = new CMultiDocTemplate(
              IDR_PICTURETEMPLATE,
              RUNTIME_CLASS(CPictureDoc),     // document class
              RUNTIME_CLASS(CChildFrame),     // frame class
              RUNTIME_CLASS(CPictureView));   // view class
        AddDocTemplate(pNewDocTemplate);

        // create main MDI Frame window
        CMainFrame* pMainFrame = new CMainFrame;
        if (!pMainFrame->LoadFrame(IDR_MAINFRAME))
                return FALSE;
        m_pMainWnd = pMainFrame;

        // Parse command line for standard shell commands, DDE, file open
        CCommandLineInfo cmdInfo;
        ParseCommandLine(cmdInfo);

        // Dispatch commands specified on the command line
        // We're disabling this so empty picture documents aren't shown at startup
        // if (!ProcessShellCommand(cmdInfo))
        //    return FALSE;

        // The main window has been initialized, so show and update it.
        pMainFrame->ShowWindow(m_nCmdShow);
        pMainFrame->UpdateWindow();

        return TRUE;
}
```

CHAPTER 1
DOCUMENT AND VIEW

5. Edit CPictureView::OnInitialUpdate. This little bit of code resizes the parent, in this case the *CChildFrame*, to fit snugly around the *CPictureView* content.

```
void CPictureView::OnInitialUpdate()
{
        CScrollView::OnInitialUpdate();

        OnUpdate(NULL, 0, NULL);

        // Q98598: Call ResizeParentToFit twice:
        // First time to "expand" the view and remove the scroll bars,
        // Second time to reduce the size of the view to the smallest size
        // available without scroll bars.

        ResizeParentToFit(FALSE);
        ResizeParentToFit(TRUE);
}
```

6. Build and run the app. At this point, you have enough functionality to check *OnGetMinMaxInfo*. Start the app, then load a bitmap like Clouds.bmp. The bitmap should fit squarely within the child window without any scroll bars. *CChildFrame* shouldn't let you make it any larger.

7. Insert the Split Bars component. Use the Component Gallery to insert the Split Bars component. Add the splitter bars to *CChildFrame,* making sure to add both types of splitter bars. Close the Component Gallery when you're ready to continue.

8. Edit CChildFrame::OnGetMinMaxInfo again. We have to account for the scroll bar and splitter bar sizes since they now affect the maximum size of the child frame. Since the bar sizes are never turned off, the maximum width is now the sum of the splitter width, the vertical scroll bar width, and the bitmap width.

```
void CChildFrame::OnGetMinMaxInfo(MINMAXINFO FAR* lpMMI)
{
        // The following technique works only with CScrollView derived views
        // with or without splitter panes
        CScrollView* pView = (CScrollView *) GetActiveView();

        // we might not have a view attached yet
        if (pView)
        {
                ASSERT(pView->IsKindOf(RUNTIME_CLASS(CScrollView)));
                DWORD dwExStyle = pView->GetExStyle();

                CRect rect (CPoint(0, 0), pView->GetTotalSize());
                CalcWindowRect (rect);

                CSize size;
                size.cx = rect.Width();
                size.cy = rect.Height();
```

1.2
CONTROL THE SIZE OF MY CFORMVIEWS AND CSCROLLVIEWS

```
            if (dwExStyle & WS_EX_CLIENTEDGE)
            {
                    size.cx += 4;
                    size.cy += 4;
            }

            if (GetExStyle() & WS_EX_CLIENTEDGE)
            {
                    size.cx += 4;
                    size.cy += 4;
            }

            // Use the following code if you have a splitter window:

            // The width and height of the splitter is fixed to 4 pixels
            // (judging from the constructor in winsplit.cpp). This may
            // change in the future, but m_cxSplitter and m_cySplitter aren't
            // public members so there's no programmatic way to find out.

            lpMMI->ptMaxTrackSize.x = size.cx + GetSystemMetrics(SM_CXVSCROLL) + 4;
            lpMMI->ptMaxTrackSize.y = size.cy + GetSystemMetrics(SM_CYHSCROLL) + 4;

            // Otherwise, remove the comments and use this code:
            // lpMMI->ptMaxTrackSize.x = size.cx;
            // lpMMI->ptMaxTrackSize.y = size.cy;
        }
    }
```

9. **Build and run the app.** Now when you load a bitmap, you should see splitter bars and scroll bars, even when the window is sized as large as possible. The scroll bars stick around because code inside the splitter bars keeps them visible at all times.

How It Works

OnGetMinMaxInfo is called whenever Windows needs to know the allowable size and position information of a window. However, the window in question is the MDI child frame, not the view. The only size information we have at this point is the bitmap width and height. By asking the scroll view for its total size through *GetTotalSize,* we can pass that rectangle to *CalcWindowRect* (a really cool *CWnd* method that figures out how big the frame window *should* be).

After some minor tweaking, depending on whether or not the view or the frame has the style WS_EX_CLIENTEDGE set, we set the size members in *ptMaxTrackSize* and return.

You may be wondering what the two *ResizeParentToFit* calls in *CSizeView::OnInitialUpdate* are for. Using these two calls in combination expands then shrinks the client window to just the right size to fit around the view.

Comments

To prevent users from resizing a CFormView or *CScrollView* completely, put this code in the view's MDI child window:

```
BOOL CMyChildFrame::PreCreateWindow(CREATESTRUCT& cs)
{
    cs.style &= ~WS_THICKFRAME;
    return CMDIChildWnd::PreCreateWindow(cs);
}
```

This code removes the WS_THICKFRAME style bit, which prevents the window from being created with a resizable frame.

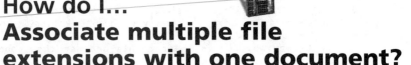

COMPLEXITY
BEGINNING

1.3 How do I... Associate multiple file extensions with one document?

Problem

My bitmap viewer uses two different extensions to refer to the same document type: *.BMP and *.DIB. Both extensions are common, and the code to handle them is the same. How do I associate these two extensions, or any extensions, with one document class?

Technique

Part of the MFC design associates a document with a particular file extension. This not only simplifies opening and saving files, but also makes it easy to launch the application associated with the file extension.

Here's the problem: More than one file extension may be associated with documents that can be handled by the same document class. *CDocument* only supports one file extension. For example, the *DibLook* sample that ships with Visual C++ displays device-independent bitmaps that have the extension *.DIB. However, most device-independent bitmaps have a file extension of *.BMP.

MDI applications use *CMultiDocTemplate* objects to keep track of the relationship between the document types and the document and view classes used by the application. To support a new file type, we'll add a new document template that has the same view and document class information but uses the new file extension. Because of these changes, the FileOpen dialog provides two choices for the file type, as shown in Figure 1-5.

1.3
ASSOCIATE MULTIPLE FILE EXTENSIONS WITH ONE DOCUMENT

Figure 1-5 Different extensions for the same document type

Steps

1. **Create a new project called DocExt using the Picture AppWizard.** You can't set any options with this custom AppWizard. It simply creates an MDI application capable of viewing bitmaps. It already supports document types with the extension *.BMP. We're going to add support for *.DIB files too.

2. **Modify the IDR_DIBTYPE string table resource.** The existing IDR_DIBTYPE string resource must be modified slightly to help the existing file type cooperate with the new BMP file type. Using App Studio, open the first string table segment and modify IDR_DIBTYPE to look like the code below.

   Change the string from

```
\nDib\nDIBLOOK Document\nDIB Files (*.dib)\n.dib\nDibFileType\nDIBLOOK File Type
```

   to:

```
\nDib\nBitmap\nDIB Files (*.dib)\n.dib\nDibFileType\nDIBLOOK File Type
```

3. **Copy the IDR_PICTURETYPE string resource to IDR_DIBTYPE.** Select the IDR_PICTURETYPE string resource, copy it to the clipboard, then paste it back into the string table. Change the copy's name from IDR_PICTURETYPE1 to IDR_DIBTYPE. Next, modify the new string to look like the following:

   Change the string from

```
\nPicture\nPict1\nPicture Files (*.bmp)\n.BMP\nPict.Document\nPict1 Document\n\n
```

   to:

```
\nPicture\n\nDIB Files (*.dib)\n.DIB\nPict.Document\nPict1 Document\n\n
```

   Notice the second "word," Pict1, should be removed from this string. MFC displays a special dialog box, *CNewTypeDlg* (implemented in DOCMGR.cpp), whenever the File New menu is activated and there is more than one

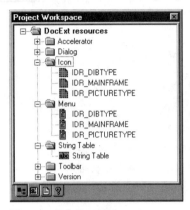

Figure 1-6 DocExt resources

document type to choose from. It loops through the document templates looking for this second string as identified by *CDocTemplate::fileNewName*. Since BMPs and DIBs use the same document, we don't want *CNewTypeDlg* displayed. We fake out *CNewTypeDlg* by leaving this part of the string empty, so it won't need to display the dialog.

4. **Copy the IDR_PICTURETYPE menu and icon resources.** There are also menu and icon resources named IDR_PICTURETYPE that should be copied to IDR_DIBTYPE. Use the copy and paste method mentioned in step 3. When you're finished, your resources should look like those in Figure 1-6.

5. **Edit CDocExtApp::InitInstance.** We need to add code that creates an additional document template during the application's initialization. This second template is identical to the first except it uses the IDR_DIBTYPE resources instead of IDR_PICTURETYPE. Edit the *CDocExtApp::InitInstance* so it looks like this:

```
BOOL CDocExtApp::InitInstance()
{
    AfxEnableControlContainer();

    // Standard initialization
    // If you are not using these features and wish to reduce the size
    // of your final executable, you should remove from the following
    //  the specific initialization routines you do not need.

#ifdef _AFXDLL
    Enable3dControls();         // Call this when using MFC in a shared DLL
#else
    Enable3dControlsStatic();   // Call this when linking to MFC statically
#endif

    LoadStdProfileSettings();   // Load standard INI file options (including MRU)
```

1.3
ASSOCIATE MULTIPLE FILE EXTENSIONS WITH ONE DOCUMENT

```
    // Register the application's document templates.  Document templates
    //  serve as the connection between documents, frame windows, and views.
    CMultiDocTemplate* pNewDocTemplate = new CMultiDocTemplate(
        IDR_PICTURETYPE,
        RUNTIME_CLASS(CPictureDoc),      // document class
        RUNTIME_CLASS(CChildFrame),      // frame class
        RUNTIME_CLASS(CPictureView));    // view class
    AddDocTemplate(pNewDocTemplate);

    pNewDocTemplate = new CMultiDocTemplate(
        IDR_DIBTYPE,
        RUNTIME_CLASS(CPictureDoc),      // document class
        RUNTIME_CLASS(CChildFrame),      // frame class
        RUNTIME_CLASS(CPictureView));    // view class
    AddDocTemplate(pNewDocTemplate);

    // create main MDI Frame window
    CMainFrame* pMainFrame = new CMainFrame;
    if (!pMainFrame->LoadFrame(IDR_MAINFRAME))
        return FALSE;
    m_pMainWnd = pMainFrame;

    // Enable drag/drop open
    m_pMainWnd->DragAcceptFiles();

    // Enable DDE Execute open
    EnableShellOpen();
    RegisterShellFileTypes(TRUE);

    // Parse command line for standard shell commands, DDE, file open
    CCommandLineInfo cmdInfo;
    ParseCommandLine(cmdInfo);

    // Dispatch commands specified on the command line
    if (!ProcessShellCommand(cmdInfo))
        return FALSE;

    // The main window has been initialized, so show and update it.
    pMainFrame->ShowWindow(m_nCmdShow);
    pMainFrame->UpdateWindow();

    return TRUE;
}
```

6. Build and test the application. Select File New from the main menu and notice that no dialog appears even though we registered more than one document. Also, select File Open and notice the "Files of Type" combo box shows *.BMP and *.DIB.

If no association exists for files with the *.BMP or *.DIB extension, running the program will register these extensions and allow them to be launched from the Explorer. DocExt can also be used as a drag-and-drop destination for *.DIB or *.BMP files from the Explorer.

How It Works

The IDR_DIBTYPE and IDR_PICTURETYPE string resource specifies attributes used by the MFC framework when running DocExt. Every SDI or MDI application built with an AppWizard has a resource string that looks something like IDR_PICTURETYPE. The resource string contains up to seven segments, each separated by \n, as shown here:

```
"\n
Picture\n
Pict1\n
Picture Files (*.bmp)\n
.BMP\n
Pict.Document\n
Pict1 Document\n
\n"
```

The first segment is not used by MDI applications. In an SDI application, it's used as the document title.

The string is all on one line in the string resource table. Each of the segments has a particular purpose, as shown in the following table.

IDR_PICTURETYPE	USED FOR	ENUM DOCSTRINGINDEX
(empty)	SDI window title	windowTitle
Picture	Root portion of the document name	docName
Pict1	Text for File New dialog	fileNewName
Picture Files (*.BMP)	File filter text for common dialog	filterName
.BMP	File extension for common dialog	filterExt
Pict.Document	Used by registration database	regFileTypeId
Pict1 Document	Used by registration database	regFileTypeName

Any segments not used can be left blank, but the \n characters act as delimiters and must be left in place. If the file filter information is omitted from the string, the menu item for File Open will be disabled. Likewise, if the default file extension is not included, the File Save As menu item will be disabled.

When *AddDocTemplate* is called from *InitInstance* (see step 5), an association is formed between the *CPictureDoc* and *CPictureView* classes. Information from the IDR_PICTURETYPE and IDR_DIBTYPE resources is used to initialize the documents and views. Instead of creating a new document or view class, the existing classes are associated with a new file type through a new template. The string, icon, and menu resources identified as IDR_DIBTYPE are just copies of the resources identified by IDR_PICTURETYPE, extending all of the functionality provided to .*DIB files to the .*BMP files.

1.3
ASSOCIATE MULTIPLE FILE EXTENSIONS WITH ONE DOCUMENT

Comments

The overhead involved in this technique is relatively small, as long as the number of extra files supported by each document remains small. If a large number of extra file types are used for a small number of documents, it might be more appropriate to provide an enhanced version of *CDocTemplate* that supports direct sharing of resources without the need to clone resources.

The advantage of this approach is that it is simple, and it allows customization of the menu and icon resources for each file type. For instance, a different icon for the DIB file type might be useful.

If you don't care about the shell drag-and-drop feature for your extra document types (DIB in this case), there's an easier solution that doesn't require any more code. The only modification you need to make from the Picture AppWizard generated code is in the string table. Simply modify the IDR_PICTURETYPE from this

```
\nPicture\nPict1\nPicture Files (*.bmp)\n.BMP\nPict.Document\nPict1 Document\n\n
```

to this,

```
\nPicture\nPict1\nPicture Files (*.bmp,*.dib)\n.BMP;*.DIB\nPict.Document\nPict1 Document\n\n
```

Two things have changed here. The drop down combo in the file open dialog will look like the one shown in Figure 1-7. Also, the dialog will display files of type BMP and DIB at the same time. If you trace into the code that parses these strings to prepare the File Open dialog, you'll see that the string segment ".BMP;*.DIB" is prepended with an asterisk and added to the filters for the dialog. By tacking on the "*.DIB" to this string, we're getting a free ride. The drawback to this approach is that the application won't support drag-and-drop from the Explorer and the DIB extension won't be registered for this application. You need to add the second document template like we did in step 5.

Figure 1-7 DocExt file types

CHAPTER 1
DOCUMENT AND VIEW

COMPLEXITY
INTERMEDIATE

1.4 How do I... Automatically scroll a view during mouse drags?

Problem

I'd like my *CScrollView* derived classes to automatically scroll when I click the mouse cursor and drag it outside of the view. For example, in Microsoft Word, you can click and drag the mouse outside of the document area and the text will scroll in that direction. You can scroll around the document easily without using the scroll bars. I'd like to use this technique in a drawing program to drag a shape into view.

Technique

Autoscrolling means the window begins to scroll as soon as the mouse cursor leaves the client area of the current view. You must press the left mouse button to autoscroll.

For this How-To, we'll write a special *CScrollView* derived class called *CAutoScrollView*. Our class doesn't do anything until it detects that the left mouse button is pressed. Then, while the mouse is outside of the client area, *CAutoScrollView* will automatically scroll the view in the direction of the mouse, as shown in Figure 1-8 and Figure 1-9.

The view creates a pattern and paints it to the screen during *OnDraw* so that we have something interesting to scroll. The pattern is created only once during *OnInitialUpdate* because it takes a noticeable amount of time to calculate. We'll create the pattern using elliptical shapes and clipping regions and store it in a bitmap.

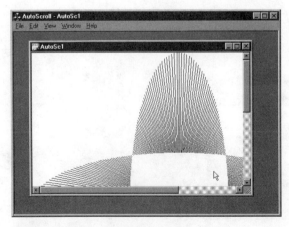

Figure 1-8 Mouse down in client area

1.4
AUTOMATICALLY SCROLL A VIEW DURING MOUSE DRAGS

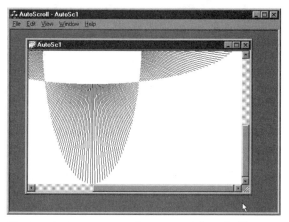

Figure 1-9 A mouse drag outside of client area scrolls in that direction

Steps

1. **Create a new project called AutoScroll using the MFC AppWizard (exe).**
   Use all the defaults, but in step 6, change the base class for *CAutoScrollView* from *CView* to *CScrollView*.

   Classes to be created:
   Application: CAutoScrollApp in AutoScroll.h and AutoScroll.cpp
   Frame: CMainFrame in MainFrm.h and MainFrm.cpp
   MDIChildFrame: CChildFrame in ChildFrm.h and ChildFrm.cpp
   Document: CAutoScrollDoc in AutoScrollDoc.h and AutoScrollDoc.cpp
   ScrollView: CAutoScrollView in AutoScrollView.h and AutoScrollView.cpp

   Features:
   + Initial toolbar in main frame
   + Initial status bar in main frame
   + Printing and Print Preview support in view
   + Uses shared DLL implementation (MFC40.DLL)

2. **Add member variables to CAutoScrollView.** Use the add member variable dialog to add these four members:

Type	Declaration	Access
CRgn	m_rgnClip	public
CDC	m_dcMem	public
CBitmap	m_bmp	public
CBitmap	*m_pOldBmp	public

3. Edit AutoScrollView.cpp. *OnInitialUpdate* is called only once—when a view is about to be displayed. It's here that we'll set up the memory device context used by *OnDraw*. Don't get caught up in the details of this method unless you're really interested in elliptical regions and fancy trigonometric functions. It's only here to give us something interesting to scroll around. Use ClassWizard to add a handler for *CAutoScrollView::OnInitialUpdate* and edit the code as follows:

```cpp
#include <math.h>
void CAutoScrollView::OnInitialUpdate()
{
    CScrollView::OnInitialUpdate();

    int cx = 600;
    int cy = 600;
    SetScrollSizes (MM_TEXT, CSize(cx, cy));

    // Build the complex clipping region
    //
    CRgn rgn[2];
    rgn[0].CreateEllipticRgn (cy / 3, 0, 2 * cx / 3, cy);
    rgn[1].CreateEllipticRgn (0, cy / 3, cx, 2 * cy / 3);
    m_rgnClip.CreateRectRgn (0, 0, 1, 1);

    m_rgnClip.CombineRgn (&rgn[0], &rgn[1], RGN_XOR);

    // Draw the design into a memory dc
    //
    CClientDC dc (NULL);
    m_dcMem.CreateCompatibleDC (&dc);
    m_bmp.CreateCompatibleBitmap (&dc, cx+1, cy+1);
    m_pOldBmp = m_dcMem.SelectObject (&m_bmp);

    // Fill the background with the system color
    CBrush* pBkgBrush = CBrush::FromHandle(::GetSysColorBrush(COLOR_WINDOW));
    CRect rc (0, 0, cx+1, cy+1);
    m_dcMem.FillRect (rc, pBkgBrush);

    // Draw with a blue pen
    CPen pen (PS_SOLID, 1, RGB(0,0,255));
    CPen* pOldPen = m_dcMem.SelectObject (&pen);

    // All lines are drawn assuming (0,0) is the center of the image
    m_dcMem.SetViewportOrg (cx / 2, cy / 2);

    // Only lines visible in the clipping region are visible
    m_dcMem.SelectClipRgn (&m_rgnClip);

    double fRadius = _hypot (cx / 2.0, cy / 2.0);

#define TWO_PI (3.14159 * 2)

    for (double fAngle = 0.0 ; fAngle < TWO_PI ; fAngle += TWO_PI / 360)
```

1.4 AUTOMATICALLY SCROLL A VIEW DURING MOUSE DRAGS

```
        {
                m_dcMem.MoveTo (0, 0);
                m_dcMem.LineTo ( (int) (fRadius * cos (fAngle) + 0.5),
                        (int) (-fRadius * sin (fAngle) + 0.5));
        }

        m_dcMem.SetViewportOrg (0, 0);
        m_dcMem.SelectObject (pOldPen);
}
```

Now that we have the design in a handy memory DC, we can just blit it to the screen in *OnDraw*. If we had to calculate this pattern and draw it from scratch for each WM_PAINT, the update time would be really slow. Insert this code in *OnDraw*:

```
void CAutoScrollView::OnDraw(CDC* pDC)
{
        CSize sz = GetTotalSize();
        pDC->BitBlt(0, 0, sz.cx, sz.cy, &m_dcMem, 0, 0, SRCCOPY);
}
```

Finally, just to clean up after ourselves, we need to select the old bitmap back into the memory DC before it's automatically deleted. Here's the code for the *CAutoScrollView* destructor:

```
CAutoScrollView::~CAutoScrollView()
{
        m_dcMem.SelectObject(m_pOldBmp);
}
```

4. **Insert the AutoScroll component.** Use the Component Gallery to insert the AutoScroll component. You'll find it under the "Visual C++ How-To" tab. Select the *CAutoScrollView* class in the list box and press the Apply button. Close the Component Gallery when you're ready to continue.

5. **Build and test the application.** Make the MDI window small and click the mouse in the client area. Notice how the client area scrolls when the mouse moves outside it. The farther the mouse moves from the client area, the faster the scrolling.

How It Works

The component inserted a big method called *AutoScroll* in *CAutoScrollView*. It's a helper method *OnLButtonDown* calls when the mouse is pressed in the view. Besides initializing a couple of Booleans, all the interesting code happens in here:

```
void CAutoScrollView::OnLButtonDown(UINT nFlags, CPoint point)
{
        AutoScroll(WM_LBUTTONUP);
}

void CAutoScrollView::AutoScroll(UINT nRefMessage)
{
```

continued on next page

CHAPTER 1
DOCUMENT AND VIEW

continued from previous page

```
    MSG     msg;                // for processing messages while autoscrolling
    CPoint  ptScrollPos,        // Current scroll position - logical units
    CPoint  ptDevScrollPos,     // Current scroll position - device units
    CPoint  ptCursorPos;        // Current mouse cursor position
    CRect   rc;                 // Client area
    long    dx, dy;             // Scrolling increment
    SIZE    sizeTotal;          // CScrollView scroll data
    SIZE    sizePage,
    SIZE    sizeLine;
    int     nMapMode;           // Mapping mode
    int     nMapFactor;         // Accounts for mapping mode
    int     xMin, xMax;
    int     yMin, yMax;         // Scroll range

    if (!m_bAutoScroll)
        return;

    msg.message = 0;    // forces at least one loop.
    SetCapture();
    GetDeviceScrollSizes(nMapMode, sizeTotal, sizePage, sizeLine);

    // We keep track of the scroll range because CScrollView::ScrollToPosition will
    // always try to scroll even if the scroll limit has been reached.
    // This results in screen flickering when ScrollWindow is called.
    GetScrollRange(SB_HORZ, &xMin, &xMax);
    GetScrollRange(SB_VERT, &yMin, &yMax);

    // Process all messages until the relevant mouse button
    // has been released. nRefMessage depends on which button
    // has been used to trigger autoscrolling.
    while (msg.message != nRefMessage)
    {
        // Process incoming messages until autoscroll button is released
        if (PeekMessage(&msg, 0, 0, 0, PM_REMOVE))
        {
            TranslateMessage(&msg);
            DispatchMessage(&msg);
        }

        ptScrollPos = GetScrollPosition();
        ptDevScrollPos = GetDeviceScrollPosition();
        GetCursorPos(&ptCursorPos);
        ScreenToClient(&ptCursorPos);
        GetClientRect(&rc);
        dx = 0L;
        dy = 0L;

        if ((ptCursorPos.y < 0) && (ptDevScrollPos.y != yMin))
                // Cursor is above client area
            dy = min(-sizeLine.cy, max(-sizePage.cy,
                    (ptCursorPos.y/10) * sizeLine.cy));
        else if ((ptCursorPos.y > rc.bottom) && (ptDevScrollPos.y != yMax))
                // Cursor is below client area
            dy = max(sizeLine.cy, min(sizePage.cy,
```

1.4
AUTOMATICALLY SCROLL A VIEW DURING MOUSE DRAGS

```
                    ((ptCursorPos.y - rc.bottom)/10) * sizeLine.cy));
        // otherwise we can't scroll anyway

    if ((ptCursorPos.x < 0) && (ptDevScrollPos.x != xMin))
        // Cursor is on the left of the client area
        dx = min(-sizeLine.cx, max(-sizePage.cx,
(ptCursorPos.x/10) * sizeLine.cx));
        else if ((ptCursorPos.x > rc.right) && (ptDevScrollPos.x != xMax))
            // Cursor is on the right of the client area
            dx = max(sizeLine.cx, min(sizePage.cx,
((ptCursorPos.x - rc.right)/10) * sizeLine.cx));
        // otherwise we can't scroll anyway

        // if mouse cursor is dragging outside the client area, scrolling occurs
        if ((dx != 0) || (dy != 0))
        {
            // Flip the Y coordinate if we're not in MM_TEXT
            nMapFactor = (nMapMode == MM_TEXT) ? 1 : -1;
            ptScrollPos.y += (int) dy * nMapFactor;
            ptScrollPos.x += (int) dx;
            m_bIsScrolling = TRUE;
            OnAutoScroll(ptCursorPos, TRUE);
            ScrollToPosition(ptScrollPos);
            OnAutoScroll(ptCursorPos, FALSE);
        } else {
            m_bIsScrolling = FALSE;
        }
    }
    ReleaseCapture();
    m_bIsScrolling = FALSE;
}
```

As soon as the left mouse button goes down, *CAutoScrollView* enters *AutoScroll*. The outer loop starts processing and distributing Windows messages while looking for the corresponding button up message (WM_LBUTTONUP in this case). Until the button up message comes through the message queue, *AutoScroll* dispatches all the Windows messages and calculates where to scroll the view.

The first section of code figures out how far the mouse has traveled outside of the client area and in which direction. From this code, a pair of delta X and Y coordinates are calculated. Then these values are passed to *ScrollToPosition* to bring the view to the right place.

The speed of the scroll depends on the distance between the window border and the mouse cursor. The greater the distance, the faster the view scrolls.

Using CAutoScrollView in Your Application

You can enable or disable the autoscroll feature by toggling the state of *m_bAutoScroll*. Call *m_bIsScrolling* to determine if autoscrolling is occurring.

To give your application's view a chance to update the screen while autoscrolling, *CAutoScrollView* calls its *OnAutoScroll* virtual member function just before and just after scrolling. Override this function in your view if you want to take some action whenever your application autoscrolls. By default, *OnAutoScroll* does nothing.

CAutoScrollView automatically adapts to the mapping mode. For example, if you have set a metric mapping mode, the *nMapFactor* will be used to reverse Y coordinates.

Comments

CAutoScrollView also corrects an annoying bug in *CScrollView::ScrollToPosition*. This method doesn't check whether the scroll limit has already been reached and always tries to scroll. *OnAutoScroll* works around this problem to avoid flicker. This bug may be fixed in MFC 4.x.

COMPLEXITY INTERMEDIATE

1.5 How do I... Open more than one document at a time?

Problem

I'd like to modify the common file dialog box to open more than one document at a time. The framework should pass all these documents to my application so they can be opened at the same time. How do I do this?

Technique

MFC encapsulates the common file dialog in a class called *CFileDialog*. Although this class has features supporting multiple file selection, as shown in Figure 1-10, the mechanism for retrieving the names of them is not straightforward. Also, *CFileDialog*'s path buffer is not big enough to hold a lot of files; the filenames are stored in a buffer just _MAX_PATH bytes long (260 bytes in Windows 95).

Figure 1-10 CFileDialog modified to support multiple selection

1.5
OPEN MORE THAN ONE DOCUMENT AT A TIME

In this How-To, we'll see how to use the *CMultiFileDialog* class that comes from the Multi File Open component that ships with this book. *CMultiFileDialog* inherits all of its functionality from its base class *CFileDialog*, but allocates a much larger buffer to hold multiple filenames.

In the first edition of *Visual C++ How-To*, I added a few methods to *CMultiFileDialog* that made it easier to loop through the selected files. Now there are two new methods in *CFileDialog* that do the job for us. We'll see how to use them and how to work around an MFC bug that occurs when we select files from the root.

To integrate *CMultiFileDialog* into the MFC framework, we need to write our own code to handle the File Open menu option. *CWinApp::OnFileOpen* normally handles the command, but that code uses *CFileDialog*. Instead, our version uses *CMultiFileDialog* then calls *CWinApp::OpenDocumentFile* for every selected file.

Steps

1. **Create a new project called MultiOpen using the Picture AppWizard.** You can't set any options with this custom AppWizard; it simply creates an MDI application capable of viewing bitmaps.

2. **Insert the Multi File Dialog component.** Use the Component Gallery to insert the Multi File Dialog component. Like all the other components in this book, you should find it under the "Visual C++ How-To" tab. There are no options for this component; it always adds MultiFileDlg.cpp and MultiFileDlg.h to your application (see Figure 1-11). Close the Component Gallery when you're ready to continue.

3. **Use the WizardBar to add a handler for ID_FILE_OPEN in CMultiOpenApp.** *CWinApp* normally handles this command for us, but it will only open one document. Our implementation is similar but it uses *CMultiFileDialog* and opens each selected file. If you normally use ClassWizard to add handlers for

Figure 1-11 Inserting the Multi File Dialog component

Figure 1-12 Use the WizardBar to add menu handlers

menus, try using the WizardBar as shown in Figure 1-12. Now insert this code:

```
void CMultiOpenApp::OnFileOpen()
{
    CMultiFileDialog dlgFile(TRUE);

    CString title, strFilter, strDefault;
    VERIFY(title.LoadString(AFX_IDS_OPENFILE));

    // do for all doc template
    POSITION pos = GetFirstDocTemplatePosition();
    BOOL bFirst = TRUE;
    while (pos != NULL)
    {
        CDocTemplate* pTemplate = GetNextDocTemplate(pos);
        AppendFilterSuffix (strFilter, dlgFile.m_ofn, pTemplate,
            bFirst ? &strDefault : NULL);
        bFirst = FALSE;
    }

    // append the "*.*" all files filter
    CString allFilter;
    VERIFY(allFilter.LoadString(AFX_IDS_ALLFILTER));
    strFilter += allFilter;
    strFilter += (TCHAR)'\0';    // next string please
    strFilter += _T("*.*");
    strFilter += (TCHAR)'\0';    // last string
    dlgFile.m_ofn.nMaxCustFilter++;

    dlgFile.m_ofn.lpstrFilter = strFilter;
    dlgFile.m_ofn.lpstrTitle = title;
    dlgFile.m_ofn.hwndOwner = AfxGetMainWnd()->GetSafeHwnd();

    if (dlgFile.DoModal() == IDOK)
    {
        POSITION pos = dlgFile.GetStartPosition();
        while (pos != NULL)
            OpenDocumentFile(dlgFile.GetNextPathName(pos));
    }
}
```

4. **Remove the extra ID_FILE_OPEN message map.** Since *CWinApp* normally handles the ID_FILE_OPEN menu, you need to remove the message map that AppWizard generated. Locate the BEGIN_MESSAGE_MAP section near the top of MultiOpen.cpp. Remove the following line from the file:

```
ON_COMMAND(ID_FILE_OPEN, CWinApp::OnFileOpen)
```

1.5
OPEN MORE THAN ONE DOCUMENT AT A TIME

Don't remove the similar line between the AFX_MSG_MAP comments; we just added that line in step 5.

5. Add the AppendFilterSuffix helper function. Add the following line of code to the top of MultiOpen.cpp:

```
static void AppendFilterSuffix(CString& filter, OPENFILENAME& ofn,
       CDocTemplate* pTemplate, CString* pstrDefaultExt);
```

Now add the body of the *AppendFilterSuffix* method to the bottom of the file. This method came straight from the MFC source code. Since it's not a public method, we can't use it directly and must write our own.

```
// taken directly from mfc\src\docmgr.cpp
static void AppendFilterSuffix(CString& filter, OPENFILENAME& ofn,
       CDocTemplate* pTemplate, CString* pstrDefaultExt)
{
    ASSERT_VALID(pTemplate);
    ASSERT_KINDOF(CDocTemplate, pTemplate);

    CString strFilterExt, strFilterName;
    if (pTemplate->GetDocString(strFilterExt, CDocTemplate::filterExt) &&
        !strFilterExt.IsEmpty() &&
        pTemplate->GetDocString(strFilterName, CDocTemplate::filterName) &&
        !strFilterName.IsEmpty())
    {
        // a file-based document template - add to filter list
        ASSERT(strFilterExt[0] == '.');
        if (pstrDefaultExt != NULL)
        {
            // set the default extension
            *pstrDefaultExt = ((LPCTSTR)strFilterExt) + 1;  // skip the '.'
            ofn.lpstrDefExt = (LPTSTR)(LPCTSTR)(*pstrDefaultExt);
            ofn.nFilterIndex = ofn.nMaxCustFilter + 1;  // 1 based number
        }

        // add to filter
        filter += strFilterName;
        ASSERT(!filter.IsEmpty());  // must have a file type name
        filter += (TCHAR)'\0';  // next string please
        filter += (TCHAR)'*';
        filter += strFilterExt;
        filter += (TCHAR)'\0';  // next string please
        ofn.nMaxCustFilter++;
    }
}
```

OnFileOpen uses *AppendFilterSuffix* to create the file filter string and the default filter extension used by the common file dialog. The common dialog displays the filter string in the drop-down combo, such as "Picture Files (*.BMP)". The default filter extension in this case would be the string "*.BMP". Both of these strings are generated from those funny looking string resources like the one shown in Figure 1-13.

Figure 1-13 The string resource parsed by AppendFilterSuffix

6. **Compile and test the application.** Launch the app and switch to a directory with a bunch of bitmap files (check the Windows directory; it's full of them). Then use File Open to select all of them and press OK. Voilà! They all open as separate documents.

How It Works

CMultiFileDialog distinguishes itself from its base class *CFileDialog* by adding to the *m_ofn.flags* variable OFN_ALLOWMULTISELECT. This style allows the user to select more than one document in the common file dialog. Without this flag, you'd wind up with a normal common file dialog that only allows you to select single files. The rest of the constructor parameters are identical to *CFileDialog*'s. Consult the MFC documentation for a full description of the parameters passed to the *CFileDialog* constructor.

Here's the header file showing the constructor with the new flag (remember, it was added to your project by the Multi File Dialog component).

```
class CMultiFileDialog : public CFileDialog
{
        DECLARE_DYNAMIC(CMultiFileDialog)

public:
        int DoModal();
        virtual ~CMultiFileDialog();
        CMultiFileDialog(BOOL bOpenFileDialog,
                LPCTSTR lpszDefExt = NULL,
                LPCTSTR lpszFileName = NULL,
                DWORD dwFlags = OFN_HIDEREADONLY | OFN_OVERWRITEPROMPT
                        | OFN_ALLOWMULTISELECT, // this lets us open
                                                // multiple files
                LPCTSTR lpszFilter = NULL,
                CWnd* pParentWnd = NULL);

protected:
        //{{AFX_MSG(CMultiFileDialog)
        //}}AFX_MSG
        DECLARE_MESSAGE_MAP()

        TCHAR* m_pszFileName;
};
```

The code for *CMultiFileDialog* is quite simple. The constructor passes all the parameters to its base class constructor, then allocates a 2K buffer to hold the selected files.

1.5 OPEN MORE THAN ONE DOCUMENT AT A TIME

DoModal makes sure you haven't removed the OFN_ALLOWMULTISELECT flag with a handy assertion. Then it sets up the pointer to the buffer and calls *CFileDialog::DoModal* to continue the show.

```
CMultiFileDialog::CMultiFileDialog(BOOL bOpenFileDialog, LPCTSTR lpszDefExt,
    LPCTSTR lpszFileName, DWORD dwFlags, LPCTSTR lpszFilter, CWnd* pParentWnd) :
    CFileDialog(bOpenFileDialog, lpszDefExt, lpszFileName, dwFlags, lpszFilter,
            pParentWnd)
{
    m_pszFileName = new TCHAR[MAXMULTIPATH];
    // new automatically throws a memory exception if it fails
    m_pszFileName[0] = '\0';
}

CMultiFileDialog::~CMultiFileDialog()
{
    if (m_pszFileName != NULL)
        delete [] m_pszFileName;
}

int CMultiFileDialog::DoModal()
{
    ASSERT_VALID(this);
    ASSERT(m_ofn.Flags & OFN_ALLOWMULTISELECT);

    m_ofn.lpstrFile = m_pszFileName;
    m_ofn.nMaxFile = MAXMULTIPATH;

    return CFileDialog::DoModal();
}
```

Earlier versions of *CMultiFileDialog* required us to parse *m_pszFileName*, but MFC 4.x introduced two new methods that make that code unnecessary. *GetStartPosition* and *GetNextPathName* are still interesting to examine. They provide an easy way to pick apart the long string returned by the common dialog. An example might look like this:

```
C:\WIN95\IMAGES clouds.bmp magritte.bmp kahlo.bmp
```

In the first edition of this book, code was written to parse this type of string. Using the C-runtime function *strtok* made it easy to pick apart the directory name and all the filenames. Windows 95 allows filenames to have embedded spaces. So Microsoft changed the delimiter character from a space to a NULL, rendering the *strtok* solution useless. Thankfully, *CFileDialog* has *GetStartPosition* and *GetNextPathName* to pick apart these strings.

OnFileOpen

Armed with a useful, generic class to handle multiple file selection, we hooked it up to *CMultiOpenApp::OnFileOpen*. Normally AppWizard hooks up ID_FILE_OPEN to the default implementation of *CWinApp::OnFileOpen*. This is fine for most people. It's not for us.

By implementing our own *OnFileOpen*, we have the freedom to use any method to open files. How about *CMultiFileDialog*? Of course, we're responsible for a few other mundane details, like handling the construction of the filter string. That's what the *AppendFilterSuffix* method is for. It constructs a special string in the format required by the common file dialog.

If the user selects a few files and presses OK, we simply loop through the filename array contained within *CMultiFileDialog* and pass each filename onto *OpenDocumentFile*.

Comments

For more information on customizing the common dialogs, search through Visual C++ Books Online using these keywords: customizing common dialogs.

You need to be aware of a bug in MFC. If you take a close look at the *GetNextPathName* method in msdev\mfc\src\dlgfile.cpp, near the bottom of the method, you'll see this line:

```
return strPath + '\\' + strFileName;
```

Now, unless they've fixed this in a release after MFC 4.0, the string returned from this method is invalid for files chosen from a root directory. For example, if you selected the files "Baked Beans.bmp" and "Spam.bmp" from the root of the C: drive, the filename returned from the first call to *GetNextPathName* is

```
C:\\Baked Beans.bmp
```

Note the double slash. Undoubtedly, *OpenDocumentFile* will complain. *GetNextPathName* added an extra slash when it didn't need to. Here's the code to fix the bug:

```
if (dlgFile.DoModal() == IDOK)
{
    POSITION pos = dlgFile.GetStartPosition();
    while (pos != NULL)
    {
        CString strPath = dlgFile.GetNextPathName(pos);
        if (strPath.Find(":\\\\") == 1 && strPath.GetLength() > 4)
        {
            // this means we have an invalid path that looks
            // like this: C:\\foo.bmp
        // We need to cut out the extra slash
            CString temp;
            temp = strPath.Left(3);
            temp += strPath.Mid(4);
            strPath = temp;
        }
        OpenDocumentFile(strPath);
    }
}
```

1.6 How do I... Show different views of a single document?

COMPLEXITY
INTERMEDIATE

Problem

There are two different views to display for a single document type. How do I show or create the second view and hook it up to the first view's document?

Technique

Think about adding a second view to your document, one that shows the "internal" view of the data in the document. This might be used during debugging to see what's going on live, behind the scenes. The only trick is figuring out how to attach this new view to an existing document.

For this example, we'll write a simple connect-the-dots drawing program (see Figure 1-14). As you click in the client area, each point is kept in a *CArray* template belonging to the document. The first kind of view, *CLinesView,* displays the shape using *CDC::Polyline*. The second view is for debugging purposes. It lists all the current points in a list control. A menu item attached to the View menu lets you switch between the two types. This menu item will also create the debugging view if it doesn't already exist.

We'll also modify the *CChildFrame* class to set the MDI titles to something more intuitive than "Lines1:1" and "Lines1:2". Instead, the lines view will display "Lines1: Polyline Drawing" and the debug view will show "Lines1: Debug Listing".

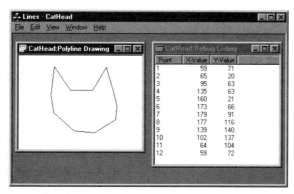

Figure 1-14 A single document with two different views

CHAPTER 1
DOCUMENT AND VIEW

Steps

1. **Create a new project called Lines using the MFC AppWizard (exe).** Use all the defaults and make sure you're creating a multiple document app.

   Classes to be created:
Application:	CLinesApp in Lines.h and Lines.cpp
Frame:	CMainFrame in MainFrm.h and MainFrm.cpp
MDIChildFrame:	CChildFrame in ChildFrm.h and ChildFrm.cpp
Document:	CLinesDoc in LinesDoc.h and LinesDoc.cpp
View:	CLinesView in LinesView.h and LinesView.cpp

   Features:
   + Initial toolbar in main frame
   + Initial status bar in main frame
   + Printing and Print Preview support in view
   + Uses shared DLL implementation (MFC40.DLL)

2. **Add a new class with ClassWizard.** The first view, *CLinesView*, was created by AppWizard in the previous step. Create the second view using ClassWizard with the following parameters:

Class name:	CDebugView
Base class:	CListView
File:	DebugView.cpp

   Hey, what's this *CListView*? If you haven't used this new MFC 4.0 class, it's a *CView* with an embedded *CListCtrl* object. It handles WM_SIZE to keep the list control sized to fit the view's client area.

3. **Add some methods with ClassWizard.** While still in ClassWizard, use the Message Maps tab to add the following methods to several classes:

Object	Function	Message
CLinesView	OnInitialUpdate	
CLinesView	OnLButtonDown	WM_LBUTTONDOWN
CDebugView	OnInitialUpdate	
CDebugView	OnUpdate	

4. **Add a string resource.** Using App Studio, make a copy of the existing string resource IDR_LINESTYPE and change the ID to IDR_DEBUGTYPE.

   The caption for the IDR_DEBUGTYPE is not identical to IDR_LINESTYPE. Modify it and remove the second section, "Lines," to prevent the framework from thinking we have more than one document type. Otherwise, you would end up with the dialog box shown in Figure 1-15.

1.6
SHOW DIFFERENT VIEWS OF A SINGLE DOCUMENT

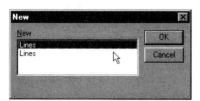

Figure 1-15 The unwanted File New dialog box

By the way, because of this trick, you'll see a trace string in the Output window that says something like "Warning: Dialog creation failed!". Because our application has more than one view, the document manager tries to display the File New dialog. However, the string for the second view, IDR_DEBUGTYPE, doesn't have the correct entry (because you just removed it) to display the dialog. The document manager bails out thinking there was an error.

5. Add and modify the menus. Besides copying the string resources, you also need to copy the menu IDR_LINESTYPE to IDR_DEBUGTYPE. At the bottom of the IDR_LINESTYPE View submenu, add an item called "&Debug Window". At the bottom of the IDR_DEBUGTYPE View submenu, add an item called "&Lines Window". Attach both of these menus to methods in *CMainFrame* using ClassWizard and call them *OnViewDebugWindow* and *OnViewLinesWindow*.

Object	Function	Message
CMainFrame	OnViewLinesWindow	ID_VIEW_LINESWINDOW
CLinesView	OnViewDebugWindow	ID_VIEW_DEBUGWINDOW

6. Edit the CLinesApp header file. We need two document templates, one for each view type. We also want to make our application object, *theApp*, global. So, add this line to the bottom of Lines.cpp:

```
extern CLinesApp NEAR theApp;
```

Now add these two member variables to the class declaration:

```
class CLinesApp : public CWinApp
{
public:
        CLinesApp();

        CMultiDocTemplate* m_pLinesTemplate;
        CMultiDocTemplate* m_pDebugTemplate;

// Overrides
    virtual BOOL InitInstance();

// Implementation
        //{{AFX_MSG(CLinesApp)
```

continued on next page

CHAPTER 1
DOCUMENT AND VIEW

continued from previous page

```
        afx_msg void OnAppAbout();
    //}}AFX_MSG
    DECLARE_MESSAGE_MAP()
};
```

Make sure the two *CMultiDocTemplates* are public because they'll be accessed directly from *CMainFrame* through the global variable *theApp*.

7. Edit CLinesApp::InitInstance. We need to add one more document template to the application's template list. This will associate the second view type, *CDebugView*, with *CLinesDoc*. Also, both views will use our modified MDI child window, *CChildFrame*, which we'll tweak later. Make these changes to *InitInstance*:

```
m_pLinesTemplate = new CMultiDocTemplate(
     IDR_LINESTYPE,
     RUNTIME_CLASS(CLinesDoc),
     RUNTIME_CLASS(CChildFrame),    // custom MDI child frame
     RUNTIME_CLASS(CLinesView));
AddDocTemplate(m_pLinesTemplate);

m_pDebugTemplate = new CMultiDocTemplate(
     IDR_DEBUGTYPE,
     RUNTIME_CLASS(CLinesDoc),
     RUNTIME_CLASS(CChildFrame),    // custom MDI child frame
     RUNTIME_CLASS(CDebugView));
AddDocTemplate(m_pDebugTemplate);
```

Also, at the top of the file, add two #include directives like this:

```
#include "stdafx.h"
#include "Lines.h"

#include "MainFrm.h"
#include "ChildFrm.h"
#include "LinesDoc.h"
#include "LinesView.h"
#include "DebugView.h"
```

8. Add a function to CMainFrame. Add the following public method for *CMainFrame* (Hint: Use the right-mouse button on *CMainFrame* and choose Add Function; it's easier because it adds an empty body to the MainFrm.cpp.):

```
// Operations
public:
     void SwitchToView(CDocTemplate* pTemplate, CRuntimeClass *pViewClass);
```

9. Edit the CMainFrame members. Fill in the two methods for handling the menu items "Debug" and "Lines" like this:

```
void CMainFrame::OnViewDebugWindow()
{
     SwitchToView(theApp.m_pDebugTemplate, RUNTIME_CLASS(CDebugView));
}
```

1.6
SHOW DIFFERENT VIEWS OF A SINGLE DOCUMENT

```
void CMainFrame::OnViewLinesWindow()
{
        SwitchToView(theApp.m_pLinesTemplate, RUNTIME_CLASS(CLinesView));
}
```

Now, edit the *SwitchToView* method at the bottom of MainFrm.cpp:

```
void CMainFrame::SwitchToView(CDocTemplate* pTemplate, CRuntimeClass ⇒
*pViewClass)
{
        CMDIChildWnd* pMDIActive = MDIGetActive();
        CDocument* pDoc = pMDIActive->GetActiveDocument();
        CView* pView;

        POSITION pos = pDoc->GetFirstViewPosition();
        while (pos != NULL)
        {
                pView = pDoc->GetNextView(pos);
                if (pView->IsKindOf(pViewClass))
                {
                        // the requested view class has already been created; show it
                        pView->GetParentFrame()->ActivateFrame();
                        return;
                }
        }

        // The requested view hasn't been created yet
        CMDIChildWnd* pNewFrame = (CMDIChildWnd*)
                pTemplate->CreateNewFrame(pDoc, NULL);

        if (pNewFrame == NULL)
                return;

        pTemplate->InitialUpdateFrame (pNewFrame, pDoc);
}
```

Add two more includes at the top of MainFrm.cpp or the compiler will complain:

```
#include "stdafx.h"
#include "Lines.h"
#include "MainFrm.h"
#include "LinesView.h"
#include "DebugView.h"
```

10. Add a member variable to CLinesDoc. Use the add member variable dialog to add this variable to hold an array of *CPoint* objects:

Type	Declaration	Access
CArray<CPoint, CPoint>	m_points	public

The first version of this program used a *CDWordArray,* one of the predefined classes in MFC, to store the points. Stuffing a *CPoint* object into a DWORD doesn't work in Win32 because the point's X and Y values are now *longs*. Besides, templates are cool, and I was looking for an excuse to use them.

CHAPTER 1
DOCUMENT AND VIEW

11. Edit LineView.h. At the top of the file, add this forward declaration for *CLinesDoc*. Without it, the compiler will complain when it pulls LinesView.h into MainFrm.h. The forward class declaration avoids unnecessary #includes, but it only works for pointers to classes.

```
class CLinesDoc;
class CLinesView : public CView
{
...
```

12. Edit CLinesView::OnLButtonDown. Add code for *OnLButtonDown* that just records the mouse down position on the document as follows:

```
void CLinesView::OnLButtonDown(UINT nFlags, CPoint point)
{
    // Add the new point to the document and notify the other views
    int index = GetDocument()->m_points.Add(point);
    GetDocument()->UpdateAllViews(NULL, 1, (CObject*) &point);
}
```

Locate *CLinesView::OnInitialUpdate* and add this single line:

```
void CLinesView::OnInitialUpdate()
{
    SetWindowText("Polyline Drawing");
}
```

Also, fill in the code for *OnDraw*. Here, we simply loop through the list of DWORD points, building a POINT array to pass to *CDC::Polyline* like so:

```
void CLinesView::OnDraw(CDC* pDC)
{
    CLinesDoc* pDoc = GetDocument();
    ASSERT_VALID(pDoc);

    CRect rc;
    GetClientRect(rc);
    int nCount = pDoc->m_points.GetSize();
    if (nCount == 0)
        return;

    // polyline requires at least 2 points
    if (nCount == 1)
    {
        // draw the point
        CPoint pt(pDoc->m_points[0]);
        pt.x++; pt.y++;
        pDC->MoveTo(pt);
        pDC->LineTo(pDoc->m_points[0]);
        return;
    }
    else
    {
```

1.6
SHOW DIFFERENT VIEWS OF A SINGLE DOCUMENT

```
        POINT* points = new POINT [nCount];
        for (int i = 0; i < nCount; i++)
                points[i] = pDoc->m_points[i];

        pDC->Polyline(points, nCount);
        delete points;
    }
}
```

13. Add a member variable to CDebugView. Use the add member variable dialog to add this variable to track the number of points added to the list control:

Type	Declaration	Access
int	m_nPoints	protected

14. Edit CDebugView::OnInitialUpdate and OnUpdate. Change the existing code to look like this:

```
void CDebugView::OnInitialUpdate()
{
    CListView::OnInitialUpdate();
    SetWindowText("Debug Listing");

    CListCtrl& ctrl = GetListCtrl();

    // change the list control style from whatever CListView used to LVS_REPORT
    SetListStyle(ctrl.GetSafeHwnd(), LVS_REPORT);

    // Setup the column headers
    ctrl.InsertColumn(0, "Point", LVCFMT_LEFT, 50, 0);
    ctrl.InsertColumn(1, "X-Value", LVCFMT_RIGHT, 50, 1);
    ctrl.InsertColumn(2, "Y-Value", LVCFMT_RIGHT, 50, 2);

    // Add the points in the document
    CLinesDoc* pDoc = (CLinesDoc *) GetDocument();
    int nCount = pDoc->m_points.GetSize();
    for (int i = 0; i < nCount; i++)
        OnUpdate(NULL, 1, (CObject *) &pDoc->m_points[i]);
}

void CDebugView::OnUpdate(CView* pSender, LPARAM lHint, CObject* pObject)
{
    // CView::OnInitialUpdate will call us with lHint set to 0 (ignore it)
    if (lHint == 1)
    {
        CPoint* pPoint = (CPoint *) pHint;
        AddPoint(m_nPoint++, *pPoint);
    }
}
```

OnInitialUpdate sets the view caption (which is normally not visible) that *CChildFrame* uses to set the MDI child window caption. *OnInitialUpdate* also loops through the existing *m_points* array, and calls a helper method to add them to the list control.

CHAPTER 1
DOCUMENT AND VIEW

OnUpdate gets the messages sent by *CLinesView* through *UpdateAllViews*. Whenever a mouse down occurs in *CLinesView*, the point is sent to *CDebugView* through this mechanism. A pointer to the point (oh boy!) is passed in through the last parameter, *pObject*.

15. **Add two helper functions to CDebugView.** Add the following protected methods to *CDebugView*:

```
// Helpers
protected:
void AddPoint(int nPoint, CPoint pt);
void SetStyle(HWND hWnd, DWORD dwView);
```

16. **Edit CDebugView::AddPoint and SetListStyle.** The code for these two helpers looks like this:

```
void CDebugView::AddPoint(int nPoint, CPoint pt)
{
    LV_ITEM item;
    memset(&item, 0, sizeof(item));
    CListCtrl& ctrl = GetListCtrl();

    CString temp;

    temp.Format("%d", nPoint);
    int index = ctrl.InsertItem(nPoint, temp);

    temp.Format("%d", pt.x);
    ctrl.SetItemText(index, 1, temp);

    temp.Format("%d", pt.y);
    ctrl.SetItemText(index, 2, temp);
}

void CDebugView::SetStyle(HWND hWnd, DWORD dwView)
{
    // Get the current window style.
    DWORD dwStyle = GetWindowLong(hWnd, GWL_STYLE);

    // Only set the window style if the view bits have changed.
    if ((dwStyle & LVS_TYPEMASK) != dwView)
        SetWindowLong(hWnd, GWL_STYLE,
            (dwStyle & ~LVS_TYPEMASK) | dwView);
}
```

AddPoint converts the point's X and Y coordinates to strings and adds the whole lot to the list control. *SetListStyle* sets the window style passed in as *dwView*.

17. **Add a function to CChildFrame.** Add the following virtual public member method. It's called whenever the framework needs to set the MDI caption.

```
// Attributes
public:
    virtual void OnUpdateFrameTitle(BOOL bAddToTitle) ;
```

1.6
SHOW DIFFERENT VIEWS OF A SINGLE DOCUMENT

18. **Edit CChildFrame::OnUpdateFrameTitle.** Add the *OnUpdateFrameTitle* code shown here:

```
void CTitleChildWnd::OnUpdateFrameTitle(BOOL bAddToTitle)
{
    CDocument* pDoc = GetActiveDocument();

    if (bAddToTitle && pDoc != NULL)
    {
        CString strCurCaption, strWindowText, strNewCaption;

        // Get the current child window caption text
        GetWindowText(strCurCaption);

        // Get the special view name through the view's window text
        GetActiveView()->GetWindowText(strWindowText);

        // Get the doc name attached to this window
        const CString& strDocTitle = pDoc->GetTitle();

        // generate our new window caption
        strNewCaption = strDocTitle;
        if (m_nWindow > 0)
        {
            strNewCaption += ":";
            strNewCaption += strWindowText;
        }

        // Only switch to the new caption if it differs from the old
        // (this reduces flickerñMFC uses AfxSetCaption)
        if (strNewCaption != strCurCaption)
            SetWindowText(strNewCaption);
    }

    // give the MDI frame window a chance to update its title
    GetMDIFrame()->OnUpdateFrameTitle(bAddToTitle);
}
```

19. **Build and test the application.** Add a few points to the main view before turning on the debugging window.

How It Works

SwitchToView is the really interesting part of this program. It's fairly trivial to create another view and add it to a new document template, but how do you actually create and show it?

When a line view has some data in it, you can select the View Debug menu, and *SwitchToView* will execute. It searches through all the views of the current document looking for a view class that matches the *CRuntimeClass* argument. If an existing object is found, the view is activated. If it is not found, the view is created using a couple of *CMultiDocTemplate* methods.

If you were to look behind the scenes at what happens when File New is selected, you'd find code similar to *SwitchToView*.

The views stay synchronized because the active view stores the mouse points in the document. It notifies the other views of the new point through *UpdateAllViews*. If *CDebugView* exists at that time, it simply adds the point to the bottom of its list box. If *CDebugView* hasn't been created yet, it doesn't matter that it misses out on the *UpdateAllViews* call. It simply uses *m_points* to initialize the list control later in *CDebugView::OnInitialUpdate*.

Changing the Autocaption Feature

By overriding *OnUpdateFrameTitle* in step 16, we gain control of the captions used in each MDI child frame. Using a little trick, *CChildFrame* asks its embedded view for its caption. Even though it's not normally displayed by MFC, we're using it in a special case here. If there is more than one view attached to a single document, we're going to use each view's caption (set by each view in *OnInitialUpdate*) as part of the MDI title string.

Without this feature, the titles would be "Line1:1" and "Line1:2," if you were currently showing a *CLinesView* and *CDebugView*. Not very useful. Instead, our *OnUpdateFrameTitle* sets the caption to "Line1:Polyline Drawing" and "Line1:Debug Listing."

Comments

SwitchToView has another interesting use. If you want to create a screen-oriented application, where one button on a screen leads to another screen, you can use *SwitchToView* to manage the different screens. For example, an order entry application might display one view to enter the customer information. After the information has been entered, *SwitchToView* would display the next screen in the chain.

COMPLEXITY
ADVANCED

1.7 How do I... Lock a splitter window containing different views?

Problem

How do I use splitter bars to separate my panes into two different views? The Split Bars component and the AppWizard option both assume the same view will be used for both panes. Also, how can I fix the scroll bar into a position so the user can't move it?

1.7
LOCK A SPLITTER WINDOW CONTAINING DIFFERENT VIEWS

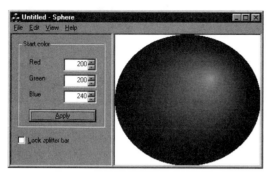

Figure 1-16 Two views separated by a splitter window

Technique

The MFC class *CSplitterWnd* supports two types of splitter windows: static and dynamic. A dynamic splitter window creates and deletes panes as the user splits and unsplits the window. A static splitter window must know the total number of horizontal and vertical panes at creation time. All of the panes are created when the static splitter window is created, and the number of panes cannot change.

We're going to write an application that contains a vertical static splitter window separating two panes. The left pane accepts an RGB color value and stores the color information in its document. The right pane renders the document's data by drawing a sphere with the color intensity specified in the document object.

The left pane also has a checkbox to allow the user to lock and unlock the splitter bar. The splitter bar cannot be moved, or even selected, if it is locked. Figure 1-16 shows the running application.

The first version of this program didn't use the spin controls, but I decided to throw them in for the second edition. Besides, they look great and only take a few more lines of code to support.

Steps

1. Create a new project called **Sphere** using the MFC AppWizard (exe).
Press the Advanced button in step 4 and turn on the Use Split Window option.

Classes to be created:
Application:	CSphereApp in Sphere.h and Sphere.cpp
Frame:	CMainFrame in MainFrm.h and MainFrm.cpp
Document:	CSphereDoc in SphereDoc.h and SphereDoc.cpp
View:	CSphereView in SphereView.h and SphereView.cpp

Features:
+ 3D Controls
+ Splitter windows in views
+ Uses shared DLL implementation (MFC40.DLL)

2. Add a member variables to CSphereDoc. The document stores the sphere's initial color in the public member *m_color*.

Type	Declaration	Access
COLORREF	m_color	public

Maybe you've been following Microsoft's philosophy of only adding "Accessor" or Get/Set functions when they add value to the class. In this case, *CSphereDoc* doesn't care when its color value changes, so making the member public makes sense. Check out the article titled "Microsoft Foundation Class Library Development Guidelines" by Jocelyn Garner in Microsoft Development Library, October 1995.

3. Edit CSphereDoc::CSphereDoc. Add the following initialization code to the constructor of the *CSphereDoc* class in the file SphereDoc.cpp:

```
CSphereDoc::CSphereDoc()
{
    m_color = RGB(255,0,100); // initial color of sphere
}
```

4. Create the splitter window class. Normally, you could just use the *CSplitterWnd* class directly, but you need a derived class if you want to stop users from moving the splitter bar. Use ClassWizard to create the class *CLockSplitter*. Supply the following information to ClassWizard:

Class name:	CLockSplitter
Base class:	generic CWnd
File:	LockSplitter.cpp

Why specify a generic *CWnd* class instead of a *CSplitterWnd* class? ClassWizard only works with certain classes, and *CSplitterWnd* is not one of them. Do a global replacement of the string *CWnd* with the string *CSplitterWnd* in the files LockSplitter.h and LockSplitter.cpp. You should only find one occurrence in each file.

5. Use ClassWizard to add message handlers in CLockSplitter. Add message-handling functions for these objects:

Object ID	Function	Message
CLockSplitter	OnLButtonDown	WM_LBUTTONDOWN
CLockSplitter	OnMouseMove	WM_MOUSEMOVE
CLockSplitter	OnSetCursor	WM_SETCURSOR

1.7
LOCK A SPLITTER WINDOW CONTAINING DIFFERENT VIEWS

6. **Add a data member to the splitter window class.** *CLockSplitter* keeps track of whether its splitter bar is locked or not through the Boolean member variable *m_bLocked*. Add the following data member to the *CLockSplitter* class:

Type	Declaration	Access
BOOL	m_bLocked	public

7. **Initialize the data member of the splitter window class.** Add the following initialization code to the constructor of the *CLockSplitter* class:

```
CLockSplitter::CLockSplitter()
{
    m_bLocked = FALSE;  // initial state of splitter bar
}
```

8. **Edit CLockSplitter::OnLButtonDown.** You need to handle the WM_LBUTTONDOWN message to prevent the user from selecting the splitter bar if it is locked. Locate the ClassWizard-generated *OnLButtonDown* and add code as shown here:

```
void CLockSplitter::OnLButtonDown(UINT nFlags, CPoint point)
{
    if (!m_bLocked)
        CSplitterWnd::OnLButtonDown(nFlags, point);
}
```

Likewise, for *OnMouseMove* and *OnSetCursor*, change the code as follows:

```
void CLockSplitter::OnMouseMove(UINT nFlags, CPoint point)
{
    if (!m_bLocked)
        CSplitterWnd::OnMouseMove(nFlags, point);
    else
        CWnd::OnMouseMove(nFlags, point);
}

BOOL CLockSplitter::OnSetCursor(CWnd* pWnd, UINT nHitTest, UINT message)
{
    if (!m_bLocked)
        return CSplitterWnd::OnSetCursor(pWnd, nHitTest, message);
    else
        return CWnd::OnSetCursor(pWnd, nHitTest, message);
}
```

For these two methods, we want the default behavior provided by *CWnd* if the splitter is locked.

9. **Create the input dialog.** This dialog will be attached to a class derived from *CFormView* and displayed in the left splitter window pane. Bring up a context menu over Dialog in the ResourceView and choose Insert. Select the IDD_FORMVIEW dialog as shown in Figure 1-17. Use App Studio to create a dialog that looks like Figure 1-18.

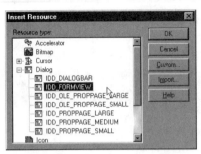

Figure 1-17 The Insert Dialog dialog

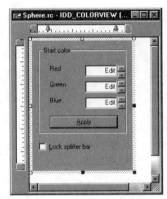

Figure 1-18 IDD_COLOR dialog

Add dialog controls using the following table:

Control	ID	Attributes
Dialog ID	IDD_COLOR	No border, not visible, child control
Red edit field	IDC_RED	Right justified, multiline, number
Green edit field	IDC_GREEN	Right justified, multiline, number
Blue edit field	IDC_BLUE	Right justified, multiline, number
Apply push button	IDC_APPLY	Default button
Lock Bar check box	IDC_LOCKBAR	Default
Spin 1	IDC_SPIN1	Right alignment, Auto buddy, Set buddy integer
Spin 2	IDC_SPIN2	Right alignment, Auto buddy, Set buddy integer
Spin 3	IDC_SPIN3	Right alignment, Auto buddy, Set buddy integer

For the spin controls to work correctly, they must come after their "buddy" edit control in the tab order as shown in Figure 1-19.

Select the default button style for the Apply push button. This allows the button to be selected when the user presses the enter key. Since this is the dialog for a *CFormView* class, make sure the dialog box is a child window, has no border, and the visible style is not selected.

10. **Create a new class called CColorView.** Use ClassWizard to create a new class using the following information:

   Class name: CColorView
   Base class: CFormView
   File: ColorView.cpp
   Dialog: IDD_COLOR

1.7
LOCK A SPLITTER WINDOW CONTAINING DIFFERENT VIEWS

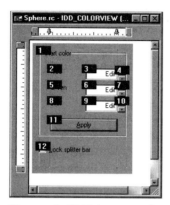

Figure 1-19 Tab control order for IDD_COLOR

11. **Add member variables to CColorView.** Add the following variables to *CColorView* using the Member Variables tab in ClassWizard:

Control ID	Type	Member
IDC_BLUE	int	m_blue
IDC_GREEN	int	m_green
IDC_RED	int	m_ged
IDC_LOCKBAR	BOOL	m_bLockBar
IDC_SPIN1	CSpinButtonCtrl	m_spin1
IDC_SPIN2	CSpinButtonCtrl	m_spin2
IDC_SPIN3	CSpinButtonCtrl	m_spin3

12. **Add message handlers in CColorView.** Add message-handling functions for these objects:

Object ID	Function	Message
IDC_LOCKBAR	OnLockBar	BN_CLICKED
IDC_APPLY	OnApply	BN_CLICKED
CColorView	OnInitialUpdate	

13. **Edit CColorView::OnInitialUpdate.** *ColorView::OnInitialUpdate* initializes its three edit controls and the check box. It also sets the valid ranges for the three spin buttons.

```
void CColorView::OnInitialUpdate()
{
    CFormView::OnInitialUpdate();
    // init the form controls with the current doc color
    // and splitter lock state
```

continued on next page

CHAPTER 1
DOCUMENT AND VIEW

continued from previous page

```
    CSphereDoc* pDoc = (CSphereDoc *) GetDocument();
    ASSERT(pDoc->IsKindOf(RUNTIME_CLASS(CSphereDoc)));

    COLORREF color = pDoc->m_color;

    m_red = GetRValue(color);
    m_green = GetGValue(color);
    m_blue = GetBValue(color);

    CLockSplitter* pSplitter = (CLockSplitter*) GetParent();
    m_bLockBar = pSplitter->m_bLocked;

    // Set the spin button ranges
    m_spin1.SetRange(0, 255);
    m_spin2.SetRange(0, 255);
    m_spin3.SetRange(0, 255);

    UpdateData(FALSE);
}
```

Include the following header files in ColorView.cpp:

```
#include "stdafx.h"
#include "Sphere.h"
#include "ColorView.h"
#include "SphereDoc.h"
#include "LockSplitter.h"
```

14. Edit **CColorView::OnLockbar**. The user specifies whether the splitter bar should be locked by clicking the Lock Bar check box. We'll handle this message here and inform the splitter window class if the splitter bar should be locked or not.

```
void CColorView::OnLockbar()
{
    UpdateData();

    // In this case, our parent is the splitter window (normally it would be
    // the child frame).
    CLockSplitter* pSplitter = (CLockSplitter*) GetParent();
    pSplitter->m_bLocked = m_bLockBar;
}
```

15. Code **CColorView::OnApply**. The user applies the new colors to the sphere by clicking the Apply button. We take the three color values and stick them in the document, then notify all other views (in this case, *CSphereView*) through *UpdateAllViews*.

```
void CColorView::OnApply()
{
    CSphereDoc* pDoc = (CSphereDoc *) GetDocument();
    ASSERT(pDoc->IsKindOf(RUNTIME_CLASS(CSphereDoc)));

    UpdateData();

    pDoc->m_color = RGB(m_red, m_green, m_blue);
    pDoc->UpdateAllViews(this);
}
```

1.7
LOCK A SPLITTER WINDOW CONTAINING DIFFERENT VIEWS

16. Edit MainFrm.h. In step 1, you told AppWizard you wanted a splitter window. It added one of type *CSplitterWnd*, but we want to use our new *CLockSplitter*. Locate the line declaring *m_wndSplitter* and change it to look like the following code:

```
// Attributes
protected:
    CLockSplitter m_wndSplitter;
```

You also need to include the *CLockSplitter* header file at the top of MainFrm.h like this:

```
#include "LockSplitter.h"
```

17. Edit CMainFrame::OnCreateClient. The framework calls *OnCreateClient* during the main frame creation process. We override this method to create a splitter window that gets embedded in the main frame window. This implementation creates a static window, creates a view window for each pane, and repositions the splitter bar to the size of the first pane.

```
BOOL CMainFrame::OnCreateClient( LPCREATESTRUCT /*lpcs*/,
    CCreateContext* pContext)
{
    // create static splitter window with 1 row and 2 columns
    VERIFY(m_wndSplitter.CreateStatic(this, 1, 2));

    // put the CColorView, on the left side
    m_wndSplitter.CreateView(0, 0,
            RUNTIME_CLASS(CColorView), CSize(0, 0), pContext);

    // and the CSphereView on the right side
    m_wndSplitter.CreateView(0, 1,
            RUNTIME_CLASS(CSphereView), CSize(0, 0), pContext);

    // Size the left pane to fit the CColorView exactly
    CColorView* pWnd = (CColorView *) m_wndSplitter.GetPane(0, 0);
    CSize size = pWnd->GetTotalSize();

    // set the left pane width
    m_wndSplitter.SetColumnInfo(0, size.cx, 0);

    return TRUE;
}
```

You need to include the definitions of *CSphereView* and *CColorView* since you are creating objects of those types. Include the following header files in the file MainFrm.cpp:

```
#include "stdafx.h"
#include "Sphere.h"
#include "MainFrm.h"
#include "SphereDoc.h"
#include "ColorView.h"
#include "SphereView.h"
```

CHAPTER 1
DOCUMENT AND VIEW

18. Edit CSphereView::OnDraw. *CSphereView* draws the sphere using the color specified in the document class. *OnDraw* paints a sphere by drawing a series of ellipses. The color intensity of each ellipse is gradually increased, the size gradually decreased, and the position moved towards the upper-right corner. When all the ellipses are drawn, it gives the illusion of a sphere.

```
void CSphereView::OnDraw(CDC* pDC)
{
        CSphereDoc* pDoc = GetDocument();
        ASSERT_VALID(pDoc);

        // draw ellipse with out any border
        pDC->SelectStockObject(NULL_PEN);

        // get the RGB color components of the sphere color
        COLORREF color = pDoc->m_color;
        BYTE byRed   = GetRValue(color);
        BYTE byGreen = GetGValue(color);
        BYTE byBlue  = GetBValue(color);

        // get the size of the view window
        CRect rect;
        GetClientRect(rect);

        // get minimum number of units
        int nUnits = min(rect.right, rect.bottom);

        // calculate the horizontal and vertical step size
        float fltStepHorz = (float)rect.right / nUnits;
        float fltStepVert = (float)rect.bottom / nUnits;

        // How many ellipses do we draw
        int nEllipse = nUnits / 3;
        int nIndex;

        CBrush    brush;       // brush used for ellipse fill color
        CBrush*   pBrushOld;   // previous brush that was selected into dc

        // draw ellipse, gradually moving towards upper right corner
        for (nIndex=0; nIndex <= nEllipse; nIndex++)
        {
                // create solid brush
                brush.CreateSolidBrush(RGB(((nIndex*byRed)/nEllipse),
                        ((nIndex*byGreen)/nEllipse), ((nIndex*byBlue)/nEllipse)));

                // select brush into dc
                pBrushOld = pDC->SelectObject(&brush);

                // draw ellipse
                pDC->Ellipse(fltStepHorz*nIndex*2, fltStepVert*nIndex,
                        rect.right-(fltStepHorz*nIndex)+1,
                        rect.bottom-(fltStepVert*(nIndex*2))+1);

                // deselect brush from dc so we can delete the brush
                pDC->SelectObject(pBrushOld);
```

1.7
LOCK A SPLITTER WINDOW CONTAINING DIFFERENT VIEWS

```
        // delete the brush
        brush.DeleteObject();
    }
}
```

19. **Build and test the application.** Change the default colors and click the Apply button. Also, reposition the splitter bar and notice how the sphere redraws to fit the pane space. Lock the splitter pane and notice that the mouse cursor doesn't change to two horizontal arrows as it passes over the splitter bar.

How It Works

This sample application displays a sphere in the right pane of a static splitter window. The color of the sphere is entered into the left pane of the splitter window. The color is stored in the document's public member *CSphereDoc::m_color* when the Apply button is pressed. Figure 1-20 shows the sample application document/view interaction.

CColorView also calls *UpdateAllViews* when Apply is pressed to inform all the views that the document has been modified (in this case *CSphereView* is notified). *OnUpdate* will be called for all of the document's views, except the view passed as the argument to *UpdateAllViews*.

A modified *CSplitterWnd* class, *CLockSplitter*, actually creates and owns the two viewer panes. It behaves just like a splitter window, but provides two additional functions to lock and unlock the splitter bar and to retrieve the lock state of the splitter bar.

CLockSplitter calls base class methods if the splitter bar is not locked. If the splitter bar is locked, *CLockSplitter* "eats" the WM_LBUTTONDOWN and WM_SETCURSOR messages by not calling any *CSplitterWnd* base methods. This technique prevents the user from selecting the splitter bar and prevents the cursor from changing as it passes over the splitter bar.

A splitter window is embedded in the main frame window. You can embed a static splitter window in the main frame window by specifying a *CSplitterWnd* class, or derived class, as a data member in your main frame window class. To do so, we

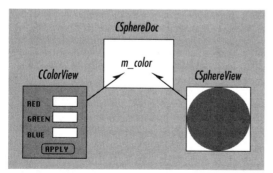

Figure 1-20 Sphere document/view interaction

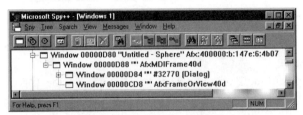

Figure 1-21 Spy++ shows the parent/child relationship

overrode the *CMainFrame::OnCreateClient* member function and called the *CSplitterWnd::CreateStatic* member function in step 17.

```
BOOL bResult = m_wndSplitter.CreateStatic(this, 1, 2);
```

Static splitter windows require that each pane's view be created individually through *CSplitterWnd::CreateView*. We added this code in step 17 too.

Embedding a splitter window into your main frame introduces a new parent/child relationship. The views are children of the splitter window, and the splitter window is a child of the main frame window. Figure 1-21 shows the parent/child relationship as displayed in the Spy++ tool.

Figure 1-22 shows a graphical representation of the parent/child relationship.

We forced the splitter window's left pane to the same width as *CColorView*'s width through *GetTotalSize*. You can reposition the splitter bar to the default size of the *CColorView* window by passing its size to *CSplitterWnd::SetRowInfo* and *CSplitterWnd::SetColumnInfo* as follows:

```
CSize size = pWnd->GetTotalSize();
m_wndSplitter.SetColumnInfo(0, size.cx, 0);
```

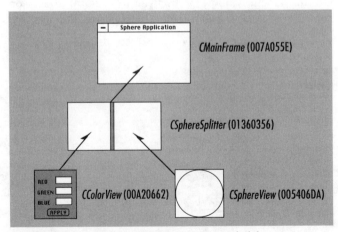

Figure 1-22 Splitter window parent/child relationship

1.7
LOCK A SPLITTER WINDOW CONTAINING DIFFERENT VIEWS

CSphereView is used as the right pane of the splitter window and is responsible for rendering the document's data. It is derived from the *CView* class and is pretty straightforward. The only new code for this class is contained in its *OnDraw* member function. It renders the document by drawing a 3D ellipse of the color specified in the document class.

The document color is first separated into RGB intensity values by calling the SDK *GetXValue* functions. The horizontal and vertical step values are calculated based on the size of the view. The sphere is created by drawing a whole bunch of ellipses, each slightly offset from the other towards the top right. The color of each ellipse is gradually changed from black to the color specified in the document class.

Comments

See the Microsoft Technical Note 29 "Splitter Windows" in Books Online for more information about splitter windows. The sample MFC application VIEWEX that comes with Visual C++ 2.0 uses splitter windows. You might find it helpful to look at this sample application as well. If you want to explore splitter windows even further, you can look at the *CSplitterWnd* source files. The class is declared in the file afxext.h and implemented in the file winsplit.cpp.

CHAPTER 2
STATUS BARS AND TOOLBARS

STATUS BARS AND TOOLBARS

How do I…

2.1 Maximize the first pane while displaying menu help?
2.2 Put the current time in the status bar?
2.3 Change the status bar font and style?
2.4 Add a status bar to my views?
2.5 Display a progress meter in the status bar?
2.6 Put bitmaps in the status bar using an image list?
2.7 Put line and column indicators on the status bar?
2.8 Customize a toolbar for display in a dialog?
2.9 Create a custom CControlBar to display static text?

If there's been any significant advance in the development of the Windows user interface (UI) since the button, it's probably been the introduction of the status bar and toolbar. Since these are features you get for free in any AppWizard-generated program, they're becoming very common controls.

This chapter illustrates techniques to extend the usefulness of the *CToolBar* and *CStatusBar* classes. By overriding parts of these classes, you can customize your application almost any way you want. Set your MFC application apart from the rest by adding some of these great features.

For instance, you'll learn how to write a special status bar that displays a progress meter in one of its panes. Other How-Tos describe techniques to display a clock in a

CHAPTER 2
STATUS BARS AND TOOLBARS

status bar pane or to create your own custom control bar class. You'll also see how to change the font and style used by the status bar.

MFC versions prior to 4.0 included complete source code for toolbars and status bars. Now since these controls are part of the operating system, MFC 4.0 simply wraps the supporting SDK functions. Because of the dramatic changes in the implementation of *CToolBar* and *CStatusBar*, techniques from the first edition no longer work. The techniques illustrated below have been reworked for MFC 4.0.

2.1   Maximize the First Pane While Displaying Menu Help

App Studio lets you add help text to menu items. But if the text is too long, it'll be clipped when shown in the first pane of the status bar. This trick shows how to make the pane bigger while it's displaying the menu help.

Additional Topics: Handling menu messages WM_INITMENUPOPUP and WM_MENUSELECT, SetPaneInfo

2.2   Put the Current Time in the Status Bar

Do you want to change the status bar to provide some useful information? Instead of showing the state of the Scroll Lock key in the status bar (who needs to know that?), display a clock instead. This How-To lets you add a special clock pane that toggles between the date and time when clicked. It's even aware of locale-specific time and date formats.

Additional Topics: CTime, message queues and idle states, timers, EnumDateFormats, EnumTimeFormats

2.3   Change the Status Bar Font and Style

With a little extra work, you can change the font used by the status bar. You'll even learn how to change the 3D style of each pane to create interesting effects.

Additional Topics: CFontDialog, fonts, status bar pane styles

2.4   Add a Status Bar to My Views

MFC already gives you a status bar for your main window. But you'll have to follow these steps to add a status bar to all your views. If you're writing an MDI application and want your views to control their own status bar or toolbar, these steps modify *CChildFrame* to do just that.

Additional Topics: WM_SETMESSAGESTRING, GetParentFrame

2.5   Display a Progress Meter in the Status Bar

You don't need to pop up a dialog box to display the progress of an operation. Instead, follow these steps to create a special *CStatusBar* that turns a pane into a progress meter to show what percentage of a task has been completed.

Additional Topics: pane styles and rectangles, CProgressCtrl

2.6 Put Bitmaps in the Status Bar Using an Image List

Jazz up your status bar with fancy bitmap indicator lights instead of "NUM" or "CAPS." We'll put a red and green light in a pane to indicate the status of an operation.

Additional Topics: SBT_OWNERDRAW, clipping regions, CImageList

2.7 Put Line and Column Indicators on the Status Bar

Using the MFC *CEditView* class, we'll see how to display the row and column position of the caret in the status bar. It even works when you highlight multiple characters.

Additional Topics: caret position and direction

2.8 Customize a Toolbar for Display in a Dialog

Sure, it's easy to add toolbars to a Document/View application, but how do you add one to a dialog? This How-To creates a new *CToolBarCtrl* that understands the toolbar resource data and handles its own tooltip messages.

Additional Topics: parsing the toolbar resource, tooltip text notification messages, AfxExtractSubString

2.9 Create a Custom CControlBar to Display Static Text

The code in this How-To creates a new control bar called *CStaticBar* you can add to your views to give them a fancier title. The InfoViewer in Developer Studio uses a similar control to display the topic's title.

Additional Topics: WM_SIZEPARENT, CalcFixedLayout, using DrawText to calculate text extents

COMPLEXITY
BEGINNING

2.1 How do I... Maximize the first pane while displaying menu help?

Problem

While editing a menu in App Studio, I can type in a text string or prompt that appears in the status bar when that menu item is highlighted. But, if the prompt is too long to fit, it's simply clipped on the right side. Microsoft Word solves this problem by hiding the normal panes when you use the menus as shown in Figure 2-1 and Figure 2-2 below. How do they do this?

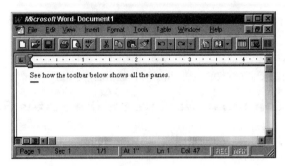

Figure 2-1 Normal Microsoft Word 7.0 status bar

Technique

We can solve this problem by resizing the first pane, the pane where the menu text appears, so it's wide enough to hide the other panes. Windows sends two messages, WM_INITMENUPOPUP and WM_MENUSELECT, that we'll capture to give *CMainFrame* a chance to resize the first pane.

In the steps below, we'll handle the WM_MENUSELECT message through *CMainFrame::OnMenuSelect* and temporarily set the first pane width to a large number. Later, when the menu is removed, WM_INITMENUPOPUP signals our *CMainFrame::OnInitMenuPopup* to restore the pane to its original width.

Steps

1. **Create a new project called PaneWidth using the MFC AppWizard (exe).** Click the option to create a single document application, then press the Finish button.

   Classes to be created:
   Application: CPaneWidthApp in PaneWidth.h and PaneWidth.cpp
   Frame: CMainFrame in MainFrm.h and MainFrm.cpp
   Document: CPaneWidthDoc in PaneWidthDoc.h and PaneWidthDoc.cpp
   View: CPaneWidthView in PaneWidthView.h and PaneWidthView.cpp

   Features:
   + Initial toolbar in main frame
   + Initial status bar in main frame
   + Printing and Print Preview support in view
   + 3D Controls
   + Uses shared DLL implementation (MFC40.DLL)

2. **Change CMainFrame's message filter type.** ClassWizard normally doesn't display the messages we want to handle in *CMainFrame*. By changing *CMainFrame*'s filter type to a more generic filter, we'll have access to a greater

2.1
MAXIMIZE THE FIRST PANE WHILE DISPLAYING MENU HELP

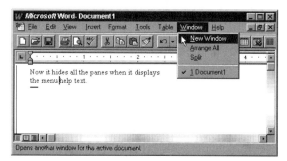

Figure 2-2 The status bar changes when you use the menus

number of Window messages. Press Ctrl+W, choose *CMainFrame* from the Class Name combo, then press the Class Info tab at the top. Change the Message filter from "Topmost Frame" to "Window" as shown in Figure 2-3.

3. **Add member variables to CMainFrame.** Use the add member variable dialog to add these four members:

Type	Declaration	Access
UINT	m_nPaneID	protected
UINT	m_nPaneStyle	protected
int	m_cxPaneWidth	protected
BOOL	m_bMenuSelected	protected

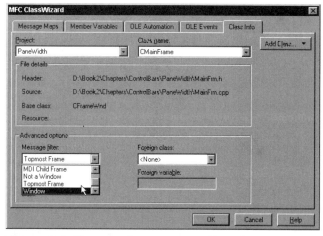

Figure 2-3 Change the message filter for CMainFrame

63

CHAPTER 2
STATUS BARS AND TOOLBARS

4. Initialize the variables in CMainFrame's constructor. Double click on the *CMainFrame* constructor in ClassView and modify the code as shown:

```
CMainFrame::CMainFrame()
{
        m_cxPaneWidth = -1;
        m_bMenuSelected = FALSE;
}
```

5. Use the WizardBar to add a handler for WM_INITMENUPOPUP in CMainFrame. Modify the code as shown here to save the first pane's width for restoration later:

```
void CMainFrame::OnInitMenuPopup(CMenu* pPopupMenu, UINT nIndex, BOOL bSysMenu)
{
        CFrameWnd::OnInitMenuPopup(pPopupMenu, nIndex, bSysMenu);

        // store width of first pane and its style
        if (m_cxPaneWidth == -1 && m_bMenuSelected)
        {
                m_wndStatusBar.GetPaneInfo(0, m_nPaneID,
                    m_nPaneStyle, m_cxPaneWidth);

                // set the first pane's width to a very large number
                m_wndStatusBar.SetPaneInfo(0, m_nPaneID,
                    SBPS_NOBORDERS|SBPS_STRETCH, 10000);
        }
}
```

6. Use the WizardBar to add a handler for WM_MENUSELECT in CMainFrame. Modify the code as shown here:

```
void CMainFrame::OnMenuSelect(UINT nItemID, UINT nFlags, HMENU hSysMenu)
{
        CFrameWnd::OnMenuSelect(nItemID, nFlags, hSysMenu);

        // Restore first pane of the status bar?
        if (nFlags == 0xFFFF && hSysMenu == 0 && m_cxPaneWidth != -1)
        {
                // The menu was closed (see help on OnMenuSelect), so restore
                // the first pane to its original value

                m_bMenuSelected = FALSE;
                m_wndStatusBar.SetPaneInfo(0, m_nPaneID,
                    m_nPaneStyle, m_cxPaneWidth);

                m_cxPaneWidth = -1;    // Set it to illegal value
        }
        else
        {
                m_bMenuSelected = TRUE;
        }
}
```

How It Works

If you create a menu in App Studio, you have an option to enter the prompt text. App Studio makes a string resource out of this pane text and adds it to the string table using the same ID as the menu item. The MFC plumbing takes care of the rest; when you select a menu item, the frame window loads the corresponding string and sends it to the status bar.

Our technique steps into the middle of this process by intercepting two key Windows messages. Right after you click a menu, but before it's actually displayed, Windows sends your frame window a WM_INITMENUPOPUP. We responded to this message in step 5 by storing the normal size of the first pane in *m_cxPaneWidth* right before blowing it out to 10,000 pixels. That should be wide enough to crowd out all the other panes.

Also, by setting the *m_cxPaneWidth* to a value other than the initialized version of −1, we lock ourselves out of resizing the pane more than once. Because Windows calls WM_INITMENUPOPUP every time you drop down a menu, our status bar would get dizzy with all our resize requests.

How do we know when to restore the status bar to its normal width? The WM_MENUSELECT message notifies the frame window, among other things, when the menu has been closed or canceled. At that point, we restore the status bar pane and set *m_cxPaneWidth* back to −1.

COMPLEXITY
BEGINNING

2.2 How do I... Put the current time in the status bar?

Problem

How do I periodically update a pane in the status bar, as you might for a clock? I've tried changing the text while processing the ON_UPDATE_CMD_UI message for the pane, but this method seems unreliable.

I'd also like to detect mouse clicks in the status bar to toggle the information displayed in one of the panes.

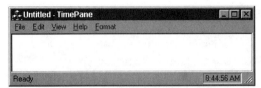

Figure 2-4 Before clicking the clock pane

Technique

There are two reasons why the ON_UPDATE_CMD_UI scheme works reliably. First, MFC only updates status bar panes when the application enters an idle state. Secondly, if the message queue is drained and stays empty, the code that handles the idle state, *CWinApp::OnIdle,* will never be called. As you'll see, it's still possible to update the pane's text by handling ON_UPDATE_CMD_UI if we force-feed messages into the queue on a regular basis.

You are going to create a sample application that uses a pane on the right side of the status bar to display the current date or time. Clicking in this "clock" pane will toggle between the date and time, as shown in Figure 2-4 and Figure 2-5.

There is also a special dialog added that allows you to choose from a list of supported time and date formats as shown here in Figure 2-6. Win32 has two functions—*EnumDateFormats* and *EnumTimeFormats*—that return a special formatted string. This string is usable by other Win32 functions which format the date and time to the user's current locale.

Visual C++ 4.0 ships with a component that adds the date and time to their own status bars. We're going a bit farther by letting the user toggle a single pane between two formats. The component also doesn't update the time if a modal dialog box is being displayed. The date and time formatting in the steps below also doesn't make any assumptions about the user's preferences. For example, an American software engineer might assume that the date May 14th, 1995 should be displayed 5/14/95, whereas a German user would prefer to see it as 14/5/95.

Steps

1. **Create a new project called TimePane using the MFC AppWizard (exe).**
   Click the option for an SDI application then press the Finish button.

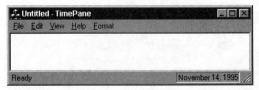

Figure 2-5 After clicking the clock pane

2.2
PUT THE CURRENT TIME IN THE STATUS BAR

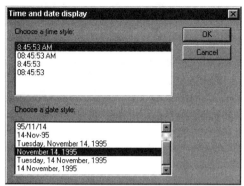

Figure 2-6 Choosing a date and time format

Classes to be created:
    Application: CTimePaneApp in TimePane.h and TimePane.cpp
    Frame: CMainFrame in MainFrm.h and MainFrm.cpp
    Document: CTimePaneDoc in TimePaneDoc.h and TimePaneDoc.cpp
    View: CTimePaneView in TimePaneView.h and TimePaneView.cpp

Features:
    + Initial toolbar in main frame
    + Initial status bar in main frame
    + Printing and Print Preview support in view
    + 3D Controls
    + Uses shared DLL implementation (MFC40.DLL)

2. Add a string resource for the status bar pane. Use App Studio to add a string resource called ID_INDICATOR_CLOCK. Put this string with all the other ID_INDICATOR strings and give it an initial caption of "00:00 AM." *CStatusBar* uses the string length to calculate the initial pane width.

3. Add a new pane to the status bar. In MainFrm.cpp, add ID_INDICATOR_CLOCK to the end of the indicators array, as shown here:

```
static UINT indicators[] =
{
    ID_SEPARATOR,           // status line indicator
    ID_INDICATOR_CLOCK
};
```

This will add a new pane on the right side of the status bar. We'll be changing the default caption of "00:00 AM" to reflect the current time in step 6.

4. Start a timer in CMainFrame::OnCreate. Add the following line to the end of the *CMainFrame::OnCreate* member function (also in MainFrm.cpp):

```
m_wndStatusBar.SetTimer(2, 1000, NULL);
```

CHAPTER 2
STATUS BARS AND TOOLBARS

Windows will fire a WM_TIMER message at TimePane every 1,000 milliseconds (commonly known as 1 second).

The first edition of this book used timer event number 2 because MFC 3.0 reserved number 1 for tooltips. Since tooltips are now handled much differently, the only timer values to avoid are the ones reserved for fly-by status bar help (0xE000 and 0xE001—see Barcore.cpp). Keep it at 2 because you should know not to change working code!

If you've skipped ahead at this point, you may notice that we never handle the timer message with *CMainFrame::OnTimer*. That's the real subtlety of this How-To, which will be fully explained in the "How It Works" section.

5. Add the update command handler for the new pane. Since you can't add command handlers for a status bar pane through ClassWizard, you'll have to do it by hand. First, add a line to the MainFrm.h like so:

```
protected:
    //{{AFX_MSG(CMainFrame)
    afx_msg int OnCreate(LPCREATESTRUCT lpCreateStruct);
    //}}AFX_MSG
    afx_msg void OnUpdateClock(CCmdUI *pCmdUI);
    DECLARE_MESSAGE_MAP()
```

Next, add an entry to the message map in MainFrm.cpp like this:

```
BEGIN_MESSAGE_MAP(CMainFrame, CFrameWnd)
    //{{AFX_MSG_MAP(CMainFrame)
    ON_WM_CREATE()
    //}}AFX_MSG_MAP
    ON_UPDATE_COMMAND_UI(ID_INDICATOR_CLOCK, OnUpdateClock)
END_MESSAGE_MAP()
```

6. Add member variables to CMainFrame. Use the add member variable dialog to add these two members. They'll hold the date and time format "pictures". For example, the string "mm/dd/yy" would generate the date "12/20/93".

Type	Declaration	Access
CString	m_strDateFormat	protected
CString	m_strTimeFormat	protected

Initialize these variables to a reasonable default in *CMainFrame's* constructor:

```
CMainFrame::CMainFrame()
: m_strDateFormat("M/d/yy"), m_strTimeFormat("h:mm:ss tt")
{
    m_wndStatusBar.m_nPaneID = ID_INDICATOR_CLOCK;
}
```

2.2
PUT THE CURRENT TIME IN THE STATUS BAR

7. Write the date or time to the status bar. Add the *OnUpdateClock* method at the bottom of MainFrm.cpp.

```
void CMainFrame::OnUpdateClock(CCmdUI *pCmdUI)
{
    // Write the date or time in the status bar pane. What
    // gets written depends on the setting of the status
    // bar's m_bPaneOn member.
    TCHAR buf[256];
    LCID lcid = GetUserDefaultLCID();

    if (m_wndStatusBar.m_bPaneOn)
            VERIFY(GetTimeFormat(lcid, 0, NULL, m_strTimeFormat, buf, 256));
    else
            VERIFY(GetDateFormat(lcid, 0, NULL, m_strDateFormat, buf, 256));

    // Update the pane's width to fit the text
    UINT nID, nStyle;
    int nWidth, nIndex = m_wndStatusBar.CommandToIndex(ID_INDICATOR_CLOCK);

    CClientDC dc(&m_wndStatusBar);
    CFont* pOldFont = dc.SelectObject(m_wndStatusBar.GetFont());
    CSize szExtent = dc.GetTextExtent(buf, strlen(buf));
    dc.SelectObject(pOldFont);

    m_wndStatusBar.GetPaneInfo(nIndex, nID, nStyle, nWidth);
    m_wndStatusBar.SetPaneInfo(nIndex, nID, nStyle, szExtent.cx);
    m_wndStatusBar.SetPaneText(nIndex, buf);

    pCmdUI->Enable();
}
```

This message-handling member function retrieves the current date and time and then writes the appropriate date or time string to the status bar pane.

OnUpdateClock executes about every second, but don't worry about unnecessary pane flashes. The code that changes the pane width doesn't do anything if the new width is the same as the old (step into the code in the debugger to see what I mean).

8. Create the date and time format dialog. We're going to create a dialog that displays a list of date and time formats that let the user customize the way each is displayed in the status bar pane. The list of possible date and time formats come from a pair of Win32 functions called *EnumTimeFormats* and *EnumDateFormats*. We'll take the format strings returned from these two functions and add them to a pair of list boxes. Use App Studio to create a dialog called IDD_CLOCK_FORMAT that looks like Figure 2-7.

Add dialog controls using the following table:

Control	ID	Attributes
Time list box	IDC_TIME_LIST	Single selection; not sorted
Date list box	IDC_DATE_LIST	Single selection; not sorted

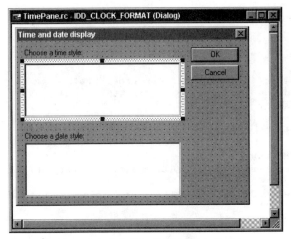

Figure 2-7 IDD_CLOCK_FORMAT dialog

9. **Create a new class called CClockFormatDlg.** Use ClassWizard to create a new class based on the new dialog IDD_CLOCK_FORMAT using the following information:

Class name:	CClockFormatDlg
Base class:	CDialog
File:	ClockFormatDlg.cpp
Dialog:	IDD_CLOCK_FORMAT

10. **Add member variables to CClockFormatDlg.** Add the following variables to *CClockFormatDlg* using the member variables tab in ClassWizard:

Control ID	Type	Member
IDC_DATE_LIST	CListBox	m_listDate
IDC_DATE_LIST	UINT	m_nDate
IDC_TIME_LIST	CListBox	m_listTime
IDC_TIME_LIST	UINT	m_nTime

11. **Edit ClockFormatDlg.h.** Add these members somewhere after the constructor. The date and time enumeration routines access the list box controls, the string arrays, and the current time and locale through the static members. If you haven't used enumeration or callback routines before, you'll quickly find you have to make them static because of the hidden "this" pointer passed as the first argument to all non-static class methods.

```
// Attributes
public:
        // These hold the date and time format "pictures", ex: "hh:mm:ss"
        // represented in the two list boxes
```

2.2
PUT THE CURRENT TIME IN THE STATUS BAR

```
        CStringArray m_timeStrings;
        CStringArray m_dateStrings;

        // These four static members give the enumeration routines access to all
        // the goodies belonging to a CClockFormatDlg object
        static LCID m_id;
        static CListBox* m_pListBox;
        static CStringArray* m_pArray;

        static BOOL CALLBACK DateFmtEnumProc(LPTSTR lpszFormatString);
        static BOOL CALLBACK TimeFmtEnumProc(LPTSTR lpszFormatString);
```

12. **Use the WizardBar to handle WM_INITDIALOG for CClockFormatDlg.** Add the following code to fill the list boxes with the possible date and time formats:

```
BOOL CClockFormatDlg::OnInitDialog()
{
        CDialog::OnInitDialog();

        m_id = GetUserDefaultLCID();

        m_pListBox = &m_listDate;
        m_pArray = &m_dateStrings;
        EnumDateFormats(DateFmtEnumProc, m_id, DATE_SHORTDATE);
        EnumDateFormats(DateFmtEnumProc, m_id, DATE_LONGDATE);

        m_pListBox = &m_listTime;
        m_pArray = &m_timeStrings;
        EnumTimeFormats(TimeFmtEnumProc, m_id, 0);

        m_pListBox = NULL;
        m_listDate.SetCurSel(0);
        m_listTime.SetCurSel(0);

        return TRUE;
}
```

13. **Add the date and time format enumerator callbacks.** Add these two methods at the bottom of ClockFormatDlg.h. By the way, these methods were derived from similar code in Datedial.cpp from the WordPad sample.

```
BOOL CALLBACK CClockFormatDlg::DateFmtEnumProc(LPTSTR lpszFormatString)
{
        ASSERT(m_pListBox != NULL);
        TCHAR buf[256];
        VERIFY(GetDateFormat(m_id, 0, NULL, lpszFormatString, buf, 256));

        // we can end up with same format because a format with leading
        // zeroes may be the same as one without when a number is big enough
        // e.g., 09/10/94 9/10/94 are different but 10/10/94 and 10/10/94 are
        // the same
        int index;
        if (m_pListBox->FindStringExact(-1,buf) == CB_ERR)
                index = m_pListBox->AddString(buf);
```

continued on next page

CHAPTER 2
STATUS BARS AND TOOLBARS

continued from previous page

```
        if (index != LB_ERR)
            m_pArray->Add(lpszFormatString);
        return TRUE;
}

BOOL CALLBACK CClockFormatDlg::TimeFmtEnumProc(LPTSTR lpszFormatString)
{
    ASSERT(m_pListBox != NULL);
    TCHAR buf[256];
    VERIFY(GetTimeFormat(m_id, 0, NULL, lpszFormatString, buf, 256));

    // we can end up with same format because a format with leading
    // zeroes may be the same as one without when a number is big enough
    // e.g., 08:15 8:15 are different but 11:15 and 11:15 are the same
    int index;
    if (m_pListBox->FindStringExact(-1,buf) == CB_ERR)
        index = m_pListBox->AddString(buf);

    if (index != LB_ERR);
        m_pArray->Add(lpszFormatString);
    return TRUE;
}
```

14. **Modify the include directives in ClockFormatDlg.cpp.** Edit the top of the file to add the static members and modify the include directives like this:

```
#include "stdafx.h"
#include "resource.h"
#include "ClockFormatDlg.h"
SYSTEMTIME CClockFormatDlg::m_time;
LCID CClockFormatDlg::m_id;
CStringArray CClockFormatDlg::m_pArray = NULL;
CListBox* CClockFormatDlg::m_pListBox = NULL;
```

15. **Edit StdAfx.h.** Before we forget, we need to add an include to StdAfx.h to pull in all the National Language Support (NLS) features for Win32 applications.

```
#define VC_EXTRALEAN

#include <afxwin.h>
#include <afxext.h>
#ifndef _AFX_NO_AFXCMN_SUPPORT
#include <afxcmn.h>
#endif

#include <winnls.h>
```

16. **Modify the IDR_MAINFRAME menu.** Add a new menu item called "Format" and a submenu labeled "Clock pane". Use ClassWizard to attach the submenu to a new method in *CMainFrame* called *OnFormatClockPane*.

Object	Function	Message
CMainFrame	OnFormatClockPane	ID_FORMAT_CLOCKPANE

2.2
PUT THE CURRENT TIME IN THE STATUS BAR

Press the "Edit Code" button and modify *OnFormatClockPane* to look like this:

```
void CMainFrame::OnFormatClockPane()
{
    CClockFormatDlg dlg;
    if (dlg.DoModal() == IDOK)
    {
        m_strDateFormat = dlg.m_timeStrings.GetAt(dlg.m_nTime);
        m_strTimeFormat = dlg.m_dateStrings.GetAt(dlg.m_nDate);

        TRACE("date:%s\n", (LPCSTR) m_strDateFormat);
        TRACE("time:%s\n", (LPCSTR) m_strTimeFormat);
    }
}
```

17. Create a new status bar class. Now we need a new type of status bar that can detect if a particular pane was clicked or not. Use ClassWizard to create the class *CToggleBar*. Supply the following information to ClassWizard:

Class name:	CToggleBar
Base class:	generic CWnd
File:	ToggleBar.cpp

After you've created the class, use the search and replace dialog to change every occurrence of *CWnd* with *CStatusBar* in ToggleBar.h and ToggleBar.cpp. It sure would be easier if the Visual C++ folks added *CStatusBar* to the list of class types.

18. Add a member to keep track of the click state. We're going to use a Boolean variable to simulate a check box for the pane. The second variable lets the owner of the status bar identify which pane to track the mouse down events.

Type	Declaration	Access
BOOL	m_bPaneOn	public
UINT	m_nPaneID	public

19. Initialize the variables in CToggleBar::CToggleBar. Edit the constructor to look like this:

```
CToggleBar::CToggleBar()
{
    m_nPaneID = 0;
    m_bPaneOn = TRUE;
}
```

20. Handle the mouse down message. Use the WizardBar to add this message-handling function for *CToggleBar*:

Object ID	Function	Message
CToggleBar	OnLButtonDown	WM_LBUTTONDOWN

CHAPTER 2
STATUS BARS AND TOOLBARS

Then modify the code to look as follows:

```
void CToggleBar::OnLButtonDown(UINT nFlags, CPoint point)
{
    ASSERT(m_nPaneID != 0);    // parent must set this

    // Get the bounding rect for our pane
    CRect r;
    ASSERT(CommandToIndex(m_nPaneID) != -1);   // this pane must exist
    GetItemRect (CommandToIndex(m_nPaneID), &r);

    // Toggle the state of m_bPaneOn if the mouse went down in this rectangle
    if (r.PtInRect(point))
        m_bPaneOn = !m_bPaneOn;
}
```

21. **Use the CToggleBar class in CMainFrame.** In MainFrm.h, change the *m_wndStatusBar* data member to type *CToggleBar* instead of type *CStatusBar,* like this:

```
protected:    // control bar embedded members
    CToggleBar    m_wndStatusBar;
    CToolBar      m_wndToolBar;
```

Also, you will need to add this line at the top:

```
#include "ToggleBar.h"
```

22. **Build and test the program.** Notice how the clock updates even while the application sits idle. Also, click the pane to toggle between the date and time and watch the pane change.

How It Works

MFC only updates toolbar buttons and status bar panes when the application enters an idle state. The framework sends out special messages that you can map to your own methods for customized handling. For instance, in step 5, we add the *CMainFrame::OnUpdateClock* method that will be called when MFC wants the status bar pane updated.

Idle States

The MFC framework is constantly updating the state of all toolbar buttons and status bar panes. All the update command handlers are called whenever your application enters an idle state, which only occurs when the application's message queue is drained. If the user does nothing and leaves the system in a quiescent state, no messages will be generated and the idle state is never entered. In this situation, the clock would freeze (more noticeable if you're displaying seconds) until the user did something to cause another message to be generated, as illustrated by Figure 2-8.

Step 4 avoids this potential problem by forcing a message to be generated periodically, regardless of the user's activity. We do this by setting a timer in *CMainFrame::OnCreate,* which sends a WM_TIMER message into the message queue every second. This

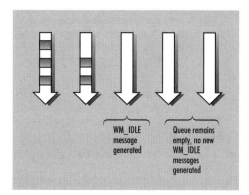

Figure 2-8 The idle state

guarantees the message queue will have something to empty (and thus enter the idle state) at least once a second if the user is just staring at the screen. This scenario is illustrated in Figure 2-9.

Detecting Mouse Clicks in the Status Bar

Step 17 creates a new status bar called *CToggleBar* to replace the normal *CStatusBar* used by the main frame. It has a public Boolean that *CMainFrame* queries to determine the clicked pane's current state (on or off). If it's on, the time is shown; otherwise the date is displayed.

How does *CToggleBar* know when a particular pane is clicked? By handling all the mouse down messages in *CToggleBar::OnLButtonDown*. *CToggleBar* retrieves the bounding rectangle using *GetItemRect* for the pane ID specified by *m_nPaneID*. *PtInRect* tests the point to see if it lies inside the rectangle; if it does, *m_bPaneOn* is toggled. Figure 2-10 illustrates the *PtInRect* call.

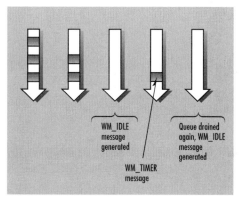

Figure 2-9 Draining the message queue with a timer message

CHAPTER 2
STATUS BARS AND TOOLBARS

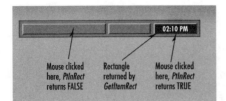

Figure 2-10 Using PtInRect

Formatting the Date and Time for a Specific Locale

Win32 offers a large number of functions to support local conventions through the National Language Support API. One of the more useful sets of NLSAPI calls—*GetDateFormat, GetTimeFormat, EnumDateFormats,* and *EnumTimeFormats*—returns formatted time and date picture strings. As their names suggest, *EnumDateFormats* and *EnumTimeFormats* enumerate all the possible date and time formats for the current locale. A user can customize these lists through the Regional Settings control panel as shown in Figure 2-11.

CClockFormatDlg uses these two functions to build two lists of available formats. *EnumDateFormats* and *EnumTimeFormats* enumerates date and time formats by making repeated calls to an application defined callback function.

EnumDateFormats and *EnumTimeFormats* pass each formatted "picture" to the callback functions *DateFmtEnumProc* and *TimeFmtEnumProc*. These methods use *GetDateFormat* and *GetTimeFormat* to turn the current date and time into a properly formatted string. We could have displayed the raw picture string, like

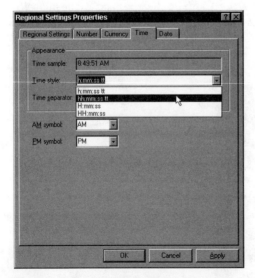

Figure 2-11 Regional Settings control panel

2.2
PUT THE CURRENT TIME IN THE STATUS BAR

"MMMM d, yyyy", in the list box, but a concrete example, like "May 14, 1994", is a little easier to decipher. A list of picture strings and their corresponding "rendered" format (in the English locale) is shown in Table 2-1.

PICTURE STRING	FORMATTED STRING
M/dd/yy	06/12/96
dd/M/yy	12/6/96
MMMM dd, yyyy	September 24, 1996
dd-MMM-yy	09-Sep-95
h:mm:ss	1:20:30
h:mm t	1:20 p
h:mm:ss tt	1:20:30 PM
HHmm	1320

Table 2-1 Sample date and time formats

CMainFrame::OnFormatClockPane displays the dialog and keeps track of the selected picture strings. *OnUpdateClock* uses the strings later when it sets the text of the status bar pane.

Comments

Windows will stop sending timer messages to your application if it's currently showing a modal dialog. To verify this for yourself, run the program again and display the About dialog. If the time is showing seconds, you'll notice the pane text doesn't change until you close the dialog. This bug was left in to see if you're reading the comments section; read on to see how to fix it.

Since we rely on WM_TIMER messages to update the time pane, we need a slightly different approach to update the pane while a dialog is displayed. The third argument to *SetTimer* allows us to specify a timer callback function to process the WM_TIMER messages. If this parameter is NULL, like it is in step 4, the WM_TIMER messages are placed in the application's message queue, triggering the idle-time processing. If we pass a pointer to a *TimerProc* function instead of NULL, the callback will be called instead.

Inside the *TimerProc* function, we'd force the *CWinApp* to perform its idle-time processing by calling *CWinApp::OnIdle* like this (add this to the bottom of MainFrm.cpp):

```
void CALLBACK EXPORT TimerProc (
    HWND hWnd,          // handle of CWnd that set the timer
    UINT nMsg,          // WM_TIMER
    UINT nIDEvent,                  // timer identification
    DWORD dwTime)                   // current time
{
```

continued on next page

continued from previous page

```
        // Force MFC to perform idle-time processing like calling
        // our pane update method.
        AfxGetApp()->OnIdle(0);
}
```

You'll also need to add this line to the top of MAINFRM.cpp:

```
extern "C"
void CALLBACK EXPORT TimerProc(HWND hWnd, UINT nMsg,
    UINT nIDEvent, DWORD dwTime);
```

Change the parameters for the time generation to include the seconds instead of the AM/PM indicator, so it's easier to tell if this method is working.

Replace the NULL argument to *SetTimer* with *TimerProc* in step 4. Rebuild the app, then bring up the About dialog and notice the seconds still ticking away.

Of course you're not limited to displaying just the date and time in the status bar. Any information you might want displayed, regardless of the idle state, could be shown using these techniques. For example, you could indicate what portion of a background task has been completed.

You Can't Find the Seconds Either?

During the writing of this program, I discovered that my list of available time formats didn't include the seconds! If you're having this problem too, bring up the Regional Settings dialog from the Control Panel. Type in "h:mm:ss tt" in the Time style area. Now you can switch back to TimePane and find the new format.

COMPLEXITY
BEGINNING

2.3 How do I... Change the status bar font and style?

Problem

How do I change the font used by the status bar? Also, how can I change the 3D style of the first pane? The keyboard indicators have an inset frame but the first pane does not.

Technique

It's a snap to change the font used by the status bar once you've created the appropriate *CFont* object. However, if you look through the documentation, you won't find an obvious *CStatusBar* method to do this. The key is to use the *CWnd::SetFont* method. Since *CStatusBar* is a *CWnd* class through inheritance, it knows how to respond to a WM_SETFONT event.

2.3
CHANGE THE STATUS BAR FONT AND STYLE

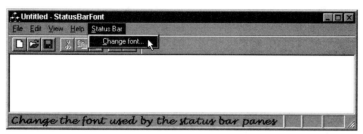

Figure 2-12 Change the font used by the status bar

We'll use the font common dialog to change the status bar font. As a bonus, we'll instruct the font dialog box to display the current status bar font, instead of the first font in alphabetical order.

By default, the first pane in the status bar doesn't have any of the fancy 3D styles applied to it. A convenient place to change the style is in *CMainFrame::OnCreate,* right after the status bar is created (but before it's shown).

Figure 2-12 shows the sample application with a great script font called Lucida Handwriting.

Steps

1. **Create a new project called StatusBarFont using the MFC AppWizard (exe).**
   Click the option for a single-document application, then press the Finish button.

   Classes to be created:
Application:	CStatusBarFontApp in StatusBarFont.h and StatusBarFont.cpp
Frame:	CMainFrame in MainFrm.h and MainFrm.cpp
Document:	CStatusBarFontDoc in StatusBarFontDoc.h and StatusBarFontDoc.cpp
View:	CStatusBarFontView in StatusBarFontView.h and StatusBarFontView.cpp

   Features:
   + Initial toolbar in main frame
   + Initial status bar in main frame
   + Printing and Print Preview support in view
   + 3D Controls
   + Uses shared DLL implementation (MFC40.DLL)

2. **Add member variables to CMainFrame.** We need two variables to keep track of the current status bar font. Use the add member variable dialog in ClassView to add these two members:

Type	Declaration	Access
CFont	m_font	protected
LOGFONT	m_lf	protected

CHAPTER 2
STATUS BARS AND TOOLBARS

3. Edit the MAINFRM.cpp file. Edit the *OnCreate* member function as shown here:

```
int CMainFrame::OnCreate(LPCREATESTRUCT lpCreateStruct)
{
    if (CFrameWnd::OnCreate(lpCreateStruct) == -1)
        return -1;
    ...

    // Create default font used by status bar
    memset(&m_lf, 0, sizeof(LOGFONT));
    m_lf.lfHeight = 8;
    strcpy(m_lf.lfFaceName, "MS Sans Serif");
    VERIFY(m_font.CreateFontIndirect(&m_lf));
    m_wndStatusBar.SetFont(&m_font);

    // put a 3D border around the first pane in the status bar
    UINT nID, nStyle;
    int cxWidth;
    m_wndStatusBar.GetPaneInfo(0, nID, nStyle, cxWidth);
    m_wndStatusBar.SetPaneInfo(0, nID, SBPS_STRETCH|SBPS_NORMAL, cxWidth);

    return 0;
}
```

4. Add a menu item. Create a menu called "Status Bar" with a submenu labeled "Change font...". Attach the menu item to a method called *CMainFrame::OnStatusBarChangeFont* using ClassWizard. Press the Edit Code button and continue to the next step.

5. Edit the OnViewChangeFont method. This method displays the font chooser dialog and changes the status bar font if the user presses OK. It needs to be edited as follows:

```
void CMainFrame::OnViewChangeFont()
{
    CFontDialog dlg(&m_lf, CF_SCREENFONTS);

    if (dlg.DoModal() == IDOK)
    {
        m_font.DeleteObject();
        if (m_font.CreateFontIndirect(&m_lf))
        {
            m_wndStatusBar.SetFont(&m_font);
            RecalcLayout();
        }
    }
}
```

6. Build and test the application. Try changing the font to something fun like Wingdings.

How It Works

In the first part of *CMainFrame::OnCreate*, we construct a new font using a LOGFONT structure. Instead of using a local variable for the LOGFONT structure, we use the member variable *m_lf* since *CFontDialog* needs the same information later to select the default font.

Next, we use *CStatusBar::SetPaneInfo* to change the style of the first pane to make it look recessed. Since you can't change a pane's style without also specifying the ID and width, *GetPaneInfo* is used first to get the other necessary details about the pane.

After changing the font, we call *CMainFrame::RecalcLayout* in case the status bar needs to be resized for a different sized font.

Comments

If you change the status bar font size to something larger than 14 points, the fixed-size panes don't get wider. That's because the size of the fixed panes is determined when the status bar is first created. For a larger size, modify the string resources for the indicators and pad them with spaces. Or use *SetPaneInfo* to change the pane size at runtime.

For a different effect, change the line that reads

```
m_wndStatusBar.SetPaneInfo(0, nID, SBPS_STRETCH|SBPS_NORMAL, cxWidth);
```

to

```
m_wndStatusBar.SetPaneInfo(0, nID, SBPS_STRETCH|SBPS_POPOUT, cxWidth);
```

and the first pane will "pop out" of the status bar.

COMPLEXITY
BEGINNING

2.4 How do I... Add a status bar to my views?

Problem

AppWizard makes it easy to add a status bar for my whole application. How do I add a status bar to each individual view in an MDI application?

Technique

The key here is to add the status bar to the view's *frame* rather than to the actual view itself. A view can own and display a status bar, but then the view would be responsible for subtracting the status bar from the client area. It's much easier to add the status bar to the frame window and let those two objects handle the real estate calculations for the view.

CHAPTER 2
STATUS BARS AND TOOLBARS

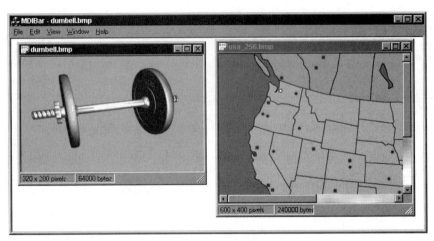

Figure 2-13 Status bar attached to a CView

You can add a status bar, or any *CControlBar* class, to a *CMDIChildWnd* derivative much as you'd add a status bar to your application's main window. Earlier versions of AppWizard attached MDI views to *CMDIChildWnd*, but Visual C++ 4.0 adds the derived class *CChildFrame* to all MDI projects. It's in this class where we'll add the status bar. By default, all views are attached to this child frame in the document template. Once you have a status bar attached to the view's frame, the view can display information specific to that view. One type of program, a bitmap viewer, could use this technique to display each bitmap's size and color depth in the status bar. Figure 2-13 shows the sample application we'll build in the following steps.

Steps

1. **Create a new project called MDIBar using the Picture AppWizard.** You can't set any options with this custom AppWizard; it simply creates an MDI application capable of viewing bitmaps.

2. **Add CPictureView and CPictureDoc to ClassWizard.** Visual C++ 4.0 Custom AppWizards don't handle the ClassWizard database properly, so we have to add *CPictureView* and *CPictureDoc* by hand. Press [CTRL]-[W] to bring up ClassWizard. If it complains about not finding *CMDIBarView*, don't be alarmed; just press OK, then the Remove button. ClassWizard thinks the class should exist because it's referenced in the MDIBar.clw file, but the Picture AppWizard didn't create it.

   Now press the Add Class button and choose the From A File option. Type "CPictureView" in Class Name and "pictureview.h" and "pictureview.cpp" should appear in the Header and Implementation file areas. See Figure 2-14 for an example. Press OK, then repeat these steps for "CPictureDoc".

2.4
ADD A STATUS BAR TO MY VIEWS

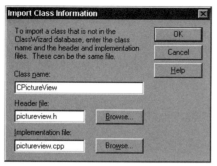

Figure 2-14 Adding a class from a file to ClassWizard

Now if you open PictureDoc.cpp and PictureView.cpp, the WizardBar will show up. We'll be using them in later steps.

3. **Add temporary menu resources.** Here's a time-saving trick. Normally when you create a new status bar pane, you follow several steps: Create a string resource, add an ON_UPDATE_COMMAND_UI handler to the message map, add a new method to the class, then add the code for the method. As it turns out, ClassWizard will do all that work for us, but we have to trick it into thinking we're dealing with menus instead of status bar panes. Add these two menus to the IDR_MAINFRAME Help menu (see Figure 2-15):

Menu ID	Caption	Prompt
ID_INDICATOR_PIXELS	pixels	9,999 x 9,999 pixels
ID_INDICATOR_BYTES	bytes	99,999 bytes

4. **Add ON_UPDATE_COMMAND_UI handlers for the two status bar panes.** Now the WizardBar will display the two new menu IDs in the Object IDs combo-box as shown in Figure 2-16. Select ID_INDICATOR_PIXELS and

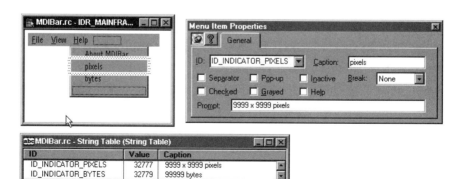

Figure 2-15 Temporary menus for panes

CHAPTER 2
STATUS BARS AND TOOLBARS

UPDATE_COMMAND_UI in the Messages tab to add a handler for this status bar pane. Do the same for ID_INDICATOR_BYTES.

Now that we got ClassWizard to add the message maps and the two member functions, we can remove the two menus added in step 3. The prompt strings are not removed from the string table. We'll use those strings as the status bar pane IDs next.

5. Edit OnUpdateIndicatorPixels and OnUpdateIndicatorBytes. Modify the two new functions as follows:

```
void CPictureView::OnUpdateIndicatorPixels(CCmdUI* pCmdUI)
{
    CSize size = GetDocument()->GetSize();

    CString msg;
    msg.Format("%d x %d pixels", size.cx, size.cy);
    pCmdUI->SetText(msg);
}
```

```
void CPictureView::OnUpdateIndicatorBytes(CCmdUI* pCmdUI)
{
    CSize size = GetDocument()->GetSize();

    // CPictureDoc only handles 8-bit per pixel images, so
    // the image size is always the width * height * 1
    DWORD dwBytes = size.cx * size.cy * 1;

    CString msg;
    msg.Format("%ld bytes", dwBytes);
    pCmdUI->SetText(msg);
}
```

6. Add a status bar to CChildFrame. Use the add member variable dialog to add this member to *CChildFrame*.

Type	Declaration	Access
CStatusBar	m_bar	protected

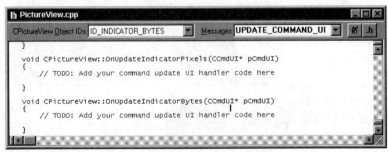

Figure 2-16 Status Bar pane IDs in the WizardBar

2.4
ADD A STATUS BAR TO MY VIEWS

7. Use the WizardBar to add a handler for WM_CREATE in CChildFrame.
We'll create the new status bar while handling the WM_CREATE message. Edit the *CChildFrame::OnCreate* code as follows:

```
static UINT BASED_CODE indicators[] =
{
        ID_INDICATOR_PIXELS,
        ID_INDICATOR_BYTES
};

int CChildFrame::OnCreate(LPCREATESTRUCT lpCreateStruct)
{
        if (CMDIChildWnd::OnCreate(lpCreateStruct) == -1)
                return -1;

        // If you pass AFX_IDW_STATUS_BAR instead of 101 as the ID, the status bar
        // can be toggled through the View Status Bar menu.
        m_bar.Create(this, WS_CHILD | WS_VISIBLE | CBRS_BOTTOM, 101);
        m_bar.SetIndicators (indicators, sizeof(indicators)/sizeof(UINT));

        return 0;
}
```

8. Build and test the application. Open a couple of 256-color bitmaps. The status bar for each view should show the bitmap dimensions in pixels and the total size in bytes.

How It Works

In an MDI application, *CView* objects are contained in a child window, usually *CChildFrame*. However, this default child window doesn't support status bars. In steps 6 and 7, we added a *CStatusBar* member and created it during WM_CREATE.

Once *CChildFrame* embeds the status bar in its client area, the view can update the status bar panes just like it would update the main frame panes—through ON_UPDATE_COMMAND_UI. The two new methods in *CPictureView*, *OnUpdateIndicatorPixels* and *OnUpdateIndicatorBytes*, use *pCmdUI* to set the text for the status bar. Note that the parent frame, *CChildFrame*, didn't need to expose its *m_bar* member variable directly to the view in order for the view to set the pane text.

Comments

The first edition version of this application didn't use ON_UPDATE_COMMAND_UI handlers to update the status bar. Instead it relied on a private MFC message WM_SETMESSAGESTRING. For example, to set the first pane in the status bar during a mouse down event, you could add this:

```
void CPictureView::OnLButtonDown(UINT nFlags, CPoint point)
{
        GetParentFrame()->SendMessage(WM_SETMESSAGESTRING, IDS_TEST_STRING);
}
```

WM_SETMESSAGESTRING is sent to the frame window to ask it to update the message line in the status bar. Since the message is private to MFC, you need to include AFXPRIV.H in PictureView.cpp.

The default handler for WM_SETMESSAGESTRING lives in *CFrameWnd::OnSetMessageString* in the file Winfrm.cpp. The first line in this function calls *GetMessageBar*, a *CFrameWnd* virtual method. The code for *CMDIChildFrame::GetMessageBar* looks like this:

```
CWnd* CMDIChildWnd::GetMessageBar()
{
    // status bar/message bar owned by parent MDI frame
    return GetMDIFrame()->GetMessageBar();
}
```

It simply asks the MDI frame window for *its* status bar. So, if you want WM_SETMESSAGESTRING to work for child frames, you have to write your own *GetMessageBar* that returns the child's status bar, not the main frame's status bar. Here's the code:

```
CWnd* CChildWnd::GetMessageBar()
{
    return &m_bar;
}
```

Microsoft Technical Note #24 explains this message and others like it used in the MFC framework.

With very little change, this sample code can be used to add a toolbar to a child window. Simply add a *CToolBar* member variable to *CChildFrame* and create it in *CChildFrame::OnCreate*. Use the toolbar creation code that AppWizard generated in MainFrm.cpp as a guide.

COMPLEXITY
INTERMEDIATE

2.5 How do I... Display a progress meter in the status bar?

Problem

How do I display progress information, such as what percent of an operation is complete, in the status bar? How can I turn one of the text panes into a Windows progress control?

2.5
DISPLAY A PROGRESS METER IN THE STATUS BAR

Technique

If we create our own *CStatusBarCtrl* called *CMeterBar*, it's easy to add a few methods that turn one of the panes into a progress meter. During a lengthy operation, you can periodically call a *CMeterBar* method to update the meter with the current percentage. The last pane in the status bar will be designated as a "meter pane" and will contain a *CProgressCtrl* object (See Figure 2-17). The embedded meter control is repositioned during *CMeterBar::OnSize* so it fits inside the last pane's bounding rectangle.

Steps

1. Create a new project called ProgressMeter using the MFC AppWizard (exe). Turn off the option for a status bar in step 4 since we'll be adding our own. The application should also be SDI instead of the default MDI.

Classes to be created:
    Application: CProgressMeterApp in ProgressMeter.h and ProgressMeter.cpp
    Frame: CMainFrame in MainFrm.h and MainFrm.cpp
    Document: CProgressMeterDoc in ProgressMeterDoc.h and ProgressMeterDoc.cpp
    View: CProgressMeterView in ProgressMeterView.h and ProgressMeterView.cpp

Features:
    + Initial toolbar in main frame
    + Printing and Print Preview support in view
    + 3D Controls
    + Uses shared DLL implementation (MFC40.DLL)

2. Create a new class called CMeterBar. Use ClassWizard to create a new class using the following information:

    Class name: CMeterBar
    Base class: CStatusBarCtrl
    File: MeterBar.cpp

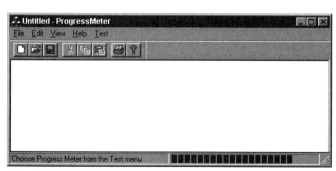

Figure 2-17 Progress pane in status bar

CHAPTER 2
STATUS BARS AND TOOLBARS

3. **Edit MeterBar.h.** Add a member variable for the progress meter and a public method to retrieve the control:

```
class CMeterBar : public CStatusBarCtrl
{
// Construction
public:
        CMeterBar();

// Attributes
public:
        CProgressCtrl& GetProgressCtrl()
                { return m_meter; }

// Implementation
public:
        virtual ~CMeterBar();

        // Generated message map functions
protected:
        //{{AFX_MSG(CMeterBar)
        //}}AFX_MSG
        DECLARE_MESSAGE_MAP()

        CProgressCtrl m_meter;
};
```

4. **Use the WizardBar to handle WM_CREATE for CMeterBar.** Add the following code:

```
int CMeterBar::OnCreate(LPCREATESTRUCT lpCreateStruct)
{
        if (CStatusBarCtrl::OnCreate(lpCreateStruct) == -1)
                return -1;

        m_meter.Create(WS_CHILD | WS_VISIBLE, CRect(0,0,0,0), this, 101);
        m_meter.SetRange(0, 10);
        m_meter.SetPos(0);
        m_meter.SetStep(1);

        return 0;
}
```

This code creates the embedded progress meter and sets some default parameters for the control.

5. **Use the WizardBar to handle WM_SIZE for CMeterBar.** Add the following code:

```
void CMeterBar::OnSize(UINT nType, int cx, int cy)
{
        CStatusBarCtrl::OnSize(nType, cx, cy);

        // Assume the last pane in the control is used for the meter
        int nTemp;
        int nCount = GetParts(0, &nTemp);
```

2.5
DISPLAY A PROGRESS METER IN THE STATUS BAR

```
    if (nCount > 0)
    {
        CRect r;
        GetRect(nCount - 1, r);
        m_meter.MoveWindow(r);
    }
}
```

Every time the status bar is resized, we have to move the embedded progress meter by hand.

6. Modify the IDR_MAINFRAME menu. Add a new menu item called "Test" and a submenu labeled "Meter Bar". Use ClassWizard to attach the submenu to a new method in *CMainFrame* called *OnTestMeterBar*. Add these other message handlers as well:

Object ID	Message	Function
ID_TEST_METERBAR	COMMAND	OnTestMeterBar
CMainFrame	WM_TIMER	OnTimer
CMainFrame	WM_SIZE	OnSize

7. Add member variables to CMainFrame. Use the add member variable dialog to add a member variable for the new status bar:

Type	Declaration	Access
CMeterBar	m_wndStatusBar	protected

Also edit MainFrm.h and add this include at the top of the file:

```
#include "MeterBar.h"
```

8. Modify CMainFrame::OnCreate. Add these lines to create the meter bar:

```
int CMainFrame::OnCreate(LPCREATESTRUCT lpCreateStruct)
{
    if (CFrameWnd::OnCreate(lpCreateStruct) == -1)
        return -1;

    if (!m_wndToolBar.Create(this) ||
        !m_wndToolBar.LoadToolBar(IDR_MAINFRAME))
    {
        TRACE0("Failed to create toolbar\n");
        return -1;      // fail to create
    }

    m_wndToolBar.SetBarStyle(m_wndToolBar.GetBarStyle() |
        CBRS_TOOLTIPS | CBRS_FLYBY | CBRS_SIZE_DYNAMIC);

    m_wndToolBar.EnableDocking(CBRS_ALIGN_ANY);
    EnableDocking(CBRS_ALIGN_ANY);
    DockControlBar(&m_wndToolBar);
```

continued on next page

CHAPTER 2
STATUS BARS AND TOOLBARS

continued from previous page

```
    m_wndMeterBar.Create (WS_CHILD | WS_BORDER | WS_VISIBLE |
        CCS_BOTTOM | SBARS_SIZEGRIP,
        CRect(0, 0, 0, 0), this, 101);

    int aWidths[2] = {0, 0};
    m_wndMeterBar.SetParts (2, aWidths);
    m_wndMeterBar.SetText ("Choose Meter Bar from the Test menu", 0, 0);
    m_wndMeterBar.SetText ("", 1, SBT_NOBORDERS);

    return 0;
}
```

9. **Code the OnTestMeterBar function.** This code is executed when the user chooses the Meter Test command from the menu:

```
void CMainFrame::OnTestMeterBar()
{
    SetTimer(1, 500, NULL);
}
```

This simply starts a half-second timer that's used to trigger the update of the status bar.

10. **Code the OnTimer function.** This code is executed every half second in response to a WM_TIMER message sent by Windows. For this example, we're updating the meter progress by 10 percent each time by stepping the control to the next increment. When we reach 100 percent, the timer is killed, and the meter is set to 0 to clear the pane.

```
void CMainFrame::OnTimer(UINT nIDEvent)
{
    static int nCount = 0;
    m_wndMeterBar. GetProgressCtrl().StepIt();

    if (++nCount == 10)
    {
        nCount = 0;
        KillTimer(1);
        m_wndMeterBar. GetProgressCtrl().SetPos(0);
    }
}
```

11. **Code the OnSize function.** When the user resizes the app, we have to layout the panes manually. In this case, the space is split evenly between the left and right panes. It's important to put the *SetParts* call before passing the WM_SIZE message to the status bar.

```
void CMainFrame::OnSize(UINT nType, int cx, int cy)
{
    CFrameWnd::OnSize(nType, cx, cy);

    if (m_wndMeterBar.GetSafeHwnd())
    {
        int aWidths[2] = {cx/2, -1};
```

2.6 PUT BITMAPS IN THE STATUS BAR USING AN IMAGE LIST

```
        m_wndMeterBar.SetParts(2, aWidths);

        m_wndMeterBar.SendMessage(WM_SIZE, nType, MAKELONG(cy, cx));
    }
}
```

12. Build and test the program. Under the Test menu, select Meter Bar and watch the first pane in the status bar change as the timer elapses.

How It Works

Think of the *CMeterBar* class as a *CStatusBarCtrl* with its own *CProgressCtrl* that just happens to follow the last pane. That is, whenever the meter bar is resized, the progress meter moves on top of the last pane.

CMeterBar captures the WM_SIZE message and asks itself how many panes are present. *GetParts* returns the number of panes, and *GetRect* returns the client coordinates of the last pane rectangle. *CMeterBar* moves the progress control to the same rectangle.

CMeterBar::GetProgressCtrl gives the owner of the meter bar a convenient method for accessing the embedded progress control. *CMainFrame* uses the standard progress meter methods like *StepIt* and *SetPos* when the timer messages fire. Remember, we added code in step 10 to start a timer when a menu option was chosen. A static variable keeps track of the number of times the timer fires. When it reaches ten, *CMainFrame* kills the timer and resets the progress control.

Comments

The first edition version subclassed *CStatusBar* instead of *CStatusBarCtrl*. That technique overrode *CStatusBar::DoPaint* to fake a progress meter by inverting part of the rectangle used to paint the pane. This newer technique gives us access to all the features supported by the Windows progress control.

If you're unclear on the differences between *CStatusBar* and *CStatusBarCtrl* and the appropriate uses of each, read the Microsoft Technote #60 in the InfoViewer.

COMPLEXITY
INTERMEDIATE

2.6 How do I...
Put bitmaps in the status bar using an image list?

Problem

It is a fairly simple matter to add text to any of the individual panes in a status bar by using the *SetWindowText* or *SetPaneText* member functions. However, the *CStatusBar* class provides no built-in member functions for drawing bitmaps in the status bar.

CHAPTER 2
STATUS BARS AND TOOLBARS

Technique

For this How-To, we're going to create a *CStatusBarCtrl* window and attach it to the MDI client. One of its panes will be marked with the status bar style SBT_OWNERDRAW using the *CStatusBarCtrl::SetText* method. However, once you mark a pane with this style, Windows will start sending the status bar WM_DRAWITEM messages, which the standard implementation doesn't understand (actually, the *CStatusBarCtrl* version simply ASSERTS). So we'll use ClassWizard to create our own version called *CBmpBarCtrl* that paints a bitmap in the last pane.

To make things a little more interesting, we'll use the *CImageList* control to manage the bitmaps. Not only can we use the toolbar editor to create our image list, but *CImageList::Draw* also handles transparency so we can place the bitmaps we draw on any color background. The finished application is shown in Figure 2-18.

Steps

1. **Create a new project called BmpPane using the MFC AppWizard (exe).**
   Click the option for a single-document application, then press the Finish button.

   Classes to be created:

Application:	CBmpPane in BmpPane.h and BmpPane.cpp
Frame:	CMainFrame in MainFrm.h and MainFrm.cpp
Document:	CBmpPaneDoc in BmpPaneDoc.h and BmpPaneDoc.cpp
View:	CBmpPaneView in BmpPaneView.h and BmpPaneView.cpp

   Features:
   + Initial toolbar in main frame
   + Initial status bar in main frame
   + Printing and Print Preview support in view
   + 3D Controls
   + Uses shared DLL implementation (MFC40.DLL)

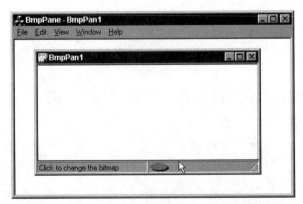

Figure 2-18 Displaying bitmaps in a status bar pane

2.6
PUT BITMAPS IN THE STATUS BAR USING AN IMAGE LIST

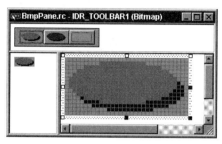

Figure 2-19 Red and green buttons

2. **Create a new toolbar control.** Switch to ResourceView and bring up the context menu for the Toolbar. Select "Insert Toolbar" from the pop-up menu. Next, display the property page for the toolbar by pressing the key combination [ALT]-[ENTER]. Change the width to 32 pixels. Now add two new toolbar buttons, a green and red circle, like the ones shown in Figure 2-19.

Although you won't see it in the Bitmap section, the toolbar editor saves a single bitmap called IDR_TOOLBAR1 in the resource file. Open BmpPane.rc as a text file and search for IDR_TOOLBAR1 if you want to see how App Studio saves the toolbar information.

3. **Create a new class called CBmpBarCtrl.** Use ClassWizard to create a new class using the following information:

   Class name: CBmpBarCtrl
   Base class: CStatusBarCtrl
   File: BmpBarCtrl.cpp

4. **Edit BmpBarCtrl.h.** You're going to add an image list to the view control in a later step. To paint the bitmaps, the status bar needs a pointer to that image list.

```
class CBmpBarCtrl : public CStatusBarCtrl
{
// Construction
public:
        CBmpBarCtrl();

// Attributes
public:
        void SetImageList(CImageList* pList)
                { m_pList = pList; }
        CImageList* m_pList;

// Implementation
public:
        virtual ~CBmpBarCtrl();
```

continued on next page

CHAPTER 2
STATUS BARS AND TOOLBARS

continued from previous page
```
        // Generated message map functions
protected:
        virtual void DrawItem(LPDRAWITEMSTRUCT lpDrawItemStruct);
        //{{AFX_MSG(CBmpBarCtrl)
        //}}AFX_MSG

        DECLARE_MESSAGE_MAP()
};
```

   5. Initialize the pointer in the constructor. Edit the *CBmpBarCtrl* constructor and set the pointer to the image list to NULL:

```
CBmpBarCtrl::CBmpBarCtrl()
{
        m_pList = NULL;
}
```

   6. Use the WizardBar to add *CChildFrame::OnGetMinMaxInfo*. Add the following code:

```
void CBmpBarCtrl::DrawItem(LPDRAWITEMSTRUCT lpDrawItemStruct)
{
        if (m_pList == NULL)
                return;

        // the item data added as the string in Add() refers should
        // refer to a valid index in m_pList
        int nIndex = lpDrawItemStruct->itemData;
        ASSERT(nIndex < m_pList->GetImageCount());

        // Turn the HDC into a CDC object
        CDC* pdcDest = CDC::FromHandle(lpDrawItemStruct->hDC);

        // Draw the bitmap transparently
        CPoint pt(lpDrawItemStruct->rcItem.left, lpDrawItemStruct->rcItem.top);
        m_pList->Draw(pdcDest, nIndex, pt, ILD_TRANSPARENT);
}
```

   7. Edit ChildFrm.h. Add the following lines to the top of the *CChildFrame* header file:

```
#include "BmpBarCtrl.h"

class CChildFrame : public CMDIChildWnd
{
        DECLARE_DYNCREATE(CChildFrame)
public:
        CChildFrame();

// Attributes
public:
        CBmpBarCtrl& GetStatusBar()
                {  return m_bar; }

        CBmpBarCtrl m_bar;
...
```

94

2.6
PUT BITMAPS IN THE STATUS BAR USING AN IMAGE LIST

8. **Use the WizardBar to handle WM_CREATE for CChildFrame.** Add the following code:

```
int CChildFrame::OnCreate(LPCREATESTRUCT lpCreateStruct)
{
        if (CMDIChildWnd::OnCreate(lpCreateStruct) == -1)
                return -1;

        m_bar.Create (WS_CHILD | WS_BORDER | WS_VISIBLE | CCS_BOTTOM | ⇒
SBARS_SIZEGRIP,
                CRect(0, 0, 0, 0), this, AFX_IDW_STATUS_BAR);

        int aWidths[4] = {0, 0};
        m_bar.SetParts (2, aWidths);
        m_bar.SetText ("Click to change the bitmap", 0, 0);
        m_bar.SetText ((LPCSTR) (DWORD) 0, 1, SBT_OWNERDRAW);

        return 0;
}
```

This code creates the status bar and sets up two panes: one for text and the other for the bitmaps.

9. **Use the WizardBar to handle WM_SIZE for CChildFrame.** Add the following code:

```
void CChildFrame::OnSize(UINT nType, int cx, int cy)
{
        CMDIChildWnd::OnSize(nType, cx, cy);

        if (m_bar.GetSafeHwnd() == NULL)
                return;

        int aWidths[4] = {cx/2, -1};
        m_bar.SetParts(2, aWidths);
        m_bar.MoveWindow(0, cy-10, cx, cy);
}
```

This code resizes the panes equally so they split the available real estate. The first pane's right edge is half the width of the client area (cx/2) and the other pane gets what's left over (signified by –1).

10. **Add a member variable to CBmpPaneView.** Use the add member variable dialog to add the variable that holds the two bitmaps created in step 2:

Type	Declaration	Access
CImageList	m_list	protected

11. **Use the WizardBar to add CBmpPaneView::OnInitialUpdate.** Here we create the image list using the toolbar image from step 2. Then we ask the parent frame (which better be a *CChildFrame*) for a reference to the *CBmpBarCtrl*. The

95

address of *m_list* is passed to the bar through *SetImageList* for use later in drawing. Add this code:

```
void CBmpPaneView::OnInitialUpdate()
{
    CView::OnInitialUpdate();

    VERIFY(m_List.Create (IDR_TOOLBAR1, 32, 1, RGB(192, 192, 192)));

    CChildFrame* pFrame = ((CChildFrame *) GetParentFrame());
    ASSERT(pFrame->IsKindOf(RUNTIME_CLASS(CChildFrame)));
    CBmpBarCtrl& bar = pFrame->GetStatusBar();

    bar.SetImageList(&m_List);

    // Fake an OnLButtonDown to toggle the status bar bitmap
    OnLButtonDown(0, CPoint(0, 0));
}
```

12. **Use the WizardBar to handle WM_LBUTTONDOWN for CBmpPaneView.**

Finally, add the following code that toggles between the two bitmaps:

```
void CBmpPaneView::OnLButtonDown(UINT nFlags, CPoint point)
{
    CChildFrame* pFrame = ((CChildFrame *) GetParentFrame());
    ASSERT(pFrame->IsKindOf(RUNTIME_CLASS(CChildFrame)));

    CStatusBarCtrl& bar = pFrame->GetStatusBar();

    // Keep a variable to toggle between the first two images
    // in the image list.
    static UINT nID = 0;
    nID = (nID == 0) ? 1 : 0;

    // Change the index for the second pane and force a repaint
    bar.SetText((LPCSTR) (DWORD) nID, 1, SBT_OWNERDRAW);
}
```

13. **Build and run the app.** If you press the mouse button anywhere in the view, the bitmap pane should toggle between the red and green ovals.

How It Works

The first version of this program used two separate bitmaps instead of the *CImageList*. However, the bitmap pane looked terrible because the oval bitmaps had a white background, while the status bar pane had a gray background. Once you have figured out that the toolbar is just a fancier bitmap editor, you can convert the code to the *CImageList*.

The transparency effect works because we specified a background color when the image list was created in *CBmpPaneView::OnInitialUpdate* (see step 10). The default background color in the toolbar editor is light gray, the same color passed as the last argument to *CImageList::Create*.

2.7
PUT LINE AND COLUMN INDICATORS ON THE STATUS BAR

The other arguments to *CImageList::Create* tell the image list where to find the bitmap (IDR_TOOLBAR1) and how big each individual bitmap is. Although you create each toolbar button separately, they're all stored side by side in one long bitmap. Each individual bitmap is 32 pixels wide, but the whole bitmap is 64 pixels wide.

CImageList assigns the first bitmap an index value of 0, and the second bitmap to 1. Since we're allowed to pass any old DWORD value to *SetText* when we use the SBT_OWNERDRAW style, we simply pass the bitmap index value. Later on, in *CBmpBarCtrl::DrawItem,* the DWORD value is interpreted as the index into the image list. The image list *Draw* method takes care of painting the correct image with transparency into the bitmap pane.

Comments

This technique focused on modifying the Windows status bar, *CStatusBarCtrl*, instead of the MFC status bar, *CStatusBar.* If you wish to draw a bitmap in the MFC status bar, please read the article in Books Online titled "Displaying a Bitmap in a CStatusBar Pane." It tells you how to override the *CStatusBar* method *DoPaint*. It's a bit messy, and I'm not sure it would even work in MFC 4.0 since *CStatusBar* now uses the Windows control to handle the status bar, instead of its own code. The How-To in the first edition of *Visual C++ How-To* used the approach outlined in this article.

COMPLEXITY
INTERMEDIATE

2.7 How do I...
Put line and column indicators on the status bar?

Problem

Most text editors and word processors show you the line and column position of the cursor as you type. I'm using the *CEditView* class as a simple text editor and want to show the current line and column in the status bar. Is there an easy way to do this?

Technique

Like the *CEdit* class, *CEditView* provides the functionality of a standard Windows edit control. In addition to simple multiline text editing, *CEditView* gives you printing, find and replace dialogs, and clipboard support—all wrapped up in an easy-to-use *CView*-style class. We'll extend the usefulness of *CEditView* by deriving our own class, *CLinePositionView*. This will include methods to display the current line and column position of the cursor (or caret) in the status bar, as shown in Figure 2-20.

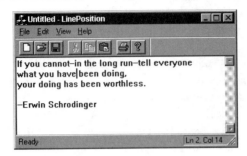

Figure 2-20 Line and column indicators

Adding a new pane to the status bar is well documented in the MFC help files. But when do you update the caret information in the pane? Every time the status bar needs updating, MFC automatically calls a special function you've specified as the update command method. This method, *OnUpdateCaretPos*, simply queries the *CEdit* control for its current position and sets the pane text with that information.

We'll write a helper function, *CLinePositionView::GetCaretPosition,* that returns the current line and column position of the caret.

Steps

1. **Create a new project called LinePosition using the MFC AppWizard (exe).** Click the option for a single-document application. In the final step, change the base class for *CLinePositionView* to *CEditView*.

    Classes to be created:
    Application: CLinePositionApp in LinePosition.h and LinePosition.cpp
    Frame: CMainFrame in MainFrm.h and MainFrm.cpp
    Document: CLinePositionDoc in LinePositionDoc.h and LinePositionDoc.cpp
    EditView: CLinePositionView in LinePositionView.h and LinePositionView.cpp

    Features:
    + Initial toolbar in main frame
    + Initial status bar in main frame
    + Printing and Print Preview support in view
    + 3D Controls
    + Uses shared DLL implementation (MFC40.DLL)

2. **Use App Studio to edit the string resource table.** Select any string table segment, and then add a new string with ID_INDICATOR_CARET as its ID and "Ln 999, Col 999" as its caption. *CStatusBar* uses the caption as both the default pane text and the determinant of initial pane width. The caption will be replaced by the actual line and column position.

2.7
PUT LINE AND COLUMN INDICATORS ON THE STATUS BAR

3. Edit the MainFrm.cpp file. Change the original *indicators* array to the following:

```
static UINT indicators[] =
{
        ID_SEPARATOR,              // first message line pane
        ID_INDICATOR_CARET,        // caret position pane
};
```

Remove the three entries that display the keyboard state.

4. Add the following function prototypes to LinePositionView.h. You must add this message-handling prototype manually because ClassWizard doesn't recognize the associated command message ID. Add the message-handling statement inside the AFX_MSG so ClassWizard will let you access and edit the code later.

```
// Generated message map functions
protected:
        //{{AFX_MSG(CLinePositionView)
        afx_msg void OnUpdateCaretPos(CCmdUI* pCmdUI);
        //}}AFX_MSG
        DECLARE_MESSAGE_MAP()
```

Also, add a helper function prototype that will be used by *OnUpdateCaretPos* under the Operations public section.

```
// Operations
public:
        void GetCaretPosition(int& nLine, int& nCol);
```

5. Edit LinePositionView.cpp. Add the following message map entries for class *CLinePositionView*. Again, ClassWizard can't add these for you because it doesn't recognize the string ID_INDICATOR_CARET as an object ID.

```
ON_UPDATE_COMMAND_UI(ID_INDICATOR_CARET, OnUpdateCaretPos)
```

Next, add the *UpdateCaretPos* method that updates the status indicator. The application framework calls this function whenever the status bar pane needs updating.

```
void CLinePositionView::OnUpdateCaretPos(CCmdUI* pCmdUI)
{
        // Get the current caret position from the helper function, then
        // format it into a string for the status bar.

        int nLine, nCol;
        GetCaretPosition(nLine, nCol);

        CString str;
        str.Format("Ln %d, Col %d", nLine, nCol);

        pCmdUI->Enable(TRUE);
        pCmdUI->SetText(str);
}
```

CHAPTER 2
STATUS BARS AND TOOLBARS

Finally, add the helper function to return the line and column position of the caret from the embedded *CEdit* control.

```cpp
void CLinePositionView::GetCaretPosition(int& nLine, int& nCol)
{
    static int oldStart = -1, oldEnd = -1;
    static enum Direction { left, right } oldDir = right;

    CEdit& theEdit = GetEditCtrl();

    // If text has been selected with the mouse, determine
    // the direction of the selection. If the user is dragging
    // to the right, the character of interest is at the end
    // of the selection. Likewise, a leftward selection means
    // we want the starting character.
    // We have to keep track of the last selection to determine
    // the current selection state.
    // If no characters are selected, newStart will equal newEnd.

    Direction newDir = right;
    int newStart, newEnd, nCurrent;
    theEdit.GetSel(newStart, newEnd);

    if ( (newEnd == oldEnd) && (newStart == oldStart))
        newDir = oldDir;
    else if (oldStart == newStart)
        newDir = right;
    else if (oldEnd == newEnd)
        newDir = left;
    else if (oldStart == newEnd)
        newDir = left;
    else if (oldEnd == newStart)
        newDir = right;

    if (newDir == right)
        nCurrent = newEnd;
    else
        nCurrent = newStart;

    oldStart = newStart;
    oldEnd = newEnd;
    oldDir = newDir;

    // Determine the current line based on the current character in
    // the selection. Add one since LineFromChar is zero-based.
    nLine = theEdit.LineFromChar(nCurrent) + 1;

    // nLineIndex is the zero-based index of the first character in
    // the nLine line.
    int nLineIndex = theEdit.LineIndex(nLine-1);

    // The caret column position is the line index subtracted from
    // the current position from GetSel.
    nCol = nCurrent - nLineIndex + 1;
}
```

2.7 PUT LINE AND COLUMN INDICATORS ON THE STATUS BAR

6. **Build and test the application.** As you type, observe that the rightmost status bar pane reflects the current position of the caret. Also, try selecting some text with the mouse. As you're dragging the mouse to the right, notice that the character at the end of the selection appears in the status bar. As you drag to the left, the leftmost character in the selection appears in the pane.

How It Works

It's fairly straightforward to add your own pane and UI command handler to the status bar. Since we've placed the command handler *OnUpdateCaretPos* in the view instead of the main frame, each edit window in an MDI application can have a different caret position. The hard part is determining just where the caret is.

If you make a drag selection with the mouse or keyboard, you want the indicator pane to display the most useful information. If the selection is moving down or to the right, the trailing end of the selection (represented by *nEnd*) is the one of interest. In a selection moving up or to the left, the starting point of the selection (*nStart*) is the one of interest.

Since there's no easy way to determine the direction of the selection, we have to do some tricky work. Using a couple of static variables, we can remember the position of the last selection. By comparing the old or previous selection with the new one, *OnUpdateCaretPos* determines the direction of the current selection. The direction (left or right) is used to pick the important character position (*nStart* or *nEnd*). Table 2-2 summarizes the cases tested before the *nStart* or *nEnd* character is used.

TEST CODE	OLD SELECTION	NEW SELECTION	RESULT
(newEnd == oldEnd) && (newStart == oldStart)	ABCDEF newDir = oldDir;	ABCDEF	Nothing has changed in the selection since last time. Use the old direction.
(oldStart == newStart)	ABCDEF newDir = right;	ABCDEF	The starting position hasn't changed, so we're moving to the right.
(oldEnd == newEnd)	ABCDEF newDir = left;	ABCDEF	The ending position hasn't changed, so we're moving to the left.
(oldStart == newEnd)	ABCDEF newDir = left;	ABCDEF	The selection has flipped directions over the starting point to the left.

continued on next page

continued from previous page

TEST CODE	OLD SELECTION	NEW SELECTION	RESULT
(oldEnd == newStart)	ABCDEF	ABCDEF	The selection has flipped
	newDir = right;		directions over the starting
			point to the right.

 Table 2-2 State table for text section

Comments

As long as the user is typing or moving the caret with the arrow keys, it's easy to determine the location of the caret. If we didn't care about updating the status bar correctly when more than one character was selected, we could have used this shorter piece of code (don't type this in):

```
void CTestView::GetCaretPosition(int& nLine, int& nCol)
{
    CEdit& theEdit = GetEditCtrl();

    // LineFromChar with no parameters returns the current line
    nLine = theEdit.LineFomChar() + 1;

    // To determine the column position, we use a combination of
    // GetSel and LineIndex. nStart and nEnd are equal if no
    // characters are selected.
    int nStart, nEnd;
    theEdit.GetSel(nStart, nEnd);

    // nLineIndex is the zero-based index of the first character in
    // the nLine line.
    int nLineIndex = theEdit.LineIndex(nLine-1);

    // The caret column position is the line index subtracted from
    // the current position from GetSel.
    nCol = nStart - nLineIndex + 1;
}
```

This code assumes *nStart* equals *nEnd*. In other words, it only works as long as the user doesn't select more than one character with the mouse.

2.8 How do I... Customize a toolbar for display in a dialog?

COMPLEXITY
ADVANCED

Problem

Toolbars and status bars are great—if you're an MDI or SDI application. How can I put a toolbar in a *dialog* and still have access to all the normal toolbar features, like tooltips and the toolbar editor.

Technique

First we'll create a new class called *CMyToolBar* which is derived from *CToolBarCtrl* instead of *CToolBar*. Because *CToolBar* normally handles all the tooltip notification messages, we'll have to add the same support to *CMyToolBar*. *CToolBarCtrl*, the wrapper class for the new Windows toolbar, doesn't support the cool toolbar editor in MFC. That's no problem. We'll simply copy the code that parses those resources straight from the MFC source code into *CMyToolBar*.

Now, to use the toolbar, all we have to do is call two methods in the dialog's WM_INITDIALOG handler. Then, just to prove it's working, we'll pop up a message box when one of the buttons is clicked. The working version looks like the dialog shown in Figure 2-21.

Steps

1. **Create a dialog-based application called BarDialog using the MFC AppWizard (exe).** Make sure you choose the option for a dialog-based application in the first step.

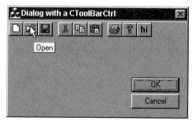

Figure 2-21 A dialog with a toolbar

CHAPTER 2
STATUS BARS AND TOOLBARS

Classes to be created:
Application: CBarDialogApp in BarDialog.h and BarDialog.cpp
Dialog: CBarDialogDlg in BarDialogDlg.h and BarDialogDlg.cpp

Features:
+ About box on system menu
+ 3D Controls
+ Uses shared DLL implementation (MFC40.DLL)

2. **Copy a toolbar resource.** Unless you're a good artist, locate any MDI or SDI application generated with AppWizard and copy its IDR_MAINFRAME toolbar resource. First, switch to the ResourceView for our project, then simply open the other application's RC file using File Open. Hold down the Control key, then drag-and-drop the IDR_MAINFRAME toolbar resource into the ResouceView window.

3. **Add another toolbar button.** Just for fun, add another button at the end of our new toolbar resouce with the text "HI" (Hint: Use the text tool to turn text into bitmapped art). Call this last button ID_HI and type "Hello dialog\nHi" as the prompt. My toolbar looks like the one shown in Figure 2-22.

4. **Create a new class called CMyToolBar.** Use ClassWizard to create a new class using the following information:

Class name: CMyToolBar
Base class: CToolBarCtrl
File: MyToolBar.cpp

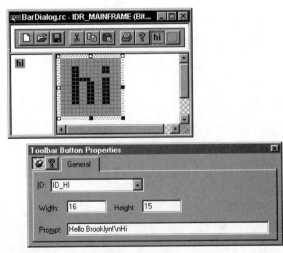

Figure 2-22 Adding a button to the toolbar

2.8
CUSTOMIZE A TOOLBAR FOR DISPLAY IN A DIALOG

5. Edit MyToolBar.h. Add all this code to MyToolBar.h. We're adding methods to support the toolbar editor resource and tooltips.

```
class CMyToolBar : public CToolBarCtrl
{
// Construction
public:
        CMyToolBar();

// Operations
public:
        BOOL LoadToolBar(UINT nIDResource);

// Overrides
        // ClassWizard generated virtual function overrides
        //{{AFX_VIRTUAL(CMyToolBar)
        //}}AFX_VIRTUAL

// Implementation
public:
        virtual ~CMyToolBar();

        // Generated message map functions
protected:
        //{{AFX_MSG(CMyToolBar)
        //}}AFX_MSG
        afx_msg void OnNeedText(NMHDR * pNotifyStruct, LRESULT* result);
        DECLARE_MESSAGE_MAP()

        BOOL SetButtons(const UINT* lpIDArray, int nIDCount);
};
```

6. Edit MyToolBar.cpp. We're going to add all the code for *CMyToolBar* in one big step, so warm up your hands and start typing.

```
BEGIN_MESSAGE_MAP(CMyToolBar, CToolBarCtrl)
        //{{AFX_MSG_MAP(CMyToolBar)
        //}}AFX_MSG_MAP
        ON_NOTIFY(TTN_NEEDTEXT, 0, OnNeedText)
END_MESSAGE_MAP()

void CMyToolBar::OnNeedText(NMHDR * pNotifyStruct, LRESULT* result)
{
        LPTOOLTIPTEXT lpTipText = (LPTOOLTIPTEXT) pNotifyStruct;
        UINT nStringID = lpTipText->hdr.idFrom;

        TCHAR szFullText[256];
        CString strTipText;
        AfxLoadString(nStringID, szFullText);
        AfxExtractSubString(strTipText, szFullText, 1, '\n');

        strcpy(lpTipText->lpszText, strTipText);

        *result = TRUE;
}
```

continued on next page

CHAPTER 2
STATUS BARS AND TOOLBARS

continued from previous page

```cpp
// The rest of the code is mostly from BARTOOL.cpp with a few modifications.

// Use this data structure to help parse the toolbar resource.
struct CToolBarData
{
        WORD wVersion;
        WORD wWidth;
        WORD wHeight;
        WORD wItemCount;
        //WORD aItems[wItemCount]

        WORD* items()
              { return (WORD*)(this+1); }
};

BOOL CMyToolBar::LoadToolBar(UINT nIDResource)
{
        ASSERT_VALID(this);
        ASSERT(nIDResource != 0);

        // determine location of the bitmap in resource fork
        HINSTANCE hInst = AfxGetInstanceHandle();
        HRSRC hRsrc = ::FindResource(hInst, MAKEINTRESOURCE(nIDResource),
               RT_TOOLBAR);
        if (hRsrc == NULL)
              return FALSE;

        HGLOBAL hGlobal = LoadResource(hInst, hRsrc);
        if (hGlobal == NULL)
              return FALSE;

        CToolBarData* pData = (CToolBarData*)LockResource(hGlobal);
        if (pData == NULL)
              return FALSE;
        ASSERT(pData->wVersion == 1);

        // Load the bitmap
        if (AddBitmap(pData->wItemCount, nIDResource) == -1)
        {
              UnlockResource(hGlobal);
              FreeResource(hGlobal);
              return FALSE;
        }

        UINT* pItems = new UINT[pData->wItemCount];
        for (int i = 0; i < pData->wItemCount; i++)
              pItems[i] = pData->items()[i];
        BOOL bResult = SetButtons(pItems, pData->wItemCount);
        delete[] pItems;

        if (bResult)
        {
              CSize sizeImage(pData->wWidth, pData->wHeight);
              CSize sizeButton(pData->wWidth + 7, pData->wHeight + 7);
```

2.8
CUSTOMIZE A TOOLBAR FOR DISPLAY IN A DIALOG

```
                SetBitmapSize(sizeImage);
                SetButtonSize(sizeButton);
        }

        UnlockResource(hGlobal);
        FreeResource(hGlobal);

        return bResult;
}

BOOL CMyToolBar::SetButtons(const UINT* lpIDArray, int nIDCount)
{
        ASSERT_VALID(this);
        ASSERT(nIDCount >= 1);   // must be at least one of them
        ASSERT(lpIDArray == NULL ||
                AfxIsValidAddress(lpIDArray, sizeof(UINT) * nIDCount, FALSE));

        // delete all existing buttons
        int nCount = GetButtonCount();
        while (nCountÑ)
                VERIFY(DeleteButton(0));

        if (lpIDArray != NULL)
        {
                // add new buttons to the common control
                TBBUTTON button; memset(&button, 0, sizeof(TBBUTTON));
                int iImage = 0;
                for (int i = 0; i < nIDCount; i++)
                {
                        button.fsState = TBSTATE_ENABLED;
                        if ((button.idCommand = *lpIDArray++) == 0)
                        {
                                // separator
                                button.fsStyle = TBSTYLE_SEP;
                                // width of separator includes 8 pixel overlap
                                button.iBitmap = 8;
                        }
                        else
                        {
                                // a command button with image
                                button.fsStyle = TBSTYLE_BUTTON;
                                button.iBitmap = iImage++;
                        }
                        if (!AddButtons(1, &button))
                                return FALSE;
                }
        }
        else
        {
                // add 'blank' buttons
                TBBUTTON button; memset(&button, 0, sizeof(TBBUTTON));
                button.fsState = TBSTATE_ENABLED;
                for (int i = 0; i < nIDCount; i++)
                {
```

continued on next page

CHAPTER 2
STATUS BARS AND TOOLBARS

continued from previous page

```
                        ASSERT(button.fsStyle == TBSTYLE_BUTTON);
                        if (!AddButtons(1, &button))
                                return FALSE;
                }
        }

        return TRUE;
}
```

Before you save this file, change the include directives to this (remove the #include "BarDialog.h"):

```
#include "stdafx.h"
#include <afxpriv.h>
#include "MyToolBar.h"
```

7. Add member variables to CBarDialogDlg. Add a member variable to hold the toolbar in the dialog (I know, *CBarDialogDlg* isn't the greatest class name).

Type	Declaration	Access
CMyToolBar	m_toolbar	protected

8. Edit BarDialogDlg.h. To appease the compiler gods, add this line to the top of BarDialogDlg.h:

```
#include "MyToolBar.h"
```

9. Edit CBarDialogDlg::OnInitDialog. Add the following code to the bottom of *OnInitDialog* to create the toolbar and load the bitmaps:

```
BOOL CBarDialogDlg::OnInitDialog()
{
        CDialog::OnInitDialog();

        // Add "About..." menu item to system menu.

        // IDM_ABOUTBOX must be in the system command range.
        ASSERT((IDM_ABOUTBOX & 0xFFF0) == IDM_ABOUTBOX);
        ASSERT(IDM_ABOUTBOX < 0xF000);

        CMenu* pSysMenu = GetSystemMenu(FALSE);
        CString strAboutMenu;
        strAboutMenu.LoadString(IDS_ABOUTBOX);
        if (!strAboutMenu.IsEmpty())
        {
                pSysMenu->AppendMenu(MF_SEPARATOR);
                pSysMenu->AppendMenu(MF_STRING, IDM_ABOUTBOX, strAboutMenu);
        }

        SetIcon(m_hIcon, TRUE);         // Set big icon
        SetIcon(m_hIcon, FALSE);        // Set small icon

        CRect r(0,0,0,0);
```

2.8
CUSTOMIZE A TOOLBAR FOR DISPLAY IN A DIALOG

```
    m_toolbar.Create(WS_BORDER | WS_VISIBLE | WS_CHILD
            | CCS_TOP | CCS_ADJUSTABLE | TBSTYLE_TOOLTIPS,
            r, this, IDR_MAINFRAME);
    m_toolbar.LoadToolBar(IDR_MAINFRAME);

    m_toolbar.AutoSize();

    return TRUE;
}
```

10. **Add the message handler for ID_HI.** Use the ClassView Add Function dialog to add the following method:

```
void CBarDialogDlg::OnHi(void)
```

11. **Edit BarDialogDlg.cpp.** Hook up the message handler and tell it to pop up a message box like this:

```
BEGIN_MESSAGE_MAP(CTestDlg, CDialog)
    //{{AFX_MSG_MAP(CTestDlg)
    ON_WM_SYSCOMMAND()
    ON_WM_PAINT()
    ON_WM_QUERYDRAGICON()
    ON_BN_CLICKED(ID_HI, OnHi)
    //}}AFX_MSG_MAP
END_MESSAGE_MAP()

void CTestDlg::OnHi()
{
    AfxMessageBox("Hello There");
}
```

12. **Reposition the OK and Cancel buttons.** If you run the app right now, the toolbar will cover up the OK button. Edit the dialog to move the OK and Cancel buttons to the bottom.

13. **Build and run the app.** You should see the standard MFC toolbar positioned at the top of the toolbar. Make sure tooltips work by leaving the mouse over one of the buttons for a few seconds. Also, click the last button labeled "hi" to make sure the message map works.

How It Works

All the interesting code is in the *CMyToolBar* class. The code in the dialog to create and load the toolbar is almost identical to the code used in a *CMainFrame* class. Our version differs slightly because dialogs don't support toolbar docking.

CMyToolBar adds two features that a normal Windows toolbar doesn't support. Our version loads toolbars from the toolbar resource (the custom resource created when you use the toolbar editor), and it handles the tooltip notification messages. If we didn't have the ability to parse the toolbar resource, you'd have to add about 20 lines of code to the dialog to load the bitmaps, set up the separator panes, set the button IDs, and so on.

LoadToolBar is pretty much an identical copy of the MFC version in BarTool.cpp. It first loads the toolbar resource into a private helper struct called *CToolBarData*. This structure contains the version or schema number of the toolbar resource, the width and height of each button, and the total number of buttons. More importantly, it contains a list of IDs to tag each bitmap in the toolbar. This is what the toolbar resource looks like in a Visual C++ 4.x RC file:

```
IDR_MAINFRAME TOOLBAR DISCARDABLE   16, 15
BEGIN
        BUTTON          ID_FILE_NEW
        BUTTON          ID_FILE_OPEN
        BUTTON          ID_FILE_SAVE
        SEPARATOR
        BUTTON          ID_EDIT_CUT
        BUTTON          ID_EDIT_COPY
        BUTTON          ID_EDIT_PASTE
        SEPARATOR
        BUTTON          ID_FILE_PRINT
        BUTTON          ID_APP_ABOUT
        BUTTON          ID_HI
END
```

We build up a list of button IDs to pass to the helper function *SetButtons*. Inside this function, all the button IDs and the appropriate styles are added to the *CToolBarCtrl*. If *SetButtons* was successful, we wrap up *LoadToolBar* by telling the Windows toolbar how big each image is and how big its containing button should be (in this case, 7 pixels wider and taller than each button image).

Now, to complete the support for the toolbar editor, we have to handle the prompt string. The file open button has a prompt string that looks like this:

```
Open an existing document\nOpen
```

We're only interested in the text after the carriage return ("Open"), since that's what should be displayed as the tooltip. But how do we handle the tooltip messages? This one took me a long time to figure out. Since the tooltip messages are sent as a WM_NOTIFY message with the code TTN_NEEDTEXT, I thought it would be simple to add a message handler in *CMyToolBar*. But if you look at the online help for ON_NOTIFY, the middle parameter is the child identifier of the control for which the notification is sent. It took me a long time to realize that tooltips have an ID of 0! Look at this code from WINCORE.cpp:

```
BOOL CWnd::OnNotify(WPARAM, LPARAM lParam, LRESULT* pResult)
{
        ASSERT(pResult != NULL);
        NMHDR* pNMHDR = (NMHDR*)lParam;
        HWND hWndCtrl = pNMHDR->hwndFrom;

        // get the child ID from the window itself
        UINT nID = _AfxGetDlgCtrlID(hWndCtrl);
        int nCode = pNMHDR->code;
        ...
```

2.9 CREATE A CUSTOM CCONTROLBAR TO DISPLAY STATIC TEXT

All WM_NOTIFY messages are first routed through this generic message handler so the LPARAM can be unpacked and sent to the appropriate message map handler. Notice the comment saying that the child ID is determined from the handle of the window sending the message. Well, this handle belongs to the tooltip control, and its ID is always going to be 0. That's why we have a 0 in our message map:

```
BEGIN_MESSAGE_MAP(CMyToolBar, CToolBarCtrl)
    //{{AFX_MSG_MAP(CMyToolBar)
    //}}AFX_MSG_MAP
    ON_NOTIFY(TTN_NEEDTEXT, 0, OnNeedText)
END_MESSAGE_MAP()
```

OnNeedText is pretty simple. It extracts the *idFrom* parameter (which is not 0, but the ID of the toolbar button in question) and uses it to load a string resource. Use two MFC helper functions, *AfxLoadString* and *AfxExtractSubString* to load the string and return the part after the carriage return "\n". The interface for these two functions is in AfxPriv.h.

Comments

Future versions of MFC beyond 4.0 might store a different toolbar resource. In that case, you'll have to modify *LoadToolBar, SetButtons,* and the *CToolBarData* struct to match the code in BARTOOL.cpp. You'll know if it changes because *LoadToolBar* will assert on the following line:

```
ASSERT(pData->wVersion == 1);
```

COMPLEXITY
ADVANCED

2.9 How do I... Create a custom CControlBar to display static text?

Problem

How do I get a title for my views in order to update through a command handler? The InfoViewer Topic window contains a window that holds the topic title (see Figure 2-23); how do I get a *CControlBar* with similar characteristics?

Technique

We're going to create a new *CControlBar* class called *CStaticBar*. You'll be able to update its caption through the same mechanism used for *CStatusBars* and menu items. The *CStaticBar* will make itself taller to accommodate long text and uses the *CDC::DrawText* method for calculating and drawing the caption (see Figure 2-24).

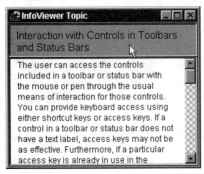

Figure 2-23 InfoViewer title in a control bar

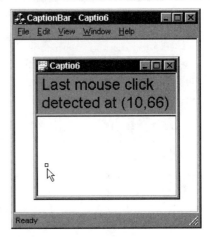

Figure 2-24 CStaticBar embedded in a child frame

Steps

1. **Create a new project called CaptionBar using the MFC AppWizard (exe).** Press the Finish button to accept all the default options.

   Classes to be created:
   Application: CCaptionBarApp in CaptionBar.h and CaptionBar.cpp
   Frame: CMainFrame in MainFrm.h and MainFrm.cpp
   MDIChildFrame: CChildFrame in ChildFrm.h and ChildFrm.cpp
   Document: CCaptionBarDoc in CaptionBarDoc.h and CaptionBarDoc.cpp
   View: CCaptionBarView in CaptionBarView.h and CaptionBarView.cpp

   Features:
   + Initial toolbar in main frame
   + Initial status bar in main frame
   + 3D Controls
   + Uses shared DLL implementation (MFC40.DLL)

2. **Create a new class called CStaticBar.** Use ClassWizard to create a new class with the following information:

   Class name: CStaticBar
   Base class: generic CWnd
   File: StaticBar.cpp

   Now replace every instance of *CWnd* with *CControlBar* in StaticBar.cpp and StaticBar.h.

2.9
CREATE A CUSTOM CCONTROLBAR TO DISPLAY STATIC TEXT

3. Edit StaticBar.h. Make the following changes to StaticBar.h:

```
class CStaticBar : public CControlBar
{
// Construction
public:
        CStaticBar();

// Attributes
public:
        void SetText(LPCTSTR lpszText);

// Overrides
        // ClassWizard generated virtual function overrides
        //{{AFX_VIRTUAL(CStaticBar)
        //}}AFX_VIRTUAL

// Implementation
public:
        virtual ~CStaticBar();

        // Generated message map functions
protected:
        //{{AFX_MSG(CStaticBar)
        //}}AFX_MSG
        afx_msg LRESULT OnSizeParent(WPARAM, LPARAM lParam);
        DECLARE_MESSAGE_MAP()

        virtual void OnUpdateCmdUI(CFrameWnd* pTarget, BOOL bDisableIfNoHndler);
        virtual CSize CalcFixedLayout(BOOL bStretch, BOOL bHorz);

        int m_cxAvailable;
        CFont m_font;
        CString m_caption;
};
```

We'll add more message map functions using the WizardBar in later steps.

4. Edit the CStaticBar constructor. The first two variables are inherited from *CControlBar* and are used internally by *CalcInsideRect*. Initialize all the member variables like this:

```
CStaticBar::CStaticBar()
{
    m_cyBottomBorder = m_cyTopBorder = 4; // l&r default to 6; t&b was 1
    m_caption = "default";                // must have some text for CalcFixedLayout
    m_cxAvailable = 0;
}
```

5. Use the WizardBar to handle WM_CREATE for CStaticBar. Add the following code:

```
int CStaticBar::OnCreate(LPCREATESTRUCT lpCreateStruct)
{
        if (CControlBar::OnCreate(lpCreateStruct) == -1)
            return -1;
```

continued on next page

CHAPTER 2
STATUS BARS AND TOOLBARS

continued from previous page

```
    // Comment out this next line for a different 3D effect
    ModifyStyleEx(0, WS_EX_CLIENTEDGE);

    // Create a font twice as tall as the system status bar font
    NONCLIENTMETRICS metrics;
    metrics.cbSize = sizeof(metrics);
    SystemParametersInfo(SPI_GETNONCLIENTMETRICS, 0, &metrics, 0);

    metrics.lfStatusFont.lfHeight *= 2;
    VERIFY(m_font.CreateFontIndirect(&metrics.lfStatusFont));

    return 0;
}
```

ModifyStyleEx adds the WS_EX_CLIENTEDGE extended style to the window to give the static bar a 3D look, a border with a sunken edge. After you finish the project, comment out that line to see an alternative look.

SystemParametersInfo returns some useful information about the current status bar font. We'll use this information to create our own font that is twice as high as the normal status font.

6. Use the WizardBar to handle WM_ERASEBKGND for CStaticBar. Replace the code with this:

```
BOOL CStaticBar::OnEraseBkgnd(CDC* pDC)
{
    CRect rect;
    GetClientRect(rect);
    pDC->FillSolidRect(rect, ::GetSysColor(COLOR_BTNFACE));

    return TRUE;
}
```

In most cases, this code will paint the background gray.

7. Use the WizardBar to handle WM_PAINT for CStaticBar. Add the following code to draw the caption:

```
void CStaticBar::OnPaint()
{
    CPaintDC dc(this); // device context for painting

    CRect r;
    GetClientRect(r);
    CalcInsideRect(r, TRUE);
    r.InflateRect(0, 2);

    CFont* pOldFont = dc.SelectObject(&m_font);

    dc.DrawText(m_caption, -1, r, DT_EDITCONTROL |
            DT_EXTERNALLEADING | DT_LEFT | DT_WORDBREAK | DT_END_ELLIPSIS);

    if (pOldFont != NULL)
            dc.SelectObject(pOldFont);
}
```

2.9
CREATE A CUSTOM CCONTROLBAR TO DISPLAY STATIC TEXT

8. Add the following code for OnSizeParent. Type in this code at the bottom of StaticBar.cpp since it's not supported by ClassWizard.

```
LRESULT CStaticBar::OnSizeParent(WPARAM, LPARAM lParam)
{
    AFX_SIZEPARENTPARAMS* lpLayout = (AFX_SIZEPARENTPARAMS*)lParam;

    // keep track of the available width for use by CalcFixedLayout later
    m_cxAvailable = lpLayout->rect.right - lpLayout->rect.left;

    return CControlBar::OnSizeParent(0, lParam);
}
```

Locate the message map and add a new entry. The ON_MESSAGE line attaches the WM_SIZEPARENT message to the *OnSizeParent* method.

```
BEGIN_MESSAGE_MAP(CStaticBar, CControlBar)
    //{{AFX_MSG_MAP(CStaticBar)
    ON_WM_CREATE()
    ON_WM_ERASEBKGND()
    ON_WM_PAINT()
    ON_MESSAGE(WM_SIZEPARENT, OnSizeParent)
    //}}AFX_MSG_MAP
END_MESSAGE_MAP()
```

Since WM_SIZEPARENT is a private message, add the following line to the top of StaticBar.cpp (you can also remove the line including CaptionBar.h).

```
#include "stdafx.h"
#include "StaticBar.h"
#include <afxpriv.h>    // for WM_SIZEPARENT
```

9. Add the SetText method. The following method will be used by the helper class *CStaticCmdUI* to set the caption for the bar. Add the following code to the bottom of StaticBar.cpp:

```
void CStaticBar::SetText(LPCTSTR lpszNew)
{
    ASSERT(lpszNew && AfxIsValidString(lpszNew));

    if (m_caption != lpszNew)
    {
        m_caption = lpszNew;
        Invalidate();
    }
}
```

10. Add two virtual helper methods. The following two methods control the size of the static bar and the caption updating.

```
// Overridden virtual helper methods

void CStaticBar::OnUpdateCmdUI(CFrameWnd* pTarget, BOOL bDisableIfNoHndler)
{
```

continued on next page

continued from previous page

```
        CStaticCmdUI state;
        state.m_pOther = this;
        state.m_nIndexMax = 1;      // there's only one thing to update
        state.m_nID = AFX_IDW_STATUS_BAR;

        // allow the statusbar itself to have update handlers
        if (CWnd::OnCmdMsg(state.m_nID, CN_UPDATE_COMMAND_UI, &state, NULL))
            return;

        // allow target (owner) to handle the remaining updates
        state.DoUpdate(pTarget, FALSE);
}

CSize CStaticBar::CalcFixedLayout(BOOL bStretch, BOOL bHorz)
{
        // Get border size (values will be negative)
        CRect rBorder; rBorder.SetRectEmpty();
        CalcInsideRect(rBorder, bHorz);

        // Based on the available width minus the border area,
        // calculate the necessary Y value to hold the text
        CRect rCalc(0, 0, m_cxAvailable - (-rBorder.Width()), 0);
        {
            CClientDC dc(this);
            CFont* pOldFont = dc.SelectObject(&m_font);

            dc.DrawText(m_caption, -1, rCalc, DT_CALCRECT | DT_EDITCONTROL |
                DT_EXTERNALLEADING | DT_LEFT | DT_WORDBREAK);

            if (pOldFont != NULL)
                dc.SelectObject(pOldFont);
        }

        // The Y value is the sum of the calculated height from DrawText,
        // plus the top and bottom border.
        CSize size;
        size.cx = 32767;
        size.cy = rCalc.Height();
        size.cy += (-rBorder.Height());

        return size;
}
```

11. **Add the CStaticCmdUI helper class.** Add the following code to the top of StaticBar.cpp:

```
// Helper class private to this file.  An instance of this object
// is passed to the UPDATE_COMMAND_UI methods to enable them
// to update the static control bar.

class CStaticCmdUI : public CCmdUI
{
public:
        virtual void SetText(LPCTSTR lpszText);
};
```

2.9
CREATE A CUSTOM CCONTROLBAR TO DISPLAY STATIC TEXT

```
void CStaticCmdUI::SetText(LPCTSTR lpszText)
{
        CStaticBar* pStaticBar = (CStaticBar*)m_pOther;
        ASSERT(pStaticBar != NULL);

        pStaticBar->SetText(lpszText);
}
```

12. Edit ChildFrm.h. Embed the static bar in the child frame by adding these lines of code:

```
#include "StaticBar.h"

class CChildFrame : public CMDIChildWnd
{
        DECLARE_DYNCREATE(CChildFrame)
public:
        CChildFrame();

// Overrides
        // ClassWizard generated virtual function overrides
        //{{AFX_VIRTUAL(CChildFrame)
        virtual BOOL PreCreateWindow(CREATESTRUCT& cs);
        //}}AFX_VIRTUAL

// Implementation
public:
        virtual ~CChildFrame();
#ifdef _DEBUG
        virtual void AssertValid() const;
        virtual void Dump(CDumpContext& dc) const;
#endif

// Generated message map functions
protected:
        //{{AFX_MSG(CChildFrame)
        //}}AFX_MSG
        DECLARE_MESSAGE_MAP()

        CStaticBar m_bar;
};
```

13. Use the WizardBar to handle WM_CREATE for CChildFrame. Add the following code to create the bar and align it to the top of the frame.

```
int CChildFrame::OnCreate(LPCREATESTRUCT lpCreateStruct)
{
        if (CMDIChildWnd::OnCreate(lpCreateStruct) == -1)
            return -1;

        m_bar.Create(NULL, NULL, WS_VISIBLE | WS_CHILD | WS_CLIPSIBLINGS | ⇒
CBRS_TOP,
            CRect(0,0,0,0), this, AFX_IDW_STATUS_BAR);
```

continued on next page

CHAPTER 2
STATUS BARS AND TOOLBARS

continued from previous page

```
        m_bar.SetBarStyle(CBRS_ALIGN_TOP);

        return 0;
}
```

14. Add a member variable to CCaptionBarView. Use the Add Member Variable dialog to add a variable which holds the last mouse point.

Type	Declaration	Access
CPoint	m_lastPoint	protected

15. Edit the CCaptionBarView constructor. Initialize the *m_lastPoint* variable like this:

```
CCaptionBarView::CCaptionBarView()
{
        m_lastPoint.x = m_lastPoint.y = -1;
}
```

16. Use the WizardBar to handle WM_LBUTTONDOWN for CCaptionBarView. This code keeps track of the last mouse click and invalidates the view.

```
void CCaptionBarView::OnLButtonDown(UINT nFlags, CPoint point)
{
        m_lastPoint = point;
        Invalidate();
}
```

17. Edit CCaptionBarView::OnDraw. Draw a small rectangle where the mouse was clicked.

```
void CCaptionBarView::OnDraw(CDC* pDC)
{
        CCaptionBarDoc* pDoc = GetDocument();
        ASSERT_VALID(pDoc);

        // Draw a rectangle at the last mouse point
        CRect r(0, 0, 5, 5);
        r += m_lastPoint;
        pDC->Rectangle(r);
}
```

18. Add the OnUpdateStaticBar helper function. Use the ClassView Add Function dialog to add the following virtual, protected method:

```
void CCaptionBarView::OnUpdateStaticBar(CCmdUI* pCmdUI)
{
        CString msg;
        msg.Format("Last mouse click detected at (%ld,%ld)",
                m_lastPoint.x, m_lastPoint.y);

        pCmdUI->SetText(msg);
}
```

2.9 CREATE A CUSTOM CCONTROLBAR TO DISPLAY STATIC TEXT

Now edit the message map to attach this method to the update handler.

```
BEGIN_MESSAGE_MAP(CCaptionBarView, CView)
    //{{AFX_MSG_MAP(CCaptionBarView)
    ON_WM_LBUTTONDOWN()
    //}}AFX_MSG_MAP
    ON_UPDATE_COMMAND_UI(AFX_IDW_STATUS_BAR, OnUpdateStaticBar)
END_MESSAGE_MAP()
```

19. Build and test the application. Click around the client area and notice the static bar text change. Try resizing the view to see how the bar reacts to smaller widths.

How It Works

A *CControlBar* is a *CWnd*-derived class that is aligned to the top or bottom of a frame window. They may also contain child controls that are either HWND-based (like *CDialogBar*), or non-HWND-based items (for example, *CToolBar, CStatusBar*). Our *CStaticBar* doesn't contain any HWND-based items; it simply draws a caption and assists with the control bar layout.

Layout

The control bar layout algorithm is very simple. The child frame window sends the WM_SIZEPARENT message to all children in the control bar range. Since *CChildFrame::OnCreate* created the *m_bar* using the AFX_IDW_STATUS_BAR control ID, WM_SIZEPARENT is sent to our control.

All control bars, including *CStaticBar*, use the client rectangle passed to WM_SIZEPARENT to position themselves and to decrease the parent's client area. In our case, we simply note the maximum available width in *m_cxAvailable*, and let the default *CControlBar::OnSizeParent* handle the rest of the operation. Eventually our implementation of *CalcFixedLayout* is called by *OnSizeParent* where we figure out how tall the bar should be.

CalcFixedLayout knows how wide the rectangle can be; it was saved in *m_cxAvailable*. Now we need to calculate the height. If we create a rectangle *m_cxAvailable* wide, *CDC::DrawText* will tell us how tall it needs to be to accommodate the caption. The resultant height is increased by the top and bottom border and returned from *CalcFixedLayout*. The view's client area is decreased by that amount.

Updating the Caption

CStaticBar::OnUpdateCmdUI is called by the framework when the application is idle. Here we create an instance of the helper class *CStaticCmdUI*, setting its *m_pOther* pointer to *this*. The MFC command routing passes the object to the view's update command handler (*CCaptionBarView::OnUpdateStaticBar*) where we simply call the virtual method *CCmdUI::SetText* with our new caption.

Because *SetText* is virtual, our implementation in *CStaticCmdUI* in turn calls *CStaticBar::SetText* using the *m_pOther* pointer. This technique separates the updating object (the view) from the object being updated (the control bar). It works the same for toolbars, status bars, and menus.

Comments

As an alternative to using *DrawText,* you could instead embed an edit control and set its caption whenever *CStaticBar::SetText* is called. You'll have to reposition the edit control by handling the WM_SIZE messages. *CalcFixedLayout* wouldn't change because you could still use *DrawText* to calculate the necessary height.

CHAPTER 3
CONTROLS

CONTROLS

How do I...

3.1 Change the cursor when it passes over a control?
3.2 Associate data with a list box item?
3.3 Limit an edit control to allow only floating-point numbers?
3.4 Color items in a list box?
3.5 Create a dynamic shortcut menu?
3.6 Create a progress meter custom control?
3.7 Create an auto-sizing multicolumn list box?
3.8 Write a custom button to display a menu?
3.9 Draw bitmaps in a list box?

This chapter uncovers little-known secrets of Windows controls by using several powerful MFC classes and C++ techniques. You'll learn how to combine classes like *CMenu* and *CButton* to come up with a completely new control, how to add a useful progress gauge to dialogs, and how to easily change the color of items in a list box. One How-To creates a new edit control that only accepts valid floating-point numbers, and another draws bitmaps in a custom list box. You'll see how easy it is to change the cursor as the mouse moves over a control. Another How-To demonstrates how to link a C++ object to an item in a list box for easy retrieval.

CHAPTER 3
CONTROLS

3.1 Change the Cursor When It Passes Over a Control

Use this popular technique to give instant feedback as the cursor moves between controls. Also learn what modifications to the registry are necessary for creating colored cursors.

Additional Topics: OnSetCursor, SetCursor, LoadStandardCursor

3.2 Associate Data with a List Box Item

Learn how to attach any C++ object to individual items in a list box. Use this method to link data to items in a list box for easy retrieval.

Additional Topics: SetItemData, LBN_SELCHANGE

3.3 Limit an Edit Control to Allow Only Floating-Point Numbers

This How-To describes how to create and use a new class of edit control, *CFloatEdit*. This new control class restricts input to floating-point numbers only, on a character-by-character basis. Illegal characters cannot be entered into the edit control.

Additional Topics: OnChar, custom character handling, strtod

3.4 Color Items in a List Box

It's possible to change the colors in a list box without resorting to a custom list box. Using just one method, you can completely change the color of not only the list boxes, but all the controls in your application.

Additional Topics: OnCtlColor, dithered vs. solid colors

3.5 Create a Dynamic Shortcut Menu

Create a menu at runtime that lists all the current tasks and displays them when the right mouse button is clicked.

Additional Topics: TrackPopupMenu, WM_CONTEXTMENU, filtering menu commands in OnCommand

3.6 Create a Progress Meter Custom Control

This custom control class lets you display text messages and change the percentage of an operation that is complete. This allows you to keep users posted during lengthy operations.

Additional Topics: custom background erasing, 3D border styles

3.7 Create an Auto-Sizing Multicolumn List Box

Use tabstops to create a multicolumn list box with a horizontal scroll bar. This list box also automatically resizes its columns so every column fits just right.

Additional Topics: proportionally spaced fonts, average character width

3.8 Write a Custom Button to Display a Menu

Sometimes you want total control over the appearance of your own customized buttons. Learn to paint a button from scratch and have it drop down a menu when pressed.

Additional Topics: self-drawn buttons, message reflection

3.9 Draw Bitmaps in a List Box

Learn how to make a self-drawn list box that paints a bitmap (with transparency) and text in a list box cell. You'll also see how to create a multicolumn custom list box.

Additional Topics: a GDI-based TransparentBlt function, focus rectangles

COMPLEXITY
BEGINNING

3.1 How do I... Change the cursor when it passes over a control?

Problem

I'd like to have the mouse cursor change when it passes over a particular control to give immediate feedback to the user. For instance, how would I change the mouse cursor to a crosshair if the user moves the mouse over a button?

Technique

The easiest way to change the cursor is by responding to the WM_SETCURSOR message. Windows sends this message to a window if the cursor moves within a window and the mouse is not currently captured. MFC applications handle this message through the *OnSetCursor* method.

The default handler passes the WM_SETCURSOR message to a parent window before processing. If the parent returns TRUE, further processing is halted. Otherwise, it's assumed that the cursor was handled by *OnSetCursor*. Passing the message to a window's parent gives the parent window responsibility for the cursor's setting in a child window.

If you want the *child* control to be responsible for the cursor, you have two choices. Either override *OnSetCursor* in the child window and set the cursor there, or register your own class with a handle to the class cursor. Both of these techniques are discussed in the Comments section.

For this How-To, we'll use *OnSetCursor* to handle the responsibility for setting the cursor for the child window controls. When you're finished with this How-To, you'll see the cursor change as you pass it over the buttons, as shown in Figure 3-1.

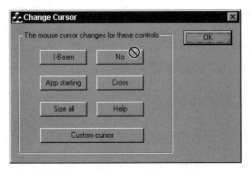

Figure 3-1 Changing the cursor for dialog controls

Steps

1. Create a new project called Cursor using the MFC AppWizard (exe).
Choose the dialog-based version and press the Finish button.

Classes to be created:
    Application: CCursorApp in Cursor.h and Cursor.cpp
    Dialog: CCursorDlg in CursorDlg.h and CursorDlg.cpp

Features:
    + About box on system menu
    + 3D Controls
    + Uses shared DLL implementation (MFC40.DLL)

2. Modify the registry to support colored cursors. Windows 3.x only supported monochromatic mouse cursors, but Windows 95 lets you create cursors in 16 or 256 colors. But for some reason, Developer Studio hides this capability. You have to add a couple of entries to the registry to enable the creation of colored cursors in App Studio.

First, run RegEdit.exe using the Run command on the Start menu. Next, locate this key in the tree: HKEY_CURRENT_USER/Software/Microsoft/Developer. Use the Edit New Key menu to add an entry called "Cursor Devices". Then, use the Edit New String Value and the table below to add two new entries to the "Cursor Devices" key. Figure 3-2 shows what my registry looks like after I make the same changes.

Key	Name	Data
Cursor Devices	32x32 16 colors	16,32,32
Cursor Devices	32x32 256 colors	256,32,32

3.1
CHANGE THE CURSOR WHEN IT PASSES OVER A CONTROL

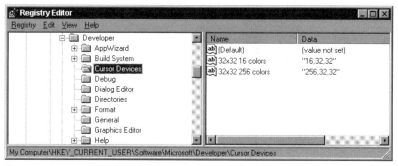

Figure 3-2 Cursor Devices registry entry

See the Knowledge Base article Q135047 for more information.

If you prefer, create a small file called "Add Cursor Devices.reg" using Notepad with the following content:

```
REGEDIT4
[HKEY_CURRENT_USER\Software\Microsoft\Developer\Cursor Devices]
"32x32 16 colors"="16,32,32"
"32x32 256 colors"="256,32,32"
```

Then double-click the file in the Explorer to add these entries to your registry.

3. **Create a colored cursor.** You have to restart Developer Studio to see the effect of the above changes. Once you've done that, switch to the ResourceView and use the Insert Resource Cursor menu to add a new cursor to your application.

A cursor can have multiple images contained in one file called device images. By default, the cursor is created with a single monochrome bitmap. To add a colored image to the cursor, press the Insert key and choose the target image "32x32 256 colors". Use the File Save All menu to save the changes so far.

Now, this may seem a little strange, but I want you to close the cursor and reopen it right away. If you don't do that, you won't see the new palette of colors. Press [ALT]+[ENTER] and choose the Palette tab. From this selection of colors and using only the Pencil tool (the other ones don't work with multi-colored cursors for some reason; maybe it's a bug), draw some colored squares. Figure 3-3 shows this.

One more thing. Use the drop-down combo to switch back to the monochrome image. Delete the unused image using the Image Delete Device Image menu option. If you don't delete it, you won't see the colored cursor.

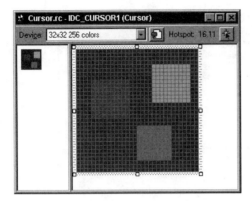

Figure 3-3 Multi-colored cursor

4. **Add controls to the IDD_CURSOR_DIALOG dialog.** Use the resource editor to add seven new buttons to the dialog, as shown in Figure 3-4. The control IDs and attributes are shown in the following table:

Control	ID	Attributes
IBeam button	IDC_BTN_IBEAM	Default
No button	IDC_BTN_NO	Default
App Starting button	IDC_BTN_APPSTARTING	Default
Cross button	IDC_BTN_CROSS	Default
Size All button	IDC_BTN_SIZEALL	Default
Help button	IDC_BTN_HELP	Default
Custom Cursor button	IDC_BTN_CUSTOM	Default

5. **Use the WizardBar to handle WM_SETCURSOR for CCursorDlg.** Add the following code to change the system cursor:

```
BOOL CCursorDlg::OnSetCursor(CWnd* pWnd, UINT nHitTest, UINT message)
{
        // The predefined cursor identifiers in WINUSER.H are
        // really numbers converted to strings using MAKEINTRESOURCE
        const char* nID;

        switch (pWnd->GetDlgCtrlID())
        {
                // Use system cursors for these buttons
                case IDC_BTN_IBEAM:         nID = IDC_IBEAM; break;
                case IDC_BTN_NO:            nID = IDC_NO; break;
                case IDC_BTN_APPSTARTING:   nID = IDC_APPSTARTING; break;
                case IDC_BTN_CROSS:         nID = IDC_CROSS; break;
                case IDC_BTN_SIZEALL:       nID = IDC_SIZEALL; break;
                case IDC_BTN_HELP:          nID = IDC_HELP; break;
```

3.1
CHANGE THE CURSOR WHEN IT PASSES OVER A CONTROL

```
            // Use our custom cursor for the Custom button
            case IDC_BTN_CUSTOM:
                        SetCursor(AfxGetApp()->LoadCursor(IDC_CURSOR1));
                        return TRUE;

            // Otherwise, let Windows handle the cursor
            default:
                        return CDialog::OnSetCursor(pWnd, nHitTest, message);
      }

      SetCursor (AfxGetApp()->LoadStandardCursor(nID));
      return TRUE;
}
```

6. **Build and test the application.** Move the mouse cursor over the buttons and observe how the cursor changes to one of the standard Windows cursors, or to our custom cursor (as shown in Figure 3-5).

How It Works

Windows sends a WM_SETCURSOR message to a window whenever the cursor moves within the window. Before it is processed by the default message handler, the window or its parent gets a chance to set the cursor. If the message is not handled (indicated by returning FALSE from *OnSetCursor*), the default message handler sets the cursor for the window.

The default handler uses the cursor specified in the window class structure. This is not a C++ class but rather a window class the framework registered with the *RegisterClass* SDK function. The MFC Technical Note "Windows Class Registration" included in Books Online describes all the default WNDCLASSes and what default cursors are used for each type of window.

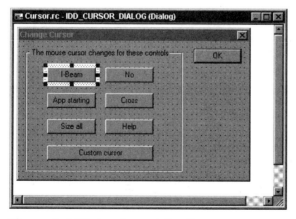

Figure 3-4 Dialog layout for the cursor project

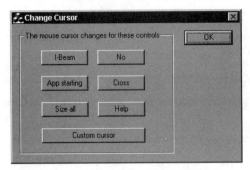

Figure 3-5 A custom color cursor

The first argument to *OnSetCursor* specifies a pointer to the window under the cursor. The *CDialog::GetDlgCtrlID* returns the identifier for that window, which we use to test against all the known controls for the *CCursorDlg* dialog. Depending on the control ID, the cursor will be set to one of the default system cursors, such as IDC_APPSTARTING or IDC_SIZEALL.

If the mouse is over one of the seven buttons, *nID* will be set and *LoadStandardCursor* will return an HCURSOR suitable for passing to *SetCursor*. *SetCursor* is an SDK function that changes the system cursor. If the mouse was not over one of the buttons, we pass the message on to our parent, and in this case, the default handler will set the cursor.

Otherwise, if the mouse was over the Custom Cursor button, we use *CWinApp::LoadCursor* instead of *LoadStandardCursor* to load IDC_CURSOR1, the colored cursor, and pass the result to *SetCursor*.

Comments

There are two other ways we could have set the cursor. The first is to handle the WM_SETCURSOR message in the child control rather than in the control's parent. By subclassing an existing control, such as a *CButton*, you would simply add the *OnSetCursor* handler and call *SetCursor*, as you did in step 3. For example, say you had a custom cursor for a new button class called *CCoolButton*. When you constructed the object, the cursor could be loaded using *LoadCursor*. Then the handle to the cursor would be used to call *SetCursor* in *OnSetCursor* like this:

```
void CCoolButton::Create(...)
{
    ...
    // Load the custom cursor
    m_hCursor = AfxGetApp()->LoadCursor(IDC_MY_CURSOR);
}

void CCoolButton::OnSetCursor(CWnd* pWnd, UINT nHitTest, UINT nMessage)
{
```

```
        SetCursor(m_hCursor);
        return TRUE;
}
```

The second way to attach a cursor to a child window is to register your own custom window class. MFC automatically registers several standard window classes, but they all define their own cursor. To help define your own class, MFC provides a helper routine for registering window classes called *AfxRegisterWndClass*. Given a set of attributes describing the window class (style, cursor, background brush, and icon), a synthetic name is generated, and the resulting window class is registered. If you save the resultant string and use it as the class name for your custom control, Windows will automatically set the cursor to the one registered for that class.

Using the *CCoolButton* example from above, you might write a Create method like this:

```
BOOL CCoolButton::Create(LPCSTR lpszWindowName, DWORD dwStyle, UINT nID,
    const RECT& rect, CWnd* pParent, UINT nID)
{
    static HCURSOR hCursor = AfxGetApp()->LoadCursor(IDC_MY_CURSOR);

    static CString sClassName = AfxRegisterWndClass (
        CS_HREDRAW | CS_VREDRAW, hCursor);

    return CWnd::Create(sClassName, lpszWindowName, dwStyle, nID,
        rect, pParent, nID);
}
```

COMPLEXITY
BEGINNING

3.2 How do I... Associate data with a list box item?

Problem

Almost every time I use a list box, I have a separate array to match each entry with some special data. How can I associate data with a list box item. For example, whenever the user selects something from the list box, I'd like to retrieve its linked data and display it.

Technique

You can associate data with a list box item by calling the *CListBox* member functions *SetItemData* and *SetItemDataPtr*. Both of these methods send a WM_SETITEMDATA message to the list box, which associates a 32-bit number with a list box index. You retrieve the data by calling *GetItemData* or *GetItemDataPtr* with the list box item's index.

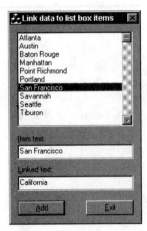

Figure 3-6 ListData program showing CString objects linked to list box items

Both functions send a WM_GETITEMDATA message to the list box, which retrieves a 32-bit number associated with the list box item.

The item index passed to *SetItemData* is usually the return value from *AddString*. So adding an item and then linking data to it is a two-step process: First call *AddString* to add the viewable list box string, then call *SetItemData,* passing the index returned from *AddString* and a pointer to an object. Retrieval of the data usually occurs when an item is selected in the list box. If you respond to the LBN_SELCHANGE message, you can query the list box for the index of the currently selected item, then pass the index to *GetItemData*.

The example program presented in this How-To links a *CString* object with each item in the list box, as shown in Figure 3-6. When you press the Add button, the content of the Item Text edit box is added to the list box. The text from the Linked Text field is used to construct a new *CString* object, which is then associated with the new item.

Steps

1. **Create a new project called ListData using the MFC AppWizard (exe).**
Choose the dialog-based version and press the Finish button.

Classes to be created:
Application: CListDataApp in ListData.h and ListData.cpp
Dialog: CListDataDlg in ListDataDlg.h and ListDataDlg.cpp

Features:
+ About box on system menu
+ 3D Controls
+ Uses shared DLL implementation (MFC40.DLL)

3.2
ASSOCIATE DATA WITH A LIST BOX ITEM

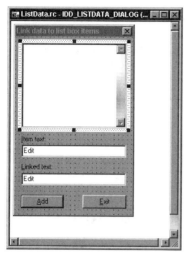

Figure 3-7 Dialog layout

2. **Add controls to the IDD_LISTDATA_DIALOG dialog.** Use the resource editor to construct a dialog similar to the one shown in Figure 3-7. The control IDs and attributes are shown in the following table:

Control	ID	Attributes
List box	IDC_LIST	Sorted, Disable no scroll
Item Text edit	IDC_TEXT	Default
Linked Text edit	IDC_DATA	Default
Add button	IDC_ADD	Default button
Done button	IDOK	Default

3. **Use ClassWizard to add message handlers and member variables.** Add message-handling functions for these objects:

Object ID	Function	Message
CListDataDlg	OnDestroy	WM_DESTROY
IDC_LIST	OnSelChangeList	LBN_SELCHANGE
IDC_ADD	OnAdd	BN_CLICKED

Switch to the Member Variables tab in ClassWizard and add the following variables:

Control ID	Type	Member
IDC_LIST	CListBox	m_list
IDC_TEXT	CString	m_strText
IDC_DATA	CString	m_strData

4. Edit the CListDataDlg::OnAdd. When the Add button is pressed, we'll get the two strings from the edit controls, add the first string to the list box, and associate the second string with the first. Add the following code to *OnAdd*:

```
void CListDataDlg::OnAdd()
{
        UpdateData();

        if (m_strText.IsEmpty())
                return;

        // add the text to the list box
        int nIndex = m_list.AddString(m_strText);

        // create a new CString object for the linked text and
        // associate it with the new list box item
        m_list.SetItemDataPtr (nIndex, new CString(m_strData));

        // Clear the edit fields
        m_strText.Empty();
        m_strData.Empty();
        UpdateData(FALSE);
        GetDlgItem(IDC_TEXT)->SetFocus();
}
```

5. Edit CListDataDlg::OnDestroy. When the dialog is destroyed, we need to cycle through the items in the list box, deleting the *CString* objects we constructed in *OnAdd*. Add the following code to *OnDestroy*:

```
void CListDataDlg::OnDestroy()
{
        int nIndex;

        // Delete the CString objects associated with each
        // list box item.
        for (nIndex = m_list.GetCount() - 1; nIndex >= 0; nIndex-)
        {
                delete (CString*) m_list.GetItemDataPtr (nIndex);
        }
        CDialog::OnDestroy();
}
```

6. Edit CListDataDlg::OnSelChangeList. When an item in the list box is selected, the item pointer will be decoded into a *CString* pointer and used to set the value of the Linked Text edit control:

```
void CListDataDlg::OnSelChangeList()
{
        int nIndex = m_list.GetCurSel();

        if (nIndex != LB_ERR)
        {
                // copy list box item to text string
                m_list.GetText (nIndex, m_strText);
```

3.2
ASSOCIATE DATA WITH A LIST BOX ITEM

```
        // get pointer to CString object
        CString* pString = (CString *) m_List.GetItemData (nIndex);
        m_strData = *pString;

        // update edit fields with new values
        UpdateData(FALSE);
    }
}
```

7. **Build and test the application.** Type in two strings in the edit controls, such as a city and its state. Press the Add button. After you add a few more cities, click on the items in the list box and you'll see the associated states.

How It Works

You associate data with a particular list box item using *SetItemData* or *SetItemDataPtr*. Both of these functions send the list box an LB_SETITEMDATA message that sets up the associated data. Call the *SetItemData* member function to associate a 32-bit number and *SetItemDataPtr* to associate a pointer.

ListData links the address of a *CString* object to a list box item. When you click the Add button, the content of the Item Text edit box is appended to the list box by calling the *AddString* member function:

```
int nIndex = m_List.AddString(m_strText);
```

A *CString* object is allocated and the contents of the Linked Text edit box are copied to the object. The list box item is associated with the pointer to the object by calling the *SetItemDataPtr* member function along with the index of the new item:

```
m_List.SetItemDataPtr(nIndex, new CString(m_strData));
```

Figure 3-8 shows the sequence of events that occur when an item is added to the list box.

You can retrieve a pointer to the associated data by calling the *GetItemDataPtr* member function. This How-To calls the *GetItemDataPtr* function whenever the current selection of the list box changes. The Item Text edit box is set to the list box item string, and the Linked Text edit box is set to the retrieved associated text. Figure 3-9 shows the sequence of events when the current selection of the list box changes.

It is your responsibility to free all the memory allocated in the *SetItemDataPtr* call. ListData deletes the associated *CString* objects during *OnDestroy*. If you try to delete the memory in the *CListDataDlg* destructor, you'll find that the list box has already been destroyed, leaking the memory as it disappeared.

OnDestroy loops through each list box item and uses *GetItemDataPtr* to fetch the pointer to the *CString* data. Since we know the pointer it returns is always a *CString*, at least for this example, it is safe to cast it to a *CString* before calling *delete*.

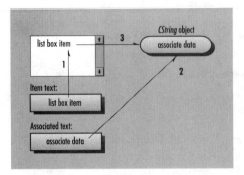
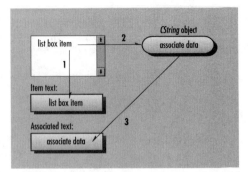

Figure 3-8 Sequence of events when item is added to list box: (1) Add string (2) Allocate object and copy associated text (3) Associate CString pointer to list box item

Figure 3-9 Sequence of events when current selection changes: (1) Set content to list box item (2) Retrieve associated pointer (3) Set content to associated CString object

Comments

You can also associate data with combo box items by taking advantage of the *SetItemData* and *GetItemData* member functions. Linking data to list box items helps you avoid using an extra array to associate list box indexes with the data objects.

COMPLEXITY
INTERMEDIATE

3.3 How do I... Limit an edit control to allow only floating-point numbers?

Problem

I need a specialized version of the *CEdit* class that only allows floating-point numbers. When the user enters a character key, it should be rejected. Is there an easy way to enhance the behavior of the *CEdit* class?

Technique

For this How-To we are going to implement an edit control class called *CFloatEdit*, which only allows entry of keystrokes that correspond to legal characters in a floating-point number. Figure 3-10 shows the floating point edit control in a dialog.

The standard Windows edit control functionality is encapsulated in a class called *CEdit*, which is a subclass of the main window class, *CWnd*.

The *CEdit* class has message-handling member functions defined for various Windows events, such as *OnPaint* (the window needs to be repainted), *OnSize* (the window size has changed), and *OnChar* (the user has hit a key).

3.3
LIMIT AN EDIT CONTROL

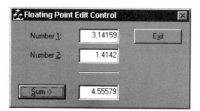

Figure 3-10 Floating point edit control

A derived class can override any of these message handlers. For this example we will only need to override *OnChar* in *CFloatEdit*. The *CFloatEdit* version of *OnChar* determines the validity of the new character. If the character is good, it passes to the base class *OnChar* message handler for processing, just like a normal edit control. If the character is invalid, the base class *OnChar* function is not called, and the invalid character is effectively tossed into the bit bucket.

We're going to write a simple program to illustrate the *CFloatEdit* control. Two edit controls take a couple of floating point numbers, which are added together with the sum displayed in another edit control. If this How-To produces incorrect results, it's not the code; you probably have one of those broken Pentiums. (Seriously, you can actually check your chip's FPU through the Device Manager area of the System control panel. Double-click the Numeric data processor item, then press the Settings tab. Mine's broken!)

Steps

1. Create a new project called FloatControl using the MFC AppWizard (exe). Choose the Dialog-based version and press the Finish button.

Classes to be created:
    Application: CFloatControlApp in FloatControl.h and FloatControl.cpp
    Dialog: CFloatControlDlg in FloatControlDlg.h and FloatControlDlg.cpp

Features:
    + About box on system menu
    + 3D Controls
    + Uses shared DLL implementation (MFC40.DLL)

2. Create a new class called CFloatEdit. Use ClassWizard to create a new class using the following information:

    Class Name: CFloatEdit
    Class Type: CEdit
    Header File: FloatEdit.h
    Implementation File: FloatEdit.cpp

While you're still in the ClassWizard, add a message handler for WM_CHAR. Press the Edit Code button and continue to the next step.

3. Edit CFloatEdit::OnChar. This code only accepts numeric characters or a decimal point separator (a period or a comma). All other characters are rejected with a resounding beep.

```
void CFloatEdit::OnChar(UINT nChar, UINT nRepCnt, UINT nFlags)
{
    // possible valid decimal point separators
    // (Remember, some countries use a comma where
    // Americans would use a period)

    static CString separators(_T(".,"));

    TCHAR tChar = (TCHAR) nChar;

    if ((IsCharAlphaNumeric(tChar) && !IsCharAlpha(tChar)) ||
        separators.Find(nChar) != -1)
    {
        CEdit::OnChar(nChar, nRepCnt, nFlags);
    }
    else
        MessageBeep(MB_ICONASTERISK);
}
```

4. Add the float operator function. Use the ClassView Add Function dialog to add the following method and code (leave the Function Type area empty; see Figure 3-11):

```
CFloatEdit::operator float()
{
    double dReturn;
    CString number;
    LPTSTR endpointer;

    GetWindowText(number);

#ifdef _UNICODE
    dReturn = wcstod((LPCTSTR) number, &endpointer);
#else
    dReturn = strtod((LPCTSTR) number, &endpointer);
#endif

    return (float) dReturn;
}
```

With this casting operator, you can now use statements of the form:

```
CFloatEdit edit1, edit2;
...    // somewhere edit1 and edit2 have been set
float val = edit1 + edit2;
```

What we are doing here is "adding" two *CFloatEdit* objects together, the result of which is a variable of type float. We can now use *CFloatEdit* objects

3.3 LIMIT AN EDIT CONTROL

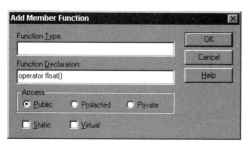

Figure 3-11 Adding an operator method using the Add Function dialog

anywhere a float would be used, such as an argument to a function or inside an arithmetic expression. We can also safely cast a *CFloatEdit* to a float.

User-defined conversions from *CFloatEdit* to other data types would also be useful. A conversion to type *CString* could, for example, extract the text from the edit control using the *GetWindowText* function.

5. Edit the include section in FloatEdit.cpp. Modify the top of the file as follows:

```
#include "stdafx.h"
#include "FloatControl.h"
#include "FloatEdit.h"
#include <stdlib.h>          // for the strtod
```

6. Edit the IDD_FLOATCONTROL_DIALOG dialog. Create a dialog like the one shown in Figure 3-12. Use the following IDs and attributes for the dialog controls:

Control	ID	Attributes
Static	IDC_STATIC	"Number &1:"
Edit #1	IDC_EDIT1	Right-aligned, multi-line
Static	IDC_STATIC	"Number &2:"
Edit #2	IDC_EDIT2	Right-aligned, multi-line
Frame	IDC_STATIC	Sunken, 1 pixel tall
Sum button	IDC_SUM	Default button
Exit button	IDOK	Turn off the Default button attribute

Hint: To get the thin line above the third edit control, use a one pixel tall frame control with the Sunken style turned on.

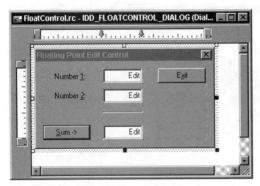

Figure 3-12 The IDD_FLOAT-CONTROL_DIALOG layout

7. **Add member variables to CFloatControlDlg.** Add the following variables to CFloatControlDlg using the Member Variables tab in ClassWizard:

Control ID	Type	Member
IDC_EDIT1	CFloatEdit	m_edit1
IDC_EDIT2	CFloatEdit	m_edit2
IDC_EDIT3	float	m_fSum

8. **Use the WizardBar to add a BN_CLICKED handler for IDC_SUM in CFloatControlDlg.** Here's where we add the two values and put the sum in IDC_EDIT3:

```
void CFloatControlDlg::OnSum()
{
    m_fSum = m_edit1 + m_edit2;
    UpdateData(FALSE);
}
```

9. **Edit FloatControlDlg.h.** Add this line to the top to include the *CFloatEdit* interface.

```
#include "FloatEdit.h"
```

10. **Build and test the application.** Try to type in letters or punctuation in the top two edit boxes; they won't be accepted. Click the Sum button to see the total in the lower edit box.

How It Works

The only difference between *CFloatEdit* and *CEdit* is the way *CFloatEdit* handles keyboard input. It only accepts numeric characters, tab, backspace, and decimal point separators (most locales use either the comma or the period). If the new character is valid, the default message handler takes care of the details. Otherwise, the edit control beeps.

Since there is no *IsCharNumeric*, I had to use a combination of *IsCharAlphaNumeric* and *IsCharAlpha*. As long as the first function returns TRUE and the second FALSE, we know the character is numeric.

The *float* operator actually converts the character string into a floating-point number using the C-runtime function *strtod* (or *wcstod* if you're compiling under Unicode). If the string is invalid and we didn't catch the problem while processing the WM_CHAR message (for example, two decimal points could have been entered), these functions might return zero.

Comments

Note that you cannot change the values passed into a base class message handler from a subclass message handler. If you wanted to map lowercase characters to uppercase for example, you might be tempted to simply change the value of *nChar*, which is passed into *CFloatEdit::OnChar* to reflect the case mapping, and then call *CEdit::OnChar* with the modified *nChar*. However, this is not allowed. If you call a base class message-handling function, you must pass through the same arguments received by the subclass message handler.

The way around this is to resend the message with the modified arguments using the *SendMessage* API call. You would want to be sure and use *SendMessage* and not *PostMessage,* as you do not want your message to wind up in the back of the message queue.

**COMPLEXITY
INTERMEDIATE**

3.4 How do I... Color items in a list box?

Problem

I'd like to change the text and background colors of my list boxes and use colors other than the default window colors. Do I have to use a custom list box, or is there a simpler alternative?

Technique

If the list box is only going to contain text, you don't need to create a custom list box. In fact, the process is fairly straightforward. Amazing as it may seem, it is possible to modify the behavior of a list box without making it a custom control.

Just before a control is drawn, Windows sends a WM_CTLCOLOR message to the control's parent in order to get information about the color of the control. *CWnd* objects handle this message by overriding the virtual method *OnCtlColor*. If you return

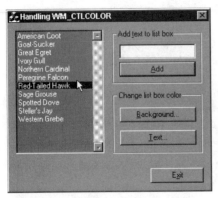

Figure 3-13 Setting the text and background colors for a list box

an HBRUSH, it will be used to paint the background of the control. This is just what we're looking for.

We'll create a background brush and set the text color before returning from *OnCtlColor*. In this How-To, we'll use two *CColorDialogs* to help us pick the colors. The list box shown in Figure 3-13 demonstrates how you can set the text and background colors.

Steps

1. **Create a new project called CtlColor using the MFC AppWizard (exe).**
   Choose the Dialog-based version and press the Finish button.

   Classes to be created:
   Application: CCtlColorApp in CtlColor.h and CtlColor.cpp
   Dialog: CCtlColorDlg in CtlColorDlg.h and CtlColorDlg.cpp

   Features:
   + About box on system menu
   + 3D Controls
   + Uses shared DLL implementation (MFC40.DLL)

2. **Add controls to the IDD_CTLCOLOR_DIALOG dialog.** Use the resource editor to construct a dialog similar to the one shown in Figure 3-14. The control IDs and attributes are shown in this table:

Control	ID	Attributes
List box	IDC_LIST	Sorted
Edit control	IDC_TEXT	Default
Add button	IDC_ADD	"&Add", default button
Background button	IDC_BACK_COLOR	"&Background..."
Text button	IDC_TEXT_COLOR	"&Text..."
Exit button	IDOK	Default

3.4
COLOR ITEMS IN A LIST BOX

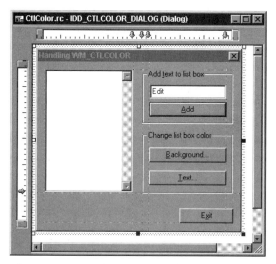

Figure 3-14 Dialog layout for the CtlColor project

3. **Use ClassWizard to add message handlers and member variables.** Add message-handling functions for these objects:

Object ID	Function	Message
CCtlColorDlg	OnCtlColor	WM_CTLCOLOR
IDC_ADD	OnAdd	BN_CLICKED
IDC_BACK_COLOR	OnBackColor	BN_CLICKED
IDC_TEXT_COLOR	OnTextColor	BN_CLICKED

Switch to the Member Variables tab in ClassWizard and add the following variables:

Control ID	Type	Member
IDC_LIST	CListBox	m_list
IDC_TEXT	CString	m_text

4. **Add a member variables to CCtlColorDlg.** Use the Add Variable dialog to add these members to keep track of the selected colors and the background brush:

Type	Declaration	Access
COLORREF	m_crText	protected
COLORREF	m_crBackground	protected
CBrush	m_brush	protected

143

5. Edit CCtlColorDlg::OnInitDialog. Locate this method using the Class View and edit it as shown here:

```
BOOL CCtlColorDlg::OnInitDialog()
{
        CDialog::OnInitDialog();
        ...

        // Provide reasonable default colors
        m_crText = GetSysColor (COLOR_WINDOWTEXT);
        m_crBackground = GetSysColor (COLOR_WINDOW);
        m_brush.CreateSolidBrush (m_crBackground);

        return TRUE;
}
```

6. Code the CCtlColorDlg::OnAdd method. This method retrieves the text from the edit control and adds it to the list box (if the string isn't empty).

```
void CCtlColorDlg::OnAdd()
{
        UpdateData();

        if (!m_text.IsEmpty())
        {
                m_list.AddString(m_text);
                m_text.Empty();
                UpdateData(FALSE);

                // Return the focus (caret) back to the edit control
                GetDlgItem(IDC_TEXT)->SetFocus();
        }
}
```

7. Code the OnBackColor and OnTextColor methods. Both of these methods use the MFC class *CColorDialog* to let the user choose a suitable color. When choosing the background color, a brush is also created based on the color. In both cases we invalidate the list box to reflect the new color scheme.

```
void CCtlColorDlg::OnBackColor()
{
        CColorDialog dlg;

        if (dlg.DoModal() == IDOK)
        {
                m_crBackground = dlg.GetColor();

                // A GDI brush might be attached to m_brush.
                // Detach returns TRUE if there was, so we need
                // to free the GDI resources with DeleteObject

                if (m_brush.Detach())
                        m_brush.DeleteObject();
```

3.4
COLOR ITEMS IN A LIST BOX

```
            // Create a brush with the background color
            m_brush.CreateSolidBrush (m_crBackground);

            m_list.Invalidate();
        }
}
void CCtlColorDlg::OnTextColor()
{
        CColorDialog dlg;

        if (dlg.DoModal() == IDOK)
        {
                m_crText = dlg.GetColor();
                m_list.Invalidate();
        }
}
```

8. **Code the CCtlColorDlg::OnCtlColor method.** Since our *m_brush* member is a *CBrush* object and not an HBRUSH, we use the *CGdiObject* method *GetSafeHandle* to return a HANDLE, which we appropriately cast to an HBRUSH.

```
HBRUSH CCtlColorDlg::OnCtlColor(CDC* pDC, CWnd* pWnd, UINT nCtlColor)
{
        if (nCtlColor == CTLCOLOR_LISTBOX)
        {
                pDC->SetBkMode(TRANSPARENT);
                pDC->SetTextColor (m_crText);
                return (HBRUSH) m_brush.GetSafeHandle();
        } else
                return CDialog::OnCtlColor(pDC, pWnd, nCtlColor);
}
```

9. **Build and test the application.** Add a few lines of text to the list box, then change the text and background colors.

How It Works

The common color dialog lets the user select an RGB color for the background or text color. Just a few lines of code in *OnTextColor* and *OnBackColor* are needed to invoke the dialogs. We just store the text color for use later in *OnCtlColor*, but we actually create a *CBrush* for the background color. That's because *OnCtlColor* expects an HBRUSH for the background, but not for the text color.

When the background color is changed, the current brush must be detached and then deleted, otherwise we will find ourselves running out of GDI resources due to one of those infamous resource leaks.

A WM_CTLCOLOR message is sent to *CCtlColorDlg* for every single child control, not just the list box. We determined in step 8 which message to handle based on the value of *nCtlColor*. If this value is CTLCOLOR_LISTBOX, then Windows is requesting a brush for all list boxes in our application. Since we only have one, we don't need to do any further processing. Otherwise, the message is sent back to the framework.

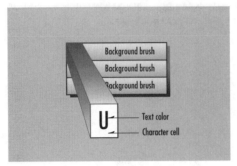

Figure 3-15 Exploded view of an item in a list box

Second, returning from *OnCtlColor* with the background brush won't completely cover all the list box control's background. Figure 3-15 shows a 3D view of a list box control with a single character, a "u" placed in it.

The large rectangular area in the background will be painted by the HBRUSH returned from *OnCtlColor*. However, the small rectangle around the text character, the character cell, can be painted in one of two ways. If we call *SetBkColor*, Windows will find the closest solid color and paint the background of the character cell with that color (if you're running Windows in 256-color mode). The problem with this method is the solid color might not match the background brush, since the brush on a paletted device might be hatched or dithered. Figure 3-16 shows what happens if the background brush is dithered and the same color is used for *SetBkColor*.

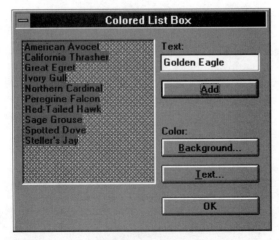

Figure 3-16 Dithered background brush

3.4 COLOR ITEMS IN A LIST BOX

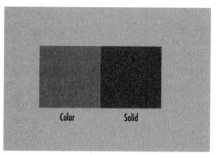

Figure 3-17 Portion of the CColorDialog showing dithering

You can see whether the color you are choosing for the background will be dithered by expanding the color dialog to view the color picker area as shown in Figure 3-17.

The second alternative is to set the background mode to TRANSPARENT by calling *SetBkMode*. The text will be drawn transparently on the list box so the background brush, whether it's solid or dithered, will show through. This way we don't have to worry about the background brush having to exactly match the character cell's background color.

Comments

If you have more than one list box in your application but only want one of the controls specially colored, you'll have to treat the *OnCtlColor* message a little differently. The second parameter passed to *OnCtlColor* is a temporary pointer to the *CWnd* object in question. If you get the control ID from this *CWnd* object using *GetDlgCtrlID*, you can compare it against a particular control. For example, we could have coded step 8 like this:

```
HBRUSH CCtlColorDlg::OnCtlColor(CDC* pDC, CWnd* pWnd, UINT nCtlColor)
{
        if (pWnd->GetDlgCtrlID() == IDC_LIST)
        {
        ...
        }
}
```

If you're curious about what effect a dithered background has when you do set the background color, modify the *OnCtlColor* method like this. Then run the program and choose a dithered color as the background. This only works on 256-color devices.

```
HBRUSH CCtlColorDlg::OnCtlColor(CDC* pDC, CWnd* pWnd, UINT nCtlColor)
{
        if (nCtlColor == CTLCOLOR_LISTBOX)
```

continued on next page

continued from previous page

```
    {
            pDC->SetBkColor (m_crBackground);
            pDC->SetTextColor (m_crText);
            return (HBRUSH) m_brush.GetSafeHandle();
    } else
            return CDialog::OnCtlColor(pDC, pWnd, nCtlColor);
}
```

Finally, you could create your own *CListBox* control and handle WM_CTLCOLOR through message reflection. Refer to Tech Note #62 "Message Reflection for Windows Controls" in Books Online for more information.

COMPLEXITY INTERMEDIATE

3.5 How do I... Create a dynamic shortcut menu?

Problem

MFC message maps provide a convenient way to handle menus designed in App Studio, but I need to display menu items that are not known at design time. How do I dynamically create and append menu items to a floating menu at runtime?

Technique

It's recommended that your Windows 95 application use the right-mouse button for displaying a shortcut menu, providing easy access to the most commonly used commands. This How-To displays a shortcut menu that contains a list of current top-level windows. A *CMenu* object is used to create, track, and modify a floating pop-up menu.

We'll display the menu if the right-mouse button is clicked within a group-box control. If an item is chosen from the pop-up menu, Windows sends the WM_COMMAND message to our dialog box. We'll process this message by overriding the *OnCommand* member function and figure out which menu item was selected. Figure 3-18 shows the sample application running.

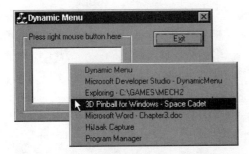

Figure 3-18 A dynamic pop-up menu showing the running applications

3.5
CREATE A DYNAMIC SHORTCUT MENU

If you don't want to change the contents of the menu at runtime, you can use the Pop-Up Menu Component Gallery to add a static menu to your application. It won't add the *OnCommand* handler for you, but it will add a default menu to the resource.

Steps

1. **Create a new project called DynamicMenu using the MFC AppWizard (exe).** Choose the Dialog-based option and press the Finish button.

   Classes to be created:
   Application: CDynamicMenuApp in DynamicMenu.h and DynamicMenu.cpp
   Dialog: CDynamicMenuDlg in DynamicMenuDlg.h and DynamicMenuDlg.cpp

   Features:
   + About box on system menu
   + 3D Controls
   + Uses shared DLL implementation (MFC40.DLL)

2. **Add controls to the IDD_DYNAMICMENU_DIALOG dialog.** Use the resource editor to construct a dialog similar to the one shown in Figure 3-19. The control IDs and attributes are shown in this table:

Control	ID	Attributes
Group	IDC_STATIC	Default
Exit button	IDOK	Default button
Picture	IDC_HERE	Type: Rectangle (White); Notify and Client Edge styles

3. **Add a member variables to CDynamicMenuDlg.** Use the Add Variable dialog to add this member to hold the pop-up menu:

Type	Declaration	Access
CMenu	m_menu	protected

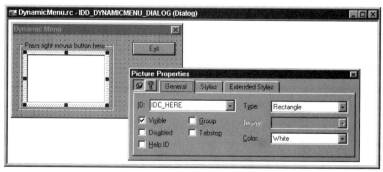

Figure 3-19 Dialog layout for DynamicMenu

4. **Add message handlers for CDynamicMenuDlg using Class Wizard.** Add message-handling functions for these objects:

Object ID	Function	Message
CDynamicMenuDlg	OnCommand	OnCommand
CDynamicMenuDlg	OnContextMenu	WM_CONTEXTMENU
CDynamicMenuDlg	OnSetCursor	WM_SETCURSOR

5. **Code the CDynamicMenuDlg::OnContextMenu method.** This code retrieves the top-level windows from the window list and dynamically appends their captions to the menu. It then uses *TrackPopupMenu* to display the menu.

```
void CDynamicMenuDlg::OnContextMenu(CWnd* pWnd, CPoint point)
{
    // add top-level window captions to menu
    UINT nMenuID = 200;     // starting menu id
    CString caption;        // string to hold window caption

    // If the cursor wasn't over the rectangle IDC_HERE, return
    if (pWnd->GetDlgCtrlID() != IDC_HERE)
        return;

    // remove existing items (if any) from pop-up menu
    for (int i = m_menu.GetMenuItemCount(); -i >= 0;)
        m_menu.RemoveMenu (i, MF_BYPOSITION);

    // get first top-most window
    CWnd* pApp = AfxGetMainWnd()->GetWindow(GW_HWNDFIRST);

    // walk entire window list
    while (pApp)
    {
        // check if window has caption and is visible
        if (pApp->GetWindowTextLength() && pApp->IsWindowVisible())
        {
            // get window caption and add it to the menu
            pApp->GetWindowText(caption);
            m_menu.AppendMenu(MF_STRING, nMenuID++, caption);
        }
        // get next window in window list
        pApp = pApp->GetWindow(GW_HWNDNEXT);
    }

    // display and track menu item selections
    m_menu.TrackPopupMenu (TPM_LEFTALIGN | TPM_RIGHTBUTTON,
        point.x, point.y, this, NULL);
}
```

3.5
CREATE A DYNAMIC SHORTCUT MENU

6. Edit CDynamicMenuDlg::OnCommand. The following code processes the WM_COMMAND message by uncovering the window selected from the shortcut menu.

```
BOOL CDynamicMenuDlg::OnCommand(WPARAM wParam, LPARAM lParam)
{
        BOOL bRet = CDialog::OnCommand(wParam, lParam);

        UINT nID = LOWORD(wParam); // menu item ID
        int nCode = HIWORD(wParam);// notification code

        // If the dialog didn't handle the message,
        // then we'll take a shot at it assuming it is from a menu
        // (indicated by nCode == 0)

        if (bRet == FALSE && nCode == 0)
        {
                // See if nID matches a menu in m_menu
                CString caption;
                if (m_menu.GetMenuString(nID, caption, MF_BYCOMMAND) != 0)
                {
                        // get pointer to window
                        CWnd* pWnd = CWnd::FindWindow(NULL, caption);

                        // ...and bring it to the foreground
                        if (pWnd)
                                pWnd->BringWindowToTop();

                        // We processed the message
                        bRet = TRUE;
                }
        }
        return bRet;
}
```

7. Edit CDynamicMenuDlg::OnSetCursor. Give the user feedback when they're over the rectangle control by changing the mouse cursor to a cross (one of the system supplied cursors).

```
BOOL CDynamicMenuDlg::OnSetCursor(CWnd* pWnd, UINT nHitTest, UINT message)
{
        // Change the cursor to a cross if it's over the IDC_HERE control
        if (pWnd->GetDlgCtrlID() == IDC_HERE)
        {
                SetCursor(AfxGetApp()->LoadStandardCursor(IDC_CROSS));
                return TRUE;
        }

        return CDialog::OnSetCursor(pWnd, nHitTest, message);
}
```

CHAPTER 3
CONTROLS

8. **Edit CDynamicMenuDlg::OnInitDialog.** The pop-up menu must be created before items can be appended to it. Add the following code to *OnCreate*:

```
BOOL CDynamicMenuDlg::OnInitDialog()
{
    CDialog::OnInitDialog();
...
    m_menu.CreatePopupMenu();

    return TRUE;  // return TRUE  unless you set the focus to a control
}
```

9. **Build and test the application.** Click the right-mouse button over the view area, and you'll be presented with a menu of all the running applications. Select one, and it will be focused.

How It Works

The *CMenu* class can be used to create, track, and modify a floating pop-up menu. An empty pop-up menu is created by calling *CMenu::CreatePopupMenu*. You do not need to call the *DestroyMenu* member function since it is automatically called by the *CMenu* destructor.

Each menu item must have a unique identifier so an application can detect which menu item was selected. The first menu item is assigned an identifier of 200. There is nothing magical about the number 200; it just needs to be different from identifiers assigned to other menu items. The identifier is incremented for each menu item appended to the menu. See Figure 3-20.

The appended menu items are static in nature; they will not be removed from the menu until the menu is destroyed or *RemoveMenu* has been called for each menu item. In step 5, we added code that removes all items from the menu:

```
int i;
for (i=m_menu.GetMenuItemCount(); --i >= 0;)
    m_menu.RemoveMenu(i, MF_BYPOSITION);
```

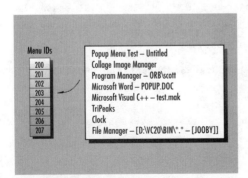

Figure 3-20 Associating menu items with identifiers

Windows maintains a list of top-level windows, commonly referred to as the "windows list." You can call *GetWindow* to retrieve windows from this list. *GetWindow*, with the relationship flag set to GW_HWNDFIRST and GW_HWNDNEXT, allows you to retrieve a list of all top-level windows. The caption of the window is appended to the menu by calling the *AppendMenu* member function.

The number of items in the menu is saved to the data member *m_nMenuItems*. This variable will be used later during processing of the WM_COMMAND message.

You can make the pop-up menu appear at the current cursor position by passing the screen coordinates of the cursor to *TrackPopupMenu*. The *OnContextMenu* member function passes the cursor position to you in screen coordinates, perfect for use in *TrackPopupMenu*.

OnCommand

Message maps provide a level of abstraction that routes menu IDs to member functions. You can use message maps with dynamic menus by reserving a block of menu IDs and associating them with menu items. This technique, however, is not useful when the number of menu items is unknown.

You'll want to process the dynamic menu items yourself and use message maps for the static menu items. You can do this by overriding the *OnCommand* member function. Menu items defined in the message map are processed by calling the base class *OnCommand* member function. The menu item is not processed by the message map if *OnCommand* returns FALSE.

Windows sends the WM_COMMAND message to your window when a menu item is selected, when a child control sends a notification message, or when an accelerator keystroke is translated. Windows packs the *wParam* and *lParam* depending on the context of the message. For menu messages, the parameters are packed like this:

Item	wParam	lParam
Menu item ID	LOWORD	—
Control handle	—	cast to HWND
Notification code	HIWORD (0 for menus)	—

If the menu item ID is found in the *m_menu*, we take the Window caption and try to associate it with a real *CWnd* object using the static method *FindWindow*. If successful, the window is brought to the top using a function called, oddly enough, *BringWindowToTop*.

Comments

Why are we using WM_CONTEXTMENU instead of WM_RBUTTONDOWN? It's a new message for Win32 applications that passes the mouse point in screen coordinates instead of client coordinates. Since *TrackPopupMenu* needs a position relative to the screen, we can use the point passed to *OnContextMenu*. The point passed to *OnRButtonDown* would need conversion through *ClientToScreen*.

TrackPopupMenu is one of the most underrated Windows API functions. It displays a floating pop-up menu that can appear anywhere on the screen. You can use the mouse cursor to specify how to align the menu, as well as which mouse button tracks menu items. It also lets you specify which window receives the WM_COMMAND messages from the menu and which screen coordinates dismiss the menu. As you can see, this is a very multifaceted function but still easy to use.

3.6 How do I... Create a progress meter custom control?

COMPLEXITY INTERMEDIATE

Problem

I'd like to create my own custom progress meter, a thermometer-style control that can display text. What's the best way to create this custom control, and how do I use it in a dialog?

Technique

OK, the above sounds pretty contrived, but a meter control is simple enough to illustrate how you might create an entirely new custom control from scratch. Although the one we'll create, *CMeterCtrl*, uses pretty much the same methods as the *CProgressCtrl*, it draws the meter differently and can display a line of text, which the other one can't.

The *CMeterCtrl* starts as a generic *CWnd,* but takes advantage of two new window styles, WS_EX_CLIENTEDGE and WS_EX_STATICEDGE, to draw the sunken border around the control. It's a cheap way to get that great 3D effect everyone loves. That leaves us to handle two events: WM_PAINT and WM_ERASEBKGND. Any *CWnd*-derived class can override these paint messages to achieve any desired effect. We'll draw the left part of the bar to indicate the percentage complete, and we'll draw the text over the bar. Figure 3-21 shows what the meter looks like while operating.

When you press the Start Timer button, a short timer triggers a simulated read from the disk drive. Every time the timer fires, the progress gauge is updated by 10 percent. The timer keeps going, but you can stop it by pressing the same button. When the percentage complete reaches 100, it starts over.

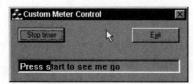

Figure 3-21 CMeter progress gauge

3.6 CREATE A PROGRESS METER CUSTOM CONTROL

Steps

1. **Create a new project called Meter using the MFC AppWizard (exe).** Choose the Dialog-based option and press the Finish button.

   Classes to be created:
   Application: CMeterApp in Meter.h and Meter.cpp
   Dialog: CMeterDlg in MeterDlg.h and MeterDlg.cpp

   Features:
   + About box on system menu
   + 3D Controls
   + Uses shared DLL implementation (MFC40.DLL)

2. **Modify the IDD_METER_DIALOG dialog.** Change the OK button's caption to Exit and remove the Cancel button. Add another button called Start Timer with an ID of IDC_START_TIMER. Place a rectangle control at the bottom of the dialog to act as a placeholder for the meter control. Disable the visible style for the rectangle since we don't want it to show up; it's just a surrogate. The dialog should look like the one shown in Figure 3-22. The dialog controls are shown below:

Control	ID	Attributes
Exit button	IDOK	Turn off the default button style
Start timer button	ID_START_TIMER	Default button
Rectangle	IDC_PLACEHOLDER	Visible style disabled

3. **Create a new class called CMeterCtrl.** Use ClassWizard to create a new class using the following information:

   Class Name: CMeterCtrl
   Class Type: generic CWnd
   Header File: MeterCtrl.h
   Implementation File: MeterCtrl.cpp

Figure 3-22 Dialog layout for the Meter project

4. **Add message handlers for CMeterCtrl using Class Wizard.** Add message-handling functions for these objects:

Object ID	Function	Message
CMeterCtrl	OnPaint	WM_PAINT
CMeterCtrl	OnEraseBkgnd	WM_ERASEBKGND
CMeterCtrl	Create	Create

5. **Edit MeterCtrl.h.** Add the following member variables and helper methods to *CMeterCtrl*. Note that I removed the first and last parameters to the *Create* method.

```
class CMeterCtrl : public CWnd
{
// Construction
public:
        CMeterCtrl();

// Attributes
public:
        // note: set the text through CWnd::SetWindowText
        UINT SetPos(UINT nPos);
        void SetRange(UINT nLower, UINT nUpper);

// Operations
public:
        void StepIt();

// Overrides
        // ClassWizard generated virtual function overrides
        //{{AFX_VIRTUAL(CMeterCtrl)
        public:
        virtual BOOL Create(LPCTSTR lpszWindowName, DWORD dwStyle, const RECT& rect,
                CWnd* pParentWnd, UINT nID);
        //}}AFX_VIRTUAL

// Implementation
public:
        virtual ~CMeterCtrl();

        // Generated message map functions
protected:
        //{{AFX_MSG(CMeterCtrl)
        afx_msg void OnPaint();
        afx_msg BOOL OnEraseBkgnd(CDC* pDC);
        //}}AFX_MSG
        DECLARE_MESSAGE_MAP()

        void InvalidateMeter();

        UINT m_nLower;   // lower bounds
        UINT m_nUpper;   // upper bounds
        UINT m_nPos;  // current position within bounds
};
```

3.6
CREATE A PROGRESS METER CUSTOM CONTROL

6. Code the helper methods in MeterCtrl.cpp. Add all this code for setting the attributes:

```cpp
void CMeterCtrl::SetRange(UINT nLower, UINT nUpper)
{
    ASSERT(nLower >= 0 && nLower < 0xffff);
    ASSERT(nUpper > nLower && nUpper < 0xffff);

    m_nLower = nLower;
    m_nUpper = nUpper;

    InvalidateMeter();
}

UINT CMeterCtrl::SetPos(UINT nPos)
{
    ASSERT(nPos >= m_nLower && nPos <= m_nUpper);
    UINT nOld = m_nPos;
    m_nPos = nPos;

    InvalidateMeter();

    return nOld;
}

void CMeterCtrl::StepIt()
{
    m_nPos++;
    if (m_nPos > m_nUpper)
        m_nPos = m_nLower;

    InvalidateMeter();
}

void CMeterCtrl::InvalidateMeter()
{
    // Small optimization that just invalidates the client area
    // (The borders don't usually need updating)

    CRect r;
    GetClientRect(r);
    InvalidateRect(r);
}
```

7. Edit CMeterCtrl::Create. Modify the parameters and add this code to the *Create* method:

```cpp
BOOL CMeterCtrl::Create(LPCTSTR lpszWindowName, DWORD dwStyle, const RECT& rect,
        CWnd* pParentWnd, UINT nID)
{
    // Create our own little class style
    static CString className = AfxRegisterWndClass(CS_HREDRAW | CS_VREDRAW);

    // We needed our own Create method so we can call CreateEx
    // internally with the WS_EX_* styles to draw the border
```

continued on next page

continued from previous page

```
        return CWnd::CreateEx(WS_EX_CLIENTEDGE | WS_EX_STATICEDGE,
            className, lpszWindowName, dwStyle,
            rect.left, rect.top, rect.right-rect.left, rect.bottom-rect.top,
            pParentWnd->GetSafeHwnd(), (HMENU) nID);
}
```

8. Edit CMeterCtrl::OnEraseBkgnd. This is an easy method. It simply fills the client area with a system brush already set to the background color in the user preferences.

```
BOOL CMeterCtrl::OnEraseBkgnd(CDC* pDC)
{
        CRect r;
        GetClientRect(r);
        CBrush* pBrush = CBrush::FromHandle(GetSysColorBrush(COLOR_BTNFACE));
        pDC->FillRect(r, pBrush);

        return TRUE;
}
```

9. Edit CMeterCtrl::OnPaint. All this code is explained in full detail later. For now, just locate *OnPaint* and type all this stuff in:

```
void CMeterCtrl::OnPaint()
{
        CPaintDC dc(this); // device context for painting
        UINT nRange = m_nUpper - m_nLower;

        CRect rClient;
        GetClientRect(rClient);

        // Figure out the left and right rectangles
        CRect rLeft = rClient;
        CRect rRight = rClient;

        rLeft.right = ((float) (m_nPos - m_nLower) / nRange) * rClient.Width();
        rRight.left = rLeft.right;

        // Create matching regions
        CRgn rgnLeft, rgnRight;
        rgnLeft.CreateRectRgnIndirect(rLeft);
        rgnRight.CreateRectRgnIndirect(rRight);

        // Draw the left part of the meter
        // (The right side was handled in OnEraseBkgnd)
        CBrush* pBrush = CBrush::FromHandle (GetSysColorBrush(COLOR_HIGHLIGHT));
        dc.FillRect(rLeft, pBrush);

        // Draw the text over the left part
        CString strCaption;
        GetWindowText(strCaption);

        dc.SelectClipRgn(&rgnLeft);
        dc.SetBkMode(TRANSPARENT);
        dc.SetTextColor(GetSysColor(COLOR_HIGHLIGHTTEXT));
        dc.DrawText(strCaption, rClient, DT_BOTTOM | DT_LEFT);
```

3.6
CREATE A PROGRESS METER CUSTOM CONTROL

```
        // Draw the text over the right part
        dc.SelectClipRgn(&rgnRight);
        dc.SetTextColor(GetSysColor(COLOR_BTNTEXT));
        dc.DrawText(strCaption, rClient, DT_BOTTOM | DT_LEFT);
}
```

10. Edit the CMeterCtrl constructor. Initialize the three member variables in the constructor like this:

```
CMeterCtrl::CMeterCtrl()
{
        m_nPos = 0;
        m_nLower = 0;
        m_nUpper = 10;
}
```

11. Add message handlers for CMeterDlg using Class Wizard. Add message-handling functions for these objects:

Object ID	Function	Message
CMeterDlg	OnTimer	WM_TIMER
IDC_START_TIMER	OnStartTimer	BN_CLICKED

12. Edit MeterDlg.h. Add a member variable for the *CMeterCtrl* class and add the include directive to the top like this:

```
#include "MeterCtrl.h"

class CMeterDlg : public CDialog
{
// Construction
public:
        CMeterDlg(CWnd* pParent = NULL);   // standard constructor

        CMeterCtrl m_meter;
...
```

13. Edit CMeterDlg::OnInitDialog. We create the window part of the meter control in the WM_INITDIALOG handler like this:

```
BOOL CMeterDlg::OnInitDialog()
{
        CDialog::OnInitDialog();

        // Add "About..." menu item to system menu.

        // IDM_ABOUTBOX must be in the system command range.
        ASSERT((IDM_ABOUTBOX & 0xFFF0) == IDM_ABOUTBOX);
        ASSERT(IDM_ABOUTBOX < 0xF000);

        CMenu* pSysMenu = GetSystemMenu(FALSE);
        CString strAboutMenu;
        strAboutMenu.LoadString(IDS_ABOUTBOX);
        if (!strAboutMenu.IsEmpty())
        {
```

continued on next page

continued from previous page

```
            pSysMenu->AppendMenu(MF_SEPARATOR);
            pSysMenu->AppendMenu(MF_STRING, IDM_ABOUTBOX, strAboutMenu);
    }

    SetIcon(m_hIcon, TRUE);         // Set big icon
    SetIcon(m_hIcon, FALSE);        // Set small icon

    // Figure out where to put the meter control
    CRect r;
    GetDlgItem(IDC_PLACEHOLDER)->GetWindowRect(r);
    ScreenToClient(r);

    m_meter.Create("Press start timer to see me go", WS_VISIBLE | ⇒
WS_CHILD, r, this, 101);
    m_meter.SetRange(10, 25);
    m_meter.SetPos(10);

    return TRUE;  // return TRUE  unless you set the focus to a control
}
```

14. **Edit CMeterDlg::OnStartTimer.** This code and the button serve double duty. They both start and stop the timer. We're using a static variable local to this method to keep track of which state we're in.

```
void CMeterDlg::OnStartTimer()
{
    static BOOL bRunning = FALSE;

    if (!bRunning)
    {
        bRunning = TRUE;
        OnTimer(1);       // force a timer event so we don't have to ⇒
wait a half sec
        SetTimer(1, 500, NULL);
        GetDlgItem(IDC_START_TIMER)->SetWindowText("Stop timer");
    } else {
        bRunning = FALSE;
        KillTimer(1);
        GetDlgItem(IDC_START_TIMER)->SetWindowText("Start timer");
    }
}
```

15. **Edit CMeterDlg::OnTimer.** It couldn't get any easier than this. We just bump the meter to the next step value. *StepIt* works just like the one in *CProgressCtrl*.

```
void CMeterDlg::OnTimer(UINT nIDEvent)
{
    m_meter.StepIt();
}
```

16. **Build and run the application.** Press the start button to see it go.

How It Works

When the main dialog box initializes, it creates the *CMeterCtrl* control *m_meter* with the same dialog box coordinates as IDC_PLACEHOLDER. By using this invisible control, you can change the position of the *CMeterCtrl* window in the resource editor instead of changing hard-coded coordinates in your application.

We're doing three basic things here. First, we calculate two rectangles: one for the left side of the meter that represents the "done" side; the right side rectangle doesn't get painted. The right side will stay the same color painted in WM_ERASEBKGND. Second, a filled rectangle is drawn using the *rLeft* rectangle to represent the current percent. Finally, the text is drawn.

How do we get that inverted text look? We use the same two rectangles to draw the window caption twice! The first time we draw the caption, the text color is set to the highlight color for text (usually white so it shows up better on a darker background). A clipping region, formed from the left side rectangle, stops the text from being drawn into the right side. The second time we draw the caption, the device context clipping region is set to the right side rectangle, preventing it from overdrawing the text from the first *DrawText*.

Comments

There are a couple of methods missing from *CMeterCtrl* that would make it a complete control: *SetStep* and *OffsetPos*. You can see what these should look like by examining the *CProgressCtrl* version in Books Online. You could extend this class even further by adding methods to return the current position and the upper and lower bounds. The progress control doesn't have those features.

COMPLEXITY
ADVANCED

3.7 How do I... Create an auto-sizing multicolumn list box?

Problem

I need to display data in a list box that should be organized in columns. I am aware of the LBS_MULTICOLUMN list box style bit which creates a multicolumn list box that scrolls horizontally, but this is not the behavior I want. I know the ListView control can display text in columns, but I want a control that dynamically resizes its columns to fit the data and one that adds new columns when necessary.

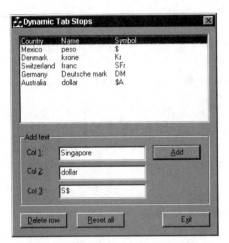

Figure 3-23 TabStop application in action

Technique

If you create a list box that has the LBS_USETABSTOPS style bit set, the list box positions the text at the tabstop when the string contains tab characters. You specify the position of the tabstops by calling the *SetTabStops* member function of the *CListBox* class.

Tabstops are defined in dialog box units. The horizontal dialog unit is one-quarter of the average character width of the current font. This can make calculating tabs a little more difficult when using proportional fonts, since each character is not the same width.

This How-To creates a new list box class called *CTabList* to support tabstops as shown in Figure 3-23. It intercepts the strings as they're added to the list box and dynamically sets the tabs to accommodate the longest string in each column. The object detects when an item is deleted from the list box and recalculates the tab settings if necessary.

Even though this sample project only uses a tab-separated string containing two tabs, the *CTabList* supports any number of tabs because it uses a dynamic array to keep track of the tab settings.

The columns will contain a space of two average characters by default. You can change this by calling the *SetColumnSpace* member function of the *CTabList* class.

Steps

1. **Create a new project called TabStop using the MFC AppWizard (exe).**
   Choose the Dialog-based option and press the Finish button.

   Classes to be created:
   Application: CTabStop in TabStop.h and TabStop.cpp
   Dialog: CTabStopDlg in TabStopDlg.h and TabStopDlg.cpp

3.7
CREATE AN AUTO-SIZING MULTICOLUMN LIST BOX

Features:
+ About box on system menu
+ 3D Controls
+ Uses shared DLL implementation (MFC40.DLL)

2. Create a new class called CTabList. Use ClassWizard to create a new class using the following information:

Class name:	CTabList
Base class:	CListBox
File:	TabList.cpp

We'll add the code for the class later. By creating the class before we modify the dialog, we'll be able to attach the list box directly to a *CTabList* in ClassWizard.

3. Modify the IDD_TABSTOP_DIALOG dialog. Switch to the Resource View and modify the dialog box as shown in Figure 3-24. The dialog options are shown below (in tab order):

Control	ID	Attributes
Dialog	IDD_TABSTOP_DIALOG	214 x 180
Edit #1	IDC_EDIT1	Default
Edit #2	IDC_EDIT2	Default
Edit #3	IDC_EDIT3	Default
Add button	IDC_ADD	Default button
Delete button	IDC_DELETE	Disabled
Reset button	IDC_RESET	Default
Exit button	IDOK	Remove default button style
List box	IDC_LIST	Use tabstops

4. Add member variables and message maps. Use ClassWizard to add the following data members to the *CTabStopDlg* class.

Control ID	Type	Member
IDC_TEXT	CString	m_strText
IDC_LIST	CTabList	m_list
IDC_DELETE	CButton	m_delete

Add the following message maps to the *CTabStopDlg* class:

Object ID	Function	Message
IDC_ADD	OnAdd	BN_CLICKED
IDC_DELETE	OnDelete	BN_CLICKED
IDC_RESET	OnReset	BN_CLICKED
IDC_LIST	OnSelChangeList	LBN_SELCHANGE

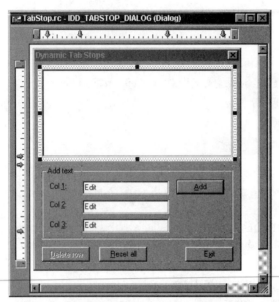

Figure 3-24 Dialog layout for the TABSTOP project

5. **Include header file.** Include the header file TabList.h to the top of the TabStopDlg.h file.

```
#include "TabList.h"
```

6. **Edit CTabStopDlg::OnAddCode.** This code adds the tab-separated string to the list box. Add the following code to the *OnAdd* member function:

```
void CTabStopDlg::OnAdd()
{
    // transfer dlg data to m_strText and add it to the list box
    UpdateData();

    CString text = m_strEdit1 + "\t" + m_strEdit2 + "\t" + m_strEdit3;
    m_List.AddString(text);

    // Reset the text boxes
    m_strEdit1.Empty();
    m_strEdit2.Empty();
    m_strEdit3.Empty();
    GetDlgItem(IDC_EDIT1)->SetFocus();
    UpdateData(FALSE);
}
```

3.7
CREATE AN AUTO-SIZING MULTICOLUMN LIST BOX

7. Code the CTabStopDlg::OnDelete method. This code deletes the currently selected string from the list box. Add the following code to the *OnDelete* function:

```
void CTabStopDlg::OnDelete()
{
    // delete the current list box selection
    m_list.DeleteString(m_list.GetCurSel());

    // disable the Delete push button
    m_delete.EnableWindow(FALSE);
}
```

8. Code the CTabStopDlg::OnReset method. This code removes all the strings from the list box. Add the following code to the *OnReset* member function:

```
void CTabStopDlg::OnReset()
{
    m_list.ResetContent();
}
```

9. Code the CTabStopDlg::OnSelchangeList method. This code is executed when the current selection of the list box changes. The Disable button is enabled since you know an item is selected in the list box. Add the following code to the *OnSelchangeList* member function:

```
void CTabStopDlg::OnSelchangeList()
{
    // enable the delete button now that an item has been selected
    m_delete.EnableWindow(TRUE);
}
```

10. Edit TabList.h. Modify the interface for *CTabList* by adding these methods and members:

```
class CTabList : public CListBox
{
// Construction
public:
    CTabList();

// Attributes
public:
    void    SetColumnSpace(int nSpacing);

// Overrides
    // ClassWizard generated virtual function overrides
    //{{AFX_VIRTUAL(CTabList)
    //}}AFX_VIRTUAL

// Implementation
public:
    virtual ~CTabList();
```

continued on next page

continued from previous page

```
        // Generated message map functions
protected:
        //{{AFX_MSG(CTabList)
        afx_msg LRESULT OnAddString(WPARAM wParam, LPARAM lParam);
        afx_msg LRESULT OnInsertString(WPARAM wParam, LPARAM lParam);
        afx_msg LRESULT OnDeleteString(WPARAM wParam, LPARAM lParam);
        afx_msg LRESULT OnResetContent(WPARAM wParam, LPARAM lParam);
        //}}AFX_MSG

        DECLARE_MESSAGE_MAP()

        // Helper methods
        void    CalculateAvgCharWidth(CDC* pDC);
        void    CalculateTabs();
        BOOL    CalculateColWidths(LPCSTR pString, BOOL bSetWidths = TRUE);
        void    InitColWidth();
        void    Recalc();

        int          m_nAvgCharWidth;   // avg character width
        int          m_nSpacing;        // number of column spaces
        CUIntArray   m_aTabs;           // array of tab settings
        CUIntArray   m_aColWidth;       // array of maximum column widths
        UINT         m_nTabs;           // number of tabs

        // character set used to calculate average character width,
        // only allocate one character set for all instances of classes
        static CString m_strCharSet;
};
```

11. **Edit TabList.cpp.** Add all these methods to the TabList.cpp file:

```
BEGIN_MESSAGE_MAP(CTabList, CListBox)
        //{{AFX_MSG_MAP(CTabList)
        ON_MESSAGE(LB_ADDSTRING,        OnAddString)
        ON_MESSAGE(LB_INSERTSTRING,     OnInsertString)
        ON_MESSAGE(LB_DELETESTRING,     OnDeleteString)
        ON_MESSAGE(LB_RESETCONTENT,     OnResetContent)
        //}}AFX_MSG_MAP
END_MESSAGE_MAP()

// initialize string to calculate average char width
CString CTabList::m_strCharSet =
        "ABCDEFGHIJKLMNOPQRSTUVWXYZabcdefghijklmnopqrstuvwxyz";

CTabList::CTabList()
{
        m_nSpacing = 2;               // init column spacing
        m_nTabs = MIN_TAB_SIZE;       // init number of tabs
        m_nAvgCharWidth = 8;          // a reasonable default

        // init size of tab setting and column width arrays
        m_aTabs.SetSize (MIN_TAB_SIZE);
        m_aColWidth.SetSize (MIN_TAB_SIZE);

        InitColWidth();               // init column width array
}
```

3.7
CREATE AN AUTO-SIZING MULTICOLUMN LIST BOX

```cpp
// Set the number of spaces to separate columns.
void CTabList::SetColumnSpace(int nSpacing)
{
    // only process if different
    if (nSpacing != m_nSpacing)
    {
        m_nSpacing = nSpacing;    // store the number of character spaces
        CalculateTabs();          // calculate new tab settings
        SetTabStops(m_nTabs,
            (LPINT) &m_aTabs[0]); // set tab settings
    }
}

// Calculate average character width. The average character width is
// calculated using the same method used by GetDialogBaseUnits function;
// average char width = (pixel width of "ABC...Zabc...z") / 52.
// The current font is used for the calculation.
void CTabList::CalculateAvgCharWidth(CDC* pDC)
{
    CFont* pCurrentFont = GetFont();  // get font currently using for list box

    // GetFont will return NULL if using System font.
    // If using system font just call GetDialogBaseUnits.
    if (!pCurrentFont)
        m_nAvgCharWidth = LOWORD(GetDialogBaseUnits());

    // if not using system font, select font into dc and
    // calculate average char width
    else
    {
        // have to select object into the dc before
        // we can calculate width of string
        CFont* pOldFont = pDC->SelectObject(pCurrentFont);

        // get width of string
        CSize size = pDC->GetTextExtent(m_strCharSet,
            m_strCharSet.GetLength());

        // calculate average char width and round result
        m_nAvgCharWidth = MulDiv(1, size.cx, m_strCharSet.GetLength());

        // select old font back into dc
        pDC->SelectObject(pOldFont);
    }
}

// calculate tabs from maximum column array
void CTabList::CalculateTabs()
{
    UINT nIndex;   // index to array

    // first tab setting is the fist col width
    m_aTabs[0] = ((m_aColWidth[0]+(m_nAvgCharWidth*m_nSpacing)) * 4) /
        m_nAvgCharWidth;
```

continued on next page

continued from previous page

```
        // calculate each tab setting
        for (nIndex=1; nIndex < m_nTabs; nIndex++)
            m_aTabs[nIndex] = m_aTabs[nIndex-1] +
            ((m_aColWidth[nIndex]+(m_nAvgCharWidth*m_nSpacing)) * 4) /
                m_nAvgCharWidth;
}

// recalculate maximum column widths
void CTabList::Recalc()
{
        // we are totally recalculating, so reset size of arrays
        m_aTabs.SetSize(MIN_TAB_SIZE);      // reset tab stop array size
        m_aColWidth.SetSize(MIN_TAB_SIZE);  // reset col width array size
        m_nTabs = MIN_TAB_SIZE;             // set number of tab settings
        InitColWidth();                     // init col width array

        // loop through list box and calculate col widths for each string
        CString str;
        for (int nItem = GetCount() - 1; nItem >= 0; -nItem)
        {
                GetText(nItem, str);        // get list box item string
                CalculateColWidths(str);    // calculate column widths of string
        }

        CalculateTabs();                    // calculate tab settings
}

// initialize column width to 0
void CTabList::InitColWidth()
{
        // initialize col width settings to a length of 0
        UINT nIndex;
        for (nIndex=0; nIndex < m_nTabs; nIndex++)
            m_aColWidth[nIndex] = 0;
}


// calculate column widths of string
BOOL CTabList::CalculateColWidths(LPCSTR pString, BOOL bSetWidths)
{
        BOOL bMaxColumn = FALSE;    // returns if this string contains max column
        CDC* pDC = GetDC();         // get dc of list box window
        UINT nCol=0;                // column currently processing

        if (pDC)
        {
                // calculate average char width
                CalculateAvgCharWidth(pDC);

                // select current font into dc so can measure width of string
                CFont* pOldFont = pDC->SelectObject(GetFont());

                CString strRow;         // row string
                CString strCol;         // column string
                CSize size;             // size of column string
                int nIndex=0;           // index to row string
```

3.7
CREATE AN AUTO-SIZING MULTICOLUMN LIST BOX

```
            strRow = pString;    // set row string to passed string

            // divide row string up into column strings
            while (nIndex != -1)
            {
                // check if need to grow tab setting and column width
                if (nCol+1 > m_nTabs)
                {
                        m_aTabs.SetSize(m_nTabs+1);
                        m_aColWidth.SetSize(m_nTabs+1);
                        m_nTabs += 1;
                }

                // parse out column string from row string
                if ((nIndex = strRow.Find('\t')) == -1)
                   strCol = strRow;
                else
                {
                        strCol = strRow.Left(nIndex);
                        strRow = strRow.Mid(nIndex+1);
                }

                // get pixel width of column string
                size = pDC->GetTextExtent(strCol, strCol.GetLength());

                // see if this is the widest column string
                if ((UINT)size.cx >= m_aColWidth[nCol])
                {
                        // this string contains a longest column string
                        bMaxColumn = TRUE;

                        // store information to column width array
                        if (bSetWidths)
                                m_aColWidth[nCol] = size.cx;
                }

                nCol++;    // move to the next column
            }

            pDC->SelectObject(pOldFont);
            ReleaseDC(pDC);
        }

        return bMaxColumn;
}


// process the LB_INSERTSTRING message
LRESULT CTabList::OnInsertString(WPARAM wParam, LPARAM lParam)
{
        // adjust the col width array for this string
        BOOL bRet = CalculateColWidths((LPCSTR)lParam);

        // set tab stop if required
        if (bRet)
        {
```

continued on next page

continued from previous page

```
            CalculateTabs();               // adjust the tab setting array
            SetTabStops(m_nTabs,
                    (LPINT)&m_aTabs[0]);   // set tab stops
    }

    return Default();
}


// process the LB_ADDSTRING message
LRESULT CTabList::OnAddString(WPARAM wParam, LPARAM lParam)
{
    // adjust the col width array for this string
    BOOL bRet = CalculateColWidths((LPCSTR)lParam);

    // set tab stop if required
    if (bRet)
    {
        CalculateTabs();                  // adjust the tab setting array
        SetTabStops(m_nTabs, (LPINT)&m_aTabs[0]);    // set tab stops
    }

    return Default();
}


// process the LB_DELETESTRING message
LRESULT CTabList::OnDeleteString(WPARAM wParam, LPARAM lParam)
{
    CString  str;
    GetText(wParam, str);

    // see if need to recalculate tab stops
    BOOL bRecalc = CalculateColWidths(str, FALSE);

    // delete string from list box
    // pass message along to list box proc
    LRESULT lRet = Default();

    // recalculate tab stops if required
    if (bRecalc)
    {
        Recalc();
        SetTabStops(m_nTabs, (LPINT)&m_aTabs[0]);
    }

    return lRet;
}

// process the LB_RESETCONTENT message
LRESULT CTabList::OnResetContent(WPARAM wParam, LPARAM lParam)
{
    m_aTabs.SetSize(MIN_TAB_SIZE);          // reset tab stop array size
    m_aColWidth.SetSize(MIN_TAB_SIZE);      // reset col width array size
    m_nTabs = MIN_TAB_SIZE;                 // set number of tab settings
```

```
        InitColWidth();                    // init column width array

        return Default();
}
```

12. Build and test the application. Enter text into the edit fields and press the Add or Insert push button. This adds the strings to the list box. Add several more strings. Notice how the columns are always aligned and their position is dynamically changed depending on the length of the strings added to the list box. If an item were deleted from the list box, the tabstops would automatically be recalculated and set.

How It Works

It is easy to align columns of data within a list box if you use a fixed-width font. Since each character has the same width, you simply insert the correct number of spaces to align each column. Figure 3-25 shows how the addition of two extra spaces to the string "Ron" will take up the same amount of pixels as the string "Cathy" when using a fixed font.

Fixed-width fonts look good for expressing some forms of data, but often data is visually more appealing when a proportionally spaced font is used. You can create a multicolumn list box and use a proportional font by using tab-separated strings. A tab-separated string is a string that contains a tab character between each column.

The tab settings must be specified in dialog units (DLUs). Dialog boxes and controls use DLUs to define their position and size. This causes the dialog box and controls to adjust their size relative to the font used for the dialog box. A horizontal dialog unit is one-quarter the width of the dialog base unit. A vertical unit is one-eighth the height of a dialog base unit. A dialog base unit is the average size of the font used for the dialog box or control. In other words, the average character contains 4 DLUs for its width and 8 DLUs for its height. Figure 3-26 shows dialog unit measurements.

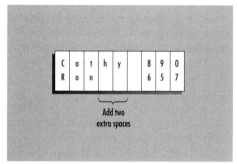

Figure 3-25 Adding space to fixed font aligns text

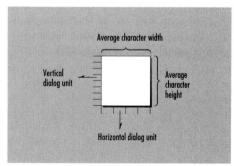

Figure 3-26 Dialog unit (DLU) measurements

CHAPTER 3
CONTROLS

It is easy to obtain the average character size if you're using the system font for a list box: Simply call the *GetDialogBaseUnits* function. The low-order word contains the average character width in pixels, and the high-order word contains the average character height in pixels.

However, this is only useful if you are using the system font. What do you do if you are using a different font for the list box? You need to calculate the average character size for the font yourself. You can do this by selecting the font into its device context, dividing the pixel length of the string containing "ABC...Zabc...z" by 52, and rounding this number to the nearest integer, like this:

```
m_strCharSet = "ABCDEFGHIJKLMNOPQRSTUVWXYZabcdefghijklmnopqrstuvwxyz";
CFont* pOldFont = pDC->SelectObject(GetFont());

Csize size = pDC->GetTextExtent(m_strCharSet, m_strCharSet.GetLength());

m_nAvgCharWidth = MulDiv(1, size.cx, m_strCharSet.GetLength());
```

You might be thinking, "This is pretty interesting, but I just want to set some tabs in my list box." Hang in there; it's important to understand how dialog units work since that's the unit of measure used to set tabs.

You call the *SetTabStops* member function to specify the tab settings. This function sends the list box an LB_SETTABSTOPS message. The first parameter is the number of tab settings. The second parameter is a pointer to the first member of an array of integers containing tabstop positions in dialog units:

```
int tabs[3];
tabs[0] = 5 * 4;    // set tab to character 5
tabs[1] = 10 * 4;   // set tab to character 10
tabs[2] = 15 * 4;   // set tab to character 15

m_list.SetTabStops(3, tabs);
```

It is easy to calculate the number of horizontal dialog units if you want to set tabstops at a certain character position. You simply multiply the character position by four:

```
nHorzDialogUnit = nCharacterPosition * 4;
```

However, this can create problems when using proportional fonts. Remember, a dialog unit is one-quarter of the average character width, so what happens if you have a string that contains a lot of characters that are wider than the average character width? The string might run over the tabstop and use the next tabstop instead. Figure 3-27 shows a situation where the first tabstop is set to the eighth character but a string with only six characters does not even fit. The strings are not that smart; they simply use the next available tab setting.

You can use this technique to set tabs if you are working with a certain type of data and you are willing to make a calculated guess. You can increase or decrease the tab setting by 20 to 30 percent to allow for wider or more narrow characters. However, you often are not working with a certain type of data, and even when you are, the data may use narrow, average, and wide characters.

3.7 CREATE AN AUTO-SIZING MULTICOLUMN LIST BOX

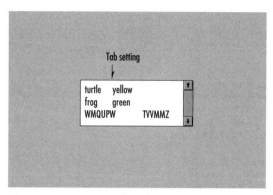

Figure 3-27 Example of long string running over the tabstop

To be sure the columns align correctly you must measure each column's text and dynamically set the tab settings. You can measure the width of the text by selecting the current font into the device context and calling the *GetTextExtent* member function:

```
CFont* pOldFont = pDC->SelectObject(GetFont());
CSize size = pDC->GetTextExtent(m_strCharSet, m_strCharSet.GetLength());
```

You can convert pixels to dialog units with the following formula:

```
nHorizontalDialogUnit = (nPixelWidth * 4) / nAvgCharWidth;
nVerticalDialogUnit = (nPixelHeight * 8) / nAvgCharWidth;
```

There is obviously a speed penalty if you have to examine every string as it is added to the list box. There is also a performance hit when a string is deleted from the list box which requires the tab settings to be recalculated. Even with these side effects, this technique may be just the answer if you need a very convenient multicolumn list box with the columns actually aligned—especially since this How-To provides a class that encapsulates this functionality for you!

Comments

There are many excellent spreadsheet and grid custom controls available, but a multicolumn list box may provide the functionality that is required for your application. It is easy to inherit from the *CListBox* class and create a new multicolumn list box class.

173

3.8 How do I...
Write a custom button to display a menu?

COMPLEXITY
ADVANCED

Problem

I need a customized button that pops up a menu when pressed. Also, I'd like to have complete control over the drawing of the button so I can add a little triangle to indicate that something shows up underneath the button when it's pressed.

Technique

Windows provides support for owner-drawn controls. Windows sends messages to the control's parent allowing it to customize the behavior and appearance of the control. MFC takes this one step further by decoding the owner-draw parameters and forwarding the messages to the control itself. This is called "self-draw" since the drawing code is in the class of the control, not in the owner window.

All this allows you to build reusable control classes in a nice object-oriented approach. For self-drawn buttons, you simply subclass off of *CButton* and handle the *DrawItem* method. The details of the structure passed to *DrawItem* are pretty hairy—that's what makes drawing custom controls difficult. The sample in this How-To will dive into *DrawItem* and come up with the code to draw a regular button with a few twists (see Figure 3-28). Not only does our new class *CMenuButtonCtrl* handle all the normal button drawing stuff, it also displays a menu when pressed. A little triangle gives a visual clue to its capabilities.

Figure 3-28 A CMenuButtonCtrl that displays a pop-up

3.8
WRITE A CUSTOM BUTTON TO DISPLAY A MENU

Steps

1. Create a new project called **MenuButton** using the MFC AppWizard (exe). Choose the Dialog-based version and press the Finish button.

Classes to be created:
  Application: CMenuButtonCtrlApp in MenuButton.h and MenuButton.cpp
  Dialog: CMenuButtonCtrlDlg in MenuButtonDlg.h and MenuButtonDlg.cpp

Features:
  + About box on system menu
  + 3D Controls
  + Uses shared DLL implementation (MFC40.DLL)

2. Create a new class called **CMenuButtonCtrl**. Use ClassWizard to create a new class using the following information:

  Class name: CMenuButtonCtrl
  Base class: CButton
  File: MenuButtonCtrl.cpp

While you're still in ClassWizard, add a handler for the *DrawItem* method to *CMenuButtonCtrl*.

3. Modify IDD_MENUBUTTON_DIALOG in App Studio. Use the dialog shown in Figure 3-29 and the following table to help you lay out the dialog. Make sure the owner-draw attribute is checked for the Fruit button.

Control	ID	Attributes
Check box	IDC_STAYDOWN	auto
Fruit button	IDC_MENU_BUTTON	owner draw
Quit button	IDOK	Default button

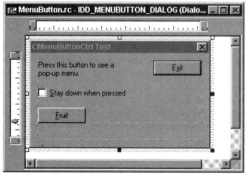

Figure 3-29 Dialog layout for the MenuButton project

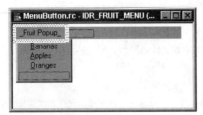

Figure 3-30 The Fruit menu

4. **Add member variables to CMenuButtonDlg.** Add the following variables to *CMenuButtonDlg* using the Member Variables tab in ClassWizard:

Control ID	Type	Member
IDC_STAYDOWN	BOOL	m_bStayDown
IDC_FRUIT	CMenuButtonCtrl	m_button

Developer Studio should warn you to include the header file MenuButtonCtrl.h to the dialog. Do that now in MenuButtonDlg.h:

```
#include "MenuButtonCtrl.h"
```

5. **Add a menu.** Add a menu with the ID IDR_FRUIT_MENU that looks like the one shown in Figure 3-30. *CMenuButtonCtrl* will display the bottom part of the pop-up menu; the Fruit caption won't be visible in the sample. Instead, the title of the button is given in the dialog layout you crafted in step 2.

Use the following IDs for the menu items: ID_BANANAS, ID_APPLES, and ID_ORANGES.

6. **Modify MenuButtonCtrl.h.** Make the following changes to MenuButtonCtrl.h and save the file when you've finished.

```
class CMenuButtonCtrl : public CButton
{
// Construction
public:
        CMenuButtonCtrl();

// Attributes
public:
        void SetPopupMenu(CMenu* pMenu) { m_pMenu = pMenu; }
    BOOL m_bStayDown;

// Operations
public:

// Overrides
        // ClassWizard generated virtual function overrides
        //{{AFX_VIRTUAL(CMenuButtonCtrl)
```

3.8
WRITE A CUSTOM BUTTON TO DISPLAY A MENU

```
public:
    virtual void DrawItem(LPDRAWITEMSTRUCT lpDrawItemStruct);
    //}}AFX_VIRTUAL

// Implementation
public:
    virtual ~CMenuButtonCtrl();

    // Generated message map functions
protected:
    //{{AFX_MSG(CMenuButtonCtrl)
    //}}AFX_MSG

    DECLARE_MESSAGE_MAP()

// Helpers
    void DisplayMenu();
    void DrawTriangle(CDC *pDC, CPoint ptTopLeft, int nWidth);

    CFont m_font;
    CMenu* m_pMenu;
    BOOL m_bDrawLockout;
};
```

7. Edit the CMenuButtonCtrl constructor. Initialize the member variables here:

```
CMenuButtonCtrl::CMenuButtonCtrl()
{
    m_bDrawLockout = FALSE;
    m_bStayDown = FALSE;
}
```

8. Add the DisplayMenu code to MenuButtonCtrl.cpp. This helper method is called to display a simple pop-up menu using *TrackPopupMenu*.

```
void CMenuButtonCtrl::DisplayMenu()
{
    if (m_pMenu)
    {
        CRect btnRect;
        GetWindowRect(btnRect);

        m_bDrawLockout = TRUE;
        m_pMenu->TrackPopupMenu(TPM_LEFTALIGN | TPM_LEFTBUTTON,
            btnRect.left, btnRect.bottom-1, GetParent(), btnRect);
        m_bDrawLockout = FALSE;

        SendMessage(WM_LBUTTONUP, 0, MAKELPARAM(1,1));

        if (m_bStayDown)
            Invalidate(FALSE);
    }
}
```

CHAPTER 3
CONTROLS

9. **Add a reflected message handler for BN_CLICKED.** Use the WizardBar to handle the =BN_CLICKED message. The equal sign indicates a message that is normally handled by the parent of the control, but in this case, our button wants to be notified when it has been clicked.

```
void CMenuButtonCtrl::OnClicked()
{
    if (!m_bStayDown)
        DisplayMenu();
}
```

10. **Add the DrawItem code in MenuButtonCtrl.cpp.** *DrawItem* is called whenever Windows needs to update the display of the button. After the button border is drawn, *DrawItem* places the text and triangle on the button and displays the menu if necessary.

```
void CMenuButtonCtrl::DrawItem(LPDRAWITEMSTRUCT lpDIS)
{
        CRect rect (&(lpDrawItemStruct->rcItem));
        CDC *pDC = CDC::FromHandle(lpDrawItemStruct->hDC);
        UINT state = lpDrawItemStruct->itemState;
        UINT action = lpDrawItemStruct->itemAction;

        if (m_bStayDown && m_bDrawLockout == TRUE)
            return;

        // Fill the entire button with the button brush
        HBRUSH hbrText = GetSysColorBrush(COLOR_BTNTEXT);
        HBRUSH hbrFace = GetSysColorBrush(COLOR_3DFACE);
        HBRUSH hOldBrush = (HBRUSH) SelectObject(pDC->m_hDC, hbrFace);
        FillRect(pDC->m_hDC, rect, hbrFace);

        CRect edgeRect(rect);
        if (state & ODS_FOCUS)
        {
            pDC->Rectangle(rect);
            edgeRect.InflateRect(-1, -1);
        }

        if (state & ODS_SELECTED)
        {
            CPen pen(PS_SOLID, 1, GetSysColor(COLOR_3DSHADOW));
            CPen* pOldPen = pDC->SelectObject(&pen);
            pDC->Rectangle(edgeRect);
            pDC->SelectObject(pOldPen);
        } else
            pDC->DrawEdge(edgeRect, EDGE_RAISED, BF_RECT | BF_SOFT);

        // Calculate the width and height of the triangle
        // based on the 'M' character
        CSize szTri = pDC->GetOutputTextExtent("M", 1);
```

3.8
WRITE A CUSTOM BUTTON TO DISPLAY A MENU

```cpp
    // Calculate the width and height of the text
    CString text;
    GetWindowText(text);
    CSize szText = pDC->GetOutputTextExtent(text, text.GetLength());

    // Calculate the total size of the text + the triangle
    CSize szTotal(szText);
    szTotal.cx += szTri.cx;

    // change the width/height of the button rect
    CRect textRect = rect;
    textRect.InflateRect(-((rect.Width() - szTotal.cx)/2),
        -((rect.Height() - szTotal.cy)/2));
    textRect.top--;

    CRect triRect = textRect;
    triRect.left = textRect.right - szTri.cx;
    triRect.InflateRect(0, -((textRect.Height() - szTri.cy)/2));

    // Draw the text
    pDC->SetBkMode(TRANSPARENT);
    if (state & ODS_SELECTED)
        textRect.OffsetRect(1, 1);
    pDC->DrawText(text, -1, textRect, DT_SINGLELINE | DT_LEFT);

    // Draw the triangle
    SelectObject(pDC->m_hDC, hbrText);
    CPoint ptTri(textRect.left + szText.cx, textRect.top + 3);
    DrawTriangle(pDC, ptTri, 11);

    // Draw the focus rectangle if necessary
    if (state & ODS_FOCUS)
    {
        CRect focusRect(rect);
        focusRect.InflateRect(-4, -4);
        pDC->DrawFocusRect(focusRect);
    }

    SelectObject(pDC->m_hDC, hOldBrush);

    if (m_bStayDown && (action & ODA_SELECT) &&
        (state & ODS_FOCUS) && (state & ODS_SELECTED))
    {
        DisplayMenu();
    }
}
```

11. **Add the DrawTriangle code in MenuButtonCtrl.cpp.** This helper method draws the triangle that looks a lot like the Windows 3.1 minimize button. The last parameter, *nWidth*, specifies how many pixels wide the triangle is at the top. For best results, this algorithm should be an odd number to produce a

nice triangle. The caller of this function, *DrawItem*, has already set the brush used to fill in the triangle.

```
void CMenuButtonCtrl::DrawTriangle(CDC *pDC, CPoint ptTopLeft, int nWidth)
{
    // Use odd widths for best results
    POINT ptArray[3];
    ptArray[0] = ptTopLeft;
    ptArray[1].x = ptTopLeft.x + nWidth - 1;
    ptArray[1].y = ptTopLeft.y;
    ptArray[2].x = ptTopLeft.x + nWidth / 2;
    ptArray[2].y = ptTopLeft.y + nWidth / 2;
    pDC->Polygon(ptArray, 3);
}
```

12. Add a member variable to CMenuButtonDlg. Use the Add Variable dialog to add a member to hold the menu that will be used by the button.

Type	Declaration	Access
CMenu	m_menu	protected

13. Edit CMenuButtonDlg::OnInitDialog. At the end of the dialog initialization, add this code to set up the menu button:

```
BOOL CMenuButtonDlg::OnInitDialog()
{
    CDialog::OnInitDialog();
...

    VERIFY(m_menu.LoadMenu(IDR_FRUIT_MENU));

    CMenu* pMenu = m_menu.GetSubMenu(0);
    ASSERT(pMenu);
    m_button.SetPopupMenu(pMenu);

    return TRUE;  // return TRUE unless you set the focus to a control
}
```

After loading the IDR_FRUIT_MENU menu, *OnInitDialog* retrieves a pointer to the first menu item to pass to the *CMenuButtonCtrl*.

14. Use the WizardBar to add a BN_CLICKED handler for IDC_STAYDOWN in CMenuButtonDlg. The following code toggles the *m_bStayDown* state of the menu button.

```
void CMenuButtonDlg::OnStayDown()
{
    UpdateData();
    m_button.m_bStayDown = m_bStayDown;
}
```

15. Build and run the application. Notice that you can bring up the menu by clicking and holding the button or by clicking and then letting go of the mouse button. It works just like a regular menu item.

3.8 WRITE A CUSTOM BUTTON TO DISPLAY A MENU

How It Works

You can divide the functionality of *CMenuButtonCtrl* into three basic parts:

- 3D button drawing (step 10)
- Triangle drawing (step 11)
- Pop-up menu display (step 8)

The pop-up menu part is actually the easiest to understand. *DisplayMenu* uses the *CMenu::TrackPopupMenu* to do all of its work. By passing the button rectangle to *TrackPopupMenu*, the user can click and release the button without dismissing the menu. If a NULL was passed as the last value, the pop-up menu would disappear as soon as the mouse was released.

DrawItem

As soon as you start messing around with the visuals in a custom control or start modifying a control's behavior, you have to completely implement all of its drawing code. You can't call *CButton::DrawItem* to draw the tricky button shadows—you have to write all the code yourself. It's what we wanted to do anyway, since it makes this How-To a little more interesting.

DrawItem first fills in the button rectangle with a button brush using the new Win32 function *GetSysColorBrush*. Then the outer frame is drawn using the another new function called *DrawEdge*. *DrawEdge* doesn't help if the button is currently pressed; a few calls to *CDC::Rectangle* are used instead. After drawing the button face, the rectangle for the text and triangle is computed, then used by *DrawText* and the helper method *DrawTriangle*. These two methods put the text and triangle in the center of the button. If necessary, the *CDC* method *DrawFocusRect* draws the focus rectangle. Finally, the menu is displayed if two conditions are met: The button is being selected, and it has the focus.

Comments

If you remove the pop-up menu functionality and triangle display, the button behaves just like a normal Windows button would. If you ever need a different customized button, you can use this code as a starting point.

CHAPTER 3
CONTROLS

COMPLEXITY
ADVANCED

3.9 How do I... Draw bitmaps in a list box?

Problem

I'd like to have a list box capable of displaying a bitmap next to a line of text. How do I draw the bitmaps and also show the selection and focus status correctly? I'd also like to have the bitmap appear transparent when the list box item is selected. I know that I need a custom list box, but I can't sort out exactly which steps to take.

Technique

Windows provides support for owner-drawn controls and menus. Windows messages are sent to a parent window of a control, allowing you to customize the visual appearance and behavior of the control. However, to use these owner-drawn controls, your *CWnd*-derived class has to implement the owner-draw behavior of the list box or any other control. This approach does not lead to reusable code. If you have two similar controls in two different dialogs, you must implement the custom control behavior in two places. MFC supports a self-drawing control architecture to solve this problem.

MFC provides a default implementation for the standard owner-draw messages. This default implementation will decode the owner-draw parameters and delegate the owner-draw messages to the control. This is called "self-draw" since drawing, measuring, or comparing the code is in the class of the control or menu, not in the owner window.

This allows you to build reusable control classes that display the control using owner-draw semantics. The code for drawing the control, not the owner of the control, is in the control class. This is an object-oriented approach to custom control programming.

In our case, we're going to implement a self-drawn list box called *CBmpListCtrl*. Each item in the list box consists of a bitmap and a text string. When it's time to draw an item in the list box, the virtual self-drawing methods take care of painting the bitmap and text. It looks like a regular list box to the client, in this case our test dialog. See Figure 3-31.

To make the code easier to follow, the actual drawing of the text and bitmap take place in a separate class representing a single item in the list box, called *CBmpListCtrlData*. If you want to customize the drawing, you can still use *CBmpListCtrl*; you'd only need to change a few methods in *CBmpListCtrlData*.

Steps

1. Create a new project called BmpList using the MFC AppWizard (exe).
Choose the Dialog-based version and press the Finish button.

3.9 DRAW BITMAPS IN A LIST BOX

Classes to be created:
Application: CBmpListCtrlApp in BmpListCtrl.h and BmpList.cpp
Dialog: CBmpListCtrlDlg in BmpListDlg.h and BmpListDlg.cpp

Features:
+ About box on system menu
+ 3D Controls
+ Uses shared DLL implementation (MFC40.DLL)

2. **Create a new class called CBmpListCtrl.** Use ClassWizard to create a new class using the following information:

   Class name: CBmpListCtrl
   Base class: CListBox
   File: BmpListCtrl.cpp

3. **Add two bitmaps.** Use the bitmap editor to add two new bitmaps labeled IDB_BITMAP1 and IDB_BITMAP2. Follow the design shown in Figure 3-32.

4. **Add controls to the IDD_BMPLIST_DIALOG dialog.** Use the resource editor to construct a dialog similar to the one shown in Figure 3-33. The control IDs and attributes are shown in this table (in tab order):

Control	ID	Attributes
Edit control	IDC_EDIT1	Default
Add button	IDC_ADD	"&Add", default button
Left radio button	IDC_BITMAP	"&Checkmark", group, tabstop
Right radio button	IDC_RADIO2	"&X-mark", tabstop
Exit button	IDOK	"&Exit"
List box	IDC_LIST	Not sorted, owner-draw variable, no integral height

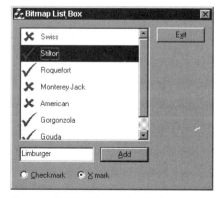

Figure 3-31 CBmpListCtrl in a dialog

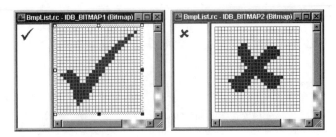

Figure 3-32 Two bitmaps used by the bitmap list box

5. **Use ClassWizard to add message handlers and member variables.** Add message-handling functions for this object:

Object ID	Function	Message
IDC_ADD	OnAdd	BN_CLICKED

Switch to the Member Variables tab in ClassWizard and add the following variables:

Control ID	Type	Member
IDC_LIST	CBmpListCtrl	m_wndBmpList
IDC_EDIT1	CString	m_sText
IDC_EDIT1	CEdit	m_wndText
IDC_BITMAP	int	m_nBitmap

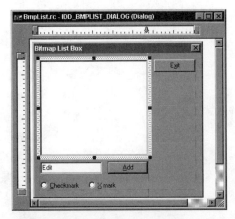

Figure 3-33 Dialog layout for the BMPLIST project

3.9
DRAW BITMAPS IN A LIST BOX

Developer Studio should warn you to include the header file BmpListCtrl.h to the dialog. Do that now in BmpListDlg.h:

```
#include "BmpListCtrl.h"
```

6. Edit BmpListDlg.h. In a later step, we'll be creating the file BmpListCtrl.h that will be used by *CBmpListDlg*, so add this line at the top of BmpListDlg.h:

```
#include "BmpListCtrl.h"
```

7. Code CBmpListDlg::OnAdd. When the Add button is pressed, we want to add the content of the edit box to the list box. We also want to pass the bitmap resource ID for the new item.

```
void CBmpListDlg::OnAdd()
{
    UpdateData(TRUE);

    int nResID = (m_nBitmap == 0) ? IDB_BITMAP1 : IDB_BITMAP2;

    if (!m_sText.IsEmpty())
    {
        m_wndBmpList.AddItem (m_sText, nResID);
        m_wndText.SetSel(0, -1);
        m_wndText.SetFocus();
    }
}
```

8. Modify the CBmpListDlg constructor. Change the initialization of the *m_nBitmap* variable to 0 so the first radio button will be selected.

```
CBmpListDlg::CBmpListDlg(CWnd* pParent /*=NULL*/)
    : CDialog(CBmpListDlg::IDD, pParent)
{
    //{{AFX_DATA_INIT(CBmpListDlg)
    m_sText = _T("");
    m_nBitmap = 0;
    //}}AFX_DATA_INIT
    m_hIcon = AfxGetApp()->LoadIcon(IDR_MAINFRAME);
}
```

9. Use ClassWizard to add message handlers for CBmpListCtrl. Add message-handling functions for these objects:

Object ID	Function
CBmpListCtrl	DeleteItem
CBmpListCtrl	DrawItem
CBmpListCtrl	MeasureItem

10. Edit BmpListCtrl.h. In addition to the *CBmpListCtrl* class you just added in step 8, we're going to add a small helper class called *CBmpListCtrlData*. This class represents an item in the list box and holds its text and bitmap ID. It also knows how to actually draw the bitmap and the text.

Add the following code to the top of BmpListCtrl.h:

```cpp
/////////////////////////////////////////////////////////////////////
// CBmpListCtrlData helper

class CBmpListCtrlData
{
public:
        CBmpListCtrlData (const char* pszText, UINT nBitmapID)
            : m_sText (pszText), m_nBitmapID (nBitmapID)
            { }

        CSize GetSize();
        void DrawItem (CDC* pDC, const CRect& rc, BOOL bSelected);
        void Focus (CDC* pDC, const CRect& rc, BOOL bAddFocus);

protected:
        CString m_sText;
        UINT    m_nBitmapID;

        CBitmap m_bmp;
        CSize   m_size;

        void LoadBitmap();
};
```

11. **Add the AddItem helper function to CBmpListCtrl.** Use the ClassView Add Function dialog to add the following method.

```cpp
public:
        int AddItem (LPCTSTR pszText, UINT nBitmapID);
```

12. **Add the CBmpListCtrlData implementation to BmpListCtrl.cpp.** Add the following methods to the top of BmpListCtrl.cpp:

```cpp
void TransparentBlt (HDC hdc, HBITMAP hBitmap, short xStart,
        short yStart, COLORREF cTransparentColor);

void CBmpListCtrlData::LoadBitmap()
{
        VERIFY (m_bmp.LoadBitmap(m_nBitmapID));
        BITMAP bmpStruct;
        m_bmp.GetObject (sizeof(BITMAP), &bmpStruct);

        m_size.cx = bmpStruct.bmWidth;
        m_size.cy = bmpStruct.bmHeight;
}

CSize CBmpListCtrlData::GetSize()
{
        ASSERT (m_nBitmapID != 0);

        if (m_bmp.m_hObject == NULL)
            LoadBitmap();
```

3.9
DRAW BITMAPS IN A LIST BOX

```cpp
        return m_size;
}

void CBmpListCtrlData::Focus (CDC* pDC, const CRect& rcDraw, BOOL bAddFocus)
{
        // We can ignore bAddFocus since DrawFocusRect uses XOR

        CRect rc(rcDraw);
        rc.left += m_size.cx + 5;

        pDC->DrawText (m_sText, m_sText.GetLength(), rc,
                DT_CALCRECT | DT_SINGLELINE | DT_VCENTER | DT_LEFT);

        // Vertically center rc in rcDraw
        rc.OffsetRect (0, (rcDraw.Height() / 2) - (rc.Height() / 2));

        // rc.bottom = rc.top + nHeight;
        pDC->DrawFocusRect(rc);
}

void CBmpListCtrlData::DrawItem (CDC* pDC, const CRect& rcDraw, BOOL bSelected)
{
        CRect rc(rcDraw);

        if (m_bmp.m_hObject == NULL)
                LoadBitmap();

        // First fill the background with the appropriate color
        //
        COLORREF crBackground, crText;
        if (bSelected)
        {
                crBackground = GetSysColor (COLOR_HIGHLIGHT);
                crText = GetSysColor (COLOR_HIGHLIGHTTEXT);
        } else {
                crBackground = GetSysColor (COLOR_WINDOW);
                crText = GetSysColor (COLOR_WINDOWTEXT);
        }
        pDC->SetBkColor(crBackground);
        ExtTextOut(pDC->GetSafeHdc(), 0, 0, ETO_OPAQUE, rc, NULL, 0, NULL);

        // Draw the bitmap
        TransparentBlt(pDC->GetSafeHdc(), (HBITMAP) m_bmp.GetSafeHandle(),
                rc.left, rc.top, RGB(255, 255, 255));

        // Shift the rectangle to the left to account for the space
        // used by blitting the bitmap
        rc.left += m_size.cx + 5;

        // Draw the text
        pDC->SetBkColor (crBackground);
        pDC->SetTextColor (crText);
        pDC->DrawText (m_sText, m_sText.GetLength(), rc,
                DT_SINGLELINE | DT_VCENTER | DT_LEFT);
}
```

CHAPTER 3
CONTROLS

13. **Code the CBmpListCtrl::AddItem method.** Add the following method at the bottom of BmpListCtrl.cpp. This method constructs a *CBmpListCtrlData* object based on the text string and bitmap resource ID, then adds it to the list box with *CListBox::AddString*. Even though the object is not a string, since we're doing all the drawing we can add anything we want to the list box.

```
int CBmpListCtrl::AddItem (LPCTSTR pszText, UINT nBitmapID)
{
        CBmpListCtrlData* pData = new CBmpListCtrlData (pszText, nBitmapID);

        int nRet = AddString ((LPCSTR) pData);
        if (nRet == LB_ERR)
                delete pData;

        return nRet;
}
```

14. **Code the three virtual methods.** Add bodies to the following three virtual methods. *DrawItem* decodes the LPDRAWITEMSTRUCT parameters and has each *CBmpListCtrlData* object draw and focus itself. *MeasureItem* and *DeleteItem* are the other two methods necessary for self-drawn list boxes.

```
void CBmpListCtrl::DrawItem(LPDRAWITEMSTRUCT lpDrawItemStruct)
{
        CDC* pDC = CDC::FromHandle(lpDrawItemStruct->hDC);
        CBmpListCtrlData *pData = (CBmpListCtrlData *) (lpDrawItemStruct->itemData);
        ASSERT(pData);
        CRect rc (lpDrawItemStruct->rcItem);

        if (lpDrawItemStruct->itemID == LB_ERR)
                return;

        if (lpDrawItemStruct->itemAction & (ODA_DRAWENTIRE | ODA_SELECT) )
                pData->DrawItem (pDC, rc, lpDrawItemStruct->itemState & ODS_SELECTED);

        if (lpDrawItemStruct->itemAction & ODA_FOCUS)
                pData->Focus(pDC, rc, lpDrawItemStruct->itemState & ODS_FOCUS);
}

void CBmpListCtrl::MeasureItem(LPMEASUREITEMSTRUCT lpMeasureItemStruct)
{
        CBmpListCtrlData *pData = (CBmpListCtrlData *) (lpMeasureItemStruct->itemData);

        // MeasureItem is called only once for fixed sized list boxes,
        // before they have any data!  So we return 26 pixels just in case;
        // otherwise we return the height of each item's bitmap.

        if (pData)
                lpMeasureItemStruct->itemHeight = pData->GetSize().cx;
        else
                lpMeasureItemStruct->itemHeight = 26; // a reasonable default
}
```

3.9
DRAW BITMAPS IN A LIST BOX

```cpp
void CBmpListCtrl::DeleteItem(LPDELETEITEMSTRUCT lpDeleteItemStruct)
{
    CBmpListCtrlData *pData = (CBmpListCtrlData *) (lpDeleteItemStruct->itemData);
    ASSERT(pData);
    delete pData;
}
```

15. Add the TransparentBlt function. Add the following code to the bottom of BmpListCtrl.cpp. This function draws a bitmap onto a device context using the transparent color to mask out the area of the destination image you want to show through the bitmap.

```cpp
void TransparentBlt (HDC hdc, HBITMAP hBitmap, short xStart,
    short yStart, COLORREF cTransparentColor)
{
    BITMAP      bm;
    COLORREF    cColor;
    HBITMAP     bmAndBack, bmAndObject, bmAndMem, bmSave;
    HBITMAP     bmBackOld, bmObjectOld, bmMemOld, bmSaveOld;
    HDC         hdcMem, hdcBack, hdcObject, hdcTemp, hdcSave;
    POINT       ptSize;

    ASSERT (hBitmap);

    hdcTemp = CreateCompatibleDC(hdc);              // Select the bitmap
    SelectObject(hdcTemp, hBitmap);                 // Get width of bitmap
    GetObject(hBitmap, sizeof(BITMAP), (LPSTR)&bm); // Get height of bitmap
    ptSize.x = bm.bmWidth;                          // Convert from device
    ptSize.y = bm.bmHeight;                         // to logical points
    DPtoLP(hdcTemp, &ptSize, 1);

    // Create some DCs to hold temporary data.
    hdcBack   = CreateCompatibleDC(hdc);
    hdcObject = CreateCompatibleDC(hdc);
    hdcMem    = CreateCompatibleDC(hdc);
    hdcSave   = CreateCompatibleDC(hdc);
    // Create a bitmap for each DC.

    // Monochrome DC
    bmAndBack   = CreateBitmap(ptSize.x, ptSize.y, 1, 1, NULL);

    // Monochrome DC
    bmAndObject = CreateBitmap(ptSize.x, ptSize.y, 1, 1, NULL);
    bmAndMem    = CreateCompatibleBitmap(hdc, ptSize.x, ptSize.y);
    bmSave      = CreateCompatibleBitmap(hdc, ptSize.x, ptSize.y);

    // Each DC must select a bitmap object to store pixel data.
    bmBackOld   = (HBITMAP) SelectObject(hdcBack, bmAndBack);
    bmObjectOld = (HBITMAP) SelectObject(hdcObject, bmAndObject);
    bmMemOld    = (HBITMAP) SelectObject(hdcMem, bmAndMem);
    bmSaveOld   = (HBITMAP) SelectObject(hdcSave, bmSave);
```

continued on next page

continued from previous page

```c
// Set proper mapping mode.
SetMapMode(hdcTemp, GetMapMode(hdc));

// Save the bitmap sent here, because it will be overwritten.
BitBlt(hdcSave, 0, 0, ptSize.x, ptSize.y, hdcTemp, 0, 0, SRCCOPY);

// Set the background color of the source DC to the color.
// contained in the parts of the bitmap that should be transparent
cColor = SetBkColor(hdcTemp, cTransparentColor);

// Create the object mask for the bitmap by performing a BitBlt
// from the source bitmap to a monochrome bitmap.
BitBlt(hdcObject, 0, 0, ptSize.x, ptSize.y, hdcTemp, 0, 0,
       SRCCOPY);

// Set the background color of the source DC back to the original
// color.
SetBkColor(hdcTemp, cColor);

// Create the inverse of the object mask.
BitBlt(hdcBack, 0, 0, ptSize.x, ptSize.y, hdcObject, 0, 0,
       NOTSRCCOPY);

// Copy the background of the main DC to the destination.
BitBlt(hdcMem, 0, 0, ptSize.x, ptSize.y, hdc, xStart, yStart,
       SRCCOPY);

// Mask out the places where the bitmap will be placed.
BitBlt(hdcMem, 0, 0, ptSize.x, ptSize.y, hdcObject, 0, 0, SRCAND);

// Mask out the transparent colored pixels on the bitmap.
BitBlt(hdcTemp, 0, 0, ptSize.x, ptSize.y, hdcBack, 0, 0, SRCAND);

// XOR the bitmap with the background on the destination DC.
BitBlt(hdcMem, 0, 0, ptSize.x, ptSize.y, hdcTemp, 0, 0, SRCPAINT);

// Copy the destination to the screen.
BitBlt(hdc, xStart, yStart, ptSize.x, ptSize.y, hdcMem, 0, 0,
       SRCCOPY);

// Place the original bitmap back into the bitmap sent here.
BitBlt(hdcTemp, 0, 0, ptSize.x, ptSize.y, hdcSave, 0, 0, SRCCOPY);

// Delete the memory bitmaps.
DeleteObject(SelectObject(hdcBack, bmBackOld));
DeleteObject(SelectObject(hdcObject, bmObjectOld));
DeleteObject(SelectObject(hdcMem, bmMemOld));
DeleteObject(SelectObject(hdcSave, bmSaveOld));

// Delete the memory DCs.
DeleteDC(hdcMem);
DeleteDC(hdcBack);
DeleteDC(hdcObject);
DeleteDC(hdcSave);
DeleteDC(hdcTemp);
}
```

16. Build and test the application. Type some text into the edit box and press the Add button. The text should be added to the list box along with the bitmap for the check mark.

How It Works

In order to better understand the way an item in the list box is drawn, you need to visualize each item as a series of planes, each of which must be rendered in a particular order. Figure 3-34 shows a 3D view of a list box.

At the bottom level, we have the list box frame itself. For the purposes of our discussion, the frame also includes any list box items that are not currently being drawn. The next layer up from the bottom is the background rectangle. This rectangle is the area that has been set aside on the surface of the list box for the display of your item. This rectangle should change color when selected, and it should have a focus rectangle drawn around it when it has the focus.

If you take a close look at some implementations of custom list boxes with bitmaps, the selection rectangle has the largest range of differences. In the File Manager, the selection rectangle does not extend from one side of the list box to the other, but is drawn only under the bitmap and the text label. In some list boxes, the selection rectangle highlights only the text label. This example draws the entire rectangle in a highlighted color when selected.

The next layer above the background rectangle is the bitmap. The bitmap is drawn after the background rectangle, so it can be made transparent and the background color will show through the bitmap. The last layer is the text label, which is centered vertically in the list box item's area, right next to the bitmap.

The heart of *CBmpListCtrl* is the *DrawItem* method. Here the DRAWITEMSTRUCT parameter is decoded and the appropriate *CBmpListCtrlData* item is instructed to draw itself, or draw a focus rectangle. The other virtual methods, *DeleteItem* and *MeasureItem* are needed so the list box can remove items and figure out how much room to allocate for each item in the list box.

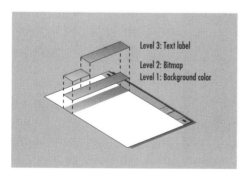

Figure 3-34 3D view of a CBmpListCtrl item

It's the *CBmpListCtrlData* object that actually draws the bitmap and text. Its *DrawItem* method you added in step 11 is called for every item in the list box. It first paints the background with one of two colors to indicate the normal or selected state.

Next, it paints the bitmap using a special function called *TransparentBlt*. The bitmaps are constructed in such a way that any white areas of the bitmap are replaced by the pixels in the destination area. Thus, if the list box selection color happens to be blue, the bitmap will be painted with blue color where there are white pixels in the source image. Finally, the text is drawn using *CDC::DrawText*.

Comments

If you want to make this a multicolumn list box like the one shown in Figure 3-35, there are a couple of modifications you have to make to the code and resource file. First, use the dialog editor to modify two properties of the list box. Change the Owner Draw option from Variable to Fixed and check the multicolumn option.

Windows imposes a strange restriction on multicolumn list boxes which makes them tricky to implement: They must have a fixed height. However, there's another restriction that self-drawn list boxes should have—a variable height! Since a multicolumn list box has a fixed height, the *MeasureItem* method is called only once, before any data is in the list box. Another twist is that when you use a subclassed list box like the one in our How-To, the list box never gets the *MeasureItem* message. So instead, you need to add two lines of code in *CBmpListCtrlData::OnInitDialog* to ensure that everything works properly:

```
m_wndBmpList.SubclassDlgItem (IDC_LIST, this);
m_wndBmpList.SetColumnWidth(100);   // 100 pixels wide
m_wndBmpList.SetItemHeight(0, 26);  // 26 pixels tall (the bitmap height)
```

SetColumnWidth is always used by multicolumn list boxes. It specifies how many pixels wide to allocate each list box item. *SetItemHeight* is necessary in this case because *MeasureItem* is not called for a list box that has already been created; we're just subclassing an existing one. If *CBmpListCtrl* was created with Create, *SetItemHeight* wouldn't be necessary.

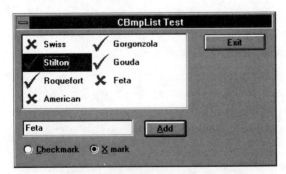

Figure 3-35 A multicolumn self-drawn list box

3.9
DRAW BITMAPS IN A LIST BOX

If you're familiar with the new common controls, you might be wondering why I didn't just use the ListView control. The solution presented here allows you to completely customize the drawing and layout of each listbox item. You can also make a *CBmpListCtrlData* an abstract base class and turn all its drawing methods into virtual ones. That would let you have radically different list box items within the same control.

```
class CListData
{
public:
        CListData() {};
        virtual ~CListData() {};

        virtual CSize GetSize() = 0;
        virtual void DrawItem (CDC* pDC, const CRect& rc, BOOL bSelected) = 0;
        virtual void Focus (CDC* pDC, const CRect& rc, BOOL bAddFocus) = 0;
};
```

CHAPTER 4
MULTIMEDIA

4

MULTIMEDIA

How do I...

4.1 **Preview an AVI file using the common file dialog?**

4.2 **Display bitmaps using the DrawDib functions?**

4.3 **Play AVI files in a CView?**

4.4 **Play large WAV files?**

4.5 **Play tracks from an audio CD?**

4.6 **Create 3D animation using OpenGL and MFC?**

Almost all new computers sold today are "multimedia ready." They come bundled with sound cards, accelerated video cards, CD-ROM drives, and speakers. But what does all that have to do with multimedia? Technically speaking, multimedia just means more than one medium, but that doesn't tell us much. For computers running Windows, multimedia has come to mean a system capable of supporting increasingly rich data types, usually including audio and video components. Microsoft has made extensions to the Windows operating system family to support these new devices and file formats such as animation, sound files, audio CD drives, MIDI devices, joysticks, laser discs, VCRs, DAT, and more.

You'll run into new hurdles when you start to tackle this world of multimedia programming. This chapter demonstrates how to work with some of the difficult aspects of multimedia. You'll learn how to create workstation-quality 3D graphics using the OpenGL (Open Graphics Library) graphics system. There is a How-To that demonstrates how to read and display a DIB (device-independent bitmap) file using new features from Video for Windows(VfW). You'll also see how to use MCI (Media Control Interface) commands to play large WAV files and to create a miniaudio CD player. You'll discover how to play AVI files by embedding a special window, MCIWnd, into your view. The first How-To demonstrates an easy way to add AVI previewing to a common file dialog.

4.1 Preview an AVI File Using the Common File Dialog

This How-To shows how to use *CFileDialog* to derive a class that employs new APIs from the Video for Windows SDK to display a small video preview window. When a video file is selected in the dialog box, a thumbnail version of the video is displayed in the lower-right corner, so you can preview the contents before opening it.

Additional Topics: CFileDialog, GetOpenFileNamePreview

4.2 Display Bitmaps Using the DrawDib Functions

This How-To shows how to create a simple class that encapsulates a device-independent bitmap (DIB). The sample lets you load a bitmap file, then stretch it to different sizes simply by resizing the application's window. We'll be using display APIs from the Video for Windows *DrawDib* family instead of the standard GDI methods. By using these new APIs, we get dithering for free.

Additional Topics: dithering, color maps, sizing a CView

4.3 Play AVI Files in a CView

Video for Windows includes a great control to ease playback of AVI movie files. With a few lines of code, you'll see how to embed this control into a *CView*, giving you a quick way to play AVI files in an MDI application.

Additional Topics: MCIWnd

4.4 Play Large WAV Files

The Windows SDK provides a simple function to play WAV files, but unfortunately it doesn't work with WAV files that are too large to fit in available memory. This sample application creates a class you can use in your application to play small or large WAV files. The class abstracts the complicated MCI commands and data structures, so you can concentrate on simpler functions such as Play and Stop. The sample application uses the class to create a small WAV file player.

Additional Topics: MM_MCINOTIFY, asynchronous playback

4.5 Play Tracks from an Audio CD

This sample application creates a mini CD player. You can play your favorite CD track, pause the CD, move to the previous or next track, and eject the CD. When a new CD is inserted into the drive, the number of available tracks is determined. The play time of the CD and the current track and position are displayed.

Additional Topics: mciSendCommand, CBitmapButton

4.6 Create 3D Animation Using OpenGL and MFC

OpenGL is an operating system independent graphics library that brings workstation-quality 3D rendering to Windows NT. You'll be able to add sophisticated, 3D graphics and animation to your applications by using the techniques described in this How-To.

Additional Topics: PreCreateWindow, quadric shapes, polar coordinates

COMPLEXITY
BEGINNING

4.1 How do I... Preview an AVI file using the common file dialog?

Problem

The Win32 Multimedia SDK replaces the common file dialog API *GetOpenFileName* with a new function called *GetOpenFileNamePreview*. The function extends the common dialog by showing a thumbnail preview of the currently selected AVI file, as illustrated in Figure 4-1. The *CFileDialog* class doesn't have any methods to display a video inside the common file dialog. How do I use the new dialog in MFC?

Technique

Since there is no MFC support for any of the multimedia APIs, there are two ways to tackle this problem. The first would be to use *GetOpenFileNamePreview* directly, as you would in a Windows program written in C. This requires initialization of the OPENFILENAME structure and some post-processing of the return values—things *CFileDialog* already does.

Figure 4-1 Opening an AVI file with a thumbnail preview

CHAPTER 4
MULTIMEDIA

A more object-oriented approach would be to derive a new class from the MFC *CFileDialog* class and override the *DoModal* virtual member function. The new implementation of *DoModal* can call the *GetOpenFilenamePreview* function instead of the normal *GetOpenFilename*. Since the new class derives from *CFileDialog*, we gain a lot of useful code through inheritance.

The amount of code required for this technique is much smaller than trying to use the straight C API. It's more reliable too, since the MFC code we'll be reusing has been well tested and is full of error checking and assertions.

Steps

1. Create a new project called VideoPreview using the MFC AppWizard (exe). Choose the dialog-based option and press the Finish button.

Classes to be created:
Application: CVideoPreviewApp in VideoPreview.h and VideoPreview.cpp
Dialog: CVideoPreviewDlg in VideoPreviewDlg.h and VideoPreviewDlg.cpp

Features:
+ About box on system menu
+ 3D Controls
+ Uses shared DLL implementation (MFC40.DLL)

2. Add a new class with ClassWizard. Create a new class called *CAviFileDialog* with *CFileDialog* as its base class:

Class name: CAviFileDialog
Base class: CFileDialog
File: AviFileDialog.cpp

3. Edit the CAviFileDialog constructor. The following two lines of code set the dialog's caption and modify the file filter to browse for AVI files.

```
CAviFileDialog::CAviFileDialog(BOOL bOpenFileDialog, LPCTSTR lpszDefExt,
    LPCTSTR lpszFileName, DWORD dwFlags, LPCTSTR lpszFilter, CWnd* pParentWnd) :
    CFileDialog(bOpenFileDialog, lpszDefExt, lpszFileName, dwFlags,
        lpszFilter, pParentWnd)
{
    // Provide reasonable default values for AVI files
    m_ofn.lpstrTitle = "Open Video File";
    m_ofn.lpstrFilter = "Video for Windows File (*.avi)\0*.avi\0";
}
```

4. Override the DoModal virtual method. Use the ClassView Add Function dialog to add the following method (choose the Virtual and Public options in the dialog). Most of this code comes from the *CFileDialog::DoModal* code in \msdev\mfc\src\DlgFile.cpp.

4.1
PREVIEW AN AVI FILE USING THE COMMON FILE DIALOG

```
int CAviFileDialog::DoModal()
{
    ASSERT_VALID(this);
    ASSERT(m_ofn.Flags & OFN_ENABLEHOOK);
    ASSERT(m_ofn.lpfnHook != NULL); // can still be a user hook

    m_ofn.hwndOwner = PreModal();
    int nResult;
    if (m_bOpenFileDialog)
        nResult = ::GetOpenFileNamePreview(&m_ofn);
    else
        nResult = ::GetSaveFileNamePreview(&m_ofn);
    PostModal();

    return nResult;
}
```

Scroll to the top of the file and add these three lines:

```
#include "stdafx.h"
#include "VideoPreview.h"
#include "AviFileDialog.h"
#include <afxpriv.h>        // for AfxHookWindowCreate
#include <vfw.h>            // for GetOpenFileNamePreview
#pragma comment(lib, "vfw32.lib")
```

The *pragma* line instructs the compiler to link to the vfw32.lib library, which includes the support for *GetOpenFileNamePreview*. Incidentally, the Windows Multimedia component adds a *#include* directive and a *#pragma* to StdAfx.h to link to <winmm.lib>, which *doesn't* include support for *GetOpenFileNamePreview* (I tried it).

5. Edit CVideoPreviewApp::InitInstance. We don't really need to use the dialog created by AppWizard since we're trying to demonstrate *CAviFileDialog*, so we modify the initialization code to display our new dialog.

```
BOOL CVideoPreviewApp::InitInstance()
{
    // Standard initialization

#ifdef _AFXDLL
    Enable3dControls();         // Call this when using MFC in a shared DLL
#else
    Enable3dControlsStatic();   // Call this when linking to MFC statically
#endif

    CAviFileDialog dlg(TRUE);
    m_pMainWnd = &dlg;
    int nResponse = dlg.DoModal();
    if (nResponse == IDOK)
    {
        CString msg;
        msg.Format("You selected: %s", (LPCSTR) dlg.GetFileName());
        AfxMessageBox(msg);
    }
```

continued on next page

continued from previous page

```
        //  Since the dialog has been closed, return FALSE so that we exit the
        //  application, rather than start the application's message pump.
        return FALSE;
}
```

Modify the *#include* lines at the top of the file like this (remove the reference to VideoPreviewDlg.h):

```
#include "stdafx.h"
#include "VideoPreview.h"
#include "AviFileDialog.h"
```

6. **Build and test the program.** The common file dialog should appear when you run the program. Select an AVI file, but don't double-click on its name. A thumbnail preview will appear in the lower-right corner of the dialog box after a few seconds, as in Figure 4-1. To preview the video, press the Play button.

How It Works

CAviFileDialog is a specialized *CFileDialog* class that handles the selection and preview of AVI files. When the class is instantiated, the constructor for *CAviFileDialog* modifies the *m_ofn* member variable to supply reasonable defaults for both the dialog caption and the file filter.

CFileDialog::DoModal initializes the OPENFILENAME structure and calls the *GetOpenFileName* SDK function. The implementation of *CAviFileDialog::DoModal* does the same thing, but *GetOpenFileNamePreview* is called instead of *GetOpenFileName*.

Comments

Most of the work in this How-To is done by the *CFileDialog* class. By deriving *CAviFileDialog* from *CFileDialog*, all of the code that handles a common file dialog is reused. Since most of the code is part of the MFC library, it is more reliable than if it was rewritten from scratch.

COMPLEXITY
INTERMEDIATE

4.2 How do I... Display bitmaps using the DrawDib functions?

Problem

I need an easy way to display bitmaps that solves a major headache: what to do about DIBs that have a bit depth different from the user's current video setup. For example, if I try to display a 24-bit or full-color image on a palettized device (for example, a 256-color display), the image looks terrible. Besides having multiple bitmaps for different color displays, what can I do? Also, how do I handle palette messages in an MDI application since they're only sent to top-level windows?

Technique

You could look long and hard for a solution using the Windows SDK only to find the answer in a little known family of Video for Windows APIs called the *DrawDib* functions. Not only are these methods fast (they're tuned to the current display just like AVI playback), they also perform dithering. Dithering is a graphics algorithm used to display a color image on a device that supports fewer colors than the image uses. It's similar to halftoning, a technique used for printing black-and-white photographs in newspapers.

Collectively, the *DrawDib* functions are similar to the *StretchDIBits* function because they provide image-stretching and dithering capabilities. But the *DrawDib* functions support image decompression, data-streaming, and a greater number of display adapters.

The *DrawDib* functions also improve the speed and quality of displaying images on display adapters with more limited capabilities. For example, when using an 8-bit display adapter, the *DrawDib* functions efficiently dither true-color images to 256 colors. They also dither 8-bit images when using 4-bit display adapters.

We create a class called CDIB that encapsulates some of the *DrawDib* functionality. It has a member function, *Draw*, which uses the *DrawDibDraw* VfW function to display the DIB in the application's client area. The DIB is initially displayed in its original size, but you can grab the edges and resize it—the image will stretch to fit the client area.

Both *CMainFrame* and our view class will share the palette responsibility. Since palette messages are only sent to top-level windows, *CMainFrame* will forward them to all current views, letting each one determine the best action.

Steps

1. Create a new project called **DrawDib** using the MFC AppWizard (exe).
Use all the defaults and make sure you're creating an MDI app. Press the Advanced button in step 4 and change the File Extension to "bmp". Change the view and document class names in the last step as shown below:

Classes to be created:
Application:	CDrawDibApp in DrawDib.h and DrawDib.cpp
Frame:	CMainFrame in MainFrm.h and MainFrm.cpp
MDIChildFrame:	CChildFrame in ChildFrm.h and ChildFrm.cpp
Document:	CDibDoc in DibDoc.h and DibDoc.cpp
View:	CDibView in DibView.h and DibView.cpp

CHAPTER 4
MULTIMEDIA

Features:
+ Initial toolbar in main frame
+ Initial status bar in main frame
+ 3D Controls
+ Document supports files with extension .BMP
+ Uses shared DLL implementation (MFC40.DLL)

2. Edit StdAfx.h. Add these two lines to the bottom of the file:

```
#include <afxwin.h>         // MFC core and standard components
#include <afxext.h>         // MFC extensions
#ifndef _AFX_NO_AFXCMN_SUPPORT
#include <afxcmn.h>         // MFC support for Windows 95 Common Controls
#endif // _AFX_NO_AFXCMN_SUPPORT

#include <vfw.h>
#pragma comment(lib, "vfw32.lib")
```

3. Declare the CDIB class. Create a new file called Dib.h for the CDIB class declaration and give it the following contents:

```
class CDIB : public CObject
{
// Construction
public:
        CDIB();
        virtual ~CDIB();

// Attributes
public:
        BYTE* GetBits();
        CSize GetSize();
        BOOL IsValid() { return (m_hDrawDib != NULL); }
        operator HDRAWDIB() { return m_hDrawDib; }

// Operations
public:
        BOOL Open(const char* pzFileName);
        void Close();
        void Draw(CDC* pDC, int nWidth, int nHeight);

// Implementation
protected:
        BYTE* m_pDIB;
        HDRAWDIB m_hDrawDib;
};
```

4. Define the CDIB class. Create a new file for the CDIB class definition. Call the file Dib.cpp and give it the following contents:

```
#include "stdafx.h"
#include "dib.h"

CDIB::CDIB()
```

4.2
DISPLAY BITMAPS USING THE DRAWDIB FUNCTIONS

```
{
    m_hDrawDib = NULL;
    m_pDIB = NULL;
}

CDIB::~CDIB()
{
    Close();
}

void CDIB::Draw(CDC* pDC, int nWidth, int nHeight)
{
    ASSERT(IsValid());

    DrawDibRealize(m_hDrawDib, pDC->GetSafeHdc(), TRUE);

    DrawDibDraw (m_hDrawDib, pDC->GetSafeHdc(),
            0,           // dest left
            0,           // dest top
            nWidth,
            nHeight,
            (BITMAPINFOHEADER*) m_pDIB,
            (LPVOID) GetBits(),
            0,           // source left
            0,           // source top
            ((BITMAPINFOHEADER*) m_pDIB)->biWidth,
            ((BITMAPINFOHEADER*) m_pDIB)->biHeight,
            DDF_BACKGROUNDPAL);
}

CSize CDIB::GetSize()
{
    return CSize( ((BITMAPINFOHEADER*) m_pDIB)->biWidth,
            ((BITMAPINFOHEADER*) m_pDIB)->biHeight);
}

void CDIB::Close()
{
    if (m_hDrawDib != NULL)
    {
        DrawDibClose(m_hDrawDib);
        m_hDrawDib = NULL;
    }

    if (m_pDIB != NULL)
        delete m_pDIB;
}

BOOL CDIB::Open(const char* pzFileName)
{
    BITMAPFILEHEADER bmpfh;
    CFile file;
    int nHeaderSize;

    Close();
```

continued on next page

continued from previous page

```
        // DrawDibOpen initializes the DrawDib library and
        // returns a handle for all DrawDib operations
        if (!(m_hDrawDib = DrawDibOpen()))
             goto bail;

        // Open and read the DIB file header
        nHeaderSize = sizeof(BITMAPFILEHEADER);

        if (!file.Open(pzFileName, CFile::modeRead | CFile::typeBinary))
             goto bail;

        if (file.Read((void *) &bmpfh, nHeaderSize) != (UINT) nHeaderSize)
             goto bail;

        // Validate the DIB file header by checking the first
        // two characters for the signature "BM"
        if (bmpfh.bfType != *((WORD*) "BM"))
             goto bail;

        // Allocate a big chunk of global memory to store the DIB
        m_pDIB = (BYTE *) new char[bmpfh.bfSize - nHeaderSize];

        if (!m_pDIB)
             goto bail;

        // Read the DIB into the buffer 32K at a time using ReadHuge
        file.ReadHuge(m_pDIB, bmpfh.bfSize - nHeaderSize);

        if (((BITMAPINFOHEADER *) m_pDIB)->biSizeImage == 0)
        {
             // The application that created this bitmap didn't fill in
             // the biSizeImage field (Photoshop 3.0x does this). Let's
             // fill it in even though the DrawDib* functions don't need it.
             BITMAPINFOHEADER* pDib = (BITMAPINFOHEADER*) m_pDIB;

             // Scan lines must be DWORD aligned, hence the strange bit stuff
             pDib->biSizeImage =
                 ((((pDib->biWidth * pDib->biBitCount) + 31) & ~31) >> 3) * pDib->biHeight;
        }

        file.Close();
        return TRUE;

bail:
        Close();
        return FALSE;


BYTE* CDIB::GetBits()
{
        // The size of the color map is determined by the number of
        // RGBQUAD structures present.  It also depends on the bit-depth
        // of the DIB.
```

4.2
DISPLAY BITMAPS USING THE DRAWDIB FUNCTIONS

```
    DWORD dwNumColors, dwColorTableSize;
    BITMAPINFOHEADER* lpDib = (BITMAPINFOHEADER *) m_pDIB;

    WORD wBitCount = lpDib->biBitCount;

    if (lpDib->biSize >= 36)
        dwNumColors = lpDib->biClrUsed;
    else
        dwNumColors = 0;

    if (dwNumColors == 0)
    {
        if (wBitCount != 24)
            dwNumColors = 1L << wBitCount;
        else
            dwNumColors = 0;
    }

    dwColorTableSize = dwNumColors * sizeof (RGBQUAD);

    return m_pDIB + lpDib->biSize + dwColorTableSize;
}
```

Press the right-mouse button over Dib.cpp and insert it into the DrawDib project.

5. Edit DibDoc.h. Add a CDIB member variable to your document like this:

```
// Attributes
public:
    CDIB m_dib;
```

Also, at the top of DibDoc.h, add a #include line like this:

```
#include "dib.h"
```

6. Use the WizardBar to add CDibDoc::OnOpenDocument. We want the CDIB class to handle the file reading, so we'll override *CDibDoc::OnOpenDocument* and pass the file name selected in the common file dialog to *m_dib*.

```
BOOL CDibDoc::OnOpenDocument(LPCTSTR lpszPathName)
{
    return m_dib.Open(lpszPathName);
}
```

7. Edit CDibDoc::OnNewDocument. We don't support empty *CDIB* objects, so return FALSE from *OnNewDocument*.

```
BOOL CDibDoc::OnNewDocument()
{
    return FALSE;
}
```

8. **Use the WizardBar to handle WM_PALETTECHANGED for CMainFrame.**
   Add the following code:

```
void CMainFrame::OnPaletteChanged(CWnd* pFocusWnd)
{
    // Tell all children to remap palettes
    SendMessageToDescendants(WM_PALETTECHANGED,
        (WPARAM)(pFocusWnd->GetSafeHwnd()));

    // Note: We don't need to handle WM_QUERYNEWPALETTE in CMainFrame.
    // Windows sends the message as part of the frame activation process.
    // However, at the time OnQueryNewPalette handles the message, there
    // is no active view to forward the message to.  Instead, since the
    // framework calls CView::OnActivateView around the same time (and
    // when you switch between MDI views), we'll realize the palette
    // in the foreground there.
}
```

Note: We don't need to handle WM_QUERYNEWPALETTE in *CMainFrame*. Windows sends the message as part of the frame activation process. ~~However, at the time *OnQueryNewPalette* handles the message, there is no~~ active view to forward the message to. Instead, we'll realize the palette in *CView::OnActivateView* since the framework calls it around the same time (and when you switch between MDI views).

9. **Edit CDibView::OnDraw.** Tell the document's *CDIB* object to draw itself in the client area of the view.

```
void CDibView::OnDraw(CDC* pDC)
{
    CDibDoc* pDoc = GetDocument();
    ASSERT_VALID(pDoc);

    CRect r;
    GetClientRect(r);

    pDoc->m_dib.Draw(pDC, r.Width(), r.Height());
}
```

10. **Use the WizardBar to add CDibView::OnInitialUpdate.** Set the initial size of the view to the bitmap's dimensions.

```
void CDibView::OnInitialUpdate()
{
    CView::OnInitialUpdate();

    CRect r (CPoint(0, 0), GetDocument()->m_dib.GetSize());
    GetParentFrame()->CalcWindowRect(r);
    GetParentFrame()->SetWindowPos(NULL, 0, 0, r.Width(), r.Height(),
        SWP_NOACTIVATE | SWP_NOMOVE | SWP_NOZORDER);
}
```

4.2
DISPLAY BITMAPS USING THE DRAWDIB FUNCTIONS

11. Add the RealizePalette helper function. Use the ClassView Add Function dialog to add the following protected method and edit the code as follows:

```
BOOL CDibView::RealizePalette(BOOL bForceBkgnd)
{
    UINT nColorsChanged;
    {
        CClientDC dc(this);
        nColorsChanged =
            DrawDibRealize(GetDocument()->m_dib, dc.GetSafeHdc(), bForceBkgnd);
    }

    if (nColorsChanged || bForceBkgnd)
        Invalidate();

    return (BOOL) nColorsChanged;
}
```

This helper function uses the *DrawDibRealize* method to realize the palette and if any of the colors change, invalidate the client area so the bitmap is redrawn.

12. Use the WizardBar to add CDibView::OnActivateView. Set the initial size of the view to the bitmap's dimensions.

```
void CDibView::OnActivateView(BOOL bActivate, CView* pActivateView, CView* pDeactiveView)
{
    if (bActivate)
    {
        // We're going active to realize our palette in
        // the foreground.
        RealizePalette(FALSE);

        // DrawDibRealize sends WM_PALETTECHANGED to all apps
        // if it realizes any new colors. If CDC::RealizePalette
        // were used instead of DrawDibRealize, this next line of code would be
        // necessary.

        // AfxGetMainWnd()->SendMessage(WM_PALETTECHANGED,
        //    (WPARAM) GetSafeHwnd(), 0);
    }
}
```

13. Change the CDibView message filter. Start ClassWizard and switch to the Class Info tab. Locate *CDibView* in the Class name combo and change the message filter to "Window". If you have DibView.cpp open in an editor, close it then reopen it in order to see the changes made to the Messages combo.

14. Use the WizardBar to handle WM_PALETTECHANGED for CDibView. Add the following code:

```
void CDibView::OnPaletteChanged(CWnd* pFocusWnd)
{
```

continued on next page

CHAPTER 4
MULTIMEDIA

continued from previous page
```
        // Ignore this message if we sent it
        if (pFocusWnd == this || IsChild(pFocusWnd))
            return;

        RealizePalette(TRUE);
}
```

15. Use the WizardBar to handle WM_QUERYNEWPALETTE for CDibView. Add the following code:

```
BOOL CDibView::OnQueryNewPalette()
{
        return RealizePalette(FALSE);
}
```

16. Build and test the program. Locate some *.BMP files and load them. The best test is to load a 24-bit color image and display it on an 8-bit (or 256-color) display. *DrawDibDraw* takes care of the dithering for you.

How It Works

Before the image is displayed in the *CDibView*, *OnInitialUpdate* is called. Here we determine how big the .DIB is in pixels. We want our client area to be just big enough to hold the DIB so stretching won't occur. *CWnd::CalcWindowRect* figures out how big an MDI child window must be to support a client rectangle of a specified size. The modified rectangle it returns is used to resize the *CDibView* parent window.

Painting the CDIB object is quite easy. *CDibView::OnDraw* passes a pointer to a device context and its width and height to *CDIB::Draw*, which draws the bitmap with a single function call to *DrawDibDraw*. It's here that any dithering will take place if necessary.

One of the parameters to *DrawDibDraw* requires a pointer to the actual pixels. The *CDIB::GetBits* helper function does this, but it's not as straightforward as you would think. Unfortunately, finding where the bitmap itself begins is not all that simple. The problem lies in the fact that the colormap sits between the *.DIB header and the bitmap. The size of the colormap needs to be computed based on the values of the *biSize*, *biClrUsed*, and *biBitCount* fields in the DIB header. Once we know how big the colormap is, we add that size to the beginning of the entire structure and end up with a pointer to the raw pixel data.

Handling palette messages in an MDI application is a bit tricky. Since the two palette messages, WM_QUERYNEWPALETTE and WM_PALETTECHANGED, are only sent to top-level windows, we can only catch them in *CMainFrame*. We only handle *OnPaletteChanged* to pass that message on to the views. Windows sends WM_QUERYNEWPALETTE at a time where the current active view is unknown. Instead, each view is responsible for handling *OnActivateView* and rendering their palette in the foreground. If the active view changes the palette, *DrawDibRealize* automatically sends out WM_PALETTECHANGED, which in turn filters back down to the other inactive views. These in turn request that their palettes be realized in the background.

Comments

Collectively, the *DrawDib* functions are similar to the *StretchDIBits* function because they provide image-stretching and dithering capabilities. However, the *DrawDib* functions support image decompression, data-streaming, and a greater number of display adapters.

Under some circumstances, *StretchDIBits* might be a better choice over the *DrawDib* functions because it supports a larger set of painting methods. If you search for the string "Do I Need DrawDib" in the Books Online, you'll find a document explaining the differences between the two functions.

COMPLEXITY
INTERMEDIATE

4.3 How do I... Play AVI files in a CView?

Problem

I'd like to use the services from Video for Windows to play AVI movies inside my application. The movies should play back in a *CView* object.

Technique

There are two ways to approach this problem. The first is to use the low-level AVI file functions to read the video streams from an AVI video file. Although this method gives you more control over the entire playback process, there's a lot more code to write.

A simpler technique uses an existing window class from the Video for Windows SDK: MCIWnd. MCIWnd (for Media Control Interface Window) is a window class for controlling multimedia devices, such as wave, MIDI, digital video, VCR, and CD audio devices. In this example, we'll use MCIWnd features for AVI playback, but it can also be adapted for other media with very little work. We only need to create a window of this class, and then send it a message to open and control an MCI device. By embedding an MCIWnd window in our standard *CView* derived class, we'll be able to access all the features of this rich API set. Figure 4-2 shows two AVI files in an MDI application. MCIWnd handles the toolbar you see below the two videos.

Figure 4-2 AVI movie files

Steps

1. Create a new project called VideoPlay using the MFC AppWizard (exe). Use all the defaults and make sure you're creating a multiple document application. Press the Advanced button in step 4 and change the file extension to "avi". Shorten the view and document names in the last step as shown below:

Classes to be created:
Application: CVideoPlayApp in VideoPlay.h and VideoPlay.cpp
Frame: CMainFrame in MainFrm.h and MainFrm.cpp
MDIChildFrame: CChildFrame in ChildFrm.h and ChildFrm.cpp
Document: CVideoDoc in VideoDoc.h and VideoDoc.cpp
View: CVideoView in VideoView.h and VideoView.cpp

Features:
+ Initial toolbar in main frame
+ Initial status bar in main frame
+ 3D Controls
+ Uses shared DLL implementation (MFC40.DLL)
+ Document supports files with extension .AVI

2. Edit StdAfx.h. By putting the include files in StdAfx.h, we benefit from having all the multimedia information inside the precompiled header. Also, since every file in the project already includes StdAfx.h, we don't need to include the multimedia files anywhere else.

```
#include <afxwin.h>         // MFC core and standard components
#include <afxext.h>         // MFC extensions (including VB)
```

4.3
PLAY AVI FILES IN A CVIEW

```
#include <vfw.h>
#pragma comment(lib, "vfw32.lib")
```

   3. Edit CVideoPlayApp::InitInstance. In order to use the MCIWnd class, we need to register the window by calling *MCIWndRegisterClass*. Also, we must check to make sure the application is running on a system with a version of Video for Windows that supports MCIWnd. Insert the following code into *CTestApp::InitInstance*:

```
BOOL CVideoPlayApp::InitInstance()
{
        // Standard initialization

        // Since we're not using MCIWndCreate, we need to register
        // MCIWND_WINDOW_CLASS by calling this function
        if (!MCIWndRegisterClass())
            return FALSE;
...
}
```

   4. Edit VideoView.h. We need a member variable to hold the embedded MCIWnd's HWND. MCIWnd sends us an important message, MCIWNDM_NOTIFYSIZE, so we'll also add a method to handle the message. Edit *CVideoView*'s interface so it looks like the following:

```
class CVideoView : public CView
{
protected: // create from serialization only
        CVideoView();
        DECLARE_DYNCREATE(CVideoView)

// Attributes
public:
        CVideoDoc* GetDocument();
        HWND m_hAVI;

// Overrides
        // ClassWizard generated virtual function overrides
        //{{AFX_VIRTUAL(CVideoView)
        public:
        virtual void OnDraw(CDC* pDC);  // overridden to draw this view
        virtual BOOL PreCreateWindow(CREATESTRUCT& cs);
        protected:
        //}}AFX_VIRTUAL

// Implementation
public:
        virtual ~CVideoView();
#ifdef _DEBUG
        virtual void AssertValid() const;
        virtual void Dump(CDumpContext& dc) const;
#endif
```

continued on next page

continued from previous page
```
// Generated message map functions
protected:
        //{{AFX_MSG(CVideoView)
        //}}AFX_MSG
        afx_msg LONG OnNotifySize(UINT wParam, LONG lParam);
        DECLARE_MESSAGE_MAP()
};
```

    5. Use the WizardBar to add CVideoView::OnInitialUpdate. *OnInitialUpdate* will create the MCIWnd window and load the selected AVI file from the dialog.

```
void CVideoView::OnInitialUpdate()
{
        CView::OnInitialUpdate();

        m_hAVI = MCIWndCreate(m_hWnd, AfxGetInstanceHandle(),
                MCIWNDF_NOTIFYSIZE | MCIWNDF_NOERRORDLG |
                WS_CHILD | WS_VISIBLE, NULL);

        if (m_hAVI == NULL)
                return;

        const CString& filename = GetDocument()->GetPathName();
        if (filename.GetLength() > 0)
                MCIWndOpen(m_hAVI, (LPCSTR) filename, 0);
}
```

    6. Edit CVideoView's constructor. Like all good programmers, we'll initialize our member variables to NULL in the constructor. Since we'll be checking to see if *m_hAVI* is NULL later, this line of code is very important.

```
CVideoView:: CVideoView()
{
        m_hAVI = NULL;
}
```

    In order to trap the MCIWNDM_NOTIFYSIZE message sent by the embedded MCIWnd, we need to add an entry to the message map (the code should be located just above the constructor):

```
BEGIN_MESSAGE_MAP(CVideoView, CView)
        //{{AFX_MSG_MAP(CVideoView)
        ON_MESSAGE(MCIWNDM_NOTIFYSIZE, OnNotifySize)
        //}}AFX_MSG_MAP
END_MESSAGE_MAP()
```

    7. Add code for OnNotifySize. *OnNotifySize* catches the messages sent by MCIWnd. Here we'll resize the parent MDI child frame so the movie and the toolbar fit inside with no extra space.

```
LONG CVideoView::OnNotifySize(UINT wParam, LONG lParam)
{
        CRect rc;
        CFrameWnd* pParent = GetParentFrame();
```

4.3
PLAY AVI FILES IN A CVIEW

```
    if (m_hAVI)
    {
        // adjust MDI child frame to movie size
        ::GetWindowRect(m_hAVI, rc);
        pParent->CalcWindowRect(rc, CWnd::adjustBorder);

        CSize size(rc.Width(), rc.Height());
        if (GetExStyle() & WS_EX_CLIENTEDGE)
        {
            size.cx += 4;
            size.cy += 4;
        }

        pParent->SetWindowPos(NULL, 0, 0, size.cx, size.cy,
            SWP_NOZORDER | SWP_NOACTIVATE | SWP_NOMOVE);
    } else {
        // No movie yet. Adjust the window so
        // the movie toolbar seems about 60 pixels tall.
        pParent->SetWindowPos(NULL, 0, 0, 200, 60,
            SWP_NOZORDER | SWP_NOACTIVATE | SWP_NOMOVE);
    }
    return TRUE;
}
```

8. **Build and test the application.** Load an AVI file and hit the Play button. Notice that we didn't need to write any code to handle the movie toolbar; MCIWnd did all the work for us.

How It Works

We're taking advantage of the MCIWnd window class that comes with Multimedia SDK to play back an AVI movie. With very little code, we're able to embed an instance of this window inside a *CView*.

MFC calls *OnIntialUpdate* before *CVideoView* is visible. It's here that we call *MCIWndCreate*. We could have created the control earlier, but by the time *OnInitialUpdate* executes, we know that the AVI file name (if any) has already been stored in *CDocument*. If the creation is successful and there is a file name (the user chose File Open instead of File New), then we make one more call to load the AVI file through *MCIWndOpen*.

If the call to *MCIWndOpen* is successful, the embedded MCIWnd control sends the message MCIWNDM_NOTIFYSIZE to *CVideoView*. MCIWnd sends this message whenever the MDI child window needs to be resized to display the movie. It's also sent if the user chooses to zoom in or out of the movie after it's loaded.

4.4 How do I... Play large WAV files?

COMPLEXITY: INTERMEDIATE

Problem

I play small WAV files with *sndPlaySound* to give users quick audio feedback when they press a certain button. However, *sndPlaySound* isn't suitable for WAV files that are too large to fit in available memory. How do I use the Media Control Interface (MCI) to play large audio files asynchronously and be notified when they're finished? Plus, I'd like to be able to stop and restart the audio while it's playing back.

Technique

Windows supports two RIFF (resource interchange file format) audio files: the RMID file for MIDI (musical instrument digital interface) and the WAV file for waveform audio. This sample application will show how to play large WAV files using MCI commands.

Only one line of code is needed to play a sound file with *sndPlaySound*. The following plays a WAV file synchronously, meaning, it plays the sound and does not return until the sound is finished playing:

```
sndPlaySound("noise.wav", SND_SYNC);
```

The following plays a WAV file asynchronously, meaning, it plays the sound but immediately returns from the function:

```
sndPlaySound("noise.wav", SND_ASYNC);
```

As you can see, *sndPlaySound* is very simple to use. So what's wrong with using *sndPlaySound* to play all your WAV files? There's one big restriction to using *sndPlaySound* to play waveform sounds: The entire sound must fit in available physical memory. Use *sndPlaySound* to play sound files that are relatively small in size—up to about 100K. For larger sound files, use the MCI services.

This How-To creates a *CWave* class that handles the MCI commands to play back audio for you. It executes many MCI commands and sets up data structures for you so that you invoke simple member functions, such as *OpenDevice*, *CloseDevice*, *Play*, and *Stop*. Figure 4-3 shows the wave player application at work.

Figure 4-3 The wave player application

4.4
PLAY LARGE WAV FILES

Steps

1. **Create a new project called BigWave using the MFC AppWizard (exe).** Choose the Dialog-based version and press the Finish button.

   Classes to be created:
   - Application: CBigWaveApp in BigWave.h and BigWave.cpp
   - Dialog: CBigWaveDlg in BigWaveDlg.h and BigWaveDlg.cpp

   Features:
   - + About box on system menu
   - + 3D Controls
   - + Uses shared DLL implementation (MFC40.DLL)

2. **Edit StdAfx.h.** By putting the include files in StdAfx.h, we benefit from having all the multimedia information inside the precompiled header. Also, since every file in the project already includes StdAfx.h, we don't need to include the multimedia files anywhere else.

```
#include <afxwin.h>              // MFC core and standard components
#include <afxext.h>              // MFC extensions (including VB)

#include <vfw.h>
#pragma comment(lib, "winmm.lib")
#pragma comment(lib, "vfw32.lib")
```

3. **Create the CWave class declaration.** Create a new file called Wave.h and add the following class definition:

```
class CWave : public CObject
{
// Construction
public:
        CWave();
        virtual ~CWave();

// Operations
public:
        DWORD     OpenDevice();
        DWORD     CloseDevice();
        DWORD     Play(CWnd* pParentWnd, LPCSTR pFileName);
        DWORD     Stop();

// Implementation
protected:
        void      DisplayErrorMsg(DWORD dwError);

// Members
protected:
        MCIDEVICEID  m_nDeviceID;
        MCIDEVICEID  m_nElementID;
};
```

CHAPTER 4
MULTIMEDIA

4. Create the CWave class implementation. The constructor of the *CWave* class initializes the private data members, and the destructor closes the waveform audio device and WAV file element. Create a new file called Wave.cpp, and add the following constructor and destructor member functions implementation:

```
#include "stdafx.h"
#include "wave.h"

CWave::CWave()
{
    // initialize private data members
    m_nDeviceID = 0;
    m_nElementID = 0;
}

CWave::~CWave()
{
    // make sure wave file is closed
    if (m_nElementID)
        Stop();

    // make sure wave device is closed
    if (m_nDeviceID)
        CloseDevice();
}
```

The *OpenDevice* member function opens the WAV audio device. For better performance, it's a good idea to open the device, open and close each WAV file element as needed, and then close the device. Append the code for *OpenDevice* to Wave.cpp.

```
DWORD CWave::OpenDevice()
{
    DWORD dwResult = 0;
    // open wave device if not already open
    if (m_nDeviceID)
    {
        MCI_OPEN_PARMS mciOpenParms;

        // set the device to a WAV audio device
        mciOpenParms.lpstrDeviceType = (LPSTR)MCI_DEVTYPE_WAVEFORM_AUDIO;

        // open the wave device
        dwResult = mciSendCommand(NULL, MCI_OPEN,
            MCI_OPEN_TYPE | MCI_OPEN_TYPE_ID | MCI_WAIT,
            (DWORD)(LPVOID)&mciOpenParms);

        // save device identifier, will use with other MCI commands
        m_nDeviceID = mciOpenParms.wDeviceID;

        // display error message if failed
        if (dwResult)
```

4.4
PLAY LARGE WAV FILES

```
            DisplayErrorMsg(dwResult);
    }

    // return result of MCI operation
    return dwResult;
}
```

The *CloseDevice* member function closed the waveform audio device. Add the following *CloseDevice* implementation to the file Wave.cpp:

```
DWORD CWave::CloseDevice()
{
    DWORD dwResult = 0;

    // close if currently open
    if (m_nDeviceID)
    {
        // close the MCI device
        dwResult = mciSendCommand(m_nDeviceID,
            MCI_CLOSE, NULL, NULL);

        // display error message if failed
        if (dwResult)
            DisplayErrorMsg(dwResult);

        // set identifier to closed state
        else
            m_nDeviceID = 0;
    }

    // return result of MCI operation
    return dwResult;
}
```

The *Play* member function plays the specified WAV file. An MM_MCINOTIFY notification message will be posted to the specified window when the play operation is completed. Add this *Play* implementation to the file Wave.cpp:

```
DWORD CWave::Play(CWnd* pWnd, LPCSTR pFileName)
{
    MCI_OPEN_PARMS mciOpenParms;

    // initialize structure
    memset(&mciOpenParms, 0, sizeof(MCI_OPEN_PARMS));

    // set the WAV file name to be played
    mciOpenParms.lpstrElementName = pFileName;

    // first open the device
    DWORD dwResult = mciSendCommand(m_nDeviceID, MCI_OPEN,
        MCI_OPEN_ELEMENT,
        (DWORD)(LPVOID)&mciOpenParms);

    // display error message if failed
    if (dwResult)
        DisplayErrorMsg(dwResult);
```

continued on next page

continued from previous page

```
        // if successful, instruct the device to play the WAV file
        else
        {
                // save element indentifier
                m_nElementID = mciOpenParms.wDeviceID;

                MCI_PLAY_PARMS mciPlayParms;

                // set the window that will receive notification message
                mciPlayParms.dwCallback = (DWORD)pWnd->m_hWnd;

                // instruct device to play file
                dwResult = mciSendCommand(m_nElementID, MCI_PLAY,
                        MCI_NOTIFY, (DWORD)(LPVOID)&mciPlayParms);

                // display error and close element if failed
                if (dwResult)
                {
                        DisplayErrorMsg(dwResult);
                        Stop();
                }
        }

        // return result of MCI operation
        return dwResult;
}
```

The *Stop* member function stops the WAV file by closing the WAV file element. Here is the *Stop* implementation you should add to the Wave.cpp file:

```
DWORD CWave::Stop()
{
        DWORD dwResult = 0;

        // close if element is currently open
        if (m_nElementID)
        {
                // close element
                dwResult = mciSendCommand(m_nElementID, MCI_CLOSE, NULL, NULL);

                // display error message if failed
                if (dwResult)
                        DisplayErrorMsg(dwResult);

                // set identifier to closed state
                else
                        m_nElementID = 0;
        }
        // return result of MCI operation
        return dwResult;
}
```

If an error occurs, the *DisplayErrorMsg* private member function displays a text string that provides information about the MCI error. Add this *DisplayErrorMsg* member function implementation to Wave.cpp:

4.4
PLAY LARGE WAV FILES

```
void CWave::DisplayErrorMsg(DWORD dwError)
{
    // check if there was an error
    if (dwError)
    {
        // character string that contains error message
        char szErrorMsg[MAXERRORLENGTH];

        // retrieve string associated with error
        if (!mciGetErrorString(dwError, szErrorMsg, sizeof(szErrorMsg)))
            strcpy(szErrorMsg, "Unknow Error");

        // display error string in message box
        AfxMessageBox(szErrorMsg);
    }
}
```

5. **Add Wave.cpp to the BigWave project.** Right-mouse click on the Wave.cpp file in the editor and select the option that says "Insert File into Project".

6. **Add member variables to CAutoScrollView.** Use the add member variable dialog to add this member:

Type	Declaration	Access
CWave	m_wave	protected

7. **Edit the IDD_BIGWAVE_DIALOG.** Modify the dialog to look like the one shown in Figure 4-4 using the attributes in the table below:

Control	ID	Attributes
Dialog	IDD_BIGWAVE_DIALOG	Accept files (under Extended Styles)
Button	IDC_FILE	"File...", default button
Button	IDC_PLAY	"Play", button, disabled
Button	IDC_STOP	"Stop", disabled
Button	IDOK	"Exit"
Edit	IDC_EDITFILE	Default

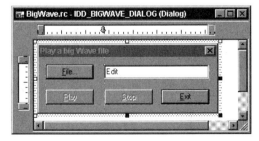

Figure 4-4 The BigWave dialog box

CHAPTER 4
MULTIMEDIA

8. **Add data members to the class.** Use ClassWizard to add the following data members to the *CBigWaveDlg* class:

Control ID	Type	Member
IDC_EDITFILE	CString	m_strFile
IDC_PLAY	CButton	m_wndPlay
IDC_STOP	CButton	m_wndStop
IDC_FILE	CButton	m_wndFile

The *m_strFile* data member stores the contents of the edit control. There are control data members for the File, Play, and Stop buttons so you can easily enable and disable the push buttons at the appropriate times.

9. **Add message handlers for the *CBigWaveDlg* class.** Use ClassWizard to add message handlers for these events:

Object ID	Function	Message
IDC_EDITFILE	OnChangeEditFile	EN_CHANGE
IDC_FILE	OnFile	BN_CLICKED
IDC_PLAY	OnPlay	BN_CLICKED
IDC_STOP	OnStop	BN_CLICKED
IDC_EXIT	OnExit	BN_CLICKED

10. **Use the WizardBar to handle EN_CHANGE for IDC_EDITFILE.** WizardBar will create a method called *CBigWaveDlg::OnChangeEditfile*. Edit the code to disable the Play button if the string is empty.

```
void CBigWaveDlg::OnChangeEditfile()
{
    UpdateData();

    // disable the play button if the string is empty
    m_wndPlay.EnableWindow(m_strFile.GetLength() ? TRUE : FALSE);
}
```

11. **Use the WizardBar to handle BN_CLICKED for IDC_FILE.** If the user clicks the File button, we'll let them browse for a WAV file. Add the following code to the message handler:

```
void CBigWaveDlg::OnFile()
{
    CFileDialog dlgFile(TRUE, NULL, NULL,
        OFN_HIDEREADONLY, "Wave Files (*.WAV) |*.WAV|");

    // if select file, copy contents to edit control
    if (dlgFile.DoModal() == IDOK)
    {
        m_strFile = dlgFile.GetPathName();
```

4.4
PLAY LARGE WAV FILES

```
            UpdateData(FALSE);
            m_wndPlay.EnableWindow(TRUE);
            m_wndPlay.SetFocus();
        }
    }
```

12. Use the WizardBar to handle BN_CLICKED for IDC_PLAY. Try to play the file specified in the edit control.

```
void CBigWaveDlg::OnPlay()
{
    UpdateData();
    // play WAV file and enable stop push button.
    // A zero return value indicates success
    if (m_wave.Play(this, m_strFile) == 0)
    {
        m_wndPlay.EnableWindow(FALSE);
        m_wndFile.EnableWindow(FALSE);
        m_wndStop.EnableWindow(TRUE);
        m_wndStop.SetFocus();
    }
}
```

13. Use the WizardBar to handle BN_CLICKED for IDC_STOP. Let the user stop play back by responding to the IDC_STOP button.

```
void CBigWaveDlg::OnStop()
{
    // stop WAV file and disable stop push button
    if (!m_wave.Stop())
    {
        m_wndPlay.EnableWindow(TRUE);
        m_wndFile.EnableWindow(TRUE);
        m_wndStop.EnableWindow(FALSE);
        m_wndPlay.SetFocus();
    }
}
```

14. Handle the MM_MCINOTIFY message. Windows sends this message to *CBigWaveDlg* when the MCI device has completed an operation that specifies the MCI_NOTIFY flag. In our case, *CWave::Play* uses this flag so the dialog can be notified when the WAV file completes.

Since ClassWizard doesn't support this message, use the Add Function dialog to add the prototype and body to *CBigWaveDlg*.

```
protected:
    LRESULT OnMCINotify(WPARAM wParam, LPARAM lParam);
```

Add the following macro in the message map for class *CBigWaveDlg*:

```
BEGIN_MESSAGE_MAP(CBigWaveDlg, CDialog)
    //{{AFX_MSG_MAP(CBigWaveDlg)
    ON_WM_SYSCOMMAND()
    ON_WM_PAINT()
```

continued on next page

continued from previous page
```
        ON_WM_QUERYDRAGICON()
        ON_EN_CHANGE(IDC_EDITFILE, OnChangeEditfile)
        ON_BN_CLICKED(IDC_FILE, OnFile)
        ON_BN_CLICKED(IDC_PLAY, OnPlay)
        //}}AFX_MSG_MAP
        ON_MESSAGE(MM_MCINOTIFY, OnMCINotify)
END_MESSAGE_MAP()
```

The framework will now invoke the *OnMCINotify* member function when the *CBigWaveDlg* window receives an MM_MCINOTIFY message. The last step is to actually create the function. Add the following function implementation file BigWaveDlg.cpp:

```
LRESULT CBigWaveDlg::OnMCINotify(WPARAM wParam, LPARAM lParam)
{
        // We've been notified that the WAV file has played to completion.
        // Call OnStop to disable the Stop button and reenable the Play button.
        OnStop();
        return FALSE;
}
```

15. Edit BigWaveDlg.h. Add the following #include to the top of WaveDlg.h:

```
#include "wave.h"
```

16. **Change the Message filter for CBigWaveDlg.** Use the Class Info tab in Class Wizard to change the message filter from Dialog to Window. When we turn on the Accept Files option in step 7, we're telling Windows to send the dialog the WM_DROPFILES message each time the user drags a file onto our dialog. Class Wizard doesn't normally offer this message to dialogs, so you need to change the filter type to Window.

17. **Use WizardBar to handle the WM_DROPFILES message in CBigWaveDlg.** You first have to close the editor then reopen BigWaveDlg.cpp for the combo-box to refresh itself with all the Window messages. Select WM_DROPFILES from the list and edit the code as follows:

```
void CBigWaveDlg::OnDropFiles(HDROP hDropInfo)
{
        // Only one file will be accepted
        if (DragQueryFile (hDropInfo, (UINT) -1, NULL, 0) != 1)
            return;

        char lpszFile[MAX_PATH];
        DragQueryFile (hDropInfo, 0, lpszFile, MAX_PATH);

        m_strFile = lpszFile;
        UpdateData(FALSE);
        m_wndPlay.EnableWindow();

        DragFinish(hDropInfo);
}
```

4.4
PLAY LARGE WAV FILES

18. Build and test the application. Select a WAV file by pressing the File button, then listen to the file play. You can press the Stop button during playback. You can also drop a WAV file from the Explorer onto the dialog.

How It Works

The *CWave* class abstracts the specific MCI commands and data structures and contains only a few simple public member functions: *OpenDevice*, *CloseDevice*, *Play*, and *Stop*.

A waveform audio device is a compound device. You will have better performance if you open the waveform device, open and close each waveform element, and then close the waveform device. You can open the waveform device by calling *CWave::OpenDevice*.

OpenDevice passes the MCI_OPEN command to the *mciSendCommand* function. If the call is successful, the waveform device identifier is returned in the *wDeviceID* member of the MCI_OPEN_PARMS data structure. This identifier is saved for later use in a private data member.

Once the *CWave* object is opened, you are ready to play WAV files through *CWave::Play*. The WAV file's name and a window pointer for MCI notification messages are passed to the Play method.

Playing a WAV file is a two-step process. First, the WAV file is opened by allocating an MCI_OPEN_PARMS structure and setting the *lpstrElementName* member to the WAV file you want to play. Passing this structure and the verb MCI_OPEN to *mciSendCommand* opens the WAV file and returns an element identifier in the *wDeviceID* member of the MCI_OPEN_PARMS structure.

The second step instructs the wave audio device to play the WAV file. An MCI_PLAY_PARMS structure is allocated, and the *dwCallback* member is set to the window handle that will receive a notification message when the device is finished playing. If you want to play the wave file synchronously, add the MCI_WAIT flag and skip the window handle. Remember, this will cause your application to wait for the WAV files to finish playing before it returns from the *mciSendCommand* function. You will most likely want to play large WAV files asynchronously by specifying the MCI_NOTIFY flag and setting the *dwCallback* member as shown here:

```
MCI_PLAY_PARMS mciPlayParms;
mciPlayParms.dwCallback = (DWORD)pWnd->m_hWnd;

dwResult = mciSendCommand(m_nDevice, MCI_PLAY,
    MCI_NOTIFY, (DWORD)(LPVOID)&mciPlayParms);
```

The WAV file will start playing, and an MM_MCINOTIFY message will be sent to the specified window when the WAV file has completed. Figure 4-5 shows the sequence of events that occurs when you play a WAV file with the MCI_NOTIFY flag.

It is your responsibility to close the WAV file element when it is finished playing. To do so, simply call the Stop member function of the *CWave* class.

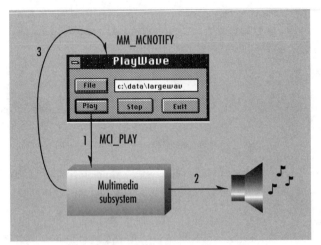

Figure 4-5 Playing a WAV file: (1) Instruction to play WAV file and return immediately (2) WAV file plays (3) Notification message is sent when complete

We've examined the Play member function, so it is only fair that we also examine the Stop member function. Stop passes the WAV file identifier and the MCI_CLOSE command to the *mciSendCommand* function. It does not need to allocate an MCI structure for this command. The following code closes the WAV file element:

```
mciSendCommand(m_nElement, MCI_CLOSE, NULL, NULL);
```

The waveform audio device must also be closed when you are finished playing all your WAV files. This is automatically done for you in the destructor of the *CWave* class by calling *CWave::CloseDevice*.

Comments

There's a simple rule to remember when you use the *CWave* class in your applications: Make sure the *CWave* object is allocated for the entire time the WAV file is being played. For example, the following code wouldn't play the wave file correctly:

```
void CMyClass::SomeEvent()
{
    CWave wave;
    wave.OpenDevice();
    wave.Play(this, "event.wav");
}
```

It would create a *CWave* object, open the audio device, and invoke the Play member function, but then it would destroy the *CWave* object when you exit the function.

4.5 PLAY TRACKS FROM AN AUDIO CD

In other words, when the wave object goes out of scope, its destructor would close the audio device and stop the playback. When you define a *CWave* object as a class member, you will not have this problem.

The *CWave* class could easily be extended to retrieve information about waveform audio devices and WAV file elements. You could also, without much modification, add MIDI file playback support to *CWave*.

For more information, refer to the section titled "Playing and Recording Audio Using MCI" in the Multimedia Services section of the Win32 SDK in Books Online.

COMPLEXITY: INTERMEDIATE

4.5 How do I... Play tracks from an audio CD?

Problem

I know how to play small WAV files, but what I really want to do is play audio CD tracks. How do I write a small CD player program?

Technique

Playing audio CD tracks is fairly simple, but a complete CD controller program takes a lot of code. This sample application creates a class to help you manipulate audio CDs and uses that class in a software CD player. The CD player stops, pauses tracks, and retrieves information about the CD device and its media.

This How-To creates a class called *CCDAudio* to abstract the Media Control Interface (MCI) and all of its functions and structures for you. You can use this class in your application, or you can make direct MCI calls. Figure 4-6 shows the CD Player program.

Steps

1. Create a new project called DiscPlayer using the MFC AppWizard (exe). Choose the Dialog-based version and press the Finish button.

Classes to be created:
Application: CDiscPlayerApp in DiscPlayer.h and DiscPlayer.cpp
Dialog: CDisCDiscPlayerDlg in DisCDiscPlayerDlg.h and DisCDiscPlayerDlg.cpp

Features:
+ About box on system menu
+ 3D Controls
+ Uses shared DLL implementation (MFC40.DLL)

Figure 4-6 CD Player in action

2. **Insert the Windows Multimedia component.** Use the Component Gallery to insert the Windows Multimedia component into your project. It adds a few lines of code to the bottom of your StdAfx.h file:

```
#include <afxwin.h>         // MFC core and standard components
#include <afxext.h>         // MFC extensions (including VB)
#include <MMSystem.h>
// CG: The following line was added by the Windows Multimedia component.
#pragma comment(lib, "winmm.lib")
```

3. **Create the CCDAudio class.** The *CCDAudio* class provides a high-level interface to CD audio devices by abstracting MCI commands and data structures. The user of the class does not have to be familiar with specific MCI information, only with operations you would perform on your own CD player like play, stop, pause, and eject.

Create a new file called CDAudio.cpp and type in the following text:

```
#include "stdafx.h"
#include "cdaudio.h"

CCDAudio::CCDAudio()
{
    m_pWnd = NULL;
    m_bOpened = FALSE;
}

CCDAudio::~CCDAudio()
{
    Close();
}

BOOL CCDAudio::Open(CWnd* pWnd)
{
    m_pWnd = pWnd;

    // if a device is already opened, close it
    if (m_bOpened)
        Close();

    // open CD audio device
    MCI_OPEN_PARMS mciOpenParms;
    mciOpenParms.lpstrDeviceType = (LPCSTR)MCI_DEVTYPE_CD_AUDIO;
```

4.5
PLAY TRACKS FROM AN AUDIO CD

```cpp
        DWORD dwResult = mciSendCommand(NULL, MCI_OPEN,
            MCI_OPEN_TYPE | MCI_OPEN_TYPE_ID | MCI_OPEN_SHAREABLE | MCI_WAIT,
            (DWORD)(LPVOID)&mciOpenParms);

        // if successful, set time format of device
        if (!dwResult)
        {
            // save opened state
            // this state is evaluated by the close function
            m_bOpened = TRUE;

            // save device identifer
            // this ID will be used in all preceding MCI calls
            m_nDeviceID = mciOpenParms.wDeviceID;

            // set time format of device
            MCI_SET_PARMS mciSetInfo;
            mciSetInfo.dwTimeFormat = MCI_FORMAT_TMSF;

            SendCommand(MCI_SET, MCI_SET_TIME_FORMAT | MCI_WAIT,
                (DWORD)(LPVOID)&mciSetInfo);
        }

        return m_bOpened;
}

void CCDAudio::Close()
{
        // check if device was ever opened
        if (m_bOpened)
        {
            // close the device
            DWORD dwResult = SendCommand(MCI_CLOSE, MCI_WAIT, NULL);

            // if successfully closed device, save this state
            if (!dwResult)
                m_bOpened = FALSE;
        }
}

CString CCDAudio::GetUniqueID()
{
        char buffer[MAX_PATH];
        MCI_INFO_PARMS info;
        memset(buffer, 0, MAX_PATH);

        info.dwCallback = (DWORD) m_pWnd->m_hWnd;
        info.lpstrReturn = buffer;
        info.dwRetSize = MAX_PATH;

        SendCommand(MCI_INFO, MCI_WAIT | MCI_INFO_MEDIA_IDENTITY,
            (DWORD) &info);

        DWORD dwValue;
        char* stopString;
```

continued on next page

continued from previous page

```
        dwValue = strtoul(buffer, &stopString, 10);
        wsprintf(buffer, "%lx", dwValue);

        return buffer;
}

CString CCDAudio::GetTrackTitle(UINT nTrackID, LPCTSTR pszUniqueID)
{
        ASSERT(pszUniqueID != NULL);
        ASSERT(nTrackID <= GetNumberOfTracks());

        TCHAR szTrack[10];
        wsprintf(szTrack, "%d", nTrackID);
        TCHAR szTitle[MAX_PATH];

        GetPrivateProfileString(pszUniqueID, szTrack, szTrack, szTitle, ⇒
MAX_PATH, "cdplayer.ini");

        return szTitle;
}

void CCDAudio::Play(int nTrack)
{
        // create position to start playing at
        m_mciPlayParms.dwFrom = MCI_MAKE_TMSF(nTrack, 0, 0, 0);

        // specify winow handle to receive mci notification message
        m_mciPlayParms.dwCallback = (DWORD)m_pWnd->m_hWnd;

        // start playing track
        SendCommand(MCI_PLAY, MCI_FROM | MCI_NOTIFY,
            (DWORD)(LPVOID)&m_mciPlayParms);
}

void CCDAudio::SetPosition(int nSeconds)
{
        int min = nSeconds / 60;
        int sec = nSeconds % 60;

        // Set the time format
        MCI_SET_PARMS parms;
        parms.dwTimeFormat = MCI_FORMAT_MSF;
        SendCommand(MCI_SET, MCI_SET_TIME_FORMAT | MCI_WAIT,
            (DWORD)(LPVOID)&parms);

        // create position to start playing at
        m_mciPlayParms.dwFrom = MCI_MAKE_MSF(min, sec, 0);

        // specify window handle to receive mci notification message
        m_mciPlayParms.dwCallback = (DWORD)m_pWnd->m_hWnd;

        // start playing track
        SendCommand(MCI_PLAY, MCI_FROM | MCI_NOTIFY,
            (DWORD)(LPVOID)&m_mciPlayParms);
```

4.5
PLAY TRACKS FROM AN AUDIO CD

```cpp
    parms.dwTimeFormat = MCI_FORMAT_TMSF;
    SendCommand(MCI_SET, MCI_SET_TIME_FORMAT | MCI_WAIT,
        (DWORD)(LPVOID)&parms);
}

void CCDAudio::Stop()
{
    SendCommand(MCI_STOP, MCI_WAIT, NULL);
}

void CCDAudio::Pause()
{
    SendCommand(MCI_PAUSE, MCI_WAIT, NULL);
}

void CCDAudio::ResumePlay()
{
    SendCommand(MCI_PLAY, MCI_NOTIFY, (DWORD)(LPVOID)&m_mciPlayParms);
}

void CCDAudio::Eject()
{
    SendCommand(MCI_SET, MCI_SET_DOOR_OPEN, NULL);
}

UINT CCDAudio::GetNumberOfTracks()
{
    return (UINT) GetStatus(MCI_STATUS_NUMBER_OF_TRACKS);
}

BOOL CCDAudio::IsMediaPresent()
{
    if (IsDeviceOpen())
        return (BOOL) GetStatus(MCI_STATUS_MEDIA_PRESENT);
    else
        return FALSE;
}

BOOL CCDAudio::IsPlaying()
{
    return (BOOL) (GetStatus(MCI_STATUS_MODE) == MCI_MODE_PLAY);
}

void CCDAudio::GetLength(int& nMinutes, int& nSeconds)
{
    DWORD dwReturn = GetStatus(MCI_STATUS_LENGTH);

    // store information in passed variables
    nMinutes = MCI_MSF_MINUTE(dwReturn);
    nSeconds = MCI_MSF_SECOND(dwReturn);
}

void CCDAudio::GetTrackLength(int nTrack, int& nMinutes, int& nSeconds)
{
```

continued on next page

continued from previous page

```
    // retrieve length of track
    DWORD dwResult = GetStatus(MCI_STATUS_LENGTH, nTrack);

    // store information in passed variables
    nMinutes = MCI_MSF_MINUTE(dwResult);
    nSeconds = MCI_MSF_SECOND(dwResult);
}

void CCDAudio::GetPosition(int& nMinutes, int& nSeconds)
{
    // Set the time format
    MCI_SET_PARMS parms;
    parms.dwTimeFormat = MCI_FORMAT_MSF;
    SendCommand(MCI_SET, MCI_SET_TIME_FORMAT | MCI_WAIT,
        (DWORD)(LPVOID)&parms);

    // retrieve current position of CD
    DWORD dwResult = GetStatus(MCI_STATUS_POSITION);

    // save information to passed variables
    nMinutes = MCI_MSF_MINUTE(dwResult);
    nSeconds = MCI_MSF_SECOND(dwResult);

    parms.dwTimeFormat = MCI_FORMAT_TMSF;
    SendCommand(MCI_SET, MCI_SET_TIME_FORMAT | MCI_WAIT,
        (DWORD)(LPVOID)&parms);
}

void CCDAudio::GetPosition(int& nTrack, int& nMinutes, int& nSeconds)
{
    // retrieve current position of CD
    DWORD dwResult = GetStatus(MCI_STATUS_POSITION);

    // save information to passed variables
    nTrack = MCI_TMSF_TRACK(dwResult);
    nMinutes = MCI_TMSF_MINUTE(dwResult);
    nSeconds = MCI_TMSF_SECOND(dwResult);
}

////////////////////////////////////////////////////
// Helpers

DWORD CCDAudio::GetStatus(DWORD dwItem, int nTrack)
{
    DWORD dwFlags = MCI_STATUS_ITEM | MCI_WAIT;
    MCI_STATUS_PARMS mciStatusInfo;

    mciStatusInfo.dwItem = dwItem;
    if (nTrack != -1)
    {
        mciStatusInfo.dwTrack = nTrack;
        dwFlags |= MCI_TRACK;
    }
```

4.5
PLAY TRACKS FROM AN AUDIO CD

```
        SendCommand(MCI_STATUS, dwFlags,
            (DWORD) (LPVOID) &mciStatusInfo);

        return mciStatusInfo.dwReturn;
}

DWORD CCDAudio::SendCommand(UINT uMsg, DWORD dwCommand, DWORD dwParam)
{
        DWORD dwError = mciSendCommand(m_nDeviceID,
                uMsg, dwCommand, dwParam);

        // check if there was an error
        if (dwError)
        {
            // character string that contains error message
            char szErrorMsg[MAXERRORLENGTH];

            // retrieve string associated with error
            if (!mciGetErrorString(dwError, szErrorMsg, sizeof(szErrorMsg)))
                strcpy(szErrorMsg, "Unknow Error");

            // display error string in message box
            AfxMessageBox(szErrorMsg, MB_ICONEXCLAMATION | MB_OK);
        }
        return dwError;
}
```

4. Create the CDAudio interface file. Now create a new file—the interface file—for *CDAudio* called CDAudio.h. Follow these steps:

```
#ifndef _CDPLAYER_
#define _CDPLAYER_

// place these lines in stdafx.h for a faster compile
#ifndef _INC_MMSYSTEM
#include <mmsystem.h>
#endif
#pragma comment(lib, "winmm.lib")

class CCDAudio : public CObject
{
// constructor, destructor
public:
        CCDAudio();
        ~CCDAudio();

// public member functions
public:
        BOOL IsDeviceOpen()
            { return m_bOpened; }

        // actions
        BOOL Open(CWnd* pWnd);
        void Close();
        void Play(int nTrack);
```

continued on next page

continued from previous page

```
        void ResumePlay();
        void Pause();
        void Stop();
        void Eject();
        void SetPosition(int nSeconds);

        // CD string information
        CString GetUniqueID();
        CString GetTrackTitle(UINT nTrackID, LPCTSTR pszUniqueID);

        // information
        UINT GetNumberOfTracks();
        BOOL IsMediaPresent();
        BOOL IsPlaying();
        void GetLength(int& nMinutes, int& nSeconds);
        void GetPosition(int& nTrack, int& nMinutes, int& nSeconds);
        void GetPosition(int& nMinutes, int& nSeconds);
        void GetTrackLength(int nTrack, int& nMinutes, int& nSeconds);

// Implementation
protected:
        DWORD GetStatus(DWORD dwItem, int nTrack = -1);
        DWORD SendCommand(UINT uMsg, DWORD dwCommand, DWORD dwParam);

// Memebers
protected:
        CWnd* m_pWnd;         // pointer to window who is using this class
        BOOL m_bOpened;       // if opened device flag

        MCIDEVICEID      m_nDeviceID;        // device identifer
        MCI_PLAY_PARMS   m_mciPlayParms;     // current play position info
};

#endif
```

5. **Add CDAudio.cpp to the project.** Click the right-mouse button while the cursor is over the file CDAudio.cpp, and choose the menu option Insert File Into Project.

6. **Create the bitmap images for the CD control buttons.** The control buttons represent the same buttons you find on a real CD player. There are buttons for play, stop, pause, previous track, next track, and eject. You can create push buttons without bitmap images if you want, but that makes for a boring looking CD player. To save time, you can copy the bitmap images from the CD-ROM, under the Multimedia\DiscPlayer directory, and paste them into your project. Figure 4-7 shows the bitmap images and their identifiers.

The easiest way to copy the bitmaps is to drag-and-drop them from one resource file into the other. Simply open both RC files, highlight the bitmaps, hold down the Control key, and drag them to the project's RC file. This works for all resources except string resources.

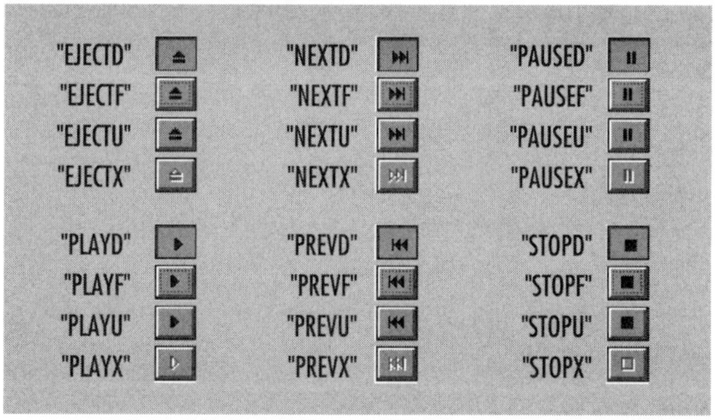

4.5
PLAY TRACKS FROM AN AUDIO CD

![CD Player button states bitmap table]

Figure 4-7 CD Player button states

Notice how the bitmap images are named. This is very important since they will be associated with *CBitmapButton* objects. There is a close relationship between the button's caption and the bitmap identifiers. You call *CBitmapButton::AutoLoad* to associate bitmap images with an owner-drawn button. The *CBitmapButton* class will automatically display the correct bitmap at the appropriate time. You can have up to four bitmap images associated with a bitmap button: up, down, focused, and disabled. Figure 4-8 shows the button and bitmap relationship for the play button.

7. **Modify the form based dialog box.** Modify the dialog box IDD_CDPLAYER_DIALOG as shown in Figure 4-9.

   The six buttons are owner-drawn, so make sure you select the Owner Drawn option in the properties dialog. Don't worry about the size of the buttons, since you will be associating them with *CBitmapButton* object later. The

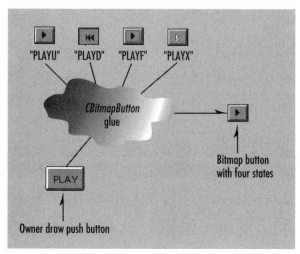

Figure 4-8 CBitmapButton

235

CHAPTER 4
MULTIMEDIA

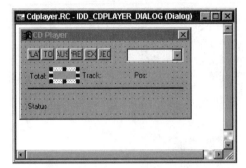

Figure 4-9 CD Player dialog box layout

CBitmapButton class will resize the button according to the size of the associated bitmaps. You only need to worry about the position of the Play button. You will later write code to calculate the position of the other buttons relative to the Play button. The buttons are too small to see their captions, but they are in the following order: Play, Stop, Pause, Prev, Next, and Eject. Here are the control identifiers and captions for the six buttons and the static controls:

Control	ID	Attributes
Push button	IDC_PLAY	"Play", owner drawn
Push button	IDC_STOP	"Stop", owner drawn
Push button	IDC_PAUSE	"Pause", owner drawn
Push button	IDC_PREV	"Prev", owner drawn
Push button	IDC_NEXT	"Next", owner drawn
Push button	IDC_EJECT	"Eject", owner drawn
Static	IDC_STATIC	"Total:"
Static	IDC_STATIC	"Track:"
Static	IDC_STATIC	"Pos:"
Static	IDC_INFO_TOTALLENGTH	
Static	IDC_INFO_TRACKLENGTH	
Static	IDC_INFO_POSITION	
Static	IDC_INFO_STATUS	
Combo box	IDC_TRACK	Drop list, no sort
Picture	IDC_STATIC	Black, frame

Notice that the information static text controls do not have a caption. They act as placeholders for information determined at runtime. Since they don't have a caption, it's not easy to see where they should be positioned on the dialog box. Figure 4-10 shows where the information static text controls should be placed.

4.5
PLAY TRACKS FROM AN AUDIO CD

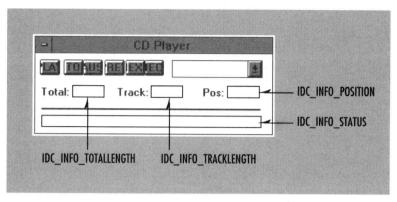

Figure 4-10 Static placement

8. **Add data members to the class.** Use ClassWizard to add member variables to the *CDiscPlayerDlg* class. The data members are created so you can easily access the control objects. Add the following data members:

Control ID	Type	Member
IDC_INFO_POSITION	CStatic	m_wndPosition
IDC_INFO_STATUS	CStatic	m_wndStatus
IDC_INFO_TOTALLENGTH	CStatic	m_wndTotalLength
IDC_INFO_TRACKLENGTH	CStatic	m_wndTrackLength
IDC_TRACK	CComboBox	m_wndTrack

9. Use ClassWizard to add message handlers in **CDiscPlayerDlg**. Add these message handlers using ClassWizard:

Object ID	Function	Message
CDiscPlayerDlg	OnCreate	WM_CREATE
CDiscPlayerDlg	OnInitDialog	WM_INITDIALOG
CDiscPlayerDlg	OnTimer	WM_TIMER
CDiscPlayerDlg	OnDestroy	WM_DESTROY
IDC_PLAY	OnPlay	BN_CLICKED
IDC_STOP	OnStop	BN_CLICKED
IDC_PAUSE	OnPause	BN_CLICKED
IDC_PREV	OnPrev	BN_CLICKED
IDC_NEXT	OnNext	BN_CLICKED
IDC_EJECT	OnEject	BN_CLICKED
IDC_TRACK	OnSelChangeTrack	CBN_SELCHANGE

CHAPTER 4
MULTIMEDIA

10. **Add member function prototypes to the dialog class.** *CDiscPlayerDlg* contains four private member functions. The *OnNewCD* function will be invoked whenever a new CD is detected in the CD drive. *UpdateInfo* updates information about the CD. *UpdateTrackInfo* updates information about an individual track on the CD, and *UpdatePosition* updates information about the current position of the CD. Add the following function prototypes to the *CDiscPlayerDlg* class in the DiscPlayerDlg.h file:

```
// private member functions
private:
     void    OnNewCD();             // called when new CD is inserted
     void    UpdateInfo();          // update information about CD
     void    UpdateTrackInfo();     // update information about current track
     void    UpdatePosition();      // update information about position
```

11. **Add data members to the dialog class.** *CDiscPlayerDlg* contains a *CCDAudio* object data member to communicate with the CD audio device. It also stores the timer identifier returned from the *CWnd::SetTimer* function so it can remove the timer later by calling *CWnd::KillTimer*. The class keeps track of whether or not a CD is inserted in the drive with the *m_bMediaPresent* data member. There is a *CBitmapButton* variable for each bitmap button. Each *CBitmapButton* object will be associated with a push button at runtime. Add the following data members to the *CDiscPlayerDlg* class in the DiscPlayerDlg.h file:

```
// private data members
private:
     CCDAudio      m_cd;              // CD audio object
     BOOL          m_bMediaPresent;   // remember if media was present
     int           m_nTimerID;        // timer identifier

     // bitmap button push buttons
     CBitmapButton  m_wndPlay;
     CBitmapButton  m_wndStop;
     CBitmapButton  m_wndPause;
     CBitmapButton  m_wndPrev;
     CBitmapButton  m_wndNext;
     CBitmapButton  m_wndEject;
```

You also need to include the declaration file for *CCDAudio* since you are using a data member of that type. Add the following #include statement at the top of the DiscPlayerDlg.h file:

```
#include "cdaudio.h"
```

12. **Add the implementation of the member functions.** *OnNewCD* is invoked by the application whenever a new CD is detected. It retrieves the number of tracks on the CD and creates an entry in the track selection combo box for each track. Add the following code to the DiscPlayerDlg.cpp file:

```
void CDiscPlayerDlg::OnNewCD()
{
     // get number of tracks on CD
     int nNumTracks = m_cd.GetNumberOfTracks();
```

4.5
PLAY TRACKS FROM AN AUDIO CD

```
        // clear contents of track combo box
    m_wndTrack.ResetContent();

        int    nIndex;          // index to combo box list
        char   szItem[12];      // string that is added to combo box

        // add a string item to track combo box for each track
        for (nIndex=1; nIndex <= nNumTracks; nIndex++)
        {
            wsprintf(szItem, "Track %i", nIndex); // create string
            m_wndTrack.AddString(szItem);         // add string to combo box
        }

        // select the first track (the first combo box item)
        m_wndTrack.SetCurSel(0);
}
```

UpdateInfo displays the length, or play time, of the CD. It is called whenever a new CD is inserted into the CD drive. Add the following code to the DiscPlayerDlg.cpp file:

```
void CDiscPlayerDlg::UpdateInfo()
{
        int nMinutes;      // number of minutes of CD
        int nSeconds;      // number of seconds of CD

        // get total length of CD
        m_cd.GetLength(nMinutes, nSeconds);

        // create string to display
        char szInfo[20];
        wsprintf(szInfo, "%02i:%02i", nMinutes, nSeconds);

        // display total length of CD
        m_wndTotalLength.SetWindowText(szInfo);
}
```

UpdateTrackInfo displays the length, or play time, of an individual track on the CD. It is called whenever a new track is played on the CD. Add the following code to the DiscPlayerDlg.cpp file:

```
void CDiscPlayerDlg::UpdateTrackInfo()
{
        // retrieve currently selected track
        int nTrack = m_wndTrack.GetCurSel();

        // make sure a track is selected !
        if (nTrack != CB_ERR)
        {
            // track is actually one more than selected item
            nTrack++;

            int nMinutes;  // number of minutes of track
            int nSeconds;  // number of seconds of track
```

continued on next page

continued from previous page

```
            // retrieve length of track
            m_cd.GetTrackLength(nTrack, nMinutes, nSeconds);

            // create string to display
            char szInfo[20];
            wsprintf(szInfo, "%02i:%02i", nMinutes, nSeconds);

            // display length of track
            m_wndTrackLength.SetWindowText(szInfo);
      }
}
```

UpdatePosition displays the current position of the CD. It is called in response to the WM_TIMER message if the CD is playing. There is no reason to call this function if the CD is not currently playing. Add the following code to the DiscPlayerDlg.cpp file:

```
void CDiscPlayerDlg::UpdatePosition()
{
      int    nTrack;     // track position of CD
      int    nMinutes;   // minutes position of track
      int    nSeconds;   // seconds position of track

      // get current position of CD
      m_cd.GetPosition(nTrack, nMinutes, nSeconds);

      // create string to display
      char szInfo[20];
      wsprintf(szInfo, "%02i:%02i", nMinutes, nSeconds);

      // display position of track
      m_wndPosition.SetWindowText(szInfo);

      // create current track string
      wsprintf(szInfo, "Playing track %i", nTrack);

      // display track information
      m_wndStatus.SetWindowText(szInfo);

      // update track selection if on new track
      if (m_wndTrack.GetCurSel() + 1 != nTrack)
      {
            m_wndTrack.SetCurSel(nTrack-1);    // select track in combo box
            UpdateTrackInfo();                 // update track information
      }
}
```

13. **Code the OnCreate method.** Here we try to open the CD audio device. If there is an error, a message is displayed to the user, and the application is terminated by returning a value of –1. Add the following code to the message handler:

```
int CDiscPlayerDlg::OnCreate(LPCREATESTRUCT lpCreateStruct)
{
      if (CDialog::OnCreate(lpCreateStruct) == -1)
            return -1;
```

4.5
PLAY TRACKS FROM AN AUDIO CD

```
    // open the cd audio device
    if (m_cd.Open(this))
    {
        // if failed, let user know we are terminating the application
        MessageBox("Application will terminate because "
            "it could not open CD-ROM device.",
            NULL, MB_OK | MB_ICONSTOP);

        // return -1 to destroy the window
        return -1;
    }

    return 0;
}
```

14. Code the OnInitDialog method. The following code attaches the *CBitmapButtons* to their dialog counterparts then recalculates their positions. The timer is used to check the status of the CD and the current track.

```
BOOL CDiscPlayerDlg::OnInitDialog()
{
    CDialog::OnInitDialog();
    CenterWindow();

    // Add "About..." menu item to system menu.
    CMenu* pSysMenu = GetSystemMenu(FALSE);
    CString strAboutMenu;
    strAboutMenu.LoadString(IDS_ABOUTBOX);
    if (!strAboutMenu.IsEmpty())
    {
        pSysMenu->AppendMenu(MF_SEPARATOR, -1, (LPCSTR)NULL);
        pSysMenu->AppendMenu(MF_STRING, IDS_ABOUTBOX, strAboutMenu);
    }

    // associate button IDs to CBitmapButton objects
    m_wndPlay.AutoLoad(IDC_PLAY, this);
    m_wndStop.AutoLoad(IDC_STOP, this);
    m_wndPause.AutoLoad(IDC_PAUSE, this);
    m_wndPrev.AutoLoad(IDC_PREV, this);
    m_wndNext.AutoLoad(IDC_NEXT, this);
    m_wndEject.AutoLoad(IDC_EJECT, this);

    // align buttons at runtime instead of App Studio
    // buttons will be aligned to the play button
    CRect rect;

    // get coordinates of play button relative to dialog box
    m_wndPlay.GetWindowRect(rect);
    ScreenToClient(rect);

    // save top position and size of button
    int nTopPos = rect.top;
    int nWidth = rect.right - rect.left;
```

continued on next page

CHAPTER 4
MULTIMEDIA

continued from previous page

```
        // set position of Stop button
        m_wndStop.SetWindowPos(NULL,
            rect.right, nTopPos, 0, 0, SWP_NOSIZE | SWP_NOZORDER);

        // set position of Pause button
        m_wndPause.SetWindowPos(NULL, rect.right + (nWidth),
            nTopPos, 0, 0, SWP_NOSIZE | SWP_NOZORDER);

        // set position of Prev button
        m_wndPrev.SetWindowPos(NULL, rect.right + (nWidth*2),
            nTopPos, 0, 0, SWP_NOSIZE | SWP_NOZORDER);

        // set position of Next button
        m_wndNext.SetWindowPos(NULL, rect.right + (nWidth*3),
            nTopPos, 0, 0, SWP_NOSIZE | SWP_NOZORDER);

        // set position of Eject button
        m_wndEject.SetWindowPos(NULL, rect.right + (nWidth*4),
            nTopPos, 0, 0, SWP_NOSIZE | SWP_NOZORDER);

        m_bMediaPresent = FALSE;    // init media present flag

        // set timer for 1 second
        m_nTimerID = SetTimer(1, 1000, NULL);

        return TRUE;
}
```

15. Code the OnPlay method. We want to play the currently selected track when the user clicks Play. Add the following code to the message handler:

```
void CDiscPlayerDlg::OnPlay()
{
        // get the currently selected track from the combo box
        int nTrack = m_wndTrack.GetCurSel();

        // make sure a track is selected !
        if (nTrack != CB_ERR)
        {
            // the track number is one more than the combo box item
            nTrack++;

            // display information about this track
            UpdateTrackInfo();

            // play the track
            m_cd.Play(nTrack);

            // since we are playing, the Stop and Pause buttons
            // should be enabled
            m_wndStop.EnableWindow(TRUE);
            m_wndPause.EnableWindow(TRUE);
        }
}
```

4.5
PLAY TRACKS FROM AN AUDIO CD

16. Code the OnStop method. The current track is stopped when the Stop button is clicked. Add the following code to the message handler:

```
void CDiscPlayerDlg::OnStop()
{
    // stop currently playing track
    m_cd.Stop();

    // disable Stop and Pause push buttons
    m_wndStop.EnableWindow(FALSE);
    m_wndPause.EnableWindow(FALSE);
}
```

17. Code the OnPause method. The current track is paused when the Pause button is pressed. The user can resume play by clicking the Pause button again. Add the following code to the message handler:

```
void CDiscPlayerDlg::OnPause()
{
    // pause or restart CD
    m_cd.IsPlaying() ? m_cd.Pause() : m_cd.ResumePlay();
}
```

18. Code the OnPrev method. The previous track is played when the Prev button is clicked. Add the following code to the message handler:

```
void CDiscPlayerDlg::OnPrev()
{
    // get the currently selected track
    int nCurTrack = m_wndTrack.GetCurSel();

    // select the previous track, or wrap around to last track
    nCurTrack = (nCurTrack == 0) ?
        m_wndTrack.GetCount()-1 : nCurTrackñ;

    // select new track
    m_wndTrack.SetCurSel(nCurTrack);

    // play new track
    OnPlay();
}
```

19. Code the OnNext method. The next track is played when the Next button is clicked. Add the following code to the message handler:

```
void CDiscPlayerDlg::OnNext()
{
    // get the currently selected track
    int nCurTrack = m_wndTrack.GetCurSel();

    // select the next track, or wrap around to first track
    if (++nCurTrack == m_wndTrack.GetCount())
        nCurTrack = 0;
```

continued on next page

continued from previous page

```
        // select new track
        m_wndTrack.SetCurSel(nCurTrack);

        // play new track
        OnPlay();
}
```

20. **Code the OnEject method.** The CD can be ejected by clicking the Eject button. Add the following code to the message handler:

```
void CDiscPlayerDlg::OnEject()
{
        // eject if media is present
        if (m_cd.IsMediaPresent())
            m_cd.Eject();
}
```

21. **Code the OnSelChangeTrack method.** The dialog box window will receive a CBN_SELCHANGE notification message whenever the user selects a new track. Add the following code to the message handler to play the next track:

```
void CDiscPlayerDlg::OnSelchangeTrack()
{
        OnPlay();    // play selected track
}
```

22. **Code the OnTimer method.** The dialog receives a WM_TIMER message when the timer has expired. The application detects the state of the CD and updates the appropriate information. Add the following code to the message handler:

```
void CDiscPlayerDlg::OnTimer(UINT nIDEvent)
{
        BOOL bMediaPresent;    // media present flag

        // check if there is a disk in the drive
        bMediaPresent = m_cd.IsMediaPresent();

        if (!bMediaPresent)
        {
            // display status of drive
            m_wndStatus.SetWindowText("No disk present");

            // clear disk and track information
            m_wndTotalLength.SetWindowText("");
            m_wndTrackLength.SetWindowText("");
            m_wndPosition.SetWindowText("");

            // since there is no disk, disable all the controls
            m_wndPlay.EnableWindow(FALSE);
            m_wndStop.EnableWindow(FALSE);
            m_wndPause.EnableWindow(FALSE);
            m_wndPrev.EnableWindow(FALSE);
            m_wndNext.EnableWindow(FALSE);
```

4.5
PLAY TRACKS FROM AN AUDIO CD

```
        m_wndEject.EnableWindow(FALSE);
        m_wndTrack.EnableWindow(FALSE);
    }

    // check if a disk has just been inserted; this is detected if
    // media is present now but not at the last timer message
    else if (bMediaPresent && !m_bMediaPresent)
    {
        // display drive status
        m_wndStatus.SetWindowText("New disk, retrieving information...");

        OnNewCD();          // retrieve information about disk
        UpdateInfo();       // update information about disk
        UpdateTrackInfo();  // update information about selected track

        // enable the play, prev, next, eject
        // and track selection controls
        m_wndPlay.EnableWindow(TRUE);
        m_wndPrev.EnableWindow(TRUE);
        m_wndNext.EnableWindow(TRUE);
        m_wndEject.EnableWindow(TRUE);
        m_wndTrack.EnableWindow(TRUE);

        // disable the stop and pause controls
        m_wndStop.EnableWindow(FALSE);
        m_wndPause.EnableWindow(FALSE);
    }

    // disk is present, check if it is playing or stopped
    else
    {
        // if disk is playing, update position information
        if (m_cd.IsPlaying())
            UpdatePosition();

        // disk is present but is not playing, display status
        else
            m_wndStatus.SetWindowText("Ready");
    }

    // save media present information
    m_bMediaPresent = bMediaPresent;
}
```

23. Handle the MM_MCINOTIFY message. This message is sent to a window when the MCI device has completed an operation that specifies the MCI_NOTIFY flag. In this sample application, the message is sent to the dialog box window when the end of the CD is reached or the play operation is interrupted. This message is not available in ClassWizard so you have to enter the message manually into the applications message map. Add the following function prototype to the *CDiscPlayerDlg* class declaration in the DiscPlayerDlg.h file:

```
afx_msg LRESULT OnMCINotify(WPARAM wParam, LPARAM lParam);
```

Add the following macro in the message map for class *CDiscPlayerDlg* in the file DiscPlayerDlg.cpp:

```
ON_MESSAGE(MM_MCINOTIFY, OnMCINotify)
```

The framework will now invoke *OnMCINotify* when the *CDiscPlayerDlg* window receives an MM_MCINOTIFY message.

The last step is to actually create the function. Add the following function implementation to the file DiscPlayerDlg.cpp:

```
LRESULT CDiscPlayerDlg::OnMCINotify(WPARAM wParam, LPARAM lParam)
{
    // check if reached end of CD successfully
    if (wParam == MCI_NOTIFY_SUCCESSFUL)
    {
        // select the first track and play it
        m_wndTrack.SetCurSel(0);
        OnPlay();
    }

    return 0;
}
```

24. **Code the OnDestroy method.** Here we kill the timer we created in *OnCreate*. Add the following code to the message handler:

```
void CDiscPlayerDlg::OnDestroy()
{
    CDialog::OnDestroy();

    // kill timer that was previously created
    if (m_nTimerID)
        KillTimer(m_nTimerID);
}
```

How It Works

Commands sent to the CD audio device go through several layers before reaching their final destination. The sample application uses *CCDAudio* to communicate with the CD audio device. *CCDAudio* provides high-level member functions to CD audio devices by abstracting MCI commands and data structures. All communication with the CD drive goes through *mciSendCommand*.

The SDK function *mciSendCommand* sends commands (or verbs) to MCI devices. You pass a device identifier, a command message, a set of flags, and a pointer to an MCI data structure specific for that command message.

You can also communicate with audio device drivers by calling the low-level audio services. These functions are part of the Win32 SDK and provide a device-independent interface to audio hardware devices. Figure 4-11 shows different levels involved in communicating with CD audio devices.

4.5
PLAY TRACKS FROM AN AUDIO CD

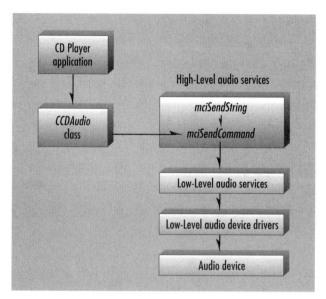

Figure 4-11 Communicating with CD audio devices

Using mciSendCommand

You can send commands to different MCI devices just as you can use the *SendMessage* function to send messages to different windows. Figure 4-12 shows the *mciSendCommand* sending commands to a CD device and a laser disc player. The destination of the command depends on the identifier passed to the *mciSendCommand*.

The second parameter to *mciSendCommand* specifies the MCI command verb. These are commands like open, close, play, stop, and get status. The third parameter is a set of flags that specifies additional operations for the command. The commands and flags are discussed in more detail in the section, "Controlling the CD Player."

The fourth parameter is a pointer to a data structure. Different commands expect a pointer to different types of data structures. Members of the structures can provide additional information and receive information returned from the MCI operation.

You can perform synchronous operations by specifying the MCI_WAIT flag. The *mciSendCommand* function will not return until the operation has completed.

You can perform asynchronous operations by specifying the MCI_NOTIFY flag. *mciSendCommand* will return immediately and post an MM_MCINOTIFY message to your window when the command has completed. This is useful when performing something like the play command. You can tell the MCI device to start playing, and your program immediately regains control. You can perform other operations while the device is playing in the background, and you will receive an MM_MCINOTIFY message when the play operation has completed.

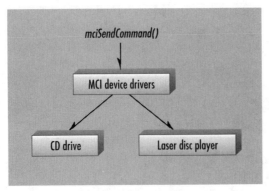

Figure 4-12 Sending commands to different MCI devices

Opening and Closing the CD Audio Device

The *CCDAudio* class provides member functions to initialize, control, and retrieve information about a CD audio device. You initialize a device by calling the *Open* member function. An MCI device must be initialized by opening it before you can communicate with the device. You open an MCI device by sending it the MCI_OPEN command. The *Open* method performs the following commands:

```
MCI_OPEN_PARMS mciOpenParms;
mciOpenParms.lpstrDeviceType = (LPCSTR)MCI_DEVTYPE_CD_AUDIO;
mciSendCommand(NULL, MCI_OPEN,
    MCI_OPEN_TYPE | MCI_OPEN_TYPE_ID | MCI_OPEN_SHAREABLE | MCI_WAIT,
    (DWORD)(LPVOID)&mciOpenParms);
```

You always pass a pointer to an MCI_OPEN_PARMS structure as the fourth parameter when opening an MCI device. The *lpstrDeviceType* member of this structure identifies the device type. The first parameter to the *mciSendCommand* function is NULL because you do not have an identifier for the device yet. The identifier will be returned in the *wDeviceID* member of the MCI_OPEN_PARMS data structure if the device is successfully opened.

The third parameter specifies additional command flags. The MCI_OPEN_TYPE and MCI_OPEN_TYPE_ID flags specify the device type that is contained in the *lpstrDeviceType* member of the MCI_OPEN_PARMS structure.

The MCI_OPEN_SHAREABLE flag specifies that the device should be opened as shareable. This means that multiple applications can access the device at the same time. The function will fail if the device is already open and is not shareable, does not have a driver, or does not exist.

The device should be closed when you are finished using it. You close the device by sending it the following MCI_CLOSE command:

```
mciSendCommand(m_nDeviceID, MCI_CLOSE, MCI_WAIT, NULL);
```

4.5
PLAY TRACKS FROM AN AUDIO CD

The first parameter specifies which device to close, and the second parameter closes the device. You do not have to close the device if you are using the *CCDAudio* class, which closes the device for you in its destructor.

The time format of the CD audio device is set to TMSF (tracks, minutes, seconds, and frames) by sending it the MCI_SET command. This is done automatically for you if you are using the *CCDAudio* class. The class performs this operation in the Open member function, as shown here:

```
MCI_SET_PARMS mciSetInfo;
mciSetInfo.dwTimeFormat = MCI_FORMAT_TMSF;
mciSendCommand(m_nDeviceID, MCI_SET,
    MCI_SET_TIME_FORMAT | MCI_WAIT,
    (DWORD)(LPVOID)&mciSetInfo);
```

Controlling the CD Player

The *CCDAudio* class provides the following control functions: *Play, Stop, Pause, ResumePlay,* and *Eject*. To play a CD, *CCDAudio::Play* passes the MCI_PLAY command to the *mciSendCommand* function, which starts the CD at the specified track position.

You specify the starting and stopping location by filling in the *dwFrom* and *dwTo* members of MCI_PLAY_PARAMS in conjunction with the MCI_FROM and MCI_TO flags.

Notice that the MCI_NOTIFY flag is specified in *Play*. When the operation completes, *mciSendCommand* will return immediately and post an MM_MCINOTIFY message to the window handle specified in the *dwCallback* member of the MCI_PLAY_PARMS structure. The *CCDAudio* class abstracts all of this for you. You simply call *Play* and pass the track to start playing.

You pause the CD by calling the *CCDAudio::Pause*. This sends the audio device an MCI_PAUSE command.

```
mciSendCommand(m_nDeviceID, MCI_PAUSE, MCI_WAIT, NULL);
```

MCI_PAUSE doesn't actually pause the CD, but in fact stops it. However, you can simulate unpausing by calling *ResumePlay*, which starts playing at the current position of the CD. As discussed earlier, you resume play by not specifying the MCI_FROM flag with the MCI_PLAY command.

You can eject the CD by calling *CCDAudio::Eject*. This function passes the MCI_SET command along with the MCI_SET_DOOR_OPEN flag to the audio device. This will open the media cover. To close the media cover, you pass the MCI_SET command along with the MCI_SET_DOOR_CLOSE flag to the audio device.

CCDAudio supports the following member functions to retrieve information about the CD: *GetNumberOfTracks, IsMediaPlaying, IsMediaPresent, GetPosition, GetLength,* and *GetTrackLength*. All of these methods query the state of the CD player using *mciSendCommand* with a pointer to the MCI_STATUS_PARAMS structure.

Error Conditions

mciSendCommand can fail for a variety of reasons. You should always check the return value for errors. It will return zero if it is successful; otherwise, it returns an error code. You can get a text description of the error code by calling *mciGetErrorString*.

Comments

CCDAudio is designed to work with CD audio devices, but it can be expanded to work with generic MCI devices. You can also easily expand this application to make a sophisticated CD player. Just look at CD equipment to get ideas for features. Here are some possibilities:

- Use a slider control with ticks to represent the current track
- Select tracks randomly
- Store titles of CDs and individual tracks using the CDPlayer.ini file maintained by the Windows 95 CD Player applet
- Sample the CD by playing a small amount of each track
- Calculate the most efficient arrangement of songs to fit on audio cassettes

COMPLEXITY
ADVANCED

4.6 How do I... Create 3D animation using OpenGL and MFC?

Problem

Windows NT 3.5 includes OpenGL, a powerful 3D graphics library that allows programmers to animate sophisticated color models complete with shading, lighting, and other effects. OpenGL functions are completely portable, but because OpenGL is independent of the operating system it runs on, getting a simple 3D graphics program up and running in MFC is difficult. What are the necessary steps to get a simple OpenGL program running using AppWizard and the MFC classes?

Technique

OpenGL is an operating system independent graphics library that supports sophisticated 3D rendering. OpenGL was originally developed by Silicon Graphics for use on their high-performance workstations. Microsoft has licensed OpenGL and is including it with Windows NT 3.5.

4.6
CREATE 3D ANIMATION USING OPENGL AND MFC

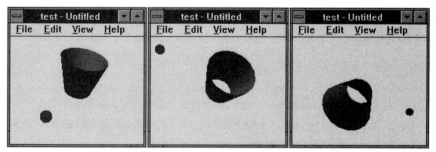

Figure 4-13 Different stages of OpenGL animation

How does it all work? Basically, you write OpenGL code that draws a scene and then displays it in a window managed by NT. Since OpenGL does all the hard work—lighting, shading, clipping, and so on—you're free to lay out the objects in the scene without worrying about the rendering details. Because OpenGL draws detailed scenes quickly, animation can be achieved by drawing and displaying scenes in rapid succession.

Manipulating the OpenGL primitives requires initialization of the OpenGL elements in a particular order, and the resources must be cleaned up in a particular order too. Also, since the library is OS-independent it has its own unique design, which doesn't mesh well with the GDI model or the way most MFC applications are built.

This How-To presents a simple SDI application that uses OpenGL to draw an animated scene in a *CView* window, as shown in Figure 4-13. The scene contains just two objects: a cylinder and a revolving light source. Every 100 milliseconds, a timer event is generated and the scene is redrawn after the cylinder and light have been repositioned to different places in 3D space. The objects appear to be moving randomly along a curved path through space, but they're really being repositioned using a clever polar coordinate system.

One warning before you dive in: OpenGL is a complex system, and learning the details of such a vast graphics library is not trivial. A big hurdle involves the connection between OpenGL and Windows NT. Some of these aspects will be covered here, but for the full treatment you should refer to the books listed in the Comments section of this How-To.

Steps

1. Create a new project called OpenGL using MFC AppWizard (exe).. The options and default class names are shown here (choose the single-document option and rename the document and view classes):

Classes to be created:
    Application: COpenGLApp in OpenGL.h and OpenGL.cpp
    Frame: CMainFrame in MainFrm.h and MainFrm.cpp
    Document: CGLDoc in GLDoc.h and GLDoc.cpp
    View: CGLView in GLView.h and GLView.cpp

251

CHAPTER 4
MULTIMEDIA

Features:
+ No toolbar or status bar
+ 3D Controls
+ Uses shared DLL implementation (MFC40.DLL)

2. Change the project settings. Change the linker options to include the two files necessary for OpenGL applications: OPENGl32.LIB and GLU32.LIB.

3. Use ClassWizard to add message handlers in CGLView. Add message-handling functions for these objects:

Object ID	Function	Message
CGLView	Create	
CGLView	PreCreateWindow	
CGLView	OnInitialUpdate	
CGLView	OnCreate	WM_CREATE
CGLView	OnDestroy	WM_DESTROY
CGLView	OnSize	WM_SIZE
CGLView	OnTimer	WM_TIMER
CGLView	OnSetCursor	WM_SETCURSOR

4. Edit the file GLView.h. At the bottom of the class declaration add these protected helper methods and member variables:

```
void SetThePixelFormat(CDC* pDC);
void DrawScene();
void DrawLight();
void PolarRotate( GLdouble dRadius, GLdouble dTwist,
         GLdouble dLatitude, GLdouble dLongitude);

HGLRC         m_hrc;
GLfloat       m_fLatitude, m_fLongitude;
GLdouble      m_dRadius;
GLUquadricObj *m_pSphere;
GLUquadricObj *m_pCylinder;
```

At the top of the file, add these two include files:

```
#include <GL/gl.h>
#include <GL/glu.h>
```

5. Edit the CGLView constructor and destructor. From this step on, we'll be editing the same file, GLView.cpp. You'll be modifying the template bodies of the methods you just added in step 3, and you'll be adding the bodies of the methods you declared in step 4. Now, locate the constructor in GLView.cpp and modify it to initialize our member variables like so:

```
#define NEARPLANE 3.0   // distance from viewpoint to front clipping plane
#define FARPLANE 7.0    // distance to back clipping plane
#define FOV 40.0        // field of view in degrees
```

4.6
CREATE 3D ANIMATION USING OPENGL AND MFC

```
CGLView::CGLView()
{
    m_pSphere = NULL;
    m_pCylinder = NULL;

    float fMaxObjectSize = (float) NEARPLANE;
    m_dRadius = NEARPLANE + fMaxObjectSize/2.0;

    m_fLatitude = 0.0f;
    m_fLongitude = 0.0f;
}
```

The memory allocated for the light sphere and the cylinder by OpenGL is released here in the destructor:

```
CGLView::~CGLView()
{
    gluDeleteQuadric (m_pSphere);
    gluDeleteQuadric (m_pCylinder);
}
```

6. Code the Create method. Every time you use the OpenGL functions, you need to attach the OpenGL device context with a Windows device context. To eliminate some extra overhead, we'll only do this attachment once in *OnCreate*. In order for that to work, we need our own device context for the whole class. By overriding Create, we register our own window class with the style CS_OWNDC that reserves a single DC for the lifetime of the *CGLView* object.

```
// Create a special window class with its own DC.
BOOL CGLView::Create(LPCTSTR lpszClassName, LPCTSTR lpszWindowName,
    DWORD dwStyle, const RECT& rect, CWnd* pParentWnd,
    UINT nID, CCreateContext* pContext)
{
    CString szClass = AfxRegisterWndClass (CS_OWNDC,
            NULL, (HBRUSH) (COLOR_WINDOW+1) );

    return CWnd::Create(szClass, lpszWindowName, dwStyle,
            rect, pParentWnd, nID, pContext);
}
```

7. Code the PreCreateWindow method. OpenGL will only work with windows whose style bits have WS_CLIPCHILDREN and WS_CLIPSIBLINGS. Without these two styles, the *SetThePixelFormat* would fail. The easiest way to ensure that our window object has these style bits set is to force them into *PreCreateWindow* like this:

```
// OpenGL doesn't work without these two class styles.
BOOL CGLView::PreCreateWindow(CREATESTRUCT& cs)
{
    cs.style |= WS_CLIPSIBLINGS | WS_CLIPCHILDREN;
    return CView::PreCreateWindow(cs);
}
```

CHAPTER 4
MULTIMEDIA

8. Code the OnCreate method. After *CGLView* has been created, we create a rendering context. First we determine a suitable pixel format for OpenGL, then we create the actual rendering context and attach it to our window's device context.

```
int CGLView::OnCreate(LPCREATESTRUCT lpCreateStruct)
{
    if (CView::OnCreate(lpCreateStruct) == -1)
        return -1;

    // Create a rendering context
    CDC* pDC = GetDC();
    SetThePixelFormat(pDC);
    m_hrc = wglCreateContext (pDC->GetSafeHdc());
    wglMakeCurrent (pDC->GetSafeHdc(), m_hrc);
    ReleaseDC (pDC);

    SetTimer (0, 100, NULL);

    return 0;
}
```

9. Code the OnDraw method. Here, we simply call our helper method *DrawScene* to execute the OpenGL functions.

```
void CGLView::OnDraw(CDC* pDC)
{
    DrawScene();
}
```

10. Code the OnInitialUpdate method. After the *CGLView* has been created, but before it's displayed, we need to set up the rendering context. This includes configuring the light attributes, setting the background color, and creating the scene's 3D objects.

```
void CGLView::OnInitialUpdate()
{
    CView::OnInitialUpdate();

    // Set the clearing color and depth. This is typical for most
    // OpenGL windows.
    glClearColor (0.0f, 0.0f, 0.0f, 1.0f);
    glClearDepth (1.0);
    glEnable (GL_DEPTH_TEST);
    glEnable (GL_LIGHTING);

    // Light attributes (short explanation)
    // vflAmbient is the amount and color of background lighting
    // in the scene. vflDiffuse is the attribute relating to any
    // light reflected from the object. vflSpecular refers to
    // highlight color.
    GLfloat     vflAmbient[] = {0.3f, 0.3f, 0.3f, 1.0f};
    GLfloat     vflDiffuse[] = {0.8f, 0.8f, 0.8f, 1.0f};
```

4.6
CREATE 3D ANIMATION USING OPENGL AND MFC

```
        GLfloat         vflSpecular[] = {1.0f, 1.0f, 1.0f, 1.0f};
        glLightfv (GL_LIGHT0, GL_AMBIENT, vflAmbient);
        glLightfv (GL_LIGHT0, GL_DIFFUSE, vflDiffuse);
        glLightfv (GL_LIGHT0, GL_SPECULAR, vflSpecular);
        glLightModelf (GL_LIGHT_MODEL_TWO_SIDE, 1.0f);
        glEnable (GL_LIGHT0);

        // Get new OpenGL objects from the library. These objects
        // must be explicitly released when the window is destroyed.
        m_pCylinder = gluNewQuadric();
        gluQuadricDrawStyle (m_pCylinder, GLU_FILL );

        m_pSphere = gluNewQuadric();
        gluQuadricDrawStyle (m_pSphere, GLU_FILL );

        // Make the client area roughly 200 x 200 pixels
        // by setting the parent frame to that size
        GetParentFrame()->SetWindowPos (NULL, 0, 0, 200, 200,
            SWP_NOMOVE | SWP_NOZORDER | SWP_NOACTIVATE);
}
```

11. Code the OnDestroy method. When the view has been destroyed, we delete the rendering context and kill the timer like so:

```
void CGLView::OnDestroy()
{
        wglDeleteContext(m_hrc);
        KillTimer(1);
        CView::OnDestroy();
}
```

12. Code the OnSize method. Every time *CGLView* is resized, we have to reconfigure the rendering context. This includes setting the new aspect ratio and viewport dimensions.

```
void CGLView::OnSize(UINT nType, int cx, int cy)
{
        CView::OnSize(nType, cx, cy);

        GLsizei  nWidth  = (GLsizei) cx;
        GLsizei  nHeight = (GLsizei) cy;
        GLdouble dAspect = (GLdouble) nWidth / (GLdouble) nHeight;

        glMatrixMode (GL_PROJECTION);
        glLoadIdentity();
        gluPerspective (FOV, dAspect, NEARPLANE, FARPLANE);
        glViewport (0, 0, nWidth, nHeight);
        glMatrixMode (GL_MODELVIEW);
}
```

13. Code the OnTimer method. When the 100-millisecond timer is triggered, we simply invalidate the entire client area, which redraws the scene. The back-

255

ground doesn't need erasing (hence the False parameter to Invalidate) since the whole client area will be repainted by OpenGL.

```
// Invalidate the window at every timer tick.
void CGLView::OnTimer(UINT nIDEvent)
{
    Invalidate(FALSE);
}
```

14. **Code the OnSetCursor method.** If the cursor is over *CGLView*, it will flash every time the scene is repainted. Here, we turn off the cursor whenever it's detected over the view's client area.

```
// To prevent the cursor from flashing, we disable the cursor when
// it's over the client area.
BOOL CGLView::OnSetCursor(CWnd* pWnd, UINT nHitTest, UINT message)
{
    if (nHitTest == HTCLIENT)
    {
        SetCursor(NULL);
        return TRUE;
    } else
        return CView::OnSetCursor(pWnd, nHitTest, message);
}
```

15. **Code the SetThePixelFormat method.** This helper method attaches a pixel format descriptor structure to the current device context.

```
void CGLView::SetThePixelFormat(CDC* pDC)
{
    static PIXELFORMATDESCRIPTOR pfd =
    {
        sizeof (PIXELFORMATDESCRIPTOR),    // size of this structure
        1,                                 // version number
        PFD_DRAW_TO_WINDOW |
        PFD_SUPPORT_OPENGL |
        PFD_DOUBLEBUFFER,                  // flags
        PFD_TYPE_RGBA,                     // RGBA pixels
        24,                                // 24-bit color
        0, 0, 0, 0, 0, 0,                  // default color bits
        0, 0,                              // no alpha channel
        0, 0, 0, 0, 0,                     // no accumulation buffer
        32,                                // 32-bit depth buffer
        0,                                 // no stencil buffer
        0,                                 // no auxiliary buffers
        PFD_MAIN_PLANE,                    // main layer
        0,                                 // reserved
        0, 0, 0                            // no layer masks
    };

    int nPixelFormat = ChoosePixelFormat (pDC->GetSafeHdc(), &pfd);
    SetPixelFormat (pDC->GetSafeHdc(), nPixelFormat, &pfd);
}
```

4.6
CREATE 3D ANIMATION USING OPENGL AND MFC

16. Code the DrawScene method. Finally, we get to the heart of the program. This is the method that's called every time the window needs repainting. We'll assume that the timer has been initiating these paint events and advance to the next "frame" of the animation.

```
void CGLView::DrawScene(void)
{
    // Float Vectors used to describe different colors
    static GLfloat vflGreenAmbient[]  = {0.1f, 0.3f, 0.1f, 1.0f};
    static GLfloat vflGreenDiffuse[]  = {0.0f, 1.0f, 0.0f, 1.0f};
    static GLfloat vflBlueAmbient[]   = {0.1f, 0.1f, 0.3f, 1.0f};
    static GLfloat vflBlueDiffuse[]   = {0.0f, 0.0f, 1.0f, 1.0f};
    static GLfloat vflBlueSpecular[]  = {0.0f, 0.0f, 1.0f, 1.0f};

    static GLfloat vflLightPosition0[] = {1.0f, 1.0f, 1.0f, 1.0f};
    static GLfloat flAngle = 0.0f;

    // Clear the depth and background buffers
    glEnable (GL_DEPTH_TEST);
    glClear (GL_COLOR_BUFFER_BIT | GL_DEPTH_BUFFER_BIT);

    glPushMatrix();
    m_fLatitude += 4.0f;
    m_fLongitude += 2.5f;
    PolarRotate (m_dRadius, 0.0, m_fLatitude, m_fLongitude);

    glPushMatrix();
    flAngle += 6.0f;
    glRotatef (flAngle, 1.0f, 0.0f, 1.0f);
    glTranslatef (0.0f, 1.5f, 0.0f);
    glLightfv (GL_LIGHT0, GL_POSITION, vflLightPosition0);
    DrawLight();
    glPopMatrix();

    glPushAttrib (GL_LIGHTING_BIT);
    // Set up the colors for the cylinder. The cylinder has
    // a blue surface and green interior.
    glMaterialfv (GL_BACK, GL_AMBIENT, vflGreenAmbient);
    glMaterialfv (GL_BACK, GL_DIFFUSE, vflGreenDiffuse);
    glMaterialfv (GL_FRONT, GL_AMBIENT, vflBlueAmbient);
    glMaterialfv (GL_FRONT, GL_DIFFUSE, vflBlueDiffuse);
    glMaterialfv (GL_FRONT, GL_SPECULAR, vflBlueSpecular);
    glMaterialf (GL_FRONT, GL_SHININESS, 50.0f);

    glPushMatrix();
    glRotatef (30.0f, 1.0f, 0.5f, 1.0f);
    gluCylinder (m_pCylinder, 0.3, 0.5, 0.8, 15, 5);
    glPopMatrix();

    glPopAttrib();
    glPopMatrix();
    glFinish();

    SwapBuffers (wglGetCurrentDC());
}
```

17. Code two helper methods. These last two methods are used exclusively by DrawScene.

```
// Rotate, twist and spin the current system, by the specified
// amount. This is what gives the model the semi-random movement
// between the cylinder and the light source.
void CGLView::PolarRotate( GLdouble dRadius, GLdouble dTwist,
        GLdouble dLatitude, GLdouble dLongitude)
{
    glTranslated (0.0, 0.0, -dRadius);
    glRotated (-dTwist, 0.0, 0.0, 1.0 );
    glRotated (-dLatitude, 1.0, 0.0, 0.0);
    glRotated (dLongitude, 0.0, 0.0, 1.0);
}

// The "light" is really just a sphere. A more sophisticated
// rendering might put a lampshade on top, but in this case,
// the primary interest is in a *quickly* moving light source.
void CGLView::DrawLight()
{
    glPushAttrib (GL_LIGHTING_BIT );
    glDisable (GL_LIGHTING );
    glColor3f (1.0f, 1.0f, 1.0f );
    gluSphere (m_pSphere, 0.1, 10, 10 );
    glPopAttrib();
}
```

18. Build and test the application. You should see a white sphere circling a cylinder which rotates in the center of the screen. The sphere represents the current, direct light source and it's visible only as a reference.

How It Works

The structure of this sample program may be similar to other graphics programs you've written. There's some initialization of the OpenGL library that's done in the creation phase. The dimensions of the scene are recalculated when WM_SIZE is received. Then the objects in the scene are repositioned and drawn in response to a timer event.

When you draw to a window using GDI functions, you use the CDC member functions. They, in turn, call SDK functions with a handle to the device context (DC). OpenGL uses an analogous handle called a rendering context (RC). The RC stores information about the current rendering environment just like a DC keeps track of the current brush, background color, and so on.

Creating the Rendering Context

Rendering contexts are created with the OpenGL function *wglCreateContext*. In our program, we create a single rendering context in *OnCreate* that's used for the lifetime of *CGLView*. The RC is destroyed using *wglDeleteContext* in *CGLView::OnDestroy*.

Creating a rendering context requires a connection to a device context. We could re-create the rendering context every time we enter *OnDraw*, but there's a lot of overhead involved in attaching the RC to the DC. So instead, we keep our device context around by creating a window with the class style bit CS_OWNDC. That way, we're guaranteed the same device context every time we enter *OnDraw*. With that assumption, we can attach the rendering context to that device context once, in *OnCreate*, then use it for the lifetime of the view.

One restriction with the Windows NT implementation of OpenGL is that it only draws in windows that have the WS_CLIPSIBLINGS and WS_CLIPCHILDREN styles. If your window doesn't have these styles, you won't see anything drawn by OpenGL. By overriding *PreCreateWindow*, we can logical-OR these window styles into the CREATESTRUCT structure to guarantee our window has these required styles.

During the creation process, *CGLView::OnCreate* handles four things: setting the pixel format structure, creating the rendering context, attaching the rendering context to the device context, and starting the animation timer.

Initializing the Rendering Context

The pixel format determines the mapping from the OpenGL graphics into a format supported by the display window. Pixel formats are just scalar values, like 1, 2, 3, 4, and so on, and are determined by first telling the OpenGL system what you want to do and where you want to do it. The first step is to fill a PIXELFORMATDESCRIPTOR structure with values that describe the sort of rendering to be done. This structure and the device context of the target window are passed to *ChoosePixelFormat*, a new Win32 function that was created to support the OpenGL implementation on Windows NT. This information is used to determine the pixel format that best matches what you want and what the system can give.

CGLView::OnInitialUpdate initializes the lighting models, the clearing color, the viewing perspective, and the quadrics used for the light sphere and the cylinder. As with most of this code, *float* arrays are used as arguments to the OpenGL library. Most OpenGL functions follow a naming convention that indicates what type of arguments they expect. For example, the function *glLightfv* is functionally equivalent to *glLightiv*, except that *glLightfv* takes a vector (that's array for normal people) of *float* as an argument, while *glLightiv* takes a vector of type *int*. Much of our initialization code creates vectors that contain lighting information to be passed to these OpenGL functions.

Drawing the Scene

When the timer fires every 100 milliseconds, the client area is invalidated to force a repaint event. This brings us to the heart of the program, *DrawScene*. Two objects are rendered here. The first is a cylinder, colored blue on the outside and green on the inside. The second represents a light source, which is just a white sphere that rotates around the cylinder. At the same time, the entire scene twists and rotates, giving the movement of the objects a sort of random effect. The last line in *DrawScene* swaps the currently visible display buffer with the buffer that has just been rendered. Double buffering enhances performance by hiding the rendering process. At any time, one buffer is displayed while the other is being rendered offscreen.

CHAPTER 4
MULTIMEDIA

Comments

This How-To is partially adapted from the AUXDEMO sample program that ships with the Windows NT OpenGL implementation. By comparing the code between the two samples, you can see how to migrate a prototype written using the higher-level auxiliary library to the lower-level GL and MFC functions.

Several factors affect the performance of an OpenGL program. For best results, stick to small scenes with a small number of objects. More complicated scenes will result in a heavier demand on system resources. Also, double buffering helps to keep animation smooth.

There are a few lines you can tweak that will change the scene in a noticeable way. First, try changing the field of view and distance parameters at the top of GLView.cpp. These determine the viewing volume of the scene and are used like a 3D clipping area. Also try changing the parameters to *gluCylinder* in *DrawScene* or the light color values in *OnInitialUpdate*.

If you'd like to learn more about OpenGL, check out the articles on the Microsoft Developers Network CD-ROM and the SDK documentation in Books Online. The two standard OpenGL references are *OpenGL Programming Guide* by Neider, Davis, and Woo (Addison-Wesley, 1993) and *OpenGL Reference Manual* by the OpenGL Architectural Review Board (Addison-Wesley, 1992).

CHAPTER 5
BITMAPS AND ICONS

BITMAPS AND ICONS

How do I…

5.1 Paint a bitmap in my MDI application's background?

5.2 Animate my application's icon?

5.3 Draw text on top of a bitmap?

5.4 Draw a bitmap with transparency?

5.5 Smoothly drag bitmaps with the mouse?

No matter what kind of Windows application you're writing, you can always make it look better with graphics. This chapter illustrates different graphic techniques using the most common graphic elements: bitmaps and icons. You'll see how to put a bitmap in the back of an MDI application or animate its icon. Another useful trick gives you the ability to add transparency to your bitmaps and display them with the ImageList control. Other How-Tos demonstrate annotating a bitmap with text and using the *CRgn* class to optimize repaint areas.

5.1 Paint a Bitmap in My MDI Application's Background

If you want to display a bitmap in the space behind your application's MDI child windows, you'll have to look a long time before you find the undocumented MDI child window. It's a member variable of the *CMDIFrameWnd* class. By subclassing this window, you can override the *OnEraseBkgnd* method to erase the background and draw a bitmap in the middle of the client area.

> **Additional Topics:** CBitmap, WM_ERASEBKGND, subclassing the MDI client window

CHAPTER 5
BITMAPS AND ICONS

5.2 Animate My Application's Icon

Here's a handy way to display progress information while your application is minimized. This How-To cycles through a short set of icons when your application is minimized. By using the special Window class (not the C++ class) members for icons, you'll see how to change the minimized icon.

Additional Topics: Icons, window class variables, using timers and LoadIcon

5.3 Draw Text on Top of a Bitmap

This How-To shows you an easy way to annotate a bitmap with text. By selecting a bitmap into a memory context, you can use any of the CDC methods to draw text essentially right on top of the bitmap. Then, you'll see how to transfer the bitmap using *BitBlt* onto the screen.

Additional Topics: CDC text drawing methods, memory device contexts

5.4 Draw a Bitmap with Transparency

Adding a bitmap to a dialog box can be almost as easy as adding an icon by following the steps in this How-To. We'll write a reusable function that simplifies handling a transparent bitmap so you can design non-rectangular shapes.

Additional Topics: BitBlt, raster operations

5.5 Smoothly Drag Bitmaps with the Mouse

Have you ever wondered how the Solitaire game works? In this How-To, we'll peer into CARDS.DLL, the library used by all Microsoft card games. We'll use its methods to display pictures of cards in a *CView* and write code to smoothly drag the images around.

Additional Topics: CRgn, runtime loading of a DLL, using the CARDS.DLL, optimized paint handling through regions, serializing methods

---

COMPLEXITY
BEGINNING

5.1 How do I... Paint a bitmap in my MDI application's background?

Problem

I'd like to put a bitmap, such as my company logo, in the background area of an MDI application. What's the easiest way to do this?

5.1
PAINT A BITMAP IN MY MDI APPLICATION'S BACKGROUND

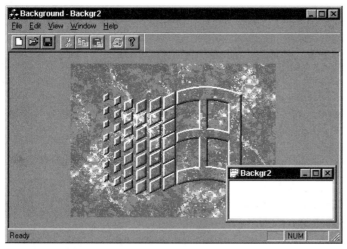

Figure 5-1 Bitmap in MDI client area

Technique

Putting a bitmap in the background of an MDI application requires doing two things: displaying a *CBitmap* object and customizing the painting of the MDI client area.

Because MFC hides a lot of the details, it's easy to forget that MDI applications are composed of two distinct window classes: the MDI frame window and the MDI client window. The client window covers the client area of the main frame window and is responsible for much of the MDI support. It's here in the client window that we'll add our hooks to paint a bitmap. We're going to subclass the default client window with one that knows how to draw a bitmap.

Every time the background needs repainting, we'll let Windows handle the message to paint the background color. Then we'll draw a bitmap in the center of the client area (see Figure 5-1).

Steps

1. Create a new project called Background using the MFC AppWizard (exe).
Use all the defaults and make sure you're creating an MDI app.

Classes to be created:
Application: CBackgroundApp in Background.h and Background.cpp
Frame: CMainFrame in MainFrm.h and MainFrm.cpp
MDIChildFrame: CChildFrame in ChildFrm.h and ChildFrm.cpp
Document: CBackgroundDoc in BackgroundDoc.h and BackgroundDoc.cpp
View: CBackgroundView in BackgroundView.h and BackgroundView.cpp

CHAPTER 5
BITMAPS AND ICONS

Features:
+ Initial toolbar in main frame
+ Initial status bar in main frame
+ 3D Controls
+ Uses shared DLL implementation (MFC40.DLL)

2. **Add a bitmap using App Studio.** Import a bitmap into your resource file from the Windows directory (press CTRL-R then the Import button). You can choose any file. Use "Windows Logo.bmp" from the Windows 95 directory. Leave the default resource ID as IDB_BITMAP1.

3. **Create a CWnd class called CBitmapClient.** Using ClassWizard, add a class to your project called *CBitmapClient* with *CWnd* as its parent. Save the files as BitmapClient.cpp and BitmapClient.h.

4. **Use ClassWizard to add message handlers.** Add message-handling functions for these objects:

Object ID	Function	Message
CBitmapClient	OnSize	WM_SIZE
CBitmapClient	OnEraseBkgnd	WM_ERASEBKGND

5. **Add member variables to CBitmapClient.** Use the add member variable dialog to add a variable which holds the background bitmap:

Type	Declaration	Access
CBitmap	m_bmp	protected

6. **Code CBitmapClient::OnEraseBkgnd.** Whenever we need to erase the background, we'll let our parent do its own erasing first. In this case, *CWnd::OnEraseBkgnd* simply fills the device context with a gray brush. Next, we *BitBlt* our bitmap into the center of the client window. Add the following code to BitmapClient.cpp:

```
BOOL CBitmapClient::OnEraseBkgnd(CDC* pDC)
{
    CWnd::OnEraseBkgnd(pDC);

    BITMAP bm ;
    CDC dcMem ;

    VERIFY(m_bmp.GetObject(sizeof(bm), (LPVOID)&bm));

    dcMem.CreateCompatibleDC(pDC);
    CBitmap* pOldBMP = (CBitmap*) dcMem.SelectObject(&m_bmp);

    CRect rect;
    GetClientRect(rect);
```

5.1
PAINT A BITMAP IN MY MDI APPLICATION'S BACKGROUND

```
        pDC->BitBlt((rect.right-bm.bmWidth) / 2,    // centered
            (rect.bottom-bm.bmHeight) / 2,
            bm.bmWidth,
            bm.bmHeight,
            &dcMem,
            0, 0,
            SRCCOPY);

        dcMem.SelectObject(pOldBMP) ;
        return TRUE;
}
```

7. **Code CBitmapClient's OnSize.** Add the following code, which forces the client window to redraw the bitmap every time its dimensions change.

```
void CBitmapClient::OnSize(UINT nType, int cx, int cy)
{
        CWnd::OnSize(nType, cx, cy);

        RedrawWindow(NULL, NULL,
            RDW_INVALIDATE|RDW_ERASE|RDW_ERASENOW|RDW_ALLCHILDREN);
        return ;
}
```

8. **Modify CBitmapClient's constructor.** The background bitmap needs to be loaded in the constructor. I originally tried loading the bitmap in *CBitmapClient::OnCreate*, but the method was never called. As it turns out, WM_CREATE isn't sent to *CWnd* objects if they're attached to HWNDs that have already been created (see step 11).

```
CBitmapClient::CBitmapClient()
{
        VERIFY(m_bmp.LoadBitmap(IDB_BITMAP1));
}
```

9. **Add member variables to CMainFrame.** Use the add member variable dialog to add the new client window to the main frame:

Type	Declaration	Access
CBitmapClient	m_wndClient	protected

Also, add the include file for our new class to the top of MainFrm.h as follows:

```
#include "BitmapClient.h"
```

10. **Modify CMainFrame::OnCreate.** In order to subclass the client window with our class, add the following code to the *OnCreate* method as shown here:

```
int CMainFrame::OnCreate(LPCREATESTRUCT lpCreateStruct)
{
        if (CMDIFrameWnd::OnCreate(lpCreateStruct) == -1)
            return -1;
```

continued on next page

continued from previous page

```
        if (!m_wndClient.SubclassWindow(m_hWndMDIClient))
        {
            TRACE("Failed to subclass MDI client window.\n");
            return -1;
        }
        ...
    }
```

m_hWndMDIClient is the *CMDIFrameWnd* member variable that contains the handle to the MDI client window. *m_wndNewClient* is our *CBitmapClient* class that will handle the *OnEraseBkgnd* and *OnSize* messages that would normally be handled by *m_hWndMDIClient*.

11. Compile and run the application. Notice how the bitmap paints itself after you change the size of the main window.

How It Works

Although it's not clearly documented in the online help, the *CMDIFrameWnd* class includes a very important member variable: *m_hWndMDIClient*. Here's an excerpt from the *CMDIFrameWnd* declaration in Afxwin.h:

```
// Implementation
public:
        HWND m_hWndMDIClient;           // MDI Client window handle
```

The first line of code in our *CMainFrame::OnCreate* calls *CMDIFrameWnd::OnCreate*. By the time control returns to our code, the client window has already been created. So to capture the window events we want like WM_ERASEBKGND, we need to subclass the client window that was just created. That's what the code in step 6 did. Now, whenever the client needs repainting or resizing, our *m_wndNewClient* object handles the events.

Previous incarnations of MFC required you to write the cryptically named *GetSuperWndProcAddr* method. If you check in Books Online, this method is now obsolete.

Painting the Bitmap

Now that our client window is all hooked up, we just need to paint the bitmap. *CBitmapClient*'s constructor loads *CBitmap* from the resource file. It's not necessary to free the bitmap; the *CBitmap* destructor takes care of the GDI bitmap resource for us.

In *CBitmapClient::OnEraseBkgnd*, you'll see that the size of the bitmap was determined by calling *CGdiObject::GetObject*. This method fills GDI-specific information in the structure passed to it—in our case, a bitmap structure. The bitmap width and height, along with the coordinates to center the bitmap, are passed to *CDC::BitBlt* to draw the bitmap in the middle of the client area.

The frame window sends a WM_SIZE message to our client window after the user has resized the application, but WM_ERASEBKGND isn't necessarily sent. That's why we need to force the repainting of the bitmap by calling *RedrawWindow* in *CBitmapClient::OnSize*.

5.1
PAINT A BITMAP IN MY MDI APPLICATION'S BACKGROUND

Comments

When first approaching this problem, you might think, "Easy, just override *CMDIFrameWnd*'s *OnEraseBkgnd*." Obviously, that doesn't work. Since MFC conveniently hides much of the confusing MDI details, it's easy to forget about the embedded MDI client window. Using *m_hWndMDIClient* leads to a solution.

If you want to color the background and paint a bitmap, *CBitmapClient::OnEraseBkgnd* is the place to do this. However, in most cases, you're probably better off letting MFC fill the background using the color selected by the user in the Control Panel. Instead of filling the background with a solid color, you could use *FillRect* to paint the background with a hatched brush.

What about CreateClient?

If you examine the documentation for *CMDIFrameWnd*, you might find a virtual function called *CreateClient*. If you override this method, you're responsible for creating the client window. We could have done just that. However, if you examine the implementation of *CMDIFrameWnd::CreateClient*, you'll see why it's easier just to subclass after the window has been created:

```
BOOL CMDIFrameWnd::CreateClient(LPCREATESTRUCT lpCreateStruct,
    CMenu* pWindowMenu)
{
    ASSERT(m_hWnd != NULL);
    ASSERT(m_hWndMDIClient == NULL);
    DWORD dwStyle = WS_VISIBLE | WS_CHILD | WS_BORDER |
        WS_CLIPCHILDREN | WS_CLIPSIBLINGS |
        MDIS_ALLCHILDSTYLES;   // allow children to be created invisible
    DWORD dwExStyle = 0;
    // will be inset by the frame

    if (afxData.bWin4)
    {
        // special styles for 3D effect on Win4
        dwStyle &= ~WS_BORDER;
        dwExStyle = WS_EX_CLIENTEDGE;
    }

    CLIENTCREATESTRUCT ccs;
    ccs.hWindowMenu = pWindowMenu->GetSafeHmenu();
        // set hWindowMenu for MFC V1 backward compatibility
        // for MFC V2, window menu will be set in OnMDIActivate
    ccs.idFirstChild = AFX_IDM_FIRST_MDICHILD;

    if (lpCreateStruct->style & (WS_HSCROLL|WS_VSCROLL))
    {
        // parent MDIFrame's scroll styles move to the MDICLIENT
        dwStyle |= (lpCreateStruct->style & (WS_HSCROLL|WS_VSCROLL));

        // fast way to turn off the scrollbar bits (without a resize)
        ModifyStyle(WS_HSCROLL|WS_VSCROLL, 0, SWP_NOREDRAW|SWP_FRAMECHANGED);
    }
```

continued on next page

continued from previous page

```
        // Create MDICLIENT control with special IDC
        if ((m_hWndMDIClient = ::CreateWindowEx(dwExStyle, _T("mdiclient"), NULL,
                dwStyle, 0, 0, 0, 0, m_hWnd, (HMENU)AFX_IDW_PANE_FIRST,
                AfxGetInstanceHandle(), (LPVOID)&ccs)) == NULL)
        {
                TRACE0("Warning: CMDIFrameWnd::OnCreateClient:failed to ⇒
create MDICLIENT.\n");
                return FALSE;
        }
        // Move it to the top of z-order
        ::BringWindowToTop(m_hWndMDIClient);

        return TRUE;
}
```

You could replace the line that calls *CreateWindowEx* with code to create an instance of *CBitmapClient,* but you'd still need all that other style manipulation stuff. (Some of the MFC classes are just full of bit twiddling to manage styles, especially *CScrollView.*)

A Faster Fill

There's an ongoing debate as to whether *CDC*'s *FillRect* or *ExtTextOut* is faster when drawing colored rectangles. Yes, *ExtTextOut* can fill rectangles—don't be fooled by its name. If you dig deep into MFC, you'll discover that the AFX engineers used *ExtTextOut* instead of *FillRect.* So maybe it is faster; it's just not documented well. Here's how you'd use it:

```
pDC->ExtTextOut(0, 0, ETO_OPAQUE, rect, NULL, 0, NULL);
```

ExtTextOut fills the rectangle with the current background color, so you may have to call *CDC::SetBkColor* to get the color you want.

For more information, check out the Microsoft Knowledge Base article Q103786, "Changing Window Background Color with Foundation Classes."

COMPLEXITY
BEGINNING

5.2 How do I... Animate my application's icon?

Problem

I'd like to change the icon when my application is minimized. For example, it might be useful to loop through an icon sequence, simulating animation, while my application services some background task. How do I load different icons and change the text displayed for the minimized app?

5.2
ANIMATE MY APPLICATION'S ICON

Technique

First, we'll need some additional icon artwork to display in place of the default icon generated by AppWizard. Any single icon can be chosen from our pool of available icons to replace the current one at runtime. In this How-To, a half-second timer notifies the application when it's time to change the icon. To simulate animation, we make each icon in the sequence slightly different from the previous one. If your artistic skills are as limited as mine, you can use a few simple techniques to generate a "filmstrip," as I'll show below.

The icon can be changed at runtime by using a new method we'll write called *LoadNewIcon*. It takes a handle to the new icon and substitutes it for the one stored by the main window class. The animation occurs only when the application is minimized.

Steps

1. **Create a new project called AnimateIcon using the MFC AppWizard (exe).** Choose the Single Document option then press the Finish button.

Classes to be created:
- Application: CAnimateIconApp in AnimateIcon.h and AnimateIcon.cpp
- Frame: CMainFrame in MainFrm.h and MainFrm.cpp
- Document: CAnimateIconDoc in AnimateIconDoc.h and AnimateIconDoc.cpp
- View: CAnimateIconView in AnimateIconView.h and AnimateIconView.cpp

Features:
+ Initial toolbar in main frame
+ Initial status bar in main frame
+ 3D Controls
+ Uses shared DLL implementation (MFC40.DLL)

2. **Use App Studio to create six icons.** Don't worry, these icons are pretty easy to make. First, create six empty icons by right-clicking on Icon in the ResourceView and choosing Insert Icon (do this six times—this gives you IDI_ICON1 through IDI_ICON6).

Since the icons will only be used when the application is minimized, you only need to worry about the smaller, 16x16 pixel icons. Since they're not created by default, you have to double-click each icon and press the New Device Image button (see Figure 5-2) to add the 16x16 version.

Select the yellow brush and choose the Filled Ellipse tool in the Graphics toolbar. We're going to create a filled yellow circle that gets larger with each icon. Use the table below to help you center each ellipse (put the cursor at the position

Figure 5-2 Using the New Device Image dialog

shown below and drag out the circle to the correct size). Figure 5-3 shows the position and size indicators in Developer Studio to help draw the circles.

Icon	Position	Size
IDI_ICON1	(5,5)	4x4
IDI_ICON2	(4,4)	6x6
IDI_ICON3	(3,3)	8x8
IDI_ICON4	(2,2)	10x10
IDI_ICON5	(1,1)	12X12
IDI_ICON6	(0,0)	14X14

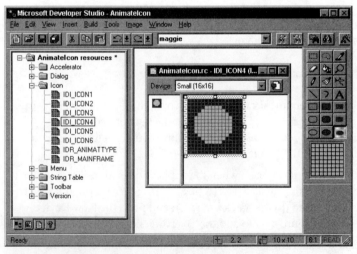

Figure 5-3 Using the position and size indicators to draw the circles

5.2
ANIMATE MY APPLICATION'S ICON

3. Use ClassWizard to add message handlers. Add message-handling functions for these objects:

Object ID	Function	Message
CMainFrame	OnTimer	WM_TIMER
CMainFrame	OnDestroy	WM_DESTROY

4. Add the LoadNewIcon helper function. Use the ClassView Add Function dialog to add the following method.

```
protected:
    void LoadNewIcon(UINT nNewIconID);
```

5. Edit CMainFrame::OnCreate. Add this line to start the timer.

```
int CMainFrame::OnCreate(LPCREATESTRUCT lpCreateStruct)
{
    if (CFrameWnd::OnCreate(lpCreateStruct) == -1)
        return -1;

    SetTimer(2, 500, NULL);
...
}
```

6. Code the OnTimer message handler. Locate the body for *OnTimer* in MainFrm.cpp and change it to look like the following code:

```
// determine number of elements in an array (not bytes) (taken ⇒
from AFXIMPL.H)
#define _countof(array) (sizeof(array)/sizeof(array[0]))

void CMainFrame::OnTimer(UINT nIDEvent)
{
    static int icons[] =
        {IDI_ICON1, IDI_ICON2, IDI_ICON3, IDI_ICON4, IDI_ICON5, IDI_ICON6,
         IDI_ICON5, IDI_ICON4, IDI_ICON3, IDI_ICON2};

    static long index = 0;

    if (IsIconic())
    {
        SetWindowText("Icon Animation");
        LoadNewIcon (icons[index++ % _countof(icons)]);
    } else {
        index = 0;
        SetWindowText("Minimize to see icon animation");
        LoadNewIcon(IDR_MAINFRAME);
    }
}
```

CHAPTER 5
BITMAPS AND ICONS

7. Edit CMainFrame::OnDestroy. This line of code stops the timer when the main window is destroyed:

```
void CMainFrame::OnDestroy()
{
    CMainFrame::OnDestroy();
    KillTimer(2);
}
```

8. Add the body for CMainFrame::LoadNewIcon. Add this code to swap the current icon:

```
void CMainFrame::LoadNewIcon(UINT nIconID)
{
    // Get a handle to the new and current icon
    HICON hIconNew = AfxGetApp()->LoadIcon(nIconID);
    HICON hIconOld = (HICON) GetClassLong(m_hWnd, GCL_HICON);

    ASSERT(hIconNew);
    ASSERT(hIconOld);

    // Substitute the new icon for the old and redraw the window
    if (hIconNew != hIconOld)
    {
        DestroyIcon(hIconOld);
        SetClassLong (m_hWnd, GCL_HICON, (long) hIconNew);
        RedrawWindow (NULL, NULL, RDW_FRAME | RDW_ERASE | RDW_INVALIDATE);
    }
}
```

9. Edit CAnimateIconApp::InitInstance. Add the following code to *CAnimateIcon::InitInstance* to force the application to start in a minimized state:

```
BOOL CAnimateIconApp::InitInstance()
{
    // Standard initialization
    Enable3dControls();       // Call this when using MFC in a shared DLL
    LoadStdProfileSettings(); // Load standard INI file options (including MRU)

    // Register document templates

    CSingleDocTemplate* pDocTemplate;
    pDocTemplate = new CSingleDocTemplate(
        IDR_MAINFRAME,
        RUNTIME_CLASS(CAnimateIconDoc),
        RUNTIME_CLASS(CMainFrame),      // main SDI frame window
        RUNTIME_CLASS(CAnimateIconView));
    AddDocTemplate(pDocTemplate);

    // Parse command line for standard shell commands, DDE, file open
    CCommandLineInfo cmdInfo;
    ParseCommandLine(cmdInfo);

    // Minimize the app when it starts
    m_nCmdShow = SW_MINIMIZE;
```

5.2
ANIMATE MY APPLICATION'S ICON

```
    // Dispatch commands specified on the command line
    if (!ProcessShellCommand(cmdInfo))
        return FALSE;

    return TRUE;
}
```

10. **Build and run the application.** While the application is minimized, you should see the icon looping through a six-frame animation at a rate of two frames per second.

How It Works

The timer for *AnimateIcon* starts in *CMainFrame::OnCreate* through a call to *SetTimer*. This sends a WM_TIMER message to *CMainFrame::OnTimer* every half-second.

OnTimer keeps track of the current icon and as long as the application is minimized, loads the next icon in the sequence. The *_countof* macro makes it easy to change the number of elements in the *icons* array without worrying about side effects. If the frame window is *not* minimized, the icon is reset to the default IDR_MAINFRAME icon created by AppWizard. The text of the window changes depending on the minimized state.

The Window Class Word

The window class word doesn't hold information about the application class in the C++ sense. Instead, it holds class-specific information about the window's icon, cursor, brush, and window styles. *LoadNewIcon* uses *GetClassLong* and *SetClassLong* to change the icon for this window. The icon resource handle determines what icon will be painted.

Swapping the Icons

LoadNewIcon simply loads the requested icon and swaps it for the current window icon. The old window icon is then deleted.

If you use *SetClassLong* to set the window's icon, but the icon is already loaded, the same handle is returned. For that reason we must check if *hIconNew* and *hIconOld* are the same by using *GetClassLong*. If they are, there's no reason to continue since the requested icon is already in place. Otherwise, the new icon is registered with *SetClassLong* and the window is redrawn to show the new icon.

Comments

LoadNewIcon can be used to change the application icon at any time, not just after a timer message. For example, a terminal program could show the status of a download operation, or a print spooler might animate a piece of paper moving through a printer.

5.3 How do I... Draw text on top of a bitmap?

COMPLEXITY INTERMEDIATE

Problem

I need to put different titles on a single bitmap. However, I won't know its caption until the program is already running and the bitmap has already been created. What's the best technique for annotating a bitmap at runtime?

Technique

All the methods for text and bitmap manipulation are wrapped by the device context class, *CDC*. The text methods operate on any kind of device context, but the bitmap operations only work on memory device contexts. To combine the text and bitmap operations we'll first select a bitmap into a memory device context, then use the text methods on the same DC to annotate the bitmap with text.

Any drawing performed on the memory DC will actually be drawn on the bitmap. After we're finished drawing on the memory DC, *BitBlt* will tranfer it to an actual display device context, as shown in Figure 5-4.

Steps

1. Create a new project called **TextOnBitmap** using the MFC AppWizard (exe). Choose the dialog-based version and press the Finish button.

Classes to be created:
Application: CTextOnBitmapApp in TextOnBitmap.h and TextOnBitmap.cpp
Dialog: CTextOnBitmapDlg in TextOnBitmapDlg.h and TextOnBitmapDlg.cpp

Features:
+ About box on system menu
+ 3D Controls
+ Uses shared DLL implementation (MFC40.DLL)

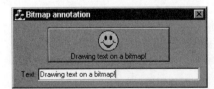

Figure 5-4 A bitmap with text annotation

5.3
DRAW TEXT ON TOP OF A BITMAP

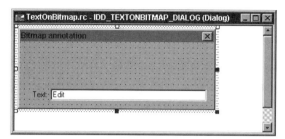

Figure 5-5 Text on Bitmap dialog

2. **Edit the IDD_TEXTONBITMAP_DIALOG dialog.** Use App Studio to modify the dialog to look like the one shown in Figure 5-5. Remove the OK and Cancel buttons and change the dimensions to 202x63. Make the ID for the edit control IDC_EDIT.

3. **Create a bitmap.** Use App Studio to create a bitmap, as shown in Figure 5-6 (it doesn't have to be perfect). Set the bitmap's dimensions to 192x54 and its ID to IDB_BITMAP.

4. **Add member variable to the dialog box class.** Use ClassWizard to add the following member variable to the *CTextOnBmpDlg* class:

Control ID	Type	Member
IDC_EDIT	CString	m_edit

5. **Use ClassWizard to add message handlers.** Add a message-handling function for the edit control:

Object ID	Function	Message
IDC_EDIT	OnChangeEdit	EN_CHANGE

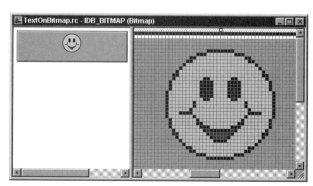

Figure 5-6 Bitmap used for the TextOnBitmap sample

CHAPTER 5
BITMAPS AND ICONS

6. **Add member variables to CTextOnBitmapDlg.** Use the Add Variable dialog to add these members:

Type	Declaration	Access
CFont	m_font	protected
CPoint	m_posBitmap	protected
CSize	m_sizeBitmap	protected

The variable *m_font* stores the font used to write text on top of the bitmap. The *m_posBitmap* and *m_sizeBitmap* variables store the position and size of the bitmap.

7. **Modify the CTextOnBitmapDlg::OnInitDialog member function.** Add code in the TODO section that creates and stores the font used to annotate the bitmaps. We also store the position and size of the bitmap for repainting in *OnPaint*.

```
BOOL CTextOnBitmapDlg::OnInitDialog()
{
    CDialog::OnInitDialog();

    // Add "About..." menu item to system menu.

    // IDM_ABOUTBOX must be in the system command range.
    ASSERT((IDM_ABOUTBOX & 0xFFF0) == IDM_ABOUTBOX);
    ASSERT(IDM_ABOUTBOX < 0xF000);

    CMenu* pSysMenu = GetSystemMenu(FALSE);
    CString strAboutMenu;
    strAboutMenu.LoadString(IDS_ABOUTBOX);
    if (!strAboutMenu.IsEmpty())
    {
        pSysMenu->AppendMenu(MF_SEPARATOR);
        pSysMenu->AppendMenu(MF_STRING, IDM_ABOUTBOX, strAboutMenu);
    }

    SetIcon(m_hIcon, TRUE);        // Set big icon
    SetIcon(m_hIcon, FALSE);       // Set small icon

    // Set up the font used for drawing the text. Get the bitmap info.
    LOGFONT lf;
    SystemParametersInfo(SPI_GETICONTITLELOGFONT,
         sizeof(LOGFONT), &lf, SPIF_SENDWININICHANGE);
    m_font.CreateFontIndirect(&lf);

    // store the size of the bitmap
    BITMAP   bm;
    CBitmap bitmap;
    bitmap.LoadBitmap(IDB_BITMAP);
    bitmap.GetObject(sizeof(BITMAP), &bm);
```

5.3
DRAW TEXT ON TOP OF A BITMAP

```
    m_sizeBitmap.cx = bm.bmWidth;      // store width of bitmap
    m_sizeBitmap.cy = bm.bmHeight;     // store height of bitmap

    // Center the bitmap horizontally in the dialog
    m_posBitmap.y = 10;   // init bitmap y position
    CRect r;
    GetClientRect(r);
    m_posBitmap.x = (r.Width() / 2) - (m_sizeBitmap.cx / 2);

    return TRUE;  // return TRUE  unless you set the focus to a control
}
```

8. Modify CTextOnBmpDlg::OnPaint. This code will be executed whenever a portion of your window becomes invalid and needs repainting. The code creates a memory device context, selects the bitmap into the device context, draws text on the device context, then copies its contents to the display.

```
void CTextOnBitmapDlg::OnPaint()
{
    if (IsIconic())
    {
        CPaintDC dc(this); // device context for painting

        SendMessage(WM_ICONERASEBKGND, (WPARAM) dc.GetSafeHdc(), 0);

        // Center icon in client rectangle
        int cxIcon = GetSystemMetrics(SM_CXICON);
        int cyIcon = GetSystemMetrics(SM_CYICON);
        CRect rect;
        GetClientRect(&rect);
        int x = (rect.Width() - cxIcon + 1) / 2;
        int y = (rect.Height() - cyIcon + 1) / 2;

        // Draw the icon
        dc.DrawIcon(x, y, m_hIcon);
    }
    else
    {
        CPaintDC dc(this);   // device context for painting
        CDC dcMem;           // memory device context
        CBitmap bitmap;

        dcMem.CreateCompatibleDC(&dc);
        bitmap.LoadBitmap(IDB_BITMAP);

        // select the bitmap into the memory device context
        CBitmap* pOldBitmap = dcMem.SelectObject(&bitmap);

        // select the font into the memory device context
        CFont* pOldFont = dcMem.SelectObject(&m_font);

        // Set the text attributes to be center and bottom aligned
        // and to draw the text with a transparent background.
        dcMem.SetTextAlign(TA_CENTER | TA_BOTTOM);
        dcMem.SetBkMode(TRANSPARENT);
```

continued on next page

continued from previous page

```
        // draw the text on the memory device context (the bitmap)
        dcMem.TextOut(m_sizeBitmap.cx / 2, m_sizeBitmap.cy - 3, m_edit);

        // transfer the memory device context to the display context
        dc.BitBlt(m_posBitmap.x, m_posBitmap.y,
            m_sizeBitmap.cx, m_sizeBitmap.cy, &dcMem, 0, 0, SRCCOPY);

        dcMem.SelectObject(pOldFont);       // unselect font
        dcMem.SelectObject(pOldBitmap);     // unselect bitmap
    }
}
```

9. **Code CTextOnBitmapDlg::OnChangeEdit.** As the user types in the text, we want to show what the text looks like on the bitmap. Locate the *OnChangeEdit* code in TextOnBitmapDlg.cpp and change it to look like this:

```
void CTextOnBitmapDlg::OnChangeEdit()
{
    UpdateData();   // update control data members

    // create bitmap bounding rectangle
    CRect rect (CPoint(0,0), m_sizeBitmap);
    rect.OffsetRect (m_posBitmap);

    // invalidate dialog, causing bitmap to be redrawn with new text
    InvalidateRect(rect, FALSE);
}
```

10. **Compile and run the application.** The text you enter into the edit field will be displayed on top of the bitmap. *OnChangeEdit* handles the EN_CHANGE notification message to update the bitmap whenever a new character is entered into the edit field. Notice that the text is not drawn outside the bitmap.

How It Works

You can't do anything with a bitmap until you select it into a memory device context. A memory device context is a block of memory that represents a display surface. When you draw to a memory device context, the output is not drawn to the display but rather to a block of memory representing the display. In most cases, the memory is really the bitmap.

You can make the display surface the same size and contain the same color layout of a bitmap by selecting a bitmap into the memory device context.

Once the bitmap is selected into the memory DC, you can draw on the DC as if you were drawing directly on the bitmap. The output of any text methods, such as *DrawText*, will be stored directly on the bitmap. After annotating the memory DC, we use *BitBlt* to transfer its contents directly to the screen.

The default background drawing mode for a device context is OPAQUE. This will fill in the background rectangle of the text with the current background color. If you specify a TRANSPARENT background mode, the background color will not change.

DRAW A BITMAP WITH TRANSPARENCY

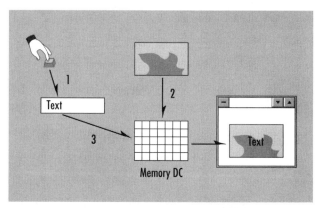

Figure 5-7 Drawing Process (1) User enters text into edit field (2) Create and select bitmap into memory device (3) Draw text on top of bitmap (4) Copy contents to display context

This How-To uses the same font that is used for the current icon-title. The *SystemParametersInfo* function retrieves logical font information by filling in a LOGFONT structure. That structure is passed to the *CreateFontIndirect* member function to create the font used by the annotation code.

Figure 5-7 illustrates an overview of the entire drawing process.

Comments

As you can see, it is pretty simple to draw text on top of a bitmap. You are not limited to drawing only text on bitmaps; you can perform any GDI operation on a bitmap. For example, you could use other primitive drawing methods like *Ellipse* or *Rectangle* to draw shapes on the bitmap before it's displayed.

COMPLEXITY
ADVANCED

5.4 How do I... Draw a bitmap with transparency?

Problem

Even though icons are limited in size and bit depth, they do support transparency. This is a feature I'd like to have with bitmaps. With icons, can I mark some of the pixels as transparent so the background color or pattern will always show through? Is there a way to do this with bitmaps?

281

CHAPTER 5
BITMAPS AND ICONS

Technique

Prior versions of Visual C++ didn't have the support for placing bitmaps in a dialog like version 4.x allows. However, you'll always be stuck with rectangular images because you don't know the background color until runtime. If you have a round image, you could paint the corners with a special color that can be used to calculate a mask. This mask identifies the transparent portions of the bitmap. *CImageList* handles a lot of this work for you.

We're going to create a special static control called *CImageWell* to assist us in illustrating the *CImageList* class. The image well will display two types of patterned backgrounds (a checkerboard and a gray-scale ramp) with the bitmap centered to illustrate the transparency (see Figure 5-8). If the transparency color doesn't exist in the bitmap the effect is no transparency, as shown in Figure 5-9.

To prove that this technique really works, we'll paint a checkerboard pattern and see how those colors show through our source bitmap, as shown in Figure 5-10.

Steps

1. **Create a new project called TransBitmap using the MFC AppWizard (exe).**
   Choose the Dialog-based version and press the Finish button.

   Classes to be created:
   Application: CTransBitmapApp in TransBitmap.h and TransBitmap.cpp
   Dialog: CTransBitmapDlg in TransBitmapDlg.h and TransBitmapDlg.cpp

   Features:
   + About box on system menu
   + 3D Controls
   + Uses shared DLL implementation (MFC40.DLL)

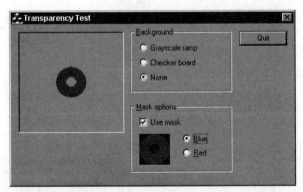

Figure 5-8 Using CImageList::Draw to paint the bitmap using a mask

5.4
DRAW A BITMAP WITH TRANSPARENCY

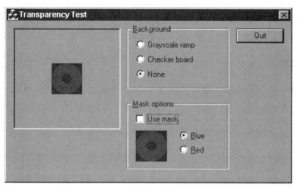

Figure 5-9 Drawing without the transparency mask

2. Add a new class with ClassWizard. Create the new class *CImageWell* using the following parameters:

Class name:	CImageWell
Base class:	CStatic
File:	ImageWell.cpp

3. Edit ImageWell.h. Modify the constructor and add a few member variables like this:

```
class CImageWell : public CStatic
{
// Construction
public:
        CImageWell(UINT nBitmapID, CSize sizeBitmap);

// Attributes
public:
        enum Background { NONE, GRAYSCALE, CHECKERBOARD };
        Background m_bkg;
        COLORREF m_color;     // mask color

        UINT m_nBitmapID;
        CSize m_sizeBitmap;
...
```

Since there are three possible background styles, the *enum* type *Background* lists the choices. The background color is specified through *m_color*, and the bitmap resource ID and size are set through the constructor.

283

CHAPTER 5
BITMAPS AND ICONS

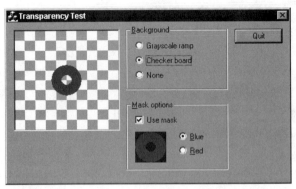

Figure 5-10 A more complicated background pattern

4. Use the WizardBar to handle WM_ERASEBKGND for CImageWell. Add the following code:

```
BOOL CImageWell::OnEraseBkgnd(CDC* pDC)
{
    CRect rClient;
    GetClientRect(rClient);

    switch (m_bkg)
    {
    case NONE:
        {
            CBrush* pBrush = CBrush::FromHandle(GetSysColorBrush(COLOR_BTNFACE));
            pDC->FillRect(rClient, pBrush);
            return TRUE;
        }
        break;

    case CHECKERBOARD:
        {
            int state = pDC->SaveDC();          // what a cool function!
            ASSERT(state != 0);

            int nBlocks = 10;

            pDC->SetMapMode(MM_ANISOTROPIC);
            pDC->SetWindowExt(nBlocks, nBlocks);
            pDC->SetViewportExt(rClient.Size());
            pDC->SetViewportOrg(rClient.left, rClient.top);

            CBrush white(RGB(255, 255, 255));
            CBrush gray(RGB(192, 192, 192));

            pDC->FillRect(CRect(0, 0, nBlocks, nBlocks), &white);
```

5.4
DRAW A BITMAP WITH TRANSPARENCY

```
            int x, y;
            for (x = 0; x < nBlocks; x += 2)
                for (y = 0; y < nBlocks; y += 2)
                {
                    pDC->FillRect(CRect(x, y, x+1, y+1), &gray);
                    pDC->FillRect(CRect(x+1, y+1, x+2, y+2), &gray);
                }

                pDC->RestoreDC(state);
            }
            break;

        case GRAYSCALE:
            {
                // Create brushes and pens
                int nSteps = rClient.Width();
                float fIncrement = (float) (255.0 / rClient.Width());
                float fColor = 0.0f;

                CBrush br;
                CRect r(rClient);
                r.right = r.left+1;
                for (int x = rClient.left; x < rClient.right; x++)
                {
                    br.CreateSolidBrush(RGB( (int) fColor,
                        (int) fColor, (int) fColor) );
                    pDC->FillRect(r, &br);
                    br.DeleteObject();
                    fColor += fIncrement;
                    r.right++;
                    r.left++;
                }
            }
            break;
    }

    return TRUE;
}
```

5. Use the WizardBar to handle WM_PAINT for **CImageWell**. Add the following code:

```
void CImageWell::OnPaint()
{
    CPaintDC dc(this); // device context for painting

    // Assume there's only one image in m_nBitmapID
    CImageList list;
    list.Create (m_nBitmapID, m_sizeBitmap.cx, 1, m_color);

    // Center the bitmap in the well
    CRect r;
    GetClientRect(r);
```

continued on next page

continued from previous page

```
        CPoint pt;
        pt.x = ((r.Width() / 2) - (m_sizeBitmap.cx/2));
        pt.y = ((r.Height() / 2) - (m_sizeBitmap.cy/2));

        list.Draw(&dc, 0, pt, ILD_TRANSPARENT);
}
```

6. **Edit CImageWell::CImageWell.** Modify the constructor to initialize its member variables like this:

```
CImageWell::CImageWell(UINT nBitmapID, CSize sizeBitmap)
{
        m_nBitmapID = nBitmapID;
        m_sizeBitmap = sizeBitmap;

        m_bkg = CHECKERBOARD;
        m_color = RGB(255, 255, 255);
}
```

7. **Add a bitmap called IDB_CIRCLE.** We'll use this bitmap to put in the image well. It doesn't need to be too precise, just make sure you use the pure red (RGB(255, 0, 0)) and pure blue (RGB(0, 0, 255)) colors somewhere to indicate two possible transparent colors.

   To add the bitmap to your resource file, select New from the Resource menu and choose Bitmap from the list box. Keep the default size of 48x48 pixels. First fill the background with blue. Then draw a red circle so it touches all four edges of the bitmap. Now turn it into a doughnut by drawing a smaller blue circle in the middle. It should look like Figure 5-11 when you've finished.

8. **Edit the IDD_TRANSBITMAP_DIALOG dialog resource.** Before you start adding controls to this dialog, first resize it to approximately 294x154 dialog units. Remove the Cancel button and rename OK to Quit. Then add the following controls, in this order, to make the dialog look like Figure 5-12:

Control	ID	Attributes
Picture	IDC_WELL	Black frame @ 7,7 (112x97), Client edge on
Background group	IDC_STATIC	"&Background", Group
Radio button	IDC_GRAYSCALE=2001	"Grayscale ramp"
Radio button	IDC_CHECKER=2002	"Checker board"
Radio button	IDC_NONE=2003	"None"
Mask group	IDC_STATIC	"&Mask options"
Check box	IDC_USE_MASK=2004	"Use mask", Group, Tabstop
Radio button	IDC_BLUE=2005	"Blue", Group, Tabstop
Radio button	IDC_RED=2006	"Red", Group, Tabstop
Picture	IDC_STATIC	Bitmap type, Image IDB_BITMAP1

Setting the IDs is important since we're going to handle all the button controls with one method.

5.4
DRAW A BITMAP WITH TRANSPARENCY

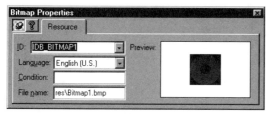

Figure 5-11 IDB_CIRCLE bitmap

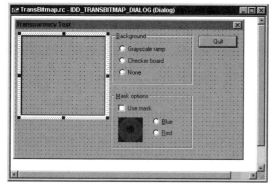

Figure 5-12 Dialog layout

9. **Add member variables to CTransBitmapDlg.** Add the following member variables using ClassWizard:

Control ID	Type	Member
IDC_WELL	CImageWell	m_well
IDC_GRAYSCALE	int	m_nBackground
IDC_BLUE	int	m_nColor
IDC_USE_MASK	BOOL	m_bUseMask

10. **Edit the CTransBitmapDlg constructor.** Change the default values used to initialize the dialog controls like this:

```
CTransBitmapDlg::CTransBitmapDlg(CWnd* pParent /*=NULL*/)
    : CDialog(CTransBitmapDlg::IDD, pParent), m_well(IDB_BITMAP1, CSize(48, 48))
{
    //{{AFX_DATA_INIT(CTransBitmapDlg)
    m_nBackground = 1;
    m_bUseMask = TRUE;
    m_nColor = 0;
    //}}AFX_DATA_INIT
    m_hIcon = AfxGetApp()->LoadIcon(IDR_MAINFRAME);
}
```

11. **Modify the CTransBitmapDlg message map.** Insert the following line that will reroute all the BN_CLICKED messages for the important dialog controls:

```
BEGIN_MESSAGE_MAP(CTransBitmapDlg, CDialog)
    //{{AFX_MSG_MAP(CTransBitmapDlg)
    ON_WM_PAINT()
    ON_WM_QUERYDRAGICON()
    ON_CONTROL_RANGE(BN_CLICKED, IDC_GRAYSCALE, IDC_RED, OnClick)
    //}}AFX_MSG_MAP
END_MESSAGE_MAP()
```

12. **Modify CTransBitmapDlg::OnInitDialog.** Fake a button press to get things rolling here.

```
BOOL CTransBitmapDlg::OnInitDialog()
{
    CDialog::OnInitDialog();

    SetIcon(m_hIcon, TRUE);     // Set big icon
    SetIcon(m_hIcon, FALSE);    // Set small icon

    OnClick(0);    // fake a click message to update the well

    return TRUE;   // return TRUE  unless you set the focus to a control
}
```

13. **Add the OnClick helper function.** Use the ClassView Add Function dialog to add the following method to the interface file and edit the body like so:

```
void CTransBitmapDlg::OnClick (UINT nID)
{
    UpdateData(TRUE);

    switch (m_nBackground)
    {
    case 0: m_well.m_bkg = CImageWell::GRAYSCALE; break;
    case 1: m_well.m_bkg = CImageWell::CHECKERBOARD; break;
    case 2: m_well.m_bkg = CImageWell::NONE; break;
    }

    switch (m_nColor)
    {
    case 0: m_well.m_color = RGB(0, 0, 255); break;
    case 1: m_well.m_color = RGB(255, 0, 0); break;
    }

    if (m_bUseMask == FALSE)
        m_well.m_color = RGB(1, 2, 3);

    m_well.Invalidate();
}
```

14. **Build and test the application.** Change some of the options and notice how they affect the bitmap transparency. You'll be able to see what the whole

bitmap looks like if you turn off the Use Mask option. With transparency on, you can see what happens while using different colors to represent the clear pixels in the source bitmap.

To see what the bitmap looks like when you identify red as the transparent color, press the Red radio button and the grayscale ramp button. You should see something like Figure 5-13.

How It Works

The first version of this How-To relied on a very long function I wrote called *TransparentBlt* (no, that's not a clear sandwich, it's a function). It used no less than five HDCs and nine *BitBlts* to achieve the same transparency effects that a single call to *CImageList::Draw* now supports.

The version presented here in the second edition is so much cleaner. With the addition of the image list control in Windows 95, Microsoft has made it much easier to manipulate bitmaps and create masks on the fly. By designating different colors as the background, as we did with the blue and red radio buttons, you can achieve some interesting effects.

CImageWell::OnPaint creates a new *CImageList* each time it receives a WM_PAINT message. I wouldn't normally recommend this method. However, in this case, we have to generate a new image list if the background color changes. That's because the image list creates a monochrome mask image based on the color value passed to *CImageList::Create*. Draw uses the mask to combine the source bitmap with the destination to achieve the transparency effect.

Comments

When I was working on the checkerboard algorithm, I forgot that the device context passed to *OnEraseBkgnd* might be in other places. Because I set up some funky mapping modes and didn't restore them, the rest of the dialog looked awfully funny. That's

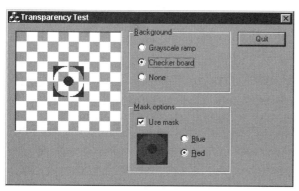

Figure 5-13 Using red to identify the transparent color

when I realized you can stash the device context away and restore it to its original state through *CDC::SaveDC* and *CDC::RestoreDC*. Remove those lines in *OnEraseBkgnd* to see what happens if you forget to use them.

You might be wondering why I set the background color to RGB(1, 2, 3) when I turned off the Use Mask option. It's because I know those colors aren't used in the bitmap, so the mask that *CImageList* creates won't ever apply to this image.

COMPLEXITY
ADVANCED

5.5 How do I... Smoothly drag bitmaps with the mouse?

Problem

I'm writing yet another card game for Windows. To make my application a little more interactive, I'd like to let the user drag the cards around on the screen. Is there a way to optimize the repaint messages to avoid a lot of flashing?

Technique

If you've ever tried to move bitmaps smoothly around the screen, you've probably become quite frustrated by all the paint messages slowing down the update time. However, with some clever painting techniques involving complex regions using *CRgn,* you can overcome this.

To illustrate these painting techniques, we're going to enlist the help of the library used by Solitaire and other Windows card games: the CARDS.DLL library. When we're finished, the How-To program will look like Figure 5-14.

All Microsoft card games get their card images from this library through a few simple APIs. For example, to draw an ace of clubs at coordinates (40, 50), you simply call the CARDS.DLL exported function *cdtDraw* like this:

```
cdtDraw(hDC, 40, 50, 1, 0, RGB(255, 255, 255));
```

It's that simple! The first parameter is the handle to the device context where the card should appear. The second and third parameters specify the X and Y client coordinates of the upper-left corner of the card. The fourth parameter is a number between 1 and 52—an ordinal number for each card in the deck.

We'll encapsulate the CARDS.DLL functionality into two classes: the *Card* class to store information about the state of a card (face showing, position, back design, and the suit/rank number) and a private class, CARDS_DLL, to manage the dynamic loading and unloading of the CARDS.DLL file.

5.5
SMOOTHLY DRAG BITMAPS WITH THE MOUSE

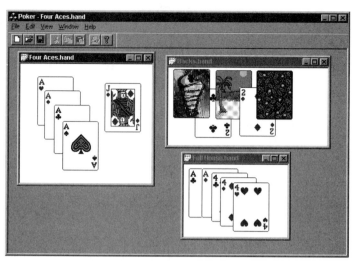

Figure 5-14 Cards in MFC

Since simply displaying static bitmaps would be too boring, we're going to spice up this How-To by allowing you to drag the cards around in a *CView*. While this might seem simple at first, we're going to do some intelligent management of the dirty rectangles using *regions* to get the quickest redraw times. A region is an elliptical or polygonal area in a window and is encapsulated by the *CRgn* class. The areas exposed as you drag cards around the screen are not necessarily rectangular. Regions make it easy to express these exposed areas.

As an added bonus, we're going to pop up a menu when you click a card with the right-mouse button. The menu choices let you delete the card, flip it over, and change the back design. A dialog class, *CBackDlg*, gives you immediate feedback as you scroll through the possible card back designs included with CARDS.DLL, as shown in Figure 5-15, with a slider control.

Figure 5-15
Drawing the card backs in a dialog

CHAPTER 5
BITMAPS AND ICONS

Also, since each *Card* object knows how to save itself to a file through *CArchive::Serialize*, it's trivial to add file opening and saving to our sample application. We'll add one line of code in our *CDocument* class to serialize the card list, which in turn saves each *Card* object to a file. Whew, that's a lot of code to write. Let's get started.

Steps

1. **Create a new project called Poker using the MFC AppWizard (exe).**
   Use all the defaults and make sure you're creating a multiple document application. Press the Advanced button in step 4 and change the File Extension to "hnd".

   Classes to be created:
Application:	CPokerApp in Poker.h and Poker.cpp
Frame:	CMainFrame in MainFrm.h and MainFrm.cpp
MDIChildFrame:	CChildFrame in ChildFrm.h and ChildFrm.cpp
Document:	CPokerDoc in PokerDoc.h and PokerDoc.cpp
View:	CPokerView in PokerView.h and PokerView.cpp

   Features:
   + Initial toolbar in main frame
   + Initial status bar in main frame
   + 3D Controls
   + Uses shared DLL implementation (MFC40.DLL)
   + Document supports files with extension .HND

2. **Edit the string table.** This is a minor point, but it really bugs me that you can only enter three characters in the File Extension field in the previous step. Only Visual C++ 4.0 limits us to three character extensions; Windows 95 couldn't care less. Let's change the extension to "hand" (for those of you that don't know Poker, a hand is not only what you use to hold the cards, it's the expression used for the group of cards in your hand). Edit IDR_POKERTYPE to look like this:

`\nPoker\nPoker\nPoker Hands (*.hand)\n.HAND\nPoker.Document\nPoker Document`

3. **Create the Card.h file.** The *Card* and *CardList* objects are used by the *CPokerDoc* class to manage the cards displayed by the CARDS.DLL file. Add the following code to a new file and save it as Card.h.

```
#ifndef _CARD_H_
#define _CARD_H_

class Card : public CObject
{
        DECLARE_SERIAL(Card);

public:
        Card();
```

5.5
SMOOTHLY DRAG BITMAPS WITH THE MOUSE

```cpp
        void Draw(CDC* pDC);
        void Erase(CDC* pDC);

        BOOL IsFaceUp(void) { return m_bFaceUp; }
        void SetFaceUp(BOOL bUp) { m_bFaceUp = bUp; }

        void ButtonDownAt(const CPoint& pt);
        void ButtonUp() { m_bDrag = FALSE; }

        void SetPos(const CPoint& ptNew);
        CPoint GetPos() { return m_ptAt; }

        void SetType(WORD num) { m_type = num; }
        WORD GetType() { return m_type; }

        void SetBack(WORD back) { m_back = back; }
        WORD GetBack() { return m_back; }

        CRect GetRect() { return CRect(m_ptAt, m_size); }

        BOOL PtInCard(const CPoint& pt)
              { return GetRect().PtInRect(pt); }

        virtual void Serialize(CArchive& ar);

// Class level static members
        static BOOL Initialize();
        static void Release();

protected:
        BOOL m_bFaceUp;
        BOOL m_bDrag;
        WORD m_type;
        CPoint m_ptAt;
        CPoint m_ptOffset;
        WORD m_back;

        static CSize m_size;
};

class CardList : public CObList
{
public:
        void AddHeadCard( Card* pCard)
              { AddHead(pCard); }

        Card* GetHeadCard()
              { return (Card*) GetHead(); }

        Card* GetNextCard(POSITION& pos)
              { return (Card*) GetNext(pos); }
};

#endif
```

CHAPTER 5
BITMAPS AND ICONS

4. Create the Card.cpp file. The CARDS_DLL class in the code below wraps up the functions provided by the CARDS.DLL file. Since it's a private class local to the Card.cpp file, the interface doesn't appear in Card.h. Create a new text file and add the following code to it, then save it as Card.cpp.

```
#include "stdafx.h"
#include "card.h"

IMPLEMENT_SERIAL(Card, CObject, 0);

class CARDS_DLL
{
public:
        CARDS_DLL();
        ~CARDS_DLL();

        // These function pointers will be set in the class constructor
        BOOL (WINAPI* pfnInit)(int*, int*);
        BOOL (WINAPI* pfnDraw)(HDC, int, int, int, int, COLORREF);
        BOOL (WINAPI* pfnTerm)(void);

        HINSTANCE m_hLib;
};

CARDS_DLL::CARDS_DLL()
{
        if (m_hLib = LoadLibrary("CARDS.DLL"))
        {
                (FARPROC&) pfnInit = GetProcAddress(m_hLib, "cdtInit");
                (FARPROC&) pfnDraw = GetProcAddress(m_hLib, "cdtDraw");
                (FARPROC&) pfnTerm = GetProcAddress(m_hLib, "cdtTerm");
        }
}

CARDS_DLL::~CARDS_DLL()
{
        if (m_hLib)
                FreeLibrary(m_hLib);
}

CARDS_DLL _cards;

CSize Card::m_size(0, 0);

BOOL Card::Initialize()
{
        if (_cards.m_hLib)
                return (*_cards.pfnInit)((int *) &m_size.cx, (int *) &m_size.cy);
        else
                return FALSE;
}
```

5.5
SMOOTHLY DRAG BITMAPS WITH THE MOUSE

```cpp
void Card::Release()
{
    if (_cards.m_hLib)
        (*_cards.pfnTerm)();
}

Card::Card()
{
    m_bFaceUp = TRUE;
    m_type = 0;
    m_ptAt.x = m_ptAt.y = 0;
    m_bDrag = FALSE;
    m_back = 62;
}

void Card::Draw(CDC* pDC)
{
    if (m_bFaceUp)
        (*_cards.pfnDraw)(pDC->GetSafeHdc(), m_ptAt.x, m_ptAt.y,
            m_type, 0, RGB(255,255,255));
    else
        (*_cards.pfnDraw)(pDC->GetSafeHdc(), m_ptAt.x, m_ptAt.y,
            m_back, 1, RGB(255,255,255));
}

void Card::Erase(CDC* pDC)
{
    (*_cards.pfnDraw)(pDC->GetSafeHdc(), m_ptAt.x, m_ptAt.y,
        0, 4, -1);
}

void Card::ButtonDownAt(const CPoint& pt)
{
    m_bDrag = TRUE;
    m_ptOffset = (CPoint) (pt - m_ptAt);
}

void Card::SetPos(const CPoint& ptNew)
{
    if (m_bDrag)
        m_ptAt = (CPoint) (ptNew - m_ptOffset);
    else
        m_ptAt = ptNew;
}

void Card::Serialize(CArchive& ar)
{
    if (ar.IsStoring())
    {
        ar << (WORD) m_bFaceUp;
        ar << m_ptAt;
        ar << m_type;
        ar << m_back;
    } else {
```

continued on next page

continued from previous page

```
            WORD wFaceUp;
            ar >> wFaceUp;
            m_bFaceUp = (BOOL) wFaceUp;
            ar >> m_ptAt;
            ar >> m_type;
            ar >> m_back;
      }
}
```

5. **Add member variables to CPokerDoc.** The member variable *m_list* is used to hold the current list of *Card* objects displayed by the views. Add these lines to the public section of PokerDoc.h:

```
// Attributes
public:
        CardList* GetCardList() { return &m_list; }
        CardList m_list;
```

Also, add this line to the top of PokerDoc.h:

```
#include "Card.h"
```

6. **Modify the CPokerDoc.cpp file.** Change the *CPokerDoc* constructor and destructor to look like the following:

```
CPokerDoc::CPokerDoc()
{
        SetModifiedFlag(FALSE);
}

CPokerDoc::~CPokerDoc()
{
        Card *pCard;
        POSITION pos = m_list.GetHeadPosition();
        while (pos != NULL)
        {
                pCard = m_list.GetNextCard(pos);
                delete pCard;
        }
        m_list.RemoveAll();
}

void CPokerDoc::Serialize(CArchive& ar)
{
        m_list.Serialize(ar);
}
```

7. **Add message handlers to CPokerView.** Using ClassWizard, add the following mouse handlers to *CPokerView*:

Object ID	Message	Function
CPokerView	WM_LBUTTONDOWN	OnLButtonDown
CPokerView	WM_LBUTTONUP	OnLButtonUp

5.5
SMOOTHLY DRAG BITMAPS WITH THE MOUSE

Object ID	Message	Function
CPokerView	WM_MOUSEMOVE	OnMouseMove
CPokerView	WM_RBUTTONDOWN	OnRButtonDown
ID_POPUP_CHANGEBACK	BN_CLICKED	OnChangeBack
ID_POPUP_DELETECARD	BN_CLICKED	OnDeleteCard
ID_POPUP_FLIPCARD	BN_CLICKED	OnFlipCard

8. Modify PokerView.h. Change the interface to *CPokerView* as follows:

```
class Card;
class CPokerView : public CView
{
protected: // create from serialization only
        CPokerView();
        DECLARE_DYNCREATE(CPokerView)

// Attributes
public:
CPokerDoc* GetDocument();

// Operations
public:

// Implementation
public:
        virtual ~CPokerView();
        virtual void OnDraw(CDC* pDC);  // overridden to draw this view
#ifdef _DEBUG
        virtual void AssertValid() const;
        virtual void Dump(CDumpContext& dc) const;
#endif

// Generated message map functions
protected:
        int m_nType;      // current card rank/suit
        Card* m_pCard;    // pointer to card being dragged

        //{{AFX_MSG(CPokerView)
        afx_msg void OnLButtonDown(UINT nFlags, CPoint point);
        afx_msg void OnMouseMove(UINT nFlags, CPoint point);
        afx_msg void OnLButtonUp(UINT nFlags, CPoint point);
        afx_msg void OnRButtonDown(UINT nFlags, CPoint point);
        afx_msg void OnChangeBack();
        afx_msg void OnDeleteCard();
        afx_msg void OnFlipCard();
        //}}AFX_MSG
        DECLARE_MESSAGE_MAP()

        Card* CardUnderPoint(const CPoint& pt);
};
```

CHAPTER 5
BITMAPS AND ICONS

9. Edit PokerView.cpp. Add the following code to PokerView.cpp. The mouse message handlers and drawing code will be explained in the How It Works section.

```
#include "stdafx.h"
#include "Poker.h"
#include "PokerDoc.h"
#include "PokerView.h"
#include "Card.h"
#include "BackDlg.h"


/////////////////////////////////////////////////////////////////////////////
// CPokerView

IMPLEMENT_DYNCREATE(CPokerView, CView)

BEGIN_MESSAGE_MAP(CPokerView, CView)
        //{{AFX_MSG_MAP(CPokerView)
        ON_WM_LBUTTONDOWN()
        ON_WM_MOUSEMOVE()
        ON_WM_LBUTTONUP()
        ON_WM_RBUTTONDOWN()
        ON_COMMAND(ID_POPUP_CHANGEBACK, OnChangeBack)
        ON_COMMAND(ID_POPUP_DELETECARD, OnDeleteCard)
        ON_COMMAND(ID_POPUP_FLIPCARD, OnFlipCard)
        //}}AFX_MSG_MAP
END_MESSAGE_MAP()

/////////////////////////////////////////////////////////////////////////////
// CPokerView construction/destruction

CPokerView::CPokerView()
{
        m_nType = 0;
        m_pCard = NULL;
}


CPokerView::~CPokerView()
{
}


/////////////////////////////////////////////////////////////////////////////
// CPokerView drawing

void CPokerView::OnDraw(CDC* pDC)
{
        CRect rcClip;
        CRgn rgnClipBox;
        Card* pCard;
        CPokerDoc* pDoc = GetDocument();
        CardList* pList = pDoc->GetCardList();

        // Get the current clipping region from the device context
```

5.5
SMOOTHLY DRAG BITMAPS WITH THE MOUSE

```
        pDC->GetClipBox(rcClip);
        rgnClipBox.CreateRectRgnIndirect(rcClip);
#ifdef _WIN32
        GetClipRgn(pDC->GetSafeHdc(), (HRGN) rgnClipBox.GetSafeHandle());
#endif

        // Walk the card list from the bottom of the pile to the top.
        // Redraw the cards that intersect with the invalid region.

        POSITION pos = pList->GetHeadPosition();
        while (pos != NULL)
        {
                pCard = (Card *) pList->GetNext(pos);
                CRect rcCard(pCard->GetRect());

                if (rgnClipBox.RectInRegion(rcCard))
                {
                        CRgn rgnCard;

                        pDC->SelectClipRgn(&rgnClipBox);
                        pCard->Draw(pDC);

                        // Now remove the area just painted by the card from
                        // what's left of the invalid region.

                        rgnCard.CreateRectRgnIndirect(pCard->GetRect());
                        if (rgnClipBox.CombineRgn(&rgnClipBox, &rgnCard, RGN_DIFF)
                            == NULLREGION)
                        {
                                // The region is empty, so we're done.
                                return;
                        }
                }
        }
}

/////////////////////////////////////////////////////////////////////
// CPokerView message handlers

void CPokerView::OnLButtonDown(UINT nFlags, CPoint point)
{
        CardList* pList = GetDocument()->GetCardList();

        if ((m_pCard = CardUnderPoint(point)) != NULL)
        {
                // Start moving this card

                SetCapture();
                m_pCard->ButtonDownAt(point);

                // Move card to top of list
                POSITION pos = pList->Find(m_pCard);
                pList->RemoveAt(pos);
                pList->AddHeadCard(m_pCard);
```

continued on next page

continued from previous page

```
                InvalidateRect(m_pCard->GetRect());
        } else {
                // Drop the next card in the series

                Card *pCard = new Card();
                pCard->SetType(m_nType++ % 52);
                pCard->SetPos(point);
                pList->AddHeadCard(pCard);
                InvalidateRect(pCard->GetRect());

                GetDocument()->SetModifiedFlag();
                GetDocument()->UpdateAllViews(this);
        }
        UpdateWindow();
}

void CPokerView::OnMouseMove(UINT nFlags, CPoint point)
{
        if (this == GetCapture())
        {
                ASSERT(m_pCard != NULL);
                CClientDC dc(this);

                // Move the card to the new point and draw it
                CRect rcBefore(m_pCard->GetRect());
                m_pCard->SetPos(point);
                m_pCard->Draw(&dc);
                CRect rcAfter(m_pCard->GetRect());

                // Redraw the exposed region (before - after)
                CRgn rgnBefore, rgnAfter, rgnResult;
                VERIFY(rgnBefore.CreateRectRgnIndirect(rcBefore));
                VERIFY(rgnAfter.CreateRectRgnIndirect(rcAfter));
                rgnResult.CreateRectRgnIndirect(rcAfter);
                rgnResult.CombineRgn(&rgnBefore, &rgnAfter, RGN_DIFF);

                InvalidateRgn(&rgnResult);
                UpdateWindow();
        }
}

void CPokerView::OnLButtonUp(UINT nFlags, CPoint point)
{
        if (this == GetCapture())
        {
                m_pCard = NULL;
                ReleaseCapture();
                GetDocument()->UpdateAllViews(this);
        }
}

void CPokerView::OnRButtonDown(UINT nFlags, CPoint point)
{
        // Display a context menu if a card was clicked
        if ((m_pCard = CardUnderPoint(point)) != NULL)
        {
```

5.5
SMOOTHLY DRAG BITMAPS WITH THE MOUSE

```
        CMenu mainMenu;
        VERIFY(mainMenu.LoadMenu(IDR_CARD_POPUP));
        CMenu* pMenu = mainMenu.GetSubMenu(0);
        ASSERT(pMenu);

        ClientToScreen(&point);
        pMenu->TrackPopupMenu(TPM_LEFTALIGN | TPM_RIGHTBUTTON,
            point.x, point.y, this);
        GetDocument()->UpdateAllViews(this);
    }
}

void CPokerView::OnChangeBack()
{
    CBackDlg dlg;

    dlg.m_back = m_pCard->GetBack();
    if (dlg.DoModal() == IDOK)
    {
        m_pCard->SetFaceUp(FALSE);
        m_pCard->SetBack(dlg.m_back);
        InvalidateRect(m_pCard->GetRect());
    }
}

void CPokerView::OnDeleteCard()
{
    ASSERT(m_pCard);

    // Delete the current card and invalidate the space it was occupying
    CardList* pList = GetDocument()->GetCardList();
    POSITION pos = pList->Find(m_pCard);
    ASSERT(pos != NULL);
    pList->RemoveAt(pos);
    InvalidateRect(m_pCard->GetRect());
    delete m_pCard;
    m_pCard = NULL;

    // If there are no more cards, mark the document clean
    // because there's nothing to save
    if (pList->IsEmpty())
        GetDocument()->SetModifiedFlag(FALSE);
}

void CPokerView::OnFlipCard()
{
    ASSERT(m_pCard);
    m_pCard->SetFaceUp(!m_pCard->IsFaceUp());
    InvalidateRect(m_pCard->GetRect());
}

Card* CPokerView::CardUnderPoint(const CPoint& pt)
{
```

continued on next page

continued from previous page

```
Card* pCard;
CardList* pList = GetDocument()->GetCardList();

POSITION pos = pList->GetHeadPosition();
while (pos != NULL)
{
    pCard = pList->GetNextCard(pos);
    if (pCard->PtInCard(pt))
        return pCard;
}
return (Card*) NULL;
}
```

10. **Create a pop-up menu.** Use the menu editor to add a new menu called IDR_CARD_POPUP. The menu captions and IDs are shown below:

Menu Item	ID
&Flip Card	ID_POPUP_FLIPCARD
&Delete Card	ID_POPUP_DELETECARD
&Change Back...	ID_POPUP_CHANGEBACK

When finished, the pop-up menu should look something like the one shown in Figure 5-16.

11. **Add a new dialog to change the card design.** Create a new dialog called IDD_BACK in the resource editor that has three controls: an OK button, a Cancel button, and a scroll bar. The table below summarizes the controls:

Control	ID	Attributes
OK button	IDOK	"OK"
Cancel button	IDCANCEL	"Cancel"
Slider	IDC_SLIDER	
Scroll bar	IDC_SCROLLBAR	no alignment

Figure 5-17 shows the finished dialog box.

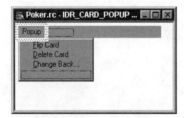

Figure 5-16 Pop-up menu for Cards

5.5
SMOOTHLY DRAG BITMAPS WITH THE MOUSE

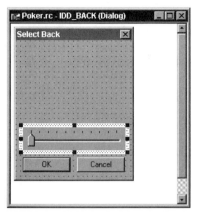

Figure 5-17 Dialog to select the card design

12. **Create a dialog class called CBackDlg.** Use ClassWizard to generate a new dialog based on IDD_BACK using the following information:

Class name:	CBackDlg
Base class:	CDialog
File:	BackDlg.cpp
Dialog:	IDD_BACK

13. **Use ClassWizard to add message handlers.** Add message-handling functions for these objects:

Object ID	Function	Message
CBackDlg	OnHScroll	WM_HSCROLL
CBackDlg	OnInitDialog	WM_INITDIALOG
CBackDlg	OnPaint	WM_PAINT

14. **Edit BackDlg.h.** Add two member variables to *CBackDlg*'s declaration, one representing the current back design and the other a *Card* instance to draw the design in the dialog.

```
#include "card.h"
class CBackDlg : public CDialog
{
// Construction
public:
        CBackDlg(CWnd* pParent = NULL);   // standard constructor
        int m_back;
        Card m_card;
        ...
};
```

CHAPTER 5
BITMAPS AND ICONS

15. Edit BackDlg.cpp. This dialog paints the *m_card* member in response to WM_PAINT messages in *OnPaint*. The card back design is picked using the scroll bar to cycle through the list of choices. *OnHScroll* handles the scroll bar and notifies the *m_card* member when a new design is picked. When the dialog is initialized, the scroll bar is set to the range of card numbers representing the valid backs (53 through 65).

Modify the existing code in BackDlg.cpp to look like the following body of code:

```
void CBackDlg::OnHScroll(UINT nSBCode, UINT nPos, CScrollBar* pScrollBar)
{
    // In this case, pBar is really a CSliderCtrl (see the docs)
    CSliderCtrl* pSlider = (CSliderCtrl*) pBar;

    if (pSlider == NULL)
        return;

    int  currentPos = pSlider->GetPos();
    int  minPos, maxPos;
    pSlider->GetRange (minPos, maxPos);

    switch (nSBCode)
    {
    case TB_BOTTOM:
        m_back = minPos; break;

    case TB_TOP:
        m_back = maxPos; break;

    case TB_PAGEDOWN:
    case TB_LINEDOWN:
        if (currentPos > minPos)
            m_back = currentPos - 1;
        break;

    case TB_PAGEUP:
    case TB_LINEUP:
        if (currentPos < maxPos)
            m_back = currentPos + 1;
        break;

    case TB_THUMBPOSITION:
    case TB_THUMBTRACK:
        m_back = currentPos;

    default:
        m_back = currentPos;
        break;
    }
    pSlider->SetPos (m_back);

    if (m_card.GetBack() != (WORD) m_back)
    {
```

5.5
SMOOTHLY DRAG BITMAPS WITH THE MOUSE

```
            m_card.SetBack(m_back);
            InvalidateRect(m_card.GetRect());
        }
}

BOOL CBackDlg::OnInitDialog()
{
        CDialog::OnInitDialog();

        m_card.SetFaceUp(FALSE);
        m_card.SetPos(CPoint(10, 10));
        m_card.SetBack(m_back);

        CSliderCtrl* pSlider = (CSliderCtrl *) GetDlgItem(IDC_SLIDER);
        pSlider->SetRange(53, 65);
        pSlider->SetPos(m_back);

        return TRUE;
}

void CBackDlg::OnPaint()
{
        CPaintDC dc(this); // device context for painting
        m_card.Draw(&dc);
}
```

16. Edit **CPokerApp::InitInstance**. Initialize the CARD_DLL class in this method as shown:

```
BOOL CPokerApp::InitInstance()
{
        // Standard initialization
        if (!Card::Initialize())
        {
            AfxMessageBox("Couldn't find CARDS.DLL");
            return FALSE;
        }
...
```

17. Use the WizardBar to add **CPokerApp::ExitInstance**. Add the following code:

```
int CPokerApp::ExitInstance()
{
        Card::Release();
        return CWinApp::ExitInstance();
}
```

InitInstance calls the static method *Card::Initialize* that sets up the connection to the CARDS.DLL file. The corresponding *Card::Release* call in *ExitInstance* unloads the DLL.

18. **Compile and run the sample application.** Try adding a new view using the New Window item under the Window menu and dragging some cards around. As you do, watch the changes reflected in the other view.

How It Works

In addition to the standard document and view classes you've come to know and love, we've written a few new classes that should be explained before we get into the meat of the How-To.

CARDS_DLL

Let's start at the lowest level: the interface to the DLL. For variety, we chose to dynamically link to CARDS.DLL. This way, if the card library is not found, we can show a more informative dialog box and exit gracefully.

CARDS_DLL creates three function pointers to the APIs in the CARDS.DLL library. The CARDS_DLL constructor first loads the library with *LoadLibrary,* then gets the addresses of the APIs and stores them in its function pointer members. If the library was loaded successfully, the destructor takes care of unloading the library with a call to *FreeLibrary.*

By encapsulating the functionality of a DLL in a class, you don't have to worry about freeing the library when you've finished with the class. The destructor takes care of all the housekeeping. Of course, you should still make sure the library was loaded successfully by checking the value of *m_hLib.* That's exactly what we do in *Card::Initialize,* which brings us to our next class.

The Card Class

The *Card* object keeps track of everything related to a card visible in the view:

- X and Y position (a *CPoint*) of the card
- Face-up or face-down state
- Card rank/suit ID (a number from 1 to 52)
- Card back design ID (a number from 53 to 65)
- Card width and height

Since every card has the same width and height, we make this information the static member variable *m_size.* Static member variables are shared among all instances of the class. Our values are set when the library is initialized with the *cdtInit* method.

Two other static member methods, *Initialize* and *Release,* take care of calling the two CARDS.DLL methods *cdtInit* and *cdtTerm.* These methods are called only once during *InitInstance* and *ExitInstance.* In case the DLL can't be located, we check the return value of *Initialize* and exit gracefully. By the time *Initialize* is called though, the library has already been loaded (or not found); *Initialize* simply checks to see whether or not *CARD_DLL:: m_hLib* is NULL.

CPokerDoc and CardList

Our *CDocument* derived class, *CPokerDoc,* simply holds a type-safe list of *Card* objects through the *m_list* data member. When the MFC frameworks asks our document to save itself, *CPokerDoc* archives the *CObList*-derived *CardList*. *CardList,* in turn, serializes each *Card* object it holds.

Any cards that haven't been removed through the pop-up menu are deleted in the *CDocument* destructor. Since cards are dynamically allocated by each *CView,* this is the best place to free them. Also, by keeping the card list in *CDocument* instead of *CView,* it's easy to support multiple views of the same card list.

One more thing about the cards in the list: They're stored in Z-order. In other words, the first card in the list is the topmost card on the screen. Whenever a card is selected for dragging, it is first moved to the head of the list. That way, *OnDraw* paints it last so it appears on top of all the other cards.

CPokerView

We've saved the best class for last. To understand how our optimized drawing occurs, think of the class in two parts: the code that handles the mouse down events for dragging and displaying the pop-up menu, and the code that repaints the cards.

Two possible things can happen when our view detects a mouse click. If the user clicks on empty space, we create a new card at the current mouse position. We then add the new card to the head of *CardList* and invalidate the rectangle that the new card now occupies. Since we've changed the document, *CDocument::SetModifiedFlag* is called followed by *UpdateAllViews* so other views (if there are any) will repaint the new card.

If the user clicks on an existing card, we enter the drag state. First we tell the card where the mouse down occurred so future *Card::SetPos* calls will be taken relative to that point. Then we move the card to the top of *CardList* and Invalidate ourselves. To ensure that the current view has the quickest response time, we don't call *UpdateAllViews* for drag operations until the drag has completed.

OnMouseMove

Here's where the code starts to get interesting. The card is immediately redrawn in the new location through *Card::Draw* using the point passed to *OnMouseMove*. Two rectangles are initialized with the old and new card positions. The difference between the old and new rectangles determines the new update region. Since taking the difference of two rectangles usually produces a region, we must convert them to regions using *CRgn::CreateRectRgnIndirect*. *CombineRgn* calculates the difference between the two regions that we pass to *InvalidateRgn*.

OnDraw

OnDraw first gets the clipping region from the device context. If you are in the habit of getting the clipping rectangle using *GetClipRect*, you may think there's a corresponding

GetClipRgn function. Well, this function exists only under Win32 and there is no corresponding MFC wrapper for it, hence the #ifdef_WIN32 surrounding part of the code:

```
// Get the current clipping region from the device context
pDC->GetClipBox(rcClip);
rgnClipBox.CreateRectRgnIndirect(rcClip);
#ifdef _WIN32
GetClipRgn(pDC->GetSafeHdc(), (HRGN) rgnClipBox.GetSafeHandle());
#endif
```

The code will work just fine on Win16 or Win32s without *GetClipRgn*. It's just a little more efficient to use *GetClipRgn* if we can, since the clipping rectangle returned from *GetClipBox* is the smallest rectangle completely encompassing the clipping region. We might be repainting areas that don't really need repainting under Win16 and Win32s.

As we loop through the cards in *CardList,* we only repaint cards whose rectangles intersect the clipping region. If a card intersects the clipping region, the region is selected into the device context and *Card::Draw* is called. Then, the area the card covers is subtracted from the clipping region, and the process continues until there are no more cards or the clipping region is empty.

Icing

Now that you've mastered drawing with regions, you get a break with a simple popup menu and a dialog. When the right-mouse button is clicked over a card, *TrackPopupMenu* gives you a choice of flipping the card, deleting the card, or changing the card backing.

CBackDlg uses a slider to let you browse the available card back designs. Since we already have a class to display the cards, it's pretty easy to just paint the card in the dialog in response to slider events. By the way, sliders communicate with the parent just like scroll bars, through the WM_HSCROLL message. One warning though: MFC's *OnHScroll* sets up a pointer to a *CScrollBar* instead of a *CSliderCtrl*. Even though the pointer is referring to a slider control, we have to cast it back to a *CSliderCtrl*.

Comments

There's another reason why we chose to dynamically link to CARDS.DLL: We couldn't figure out how to build an import library for the 32-bit CARDS.DLL under Windows NT.

There was a nice program called IMPLIB.EXE that came with the Windows SDK. It let you make an import library directly from a DLL, even if you didn't have the source code to the DLL. You could then just include the library on the linker command line and make calls to it as you would any other library. There doesn't seem to be an equivalent method under Windows NT. So you get to learn how to dynamically load and unload a DLL.

If you want to apply some of these techniques to your application but you really have no interest in card games, concentrate on the code dealing with the region

5.5
SMOOTHLY DRAG BITMAPS WITH THE MOUSE

objects—namely, *OnDraw, OnMouseMove,* and the other methods in *CPokerView*. Instead of using CARDS.DLL, you might have your own library that returns an arbitrary shape. Some of the techniques presented here will still work when you want to move objects around on the screen.

CHAPTER 6
DIALOGS

DIALOGS

How do I...

6.1 Display help for dialog controls on the status bar?

6.2 Open multiple files with the FileOpen common dialog?

6.3 Customize the common file dialog?

6.4 Expand and contract dialog boxes?

6.5 Display a dialog as either modal or modeless?

6.6 Write customized DDX/DDV routines?

This chapter dives into dialogs, uncovering tricks and techniques to extend the usefulness of the MFC *CDialog* class and the related common file dialog. You'll learn how to turn a normal dialog into a modeless one, expand a dialog into a larger one when a button is pressed, and write your own customized DDX/DDV routines. Two How-To's modify the *CFileDialog* to make a directory picker dialog and a common file dialog that display the current file's size. The final How-To takes apart the dialog resource format to dynamically switch the contents of a dialog on demand.

6.1 Display Help for Dialog Controls on the Status Bar

Normally you can only display help for toolbar buttons and menu items. Here, you'll learn how to do the same for dialog boxes.

Additional Topics: OnSetCursor, GetDescendantWindow, WM_SETMESSAGESTRING

6.2 Open Multiple Files with the FileOpen Common Dialog

The standard file selection dialog class, *CFileDialog*, provides a mechanism for allowing the selection of multiple files. However, no straightforward way exists for retrieving the names of the multiple selected files. This example demonstrates a component that creates a class called *CMultiFileDlg* which you can use in your applications to let users open more than one document at a time.

Additional Topics: OnFileOpen, OFN_ALLOWMULTISELECT flag

6.3 Customize the Common File Dialog

Change the look of the File Open common dialog to display the size in bytes of the selected file.

Additional Topics: OnLBSelChangeNotify, file information through _stat

6.4 Expand and Contract Dialog Boxes

Add a "More>>" button that expands a smaller dialog into a larger one containing more, but less frequently used, controls.

Additional Topics: EnableWindow, GetWindow, mnemonic keys

6.5 Display a Dialog as Either Modal or Modeless

Learn how to turn regular dialogs into modeless ones and remove them when a timer expires.

Additional Topics: PostNcDestroy, DoModal versus Create

6.6 Write Customized DDX/DDV Routines

MFC provides a standard mechanism for validation, reading, and writing of data from dialogs. Learn how to exploit and customize these features by writing your own DDX/DDV routines.

Additional Topics: ClassWizard information file, CDataExchange

COMPLEXITY
INTERMEDIATE

6.1 How do I... Display help for dialog controls on the status bar?

Problem

I'd like to use the status bar to display extra help for dialog controls. For instance, if the user passes the mouse over a button, extra help text for that button should appear

6.1
DISPLAY HELP FOR DIALOG CONTROLS ON THE STATUS BAR

in the status bar. Since the status bar is usually visible when a dialog is running, how can I use a pane to display extra help for my controls?

Technique

Every time the mouse passes over a window, the WM_SETCURSOR message is sent to the window's owner. If we catch the message through *OnSetCursor*, we can easily determine if the mouse is over a dialog control. Then, assuming the control has a string resource with the same ID, we pass the ID to a special function that sets the text in the first status bar pane.

To illustrate this technique, we're going to modify the About dialog that App Studio creates for MFC applications. We will add two buttons and an edit control along with string resources that share the same ID. Figure 6-1 shows the help text when the mouse passes over a dialog control.

Steps

1. Create a new project called DialogHelp using the MFC AppWizard (exe). Select the Single-Document type and press the Finish button.

    Classes to be created:
    Application: CDialogHelpApp in DialogHelp.h and DialogHelp.cpp
    Frame: CMainFrame in MainFrm.h and MainFrm.cpp
    Document: CDialogHelpDoc in DialogHelpDoc.h and DialogHelpDoc.cpp
    View: CDialogHelpView in DialogHelpView.h and DialogHelpView.cpp

    Features:
    + Initial toolbar in main frame
    + Initial status bar in main frame
    + 3D Controls
    + Uses shared DLL implementation (MFC40.DLL)

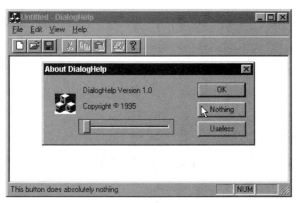

Figure 6-1 Help text in the status bar

CHAPTER 6
DIALOGS

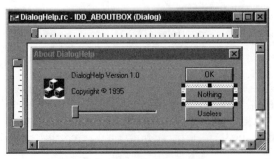

Figure 6-2 Layout for help dialog

2. **Add controls to the IDD_ABOUTBOX dialog.** Use App Studio to add two buttons and a slider to the About dialog using the following table:

Control	ID	Attributes
Button	IDC_NOTHING	"Nothing"
Button	IDC_EMPTY	"Empty"
Slider	IDC_SLIDER1	Default

Your dialog should look something like the dialog shown in Figure 6-2.

3. **Add string resources.** Use App Studio to add help text for the new controls. Give the string resources the same names as the controls. Refer to Figure 6-3 for the string text.

4. **Use the WizardBar to handle WM_SETCURSOR for CAboutDlg.** Add the following code to the body created by WizardBar:

```
BOOL CAboutDlg::OnSetCursor(CWnd* pWnd, UINT nHitTest, UINT message)
{
    // If the cursor is not over a child window control, revert
    // to the default status bar text

    if (pWnd == this)
        SetPaneText();
    else
        SetPaneText(pWnd->GetDlgCtrlID());

    return CDialog::OnSetCursor(pWnd, nHitTest, message);
}
```

ID	Value	Caption
IDR_MAINFRAME	128	DialogHelp\n\nDialog\n\n\nDialogHelp.Document\nDialog Document
IDC_SLIDER1	1000	This slider isn't attached to any code
IDC_NOTHING	1001	This button does absolutely nothing
IDS_USELESS	1002	This button doesn't do anything either

Figure 6-3 String resources for the dialog controls

6.1
DISPLAY HELP FOR DIALOG CONTROLS ON THE STATUS BAR

5. Use the WizardBar to handle WM_DESTROY for CAboutDlg. The dialog resets the status bar during the handling of the WM_DESTROY message by calling *SetPaneText* with no arguments:

```
void CAboutDlg::OnDestroy()
{
    SetPaneText();
    CDialog::OnDestroy();
}
```

6. Add the SetPaneText helper function. Use the ClassView Add Function dialog to add the following method.

```
protected:
    void SetPaneText(UINT nID = 0);
```

Edit the body as follows. You'll have to edit the first line to remove the "= 0" part since the Add Function dialog doesn't handle default values correctly.

```
void CAboutDlg::SetPaneText(UINT nID)
{
    if (nID == 0)
        nID = AFX_IDS_IDLEMESSAGE;

    CWnd* pWnd = AfxGetMainWnd()->GetDescendantWindow(AFX_IDW_STATUS_BAR);
    if (pWnd)
    {
        AfxGetMainWnd()->SendMessage(WM_SETMESSAGESTRING, nID);
        pWnd->SendMessage(WM_IDLEUPDATECMDUI);
        pWnd->UpdateWindow();
    }
}
```

7. Edit DialogHelp.cpp. Add the following two lines to the include directives at the top of DialogHelp.cpp:

```
#include "stdafx.h"
#include "DialogHelp.h"

#include "MainFrm.h"
#include "DialogHelpDoc.h"
#include "DialogHelpView.h"

#include <afxpriv.h>    // for WM_SETMESSAGESTRING and WM_IDLEUPDATECMDUI
#include <afxres.h>     // for AFX_IDW_STATUS_BAR
```

8. Recompile and run the application. Bring up the About box and notice how the status bar changes as you pass the mouse over the dialog controls. The status bar should revert to the default text of "Ready" when you close the dialog.

How It Works

For all this to work, we need to track the mouse and detect when it passes over a control. At first glance, it might seem that the WM_MOUSEMOVE message would be able to provide us with the necessary information. However, since WM_MOUSEMOVE messages go to the actual window that contains the mouse pointer, we would need an *OnMouseMove* message handler for each control in the dialog that requires help text. Needless to say, that would require a lot of code, and it wouldn't be a general solution that handles every type of control.

A much better way is to handle the WM_SETCURSOR message. This message is normally used to set a custom cursor as the cursor passes over child windows. The message serves our purpose because it tracks the movement of the cursor anywhere within a window and, more importantly, it reports which child window the mouse is directly over.

The first parameter to *OnSetCursor* is a *CWnd* pointer that refers to the window that has the mouse in its boundaries. In our case, this will be either a pointer to the dialog window itself or a child window control inside the dialog.

If the *CWnd* pointer is not equal to *this,* we know the cursor is over a child window control. Here, we simply get the dialog control ID through *GetDlgCtrlID* and pass that ID to our helper function *SetPaneText*. A word of warning: If you have controls that have the same ID but exist in different dialogs, they will display the same help text. So if you want the two controls to have different help text, they will need to have different resource IDs.

SetPaneText takes advantage of (count 'em) three undocumented or slightly documented #defines. First, if the ID passed in to *SetPaneText* is zero, we know we want to reset the status bar to its default text. This is by AppWizard and is given the ID of AFX_IDS_IDLEMESSAGE. Then, using a little-known *CWnd* method called *GetDescendantWindow,* we have the main window return us a pointer to the status bar. Since App Studio wrote the code in MainFrm.cpp to create a status bar with the ID of AFX_IDW_STATUS_BAR, we're going to get a pointer to that very status bar.

After we obtain a pointer to the status bar window, we send a message to the main window instructing it to change the status bar text. This message, WM_SETMESSAGESTRING, takes either a string resource ID or a pointer to a string. Either way, it sets the text for the status bar. It's not updated immediately though. Instead, we have to force an update by sending the status bar the WM_IDLEUPDATECMDUI message and calling *UpdateWindow* to repaint the status bar right away.

Finally, our implementation of *OnAppAbout* resets the contents of the status bar after the dialog has been closed. This assures that no residual help text remains after the dialog is dismissed.

6.2 How do I... Open multiple files with the FileOpen common dialog?

COMPLEXITY: INTERMEDIATE

Problem

I'd like to modify the common file dialog box to let me open more than one document at once. The framework should pass all these documents to my application so they can be opened at the same time. How do I do this?

Technique

MFC encapsulates the common file dialog in a class called *CFileDialog*. Although this class provides facilities for selecting multiple files, as shown in Figure 6-4, the mechanism for retrieving the names of the selected files is not particularly straightforward. Also, *CFileDialog*'s path buffer is not big enough to hold a lot of files; the filenames are stored in a buffer just _MAX_PATH bytes long (260 bytes in Windows 95).

In this How-To, we'll see how to use the *CMultiFileDialog* class which comes from the Multi File Open component that ships with this book. *CMultiFileDialog* inherits all of its functionality from its base class *CFileDialog*, but it allocates a much larger buffer to hold multiple filenames.

In the first edition of *Visual C++ How-To*, I added a few methods to *CMultiFileDialog* that made it easier to loop through the selected files. Now, there are two new methods in *CFileDialog* that do the job for us. We'll see how to use them and how to work around an MFC bug that occurs when files from the root are selected.

To integrate *CMultiFileDialog* into the MFC framework, we need to write our own code to handle the File Open menu option. *CWinApp::OnFileOpen* normally handles the command, but that code uses *CFileDialog*. Our version uses *CMultiFileDialog* instead, then calls *CWinApp::OpenDocumentFile* for every selected file.

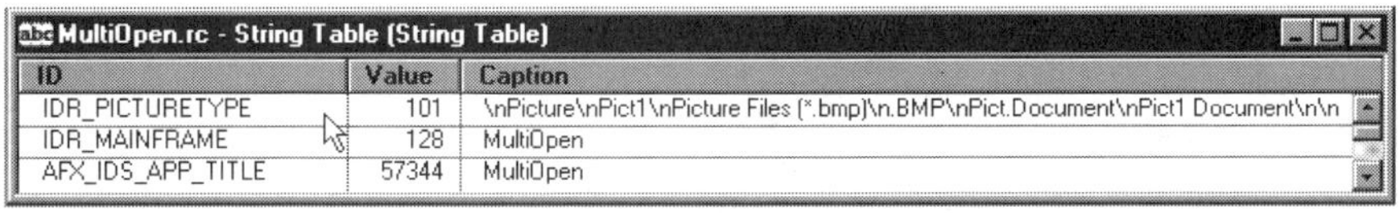

ID	Value	Caption
IDR_PICTURETYPE	101	\nPicture\nPict1\nPicture Files (*.bmp)\n.BMP\nPict.Document\nPict1 Document\n\n
IDR_MAINFRAME	128	MultiOpen
AFX_IDS_APP_TITLE	57344	MultiOpen

Figure 6-4 CFileDialog modified to support multiple selection

CHAPTER 6
DIALOGS

Figure 6-5 Inserting the Multi File Dialog component

Figure 6-6 Use the WizardBar to add menu handlers

Steps

1. **Create a new project called MultiOpen using the Picture AppWizard.** You can't set any options with this custom AppWizard; it simply creates an MDI application capable of viewing bitmaps.

2. **Insert the Multi File Open Dialog component.** Use the Component Gallery to insert the Multi File Dialog component. Like all the other components in this book, you should find it under the Visual C++ How-To tab. There are no options for this component; it always adds MultiFileDlg.cpp and MultiFileDlg.h to your application (see Figure 6-5). Close the Component Gallery when you're ready to continue.

3. **Use the WizardBar to add a handler for ID_FILE_OPEN in CMultiOpenApp.** *CWinApp* normally handles this command for us, but it will only open one document. Our implementation is similar, but it uses *CMultiFileDialog* and opens each selected file. If you normally use ClassWizard to add handlers for menus, try using the WizardBar as shown in Figure 6-6, then insert this code:

```
void CMultiOpenApp::OnFileOpen()
{
    CMultiFileDialog dlgFile(TRUE);

    CString title, strFilter, strDefault;
    VERIFY(title.LoadString(AFX_IDS_OPENFILE));
```

6.2
OPEN MULTIPLE FILES WITH THE FILEOPEN COMMON DIALOG

```cpp
    // do for all doc template
    POSITION pos = GetFirstDocTemplatePosition();
    BOOL bFirst = TRUE;
    while (pos != NULL)
    {
        CDocTemplate* pTemplate = GetNextDocTemplate(pos);
        AppendFilterSuffix (strFilter, dlgFile.m_ofn, pTemplate,
                bFirst ? &strDefault : NULL);
        bFirst = FALSE;
    }

    // append the "*.*" all files filter
    CString allFilter;
    VERIFY(allFilter.LoadString(AFX_IDS_ALLFILTER));
    strFilter += allFilter;
    strFilter += (TCHAR)'\0';    // next string please
    strFilter += _T("*.*");
    strFilter += (TCHAR)'\0';    // last string
    dlgFile.m_ofn.nMaxCustFilter++;

    dlgFile.m_ofn.lpstrFilter = strFilter;
    dlgFile.m_ofn.lpstrTitle = title;
    dlgFile.m_ofn.hwndOwner = AfxGetMainWnd()->GetSafeHwnd();

    if (dlgFile.DoModal() == IDOK)
    {
        POSITION pos = dlgFile.GetStartPosition();
        while (pos != NULL)
            OpenDocumentFile(dlgFile.GetNextPathName(pos));
    }
}
```

4. **Remove the extra ID_FILE_OPEN message map.** Since *CWinApp* normally handles the ID_FILE_OPEN menu, you need to remove the message map that AppWizard generated. Locate the BEGIN_MESSAGE_MAP section near the top of MultiOpen.cpp. Remove the following line from the file:

```cpp
ON_COMMAND(ID_FILE_OPEN, CWinApp::OnFileOpen)
```

Don't remove the similar line between the AFX_MSG_MAP comments; we just added that line in step 5.

5. **Add the AppendFilterSuffix helper function.** Add the following line of code to the top of TEST.CPP:

```cpp
static void AppendFilterSuffix(CString& filter, OPENFILENAME& ofn,
    CDocTemplate* pTemplate, CString* pstrDefaultExt);
```

Now add the body of the *AppendFilterSuffix* method to the bottom of the file. This method came straight from the MFC source code. Since it's not a public method, we can't use it directly and must write our own.

```cpp
// taken directly from mfc\src\docmgr.cpp
static void AppendFilterSuffix(CString& filter, OPENFILENAME& ofn,
    CDocTemplate* pTemplate, CString* pstrDefaultExt)
```

continued on next page

continued from previous page

```
{
    ASSERT_VALID(pTemplate);
    ASSERT_KINDOF(CDocTemplate, pTemplate);

    CString strFilterExt, strFilterName;
    if (pTemplate->GetDocString(strFilterExt, CDocTemplate::filterExt) &&
        !strFilterExt.IsEmpty() &&
        pTemplate->GetDocString(strFilterName, CDocTemplate::filterName) &&
        !strFilterName.IsEmpty())
    {
        // a file based document template - add to filter list
        ASSERT(strFilterExt[0] == '.');
        if (pstrDefaultExt != NULL)
        {
            // set the default extension
            *pstrDefaultExt = ((LPCTSTR)strFilterExt) + 1; // skip the '.'
            ofn.lpstrDefExt = (LPTSTR)(LPCTSTR)(*pstrDefaultExt);
            ofn.nFilterIndex = ofn.nMaxCustFilter + 1; // 1 based number
        }

        // add to filter
        filter += strFilterName;
        ASSERT(!filter.IsEmpty());   // must have a file type name
        filter += (TCHAR)'\0';   // next string please
        filter += (TCHAR)'*';
        filter += strFilterExt;
        filter += (TCHAR)'\0';   // next string please
        ofn.nMaxCustFilter++;
    }
}
```

OnFileOpen uses *AppendFilterSuffix* to create the file filter string and the default filter extension used by the common file dialog. The common dialog displays the filter string in the drop-down combo, like "Picture Files (*.bmp)". The default filter extension in this case would be the string "*.bmp". Both of these strings are generated from those funny-looking string resources like the one shown in Figure 6-7.

Figure 6-7 The string resource parsed by AppendFilterSuffix

6.2
OPEN MULTIPLE FILES WITH THE FILEOPEN COMMON DIALOG

6. Compile and test the application. Launch the app and switch to a directory with a bunch of bitmap files (check the Windows directory; it's full of them). Then use File Open to select all of them and press OK. They should all open as separate documents.

How It Works

CMultiFileDialog distinguishes itself from its base class *CFileDialog* by adding to the *m_ofn.flags* variable OFN_ALLOWMULTISELECT. This style allows the user to select more than one document in the common file dialog. Without this flag, you'd wind up with a normal common file dialog that allows only single files to be selected. The rest of the constructor parameters are identical to *CFileDialog*'s. Consult the MFC documentation for a full description of the parameters passed to the *CFileDialog* constructor.

Here's the header file showing the constructor with the new flag (remember it was added to your project by the Multi File Dialog component).

```
class CMultiFileDialog : public CFileDialog
{
        DECLARE_DYNAMIC(CMultiFileDialog)

public:
        int DoModal();
        virtual ~CMultiFileDialog();
        CMultiFileDialog(BOOL bOpenFileDialog,
            LPCTSTR lpszDefExt = NULL,
            LPCTSTR lpszFileName = NULL,
            DWORD dwFlags = OFN_HIDEREADONLY | OFN_OVERWRITEPROMPT
                | OFN_ALLOWMULTISELECT,  // this lets us open multiple files
            LPCTSTR lpszFilter = NULL,
            CWnd* pParentWnd = NULL);

protected:
        //{{AFX_MSG(CMultiFileDialog)
        //}}AFX_MSG
        DECLARE_MESSAGE_MAP()

        TCHAR* m_pszFileName;
};
```

The code for *CMultiFileDialog* is quite simple. The constructor passes all the parameters to its base class constructor, then allocates a 2K buffer to hold the selected files. *DoModal* makes sure you haven't removed the OFN_ALLOWMULTISELECT flag with a handy assertion. Then it sets up the pointer to the buffer and calls *CFileDialog::DoModal* to continue the show.

```
CMultiFileDialog::CMultiFileDialog(BOOL bOpenFileDialog, LPCTSTR lpszDefExt,
    LPCTSTR lpszFileName, DWORD dwFlags, LPCTSTR lpszFilter, CWnd* pParentWnd) :
        CFileDialog(bOpenFileDialog, lpszDefExt, lpszFileName, dwFlags, lpszFilter,
            pParentWnd)
{
```

continued on next page

continued from previous page

```
        m_pszFileName = new TCHAR[MAXMULTIPATH];
        // new automatically throws a memory exception if it fails
        m_pszFileName[0] = '\0';
}

CMultiFileDialog::~CMultiFileDialog()
{
        if (m_pszFileName != NULL)
                delete [] m_pszFileName;
}

int CMultiFileDialog::DoModal()
{
        ASSERT_VALID(this);
        ASSERT(m_ofn.Flags & OFN_ALLOWMULTISELECT);

        m_ofn.lpstrFile = m_pszFileName;
        m_ofn.nMaxFile = MAXMULTIPATH;

        return CFileDialog::DoModal();
}
```

Earlier versions of *CMultiFileDialog* required us to parse *m_pszFileName,* but MFC 4.x introduced two new methods that make that code unnecessary. *GetStartPosition* and *GetNextPathName* are still interesting to examine. They provide an easy to way to pick apart the long string returned by the common dialog that might look something like this:

`C:\WIN95\IMAGES clouds.bmp magritte.bmp kahlo.bmp`

The code for the first edition of this book was written to parse this type of string. Using the C-runtime function *strtok* made it easy to pick apart the directory name and all the filenames. But now filenames can have embedded spaces, so Microsoft changed the delimiter character from a space to a NULL, rendering the *strtok* solution useless. Thankfully, *CFileDialog* has *GetStartPosition* and *GetNextPathName* to pick apart these strings.

OnFileOpen

Armed with a useful, generic class to handle multiple file selection, we hooked it up to *CMultiOpenApp::OnFileOpen*. Normally, AppWizard hooks up ID_FILE_OPEN to the default implementation of *CWinApp::OnFileOpen*. This is fine for most people. It's not for us.

By implementing our own *OnFileOpen,* we have the freedom to use any method to open files. How about *CMultiFileDialog*? Of course, we're responsible for a few other mundane details, like handling the construction of the filter string. That's what the *AppendFilterSuffix* method is for. It constructs a special string in the format required by the common file dialog.

If the user selects a few files and presses OK, we simply loop through the file name array contained within *CMFileDialog* and pass each file name onto *OpenDocumentFile*.

Comments

For more information on customizing the common dialogs, search through Visual C++ Books Online using these keywords: customizing common dialogs.

You should be aware of a bug in MFC. If you take a close look at the *GetNextPathName* method in msdev\mfc\src\dlgfile.cpp, near the bottom of the method, you'll see this line:

```
return strPath + '\\' + strFileName;
```

Now unless they've fixed this in a release after MFC 4.0, the string returned from this method is invalid for files chosen from a root directory. For example, if you selected the files "Baked Beans.bmp" and "Spam.bmp" from the root of the C: drive, the filename returned from the first call to *GetNextPathName* is

```
C:\\Baked Beans.bmp
```

Note the double slash. I'll bet you *OpenDocumentFile* complains. *GetNextPathName* added an extra slash when it didn't need to. Here's the code to fix the bug:

```
if (dlgFile.DoModal() == IDOK)
{
    POSITION pos = dlgFile.GetStartPosition();
    while (pos != NULL)
    {
        CString strPath = dlgFile.GetNextPathName(pos);
        if (strPath.Find(":\\\\") == 1 && strPath.GetLength() > 4)
        {
            // this means we have an invalid path that looks like this:
            // C:\\foo.bmp
            // We need to cut out the extra slash
            CString temp;
            temp = strPath.Left(3);
            temp += strPath.Mid(4);
            strPath = temp;
        }
        OpenDocumentFile(strPath);
    }
}
```

COMPLEXITY
INTERMEDIATE

6.3 How do I... Customize the common file dialog?

Problem

I need to modify the common dialog displayed by *CFileDialog*. How do I write my own custom class that adds its own controls and knows when the current folder and file have changed?

Technique

MFC includes several convenient C++ wrappers for the Windows common dialog boxes. In particular, *CFileDialog* lets you easily manipulate the common file dialog using familiar *CDialog* methods like *DoModal*.

In Windows version 3.x, customizing the appearance of the FileOpen common dialog meant providing a custom dialog box template. This template was created by modifying the standard FileOpen dialog box template that shipped with the SDK (in the file FileOpen.dlg) as shown in Figure 6-8.

Windows 95 no longer allows modification to the standard dialog box templates. Instead, you design a dialog template that includes only the items to be added to the standard dialog box (like the one shown in Figure 6-11). COMMDLG will then create this dialog as a child of the standard dialog box (which means your template must have the WS_CHILD style).

To demonstrate the steps necessary to customize a common dialog, we'll derive a new class from *CFileDialog* called *CFileIconDlg*, which displays the icon for the currently selected file and shows the entire path for the current directory (see Figure 6-9). Several new *CFileDialog* methods (documented only in the README in Books Online) will be used to handle folder and file changes.

Steps

1. **Create a new project called CustomOpen using the MFC AppWizard (exe).** Select the Single-Document type and press the Finish button.

   Classes to be created:
   Application: CCustomOpenApp in CustomOpen.h and CustomOpen.cpp
   Dialog: CCustomOpenDlg in CustomOpenDlg.h and CustomOpenDlg.cpp

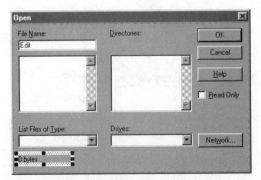

Figure 6-8 Windows 3.x custom file dialog

6.3
CUSTOMIZE THE COMMON FILE DIALOG

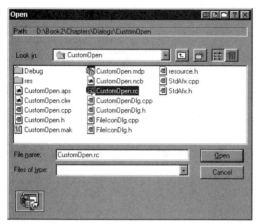

Figure 6-9 Custom file dialog shows the currently selected file's icon and the path

Features:
+ About box on system menu
+ 3D Controls
+ Uses shared DLL implementation (MFC40.DLL)

2. **Edit the symbol directives.** Switch to the ResourceView and select Resource Includes from the File menu. This will display a dialog similar to the one shown in Figure 6-10. Add a line to the read-only symbol directives that includes the <Dlgs.h> file. Now to force Developer Studio to use this new file, close the workspace, then immediately reopen the project. Switch back to the resource view and continue on to the next step.

3. **Add a form-view dialog called IDD_CUSTOM_FILEOPEN.** Use the Insert Resource menu ([CTRL]+[R]) to add a form-view style dialog (IDD_FORMVIEW). Open the dialog and rename it to IDD_CUSTOM_FILEOPEN. Modify the dialog style bits and add controls using the table below and Figure 6-11 as a guide:

Control	ID	Attributes
Dialog	IDD_CUSTOM_FILEOPEN	Child, Clip siblings, Visible, 3D Look, Control
Static	IDC_PATH	Sunken
Frame	stc32	Not visible
Button	IDC_FILEICON	Flat, Icon

4. **Resize the frame control.** Switch to the grid mode (as opposed to the guides mode) and resize the frame control so its left and right edges touch the edges of the dialog. If you didn't size the control flush with the dialog, there would be extra space on either side of the standard controls.

Figure 6-10 Adding a read-only symbol directive

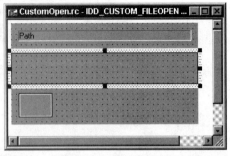

Figure 6-11 IDD_CUSTOM_FILEOPEN dialog used to customize an Open common dialog

5. **Add a string resource.** Create a new string resource called IDS_PATH with the caption "Path:\t%1". Later we'll use *AfxFormatString1* to replace "%1" with the current path.

6. **Create a new class called CFileIconDlg.** Use ClassWizard to create a new class using the following information:

Class name:	CFileIconDlg
Base class:	CFileDialog
File:	FileIconDlg.cpp

7. **Override the OnInitDone method in CFileIconDlg.** Use the ClassView Add Function dialog to add the following method:

```
void CFileIconDlg::OnInitDone()
{
    CFileDialog::OnInitDone();

    CRect r, rPath;

    // Resize the IDC_PATH control so its right edge
    // is flush with the list view control.
    CWnd* pList = GetParent()->GetDlgItem(lst1);
    pList->GetWindowRect(r);
    GetParent()->ScreenToClient(r);

    CWnd* pWnd = GetDlgItem(IDC_PATH);
    pWnd->GetWindowRect(rPath);
    GetParent()->ScreenToClient(rPath);

    pWnd->SetWindowPos(NULL, r.left, rPath.top, r.Width(), rPath.Height(),
        SWP_NOACTIVATE | SWP_NOZORDER);
}
```

This code simply resizes the IDC_PATH static to match the size of the list view.

6.3
CUSTOMIZE THE COMMON FILE DIALOG

8. Override the OnFileNameChange method in CFileIconDlg. Again, use the ClassView Add Function dialog to add the following code:

```
void CFileIconDlg::OnFileNameChange()
{
    // Get the currently selected file name
    CString strFilePath = GetPathName();

    // Get the big icon associated with this file
    SHFILEINFO fi;
    SHGetFileInfo(strFilePath, 0, &fi, sizeof(SHFILEINFO), SHGFI_ICON);

    // Use the icon in the button (assumes IDC_FILEICON has BS_ICON style set)
    CButton* pButton = (CButton*) GetDlgItem(IDC_FILEICON);
    pButton->SetIcon(fi.hIcon);
}
```

When the selected file changes, we retrieve its icon and pass it to the button.

9. Override the OnFolderChange method in CFileIconDlg. For the last time, use the ClassView Add Function dialog to add the following handler:

```
void CFileSizeDlg::OnFolderChange()
{
    // Set the IDC_PATH caption to the current folder path

    CString strFolderPath;
    AfxFormatString1(strFolderPath, IDS_PATH, GetFolderPath());

    SetDlgItemText(IDC_PATH, strFolderPath);
}
```

Here, we set the IDC_PATH static control to show the current directory.

10. Edit the CFileIconDlg constructor. Add this line to the constructor to attach our custom dialog template.

```
CFileSizeDlg::CFileSizeDlg(BOOL bOpenFileDialog, LPCTSTR lpszDefExt, ⇒
LPCTSTR lpszFileName,
        DWORD dwFlags, LPCTSTR lpszFilter, CWnd* pParentWnd) :
        CFileDialog(bOpenFileDialog, lpszDefExt, lpszFileName,
                dwFlags, lpszFilter, pParentWnd)
{
    SetTemplate(0, IDD_CUSTOM_FILEOPEN);
}
```

What an ugly looking constructor. Aren't you glad ClassWizard wrote all that code for you?

11. Edit the include directives in FileIconDlg.cpp. Add this line at the top of FileIconDlg.cpp.

```
#include "stdafx.h"
#include "CustomOpen.h"
#include "FileIconDlg.h"
#include <Dlgs.h>
```

12. **Modify CCustomOpenApp::InitInstance.** We might as well display the *CFileIconDlg* when the application starts, instead of the empty *CCustomOpenDlg* created by AppWizard.

```
BOOL CCustomOpenApp::InitInstance()
{
        // Standard initialization

#ifdef _AFXDLL
        Enable3dControls();             // Call this when using MFC in a shared DLL
#else
        Enable3dControlsStatic();       // Call this when linking to MFC statically
#endif

        CFileIconDlg dlg(TRUE);
        m_pMainWnd = &dlg;
        int nResponse = dlg.DoModal();
        if (nResponse == IDOK)
        {
        }
        else if (nResponse == IDCANCEL)
        {
        }

        // Since the dialog has been closed, return FALSE so that we exit the
        // application, rather than start the application's message pump.
        return FALSE;
}
```

Also, modify the include directives at the top to look like this:

```
#include "stdafx.h"
#include "CustomOpen.h"
#include "CustomOpenDlg.h"
#include "FileIconDlg.h"
```

13. **Build and test the application.** The selected file's icon should show up at the bottom of the dialog. The full path to the selected file should be displayed at the top.

How It Works

Why did we create IDD_CUSTOM_FILEOPEN as a form-based dialog instead of a regular dialog? Normal dialogs created in App Studio have the WS_POPUP style, but form-based dialogs use the WS_CHILD. Without it, the *CFileDialog::DoModal* call would have failed. The common dialog library creates IDD_CUSTOM_FILEOPEN as a *child* of the standard FileOpen dialog box. As a result, *CFileIconDlg* must use *GetParent* to access the "outer" containing dialog to reach the common controls, like we did in *OnInitDone*.

OnInitDone got a pointer to the list view control so it could calculate the necessary width for the IDC_PATH control at runtime. Since it's not possible to know at design time how big the list view control is, the virtual method *OnInitDone* is a convenient place to add those calculations. Incidentally, the MFC wrapper for the common dialog, *CFileDialog*, handles all the common dialog notification messages (like CDN_INITDONE) and dispatches them to empty virtual methods like *OnInitDone*.

After the dialog is up and running, *CFileIconDlg* is notified of two events: when a file is selected, and when the current folder changes. *OnFileNameChange* gets a fully qualified path to the current file when you select a new file in the list view. It uses a Windows shell function *SHGetFileInfo* to retrieve the Explorer-style icon for that file and sticks it in the button for display.

When the user navigates to a new folder, *OnFolderChange* is called. Here, we simply call *GetFolderPath* and display the result in the static control at the top of the dialog.

Comments

Although you can't change the appearance of the standard controls, like the list view—at design time—you can access them at runtime using their predefined control IDs. You'll find the complete list in Dlgs.h. Then, for example, you could change the caption of one of the controls in *OnInitDone* like this:

```
GetParent()->SetControlText(stc4, "Save here:");
```

This code would change the static text in the upper left corner that usually reads "Save in:".

6.4 How do I...
Expand and contract dialog boxes?

**COMPLEXITY
INTERMEDIATE**

Problem

I need an easy, elegant way to simplify a complex dialog. A few of my dialog controls display frequently used information, but most of the other fields are rarely needed. What I'd like is a technique that lets the user *expand* the dialog to get to the extra controls. That way, if the controls aren't needed, the dialog is smaller and less cluttered. Of course, once the dialog is expanded, there needs to be a way to *contract* it.

Technique

To illustrate our expanding and contracting dialog, we're going to prototype a simple reservation dialog like the one shown in Figure 6-12. When the More>> button is pressed, the dialog expands to show the extra controls below (see Figure 6-13).

During the dialog design, we'll add an extra, invisible control to act as a landmark that divides the normal, contracted dialog controls from the extra, expanded ones. Controls above the landmark are the ones frequently used, while the bottom controls are seldom used.

CHAPTER 6
DIALOGS

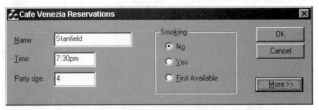

Figure 6-12 Contracted reservation dialog

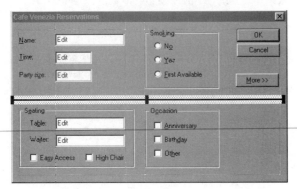

Figure 6-13 Expanded reservation dialog

The contracted and expanded dialog rectangles are calculated during initialization. The dialog is resized to the small or large rectangle depending on whether the <<Less or More>> button is pressed. Then we walk through the child window list, disabling controls outside of the new dialog rectangle. Controls that are inside the dialog boundary are enabled.

Steps

1. Create a new project called Expand using the MFC AppWizard (exe).
Choose the dialog-based version and press the Finish button.

Classes to be created:
    Application: CExpandApp in Expand.h and Expand.cpp
    Dialog: CExpandDlg in ExpandDlg.h and ExpandDlg.cpp

Features:
    + About box on system menu
    + 3D Controls
    + Uses shared DLL implementation (MFC40.DLL)

2. **Edit the IDD_EXPAND_DIALOG dialog box.** Modify the dialog box to look like the one in Figure 6-14. The exact contents of the dialog are not important.

6.4 EXPAND AND CONTRACT DIALOG BOXES

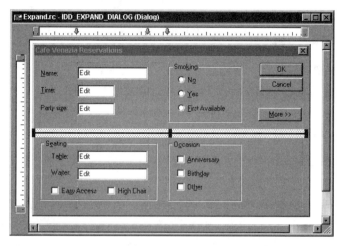

Figure 6-14 Reservation dialog layout

Only the separator (a black rectangle) and the More button are used in the code. Use the control information in the following table:

Control	ID	Attributes
Button	IDC_MORE	" &More >>"
Rectangle	IDC_DIVIDER	Black rectangle, not visible

3. Use WizardBar to add a BN_CLICKED handler for IDC_MORE in CExpandDlg. Edit the code to handle the More/Less button as follows:

```
void CExpandDlg::OnMore()
{
    // bExpand keeps track of the expanded (vs. contracted) state
    static BOOL bExpand = TRUE;

    ExpandDialog (IDC_DIVIDER, bExpand);
    bExpand = !bExpand;
}
```

4. Add the ExpandDialog helper function to CExpandDlg. Use the ClassView Add Function dialog to add the following method:

```
void CExpandDlg::ExpandDialog (int nResourceID, BOOL bExpand)
{
    // Expand the dialog to full size if bExpand is TRUE; otherwise
    // contract, with the new bottom set to the bottom of the
    // divider control specified in nResourceID.

    static  CRect rcLarge;
    static  CRect rcSmall;
    CString sExpand;
```

continued on next page

continued from previous page

```
        // First time through, save the dialog's large
        // and small sizes
        if (rcLarge.IsRectNull())
        {
            CRect rcLandmark;
            CWnd* pWndLandmark = GetDlgItem (nResourceID);
            ASSERT(pWndLandmark);

            GetWindowRect (rcLarge);
            pWndLandmark->GetWindowRect (rcLandmark);

            rcSmall = rcLarge;
            rcSmall.bottom = rcLandmark.top;
        }

        if (bExpand)
        {
            // Expand the dialog: resize the dialog
            // to its original size (rcLarge)
            SetWindowPos(NULL, 0, 0, rcLarge.Width(), rcLarge.Height(),
                SWP_NOMOVE | SWP_NOZORDER);

            sExpand = "<< &Less";
            EnableVisibleChildren();
        }
        else
        {
            // Contract the dialog to the small size
            SetWindowPos(NULL, 0, 0, rcSmall.Width(), rcSmall.Height(),
                SWP_NOMOVE | SWP_NOZORDER);

            sExpand = "   &More >>";
            EnableVisibleChildren();
        }

        SetDlgItemText (IDC_MORE, sExpand);
}
```

The first time *ExpandDialog* is called, it initializes two rectangles: *rcLarge* and *rcSmall*. The large, expanded rectangle is determined by the size in the dialog template. The small, contracted rectangle is the same as the large rectangle except that the bottom stops at the IDC_DIVIDER control.

5. Add the EnableVisibleChildren helper function to CExpandDlg. Use the ClassView Add Function dialog to add the following method:

```
void CExpandDlg::EnableVisibleChildren()
{
        // Disable all children not in the current dialog. This prevents
        // tabbing to hidden controls and disables accelerators.

        // Get the first child control
        CWnd *pWndCtl = GetWindow (GW_CHILD);
```

6.4
EXPAND AND CONTRACT DIALOG BOXES

```
    CRect rcTest;
    CRect rcControl;
    CRect rcShow;

    GetWindowRect(rcShow);

    while (pWndCtl != NULL)
    {
        pWndCtl->GetWindowRect (rcControl);

        if (rcTest.IntersectRect (rcShow, rcControl))
            pWndCtl->EnableWindow(TRUE);
        else
            pWndCtl->EnableWindow(FALSE);

        // Get the next sibling window in this chain.
        pWndCtl = pWndCtl->GetWindow (GW_HWNDNEXT);
    }
}
```

EnableVisibleChildren walks the child control list for the dialog using the SDK function *GetWindow*. Any child window whose coordinates fall outside the new dialog rectangle is disabled through *EnableWindow*.

6. Edit CExpandDlg::OnInitDialog. Edit the code for *OnInitDialog* so it looks like this:

```
BOOL CExpandDlg::OnInitDialog()
{
    CDialog::OnInitDialog();
...

    // Start the dialog in its contracted phase
    ExpandDialog (IDC_DIVIDER, FALSE);

    return TRUE;  // return TRUE  unless you set the focus to a control
}
```

When the dialog is initialized, *ExpandDialog* is called with a value of FALSE to set the dialog in the contracted state.

7. Build and test the application. Enter a few values in the contracted dialog, then press the More button. The dialog should get bigger and the other controls should appear. The More button should have changed to Less. Press the Less button, and notice that you can't tab to any of the expanded controls nor can you activate them through a mnemonic key.

How It Works

The dialog is expanded and contracted through a call to *ExpandDialog*. The first parameter specifies the divider control. This control divides the dialog in half with the extra controls in the lower part of the dialog. The second parameter, a Boolean, determines whether the dialog should expand or contract.

If the dialog should expand, the dialog is first resized to the *rcLarge* rectangle that was calculated the first time *ExpandDialog* was called. Resizing the dialog to be larger exposes the extra controls. *EnableVisibleChildren* makes sure that all the visible controls (not WS_VISIBLE, but within the dialog's client area) are enabled.

If the dialog should contract, the dialog is resized to the rectangle given in *rcSmall*. After resizing the dialog through *SetWindowPos*, all the child windows are checked to see if they're still visible. If not, they're disabled by using *EnableWindow*. Disabled windows won't receive the focus, so you can't tab to them, and their mnemonic keys won't function either.

Comments

You can apply this same technique to a dialog that expands to the right instead of down. Simply modify the *ExpandDialog* code to calculate the *rcSmall* control based on a rectangle control that runs north-south instead of east-west in the dialog. You'd need to change the code from

```
rcSmall = rcLarge;
rcSmall.bottom = rcLandmark.top;
```

to

```
rcSmall = rcLarge;
rcSmall.left = rcLandmark.right;
```

Using a dialog that initially shows only a subset of the total number of controls can be a simple way to make your application easier to use. Remember to take some care in designing the dialog, however, so the controls that are initially hidden really aren't needed much of the time. Otherwise, you might be better off reducing the total number of controls or using two different dialogs.

COMPLEXITY
INTERMEDIATE

6.5 How do I... Display a dialog as either modal or modeless?

Problem

I know the steps necessary to display a regular, modal dialog: Create an instance of my dialog class and call *CDialog::DoModal*. But how do I turn that same dialog into a modeless one? Also, how do I dismiss this modeless dialog through code?

6.5
DISPLAY A DIALOG AS EITHER MODAL OR MODELESS

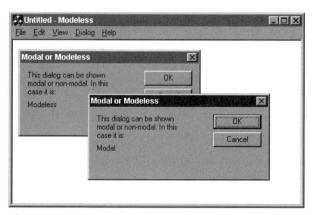

Figure 6-15 Modal and modeless dialogs

Technique

We are going to create a sample application that displays the same dialog as either modal or modeless, as shown in Figure 6-15. The modal dialog will be shown via *CDialog::DoModal*, while the modeless dialog will be created and shown through *CWnd::Create*.

You usually create modal dialogs on the stack as automatic variables; there's no need to do any memory management with new or delete. Modeless dialogs, however, are always created on the heap via new. If the modeless dialog was an automatic variable, it would exhibit some strange behavior: It would flash on the screen, then quickly disappear. Because the function that created the modeless dialog went out of scope, the automatic *CDialog* object was deleted and removed from the screen.

So how do we manage the memory allocated for modeless dialogs? To make things easy, we're going to have the modeless dialog actually delete itself when it's destroyed. In order to make this same code work for both modal and modeless dialogs, a Boolean variable indicates whether or not the dialog should delete itself. If the Boolean member is FALSE, the client is responsible for deleting the memory.

Modeless dialogs also handle the Cancel and OK buttons differently: they call *CWnd::DestroyWindow* instead of *CWnd::EndDialog*. If *OnCancel* and *OnOK* weren't overridden, the dialog would go away, but you'd get Windows resource leaks.

To illustrate how to control a modeless dialog via code, our program starts a timer to delete a modeless dialog after a few seconds have expired.

Steps

1. Create a new project called **Modeless** using the MFC AppWizard (exe).
Select the Single-Document type and press the Finish button.

Classes to be created:

Application:	CModelessApp in Modeless.h and Modeless.cpp
Frame:	CMainFrame in MainFrm.h and MainFrm.cpp
Document:	CModelessDoc in ModelessDoc.h and ModelessDoc.cpp
View:	CModelessView in ModelessView.h and ModelessView.cpp

Features:
+ Initial toolbar in main frame
+ Initial status bar in main frame
+ 3D Controls
+ Uses shared DLL implementation (MFC40.DLL)

2. **Create a dialog using App Studio.** Create a new dialog, as shown in Figure 6-16, and call it IDD_DIALOG1. Notice how the word "<placeholder>" appears in a separate static text control called IDC_TYPE. The application changes this text to modeless or modal depending on the style of the dialog.

   Be sure to switch to the More Styles tab and check the Visible option; otherwise you won't see the dialog when it's created as modeless.

3. **Create a new class called CMyDialog.** Use ClassWizard to create a new class using the following information:

Class name:	CMyDialog
Base class:	CDialog
File:	MyDialog.cpp
Dialog:	IDD_DIALOG1

4. **Add a member variable to CMyDialog.** Use the Member Variables tab in ClassWizard to add a string representing the IDC_TYPE static control.

Control ID	Type	Member
IDC_TYPE	CString	m_sType

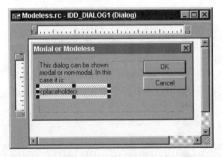

Figure 6-16 IDD_DIALOG1 dialog layout

6.5
DISPLAY A DIALOG AS EITHER MODAL OR MODELESS

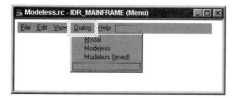

Figure 6-17 Menu items to show CMyDialog

5. **Add command handlers for CMyDialog.** Use ClassWizard to add the following button handlers:

Object ID	Message	Function
IDOK	COMMAND	OnOK
IDCANCEL	COMMAND	OnCancel

6. **Add menu items.** Add a menu called Dialog to the main menu. Add three menu items labeled Modal, Modeless, and Modeless [timed], as shown in Figure 6-17.

7. **Add command handlers for CMainFrame.** Using ClassWizard, add the following command handlers for the menu items and for the timer:

Object ID	Function	Message
CMyDialog	PostNcDestroy	
CMainFrame	OnTimer	WM_TIMER
ID_DIALOG_MODAL	OnDialogModal	COMMAND
ID_DIALOG_MODELESS	OnDialogModeless	COMMAND
ID_DIALOG_TIMED	OnDialogTimed	COMMAND
ID_DIALOG_TIMED	OnUpdateDialogTimed	UPDATE_COMMAND_UI

8. **Edit MyDialog.h** Add the public method *Create* and a Boolean to the class, like this:

```
public:
     CMyDialog(CWnd* pParent = NULL);   // standard constructor
     BOOL Create();
     BOOL m_bModeless;
```

9. **Edit the CMyDialog constructor.** Initialize the *m_bModeless* member variable to FALSE in the constructor, like this:

```
CMyDialog::CMyDialog(CWnd* pParent /*=NULL*/)
     : CDialog(CMyDialog::IDD, pParent)
{
```

continued on next page

continued from previous page
```
        //{{AFX_DATA_INIT(CMyDialog)
        m_sType = "";
        //}}AFX_DATA_INIT
        m_bModeless = FALSE;
}
```

Edit or add the following four methods:

```
void CMyDialog::OnCancel()
{
        if (m_bModeless)
                DestroyWindow();
        else
                CDialog::OnCancel();
}

void CMyDialog::OnOK()
{
        if (!UpdateData(TRUE))
                return;

        if (m_bModeless)
                DestroyWindow();
        else
                CDialog::OnOK();
}

BOOL CMyDialog::Create()
{
        return CDialog::Create(CMyDialog::IDD);
}

void CMyDialog::PostNcDestroy()
{
        CDialog::PostNcDestroy();

        if (m_bModeless)
                delete this;
}
```

10. **Edit MainFrm.h.** Add the following line of code near the top of the file. This forward declaration of *CMyDialog* frees other files that include MainFrm.h from an unnecessary dependency to MyDialog.h.

```
class CMyDialog;
class CMainFrame : public CFrameWnd
```

Add the following members to the *CMainFrame* class:

```
protected:
        CMyDialog*  m_pDlg;       // pointer to modeless, timed dialog
        int         m_nSeconds;   // # of seconds until dialog is killed
```

The first member variable, *m_pDlg*, holds a pointer to the timed, modeless version of *CMyDialog*. The second variable, *m_nSeconds*, keeps track of the number of seconds left before the timed dialog is destroyed.

6.5
DISPLAY A DIALOG AS EITHER MODAL OR MODELESS

11. Edit the CMainFrame constructor. Add the following lines to the constructor of the *CMainFrame* class:

```
CMainFrame::CMainFrame()
{
    m_pDlg = NULL;
    m_nSeconds = 0;
}
```

Include the necessary files at the top of the file:

```
#include "stdafx.h"
#include "Modeless.h"
#include "MainFrm.h"
#include "MyDialog.h"
```

Fill in the methods you added in step 7.

```
void CMainFrame::OnDialogModal()
{
    CMyDialog dlg;

    // Change the static text box to indicate the
    // state of the dialog
    dlg.m_sType = "Modal";

    // DoModal creates the dialog and doesn't return
    // until the user closes the dialog, usually either
    // through OK or Cancel
    dlg.DoModal();
}

void CMainFrame::OnDialogModeless()
{
    CMyDialog* pDlg = new CMyDialog();

    // Setting m_bModeless to TRUE forces the dialog
    // to delete 'this' in PostNcDestroy.  Therefore,
    // we're not responsible for deleting pDlg
    pDlg->m_bModeless = TRUE;

    // Change the static text box to indicate the
    // state of the dialog
    pDlg->m_sType = "Modeless";

    // Calling Create will display the dialog
    pDlg->Create();
}

void CMainFrame::OnDialogTimed()
{
    m_pDlg = new CMyDialog();
    m_pDlg->m_sType = "Modeless and Timed";
    m_pDlg->m_bModeless = TRUE;
    m_pDlg->Create();
```

continued on next page

continued from previous page

```
        // Disable the OK and Cancel buttons
        // so the user can't dismiss the dialog
        // before the timer has expired
        m_pDlg->GetDlgItem(IDOK)->EnableWindow(FALSE);
        m_pDlg->GetDlgItem(IDCANCEL)->EnableWindow(FALSE);

        // Change the dialog caption to indicate
        // how long the dialog has left to live
        m_nSeconds = 5;
        CString message;

        message.Format(IDS_COUNTDOWN, m_nSeconds);
        m_pDlg->SetWindowText(message);

        // Set a one second timer to kill the dialog
        // if m_nSeconds has elapsed.
        SetTimer(0, 1000, NULL);
}

void CMainFrame::OnUpdateDialogTimed(CCmdUI* pCmdUI)
{
        pCmdUI->Enable(m_nSeconds == 0);
}

void CMainFrame::OnTimer(UINT nIDEvent)
{
        if (--m_nSeconds == 0)
        {
                // Out of time; destroy the dialog
                KillTimer(0);
                m_pDlg->DestroyWindow();
                m_pDlg = NULL;
        } else {
                // Update the dialog caption to show the
                // number of seconds remaining
                CString message;
                message.Format(IDS_COUNTDOWN, m_nSeconds);
                m_pDlg->SetWindowText(message);
        }
}
```

12. **Add a string resource.** Add a string resource called IDS_COUNTDOWN with the caption "%d second(s) left."

13. **Recompile and run the application.** Notice that you can instantiate more than one modeless dialog and that there are no memory leaks even though we never delete any of our pointers. Also, try the timed dialog and notice that you can't bring up another timed dialog until the current one has expired.

How It Works

The main thing that distinguishes modal dialogs from modeless ones is the use of *CDialog::Create* versus *CDialog::DoModal* to display the dialog.

6.5
DISPLAY A DIALOG AS EITHER MODAL OR MODELESS

When any object of class *CWnd* is created, the constructor creates only the C++ encapsulation object. The actual window that appears on the screen is controlled by an internal Windows data structure, which must be created explicitly and attached to the *CWnd* object. The "real" window, in the case of our *CMyDialog* object, is created when either the *DoModal* or *Create* member function is called.

In the case of *DoModal*, the member function will not return until the corresponding window is destroyed. In the case of *Create*, the *DestroyWindow* member function must be called to remove the window.

Auto-cleanup

Since modal dialogs are usually created as automatic variables—that is, they're created on the stack—there's no extra C++ or Windows memory cleanup involved. Everything is neatly cleaned up when the method that instantiated the class goes out of scope.

Modeless dialogs, on the other hand, are never created on the stack. Instead, they're created on the heap with a call to new. Otherwise, when the method that called new goes out of scope, the *CDialog* object's destructor would be called, and the modeless dialog would instantly disappear.

In order to free the C++ memory allocated for the *CMyDialog* object and free the Windows resource handles allocated for the dialog object, we have to write a little more code. Since we added a special *CMyDialog* member variable, *m_bModeless* we can determine what to do when the user clicks OK or Cancel. In the case of a modeless dialog, we don't call *CDialog::EndDialog;* instead, we call it *DestroyWindow*. Otherwise, the Window's resources allocated to display the dialog will never be freed.

The very last message to be sent to a window is WM_NCDESTROY. The default handler for *CWnd* calls the virtual method *PostNcDestroy,* which we've overridden in *CMyDialog*. Here, if *m_bModeless* is FALSE, we do nothing and exit. Otherwise, we call delete this to clean up any C++ memory allocated for *CMyDialog*. Without this trick, we'd have to somehow keep track of our modeless dialogs (there may be more than one) and free the memory allocated with delete when the modeless dialog is closed. By using this technique, we can "fire and forget" the modeless dialog and let it clean up after itself.

Comments

If you wanted to create a "modeless-only" version of the dialog, you could have the constructor call Create for you. You would then need to set a flag in your dialog object, so the destructor could detect whether or not it is necessary to call *DestroyWindow*.

For more information on how to use modeless dialogs with MFC, refer to Microsoft Knowledge Base article #Q103788. *PostNcDestroy* and the reasons for using it are discussed in the Visual C++ Technical note 17.

6.6 How do I... Write customized DDX/DDV routines?

COMPLEXITY: ADVANCED

Problem

I need an easy way to transfer data between my dialog controls and their corresponding member variables. Of course, I want to take advantage of MFC's Dialog Data Exchange (DDX) and its cousin, Dialog Data Validation (DDV), to handle the data transfer and content validation. However, DDX and DDV only work with certain simple data types like *ints, longs,* and *CStrings*. How can I extend the power of DDX/DDV to handle my own data types?

Technique

As long as you use the standard DDX/DDV routines, you won't have to write a line of code for data transfer and validation—MFC and ClassWizard take care of that for you. When you use ClassWizard to add a member variable for a dialog control, you select the DDX data type and the DDV processing to apply to the data.

When you select the Add Variable button, the dialog shown in Figure 6-18 lets you choose from a set of member variable types to link to the dialog control. After you've chosen one of the built-in data types for the DDX routine, you can specify range constraints for the data. For example, you might want to limit an edit control linked to a *CString* variable so that it accepts no more than 50 characters (see Figure 6-19).

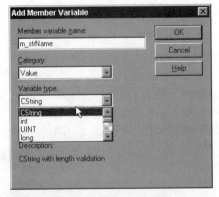

Figure 6-18 Add Member Variable dialog

6.6
WRITE CUSTOMIZED DDX/DDV ROUTINES

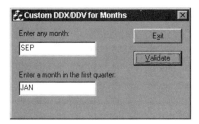

Figure 6-19 Setting the maximum characters for a DDV routine

Your normal choices for member variable types are limited to the atomic data types provided by C++ (*int, long, float,* and so on) and *CString*. Your choice of DDV validation is limited to simple numeric ranges for the atomic data types and a maximum length validation for the *CString* case.

It's likely your application has either abstract data types or custom validation requirements for the existing data types not covered by the built-in DDX/DDV routines. We're going to extend ClassWizard to add support for our own customized DDX/DDV methods.

Our DDX routine will map three-character month abbreviations to an integer member variable. For example, JAN maps to 1, FEB maps to 2, and so on. A DDX error results if the user enters a string that cannot be mapped to a month value.

Our DDV routine will validate a calendar quarter. The quarter is specified as a number from 1 to 4. Months in the first quarter are JAN, FEB, MAR; months in the second quarter are APR, MAY, JUN, and so on. If the user enters a month outside the specified quarter, a DDV error will result.

To test the month DDX and DDV routines, we'll create a dialog-based application with two edit controls that accept month strings (see Figure 6-20). The second edit control only accepts months that fall in the first quarter of the year: JAN, FEB, and MAR.

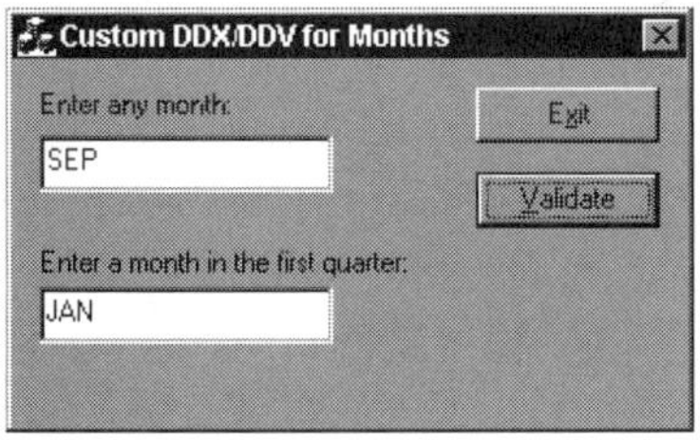

Figure 6-20 A dialog that accepts months

345

Steps

1. Create a new project called CustomDDX using the MFC AppWizard (exe). Choose the dialog-based version and press the Finish button.

Classes to be created:
Application: CCustomDDXApp in CustomDDX.h and CustomDDX.cpp
Dialog: CCustomDDXDlg in CustomDDXDlg.h and CustomDDXDlg.cpp

Features:
+ About box on system menu
+ 3D Controls
+ Uses shared DLL implementation (MFC40.DLL)

2. Modify the ClassWizard file CustomDDX.clw. The project's configuration data for ClassWizard is stored in the ASCII text file CustomDDX.clw. Open the file with the text editor for Visual C++ and add the following lines to the "General Info" section:

```
; CLW file contains information for the MFC ClassWizard

[General Info]
Version=1
LastClass=CCustomDDXDlg
LastTemplate=CDialog
NewFileInclude1=#include "stdafx.h"
NewFileInclude2=#include "CustomDDX.h"
ExtraDDXCount=1
ExtraDDX1=E;;Month;int;0;month;A month abbrev.;month;&Quarter;d
```

3. Edit the IDD_CUSTOMDDX_DIALOG dialog box. Use App Studio to edit the AppWizard-generated default dialog. Add two edit controls named IDC_ANY_MONTH and IDC_1Q_MONTH, as shown in Figure 6-21.

Control	ID	Attributes
Edit #1	IDC_ANY_MONTH	Default
Edit #2	IDC_1Q_MONTH	Default
Exit button	IDOK	Remove default button style
Validate button	IDC_VALIDATE	Add default button style

4. Add code for the Validate button. Hold down the Control key and double-click the Validate button. This adds an empty BN_CLICKED handler to which you should add the following code:

```
void CCustomDDXDlg::OnValidate()
{
        if (UpdateData())
                AfxMessageBox("Months entered are valid");
}
```

6.6
WRITE CUSTOMIZED DDX/DDV ROUTINES

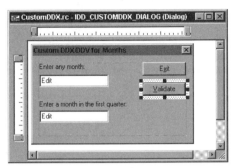

Figure 6-21 Layout for DDX/DDV dialog

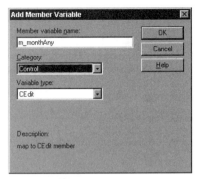

Figure 6-22 Month member variables dialog

5. **Add member variables.** Use ClassWizard to add member variables for both edit controls. Both controls use our custom month DDX routines. IDC_1Q_MONTH uses the DDV routine to allow only first quarter months. Use the Add Variable button to add variables for these controls as shown in the following table and in Figure 6-22.

Control ID	Type	Member	Validation
IDC_ANY_MONTH	int (month)	m_monthAny	None
IDC_1Q_MONTH	int (month)	m_monthFirstQuarter	1 (first quarter)

To set the validation for the IDC_1Q_MONTH control, enter a value of 1 in the Quarter edit control at the bottom of the Member Variables tab, as shown in Figure 6-23.

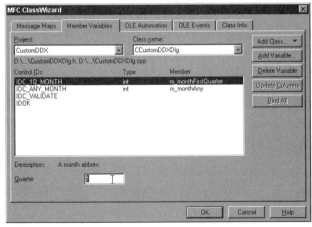

Figure 6-23 Setting the valid quarter

CHAPTER 6
DIALOGS

6. **Create the Months.h file.** Create a new source file called Months.h and add these two lines of code to it:

```
void WINAPI DDX_month(CDataExchange* pDX, int nIDC, int& month);
void WINAPI DDV_month(CDataExchange* pDX, int month, int quarter);
```

Then edit CustomDDXDlg.cpp and add a new include directive at the top:

```
#include "stdafx.h"
#include "CustomDDX.h"
#include "CustomDDXDlg.h"
#include "Months.h"
```

7. **Create the DDX/DDV routines in Months.cpp.** Create another source file called Months.cpp and insert the file into the project (Hint: Use the right-mouse button). Add the following code to the file:

```
#include "stdafx.h"
#include "Months.h"

static char *g_months[] =
{
        "JAN", "FEB", "MAR",
        "APR", "MAY", "JUN",
        "JUL", "AUG", "SEP",
        "OCT", "NOV", "DEC"
};

// DDX routine for month abbreviations
void WINAPI DDX_month(CDataExchange* pDX, int nIDC, int& month)
{
        // From dialog to class?
        if (pDX->m_bSaveAndValidate)
        {
                CString val;             // String entered in control
                BOOL bValid = FALSE;     // Month is valid
                int nMonth;              // Equivalent month

                // Get text from control and change to uppercase
                pDX->m_pDlgWnd->GetDlgItem(nIDC)->GetWindowText(val);
                val.MakeUpper();

                // See if text matches the valid month abbreviations
                for (nMonth = 0; nMonth < 12; nMonth++)
                {
                        if (!val.Compare(g_months[nMonth]))
                        {
                                bValid = TRUE;
                                break;
                        }
                }

                if (bValid)
                        month = nMonth + 1;
                else
                {
```

6.6
WRITE CUSTOMIZED DDX/DDV ROUTINES

```
                pDX->m_pDlgWnd->MessageBox
                        ("Please enter a valid month\nJAN, FEB, etc.");
                pDX->PrepareEditCtrl(nIDC);
                pDX->Fail();
        }
    } else {
            // If the value in the control is a valid month,
            // store it in the child control

            if ((month >= 1) && (month <= 12))
            {
                    pDX->m_pDlgWnd->GetDlgItem(nIDC)->
                        SetWindowText (g_months[month]);
            }
    }
}

// DDV routine to check a month in a quarter
void WINAPI DDV_month(CDataExchange* pDX, int month, int quarter)
{
        if (pDX->m_bSaveAndValidate)
        {
                // Fail if the month is not in the quarter
                if ( ((int) month / 4) != (quarter - 1) )
                {
                        pDX->m_pDlgWnd->MessageBox
                                ("Month is not in the correct quarter");
                        pDX->Fail();
                }
        }
}
```

8. **Build and test the program.** You can enter any valid month, JAN through DEC, in the first edit control, but you can enter only JAN, FEB, or MAR in the second control. Try entering a number in the first control, then pressing OK. Next, try entering DEC in the control that expects a month in the first quarter. In both cases, you'll get different message boxes indicating a DDX or DDV error.

How It Works

When DDX/DDV is applied to a dialog, several routines come into play. First, a DDX routine is called to translate the text from the dialog control to an appropriate data type. In the example shown in Figure 6-24, a DDX routine translates the edit control's characters to a *float* variable.

The DDX routine is not always successful. For example, the user may have entered characters that are illegal for a textual representation of a floating-point number. If this is the case, the DDX routine will fail, and the user will be presented with an informative error dialog indicating why the input was illegal.

If the DDX routine succeeds, a DDV routine may then be called. DDV functions are used when only a subset of the valid inputs to the DDX routine are actually valid

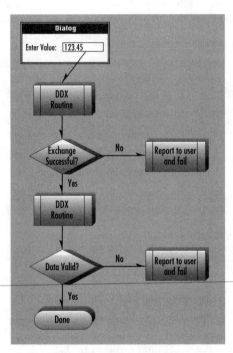

Figure 6-24 DDX/DDV Routines

for the given control. For example, it may be desirable to have a given edit control only accept floating-point numbers within a certain range. The DDX function will accept any legal floating-point number. It would be the job of the DDV to determine whether or not the entered number falls within the specified range.

If the DDV fails, the user is presented with an error dialog much in the same way as when the DDX routine fails.

When adding a mapping between a child window control and a member variable, ClassWizard consults the project's appname.CLW file (where *appname* is the name of your project) for information about custom DDX/DDV routines. In our example, we added the following lines to our project's CustomDDX.clw file:

```
ExtraDDXCount=1
ExtraDDX1=E;;Month;int;0;month;A month abbrev.;month;&Quarter;d
```

The number given for *ExtraDDXCount* indicates the number of *ExtraDDX* lines that follow. Each of the following lines is preceded by an indicator of the form *ExtraDDXn* where n indicates the entry's position in the list of DDX entries being defined.

6.6
WRITE CUSTOMIZED DDX/DDV ROUTINES

The remainder of the line consists of a number of fields separated by semicolons. For more detailed field information, refer to the Visual C++ Technical Note 26. The meanings of the fields are shown in Table 6-1.

FIELD	VALUE	DESCRIPTION
1	E	A string consisting of one or more special characters indicating the type of control this DDX/DDV routine can be used with. In our case the "E" is for edit controls.
2	(empty)	Only necessary for Visual Basic controls.
3	Month	A string to place in the Property combo box.
4	int	Data type of the variable being described. In our example, we map the strings entered by the user to integer values, so we set this field to int.
5	0	Initial value for the variable. Leave blank for classes with default constructors like CTime or CString.
6	month	The name of the DDX routine. DDX_ is appended to this string, resulting in a function called DDX_month.
7	(comment)	A comment that appears in the Add Variable dialog.
8	month	Identifies the DDV procedure (DDV_month).
9	&Quarter	String used to label the edit control in the ClassWizard Add Variable dialog where the DDV parameter is set.
10	d	A character to indicate the type of the parameter passed to the DDV routine.

Table 6-1 ExtraDDX string segments

Alternatively, you can define a second parameter to your DDV routine by including an eleventh and twelfth field which are similar to the ninth and tenth fields for the second parameter. Remember, all DDV routines must have at least one parameter, so if you specify a DDV routine in the eighth field, the ninth and tenth fields are required.

Now let's consider the DDX and DDV routines themselves. The DDX routine is actually called for both dialog read and write operations. The direction of data transfer is indicated by *m_bSaveAndValidate*. This variable is a member of the *CDataExchange* object, which is passed as the first parameter to the DDX routine. If TRUE, data is being transferred from the dialog controls to the member variables. If FALSE, the opposite is the case—the DDX routine is to transfer data from the data member to the dialog control.

CDataExchange has another public member called *m_pDlgWnd* that points to the dialog's *CWnd* object. We use this pointer in the DDX routine along with the child window control ID to get a pointer to the dialog control's object. Using this pointer, we can call *GetWindowText* to extract the text entered by the user.

We then force the text to uppercase and search the *g_months* array for a matching string. If a match is found, we set the dialog member variable to the array index where the string match is found. Otherwise, the DDX routine fails. In order to make the DDX routine fail, the *CDataExchange* object provides two member functions. The *PrepareEditCtrl* member function sets the focus to the offending child window control. The *Fail* member function resets the focus and throws an exception. Before calling *Fail,* we put up a message box informing the user that a DDX error occurred.

That covers the case where we are writing to the dialog object's data member. What about the other way around? If m_*bSaveAndValidate* is FALSE, that indicates to the DDX routine that we should be writing to the dialog window from the data member. In our case, it is simply a matter of checking whether the value of the data member corresponds to a valid month (it is between 1 and 12). If the value is valid, we set the value of the child window control to the corresponding position in the *g_months* array.

Comments

A separate DDV routine is necessary only when the validation is parameterized, as in the above example. When the DDV logic does not require any parameters, then it must be incorporated into the DDX routine. ClassWizard cannot generate calls to parameterless DDV routines.

If you want to use the DDX/DDV routines for all projects, create a file called DDX.clw in the \msdev\bin directory that looks like this:

```
[ExtraDDX]
ExtraDDXCount=1
ExtraDDX1=E;;Month;int;0;month;A month abbreviation;month;&Quarter;d
```

Then extract the *DDX_month* and *DDV_month* routines from the CustomDDX and put them in a separate file for compilation.

CHAPTER 7
OLE AND DDE

OLE AND DDE

How do I...

7.1 Create a simple OLE object and automation server?

7.2 Use OLE's drag-and-drop features?

7.3 Use structured storage?

7.4 Create a DDE object to talk to other applications?

7.5 Write an OLE spin control?

7.6 Create a color cell OLE control?

As an application developer, sooner or later you will realize that your application can't do everything. Users will want your application to do things that you never envisioned. There may be a key area of functionality that is performed better by a "specialist" application, or another application may have access to a data source that your application doesn't.

Object Linking and Embedding (OLE) and Dynamic Data Exchange (DDE) are mechanisms that can be used to share data and functionality among applications. They provide for *component-based development*, whereby individual pieces of functionality are farmed out to isolated component modules that can be dropped into any OLE-enabled application.

For many years, DDE was the only "official" mechanism for linking data between applications. Recently, with the introduction of OLE 2.0, Microsoft has positioned OLE as the strategic mechanism for implementing this type of functionality. However, a large installed base of software already uses DDE, so it is very possible that you may need DDE support in your application.

CHAPTER 7
OLE AND DDE

This chapter provides a sampling of what is involved in using OLE and DDE in your MFC applications. It cannot and does not provide a comprehensive guide to using OLE or DDE. For a more comprehensive guide to OLE containers, object servers, and automation servers, follow the excellent online documentation and tutorial provided with Visual C++.

In this chapter, you'll start by creating a simple OLE object that draws colored ovals. Then you'll see what steps are necessary to add OLE automation so the oval can be controlled through another application, such as Excel. The next How-To shows how to add drag-and-drop support to standard list boxes. Structured storage is explored in another How-To, in which you substitute the standard *CDocument* class with another that uses compound files. Writing a class for DDE communication is the topic of How-To 7.4. The last How-To is the most exciting: It shows you how to write a practical OLE custom control that you can use in any application.

7.1 Create a Simple OLE Object and Automation Server

Learn how to combine two powerful OLE features, object and automation server, into one simple MFC application. This object server handles colored circles and exposes methods to client applications that change the color of the circle. It even supports in-place editing with a little extra work.

Additional Topics: COleIPFrameWnd, COleServerItem, CColorDialog, Excel macros

7.2 Use OLE's Drag-and-Drop Features

This How-To creates a sample ToDo application. You will see how to use the OLE MFC classes to drag-and-drop items between two list boxes. You can drag-and-drop items within the same application, between instances of the application, or between other applications that participate in OLE 2.0 drag-and-drop with text (CF_TEXT) data.

Additional Topics: text clipboard format, subclassed list boxes

7.3 Use Structured Storage

OLE 2.0 offers a robust file-handling scheme allowing transaction control, incremental saves, and multilevel commits. The MFC classes can be serialized to an OLE compound file in much the same way that they are serialized to normal files. This How-To shows how you can use the OLE structured storage APIs to implement simple transacted storage.

Additional Topics: CArchive, COleStreamFile, COleDocument, creating storages

7.4 Create a DDE Object to Talk to Other Applications

Dynamic Data Exchange is a proven mechanism that allows applications to share data. Since MFC does not encapsulate the DDE library (DDEML), this How-To describes a simple class that supports DDE communication. We'll use Excel to communicate with our DDE-enabled application.

Additional Topics: DDEML, static member callbacks

7.5 Write an OLE Spin Control

Learn how to write a fully functional OLE custom control that you can use in any application. You'll create a spin button control with property pages, custom methods, and notification events. You'll see how to use the Test Container application that comes with the Control Development Kit to test your new control.

Additional Topics: CDK, ControlWizard, property pages

7.6 Create a Color Cell OLE Control

This How-To shows you how to create a useful reusable OLE color cell control that can be grouped together to create a color well control. The control handles the WM_NCPAINT message and draws its own frame. You will also see how to detect when the mouse first enters and leaves the control.

Additional Topics: WM_NCPAINT, WM_NCCALCSIZE, SetCapture, ReleaseCapture

COMPLEXITY
INTERMEDIATE

7.1 How do I... Create a simple OLE object and automation server?

Problem

I need a simple way to combine an OLE server with automation features using the MFC classes. Ideally, I'd like to access the server's features through another application like Excel using its built-in macro language (a subset of Visual Basic).

Technique

This How-To probably has the highest coolness-to-code ratio. After a few well-placed mouse clicks and a trivial amount of programming, you'll have a simple application that shows off some great OLE features.

For illustration purposes, this OLE sample draws a colored circle using *CDC::Ellipse* (hence the program name, OVAL.EXE). When you run OVAL stand-alone (see

CHAPTER 7
OLE AND DDE

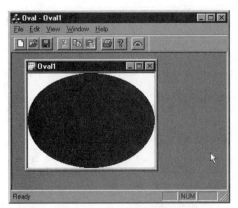

Figure 7-1 Running OVAL stand-alone

Figure 7-1), it behaves like a normal, non-OLE aware MDI application. That is, you can create as many OVAL documents as you like, each with its own color. It even supports file saving. The real fun begins when you copy one of the documents to the clipboard.

Using any OLE container program (such as Excel or OCLIENT.EXE from Visual C++), you can paste this oval object from the clipboard into the container's client area (see Figure 7-2). While the object is active in the container's document, you can change the color of the circle using an item on the toolbar (see Figure 7-3). If the object isn't on the clipboard, or even if OVAL.EXE is not running, you can insert a new oval document into your container through a standard "Insert OLE Object" dialog available in most container applications.

This might be enough to satisfy your curiosity, but we'll go beyond a simple server and add support for OLE automation. An automation server is not necessarily an OLE object server, but in this case it is. We'll expose a set of methods to let clients

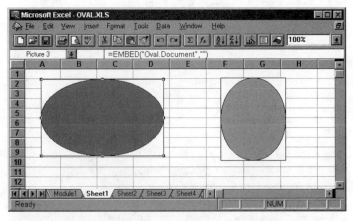

Figure 7-2 Two oval objects embedded in Excel

7.1
CREATE A SIMPLE OLE OBJECT AND AUTOMATION SERVER

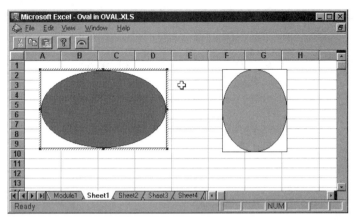

Figure 7-3 In-place activation of an oval object

"automate" certain functions by programming the oval documents. Granted, you won't be able to do anything fancy with this sample, but it'll point you in the right direction if you want to add automation to your applications. Using a high-level language like Visual Basic (which, conveniently, is the macro language of Excel and Word), we'll see how to change the color of the circle with just a few lines of Visual Basic code.

Steps

1. **Create a new project called Oval using the MFC AppWizard (exe).** In step 3, choose the Full Server option and turn on the OLE automation option (see Figure 7-4). In step 4, press the Advanced button and type in "ovl" for the file extension.

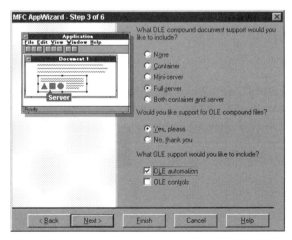

Figure 7-4 OLE settings for Oval

359

CHAPTER 7
OLE AND DDE

Classes to be created:

Application:	COvalApp in Oval.h and Oval.cpp
Frame:	CMainFrame in MainFrm.h and MainFrm.cpp
MDIChildFrame:	CChildFrame in ChildFrm.h and ChildFrm.cpp
Document:	COvalDoc in OvalDoc.h and OvalDoc.cpp
View:	COvalView in OvalView.h and OvalView.cpp
In-place Frame:	CInPlaceFrame in IpFrame.h and IpFrame.cpp
Server Item:	COvalSrvrItem in SrvrItem.h and SrvrItem.cpp

Features:
+ Initial toolbar in main frame
+ Initial status bar in main frame
+ Printing and Print Preview support in view
+ 3D Controls
+ Uses shared DLL implementation (MFC40.DLL)
+ Document supports files with extension .OVL
+ OLE Full-Server support enabled
+ OLE Compound File support enabled
+ OLE Automation support enabled

2. **Add the Change Color menu item.** We need to let the user do something to the object, so we'll add a menu item that pops up a color browser. The circle will be filled with the chosen color. Since OLE full servers can be run stand-alone, in-place, or embedded, there are three menus for each mode. For the menus IDR_OVALTYPE, IDR_OVALTYPE_SRVR_EMB, and IDR_OVALTYPE_SRVR_IP, add a menu item with the caption "Change Color..." at the bottom of each Edit menu. Use ID_EDIT_CHANGECOLOR as the new menu item ID. (Hint: You can create the new menu item in IDR_OVALTYPE, copy the item to the clipboard, and paste it at the bottom of the other two menus).

3. **Add a toolbar button.** Besides there being multiple menus for OLE servers, there are two toolbars. The first toolbar, IDR_MAINFRAME, is displayed when OVAL is run stand-alone. The second toolbar, IDR_OVALTYPE_SRVR_IP, is displayed when the object is activated in-place. Replace the last button in both toolbars with a "rainbow" button. The user can press this button to change the circle color, as shown in Figure 7-5. Give each button the same ID used in the new menu in step 2, ID_EDIT_CHANGECOLOR.

   Note: You can't tell from the grayscale picture, but the rainbow is formed from six main colors: red, orange, yellow, green, blue, and violet.

4. **Use WizardBar to handle ID_EDIT_CHANGECOLOR in COvalDoc.** Call the new handler *COvalDoc::OnEditChangeColor* and edit the code as follows:

```
void COvalDoc::OnEditChangeColor()
{
    CColorDialog dlg( RGB(m_red, m_green, m_blue), CC_RGBINIT);
```

7.1
CREATE A SIMPLE OLE OBJECT AND AUTOMATION SERVER

```
    if (dlg.DoModal() == IDOK)
    {
        COLORREF cr = dlg.GetColor();
        m_red = GetRValue(cr);
        m_green = GetGValue(cr);
        m_blue = GetBValue(cr);
        UpdateAllViews(NULL);
        NotifyChanged();
    }
}
```

The color dialog is initialized with the document's red, green, and blue components. Then, if the user selects OK, the values are saved using *SetRGB*, a method we'll code later.

5. Edit the file OvalDoc.h The circle's color is stored in three *COvalDoc* member variables called *m_red*, *m_green*, and *m_blue*. Later, we'll add access methods through the ClassWizard.

```
// Attributes
public:
    COvalSrvrItem* GetEmbeddedItem()
        { return (COvalSrvrItem*)COleServerDoc::GetEmbeddedItem(); }
    BYTE    m_red, m_blue, m_green;
```

Don't let the *GetEmbeddedItem* inline method scare you. It's one of the OLE details the AppWizard handles for you.

6. Code COvalDoc's constructor. By default, we'll make each circle blue. Change the *COvalDoc*'s constructor to look like this:

```
COvalDoc::COvalDoc()
{
    EnableCompoundFile();
    EnableAutomation();
    AfxOleLockApp();

    m_blue = 255;
    m_red = m_green = 0;
}
```

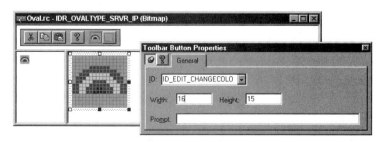

Figure 7-5 Rainbow toolbar button

CHAPTER 7
OLE AND DDE

EnableAutomation does just that: It turns on the machinery necessary to manipulate the document through OLE automation. *AfxOleLockApp* keeps track of the number of active objects in an application. Again, these are OLE details that AppWizard adds for you.

7. Edit COvalDoc::Serialize. For file saving and clipboard operations to work, fill in the *Serialize* method like this:

```
void COvalDoc::Serialize(CArchive& ar)
{
    if (ar.IsStoring())
    {
        ar << m_red << m_green << m_blue;
    }
    else
    {
        ar >> m_red >> m_green >> m_blue;
    }
}
```

Notice that the code inside doesn't care whether we're saving to a file or copying to the clipboard. Just this one set of code supports disk and clipboard storage. Once you've added one more method in the next step, OLE clipboard support will be complete.

8. Use ClassWizard to add clipboard support. All you need to do is map ID_EDIT_COPY to *COvalDoc::OnEditCopy* using the WizardBar, then edit the code to look like this:

```
void COvalDoc::OnEditCopy()
{
    COvalSrvrItem* pItem = GetEmbeddedItem();
    pItem->CopyToClipboard(TRUE);
}
```

The first line gets a pointer to the data item representing the entire document. This *COvalSrvrItem* object is what gets passed back and forth between an OLE client and server. *CopyToClipboard* uses the *Serialize* method we just wrote to put the object's data on the clipboard, along with other OLE-specific data.

9. Edit COvalView::OnDraw. Just as you would for any other application that uses views, you need to write the display code. In this case, it's quite simple. You fill a circle representing the entire client area with a colored brush. The brush color comes from the document's *m_red, m_blue,* and *m_green* components, as you can see here:

```
void COvalView::OnDraw(CDC* pDC)
{
    COvalDoc* pDoc = GetDocument();
    ASSERT_VALID(pDoc);

    COLORREF cr = RGB(pDoc->m_red, pDoc->m_green, pDoc->m_blue);
    CBrush brush (cr);
```

7.1
CREATE A SIMPLE OLE OBJECT AND AUTOMATION SERVER

```
        CBrush* pOldBrush = pDC->SelectObject(&brush);

        CRect rc;
        GetClientRect(rc);
        pDC->Ellipse(rc);

        pDC->SelectObject(pOldBrush);
}
```

10. **Code COvalSrvrItem::OnDraw.** If you're alert, you might have anticipated this step. Since an oval OLE object can have a different appearance when it's inactive versus active, we need to write the drawing code for the inactive state. The device context passed to *COvalSrvrItem::OnDraw* really represents a metafile. Since metafiles only work in MM_ANISOTROPIC mapping mode, our drawing code will look a little different than it did before. Here's the new version:

```
BOOL COvalSrvrItem::OnDraw(CDC* pDC, CSize& rSize)
{
        COvalDoc* pDoc = GetDocument();
        ASSERT_VALID(pDoc);

        pDC->SetMapMode(MM_ANISOTROPIC);
        pDC->SetWindowOrg(0,0);
        pDC->SetWindowExt(3000, 3000);

        COLORREF cr = RGB(pDoc->m_red, pDoc->m_green, pDoc->m_blue);
        CBrush brush (cr);
        CBrush* pOldBrush = pDC->SelectObject(&brush);
        CRect rc(0,0,3000,3000);
        pDC->Ellipse(rc);
        pDC->SelectObject(pOldBrush);

        return TRUE;
}
```

By default, AppWizard sets the device context to MM_ANISOTROPIC for us, with the logical window size set to 3,000x3,000 units. Then we create a circle using a rectangle with the same dimensions, which effectively draws a circle filling the entire OLE object.

11. **Compile and run OVAL.EXE.** That's right! Even though we haven't added OLE automation support, you now have a full-fledged OLE server. Run it at least once so it can register its OLE information in the system registry.

After you tire of colored circles, copy one of them to the clipboard and paste it into a suitable client like Excel or Word. By double-clicking on the oval, you can edit the document in-place. Of course, the only thing you can do is change the color using the rainbow toolbar button or the Edit menu.

CHAPTER 7
OLE AND DDE

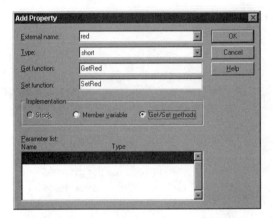

Figure 7-6 Adding properties to OVAL

12. **Add OLE automation methods through ClassWizard.** Select the OLE Automation tab in ClassWizard and choose *COvalDoc* as the class name. In this dialog, we'll add methods "exposing" *COvalDoc* to the outside world.

    Click the Add Property button and type in blue as the external name. In the implementation group, select Get/Set Methods. For the parameter type, choose short from the combo box (see Figure 7-6). Click OK, then repeat the same steps for red and green.

    Now we'll add three methods using the Add Method button. This brings up a similar dialog, but in this case, we need to provide return types and a parameter for each method. Use the following information to fill in the dialog for each of the three methods:

External Name	Internal Name	Return Type	Parameter Name	Parameter Type
RefreshWindow	RefreshWindow	void	None	None
ShowWindow	ShowWindow	void	None	None
SetRGB	SetRGB	void	red	short
			green	short
			blue	short

    When you are finished, the OLE Automation tab should look like Figure 7-7.

13. **Code the automation methods.** The Get/Set methods in OvalDoc.cpp are straightforward, as you can see here:

```
short COvalDoc::GetRed()
{
    return m_red;
}

void COvalDoc::SetRed(short nNewValue)
```

7.1
CREATE A SIMPLE OLE OBJECT AND AUTOMATION SERVER

```
{
    m_red = (BYTE) nNewValue;
    RefreshWindow();
}

short COvalDoc::GetGreen()
{
    return m_green;
}

void COvalDoc::SetGreen(short nNewValue)
{
    m_green = (BYTE) nNewValue;
    RefreshWindow();
}

short COvalDoc::GetBlue()
{
    return m_blue;
}

void COvalDoc::SetBlue(short nNewValue)
{
    m_blue = (BYTE) nNewValue;
    RefreshWindow();
}
```

For each Set method, *RefreshWindow* is called to immediately update the display and any linked object. Code the *RefreshWindow* method as follows:

```
void COvalDoc::RefreshWindow()
{
    UpdateAllViews(NULL);
    NotifyChanged();
    SetModifiedFlag();
}
```

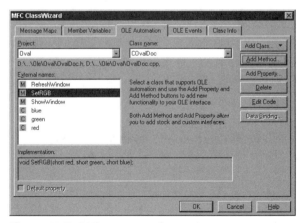

Figure 7-7 OLE Automation tab

UpdateAllViews should be familiar; it tells all the views to repaint themselves. *NotifyChanged* is a *COleDocument* method that updates any linked object. *SetModifiedFlag* marks the document as modified so the MFC framework will prompt you to save the document before exiting the application.

It's possible to use OLE automation in a client without actually having an embedded object. Basically, the application runs stand-alone but is controlled by the automation client.

The next method, *ShowWindow*, lets the client display Oval.exe, since it's hidden by default when run via OLE automation.

```
void COvalDoc::ShowWindow()
{
    POSITION pos = GetFirstViewPosition();
    CView* pView = GetNextView(pos);
    if (pView != NULL)
    {
        CFrameWnd* pFrame = pView->GetParentFrame();
        pFrame->ActivateFrame(SW_SHOW);
        pFrame = pFrame->GetParentFrame();
        if (pFrame != NULL)
            pFrame->ActivateFrame(SW_SHOW);
    }
}
```

SetRGB lets the automation client change all the colors at once with one line of code. Change the stub *SetRGB* method that ClassWizard added to look like this:

```
void COvalDoc::SetRGB(short red, short green, short blue)
{
    m_red = (BYTE) red;
    m_green = (BYTE) green;
    m_blue = (BYTE) blue;
    RefreshWindow();
}
```

Now that we have this handy *SetRGB* method, go back to *OnEditChangeColor*, and change it as follows:

```
void COvalDoc::OnEditChangeColor()
{
    CColorDialog dlg( RGB(m_red, m_green, m_blue), CC_RGBINIT);

    if (dlg.DoModal() == IDOK)
    {
        COLORREF cr = dlg.GetColor();
        SetRGB (GetRValue(cr), GetGValue(cr), GetBValue(cr));
    }
}
```

14. Recompile but don't run. Nothing has changed from a visual point of view. What we need to do now is program the application by remote control—in our case, through Excel. Don't worry if you don't have Excel. Skip to step 17

7.1
CREATE A SIMPLE OLE OBJECT AND AUTOMATION SERVER

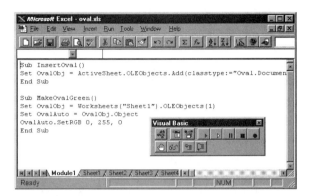

Figure 7-8 Excel macros to insert an OVAL object

to run this cool program called DispTest which is a stripped down version of Visual Basic that Microsoft ships with Developer Studio for OLE automation testing.

15. Launch Excel. Select Macro Module from the Insert menu. This will add a new tab at the bottom called Module 1. Select it and add the following Visual Basic code (see Figure 7-8):

```
Sub InsertOval()
Set OvalObj = ActiveSheet.OLEObjects.Add(classtype:="Oval.Document")
End Sub

Sub MakeOvalGreen()
Set OvalObj = Worksheets("Sheet1").OLEObjects(1)
Set OvalAuto = OvalObj.Object
OvalAuto.SetRGB 0, 255, 0
End Sub
```

The first subroutine, *InsertOval,* uses Visual Basic commands to add a new OLE object named Oval.Document to the spreadsheet. The "Oval.Document" string is looked up in the class registry and mapped to the Oval application. Then, through the magic of OLE (and about 300 pages of code later), a new Oval object is added to our spreadsheet.

The second subroutine works only after you've inserted an Oval object. It gets the OLE automation object from the oval, and then calls the exposed *SetRGB* method.

16. Execute the two macros. Switch back to the Sheet 1 tab. Then, from the Tools Macro menu, run the *InsertOval* macro. If all goes well, you'll have a new, blue circle embedded in your spreadsheet similar to the one shown in Figure 7-2.

Run the other macro, and it will change to green. To illustrate the other exposed properties, you could change the *MakeOvalGreen* to look like this:

```
Sub MakeOvalGreen()
Set OvalObj = Worksheets("Sheet1").OLEObjects(1)
Set OvalAuto = OvalObj.Object
OvalAuto.green = 255
OvalAuto.blue = 0
OvalAuto.red = 0
End Sub
```

If you watch closely, the circle will flash three times before the macro finishes. This is because OLE is secretly calling the *SetRed/Green/Blue* methods. Each one of those makes a call to *Refresh,* forcing a repaint of the *COvalSrvrItem* object which causes the flash.

17. Run DispTest.exe from the \MSDEV\Bin directory. Create two buttons called "Create Oval" and "Change Color". Double-click the Create button and edit the code to this:

```
Sub Create_Click ()
Set oval = CreateObject("Oval.Document")
oval.ShowWindow
End Sub
```

Double-click the Change button and edit the code as follows:

```
Sub Change_Click ()
oval.SetRGB 0, 255, 0
End Sub
```

Finally, select the (general) option from the Object combo and add the following line of code:

```
Dim oval As Object
```

Press [F5] to run the program then press the Create button. After a short pause, you should see Oval.exe running in its own window, but under the spell of our little Dispatch Test program (see Figure 7-9). If you press the Change color button, the blue circle should change color to green.

How It Works

This How-To illustrates two separate topics: OLE object servers and OLE automation. You've seen how to implement both and discovered that they can be developed independently. In other words, you can have a fully functional OLE server before adding OLE automation. Of course, most of the OLE details were done for you through MFC and AppWizard.

When you selected the fullserver option in AppWizard in the first step, two extra files were added that you normally don't get in a non-OLE MDI application: IpFrame.cpp and SrvrItem.cpp.

7.1
CREATE A SIMPLE OLE OBJECT AND AUTOMATION SERVER

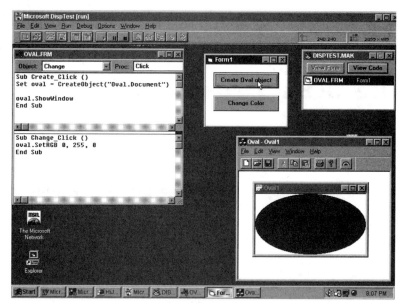

Figure 7-9 Using DispTest to control Oval

IpFrame.cpp implements a special version of a *CFrameWnd* called *COleIPFrameWnd*. This class creates and positions the control bars within the container application's document window. It also handles events when the user resizes the embedded object.

SrvrItem.cpp implements the object shared between the client and server, *COvalSrvrItem*. See the online documentation on *COleIPFrameWnd* and *COleServerItem* for more information. The *OnDraw* method provides the metafile representation of an item, allowing it to be displayed when a container application opens a compound document.

An automation client can manipulate an OLE object in two ways: by calling exposed methods or by changing exposed properties. It might be easier to think of OLE properties as C++ public member variables and OLE methods as public methods. Anything a C++ object can do through those methods, an OLE client can do too.

Comments

Can you believe we have a fully functional OLE object and automation server and we didn't even write a line of OLE code? That's because the code wizards at Microsoft wrote most of it for you and wrapped it up in some nice MFC classes.

If you want to explore OLE further, follow the excellent OLE classes tutorial that comes with Visual C++.

CHAPTER 7
OLE AND DDE

COMPLEXITY
INTERMEDIATE

7.2 How do I...
Use OLE's drag-and-drop features?

Problem

I need to drag-and-drop strings between two list boxes. I considered implementing my own communication mechanism, but I thought I might be able to use the drag-and-drop features of OLE. How do I use MFC to implement drag-and-drop between a couple of list boxes and other drop targets?

Technique

Implementing drag-and-drop between two windows is actually quite easy with MFC. Normally, you'd have to wade through hundreds of lines of the OLE SDK, but with MFC, you'll just need three classes: *COleDataSource, COleDropTarget,* and *COleDataObject*. The *COleDataSource* class is used as the data source, *COleDropTarget* represents the destination, and the data is transferred via the *COleDataObject* class. These three classes provide a relatively easy interface by abstracting a lot of the OLE SDK functions.

This How-To creates a sample application to track your ToDo tasks. You enter tasks in one list box, then drag them to another as they're completed. The drag-and-drop functionality is implemented using the three MFC classes mentioned above. You can even drag the strings right out of the listbox and into another application like Word.

Figure 7-10 shows what the ToDo application looks like when it is running. Since it uses OLE to transfer data, you'll notice that the drag-and-drop operations work between multiple instances of the application.

Steps

1. **Create a new project called ToDo using the MFC AppWizard (exe).**
Choose the Dialog-based version and press the Finish button.

Classes to be created:
Application: CToDoApp in ToDo.h and ToDo.cpp
Dialog: CToDoDlg in ToDoDlg.h and ToDoDlg.cpp

Features:
+ About box on system menu
+ 3D Controls
+ Uses shared DLL implementation (MFC40.DLL)

7.2
USE OLE'S DRAG-AND-DROP FEATURES

Figure 7-10 ToDo in action

2. Edit StdAfx.h. Add a line at the bottom to include support for OLE:

```
#include <afxole.h>
```

3. Create the new list box class. Create a subclass of *CListBox* to handle the WM_LBUTTONDOWN message and contain the OLE drop target and data source classes. Supply the following information to ClassWizard:

Class name:	CListBox
Base class:	CDragList
File:	DragList.cpp

4. Edit the dialog IDD_TODO_DIALOG. Add the controls in the following table to the IDD_TEST_DIALOG box to look like Figure 7-11. This dialog box will be used as the main window.

Control	ID	Attributes
ToDo list box	IDC_TODO	Default
Completed list box	IDC_COMPLETED	Default
Task edit field	IDC_TASK	Default, first in tab order
Add push button	IDC_ADD	Default button
Exit push button	IDOK	Default

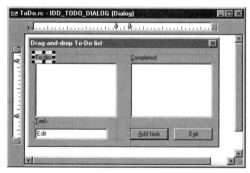

Figure 7-11 ToDo dialog layout

371

Turn on the "default button" style for the Add button, so the user can press ENTER to add the new task to the ToDo list box. Notice that the Exit push button's ID is IDOK. This will cause the dialog box to be destroyed without writing any additional code, because the *CDialog::OnOK* member function is called when you click the Exit button.

5. Use ClassWizard to add member variables for CToDoDlg. Add these member variables to attach the list boxes to *CDragList* objects, and the edit control to a window and a string.

Control ID	Type	Member
IDC_TODO	CDragList	m_listToDo
IDC_COMPLETE	CDragList	m_listComplete
IDC_TASK	CString	m_strTask
IDC_TASK	CEdit	m_wndTask

ClassWizard displays a message box reminding you to add the header file for *CDragList* to ToDoDlg.h. Do it now before continuing.

```
#include "DragList.h"
```

6. Declare the drop target class. Create a class to handle the communication between OLE and your dialog. This class is derived from the *COleDropTarget* class and will be an embedded data member of the list box class you will create later. Add the following to the top of DragList.h:

```
class CListOleDropTarget : public COleDropTarget
{
public:
        virtual DROPEFFECT OnDragEnter(CWnd* pWnd,
            COleDataObject* pDataObject, DWORD dwKeyState, CPoint point);

        virtual DROPEFFECT OnDragOver(CWnd* pWnd,
            COleDataObject* pDataObject, DWORD dwKeyState, CPoint point);

        virtual BOOL OnDrop(CWnd* pWnd,
            COleDataObject* pDataObject, DROPEFFECT dropEffect, CPoint point);
};
```

7. Define the drop target class. This file contains the code that handles the overridden functions called by the framework when a data object is first dragged, dragged over, and dropped in the list box window. Add the following class implementation near the top of DragList.cpp:

```
DROPEFFECT CListOleDropTarget::OnDragEnter(CWnd* pWnd,
    COleDataObject* pDataObject, DWORD dwKeyState, CPoint point)
{
        return OnDragOver(pWnd, pDataObject, dwKeyState, point);
}
```

7.2
USE OLE'S DRAG-AND-DROP FEATURES

```cpp
DROPEFFECT CListOleDropTarget::OnDragOver(CWnd* pWnd,
    COleDataObject* pDataObject, DWORD dwKeyState, CPoint point)
{
    // initialize the drop effect to none
    DROPEFFECT  dropEffect = DROPEFFECT_NONE;

    // check if the data object contains text data
    if (pDataObject->IsDataAvailable(CF_TEXT))
    {
        // Set effect to copy if control key is being pressed;
        // otherwise set to move if control key is not being pressed.
        dropEffect = (dwKeyState & MK_CONTROL) ?
            DROPEFFECT_COPY : DROPEFFECT_MOVE;
    }

    return dropEffect;
}

BOOL CListOleDropTarget::OnDrop(CWnd* pWnd,
    COleDataObject* pDataObject, DROPEFFECT dropEffect, CPoint point)
{
    // BUG: If we didn't pass a FORMATETC pointer, GetGlobalData would
    // have created identical to the one below except the last variable
    // would by TYMED_HGLOBAL | TYMED_MFPICT. For some reason, if you
    // use GetGlobalData in response to data dropped from a selection
    // in a Windows 95 help file, the call will fail. If you remove
    // the TYMED_MFPICT option, the call is successful. It might be
    // an OLE bug.

    // Get a handle to the clipboard text
    FORMATETC fmt = {CF_TEXT, NULL, DVASPECT_CONTENT, -1, TYMED_HGLOBAL};
    HGLOBAL hGlobal = pDataObject->GetGlobalData(CF_TEXT, &fmt);

    if (hGlobal == NULL)
        return FALSE;

    // Get a pointer to the memory
    LPCSTR pText = (LPCSTR) GlobalLock(hGlobal);

    // make sure to have valid pointer to text data
    if (AfxIsValidString(pText))
    {
        // add text to list box
        SendMessage(m_hWnd, LB_ADDSTRING, 0, (LPARAM) (LPCSTR) pText);

        // We're responsible for freeing the data
        GlobalFree(hGlobal);
        return TRUE;
    }

    return FALSE;
}
```

CHAPTER 7
OLE AND DDE

8. **Add data members to CDragList.** Add an OLE drop target class and OLE data source class to the list box class. Add the following data members to the *CToDoList* class in the file DragList.h:

```
// Operations
public:
        // Call Register usually in OnInitDialog
        void    Register ()
                { m_dropTarget.Register(this); }

protected:
        CListOleDropTarget      m_dropTarget;   // OLE drop target
        COleDataSource          m_dataSource;   // OLE data source
```

9. **Use the WizardBar to handle WM_LBUTTONDOWN for CDragList.** We need to start the drag-and-drop operation when the user presses the left-mouse button in the list box. If the current selection contains a non-empty string, we copy the string into memory allocated with the GMEM_SHARE flag. Next we give the *m_dataSource* object the memory handle using *CacheGlobalData*, then start the drag-and-drop sequence by calling *DoDragDrop*. If *DoDragDrop* returns DROPEFFECT_MOVE, it means the string was moved instead of copied, so we delete it from the list box before returning.

```
void CDragList::OnLButtonDown(UINT nFlags, CPoint point)
{
        CListBox::OnLButtonDown(nFlags, point);

        // get current selection
        int nCurSel = GetCurSel();
        if (nCurSel == LB_ERR)
            return;

        // get length of current selection
        int nLength = GetTextLen(nCurSel);
        if (nLength)
        {
                // allocate memory and get address to memory
                HGLOBAL hStr = GlobalAlloc(GMEM_FIXED | GMEM_SHARE, nLength+1);
                LPSTR pStr = (LPSTR)GlobalLock(hStr);

                if (pStr)
                {
                        GetText(nCurSel, pStr);    // copy selection from list box
                        GlobalUnlock(hStr);        // done modifying memory

                        // cache the text data
                        m_dataSource.CacheGlobalData(CF_TEXT, hStr);

                        // perform the drag and drop operation
                        DROPEFFECT dropEffect =
                            m_dataSource.DoDragDrop(
                            DROPEFFECT_COPY | DROPEFFECT_MOVE);
```

7.2
USE OLE'S DRAG-AND-DROP FEATURES

```
            // remove the selection if this was a move operation
            if (dropEffect == DROPEFFECT_MOVE)
                DeleteString(nCurSel);

            // The OLE library eats the button up message; make the list
            // box happy by simulating another button up message.
            PostMessage(WM_LBUTTONUP, nFlags, MAKELONG(point.x, point.y));
        }
    }
}
```

10. **Edit CToDoDlg::OnInitDialog.** Both *CDragList* controls must register themselves with their embedded drop target objects. We could have handled WM_CREATE in *CDragList* and called *Register* there, but that message isn't sent to subclassed controls. Since subclassed controls are attached to existing controls, Windows doesn't resend the WM_CREATE message.

```
BOOL CToDoDlg::OnInitDialog()
{
    CDialog::OnInitDialog();

    // Add "About..." menu item to system menu.

    // IDM_ABOUTBOX must be in the system command range.
    ASSERT((IDM_ABOUTBOX & 0xFFF0) == IDM_ABOUTBOX);
    ASSERT(IDM_ABOUTBOX < 0xF000);

    CMenu* pSysMenu = GetSystemMenu(FALSE);
    CString strAboutMenu;
    strAboutMenu.LoadString(IDS_ABOUTBOX);
    if (!strAboutMenu.IsEmpty())
    {
        pSysMenu->AppendMenu(MF_SEPARATOR);
        pSysMenu->AppendMenu(MF_STRING, IDM_ABOUTBOX, strAboutMenu);
    }

    SetIcon(m_hIcon, TRUE);         // Set big icon
    SetIcon(m_hIcon, FALSE);        // Set small icon

    m_listTodo.Register();
    m_listComplete.Register();

    return TRUE;  // return TRUE  unless you set the focus to a control
}
```

11. **Add a BN_CLICKED handler for IDC_ADD using WizardBar.** When you click the Add button, the contents of the Task edit field are added to the ToDo list box. Since the Add push button is the default push button, this event also occurs when you press ENTER. Add the following code to the message handler:

```
void CToDoDlg::OnAdd()
{
    // transfer contents of controls to data members
    UpdateData();
```

continued on next page

continued from previous page

```
    // process if entered a task in the task edit field
    if (m_strTask.GetLength())
    {
        // add task to the Todo list box
        m_ListTodo.AddString(m_strTask);

        // Set the focus back to the edit control
        m_wmdTask.SetSel(0, -1);
        m_wndTask.SetFocus();
    }
}
```

12. Edit CToDoApp::InitInstance. We have to initialize the OLE libraries by calling the *AfxOleInit* function in *CTestApp::InitInstance*. Add the following code to the top of the *InitInstance* method:

```
BOOL CToDoApp::InitInstance()
{
    // initialize the OLE libraries
    if (!AfxOleInit())
        return FALSE;
    ...
}
```

13. **Build and test the application.** Enter something in the Task edit control, then press the Add button. Now, click and hold the item in the left list box; the cursor should change to indicate it's suitable for dragging. Next, drop it over the right-hand list box. Drag it back to the left side, but hold the CTRL key to copy instead of move. Launch WordPad and drop some list box text into a new document.

How It Works

Clearly, there are two parts to OLE drag-and-drop: dragging and dropping. To implement the drag part, ToDo does the following:

1. Creates an instance of a *COleDataSource* class

2. Detects when the user presses the left-mouse button

3. Allocates memory for the data to be transferred (in this case, the task string)

4. Calls *COleDataSource::CacheGlobalData* to cache the data in the OLE subsystem

5. Calls *COleDataSource::DoDragDrop* to start the drag-and-drop operation

6. Removes the data from the list box if a move drop operation was performed

We created an instance of *COleDataSource* to support the source side of the data transfer. The same class could be used in other windows, like an edit control, to support drag-and-drop.

Any event can trigger a drag-and-drop operation. Our application, like most, starts the process when the left-mouse button is clicked while being held over the list item

7.2
USE OLE'S DRAG-AND-DROP FEATURES

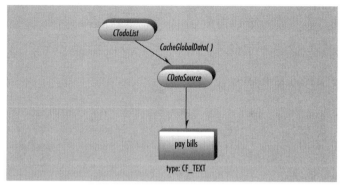

Figure 7-12 Using COleDataSource::CacheGlobalData

to be transferred. We simply detect this by handling the WM_LBUTTONDOWN message in the *CDragList* class. All this drag-and-drop business happens without help from *CDragList*'s owner, *CToDoDlg*.

You specify the data you want transfered by calling either the *CacheData* or *CacheGlobalData* member functions of the *COleDataSource* class. There are a few other methods to support delayed rendering of the data, but this sample uses *CacheGlobalData* since it is transferring a small text string. You should call the *CacheData* member function if you are transferring a large amount of data or you require a structured storage medium. Figure 7-12 illustrates this procedure.

The *COleDataSource* object caches the data until it is needed. It has a list of different cached data types, and it is responsible for freeing the cached data. The data is freed whenever it is being replaced by the same data type or it's in the destructor of the *COleDataSource* class. In this project, one data object of the data type CF_TEXT is always cached. When the application calls the *CacheGlobalData* member function, the cached data is freed and the new data takes its place. Even though you are responsible for allocating the memory for the cached data, make sure you don't free the memory. This is the responsibility of the *COleDataSource* class.

Call the *COleDataSource::DoDragDrop* member function to start a drag-and-drop operation. The function will remain in a loop until a drop occurs or until the operation is canceled. See Figure 7-13 for an illustration of this process.

The return value will indicate the drop effect generated by the drop operation. If the drop effect is DROPEFFECT_MOVE, then the data is removed from the data source list box by calling the *DeleteString* member function of the *CListBox* class.

Notice that a WM_LBUTTONUP message is posted to the list box after the drag-and-drop operation. The OLE subsystem detects and eats the WM_LBUTTONUP message in its drag-and-drop loop. This leaves the list box confused. It received a WM_LBUTTONDOWN message, but it never received a WM_LBUTTONUP message. To restore the list box to the correct state, a WM_LBUTTONDOWN message is placed in its message queue by calling the *PostMessage* function.

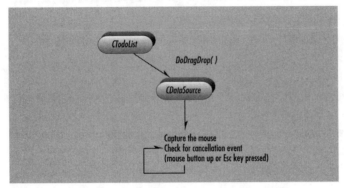

Figure 7-13 Using COleDataSource::DoDragDrop

Dropping on a Target

The other half of drag-and-drop is—you guessed it—dropping. To implement the drop operation, ToDo does the following:

1. Instantiates an object derived from *COleDropTarget* to customize the drag-and-drop handling for the list box class

2. Calls the *COleDropTarget::Register* function to register the list box window as a valid drop target window

3. Overrides *OnDragEnter* and *OnDragOver* and returns the appropriate drop effect

4. Determines whether the data object contains the CF_TEXT data format by calling the *COleDataObject::IsDataAvailable* member function

5. Overrides *OnDrop* to detect a drop operation

6. Calls *GetGlobalData* to allocate and retrieve a handle to the data being transferred

7. Adds the data string to the list box and frees the memory block storing the data

You can implement the dropping operation by using a *COleDropTarget* or derived class. *COleDropTarget* represents the target side of the data transfer. This class provides the communication mechanism between your window and the OLE subsystem.

Before you do anything, you must register windows that will participate in drag-and-drop with the OLE library. You do this by passing a pointer to the desired window to the *COleDropTarget::Register* member function. This is usually performed when handling the WM_CREATE message, but since this application subclasses the list boxes it never sees that message. This is why it provides a public member function to register the list box window as a valid drop target window. The dialog box calls this member function right after it subclasses the list boxes.

7.2
USE OLE'S DRAG-AND-DROP FEATURES

When you register a window as a drop target, the framework assigns the window to the *m_pDropTarget* protected data member of the *CWnd* class. The window must be unregistered as a drop target by calling the *COleDropTarget::Revoke* member function. The framework will automatically call this function for you when handling the WM_NCDESTROY message, so you do not need to explicitly call the function.

To allow drop operations to occur in your window, you must override two *COleDropTarget* methods: *OnDragEnter* and *OnDragOver*. They both return a code representing a cursor that illustrates either copy, move, or link.

The return drop effect depends on two things: whether the data object contains a particular format you understand and whether the [CTRL] key was pressed. You can determine whether a particular format is available in the data object by calling *IsDataAvailable*. A return value of TRUE indicates the requested data format is available; FALSE indicates it is not.

The default drop operation moves data from the source to the target. The user performs this operation by selecting the source data, dragging it, and releasing it on the drop target. The user can copy (instead of move) the data by holding down the [CTRL] key while performing the drag-and-drop operation. You can check whether the [CTRL] key is being pressed by evaluating the MK_CONTROL bit in the *dwKeyState* parameter.

The *COleDropTarget::OnDrop* member function is called when a drop operation occurs. Our application calls *GetGlobalData* to get a global memory handle to the string data. Once retrieved, we add the string to the list box by sending it the LB_ADDSTRING message. It is important to understand that the *COleDataObject* class has allocated memory for us, but we're responsible for freeing the memory. Figure 7-14 shows a diagram of this procedure.

Comments

You may want to extend other Windows controls to add drag-and-drop functionality. For instance, instead of subclassing *CListBox*, you could add drag-and-drop to *CEdit* or one of your own custom controls.

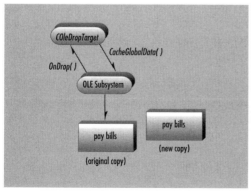

Figure 7-14 Handling OnDrop

CHAPTER 7
OLE AND DDE

COMPLEXITY
ADVANCED

7.3 How do I...
Use structured storage?

Problem

I'd like to start using the structured storage features of OLE to turn my flat-file documents into compound files. Is there a reason why I'd use structured storage over traditional file methods? How do I add compound files to an MFC application?

Technique

The OLE 2.0 structured storage specification attempts to solve several problems that have plagued traditional flat files. When the usual file I/O methods are used to store complex data, problems pop up in several areas. For example, when part of a file needs modification, the scope of the operation involves the entire file. When large files have many small updates that need to be performed quickly, performance issues often lead to splitting up the data file into smaller sections, increasing the file handling complexity in other ways. Microsoft has implemented the structured storage model with an interface called *compound files*.

Traditional file I/O techniques weigh down code when they attempt to manage the physical storage of data on the file system, instead of concentrating on the logical structure of the document. OLE 2.0 compound files alleviates some of these problems.

The OLE structured storage interface creates compound files that are organized like a file system within a file. Once the root or top-level storage is created, it can contain streams, which look and act like data files, and storages, which are similar to subdirectories. These storages can in turn contain either more storages, or streams that hold data.

A compound file breaks the different data elements into individual streams. You can update an individual stream simply by rewriting it to the underlying file system. Different data types can be grouped in the hierarchy in ways that make storage easier for the application, since the OLE storage functions will keep track of the actual bytes on the hard disk (through the *ILockBytes* interface). This allows the application to focus on content, rather than layout.

If you enable the transaction features of compound files, modifications are cached and committed later in batches. This lets you revoke changes to a file if necessary. Although this How-To doesn't cover transaction rollback, it wouldn't be too difficult to add this capability to the code.

To illustrate some of the structured storage features, the sample program for this How-To creates a new *CDocument* class called *COleDoc*. MFC already includes a *CDocument* class to handle compound files called *COleDocument*, but access to the file is limited to the constraints of *CArchive*, which doesn't know about storages and streams.

7.3
USE STRUCTURED STORAGE

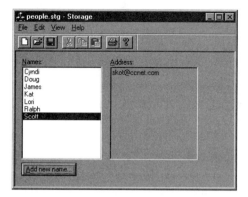

Figure 7-15 A simple database storing names and addresses

COleDoc differs from *COleDocument* in two ways: It always creates compound files (it's an option with *COleDocument*), and it doesn't use *CArchive*.

The steps show you how to create a very simple database. It associates an e-mail address with a person's name as shown in Figure 7-15. A simple dialog allows you to add new names to the view, and the standard file save and load architecture allows the data to be saved. The big difference between the traditional MFC implementation of this is the use of two new methods to take the place of Serialize.

Each name in the database corresponds to a storage of the same name. Underneath each storage is a stream named "address". The stream data contains the e-mail address. Visual C++ 4.0 includes a sample docfile viewer called DFVIEW.EXE. It was used to show the structure of a sample database as seen in Figure 7-16.

Steps

1. Create a new project called Storage using the MFC AppWizard (exe). Select the Single-Document type; press the Advanced button in step 4 and change the file extension to "stg". At the final step, make sure you change the

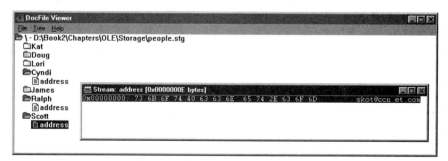

Figure 7-16 The compound file layout shown in DFVIEW.EXE

CHAPTER 7
OLE AND DDE

base class for *CStorageView* to *CFormView*, or you'll kick yourself for having to start over again when you get to step 15.

Classes to be created:
Application: CStorageApp in Storage.h and Storage.cpp
Frame: CMainFrame in MainFrm.h and MainFrm.cpp
Document: CStorageDoc in StorageDoc.h and StorageDoc.cpp
FormView: CStorageView in StorageView.h and StorageView.cpp

Features:
+ Initial toolbar in main frame
+ Initial status bar in main frame
+ Printing and Print Preview support in view
+ 3D Controls
+ Uses shared DLL implementation (MFC40.DLL)
+ Document supports files with extension .STG

Even though our application will be using OLE, don't select any of the OLE options in AppWizard. We'll add by hand the few lines of code that enable OLE support in an MFC application.

2. Create a new class called COleDoc. Use ClassWizard to create a new class using the following information:

Class name: COleDoc
Base class: CDocument
File: OleDoc.cpp

3. Use ClassWizard to add virtual functions to COleDoc. Use the ClassWizard to add support for the following virtual methods in *COleDoc*:

Object ID	Function
COleDoc	OnCloseDocument
COleDoc	OnOpenDocument
COleDoc	OnSaveDocument
COleDoc	OnNewDocument

4. Edit the OleDoc.h file. Add the following member variables and methods to OleDoc.h:

```
class COleDoc : public CDocument
{
protected:
        COleDoc();                      // protected constructor used by dynamic creation
        DECLARE_DYNCREATE(COleDoc)

//      Overrides
        // ClassWizard generated virtual function overrides
        //{{AFX_VIRTUAL(COleDoc)
```

7.3
USE STRUCTURED STORAGE

```
    public:
    virtual void Serialize(CArchive& ar);    // overridden for document i/o
    virtual void OnCloseDocument();
    virtual BOOL OnOpenDocument(LPCTSTR lpszPathName);
    virtual BOOL OnSaveDocument(LPCTSTR lpszPathName);
    protected:
    virtual BOOL OnNewDocument();
    //}}AFX_VIRTUAL

// Implementation
public:
    virtual ~COleDoc();
#ifdef _DEBUG
    virtual void AssertValid() const;
    virtual void Dump(CDumpContext& dc) const;
#endif

    // Generated message map functions
protected:
    //{{AFX_MSG(COleDoc)
    //}}AFX_MSG
    DECLARE_MESSAGE_MAP()

    LPSTORAGE m_lpRootStg;    // root storage for the document
    BOOL m_bSameAsLoad;

    // Helper methods
    DWORD AfxRelease(LPUNKNOWN* pIpUnknown);
    virtual void SaveToStorage(LPSTORAGE lpRootStg);
    virtual void LoadFromStorage(LPSTORAGE lpRootStg);
};
```

m_lpRootStg holds the top-level *IStorage* interface pointer for loading and saving the document. The *OnSave/Load/Close/OpenDocument* methods are similar to ones found in MFC's *COleDocument*.

AfxRelease is the same as the protected AFX function *_AfxRelease*. It allows you to release an OLE interface pointer while making sure the pointer is not NULL.

The two virtual methods *SaveToStorage* and *LoadFromStorage* replace the traditional serialization methods. They're called during *OnSaveDocument* and *OnLoadDocument* and are meant to be overridden by a derived class, in this case *CTestDoc*.

5. **Edit COleDoc's constructor and destructor in OleDoc.cpp.** *COleDoc's* constructor first ensures that the OLE libraries have been correctly initialized by trying to access the *IMalloc* interface exported by *CoGetMalloc*. A failure usually means *AfxOleInit* wasn't called prior to the document's creation. The normal place for *AfxOleInit* is in *CTestApp::InitInstance*. Since we didn't choose any of the OLE options in AppWizard, we'll have to add a call to *AfxOleInit* in a later step. For now, add the following code to the empty constructor body of *COleDoc*:

```
COleDoc::COleDoc()
{
```

continued on next page

continued from previous page

```
    // The CoGetMalloc trick comes straight from OLEDOC1.CPP
#ifdef _DEBUG
    // check for common mistake of not initializing OLE libraries before
    //   creating an OLE document.
    LPMALLOC lpMalloc = NULL;
    if (::CoGetMalloc(MEMCTX_TASK, &lpMalloc) != NOERROR)
    {
        TRACE0("Warning: CoGetMalloc(MEMCTX_TASK, ...) failed,\n"
            "\tperhaps AfxOleInit() has not been called.\n");
    }
    AfxRelease((LPUNKNOWN*)&lpMalloc);
#endif
    m_lpRootStg = NULL;
    m_bSameAsLoad = TRUE;
}
```

The destructor simply releases its hold on the *IStorage* interface by calling *AfxRelease* like this:

```
COleDoc::~COleDoc()
{
    // release the hold on the document storage
    AfxRelease((LPUNKNOWN*)&m_lpRootStg);
}
```

6. Edit COleDoc::OnNewDocument. The following four virtual functions take care of loading and saving documents. The first, *OnNewDocument*, is the easiest. It creates a temporary compound file by passing NULL as the first parameter to *StgCreateDocfile* and saves the resulting *IStorage* pointer in *m_lpRootStg*. Add the following code to *OnNewDocument*:

```
BOOL COleDoc::OnNewDocument()
{
    // call base class, which destroys all items
    if (!CDocument::OnNewDocument())
        return FALSE;

    // for file-based compound files, need to create temporary file
    // abort changes to the current docfile
    AfxRelease((LPUNKNOWN*)&m_lpRootStg);

    // create new temporary docfile
    LPSTORAGE lpStorage;
    HRESULT hr = StgCreateDocfile(NULL, STGM_DELETEONRELEASE|
        STGM_READWRITE|STGM_TRANSACTED|STGM_SHARE_EXCLUSIVE|STGM_CREATE,
        0, &lpStorage);
    if (hr != NOERROR)
        return FALSE;

    ASSERT(lpStorage != NULL);
    m_lpRootStg = lpStorage;

    return TRUE;
}
```

7.3
USE STRUCTURED STORAGE

7. Code *COleDoc::OnCloseDocument*. Before *OnCloseDocument* calls its parent's version of *OnCloseDocument*, it first saves the state of the auto-delete flag, *m_bAutoDelete*. If the flag wasn't set to FALSE, *CDocument::OnCloseDocument* does a "delete this" and would render any references to *m_lpRootStg* invalid. The next bit of code frees our hold in *m_lpRootStg* through a call to *AfxRelease*.

```
void COleDoc::OnCloseDocument()
{
    // close the document without deleting the memory
    BOOL bAutoDelete = m_bAutoDelete;
    m_bAutoDelete = FALSE;
    CDocument::OnCloseDocument();

    // release storage since document has been closed
    AfxRelease((LPUNKNOWN*)&m_lpRootStg);

    // delete the document if necessary
    if (bAutoDelete)
        delete this;
}
```

8. Modify *COleDoc::OnSaveDocument*. Here's where the code starts to get complicated. If the document's current filename differs from the filename passed to *OnSaveDocument*, the following code temporarily detaches the current storage object to create a new one using *StgCreateDocfile*. If all goes well, the virtual method *SaveToStorage* is used to save the bulk of the document. Since *COleDoc* was not meant to be used by itself, but as a base class, *SaveToStorage* doesn't do anything. *OnSaveDocument* is just a convenient place to create the top-level *IStorage* object.

```
BOOL COleDoc::OnSaveDocument(LPCTSTR lpszPathName)
{
    ASSERT(lpszPathName == NULL || AfxIsValidString(lpszPathName));

    LPSTORAGE lpOrigStg = NULL;
    m_bSameAsLoad = (m_strPathName == lpszPathName);

    USES_CONVERSION;

    BOOL bResult = FALSE;
    TRY
    {
        // open new root storage if necessary
        if (!m_bSameAsLoad)
        {
            // temporarily detach current storage
            lpOrigStg = m_lpRootStg;
            m_lpRootStg = NULL;

            LPSTORAGE lpStorage;
            HRESULT hr = StgCreateDocfile(T2OLE(lpszPathName),
                STGM_READWRITE | STGM_TRANSACTED |
                STGM_SHARE_EXCLUSIVE | STGM_CREATE,
                0, &lpStorage);
```

continued on next page

continued from previous page

```
                if (hr != NOERROR)
                        AfxThrowOleException(hr);

                ASSERT(lpStorage != NULL);
                m_lpRootStg = lpStorage;
        }
        ASSERT(m_lpRootStg != NULL);

        // commit the root storage
        SaveToStorage(m_lpRootStg);

        // mark document as clean if remembering the storage
        SetModifiedFlag(FALSE);

        // remember correct storage or release save copy as storage
        if (!m_bSameAsLoad)
        {
            // Save As case Ñ m_stgRoot is new storage,
            // forget old storage
            lpOrigStg->Release();
        }
        bResult = TRUE;
    }
    CATCH_ALL(e)
    {
        if (lpOrigStg != NULL)
        {
            // save as failed: abort new storage,
            // and re-attach original
            AfxRelease((LPUNKNOWN*)&m_lpRootStg);
            m_lpRootStg = lpOrigStg;
        }
        ReportSaveLoadException(lpszPathName, e,
                TRUE, AFX_IDP_FAILED_TO_SAVE_DOC);
    }
    END_CATCH_ALL

    // cleanup
    m_bSameAsLoad = TRUE;

    return bResult;
}
```

9. **Edit COleDoc::OnOpenDocument.** *OnOpenDocument* attempts to open the top-level *IStorage* object by calling *StgOpenStorage*. If the first try fails, *StgOpenStorage* is called again, but in read-only mode. The virtual helper function *LoadFromStorage* takes the top-level *IStorage* object and continues the open task. Like *SaveToStorage*, *LoadFromStorage* is a virtual function meant to be overridden by derived classes.

```
BOOL COleDoc::OnOpenDocument(LPCTSTR lpszPathName)
{
    ASSERT(lpszPathName == NULL || AfxIsValidString(lpszPathName));

    if (IsModified())
        TRACE0("Warning: OnOpenDocument replaces an unsaved document\n");
```

7.3
USE STRUCTURED STORAGE

```
    // abort changes to current docfile
    DeleteContents();
    AfxRelease((LPUNKNOWN*) &m_lpRootStg);
    SetModifiedFlag(TRUE);   // dirty during de-serialize

    USES_CONVERSION;

    BOOL bResult = FALSE;
    TRY
    {
        if (m_lpRootStg == NULL)
        {
            // open new storage file
            LPSTORAGE lpStorage;
            HRESULT hr = StgOpenStorage(T2OLE(lpszPathName), NULL,
                    STGM_READWRITE | STGM_TRANSACTED |
                    STGM_SHARE_EXCLUSIVE,
                    0, 0, &lpStorage);

            if (hr != NOERROR)
            {
                    hr = StgOpenStorage(T2OLE(lpszPathName), NULL,
                            STGM_READ | STGM_TRANSACTED |
                            STGM_SHARE_EXCLUSIVE,
                            0, 0, &lpStorage);
            }

            if (hr != NOERROR)
            {
                    AfxThrowOleException(hr);
            }

            ASSERT(lpStorage != NULL);
            m_lpRootStg = lpStorage;
        }

        // here's where you'd load the document
        LoadFromStorage(m_lpRootStg);

        SetModifiedFlag(FALSE); // start off with unmodified
        bResult = TRUE;
    }
    CATCH_ALL(e)
    {
        DeleteContents();   // removed failed contents
        AfxRelease((LPUNKNOWN*)&m_lpRootStg);

        // if not file-based load, return exceptions to the caller
        ReportSaveLoadException(lpszPathName, e,
                    FALSE, AFX_IDP_FAILED_TO_OPEN_DOC);
    }
    END_CATCH_ALL

    return bResult;
}
```

CHAPTER 7
OLE AND DDE

10. **Code the helper methods in OleDoc.cpp.** Add the following three methods to the bottom of OleDoc.cpp:

```
// taken verbatim from _AfxRelease (it was such a useful function!)
DWORD COleDoc::AfxRelease(LPUNKNOWN* plpUnknown)
{
    ASSERT(plpUnknown != NULL);
    if (*plpUnknown != NULL)
    {
        DWORD dwRef = (*plpUnknown)->Release();
        *plpUnknown = NULL;
        return dwRef;
    }
    return 0;
}

void COleDoc::SaveToStorage(LPSTORAGE lpRootStg)
{
    ASSERT(lpRootStg != NULL);
}

void COleDoc::LoadFromStorage(LPSTORAGE lpRootStg)
{
    ASSERT(lpRootStg != NULL);
}
```

11. **Change CStorageDoc's base class.** Replace every occurrence of *CDocument* in StorageDoc.cpp and StorageDoc.h with *COleDoc* using Visual C++'s search and replace dialog.

12. **Edit the StorageDoc.h file.** Modify the interface for *CTestDoc* to look like the following:

```
#include "oledoc.h"

class CStorageDoc : public COleDoc
{
protected: // create from serialization only
    CStorageDoc();
    DECLARE_DYNCREATE(CStorageDoc)

// Overrides
    // ClassWizard generated virtual function overrides
    //{{AFX_VIRTUAL(CStorageDoc)
    public:
    virtual BOOL OnNewDocument();
    virtual void Serialize(CArchive& ar);
    //}}AFX_VIRTUAL

// Implementation
public:
    virtual ~CStorageDoc();
#ifdef _DEBUG
    virtual void AssertValid() const;
    virtual void Dump(CDumpContext& dc) const;
#endif
```

7.3
USE STRUCTURED STORAGE

```
    // Generated message map functions
protected:
    //{{AFX_MSG(CStorageDoc)
    //}}AFX_MSG
    DECLARE_MESSAGE_MAP()

public:
    CMapStringToString   m_map;

protected:
    virtual void LoadFromStorage(LPSTORAGE lpRootStg);
    virtual void SaveToStorage(LPSTORAGE lpRootStg);

    // helper function for LoadFromStorage
    BOOL ReadName(LPSTORAGE lpRootStg, const char* pSubStgName);
};
```

13. Edit StorageDoc.cpp. The following three methods are used for loading and saving the *CStorageDoc* object. Add this code to the end of StorageDoc.cpp:

```
void CStorageDoc::SaveToStorage(LPSTORAGE lpRootStg)
{
    ASSERT(lpRootStg != NULL);
    DWORD dwCScode = STGM_WRITE | STGM_DIRECT |
        STGM_SHARE_EXCLUSIVE | STGM_CREATE;

    USES_CONVERSION;

    POSITION pos = m_map.GetStartPosition();
    while (pos != NULL)
    {
        COleStreamFile file;
        LPSTORAGE lpNameStorage;
        CString name;
        CString address;
        m_map.GetNextAssoc(pos, name, address);

        // Create a storage named name
        // With a stream called "Address" with address as its contents

        // Create name storage.
        if (FAILED(lpRootStg->CreateStorage(T2OLE(name),
                dwCScode, 0, 0, &lpNameStorage)))
            break;

        // Create address stream under lpNameStorage;
        if (file.CreateStream(lpNameStorage, "address",
                CFile::modeWrite|CFile::shareExclusive|CFile::modeCreate,
                NULL))
        {
            file.Write(address, address.GetLength());
            file.Close();
        }
```

continued on next page

CHAPTER 7
OLE AND DDE

continued from previous page

```
            lpNameStorage->Release();
        }
        m_lpRootStg->Commit(STGC_ONLYIFCURRENT);
}

void CStorageDoc::LoadFromStorage(LPSTORAGE lpRootStg)
{
        ASSERT(lpRootStg != NULL);

        m_map.RemoveAll();

        // Enumerate the storages under lpRootStg
        LPENUMSTATSTG lpEnum;
        STATSTG ss;
        ULONG ulCount;
        ULONG size;
        CString storageName;
        CString address;
        USES_CONVERSION;

        // Assume we have a valid IStorage instance in lpStorage,
        // so get the enumerator

        if (lpRootStg->EnumElements(0, NULL, 0, &lpEnum) != NOERROR)
                return;    // unable to get storage enumerator

        // Continue enumeration until IEnumStatStg->Next returns non-S_OK
        while (TRUE)
        {
                // Enumerate one element at a time
                if (FAILED(lpEnum->Next(1, &ss, &ulCount)))
                {
                        lpEnum->Release();
                        return;
                }

                // Possible values for ss.type are:
                // STGTY_... STREAM|STORAGE|LOCKBYTES|PROPERTY
                // For our particular format, we only care about STORAGE types
                if (ss.type != STGTY_STORAGE)
                        break;

                storageName = OLE2T(ss.pwcsName);

                VERIFY(ReadName(lpRootStg, storageName));

                // lots of work just to free the storage name
                LPMALLOC pIMalloc;
                CoGetMalloc(MEMCTX_TASK, &pIMalloc);
                pIMalloc->Free((LPVOID)ss.pwcsName);
                pIMalloc->Release();
        }
        lpEnum->Release();
}
```

7.3
USE STRUCTURED STORAGE

```
BOOL CStorageDoc::ReadName(LPSTORAGE lpRootStg, const char* pSubStgName)
{
    ASSERT(lpRootStg != NULL);
    ASSERT(pSubStgName != NULL);

    LPSTORAGE lpStorage;

    USES_CONVERSION;

    // Open the storage object named pSubStgName
    if (FAILED(lpRootStg->OpenStorage(T2OLE(pSubStgName), NULL,
        STGM_READ | STGM_SHARE_EXCLUSIVE, NULL, 0, &lpStorage)))
    {
        return FALSE;
    }

    // Now that the substorage for the name is opened,
    // open the stream named "address" (there better be one)
    COleStreamFile file;
    if (file.OpenStream (lpStorage, "address",
        CFile::modeRead | CFile::shareExclusive) == FALSE)
    {
        lpStorage->Release();
        return FALSE;
    }

    // Read in the actual stream data
    CString address;
    DWORD dwLen = file.GetLength();
    char* pAddress = address.GetBufferSetLength(dwLen);
    file.Read(pAddress, dwLen);
    address.ReleaseBuffer();
    file.Close();

    // All done with this storage, so Release it
    lpStorage->Release();

    // Add the data to the map
    m_map.SetAt(pSubStgName, address);

    return TRUE;
}
```

14. Edit CStorageDoc::OnNewDocument. Since this application is SDI, we have to empty the map when the framework creates a new document. Add the following line of code to *OnNewDocument*:

```
BOOL CStorageDoc::OnNewDocument()
{
    if (!COleDoc::OnNewDocument())
        return FALSE;

    m_map.RemoveAll();
    return TRUE;
}
```

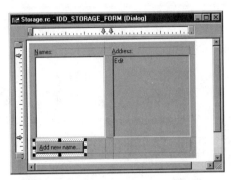

Figure 7-17 Dialog layout for the STORAGE application

15. **Edit the IDD_STORAGE_FORM dialog.** Use the resource editor to modify the dialog template created by AppWizard. The control should have two list boxes and a button as shown in Figure 7-17 and the following table:

Control	ID	Attributes
Names list box	IDC_NAME_LIST	sorted
Address edit control	IDC_ADDRESS	read-only
Button	IDC_ADD_NAME	"&Add new name...", default button

16. **Add a new dialog.** Press the right-mouse button over Dialog and choose Insert Dialog from the pop-up menu. Rename the new dialog from IDD_DIALOG1 to IDD_ADD_NAME. *CStorageView* will use this dialog to get a name and e-mail address from the user. The control should have two edit controls as shown in Figure 7-18 and the following table:

Control	ID	Attributes
Name edit	IDC_NAME	default
Address edit	IDC_ADDRESS	multiline, vertical scroll bar

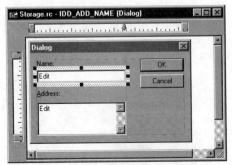

Figure 7-18 Add Name dialog layout

7.3 USE STRUCTURED STORAGE

17. Create a dialog class for IDD_ADD_NAME. Use ClassWizard to create a class representing IDD_ADD_NAME using the following information:

Class name:	CAddName
Base class:	CDialog
File:	AddName.cpp
Dialog:	IDD_ADD_NAME

18. Add message handlers and member variables for CStorageView. Using the first two tabs in ClassWizard, add the following message handlers and member variables for *CTestView*:

Object ID	Function	Message
CTestView	OnInitialUpdate	
IDC_ADD_NAME	OnAddName	BN_CLICKED
IDC_NAME_LIST	OnSelchangeNameList	LBN_SELCHANGE

Control ID	Type	Member
IDC_ADDRESS	CString	m_sAddress
IDC_NAME_LIST	CListBox	m_wndNameList

19. Add member variables for CAddName. Use ClassWizard to add these two variables to the *CAddName* dialog:

Control ID	Type	Member
IDC_ADDRESS	CString	m_sAddress
IDC_NAME	CString	m_sName

20. Edit the StorageView.cpp file. First, add the following line to the top of StorageView.cpp to pull in the interface file for *CAddName*:

```
#include "AddName.h"
```

Write the code that corresponds to the Add Names to List button on the *CFormView*. The following method simply displays the *CAddName* dialog, pulls the name and address fields out of the dialog, then adds them to the document and the list box.

```
void CStorageView::OnAddName()
{
    CAddName dlg;

    if (dlg.DoModal())
    {
        CMapStringToString& map = GetDocument()->m_map;
        map.SetAt(dlg.m_sName, dlg.m_sAddress);
```

continued on next page

continued from previous page

```
            m_wndNameList.AddString(dlg.m_sName);
            GetDocument()->SetModifiedFlag();
    }
}
```

OnSelchangeNameList is called when a new selection is made in the names list box. It retrieves the address associated with the selected name, and displays it in the IDC_ADDRESS edit control.

```
void CStorageView::OnSelchangeNameList()
{
    CString sText;
    int nSel = m_wndNameList.GetCurSel();
    m_wndNameList.GetText(nSel, sText);

    // Lookup name in the document map
    CString sAddress;
    if (GetDocument()->m_map.Lookup(sText, sAddress))
    {
        m_sAddress = sAddress;
        UpdateData(FALSE);
    }
}
```

OnInitialUpdate enumerates the strings in the document's map and adds them to the list box.

```
void CStorageView::OnInitialUpdate()
{
    m_sAddress.Empty();
    CFormView::OnInitialUpdate();

    CMapStringToString& map = GetDocument()->m_map;

    m_wndNameList.ResetContent();
    POSITION pos = map.GetStartPosition();
    while (pos != NULL)
    {
        CString name;
        CString address;

        map.GetNextAssoc(pos, name, address);

        m_wndNameList.AddString(name);
    }

    // artificially select the first item in the list box
    if (!map.IsEmpty())
    {
        m_wndNameList.SetCurSel(0);
        OnSelchangeNameList();
    }
}
```

7.3
USE STRUCTURED STORAGE

21. Edit StdAfx.h. Add the following line to the bottom of the file to pull in the OLE files:

```
#include <afxwin.h>      // MFC core and standard components
#include <afxext.h>      // MFC extensions
#include <afxole.h>      // MFC OLE classes
#include <afxpriv.h>     // for Unicode translation halpers (see TN59)
```

22. Edit CStorageApp::InitInstance. Add this one line of code to *InitInstance* to initialize the OLE libraries:

```
BOOL CStorageApp::InitInstance()
{
    // Standard initialization
    AfxOleInit();
```

23. Build and test the application. Add a few names and addresses to the document using the Add Names button. Then save the document and convince yourself that it worked by reloading the file. To really see how the file is structured (no pun intended), use the docfile viewer program DFVIEW.EXE that comes with Developer Studio (it should be in \MSDEV\BIN). It will show you something similar to Figure 7-13.

How It Works

The program starts off with an empty document. When you press the Add Names to List button, the *CAddName* dialog prompts you for a name and address. These are then added to the document's *CMapStringToString* container and the name is appended to the list box. This part is simple; the *CTestView* object has no idea that structured storage will be used to save the data.

Saving the Document

When the empty document is first created, *COleDoc::OnNewDocument* sets up a temporary compound file and saves a pointer to the top-level or root storage object. Later, when the document is saved with a different name, the temporary storage is disposed of and a new storage is saved under the name chosen by the user. *COleDoc::OnSaveDocument* differs from the *CDocument* version here because it doesn't create a *CArchive* object for use in a *Serialize* call. Instead, the virtual method *SaveToStorage* is invoked and *CTestDoc* gets a chance to write the names and addresses to the file.

SaveToStorage takes as its only argument the root storage object—actually a pointer to an instance of the *IStorage* interface. *COleDoc* doesn't care what you do inside *SaveToStorage*, because it's up to the derived classes to manage the content of the compound file. *COleDoc* is only responsible for the root storage object; what's underneath the root storage object is the responsibility of the derived class.

Each name is saved in the string map as its own storage object. Underneath each storage is a single stream named "address". To create the substorages, *SaveToStorage* enumerates the names and calls *IStorage::CreateStorage* for each one. If the storage creation was successful, a stream named "address" is created under the storage using the MFC class *COleStreamFile*. If the stream creation worked, the address is saved to the file and the file is closed. After all of the named storages are created, the root storage object is committed to the disk using *IStorage::Commit*.

Loading the Document

When you open a file, *COleDoc::OnLoadDocument* takes over. It tries to open the root storage with read-write permissions. After that, content loading takes place through the virtual method *LoadFromStorage*.

CTestDoc::LoadFromStorage is a little more complicated than *SaveToStorage* because it uses another OLE interface, *IEnum*, to enumerate the substorages in the document. *IStorage::EnumElements* returns a LPENUMSTATSTG pointer that allows us to enumerate the storages under the root level. Each storage name is passed to a helper function named *ReadName*, where the storage and "address" stream are opened, and the data is added directly to the *CMapStringToString* object.

When *ReadName* returns, the string data created by the *IEnum* object is freed using the *IMalloc* interface.

Comments

One of the benefits of compound files is that you can add new storages to a file and maintain backwards compatibility. For example, if we had used the standard *CArchive* method for saving the names and addresses, we would have a problem if a newer version saved phone numbers too. Older versions of the program wouldn't be able to read the new data format. Using compound files, a whole new substorage could be created to save the phone numbers, without disturbing the format for the names and addresses.

One more thing: The Oval program created in the first How-To for this chapter saves its data in compound files. I created a green oval and saved it as green.ovl. Since it archives only three bytes of information (the red, green, and blue colors), it's pretty easy to decode using DFVIEW.EXE (see Figure 7-19). Since Oval used the default *COleDocument* methods for creating a compound file, a generic storage called "Contents" was created automatically to hold the output from *Serialize*.

Figure 7-19 Using DFVIEW on a green Oval object

CREATE A DDE OBJECT TO TALK TO OTHER APPLICATIONS

COMPLEXITY
INTERMEDIATE

7.4 How do I... Create a DDE object to talk to other applications?

Problem

DDE might not be the cutting edge of interprocess communication—OLE fills that role nicely. However, there are still many applications that support DDE: The Program Manager uses it to create icons and program groups, and Excel has utilized DDE support for a long time. How can I use DDE with my MFC applications to communicate with other DDE-aware programs?

Technique

Dynamic Data Exchange (DDE) has been around for a while and has proven to be a very useful way for two programs to interact. Microsoft introduced the DDE Management Library (DDEML) to make DDE easier to use. DDEML is a set of functions that provides an easier, higher-level interface so applications can take advantage of DDE.

MFC does not encapsulate DDEML, nor does MFC provide any other special facilities for using DDE. This How-To describes the creation of a simple class for a DDE support object: *CDDEObj*. We'll use this class to create a DDE server application that answers two very important questions: What are the names of Santa's reindeer? And, who are the Seven Dwarfs?

Steps

1. Create a new project called DDE using the MFC AppWizard (exe).
Choose the dialog-based version and press the Finish button.

Classes to be created:
Application: CDDEApp in DDE.h and DDE.cpp
Dialog: CDDEDlg in DDEDlg.h and DDEDlg.cpp

Features:
+ About box on system menu
+ 3D Controls
+ Uses shared DLL implementation (MFC40.DLL)

CHAPTER 7
OLE AND DDE

2. Declare the CDDEObj Class. Create a new file called DDEObj.h and insert the following class declaration for the *CDDEObj* class like this:

```
// Declaration of CDDEObj respect.

#include <ddeml.h>

class CDDEObj
{
public:
    // Static callback member function.
    static HDDEDATA CALLBACK EXPORT DdeCallback(UINT iType, UINT iFmt,
        HCONV hCconv,
        HSZ hsz1, HSZ hsz2,
        HDDEDATA hData,
        DWORD dwData1,
        DWORD dwData2);

    // Extra copy of the first object's 'this' pointer for use
    // by the DdeCallback static member function.
    static CDDEObj* fakeThis;

    // Constructor sets up fakeThis pointer,
    // establishes DDE connection.
    CDDEObj();

private:
    // DDE instance ID
    DWORD idInst;

    // Service Name
    CString AppName;
};
```

3. Define the CDDEObj class. Create a new file called DDEObj.cpp and insert the following code:

```
// Implementation of the CDDEObj class.

#include "stdafx.h"
#include "ddeobj.h"

// Dwarf and Reindeer data that this DDE server provides.

char* Dwarfs[] = {
    "Grumpy",
    "Sleepy",
    "Sneezy",
    "Bashful",
    "Dopey",
    "Happy",
    "Doc"
};
```

7.4
CREATE A DDE OBJECT TO TALK TO OTHER APPLICATIONS

```cpp
char* Reindeer[] = {
        "Dasher",
        "Dancer",
        "Prancer",
        "Vixen",
        "Comet",
        "Cupid",
        "Donner",
        "Blitzen"
};

// Define the static fakeThis object.
CDDEObj* CDDEObj::fakeThis = NULL;

CDDEObj::CDDEObj()
{
        fakeThis = this;

        // Setup DDE
        DdeInitialize(&idInst, DdeCallback, APPCLASS_STANDARD |
                CBF_FAIL_ADVISES |
                CBF_FAIL_EXECUTES |
                CBF_FAIL_POKES |
                CBF_SKIP_REGISTRATIONS |
                CBF_SKIP_UNREGISTRATIONS, 0L);

        // Register this program as a DDE server with the service name
        // MyDDEApp.

        HSZ hszService;
        AppName = "MyDDEApp";

        hszService = DdeCreateStringHandle(idInst, AppName, 0);
        DdeNameService(idInst, hszService, NULL, DNS_REGISTER);
}

// Static callback member function.
HDDEDATA CALLBACK EXPORT CDDEObj::DdeCallback(UINT iType, UINT iFmt,
        HCONV hCconv, HSZ hsz1, HSZ hsz2, HDDEDATA hData,
        DWORD dwData1, DWORD dwData2)
{
        // Topic = hsz1;
        // Item = hsz2;

        char szBuffer[32];

        switch(iType) {
                // Handle the 'connect' transaction.
                case XTYP_CONNECT:
                // Get the application name.
                DdeQueryString(fakeThis->idInst, hsz2,
                        szBuffer, sizeof(szBuffer), 0);

                // If the application name is not supported by this server
                // return FALSE.
```

continued on next page

continued from previous page

```
                if (fakeThis->AppName != szBuffer)
                    return FALSE;

                // Get the topic name.
                DdeQueryString(fakeThis->idInst, hsz1,
                    szBuffer, sizeof(szBuffer), 0);

                // If the topic is not either 'Dwarfs' or 'Reindeer',
                // return with an error.
                if (strcmp(szBuffer, "Dwarfs") &&
                    strcmp(szBuffer , "Reindeer"))
                        return FALSE;

                // Return TRUE to indicate a successful connection.
                return (HDDEDATA) TRUE;
                break;

                // Process the 'request' transaction type.
                case XTYP_REQUEST:

                // Get the topic name.
                DdeQueryString(fakeThis->idInst, hsz1,
                    szBuffer, sizeof(szBuffer), 0);

                // Is the topic "Dwarfs"?
                if (strcmp(szBuffer, "Dwarfs") == 0)
                {
                    // Get the item name.
                    DdeQueryString(fakeThis->idInst, hsz2,
                        szBuffer, sizeof(szBuffer), 0);

                    // Convert the item name into a 'dwarfcode'.
                    int dwarfcode = atoi(szBuffer);

                    // If the dwarfcode is out of range, return failure.
                    if ((dwarfcode < 0) || (dwarfcode > 6))
                        return FALSE;

                    // Return the dwarf name which matches the dwarfcode.
                    return DdeCreateDataHandle(fakeThis->idInst,
                        (LPBYTE) Dwarfs[dwarfcode],
                        strlen(Dwarfs[dwarfcode])+1,
                        0, hsz2, CF_TEXT, 0);
                }

                // Is the topic "Reindeer"?
                if (strcmp(szBuffer, "Reindeer") == 0)
                {
                    // Get the item name.
                    DdeQueryString(fakeThis->idInst, hsz2,
                        szBuffer, sizeof(szBuffer), 0);

                    // Convert the item name into a 'deercode'.
                    int deercode = atoi(szBuffer);
```

7.4
CREATE A DDE OBJECT TO TALK TO OTHER APPLICATIONS

```
                // If the deercode is out of range, return failure.
                if ((deercode < 0) || (deercode > 7))
                    return FALSE;

                // Return the reindeer that matches the deercode
                return DdeCreateDataHandle(fakeThis->idInst,
                    (LPBYTE) Reindeer[deercode],
                    strlen(Reindeer[deercode])+1,
                    0, hsz2, CF_TEXT, 0);
            }
            break;
        }
        return NULL;
    }
```

Insert the DDEObj.cpp file into the DDE project.

4. Declare a CDDEObj object. Add the following line to the beginning of the application's main file DDE.CPP:

```
#include "ddeobj.h"
```

In addition, add the following declaration of a *CDDEObj* object:

```
// The one and only CDDEObj object
CDDEObj theDDEObj;
```

5. Add the DDEML library to the project. Since the DDE libraries aren't normally added to the linker when you use App Studio, change the linker to include DDEML.LIB.

6. Build the application. Since the program is a DDE server, it won't do anything by itself. Read on to see how to use it with a DDE client, Microsoft Excel.

How It Works

Our application is a DDE server, which means that it is up to a client application to make the data requests. Simply start up the application.

Next, we need to run our client application, Excel, and have it make requests to our server. Enter a remote reference formula in the first cell of the worksheet like this:

```
=MyDDEApp|Dwarfs!'3'
```

The remote reference formula contains a specification for a service name (MyDDEApp in this case), a topic name (Dwarfs), and an item name (here, a code of 3). The external reference in this formula causes Excel to behave as a DDE client and make a request of our DDE server for data as shown in Figure 7-20.

When this formula is evaluated, two DDE transactions are made: CONNECT and REQUEST. The CONNECT transaction calls the DDE callback function with both the service name and topic name. Although a server can handle requests for more than one service name, this is not typical. Our callback simply ensures that the requested service name is *MyDDEApp*.

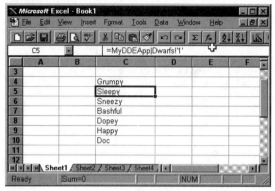

Figure 7-20 Data returned from the DDE server

The CONNECT transaction also passes the requested topic name to the callback function. Our callback function ensures that the topic name is either Dwarfs or Reindeer, which are the only two topics our application can service.

The formula evaluation also passes a REQUEST transaction to the DDE callback function. The handling of the request transaction checks for the topic (Dwarfs or Reindeer) and returns the appropriate name based on the code passed as the item name.

Comments

In step 3, we added a static member function to *CDDEObj* called *DdeCallback*. This method is what allows us to use a member function as a Windows callback function.

The problem with allowing a regular, nonstatic member function to be used as a callback lies in the fact that nonstatic member functions have an implied *this* pointer as the first, hidden argument. In other words, each normal member function is actually called with one more parameter than is actually defined. This extra parameter is the C++ this pointer. The Windows function that executes the callback obviously knows nothing about the *this* pointer. If a callback was made to an object method with a hidden this pointer, a stack fault would surely occur.

The way around this difficulty is to create a member function that is designed to omit the implied *this* pointer as an extra parameter. Such a member function is called a static member function.

Since static methods are class methods, not object methods, the concept of a *this* pointer does not apply, hence there's no access to nonstatic data members. We cheat and get around this limitation by creating a fake *this* pointer that is a static data member initialized to the value of the "real" this pointer at construction time. As long as there's only one instance of the *CDDEObj*, there's no problem using this method.

I can hear the C++ gurus groaning right now. We could have simply made the *fakeThis* pointer global, but that would have been too easy. Here, you learn how a static method can be used as a Windows callback function.

7.5 How do I... Write an OLE spin control?

COMPLEXITY: ADVANCED

Problem

OLE custom controls are poised to replace the very successful Visual Basic controls (VBXs). I understand they are built on top of OLE and are one of the driving forces behind Microsoft's component software strategy. How do I create OLE custom controls?

Technique

Microsoft has come up with some fantastic software for creating OLE custom controls and bundled it in the CDK (OLE Custom Control Development Kit). The CDK consists of development tools and MFC classes that allow you to quickly create powerful controls built on top of OLE 2.0 technology. You have probably heard or read predictions that OLE custom controls will revolutionize the software industry by taking a giant leap towards component-based software. The CDK is the tool to do it. The development kit includes ControlWizard, an extended version of ClassWizard, a Test Container application, new MFC classes, sample source code, online documentation, and a tutorial. However, one of the things it doesn't have is a truly useful control like the spin control we're going to make in this How-To.

This How-To shows you how to create an OLE custom control by building a spin button control that you can actually use in your application. A spin button control is a square window divided into two triangular buttons, each containing an arrow to indicate direction. Figure 7-21 shows two such controls, one containing up and down arrows and the other containing left and right arrows.

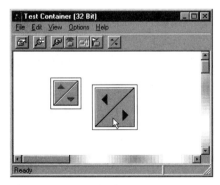

Figure 7-21 Spin button custom controls

CHAPTER 7
OLE AND DDE

First, some background. An OLE custom control is an embeddable OLE object that supports in-place activation and OLE automation. A *control* defines its interface by exposing properties and methods, and fires events to notify its container when important things happen.

Properties

Properties are the attributes of the OLE control—they're similar to public C++ members. OLE controls can define stock or custom properties. Stock properties are standard properties that are common to most OLE custom controls. Some examples of stock properties are Enabled, *hWnd*, and Caption. The *COleControl* class implements the stock properties for you. If you want to expose a stock property and use the default *COleControl* implementation, you simply use ClassWizard to select the stock property from the OLE Automation tab, and you are done. You can also override any of the stock properties.

Custom properties are attributes unique to the control you wish to expose. You can allow direct access to the property by implementing the property as a member variable. If you need to know when the property has changed, you can specify a notification function that will be called whenever the property is modified.

You'll have more control over the property if you implement it using Get/Set Methods. This allows you to define the Get function, Set function, and parameter list for the property being accessed, which is useful if you need to validate conditions and parameters before returning or setting the value of a property. Just like stock properties, you add custom properties from the OLE Automation tab of ClassWizard.

Property Pages

At runtime, the properties of your control will be modified by its container, but how do you modify control properties at design time? The answer is to use property page dialogs. Property pages provide a very convenient interface to view and modify the attributes of your control. From the developer's standpoint, developing property pages is very simple since they work just like dialog boxes. You can put all your properties into one property page, or you can organize properties into categories. Properties are often divided into General, Colors, Fonts, and Picture property pages.

Methods

Another feature that defines the interface to your OLE custom control is *methods*. Methods are similar to member functions of a class. You can expose stock or custom methods that the container application can invoke. You expose methods through the OLE Automation tab of ClassWizard. There, you specify the method's external name, internal name, return type, parameter list, and whether it is a stock method or custom method. The *external name* is the name the container application will invoke. The *internal name* is the name of the member function that implements the method.

The control in this example will expose two methods: *About* and *SetToSystemColors*. The *About* method was created by the ControlWizard and displays the *About* dialog box. The *SetToSystemColors* method is a custom method that allows the user to tell the spin button control to use colors that are defined in the Windows environment. This method could be called when processing the WM_WININICHANGED message to inform the button that the user changed his or her color settings and the new colors should be retrieved.

Events

Events provide a mechanism for your control to tell its container that something has happened, much like notification messages. As with properties and methods, there are two types of events: stock and custom. The *COleControl* class takes care of the stock events. You define custom events that make sense for your control.

The spin OCX in this How-To fires two events, an Up event and a Down event. The Up event is fired when the up or left button is pressed, and the Down event is fired when the down or right button is pressed. The container application can process these events and do whatever is appropriate, or it can completely ignore them. You add stock and custom events from the OLE Events tab of ClassWizard.

If you follow the steps outlined in this How-To, you'll have a fully-functional control to be proud of. To get the best use out of it, you can place it on the right side of an edit control. When you press the up button, the value in the edit field is incremented. The value in the edit field is decremented when the down button is pressed. The value continues to change as long as a button is pressed. Thus the name: spin button control. Figure 7-22 shows a diagram of this sequence.

You can customize much of the user interface, such as specifying the orientation of the arrows. You can also change the delay time and repeat time to customize the speed of the "spinning" effect. You can set the colors of the arrows when the button is enabled and disabled, the button face color, and the highlight and shadow colors. You can even enable or disable the up button, the down button, or the entire control.

The Up or Down event is fired when a user positions the cursor over an enabled button and clicks the left-mouse button for a specified amount of time. The button will start "spinning" after the initial delay time expires. An event is continuously fired as long as the user hold down the left-mouse button with the cursor positioned over the enabled button. Figure 7-23 shows the delay rate, repeat rate, and when events are fired.

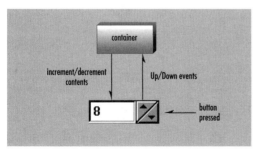

Figure 7-22 Sequence of spin button control events and actions

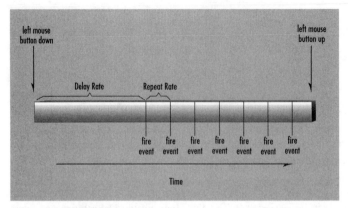

Figure 7-23 Delay rate, repeat rate, and fired events

The control exposes two methods. You can bring up the About dialog box by invoking the *About* method, and you can set the colors of the control to the colors defined in the user's Windows environment by calling *SetToSystemColors*. Normally, you'd call this method in response to a WM_WININICHANGED message.

The spin button control exposes the properties listed in the following table.

Property Name	Type	Type of Implementation
Vertical	BOOL	Member variable
UpEnabled	BOOL	Member variable
DownEnabled	BOOL	Member variable
DisableColor	OLE_COLOR	Member variable
EnableColor	OLE_COLOR	Member variable
Enabled	BOOL	Stock

The control implements the methods listed in table below.

Name	Return type	Implementation
About	void	Created by ControlWizard
SetToSystemColors	void	Custom

The control fires the events listed here:

External Name	Internal Name	Implementation
Up	FireUp	Custom
Down	FireDown	Custom

Figure 7-24 shows a spin button control along with the property page dialog box for one of the controls.

7.5
WRITE AN OLE SPIN CONTROL

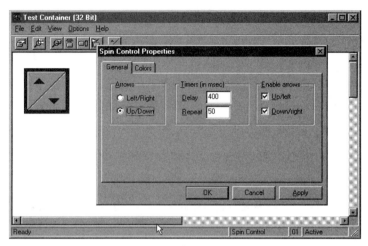

Figure 7-24 Test Container showing a spin button control

Steps

1. Create a new project workspace with the OLE ControlWizard called **Spin**. Leave all the options and press the Finish button. The options and default class names are shown here:

   DLL name: Spin.ocx
   DLL initialization code in Spin.h and Spin.cpp
   Type library source in Spin.odl

   Spin Control:
   Control class CSpinCtrl in SpinCtl.h and SpinCtl.cpp
   Property page class CSpinPropPage in SpinPpg.h and SpinPpg.cpp
   Toolbar bitmap in SpinCtl.bmp
   Activates when visible
   Has an "About" box

2. Define constants in **SpinCtl.h**. The constants are defined to indicate the hit test results, timer identifiers, and initial timer intervals. Add the following constant defines and macros to the file SpinCtl.h:

```
// Defines for hit test.
#define HIT_NOTHING      0    // did not hit up or down buttons
#define HIT_UP           1    // hit up button
#define HIT_DOWN         2    // hit down button

// Timer identifiers.
#define TIMERID_DELAY    500
#define TIMERID_REPEAT   501
```

continued on next page

continued from previous page

```
// Initial times for timers.
#define RATE_DELAY     400
#define RATE_REPEAT    50
```

3. **Add protected data members.** The spin button control can draw horizontal buttons (left and right) or vertical buttons (up and down). The orientation of the control's buttons is stored in the *m_nDirection* data member. The control can be in a variety of states; the current one is kept in the *m_wState* data member. Add the following data members to the *CSpinCtrl* declaration in the file SpinCtl.h:

```
// Implementation members
protected:
        BOOL m_bMouseOut;      // mouse outside of control area
        BOOL m_bUpClick;       // true if up button is currently pressed
        BOOL m_bDownClick;     // true if down button is currently pressed
```

4. **Edit the CSpinCtrl constructor.** The control performs three operations in its constructor: It informs the base class what interface identifiers it will be using, initializes its state, and sets its initial size. Add the following code to the constructor:

```
CSpinCtrl::CSpinCtrl()
{
        // initialize interface identifiers
        InitializeIIDs(&IID_DSpin, &IID_DSpinEvents);

        // Reset states
        m_bVertical = TRUE;
        m_bMouseOut = m_bUpClick = m_bDownClick = FALSE;

        // Set the initial size of the control.
        SetInitialSize(30,30);
}
```

5. **Add the Direction custom property.** As mentioned in the preceding step, the control can draw the direction of its buttons either as left and right or up and down. Use ClassWizard and the following attributes to add a custom property, called *Direction*, to the *CSpinCtrl* class:

External name:	Vertical
Type:	BOOL
Variable name:	m_bVertical
Notification function:	OnVerticalChanged

Edit the notification function *OnVerticalChanged* so it repaints the control when this property changes:

```
void CSpinCtrl::OnVerticalChanged()
{
        InvalidateControl();
        SetModifiedFlag();
}
```

7.5 WRITE AN OLE SPIN CONTROL

6. Add the DelayRate custom property. The control has a delay time before it starts "spinning" the spin button. In other words, a set number of milliseconds will pass after the user presses and holds down the mouse button before the control will continually fire events. This time interval is referred to as the delay rate. Use ClassWizard and the following table to add a custom property called *DelayRate* to the *CSpinCtrl* class:

External name:	DelayRate
Type:	short
Variable name:	m_nDelayRate
Notification function:	OnDelayRateChanged

7. Add the RepeatRate custom property. This property stores the number of milliseconds between firing events when the mouse button is continuously pressed. Use ClassWizard and the following table to add a property named *RepeatRate* to the class *CSpinCtrl* e:

External name:	RepeatRate
Type:	short
Variable name:	m_nRelayRate
Notification function:	OnRepeatRateChanged

8. Add the DisableColor custom property. This property stores the color of the arrow when the button is disabled. The button can be disengaged by disabling the entire control or by setting properties to disable a particular button. Add the property using the values in the following table:

External name:	DisableColor
Type:	OLE_COLOR
Variable name:	m_clrDisable
Notification function:	OnDisableColorChanged

Press the Edit code button and modify *OnDisableColorChange* so it repaints the control when the property changes.

```
void CSpinCtrl::OnDisableColorChanged()
{
        InvalidateControl();
        SetModifiedFlag();
}
```

9. Add the EnableColor custom property. This property stores the color of the arrow when the button is enabled. Add the property using the values in the following table:

External name:	EnableColor
Type:	OLE_COLOR
Variable name:	m_clrEnable
Notification function:	OnEnableColorChanged

Press the Edit code button and modify *OnEnableColorChange* so it repaints the control when the property changes.

```
void CSpinCtrl::OnEnableColorChanged()
{
    InvalidateControl();
    SetModifiedFlag();
}
```

10. Add the DownEnabled custom property. This property is TRUE if the down button is enabled and FALSE if the down button is disabled. Use ClassWizard to add a property named *DownEnabled* to the class *CSpinCtrl* using the following table:

External name:	DownEnabled
Type:	BOOL
Variable name:	m_bDownEnabled
Notification function:	OnDownEnabledChanged

Are you beginning to see a pattern here? Repaint the control when this property changes by modifying the notification method like this:

```
void CSpinCtrl::OnDownEnabledChanged()
{
    InvalidateControl();
    SetModifiedFlag();
}
```

11. Add the UpEnabled custom property. This property is TRUE if the up button is enabled and FALSE if it is is disabled. Use ClassWizard to add a property named *UpEnabled* to the class *CSpinCtrl* using the following table:

External name:	UpEnabled
Type:	BOOL
Variable name:	m_bUpEnabled
Notification function:	OnUpEnabledChanged

Again, repaint the control when this property changes by modifying the notification method like this:

```
void CSpinCtrl::OnUpEnabledChanged()
{
    InvalidateControl();
    SetModifiedFlag();
}
```

12. Add the Enabled stock property. This property is TRUE if the entire control is enabled and FALSE if the control is disabled. Use ClassWizard to add the Enabled stock property to the *CSpinCtrl* class.

7.5
WRITE AN OLE SPIN CONTROL

13. **Add the SetToSystemColors custom method.** This method allows the client to set the control's colors to the values specified in the user's Windows environment. Use ClassWizard to add a custom method to the control using the following table:

External name:	SetToSystemColors
Internal name:	SetToSystemColors
Return type:	void
Parameters:	none

Edit the *CSpinCtrl::SetToSystemColors* function as follows:

```
void CSpinCtrl::SetToSystemColors()
{
    // Initialize colors of control to
    // colors defined in Windows environment.
    m_clrEnable = GetSysColor(COLOR_BTNTEXT);
    m_clrDisable = GetSysColor(COLOR_GRAYTEXT);

    // Redraw the control.
    InvalidateControl();
}
```

14. **Add custom events to the control.** Events allow the control to notify its container when something happens. This control notifies its container when someone has clicked the up or down button. The container will receive the event and can either process or ignore it.

Use the OLE Events tab in the ClassWizard to add two events called "Up" and "Down". Neither event sends any parameters.

15. **Override the OnSetExtent member function.** The spin button control has a special condition: it must be a square. We can control the size by overriding the *OnSetExtent* member function. Since it's not handled by ClassWizard, add the following to SpinCtrl.h:

```
protected:
    // Resizing control.
    virtual BOOL OnSetExtent(LPSIZEL lpSizeL);
```

Now add the following member function implementation to the *CSpinCtrl* class:

```
BOOL CSpinCtrl::OnSetExtent(LPSIZEL lpSizeL)
{
    // Make sure control is square.
    lpSizeL->cx = min(lpSizeL->cx, lpSizeL->cy);
    lpSizeL->cy = lpSizeL->cx;
    return COleControl::OnSetExtent(lpSizeL);
}
```

16. **Serialize the properties.** Since your control is an OLE object, it can be serialized to a compound file. This means you can initialize properties when the control is being initialized, save the value of properties when the control is being saved, and restore the value of properties when the control is being loaded from storage. Fortunately, all you have to do is override the *DoPropExchange* member function of the *COleControl* class and call the appropriate PX_* functions. For example, the following line initializes the *UpEnabled* property to TRUE, writes the contents of the data member *m_bUpEnabled* when the control is being saved to storage, and loads the value of the *UpEnabled* property to the data member *m_bUpEnabled* when the control is loaded from storage:

```
PX_Bool(pPX, _T("UpEnabled"), m_bUpEnabled, TRUE);
```

The first parameter is a pointer to a *CPropertyExchange* object that is passed to the *COleControl::DoPropExchange* member function. The name of the property is specified as the second parameter. Notice the __T macro which is used for the literal string *UpEnabled*. You should use this macro with all literal strings since it provides compatibility between different string representations. The third parameter is the member variable that holds the value of the exposed property, and the last parameter is the default value of the property.

Add code to the *DoPropExchange* member function for the *CSpinCtrl* class in the file SpinCtrl.cpp, as follows:

```
void CSpinCtrl::DoPropExchange(CPropExchange* pPX)
{
    ExchangeVersion(pPX, MAKELONG(_wVerMinor, _wVerMajor));
    COleControl::DoPropExchange(pPX);

    // Our control properties.
    PX_Short(pPX, _T("Direction"), m_nDirection, DIRECTION_VERTICAL);
    PX_Bool(pPX, _T("UpEnabled"), m_bUpEnabled, TRUE);
    PX_Bool(pPX, _T("DownEnabled"), m_bDownEnabled, TRUE);
    PX_Short(pPX, _T("DelayRate"), m_nDelayRate, RATE_DELAY);
    PX_Short(pPX, _T("RepeatRate"), m_nRepeatRate, RATE_REPEAT);

    // Color properties.
    PX_Long(pPX, __T("FaceColor"),
        (long&)m_clrFaceColor, GetSysColor(COLOR_BTNFACE));

    PX_Long(pPX, __T("EnableColor"),
        (long&)m_clrEnableColor, GetSysColor(COLOR_BTNTEXT));

    PX_Long(pPX, __T("DisableColor"),
        (long&)m_clrDisableColor, GetSysColor(COLOR_GRAYTEXT));

    PX_Long(pPX, __T("HightlightColor"),
        (long&)m_clrHighlightColor, GetSysColor(COLOR_BTNHIGHLIGHT));

    PX_Long(pPX, __T("ShadowColor"),
        (long&)m_clrShadowColor, GetSysColor(COLOR_BTNSHADOW));
}
```

7.5
WRITE AN OLE SPIN CONTROL

17. Draw the control. The framework calls the *OnDraw* member function when your control needs to be drawn. There is a lot of code in this control's drawing function, but don't be alarmed. This is where all the work takes place for the spin button control. It simply draws the up and down buttons in their appropriate states. It calls the GDI command *Polyline* instead of *MoveTo/LineTo* because this command can significantly improve the performance of Win32 applications running on Windows 3.1, Windows NT, and future Windows operating systems.

It is important to remember you are living and cooperating with the container application. You draw on the DC passed to you by the container application. You need to make sure you draw within your designated rectangle, which is defined by the argument *rcBounds*. You cannot assume your upper-left corner is at location (0, 0) either. Add the following code to the *OnDraw* member function of the *CSpinCtrl* class in the file SpinCtrl.cpp:

```
void CSpinCtrl::OnDraw(
    CDC* pdc, const CRect& rcBounds, const CRect& rcInvalid)
{
    // Create brushes and pens that will be used to draw control.
    CBrush   brushFace (GetSysColor(COLOR_BTNFACE));
    CBrush   brushEnable (TranslateColor(m_clrEnable));
    CBrush   brushDisable (TranslateColor(m_clrDisable));
    CPen     penHighlight (PS_SOLID, 0, GetSysColor(COLOR_BTNHIGHLIGHT));
    CPen     penShadow (PS_SOLID, 0, GetSysColor(COLOR_BTNSHADOW));

    // Use an array of points with the GDI call Polyline
    // instead of the GDI calls MoveTo and LineTo.
    POINT pts[3];

    // Bounding rect of drawing area.
    CRect rect = rcBounds;

    // Make sure drawing area is a square.
    rect.right = rect.left + min(rect.Width(), rect.Height());
    rect.bottom = rect.top + rect.Width();

    // Even though we override OnSetExtent, sometimes the control
    // is still not square. So just fill in the unused rectangle
    // with the ambient background color.
    CRect rectUnused(rcBounds);
    rectUnused.SubtractRect(rectUnused, rect);
    CBrush brushBack(TranslateColor(AmbientBackColor()));
    pdc->FillRect(rectUnused, &brushBack);

    // Save the original pen and brushes to restore the DC after
    // you are done. Remember, this is actually the containers DC.
    CBrush* pOrgBrush =
        pdc->SelectObject(&brushFace);

    CPen* pOrgPen = pdc->SelectObject(
        CPen::FromHandle((HPEN)::GetStockObject(BLACK_PEN)));
```

continued on next page

CHAPTER 7
OLE AND DDE

continued from previous page

```
    // Draw the outer frame and fill in the face.
    pdc->Rectangle(rect);


    // Adjust the rectangle for the buttons.
    rect.left += 1;
    rect.top += 1;
    rect.right -= 2;
    rect.bottom -= 2;

    // Draw the divider line.
    SetPoint(&pts[0], rect.left, rect.bottom);
    SetPoint(&pts[1], rect.right, rect.top);
    SetPoint(&pts[2], rect.left, rect.bottom);
    pdc->Polyline(pts, 3);

    // Draw the up button.

    // Determine if we should draw the up button in the 'in' position.
    if (m_bUpClick && !m_bMouseOut)
    {
        // Draw shadow, select pen, create points, draw shadow.
        pdc->SelectObject(&penShadow);
        SetPoint(&pts[0], rect.left, rect.bottom-1);
        SetPoint(&pts[1], rect.left, rect.top);
        SetPoint(&pts[2], rect.right, rect.top);
        pdc->Polyline(pts, 3);
    }

    // Draw the up button in the 'out' position.
    else
    {
        // Draw highlight, select pen, create points, draw highlight.
        pdc->SelectObject(&penHighlight);
        SetPoint(&pts[0], rect.left, rect.bottom-1);
        SetPoint(&pts[1], rect.left, rect.top);
        SetPoint(&pts[2], rect.right-1, rect.top);
        pdc->Polyline(pts, 3);

        // Draw shadow, select pen, create points, draw shadow.
        pdc->SelectObject(&penShadow);
        SetPoint(&pts[0], rect.left, rect.bottom-1);
        SetPoint(&pts[1], rect.right-1, rect.top);
        SetPoint(&pts[2], rect.left, rect.bottom-1);
        pdc->Polyline(pts, 3);
    }


    // Draw the down button.

    // Determine if we should draw the down button in the 'in' position.
    if (m_bDownClick && !m_bMouseOut)
    {
        // Draw shadow, select pen, create points, draw shadow.
        pdc->SelectObject(&penShadow);
```

7.5
WRITE AN OLE SPIN CONTROL

```
            SetPoint(&pts[0], rect.left+1, rect.bottom);
            SetPoint(&pts[1], rect.right, rect.top+1);
            SetPoint(&pts[2], rect.left+1, rect.bottom);
            pdc->Polyline(pts, 3);
    }

    // Draw the down button in the 'out' position.
    else
    {
            // Draw shadow, select pen, create points, draw shadow.
            pdc->SelectObject(&penShadow);
            SetPoint(&pts[0], rect.left+1, rect.bottom);
            SetPoint(&pts[1], rect.right, rect.bottom);
            SetPoint(&pts[2], rect.right, rect.top+1);
            pdc->Polyline(pts, 3);

            // Draw highlight, select pen, create points, draw highlight.
            pdc->SelectObject(&penHighlight);
            SetPoint(&pts[0], rect.right, rect.top+1);
            SetPoint(&pts[1], rect.left+1, rect.bottom);
            SetPoint(&pts[2], rect.right, rect.top+1);
            pdc->Polyline(pts, 3);
    }


    // Draw the arrows.

    // If one button is depressed, set the offset variables that we use
    // to shift the small arrow image down and right.

    CPoint ptUpOffset(0,0);
    CPoint ptDownOffset(0,0);

    // Determine if up button is clicked.
    if (m_bUpClick)
            ptUpOffset.Offset(1, 1);

    // Determine if the down button is clicked.
    else if (m_bDownClick)
            ptDownOffset.Offset(1, 1);

    // Calculate placement of arrows.
    int nCenterUp = (3 * (rect.Height() + 1)) / 10;
    int nCenterDown = (7 * (rect.Height() + 1)) / 10;
    CPoint ptCenterUp(nCenterUp + rect.left, nCenterUp + rect.top);
    CPoint ptCenterDown(nCenterDown + rect.left, nCenterDown + rect.top);

    // Arrow points.
    POINT ptsUpArrow[3], ptsDownArrow[3];

    // Calculate size of arrow.
    int nSize = (int)((rect.Height()) * 3.0 / 20.0);

    // Set the points of the up and down arrows.
    if (m_bVertical)
    {
```

continued on next page

CHAPTER 7
OLE AND DDE

continued from previous page

```
        // Set up arrow points.
        SetPoint(&ptsUpArrow[0],
            ptUpOffset.x + ptCenterUp.x - nSize,
            ptUpOffset.y + ptCenterUp.y);
        SetPoint(&ptsUpArrow[1],
            ptUpOffset.x + ptCenterUp.x + nSize,
            ptUpOffset.y + ptCenterUp.y);
        SetPoint(&ptsUpArrow[2],
            ptUpOffset.x + ptCenterUp.x,
            ptUpOffset.y + ptCenterUp.y - nSize);

        // Set down arrow points.
        SetPoint(&ptsDownArrow[0],
            ptDownOffset.x + ptCenterDown.x - nSize,
            ptDownOffset.x + ptCenterDown.y);
        SetPoint(&ptsDownArrow[1],
            ptDownOffset.x + ptCenterDown.x + nSize,
            ptDownOffset.x + ptCenterDown.y);
        SetPoint(&ptsDownArrow[2],
            ptDownOffset.x + ptCenterDown.x,
            ptDownOffset.y + ptCenterDown.y + nSize);
    }

    // Set the points of the left and right arrows.
    else
    {
        // Set left arrow points.
        SetPoint(&ptsUpArrow[0],
            ptUpOffset.x + ptCenterUp.x,
            ptUpOffset.y + ptCenterUp.y - nSize);
        SetPoint(&ptsUpArrow[1],
            ptUpOffset.x + ptCenterUp.x,
            ptUpOffset.y + ptCenterUp.y + nSize);
        SetPoint(&ptsUpArrow[2],
            ptUpOffset.x + ptCenterUp.x - nSize,
            ptUpOffset.y + ptCenterUp.y);

        // Set right arrow points.
        SetPoint(&ptsDownArrow[0],
            ptDownOffset.x + ptCenterDown.x,
            ptDownOffset.y + ptCenterDown.y - nSize);
        SetPoint(&ptsDownArrow[1],
            ptDownOffset.x + ptCenterDown.x,
            ptDownOffset.y + ptCenterDown.y + nSize);
        SetPoint(&ptsDownArrow[2],
            ptDownOffset.x + ptCenterDown.x + nSize,
            ptDownOffset.y + ptCenterDown.y);
    }

    // Select the pen used for the arrow's border.
    pdc->SelectObject(CPen::FromHandle((HPEN)::GetStockObject(BLACK_PEN)));

    // Select brush to draw the up button's arrow.
    (GetEnabled() && m_bUpEnabled) ?
        pdc->SelectObject(&brushEnable) :
        pdc->SelectObject(&brushDisable);
```

7.5
WRITE AN OLE SPIN CONTROL

```
    // Draw the up arrow.
    pdc->Polygon(ptsUpArrow, 3);

    // Select brush to draw the down button's arrow.
    (GetEnabled() && m_bDownEnabled) ?
        pdc->SelectObject(&brushEnable) :
        pdc->SelectObject(&brushDisable);

    // Draw the down arrow.
    pdc->Polygon(ptsDownArrow, 3);

    // Restore state of dc.
    pdc->SelectObject(pOrgBrush);
    pdc->SelectObject(pOrgPen);
}
```

18. **Declare and implement helper methods.** The function *HitTest* determines whether a point is within the up button or down button region of the spin control. The *SetPoint* member function just sets the x and y elements of a POINT structure. Add the following function declaration to the *CSpinCtrl* class in the file SpinCtrl.h:

```
// Helper methods
protected:
    short   HitTest(const CPoint& point);
    inline void SetPoint(POINT* pPoint, int x, int y)
        {pPoint->x = x; pPoint->y = y;}
```

Now implement the *HitTest* private member function by adding the following code to the SPINCTRL.CPP file:

```
short CSpinCtrl::HitTest(const CPoint& point)
{
    // Initialize hit result to nothing.
    short nHitResult = HIT_NOTHING;

    // Perform a hit test only within the size of the control. Make sure
    // the control is a square.
    CRect rect;
    GetClientRect(rect);
    int nSize = min(rect.Width(), rect.Height());

    CPoint  ptsButton[3];                   // coordinates of button
    CRgn rgnUpButton, rgnDownButton;        // button regions

    // Perform hit test on 'up button' only if enabled.
    if (m_bUpEnabled)
    {
        // Derive coordinates of up button.
        ptsButton[0] = CPoint(0, 0);
        ptsButton[1] = CPoint(nSize, 0);
        ptsButton[2] = CPoint(0, nSize);
```

continued on next page

continued from previous page

```
            // Create polygon region from points.
            rgnUpButton.CreatePolygonRgn(ptsButton, 3, WINDING);

            // Check if point is within up button region.
            if (rgnUpButton.PtInRegion(point))
                nHitResult = HIT_UP;
    }

    // Perform hit test on 'down button' only if it is enabled.
    if (m_bDownEnabled)
    {
            // Derive coordinates of down button.
            ptsButton[0] = CPoint(nSize, 0);
            ptsButton[1] = CPoint(nSize, nSize);
            ptsButton[2] = CPoint(0, nSize);

            // Create polygon region from points.
            rgnDownButton.CreatePolygonRgn(ptsButton, 3, WINDING);

            // Check if point is within down button region.
            if (rgnDownButton.PtInRegion(point))
                nHitResult = HIT_DOWN;
    }

    return nHitResult;
}
```

19. Use WizardBar to handle WM_CANCELMODE for CSpinCtrl. Windows sends this message to inform your window that a dialog box or message box is being displayed and you can release mouse capture if necessary. Add the following code to the *OnCancelMode* function:

```
void CSpinCtrl::OnCancelMode()
{
    COleControl::OnCancelMode();

    // Reset states
    m_bDownClick = FALSE;
    m_bUpClick = FALSE;

    KillTimer(TIMERID_DELAY);
    KillTimer(TIMERID_REPEAT);

    // Release capture of mouse.
    ReleaseCapture();
}
```

20. Use WizardBar to handle WM_ERASEBKGND for CSpinCtrl. This message is intercepted to tell Windows that no further processing of this message is necessary since you will be drawing the background yourself. Add the following code to the *OnEraseBkgnd* member function:

```
BOOL CSpinCtrl::OnEraseBkgnd(CDC* pDC)
{
    return TRUE;
}
```

7.5 WRITE AN OLE SPIN CONTROL

21. **Use WizardBar to handle WM_TIMER for CSpinCtrl.** Your window will receive a WM_TIMER message every time the installed timer has expired. This time interval is specified in the *SetTimer* function. Use ClassWizard to handle the WM_TIMER message for the *CSpinCtrl* class. Add the following code to the *OnTimer* member function:

```
void CSpinCtrl::OnTimer(UINT nIDEvent)
{
    // If this is the first timer, kill it and start the repeat timer.
    if (nIDEvent == TIMERID_DELAY)
    {
        KillTimer(nIDEvent);
        SetTimer(TIMERID_REPEAT, m_nRepeatRate, NULL);
    }

    // Fire event if the mouse is still in the originally clicked area.
    if (!m_bMouseOut)
        (m_bUpClick) ? FireUp() : FireDown();

    COleControl::OnTimer(nIDEvent);
}
```

22. **Use WizardBar to handle WM_LBUTTONDOWN for CSpinCtrl.** When the user clicks the left-mouse button over the control, the control first determines where the user clicked. The control's state is saved and the control is repainted to reflect the new state. Add the following code to the *OnLButtonDown* member function:

```
void CSpinCtrl::OnLButtonDown(UINT nFlags, CPoint point)
{
    // Get hit result.
    short nHitResult = HitTest(point);

    if (nHitResult)
    {
        // Store state of control.
        if (nHitResult == HIT_UP)
            m_bUpClick = TRUE;
        else
            m_bDownClick = TRUE;

        // Cause the control to be repainted.
        InvalidateControl();
        Refresh();

        // Capture mouse and set timers.
        SetCapture();
        SetTimer(TIMERID_DELAY, m_nDelayRate, NULL);

        // Fire up or down event.
        (m_bUpClick) ? FireUp() : FireDown();
    }
}
```

CHAPTER 7
OLE AND DDE

23. Use WizardBar to handle WM_LBUTTONUP. This message indicates the user is finished pressing the up or down buttons. The installed timers are destroyed, the mouse capture is released, and the control is repainted if necessary. Add the following code to the *OnLButtonUp* member function:

```
void CSpinCtrl::OnLButtonUp(UINT nFlags, CPoint point)
{
    // Kill any installed timers.
    KillTimer(TIMERID_DELAY);
    KillTimer(TIMERID_REPEAT);

    // Release the capture of the mouse.
    ReleaseCapture();

    // Repaint if necessary, only if button is clicked and the mouse
    // is still in the boundaries of the control.
    if ((m_bUpClick || m_bDownClick) && !m_bMouseOut)
    {
        // Clear the states to allow proper repainting.
        m_bMouseOut = FALSE;
        m_bUpClick = FALSE;
        m_bDownClick = FALSE;

        // Cause the control to be redrawn.
        InvalidateControl();
        Refresh();
    }
}
```

24. Use the WizardBar to handle WM_MOUSEMOVE. The control's buttons should behave just as other types of buttons do. That is, they should be depressed when the user clicks the mouse while over the button, raised if the mouse is moved away from the button, and depressed again when the mouse is moved back over the button. The control keeps track of the state of the up and down buttons and draws them correctly. Add the following code to the *OnMouseMove* member function:

```
void CSpinCtrl::OnMouseMove(UINT nFlags, CPoint point)
{
    // Determine if the control was in the clicked state.
    if (m_bUpClick || m_bDownClick)
    {
        // Store the state of the control.
        WORD wOldState = (m_bMouseOut << 2) | (m_bUpClick << 1) | m_bDownClick;

        short nHitResult = HitTest(point);
        if (nHitResult)
        {
            // Check if currently clicking the up button.
            if (m_bUpClick)
                m_bMouseOut = (nHitResult == HIT_DOWN);

            // Check if currently clicking the down button.
            if (m_bDownClick)
```

7.5
WRITE AN OLE SPIN CONTROL

```
            m_bMouseOut = (nHitResult == HIT_UP);
    }

    // Mouse moved outside entire button.
    else
        m_bMouseOut = TRUE;

    // If the state changed, repaint the control.
    WORD wNewState = (m_bMouseOut << 2) | (m_bUpClick << 1) | m_bDownClick;
    if (wOldState != wNewState)
    {
        InvalidateControl();
        Refresh();
    }
  }
}
```

25. **Edit the IDD_PROPPAGE_SPIN dialog.** The property page dialog box allows the user to modify control properties at design time. Add the controls listed in the following table to the dialog box IDD_PROPPAGE_SPIN. Figure 7-25 shows what the IDD_PROPPAGE_SPIN dialog box should look like.

Control Type	Identifier	Options
Arrows group	IDC_STATIC	"&Arrows"
Radio button	IDC_VERTICAL	"Left/Right", Group
Radio button	IDC_RADIO2	"Up/Down"
Timers group	IDC_STATIC	"&Timers (in msec)"
Delay static	IDC_STATIC	"&Delay"
Edit	IDC_DELAY	default
Repeat static	IDC_STATIC	"&Repeat"
Edit	IDC_REPEAT	default
Enable group	IDC_STATIC	"&Enable arrows"
Check box	IDC_UP	"&Up/left"
Check box	IDC_DOWN	"&Down/right"

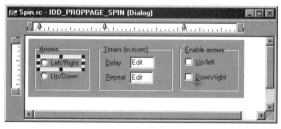

Figure 7-25 The IDD_PROPPAGE_SPIN dialog box

26. **Add data members to the property class.** Use ClassWizard to add data members listed in the following table to the *CSpinPropPage* class. This will automatically transfer the contents of the dialog box controls to the control's properties.

Identifier	Variable Name	Type	OLE Property Name
IDC_VERTICAL	m_vertical	int	Vertical
IDC_DELAY	m_delay	int	DelayRate
IDC_REPEAT	m_repeat	int	RepeatRate
IDC_UP	m_up	BOOL	UpEnabled
IDC_DOWN	m_down	BOOL	DownEnabled

27. **Add color property page.** When you created the control, *ControlWizard* created the following property page ID table in the SpinCtrl.cpp:

```
BEGIN_PROPPAGEIDS(CSpinCtrl, 1)
    PROPPAGEID(CSpinPropPage::guid)
END_PROPPAGEIDS(CSpinCtrl)
```

This displays a General page in the control's property dialog box, which allows the control's properties to be viewed and modified. It is very simple to add color, font, and picture property pages. To add a color page, modify the existing ID table for the page in the file SpinCtrl.cpp. Add the PROPPAGEID macro and change the count argument of the BEING_PROPPAGEIDS macro from 1 to 2, as follows:

```
BEGIN_PROPPAGEIDS(CSpinCtrl, 2)
    PROPPAGEID(CSpinPropPage::guid)
    PROPPAGEID(CLSID_CColorPropPage)
END_PROPPAGEIDS(CSpinCtrl)
```

Adding these lines and modifying the BEING_PROPPAGEIDS macro makes all the properties of the type OLE_COLOR available on the Color property page. Pretty neat, huh? Figure 7-26 shows the spin button control property dialog box. As you can see, all the properties of the type OLE_COLOR have been automatically added to the Property Name combo box.

28. **Modify the default dialog and bitmap resources.** You can modify the IDD_ABOUTBOX_SPIN dialog box to display the normal About dialog box type of information. ControlWizard created a default IDB_SPIN bitmap for you. You can modify this bitmap to provide an iconic representation of your control. Design tools will know how to communicate with your custom control to retrieve a copy of this bitmap. They will most likely insert the picture of your control into some type of toolbar. Notice that there is only one bitmap. You do not define up and down images, and you do not define the 3D shading. That is entirely up to the design tool. Use App Studio to modify the dialog box IDD_ABOUTBOX_SPIN and the bitmap IDB_SPIN.

7.5 WRITE AN OLE SPIN CONTROL

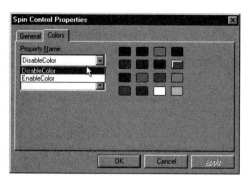

Figure 7-26 Color tab of the spin button control's property dialog box

29. **Build the control.** The last step in the build process uses RegSvr32.exe to register the control. You can manually register the control using the Tools menu, but the makefile does it for you.

30. **Test the control.** Now you've created a great OLE custom control, but how can you possibly test all the functionality of the control? Microsoft knew you would ask that question and developed an excellent application called the Test Container. This is a truly cool application and an important component of OLE control development that allows you to test all the features of your custom control. You can register, unregister, display, and set properties of OLE custom controls. You can also invoke embedded functions such as Activate, Close, and Hide. You can make sure your control renders itself correctly by moving and resizing the control's container area.

   Select Test Container from the Tools menu to run the Test Container application. Insert the spin button control into the Test Container by selecting Insert OLE Control from the Edit menu of the Test Container application. A spin button control should appear in the client area of the Test Container application. You can move the control by dragging it to a new area. You can resize the control by selecting a corner of it and dragging the mouse.

   Bring up the spin button's property dialog box by selecting Properties from the Spin Control Object menu from the Edit menu. You should see the dialog box as shown in Figure 7-24.

   Modify the properties of the spin button control by changing the values in the Properties dialog box. Notice what happens to the spin button control.

   You can see how events are fired in the Event Log dialog box. The Test Container lets you select what events to log. This can be useful when tracking down a particular problem with just one or two events. Select Event Log from the View menu. Click the spin button and notice what events are fired. Figure 7-27 shows the Event Log dialog box with Up and Down events from four spin button controls.

CHAPTER 7
OLE AND DDE

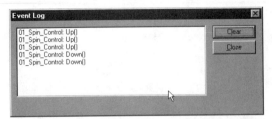

Figure 7-27 Event Log dialog box of the Test Container application

The Test Container allows you to invoke methods of your control. You can specify the parameters passed to the method and look at the value returned from the method. Select Invoke Methods from the Edit menu. Figure 7-28 shows the Invoke Control Method dialog box. Press the Invoke push button to invoke the method specified in the Name combo box.

The device context (DC) passed to the OnDraw member function will usually be a standard one, but it can also be a metafile DC. Some applications may pass a metafile DC to the *OnDraw* member function when printing your control; others, such as Microsoft Access 2.0, may simply choose to render your control using a metafile DC when in design mode. It is important to make sure your control can be rendered using a standard DC or a metafile DC. The Test Container can help you test this. Select Draw Metafile from the Edit menu. Figure 7-29 shows the spin button rendered using a metafile DC.

You can test serialization of your control's persistent properties by saving and loading the control to storage. You should modify the persistent properties of your control and make sure they are saved to storage and retrieved back from storage correctly. Go ahead and try this by changing the *FaceColor* of the spin

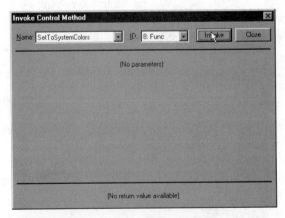

Figure 7-28 Invoke Control Method dialog box of the Test Container application

7.5 WRITE AN OLE SPIN CONTROL

Figure 7-29 Spin button control rendered using a metafile device context

button control to blue. Select Save to Substorage from the File menu. Now select Load from the File menu. A new control should appear that contains the same properties as the control you saved : in this case, a control with a blue face color.

If you need to debug your control, press the F5 key while in the debugger. Developer Studio should ask you what program to debug. Enter the full path to the Test Container. My path is d:\msdev\bin\tstcon32.exe.

How It Works

Most of the work is performed by the MFC classes. The spin button control processes the WM_CANCELMODE, WM_ERASEBKGND, WM_LBUTTONDOWN, WM_LBUTTONDBLCLK, WM_MOUSEMOVE, WM_LBUTTONUP, and WM_TIMER Windows messages.

The control receives a WM_CANCELMODE message whenever a dialog or some other modal process has started. The code kills any installed timers and releases capture of the mouse.

Windows sends the control a WM_ERASEBKGND message when it should erase its background. All the drawing, including erasing the background of the control, is performed in the *COleControl::nDraw* member function. A value of TRUE is returned when processing this message to prevent Windows from erasing the control.

The control receives a WM_LBUTTONDOWN when the left-mouse button is pressed while over the control. The control determines where the user clicked and updates its state. The control is forced to redraw itself by calling the *COleControl::InvalidateControl* member function. A left double click is treated the same as a single click. The control handles the WM_LBUTTONDBLCLK message and calls the *OnLButtonDown* member function.

The WM_MOUSEMOVE message is handled to draw the control depending on the position of the cursor. The control's buttons are drawn either raised or depressed depending on their state and the position of the mouse cursor.

CHAPTER 7
OLE AND DDE

The control receives a WM_LBUTTONUP message when the left-mouse button is released. This indicates the user has finished pushing a button. The control then kills any installed timers, repainting itself to reflect the new state and releasing the mouse capture.

Timers are installed for the *RepeatRate* and *DelayRate* properties. A WM_TIMER message is sent to the control when a timer has expired. The control fires the appropriate event when processing this message.

The control overrides the *OnDraw*, *OnSetExtent*, *DoPropExchange*, and *OnResetState* member functions of the *COleControl* class.

The *OnSetExtent* member function is overridden to make sure the control is a square. The *DoPropExchange* member function is overridden to serialize the control's properties. ControlWizard also overrides the *OnResetState* member function. The control does not perform any additional actions when overriding this member function.

Comments

This turned out to be quite a long How-To, but most of the work was in generic Windows programming and not OLE custom control development. Relatively few lines of OLE code are entered in this project. A significant amount of work was provided by the new MFC classes and ClassWizard to add properties, methods, and events.

There are some useful member functions of the *COleControl* class that you didn't get a chance to see in this exercise. Also, licensing, localization support, data binding, and subclassing an existing Windows control are some topics you might want to investigate further. Licensing allows you to say who can develop new applications using your control. Localization support allows international markets to use your control. Microsoft has recommendations on how to provide localization support with your OLE custom controls. Look up localization support in the online documentation for additional information. Data binding provides an easy way to attach a database entry to a property of your control.

Microsoft really has done an excellent job of abstracting the complexity of OLE so you can focus on control-specific issues. This How-To just skims the surface of some areas, and you may wish to learn more about the OLE controls. If so, go through the tutorial first; it touches on every aspect of OLE control development. Another resource to check out is a book by Adam Denning called *OLE Controls Inside Out*.

COMPLEXITY
BEGINNING

7.6 How do I...
Create a color cell OLE control?

Problem

I need a reusable object that can be combined together to make a color well control. It needs to be small and responsive and I would like to make it an OLE control.

7.6
CREATE A COLOR CELL OLE CONTROL

Technique

A color well is a collection of small rectangles that are displayed when the user needs to select a color. The focus changes to each individual color cell whenever the mouse moves over the cell. The collection of color cells are mutually exclusive; only one can be selected, and the color is chosen by single clicking a particular cell. A color well control is used in the Windows 95 Display control panel applette as shown in Figure 7-30.

The Windows Interface Guidelines for Software Design provides more information on color wells in Chapter 7 (Menus, Controls, and Toolbars) and Chapter 13 (Visual Design). It discusses how the color well should interact with the user, what it should look like, and the correct shading and highlighting you should use. This How-To encapsulates all of this into an OLE control and you can build a color well simply by placing several color cell controls together. Furthermore, this OLE control supports text so you can use it for other applications as you will see later when it is used in the Quick CD How-To.

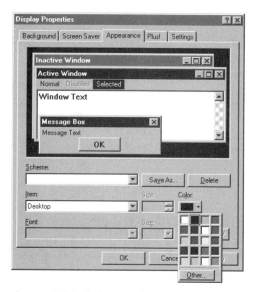

Figure 7-30 Color well control used in Display control panel applette

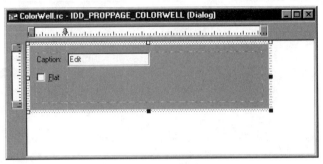

Figure 7-31 The color well properties dialog

Steps

1. Create a new project workspace with the MFC AppWizard (OLE ControlWizard) called ColorWell. Accept all the default settings and press the Finish button.

OLE Control project ColorWell.mak

DLL name: ColorWell.ocx
DLL initialization code in ColorWell.h and ColorWell.cpp
Type library source in ColorWell.odl

ColorWell Control:
   Control class CColorWellCtrl in ColorWellCtl.h and ColorWellCtl.cpp
   Property page class CColorWellPropPage in ColorWellPpg.h and ColorWellPpg.cpp
   Toolbar bitmap in ColorWellCtl.bmp
   Activates when visible
   Has an About box

2. Edit the IDD_PROPPAGE_COLORWELL dialog. Add the following controls to the dialog box as shown in Figure 7-31. This is the control's General property page and the two dialog controls let you specify the control's caption and whether it is displayed as 3D or flat.

Control	ID	Attributes
Caption label	IDC_STATIC	Defaults
Caption edit control	IDC_CAPTION	Defaults
Flat check box	IDC_FLAT	Defaults

7.6 CREATE A COLOR CELL OLE CONTROL

3. **Add member variables to CColorWellPropPage.** Use ClassWizard to add member variables to the *CColorWellPropPage* class. These variables represent the contents of the properties dialog and are used internally when drawing the control.

Name	Category	Variable type	Member	OLE property name
IDC_CAPTION	Value	CString	m_strCaption	Caption
IDC_FLAT	Value	BOOL	m_bFlat	Flat

4. **Add private data member to CColorWellCtrl.** The *CColorWellCtrl* class remembers if it is selected or not and stores this information in the private data member *m_bSelected*. This data member is used when drawing the control's border later in the WM_NCPAINT handler function.

```
private:
    BOOL m_bSelected;
```

Remember to initialize *m_bSelected* in the class constructor.

```
CColorWellCtrl::CColorWellCtrl()
{
    InitializeIIDs(&IID_DColorWell, &IID_DColorWellEvents);

    // init data members
    m_bSelected = FALSE;
}
```

5. **Add OLE control properties.** Use ClassWizard to add the following properties to the *CColorWellCtrl* class. This control exposes four stock properties: *BackColor, Caption, Font, ForeColor* and one custom property called *Flat*.

Implementation	External name
Stock	BackColor
Stock	Caption
Stock	Font
Stock	ForeColor

Implementation	External name	Type	Variable name	Notification function
Member variable	Flat	Bool	m_bFlat	OnFlatChanged

6. **Add OLE control events.** Use ClassWizard to add OLE control events to the *CColorWellCtrl* class. The *FireClickColor* event has one parameter called *color* that is the type OLE_COLOR.

Implementation	External name	Internal name
Stock	Click	FireClick
Custom	Color	FireClickColor

CHAPTER 7
OLE AND DDE

7. **Add additional property pages.** Add a color property page and font property page to the control's properties dialogs. Add the two pages inside of the PROPPAGEIDS macro group in ColorWellCtrl.cpp and remember to change the number of pages from 1 to 3.

```
// TODO: Add more property pages as needed.  Remember to increase the count!
BEGIN_PROPPAGEIDS(CColorWellCtrl, 3)
        PROPPAGEID(CColorWellPropPage::guid)
        PROPPAGEID(CLSID_CColorPropPage)
        PROPPAGEID(CLSID_CFontPropPage)
END_PROPPAGEIDS(CColorWellCtrl)
```

8. **Modify the OnResetState function.** Add the following code to *CColorWellCtrl::OnResetState*. This function is called when the control's properties should be initialized. For this control, this includes its background and foreground colors.

```
void CColorWellCtrl::OnResetState()
{
        COleControl::OnResetState();   // Resets defaults found in DoPropExchange

        SetBackColor(AmbientBackColor());
        SetForeColor(AmbientForeColor());
}
```

9. **Modify the DoPropExchange function.** Add the following code to *CColorWellCtrl::DoPropExchange*. This function is called when a control should load or store properties to persistent storage.

```
void CColorWellCtrl::DoPropExchange(CPropExchange* pPX)
{
        ExchangeVersion(pPX, MAKELONG(_wVerMinor, _wVerMajor));
        COleControl::DoPropExchange(pPX);

        PX_Bool(pPX, "Flat", m_bFlat, FALSE);
}
```

10. **Modify the OnDraw function.** Since this control does not want to draw an ellipse, replace the default code created by AppWizard with the following. This code draws a rectangle in a specified color and displays the control's caption.

```
void CColorWellCtrl::OnDraw(
                        CDC* pdc, const CRect& rcBounds, const CRect& rcInvalid)
{
        // DrawText won't take a const rect
        CRect rText(rcBounds);

        // Select font into device context
        CFont* pFontOld = SelectStockFont(pdc);

        // Paint the background color
        CBrush cbBack(TranslateColor(GetBackColor()));
        pdc->FillRect(rcBounds, &cbBack);
```

7.6
CREATE A COLOR CELL OLE CONTROL

```
    // Paint the text
    pdc->SetTextColor(TranslateColor(GetForeColor()));
    pdc->SetBkMode(TRANSPARENT);
    pdc->DrawText(InternalGetText(), -1, rcText,
        DT_CENTER | DT_VCENTER | DT_SINGLELINE);

    // Select font out of device context
    pdc->SelectObject(pFontOld);
}
```

11. Use the WizardBar to handle WM_MOUSEMOVE for CColorWellCtrl.
    The message is sent to the control whenever the cursor is moved over the control. The following code detects when the cursor is first moved into the control and when it is moved out of the control. The internal flag *m_bSelected* is set so the control can be painted in the correct state later in the *OnNcPaint* function.

```
void CColorWellCtrl::OnMouseMove(UINT nFlags, CPoint point)
{
    // Detect the first time the mouse is moved over the window
    if (GetCapture() != this)
    {
        // Capture the mouse and redraw the window
        SetCapture();
        m_bSelected = TRUE;
        RedrawWindow(NULL, NULL, RDW_FRAME | RDW_INVALIDATE | RDW_ERASE);
        return;
    }

    // Detect when the mouse moves out of our window
    CRect rcWindow;
    GetWindowRect(rcWindow);
    ClientToScreen(&point);
    if (rcWindow.PtInRect(point) == 0)
    {
        // Release mouse and redraw window
        ReleaseCapture();
        m_bSelected = FALSE;
        RedrawWindow(NULL, NULL, RDW_FRAME | RDW_INVALIDATE | RDW_ERASE);
        return;
    }
}
```

12. Use the WizardBar to handle WM_NCPAINT for CColorWellCtrl. This
    message is sent to a window when its frame needs to be painted. This control handles this message and draws the correct frame around the control and makes the control appear 3D or flat.

```
void CColorWellCtrl::OnNcPaint()
{
    // Get DC for client and nonclient areas
    CWindowDC dc(this);
```

continued on next page

431

CHAPTER 7
OLE AND DDE

continued from previous page

```
// Save the current state of the DC so we can restore it later
dc.SaveDC();

// Get the dimensions of the window
CRect rcWindow;
GetWindowRect(rcWindow);

// Select a hollow brush since we are just drawing the border
dc.SelectStockObject(HOLLOW_BRUSH);

rcWindow.OffsetRect(-rcWindow.left, -rcWindow.top);

// Draw selected border around color cell
if (m_bSelected)
{
    // Draw three concentric rectangles: black, white, then black
    CPen penDark(PS_SOLID, 1, GetSysColor(COLOR_BTNTEXT));
    CPen penLight(PS_SOLID, 1, GetSysColor(COLOR_BTNHILIGHT));

    // Draw most outer rectangle
    dc.SelectObject(&penDark);
    dc.Rectangle(rcWindow);

    // Draw middle rectangle
    dc.SelectObject(&penLight);
    rcWindow.InflateRect(-1, -1);
    dc.Rectangle(rcWindow);

    // Draw inner rectangle
    dc.SelectObject(&penDark);
    rcWindow.InflateRect(-1, -1);
    dc.Rectangle(rcWindow);
}

// Draw nonselected color cell in flat mode
else if (m_bFlat)
{
    CPen penBack(PS_SOLID, 3, TranslateColor(AmbientBackColor()));
    dc.SelectObject(&penBack);
    dc.Rectangle(rcWindow);
}

// Draw nonselected color cell in 3D mode
else
{
    // Draw 3D sunken edge
    CPen penFace(PS_SOLID, 1, GetSysColor(COLOR_BTNFACE));
    dc.SelectObject(&penFace);

    dc.Rectangle(rcWindow);

    rcWindow.InflateRect(-1, -1);
    dc.DrawEdge(rcWindow, EDGE_SUNKEN, BF_RECT);
}
```

7.6
CREATE A COLOR CELL OLE CONTROL

```
        // Restore the value of the DC
        dc.RestoreDC(-1);
}
```

13. Use the WizardBar to handle WM_NCCALCSIZE for CColorWellCtrl.
This message is sent when the client area of a window needs to be calculated.
Normally you let the default window procedure calculate this for you but the
control handles this message and subtracts enough room for the custom border.

```
void CColorWellCtrl::OnNcCalcSize(BOOL bCalcValidRects, NCCALCSIZE_PARAMS ⇒
FAR* lpncsp)
{
        // Specify a new client area size to adjust for the 3 pixel wide border
        InflateRect(lpncsp->rgrc, -3, -3);
}
```

14. Build and test the application. After you successfully compile the application, launch the OLE control test container from the Tools menu to test the control. Insert a ColorWell control and bring up its properties dialog. Enter different captions and try different background colors and fonts. Figure 7-32 shows a blue and red ColorWell control.

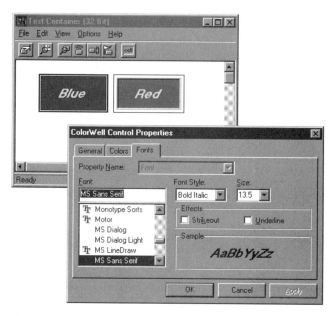

Figure 7-32 Test container with two color cell OLE controls

How It Works

The task of drawing the color cell is divided in two parts; the piece that draws the client area and the part that draws a border around the control. The code that draws the client area is contained in *CColorWellCtrl::OnDraw*. This function simply draws the rectangle by calling *CDC::FillRect* and displays the control's caption by calling *CDC::DrawText*.

The border of the control is drawn in *CColorWellCtrl::OnNcPaint*. This function is called whenever the nonclient (hence Nc) area of the control needs to be painted. Usually you just pass this along to the window's default window procedure that draws a frame around the window based on the window style.

Instead of this default behavior, we override this function and draw a custom border depending on the state of the control. If the color cell is selected, then a selected border is drawn that consists of three concentric rectangles. Note that this border is clearly documented in the Visual Design section of the Windows Interface Guidelines for Software Design documentation. If the control is not selected, the border is drawn to make the rectangle have a 3D look by calling *CDC::DrawEdge* or flat depending on the *m_bFlat* property.

We must tell Windows about the new size (it is 3 pixels wide instead of 1 pixel) since this control has a border that is thicker than a normal control Windows and sends the WM_NCCALCSIZE message when it needs to know the client size of a window. You handle this message by overriding *CWnd::OnNcCalcSize* and specify a new client size. The code for *CColorWellCtrl::OnNcCalcSize* calls *::InflateRect* to leave enough room in the window for a 3 pixel wide border.

The user interface guidelines state that a color cell should be selected simply by moving the mouse over the control and should be unselected when the mouse leaves the rectangle occupied by the color cell. In order to accomplish this behavior we must detect when the mouse first enters the control and when it leaves the control. This is accomplished by handling the WM_MOUSEMOVE message and capturing and releasing the mouse at the appropriate times.

The code in *CColorWellCtrl::OnMouseMove* detects when the mouse first enters the control by checking if it currently had the mouse captured. If the cursor is over the control (thus the WM_MOUSEMOVE message) and the mouse is not captured yet, then the mouse just entered the control. It proceeds to capture the mouse, store the new selected state and invalidate the nonclient area of the window by calling *CWnd::RedrawWindow* with the RDW_FRAME flag. This causes only the control's frame to be redrawn and not the client area.

It determines when the mouse leaves the rectangle occupied by the control by checking if the cursor position is within the bounding rectangle. If it is not, the mouse capture is released, the new selected state is updated, and the nonclient area is invalidated by calling *CWnd::RedrawWindow* again.

7.6 CREATE A COLOR CELL OLE CONTROL

Comments

This OLE control can be quite useful and it does not take very much code to implement. Depending on your application it can be beneficial to handle the WM_NCPAINT message and draw your own frame. If you need to debug this project, remember to add the path to the OLE Test Container (TSTCON32.EXE in the msdev bin directory) as the executable for debug section in the project settings dialog.

CHAPTER 8
SYSTEM

SYSTEM

How do I...

8.1 Prevent multiple instances of a running application?

8.2 Localize MFC applications using resource DLLs?

8.3 Use the Win32 registry database?

8.4 Make multiple inheritance work in MFC?

8.5 Detect when launched applications terminate under Win32?

8.6 Use system hooks under Win32?

8.7 Share data between 32-bit MFC applications?

This chapter presents techniques for using the advanced system features found in Windows 95 and Visual C++. You'll learn how to use many of the new Win32 components such as threads, synchronization objects, wait functions, the registry, memory-mapped files, hooks, and Win32 DLLs. Several advanced MFC topics are covered, including creating MFC extension DLLs, localization, and multiple inheritance.

The first How-To shows you how to prevent multiple instances of your application from running. Localization for multiple language support is the topic of another How-To that uses resource DLLs to isolate the language-specific components of an MFC program. One How-To creates a *CRegKey* class to access the registry, while the thorny problem of using multiple inheritance in a MFC program is sorted out in another How-To. Creating a multithreaded MFC application that uses several new MFC synchronization classes is the topic of a How-To that detects when a launched application terminates. Another How-To demonstrates using system-wide hooks to route all mouse

CHAPTER 8
SYSTEM

messages to your application, and the last How-To illustrates sharing data among applications using memory-mapped files.

8.1 Prevent Multiple Instances of a Running Application

If you want to make sure only one instance of your application can be started use this How-To, which illustrates a technique that works for any type of MFC-based application. It does not depend on application specific window titles nor registered window classes. Not only will the second instance terminate, it brings the first instance to the foreground.

Additional Topics: mutexes, windows properties, m_hPrevInstance

8.2 Localize MFC Applications Using Resource DLLs

By isolating all language-specific resources in special resource DLLs, a single executable can simply switch DLLs and be fluent in more than one language. This How-To creates an application in English and French. You change the locale of the application by simply installing a different language resource DLL.

Additional Topics: AfxSetResourceHandle, resource only DLLs

8.3 Use the Win32 Registry Database

The Win32 registry offers a flexible and robust way to store application information and user preferences using simple APIs. This How-To provides a new class, *CRegKey*, which makes the registration database easy to add to any Win32 application.

Additional Topics: RegCreateKeyEx, CRegKey

8.4 Make Multiple Inheritance Work in MFC

Multiple inheritance has been around for a while in Visual C++, but because MFC doesn't use it, it's been difficult to figure out how to take advantage of its powerful features. You'll see how to create special *CEdit* and *CComboBox* classes that filter keystrokes, allowing only floating-point numbers, by inheriting from a new base class.

Additional Topics: mix-in classes, ambiguous class methods, subclassing the combo box edit window

8.5 Detect When Launched Applications Terminate under Win32

Learn how to create a MFC multithreaded application that detects when launched applications terminate using the *CWinThread* class. See how to synchronize your threads by using critical sections and event objects to control access to shared resources.

Additional Topics: processes, threads, CreateProcess, CCriticalSection, CEvent, WaitForMultipleObjects

8.6 Use System Hooks under Win32

This How-To creates a useful utility that allows you to apply an action to a window by simply moving the cursor over the window and pressing the right-mouse button. A system hook routes all mouse messages to your controlling application, which determines what action to perform on the window (close, restore, minimize). A special MFC Extension DLL exports a class that handles the mouse hook. Learn what special conditions you have to consider when creating DLLs under Win32.

Additional Topics: Win32 DLLs, exporting classes from an MFC extension DLL, shared memory in Win32 DLLs

8.7 Share Data Between 32-bit MFC Applications

Learn how to take advantage of memory-mapped files to share data between two applications. As a bonus, you'll also see how to use a worker thread to monitor the state of the memory-mapped file.

Additional Topics: CreateFileMapping, AfxBeginThread, memory-mapped files

COMPLEXITY
BEGINNING

8.1 How do I... Prevent multiple instances of a running application?

Problem

I want only one instance of my application running at any time. To enforce this, I'd like the second launched instance to restore the first, then exit. I did this by checking the previous instance handle under Win16 but this does not work under Win32. What's the best solution for Win32?

Technique

Some applications are designed so that only a single instance may be running at one time. Maybe the application requires dedicated access to a unique resource, such as a modem or CD drive. Or perhaps the application requires such a large amount of system resources that only one instance of it can be brought up successfully.

Whatever the reason, it would be very rude for an application to simply terminate when a second instance is executed. Proper software etiquette dictates that the second instance should bring the first instance's window to the top of the stack before terminating.

CHAPTER 8
SYSTEM

Several techniques are often used to detect and manipulate a previous instance of a running application. One popular Win16 method simply checks the value of *CWinApp::m_hPrevInstance*, the handle to the previous instance of the application. If it's not NULL, you can use it to identify the other instance. However, this value is always NULL under Win32, so we need an alternative solution.

The technique presented here does not rely on the class or caption of a window and can be used with MDI, SDI, and Dialog-based applications.

Steps

1. Create a new project called Single using the MFC AppWizard (exe).
Select the Multiple-Document option and press the Finish button.

Classes to be created:
Application: CSingleApp in Single.h and Single.cpp
Frame: CMainFrame in MainFrm.h and MainFrm.cpp
MDIChildFrame: CChildFrame in ChildFrm.h and ChildFrm.cpp
Document: CSingleDoc in SingleDoc.h and SingleDoc.cpp
View: CSingleView in SingleView.h and SingleView.cpp

Features:
+ Initial toolbar in main frame
+ Initial status bar in main frame
+ Printing and Print Preview support in view
+ 3D Controls

2. Edit the CSingleApp::InitInstance. First you need to detect when another instance of your application has been started. The following step will fill in the TODO area. Add the following lines to the *InitInstance* function:

```
BOOL CSingleApp::InitInstance()
{
    // Standard initialization
    // If you are not using these features and wish to reduce the size
    //  of your final executable, you should remove from the following
    //  the specific initialization routines you do not need.

    // Create a mutex object. If the mutex object already exists, then
    // this is the second instance of the application. Note that the
    // mutex handle is automatically closed when the process terminates.
    ::CreateMutex(NULL, TRUE, m_pszExeName);
    if (GetLastError() == ERROR_ALREADY_EXISTS)
    {
        // TODO: set focus to previous instance
        return FALSE;
    }

    ...
}
```

8.1
PREVENT MULTIPLE INSTANCES OF A RUNNING APPLICATION

3. Implement code to find the previous instance. Next you need to find the previous instance of your application and set the focus to its main application window. Modify the *InitInstance* function to look like the following:

```
BOOL CSingleApp::InitInstance()
{
        // Standard initialization
        // If you are not using these features and wish to reduce the size
        //  of your final executable, you should remove from the following
        //  the specific initialization routines you do not need.

        // Create a mutex object. If the mutex object already exists, then
        // this is the second instance of the application. Note that the
        // mutex handle is automatically closed when the process terminates.
        ::CreateMutex(NULL, TRUE, m_pszExeName);
        if (GetLastError() == ERROR_ALREADY_EXISTS)
        {
                // Find our previous application's main window.
                CWnd* pPrevWnd = CWnd::GetDesktopWindow()->GetWindow(GW_CHILD);
                while (pPrevWnd)
                {
                        // Does this window have the 'previous instance tag' set?
                        if (::GetProp(pPrevWnd->GetSafeHwnd(), m_pszExeName))
                        {
                                // Found window, now set focus to the window.
                                // First restore window if it is currently iconic.
                                if (pPrevWnd->IsIconic())
                                        pPrevWnd->ShowWindow(SW_RESTORE);

                                // Set focus to main window.
                                pPrevWnd->SetForegroundWindow();

                                // If window has a pop-up window, set focus to pop-up.
                                pPrevWnd->GetLastActivePopup()->SetForegroundWindow();

                                return FALSE;
                        }

                        // Did not find window, get next window in list.
                        pPrevWnd = pPrevWnd->GetWindow(GW_HWNDNEXT);
                }

                TRACE(|Could not find previous instance main window!\n");
                return FALSE;
        }

#ifdef _AFXDLL
        Enable3dControls();            // Call this when using MFC in a shared DLL
#else
        Enable3dControlsStatic();      // Call this when linking to MFC statically
#endif

        LoadStdProfileSettings();      // Load standard INI file options (including MRU)
```

continued on next page

continued from previous page

```
    // Register the application's document templates.  Document templates
    //  serve as the connection between documents, frame windows, and views.

    CMultiDocTemplate* pDocTemplate;
    pDocTemplate = new CMultiDocTemplate(
        IDR_SINGLETYPE,
        RUNTIME_CLASS(CSingleDoc),
        RUNTIME_CLASS(CChildFrame), // custom MDI child frame
        RUNTIME_CLASS(CSingleView));
    AddDocTemplate(pDocTemplate);

    // create main MDI Frame window
    CMainFrame* pMainFrame = new CMainFrame;
    if (!pMainFrame->LoadFrame(IDR_MAINFRAME))
        return FALSE;
    m_pMainWnd = pMainFrame;

    // Parse command line for standard shell commands, DDE, file open
    CCommandLineInfo cmdInfo;
    ParseCommandLine(cmdInfo);

    // Dispatch commands specified on the command line
    if (!ProcessShellCommand(cmdInfo))
        return FALSE;

    // The main window has been initialized, so show and update it.
    pMainFrame->ShowWindow(m_nCmdShow);
    pMainFrame->UpdateWindow();

    // Associate a 'tag' with the window so we can locate it later.
    ::SetProp(pMainFrame->GetSafeHwnd(), m_pszExeName, (HANDLE)1);

    return TRUE;
}
```

4. **Use the WizardBar to handle WM_DESTROY for CMainFrame.** The only step left is to remove the property from the main application window. Add the following lines to *CMainFrame::OnDestroy*:

```
void CMainFrame::OnDestroy()
{
    // Remove 'previous instance tag' from window.
    ::RemoveProp(GetSafeHwnd(), AfxGetApp()->m_pszExeName);

    CMDIFrameWnd::OnDestroy();
}
```

5. **Build and test the application.** Launch Single.exe after you successfully compile the application. Then launch the program again. The first instance of Single.exe should come to the foreground. Try minimizing the application and launching it again. The first instance should restore itself to the normal size and come to the front.

8.1
PREVENT MULTIPLE INSTANCES OF A RUNNING APPLICATION

How It Works

To limit your application to one instance, you need to accomplish two tasks: Detect when a second instance is being instantiated, and set the focus to the previous instance. First, let's review how we detect the second instance of an application.

Every MFC application implements the virtual *CWinApp::InitInstance* method. If *InitInstance* returns FALSE, the application will terminate. This function is a good place to insert any application-specific initialization code, which is what we do in this example. You cannot check the *CWinApp::m_hPrevInstance* data member for Win32 applications since it is always NULL. One suggested way for detecting another instance under Win32 is to create a named *mutex*. Mutexes are like critical sections, except they can be used to synchronize data access across multiple processes. If the named mutex already exists, then we know there's another instance of our application running. You name the mutex by passing any unique name, such as the third parameter, to *::CreateMutex*. This example just uses the *m_pszExeName* data member of the application object to name the mutex.

```
::CreateMutex(NULL, TRUE, m_pszExeName);
```

Using mutexes is safer than using *CWnd::FindWindow* to locate a previous window, because a second instance of the application could be started before the first instance has finished creating its main window. Using mutexes guards against this scenario. Note that you could have used the MFC synchronization class *CMutex* in our situation, but it was easier to just call *CreateMutex*.

Activation of the Previous Instance

What do you do when you determine that another instance of your application is running? You should make the previous instance very obvious to the user by bringing it to the foreground and giving it the focus. If the previous instance is currently iconic, you should restore the window first.

There are several techniques for locating the application's previous instance main window. You can use *CWnd::FindWindow* to find a window with a specific caption. This technique requires that you know the caption of your main application window. This might be true for a simple Dialog-based application but it will not work if your application dynamically updates its caption—such as displaying the active document like SDI and MDI applications should do.

You can also use *CWnd::FindWindow* to find a window with a specific registered window class. This requires that you override *CWnd::PreCreateWindow* and register your own window class. This technique is better than the previous method but you still have to register your own window class, and you might have to modify your code when you upgrade to future versions of MFC.

This example in this How-To uses a technique that "tags" a window so it can be found later. You tag a window by calling the SDK function *SetProp* to add a character string / data handle combination pair to a window handle. This example tags the

CHAPTER 8
SYSTEM

main application window in the *InitInstance* function. Once again, it just uses the *m_pszExeName* data member of the application object to identify the window property.

```
::SetProp(pMainFrame->GetSafeHwnd(), m_pszExeName, (HANDLE)1);
```

Window properties are a convenient way to store information with a window. The MFC framework uses window properties when it subclasses a window by storing the original window procedure as a window property. When the window is unsubclassed, it simply retrieves the original window procedure from the window property. Our example uses windows properties to store a Boolean value, not a data handle.

When we detect that another instance is already running, we find the previous application's main window by searching all the top-level windows for our tag. You search all top-level windows by calling *CWnd::GetDesktopWindow* and *CWnd::GetWindow* with the GW_CHILD and GW_HWNDNEXT arguments. For each window, we look for our previous instance tag by calling the SDK function *GetProp*. If the window contains the property, then we've found our window.

When the window is found, it should be brought to the foreground. This How-To makes the window visible by first calling *CWnd::IsIconic* to determine if the window is iconic, and then *CWnd::ShowWindow* to restore the window. Next, it brings the window to the top of the window stack by calling *SetForegroundWindow*. The position of the various windows in the window stack is referred to as the Z-order in Windows terminology. The topmost window is, therefore, the first window in the Z-order. This is illustrated in Figure 8-1, where Explorer is at the bottom of the Z-order and Calc is at the top.

The previous instance might have had a dialog open at the time the user attempted to run a second instance. To account for this event, a check is made for an open

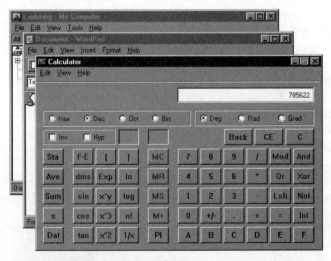

Figure 8-1 Windows Z-ordering

dialog through *CWnd::GetLastActivePopup*. The dialog is brought to the top of the stack using the same method for the application's main window. By bringing the dialog to the top, we make sure the application doesn't hide the dialog.

Finally, we return FALSE from *InitInstance*. This terminates the current (second) instance of the application. Since *InitInstance* is returning before any of the application's views are constructed, no windows for the second instance will ever be created.

Comments

There are other alternatives to using mutexes to detect another instance: creating a uniquely named pipe, creating or testing for a named semaphore, or broadcasting a unique message. You should use one of these techniques under Win32 instead of relying on *FindWindow* to determine if a previous instance is running.

COMPLEXITY
INTERMEDIATE

8.2 How do I... Localize MFC applications using resource DLLs?

Problem

I need a technique that simplifies support for multiple languages using a single set of source code. How can I dynamically switch to different localized resources without modifying any code?

Technique

For obvious reasons, your software will be more successful if it has been translated to the local language. The process of translating an application from one language to another is known as *localization*. Localization often includes more than just translating the text contained in the menu bars and dialogs. Culture-specific bitmaps or icons might not have the same meaning to other people. For instance, icons of stop signs or traffic lights colored red, yellow, and green might have different meanings to people in different countries.

Keeping all the visual resources in a resource-only DLL makes localization easier because it isolates the language-specific components in one file. Several different languages can be shipped along with one executable, and the setup program can install the appropriate language-specific DLL.

You'll also make the translation process easier if all the text strings your program uses are in the string resource table. Finding and converting the text strings can be trivial when text is embedded into the source code for a small program of a few hundred lines. However, if the application is very large, it is much easier to translate text when

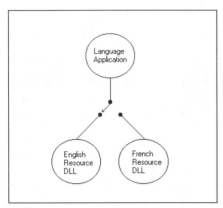

Figure 8-2 Application can use different language resource DLLs

all of it is in the string table. Instead of hard-coding strings, simply instantiate a *CString* object and call *LoadString* with the string's resource ID.

Normally, resources are contained in the application module, but you can point to a different module by calling *AfxSetResourceHandle*. This example calls this function to pick up all application resources from a resource DLL. Just by replacing the resource DLL, the application uses a totally different set of resources (strings, dialogs, bitmaps, and menus). Figure 8-2 shows how the application called Language can switch between an English-based resource DLL and a French-based resource DLL.

To illustrate this technique, this example creates an application called Language that does not contain any resources. We'll create an English DLL that contains all of the resource in English, and you will see that the application appears in English when it uses this DLL. Then we'll create a French version of the resource DLL. The program

Figure 8-3 Example application using English version of resource DLL

8.2
LOCALIZE MFC APPLICATIONS USING RESOURCE DLLS

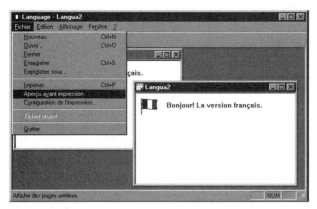

Figure 8-4 Same example application using French version of resource DLL

will then appear in French when it is executed again—even though the application was not recompiled. Figure 8-3 shows the Language application using the English version of the resource DLL. The same application is shown in Figure 8-4 when it uses the French version of the resource DLL.

Steps to Create the Language Executable

1. Create a new project workspace with the MFC AppWizard (exe) called **Language.** Select the Multiple-Document type and press the Finish button.

Classes to be created:
    Application: CLanguageApp in Language.h and Language.cpp
    Frame: CMainFrame in MainFrm.h and MainFrm.cpp
    MDIChildFrame: CChildFrame in ChildFrm.h and ChildFrm.cpp
    Document: CLanguageDoc in LanguageDoc.h and LanguageDoc.cpp
    View: CLanguageView in LanguageView.h and LanguageView.cpp

Features:
    + Initial toolbar in main frame
    + Initial status bar in main frame
    + Printing and Print Preview support in view
    + 3D Controls

2. Add a string resource. This part is a little confusing—why are we adding a string resource when the application does not contain any resources? Later, you will remove Language.rc from this project and copy it to the English resource DLL project. So, the resource string you are adding is actually for the English resource DLL—not the Language executable. The Language executable will reference this new string, but it will be contained in resource DLL.

Add the following string resource to the project. Notice that "=200" is appended to the end of the string ID. This tells the framework to define IDS_HELLO to 200. Figure 8-5 shows the string properties dialog box.

ID	Caption
IDS_HELLO=200	Hello! The English version.

3. Add data member to the CLanguageApp class. This example dynamically loads a DLL that contains all of the resources. It needs to store a handle to this DLL to free it later. Add the following data member to the *CLanguageApp* class:

```
private:
        HINSTANCE m_hLangDLL;   // resource DLL handle
```

4. Modify the CLanguageApp::InitInstance function. The application needs to load a DLL that contains all of the resources. Add the following code to the top of *InitInstance*:

```
BOOL CLanguageApp::InitInstance()
{
        // Standard initialization
        // If you are not using these features and wish to reduce the size
        //  of your final executable, you should remove from the following
        //  the specific initialization routines you do not need.

        // Load the language resource DLL.
        m_hLangDLL = AfxLoadLibrary(_T("Resource.dll"));
        if (!m_hLangDLL)
        {
                AfxMessageBox(_T("Unable to load resource DLL!"));
                return FALSE;
        }

        // Tell application what module contains our resources.
        AfxSetResourceHandle(m_hLangDLL);

...
}
```

5. Use the WizardBar to handle the ExitInstance function for CLanguageApp. You need to free the DLL you previously loaded with *AfxLoadLibrary*. Add the following code to the *ExitInstance* function:

```
int CLanguageApp::ExitInstance()
{
        // Free language resource library.
        if (m_hLangDLL)
                AfxFreeLibrary(m_hLangDLL);

        return CWinApp::ExitInstance();
}
```

8.2
LOCALIZE MFC APPLICATIONS USING RESOURCE DLLS

Figure 8-5 Adding IDS_HELLO string resource

6. **Modify CLanguageView::OnDraw.** To demonstrate that this example is dynamically retrieving values from the resource DLLs instead of its own executable, the example gets an icon and string from the DLL and draws them on the screen. Add the following code to the *OnDraw* function:

```
void CLanguageView::OnDraw(CDC* pDC)
{
    CLanguageDoc* pDoc = GetDocument();
    ASSERT_VALID(pDoc);

    // Draw icon loaded from resource DLL.
    pDC->DrawIcon(10, 10, AfxGetApp()->LoadIcon(IDR_MAINFRAME));

    // Display string from resource DLL.
    CString strMessage;
    strMessage.LoadString(IDS_HELLO);
    pDC->TextOut(60, 15, strMessage);
}
```

7. **Remove Language.rc from project.** Remember that this project will not contain any resources itself. Remove Language.rc from the list of project files. This will not delete the file—it will only remove it from this project.

   Note that ClassWizard will be disabled when a project does not contain a resource file. If you want, you can create an empty file called Empty.rc and add it to the project. ClassWizard will be enabled again after it rebuilds its information file (the .CLW file). It is not necessary to create the empty resource file for this example project.

8. **Build the project.** Build and run the project. Notice the error dialog indicating the project could not find the resource DLL. This is because the application does not contain any resources—it depends on a resource DLL to provide all of the resources. The next series of steps creates an English resource DLL for this project. When this DLL is built, you can copy the resource DLL back to this project and run the application.

Steps to Create the English Resource DLL

9. Create a new project workspace with the MFC AppWizard (dll) called English. Select the location to the Language executable project you just created. For example, if you created the Language project in C:\Projects\Language then select C:\ Projects\Language\English for this project location. Choose a Regular DLL-based application and press the Finish button.

10. Remove all files from the project. This DLL will just contain resources so all of the other files are not necessary. You can remove all the files from the project by selecting the files and pressing the DELETE key.

11. Copy resource files from the Language project. Remember when you added a resource string to the Language.rc file in the previous steps. Copy Language.rc and Resource.h file into the English project directory. Also copy all of the files from the Language\res directory into the English\res directory. The following table shows what files you need to copy from the Language project into the English project.

File	Comment
Language.rc	resource description file
resource.h	file that contains resource defines
res\Language.ico	icon for main application
res\Language.rc2	your own resource description file
res\LanguageDoc.ico	icon for documents
res\Toolbar.bmp	bitmap for toolbar

12. Add the resource file to the project. Add Language.rc to the project. You can add files to the project by selecting the Files into Project... item from the Insert menu. The only file in the English project is Language.rc—that's why this is a resource DLL!

13. Modify IDR_MAINFRAME icon. Modify the IDR_MAINFRAME icon to represent the United States flag as shown in Figure 8-6. Remember to modify both the 32x32 and 16x16 versions. This icon will appear in the view of the Language application.

14. Modify link builds settings. The only thing left to do is modify a few build settings. You modify the build settings by selecting the Settings... item from the Build menu. First you need to change some settings under the Link tab. Change the output file name from English.dll to Resource.dll. Also, add the /NOENTRY option to the link command line. This option tells the linker that this is a resource-only DLL, and it does not contain an entry point. Figure 8-7 shows the Project Settings dialog with the modified link options. Notice that you have to add the /NOENTRY option to the common options edit control.

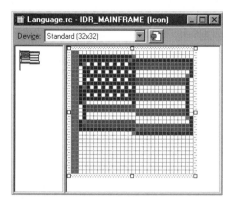

Figure 8-6 English version of the icon resource

15. **Build the project.** Copy Resource.dll to the same directory as Language.exe (probably in the Language\Debug directory). Now run Language.exe. The application should run and appear in English as shown in Figure 8-3.

Steps to Create the French Resource DLL

16. **Generate the French version of resource files.** Next, we'll create a French version of the resource DLL. The quickest way to generate a French version of the resource files is to create a temporary project based on the French locale and then copy the resource files into the French DLL project. Create a new project workspace with the MFC AppWizard (exe) called Language. Create the project in a temporary directory, such as C:\Temp\Language. Select French

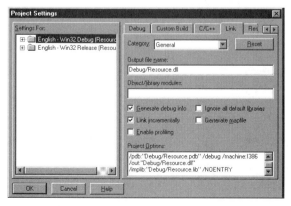

Figure 8-7 Link options for resource-only DLL

resources and the Multiple-Document type and press the Finish button. Figure 8-8 shows how to specify French resources in AppWizard.

Classes to be created:
   Application: CLanguageApp in Language.h and Language.cpp
   Frame: CMainFrame in MainFrm.h and MainFrm.cpp
   MDIChildFrame: CChildFrame in ChildFrm.h and ChildFrm.cpp
   Document: CLanguageDoc in LanguageDoc.h and LanguageDoc.cpp
   View: CLanguageView in LanguageView.h and LanguageView.cpp

Features:
   + Initial toolbar in main frame
   + Initial status bar in main frame
   + Printing and Print Preview support in view
   + 3D Controls
   + Uses shared DLL implementation (MFC40.DLL)
   + Localizable text in:
      French [Standard]

17. Create a new project called French using the MFC AppWizard (dll).
Use the location of the Language project created earlier. For example, if you created the Language project in C:\Projects\Language, then select C:\Projects\Language\French for this project location. Choose a Regular DLL-based application and press the Finish button.

18. Remove all files from the project. This DLL will just contain the French resources so all of the other files are not required. You can remove all the files from the project by selecting the files and pressing [DELETE].

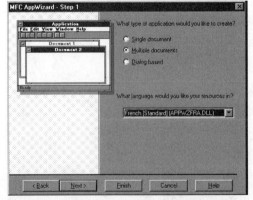

Figure 8-8 Using AppWizard to create default version of resources in French

8.2
LOCALIZE MFC APPLICATIONS USING RESOURCE DLLS

19. **Copy resource files from the French Language project.** Copy the Language.rc and Resource.h files from the temporary project you created in step 16 to the French DLL project directory. Also copy all of the resources files under the res directory. The following table shows what files you need to copy from the temporary project into the French project.

File	Comment
Language.rc	resource description file
resource.h	file that contains resource defines
res\Language.ico	icon for main application
res\Language.rc2	your own resource description file
res\LanguageDoc.ico	icon for documents
res\Toolbar.bmp	bitmap for toolbar

20. **Add the resource file to project.** Add Language.rc to the project. You add files to the project by selecting the Files into Project... item from the Insert menu.

21. **Modify the IDR_MAINFRAME icon.** Modify the IDR_MAINFRAME icon to represent the French flag. The icon will be displayed in the Language application's view. Figure 8-9 shows the French version of the application icon.

22. **Add the resource string.** Add the following string to the resource. Remember that the French version needs to have all of the same resources as the English.dll. Figure 8-10 shows the French version of the hello string resource.

ID	Caption
IDS_HELLO=200	Bonjour! La version français.

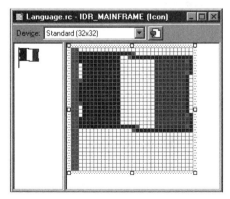

Figure 8-9 French version of the icon resource

CHAPTER 8
SYSTEM

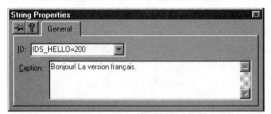

Figure 8-10 Adding the French version of the IDS_HELLO string resource

23. **Modify link builds settings.** You need to modify the link build settings just like you did with the English.dll project. You modify the build settings by selecting the Settings... item from the Build menu. Change the output file name from English.dll to Resource.dll. Since this is a resource only DLL, add the /NOENTRY option to the link command line as shown in Figure 8-7.

24. **Modify resource build settings.** You need to change three setting in the Resource tab of the Build Settings dialog. First change the default language to French. Next remove the _AFXDLL preprocessor definition, and finally, enter the path to the l.fra directory installed by Visual C++. For example, if you installed Visual C++ in the directory C:\Msdev, you would enter C:\Msdev\Mfc\include\l.fra. Figure 8-11 shows the resource build settings.

You remove the _AFXDLL preprocessor and enter the path to the French resources so your DLL will also contain the common MFC resources. If you did not do this, the application would pick up common MFC resources from the MFC runtime DLLs installed on the system. Application specific resources would be localized, but common MFC resources (such as cursors, print preview, and common property pages) would not.

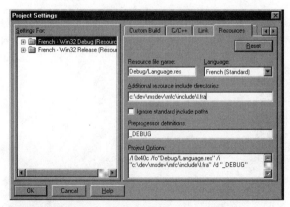

Figure 8-11 Resource settings for French resource DLL

8.2
LOCALIZE MFC APPLICATIONS USING RESOURCE DLLS

Figure 8-12 Print preview of French resource DLL

25. Build the project. Build the project and make sure there are not any compiler errors. Notice that the French resource DLL is larger than the English DLL since it also contains all of the common MFC resources. Now copy Resource.dll to the Language executable directory and run Language.exe again. Presto! Just by replacing the DLL, the application is now localized to France: All resources are in French. All the menu items and status messages are in French. Notice that the icon displayed is the French flag from the resource DLL. Select Print Preview from the File menu (Aperçu avant impression item from the Fichier menu). Notice that the buttons at the top of the window are in French as shown in Figure 8-12.

Close the application. Copy the English version of Resource.dll and run the application again. Now it is in English again. You can change all the resources the application uses simply by changing the DLL.

How It Works

The resources for a Windows application are usually bound to the executable, but are not loaded until they are needed. When a resource is needed, two things must be supplied to Windows: the instance handle of the application and the identifier for the resource.

When a DLL is loaded, Windows returns an instance handle for the DLL, just like the instance handle that belongs to an application. If the DLL contains resources, they can be referenced by using the DLL's instance handle.

In this example, the resources have been completely removed from the main executable file and placed into a DLL. When MFC classes refer to any resources, such as *CString::LoadString,* the current resource handle is used. Normally the current resource handle is the same as the application's resource handle, but we changed that through *AfxSetResourceHandle.* This function instructs MFC to extract all its resources through the handle passed as the only argument to *AfxSetResourceHandle.*

When the English-language DLL is replaced by the French version of the DLL, the resource IDs refer to resources that are located in the French-language DLL. Since the DLL was translated from an exact copy of the original DLL, all the resources should be intact and differ only by being translated into French.

CHAPTER 8
SYSTEM

Comments

Even though this example has a lot of steps, the concept is very easy. Testing the original DLL before translating it is very important. The only thing worse than an application with messed-up resources in one DLL is an application with messed-up resources in twenty DLLs.

It is possible for a resource load to fail, due to lack of memory or some other resource problem. In error conditions, it is a good idea to hard-code the error message and stay out of the string table. For example, if an application determines that no memory can be allocated, the error message should not be stored in the string table, since the call to *LoadString* may fail.

The localization of resources in a Windows application can include not only the text strings, but also bitmaps, icons, menus, and accelerator keys. When localizing an application for use in another country, keep in mind that some icons and bitmaps may have to be changed to fit local customs. Also, it's a good idea to enlist the aid of a native speaker for the translation.

COMPLEXITY
INTERMEDIATE

8.3 How do I...
Use the Win32 registry database?

Problem

I want to use the new Win32 APIs to store private information about my program such as user preferences, a list of the last files loaded, the current window position, and so on. I was using the Win16 functions *Get/WriteProfileString* to write to an INI file, but I understand this technique is being replaced by the Win32 registration database. How do I use this new feature?

Technique

First of all, I want to point out that you can read and write application specific information to the registry by calling the registry related functions of the *CWinApp* class. These are the *GetProfileInt, WriteProfileInt, GetProfileString, WriteProfileString, GetProfileBinary,* and *WriteProfileBinary* functions. Note that *GetProfileBinary* and *WriteProfileBinary* are not officially documented, but they are public members and declared in Afxwin.h. These functions are designed to store and access application specific information from the registry. Be warned: If you don't call *SetRegistryKey* first, these methods will use your application's private INI file instead of the registry.

8.3 USE THE WIN32 REGISTRY DATABASE

Figure 8-13 The Registry application displaying a value from the registry

Sometimes you need to read and write data to the registry that is not your own application specific data. This How-To creates a *CRegKey* class that you can use to read and write data to any location in the registry—not just your own application area.

Win16 programs store private information in plain text INI files, which leads to many problems. For example, INI files don't have any security mechanism. Users can modify entries in these files, sometimes with unpredictable results. Multiple installations of the same application might require multiple copies of the INI file. INI files only support text data; binary data can't be saved. The registration database was created to solve some of these problems regarding OLE in Windows 3.1. For Win32 applications, the registration database was improved through new APIs.

The Win32 API calls used to access the registry are much more flexible than the Win16 calls that manipulate INI files. Unfortunately, this also makes the API more difficult to use since there are some new rules about using the registry API that might be a little confusing if you haven't used them before.

To reduce the complexity of the registry APIs, a class can be created that wraps most of the registry functionality while presenting a simple interface. This How-To writes the *CRegKey* class, which allows easy access to registry information while handling the housekeeping details. The example program uses the *CRegKey* class to read and write the registered owner's name for Windows. This is the name that appears in the About box in any of the Windows applet applications. You would not be able to access this registry key using the *CWinApp* registry functions mentioned earlier. Figure 8-13 shows the example application in action. The Windows registry key and subkeys are shown in Figure 8-14.

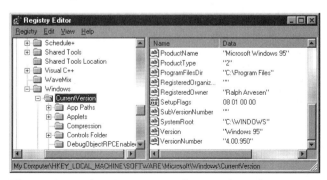

Figure 8-14 The CurrentVersion registry key

459

Steps

1. Create a new project called Registry using MFC AppWizard (exe). Create a Dialog-based application and press the Finish button.

Classes to be created:
Application: CRegistryApp in Registry.h and Registry.cpp
Dialog: CRegistryDlg in RegistryDlg.h and RegistryDlg.cpp

Features:
+ About box on system menu
+ 3D Controls
+ Uses shared DLL implementation (MFC40.DLL)

2. Edit the IDD_REGISTRY _DIALOG dialog. Add the following controls to the dialog box as shown in Figure 8-15. The edit control will display the contents of the RegisteredOwner value of the CurrentVersion registry key.

Control	ID	Attributes
System Information group box	IDC_STATIC	Defaults
Registered Owner: label	IDC_STATIC	Defaults
Edit control	IDC_OWNER	Defaults
Apply button	IDC_APPLY	Defaults
Exit button	IDCANCEL	Defaults

3. Add a member variable to CRegistryDlg. Add the following member variable to *CRegistryDlg* using the Member Variables tab in ClassWizard. The *m_strOwner* variable stores the contents of the edit control.

Control ID	Type	Member
IDC_OWNER	CString	m_strOwner

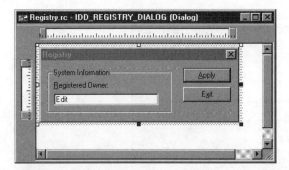

Figure 8-15 Creating the Registry example dialog box

8.3 USE THE WIN32 REGISTRY DATABASE

4. Declare the CRegKey class. Create a new file called Regkey.h and add the following code. Notice that the header file winreg.h is included since we are using the registry functions.

```
#include "winreg.h"

class CRegKey
{
// Construction
public:
        CRegKey();
        virtual ~CRegKey();

// Operations
public:
        LONG Open (HKEY hKeyRoot, LPCTSTR pszPath);
        void Close();

        LONG Write (LPCTSTR pszKey, DWORD dwVal);
        LONG Write (LPCTSTR pszKey, LPCTSTR pszVal);
        LONG Write (LPCTSTR pszKey, const BYTE* pData, DWORD dwLength);

        LONG Read (LPCTSTR pszKey, DWORD& dwVal);
        LONG Read (LPCTSTR pszKey, CString& sVal);
        LONG Read (LPCTSTR pszKey, BYTE* pData, DWORD& dwLength);

protected:
        HKEY    m_hKey;
        CString m_sPath;
};
```

5. Define the CRegKey class. Create a new file called Regkey.cpp as follows:

```
#include "stdafx.h"
#include "Regkey.h"

CRegKey::CRegKey()
{
    m_hKey = NULL;
}

CRegKey::~CRegKey()
{
        Close();
}

LONG CRegKey::Open (HKEY hKeyRoot, LPCTSTR pszPath)
{
    DWORD dw;
    m_sPath = pszPath;

    return RegCreateKeyEx (hKeyRoot, pszPath, 0L, NULL,
          REG_OPTION_VOLATILE, KEY_ALL_ACCESS, NULL,
          &m_hKey, &dw);
}
```

continued on next page

continued from previous page

```cpp
void CRegKey::Close()
{
    if (m_hKey)
    {
        RegCloseKey (m_hKey);
        m_hKey = NULL;
    }
}

LONG CRegKey::Write (LPCTSTR pszKey, DWORD dwVal)
{
    ASSERT(m_hKey);
    ASSERT(pszKey);
    return RegSetValueEx (m_hKey, pszKey, 0L, REG_DWORD,
            (CONST BYTE*) &dwVal, sizeof(DWORD));
}

LONG CRegKey::Write (LPCTSTR pszKey, LPCTSTR pszData)
{
    ASSERT(m_hKey);
    ASSERT(pszKey);
    ASSERT(pszData);
    ASSERT(AfxIsValidAddress(pszData, strlen(pszData), FALSE));

    return RegSetValueEx (m_hKey, pszKey, 0L, REG_SZ,
            (CONST BYTE*) pszData, strlen(pszData) + 1);
}

LONG CRegKey::Write (LPCTSTR pszKey, const BYTE* pData,
    DWORD dwLength)
{
    ASSERT(m_hKey);
    ASSERT(pszKey);
    ASSERT(pData && dwLength > 0);
    ASSERT(AfxIsValidAddress(pData, dwLength, FALSE));

    return RegSetValueEx (m_hKey, pszKey, 0L, REG_BINARY,
            pData, dwLength);
}

LONG CRegKey::Read (LPCTSTR pszKey, DWORD& dwVal)
{
    ASSERT(m_hKey);
    ASSERT(pszKey);

    DWORD dwType;
    DWORD dwSize = sizeof (DWORD);
    DWORD dwDest;

    LONG lRet = RegQueryValueEx (m_hKey, (LPSTR) pszKey, NULL,
            &dwType, (BYTE *) &dwDest, &dwSize);

    if (lRet == ERROR_SUCCESS)
        dwVal = dwDest;
```

8.3
USE THE WIN32 REGISTRY DATABASE

```
        return lRet;
}

LONG CRegKey::Read (LPCTSTR pszKey, CString& sVal)
{
        ASSERT(m_hKey);
        ASSERT(pszKey);

        DWORD dwType;
        DWORD dwSize = 200;
        char  string[200];

        LONG lReturn = RegQueryValueEx (m_hKey, (LPSTR) pszKey, NULL,
            &dwType, (BYTE *) string, &dwSize);

        if (lReturn == ERROR_SUCCESS)
            sVal = string;

        return lReturn;
}

LONG CRegKey::Read (LPCTSTR pszKey, BYTE* pData, DWORD& dwLen)
{
        ASSERT(m_hKey);
        ASSERT(pszKey);

        DWORD dwType;

        return RegQueryValueEx (m_hKey, (LPSTR) pszKey, NULL,
            &dwType, pData, &dwLen);
}
```

Add Regkey.cpp to the project when you're finished.

6. Modify the CRegistryDlg::OnInitDialog function. Before the dialog is shown, the current value from the registry must be extracted. Locate *OnInitDialog* in RegistryDlg.cpp and modify it as shown here:

```
BOOL CRegistryDlg::OnInitDialog()
{
        CDialog::OnInitDialog();

        // Add "About..." menu item to system menu.

        // IDM_ABOUTBOX must be in the system command range.
        ASSERT((IDM_ABOUTBOX & 0xFFF0) == IDM_ABOUTBOX);
        ASSERT(IDM_ABOUTBOX < 0xF000);

        CMenu* pSysMenu = GetSystemMenu(FALSE);
        CString strAboutMenu;
        strAboutMenu.LoadString(IDS_ABOUTBOX);
        if (!strAboutMenu.IsEmpty())
        {
            pSysMenu->AppendMenu(MF_SEPARATOR);
            pSysMenu->AppendMenu(MF_STRING, IDM_ABOUTBOX, strAboutMenu);
        }
```

continued on next page

CHAPTER 8
SYSTEM

continued from previous page

```
    // Set the icon for this dialog.  The framework does this automatically
    //   when the application's main window is not a dialog
    SetIcon(m_hIcon, TRUE);          // Set big icon
    SetIcon(m_hIcon, FALSE);         // Set small icon

    // Open registry key.
    CRegKey regKey;
    long lResult = regKey.Open(HKEY_LOCAL_MACHINE,
         _T("SOFTWARE\\Microsoft\\Windows\\CurrentVersion"));

    // Get contents of registered owner value.
    if (lResult == ERROR_SUCCESS)
    {
        regKey.Read(_T("RegisteredOwner"), m_strOwner);
        UpdateData(FALSE);
    }

    return TRUE;  // return TRUE  unless you set the focus to a control
}
```

7. **Use the WizardBar to handle BN_CLICKED for the Apply push button.**
   The contents of the edit control is saved to the registry when the Apply button is pressed. Use the WizardBar to handle the BN_CLICKED message for the IDC_APPLY object ID for the *CRegistryDlg* class. Add the following code to the message handler:

```
void CRegistryDlg::OnApply()
{
    // Open registry key.
    CRegKey regKey;
    long lResult = regKey.Open(HKEY_LOCAL_MACHINE,
         _T("SOFTWARE\\Microsoft\\Windows\\CurrentVersion"));

    // Write contents of edit control to registry.
    if (lResult == ERROR_SUCCESS)
    {
        UpdateData(TRUE);
        regKey.Write(_T("RegisteredOwner"), m_strOwner);
    }
}
```

8. **Add an include file for the CRegKey class.** Since the *CRegistryDlg* class uses *CRegKey*, you have to include the declaration for *CRegKey*. At the top of RegistryDlg.cpp, add an include file for Regkey.h as shown here:

```
#include "stdafx.h"
#include "Registry.h"
#include "RegistryDlg.h"
#include "Regkey.h"
```

9. **Build and test the application.** Run the application. Notice that the registered owner is the same name as displayed in the About box in Explorer. Enter a new name and press Apply. The About box for Explorer should display the

new name. Run RegEdit and look at the RegisteredOwner value for the HKEY_LOCAL_MACHINE \SOFTWARE\Microsoft\Windows\CurrentVersion key. The value should be the same as displayed in the example application.

How It Works

The registry database is arranged as a hierarchy, with user, application, and system-level information separated into different nodes of the database. Information about the current user is kept separate from system information.

When the *CRegistryDlg* object is constructed, it creates a *CRegKey* object and opens a path to the current version information for Windows in the registry. Information fetched from the registry populates the edit control with the RegisteredOwner value. Of course, we're using *UpdateData* to make the data transfer easier.

Before it can be used, *Open* must be called for the *CRegKey* object. *CRegKey::Open* takes two parameters: an HKEY that specifies which root of the registry to access, and a path to the information in the registry. If the path does not exist, it is created. The HKEY returned from *RegCreateKeyEx* is stored as *m_hKey*. Note that some assumptions are made about access rights and other parameters passed to *RegCreateKeyEx*.

CRegKey::Read retrieves the value of a specific key from the registry. The first parameter represents the key text, and the second is either a DWORD reference, a *CString* reference, or a pointer to a section of memory. The *Read* method is overloaded for all three types.

After fetching the information from the registry, the open key must be closed by calling *CRegKey::Close*. If the key is not explicitly closed, the destructor will take care of it when the object goes out of scope.

Storing information back in the registry is similar to reading from it. We instantiate a *CRegKey* object in the *CRegisterDlg::OnApply* method. After transferring the dialog control data to member variables through *UpdateData*, they're saved using *CRegKey::Write*.

Comments

Using the registry instead of INI files makes Win32 applications more robust. For example, it is much easier to store information about a particular version of an application in a unique location. Also, information can now be stored in a variety of formats, without the need for conversions once required with Win16. The registry also makes it easier to write an uninstall program, since removing a branch from the registry can be done with one function call.

8.4 How do I... Make multiple inheritance work in MFC?

COMPLEXITY: INTERMEDIATE

Problem

I have two similar classes that share some code. I'd like to make a new superclass out of the shared code, but the two classes inherit from different parts of the MFC tree. How do I use multiple inheritance to solve this problem and still have working MFC classes?

Technique

Even though Visual C++ supports multiple inheritance, you won't see it used anywhere in MFC—MFC is a single-inheritance class hierarchy. This is sometimes called a Smalltalk-style class hierarchy, because the Smalltalk language does not support multiple inheritance, and all classes ultimately descend from a single base class, an abstract superclass. In the case of MFC, this class is *CObject*.

The combination of an abstract superclass with multiple inheritance presents a problem. When a class has more than one base class derived from the abstract superclass, some methods become ambiguous.

Consider the *CObject* class, which has a *Dump* method for diagnostic output. If we defined a class *CMyClass*, which has both *CWnd* and *CObject* as its base classes, calls to the *Dump* method would be ambiguous (does the compiler use *CWnd*'s or *CObject*'s *Dump*?). We would need to use the class scope operator (::) to specify the reference to *Dump*. More specifically, we would need to call *CWnd::Dump* or *CObject::Dump* when calling *Dump* from a member function of *CMyClass*, as illustrated in Figure 8-16.

The problem of ambiguous members only arises when a class has more than one base class derived from a common superclass. Only one of the base classes derives from *CObject* in this How-To.

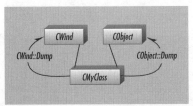

Figure 8-16 Ambiguous Dump methods

8.4 MAKE MULTIPLE INHERITANCE WORK IN MFC

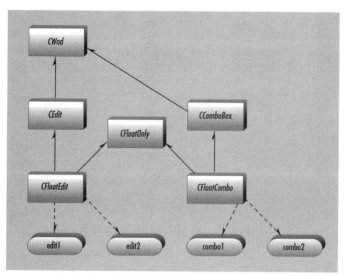

Figure 8-17 Multiple inheritance for CFloatCombo and CFloatEdit

A How-To in Chapter 3 presents a class called *CFloatEdit*, which is derived from *CEdit*. This class provided character-by-character validation of the user's input to ensure that the character was valid for a floating-point number.

For this example, we will reimplement *CFloatEdit*. But this time it will have two base classes: *CEdit* as before and a new class, *CFloatOnly*. The new *CFloatOnly* is an abstract base class designed for derivation in conjunction with one or more base classes. Classes of this type are called mix-in classes.

CFloatOnly has only one method that validates characters as floating-point numbers. Just to emphasize that multiple inheritance assists in reuse of code, we will derive a *CFloatCombo* class from *CFloatOnly*. The class *CFloatCombo* implements a combo box with the same character validation properties as *CFloatEdit*. This class and object hierarchy are illustrated in the Figure 8-17. After you successfully build and run this example program, you will see a dialog like the one shown in Figure 8-18.

Steps

1. Create a new project called Inherit using the MFC AppWizard (exe).
Choose the Dialog-based version and press the Finish button.

Classes to be created:
Application: CInheritApp in Inherit.h and Inherit.cpp
Dialog: CInheritDlg in InheritDlg.h and InheritDlg.cpp

Figure 8-18 The edit and combo box controls are both derived from base control classes as well as CFloatOnly

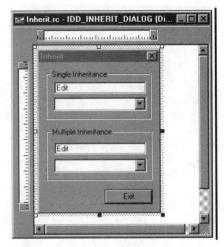

Figure 8-19 Creating the Inherit dialog box

Features:
- + About box on system menu
- + 3D Controls
- + Uses shared DLL implementation (MFC40.DLL)

2. **Edit the IDD_INHERIT_DIALOG dialog.** Add the following controls to the dialog box as shown in Figure 8-19. The controls in the single-inheritance group will only derive from MFC control classes, whereas the controls in the multiple-inheritance group will derive from multiple classes.

Control	ID	Attributes
Single-Inheritance group box	IDC_STATIC	Defaults
Edit box	IDC_EDIT	Defaults
Combo box	IDC_COMBO	Drop-down
Multiple-Inheritance group box	IDC_STATIC	Defaults
Edit box	IDC_FLTEDIT	Defaults
Combo box	IDC_FLTCOMBO	Drop-down
Exit button	IDCANCEL	Default button

3. **Create the CFloatOnly class.** Declare the new class by creating a file called FloatOnly.h and insert the following contents:

```
#ifndef _FLOATONLY_
#define _FLOATONLY_

class CFloatOnly
{
```

8.4
MAKE MULTIPLE INHERITANCE WORK IN MFC

```cpp
public:
    BOOL IsFloatChar(UINT nChar, CString& currentString);
};

#endif
```

4. Define the CFloatOnly class. Create a new file called FloatOnly.cpp and add the following code:

```cpp
#include "stdafx.h"
#include "FloatOnly.h"

#include <ctype.h>
#include <math.h>
#include <stdlib.h>

BOOL CFloatOnly::IsFloatChar(UINT nChar, CString& currentString)
{
    // Check to see if the character is valid for a floating point
    // number (the character must be either a 0-9 or a decimal point) or
    // a control character was entered.

    // If the character is valid, return TRUE, which indicates to the
    // caller that the character was valid. Otherwise
    // if the character is invalid, drop it and beep
    // the speaker.


    // If the character is a decimal point, and there is already a
    // decimal point in the string, then beep and exit.
    if (nChar == '.')
    {
        if (currentString.Find('.') != -1)
        {
            MessageBeep(MB_ICONASTERISK);
            return FALSE;
        }
    }

    if (isdigit(nChar) || (nChar == '.') || (nChar < 0x20))
        return TRUE;

    else
    {
        MessageBeep(MB_ICONASTERISK);
        return FALSE;
    }
}
```

This is where we implement the character-by-character input validation. Since *CFloatEdit* and *CFloatCombo* inherit from *CFloatOnly*, both classes have access to this code. The *IsFloatChar* member function performs the character-by-character input validation. It is passed the keypress code and the contents of the control as a string. If the character is legal for input, *IsFloatChar* returns TRUE, and the caller should then call its base class *OnChar* message handler.

Make sure you remember to add FloatOnly.cpp to your project before you continue to the next step.

5. **Create the new floating number edit class.** Create a subclass of *CEdit* that will be used in the dialog later. Supply the following information to ClassWizard:

Class name:	CFloatEdit
Base class:	CEdit
File:	FloatEdit.cpp

   Now, modify the class to also inherit from *CFloatOnly* by changing a few lines at the top of FloatEdit.h to look like this:

```
// FloatEdit.h file
#include "FloatOnly.h"
class CFloatEdit : public CEdit, public CFloatOnly
...
```

   Here, you can see multiple inheritance, live and in-person. We have derived the *CFloatEdit* class from both the *CEdit* and the *CFloatOnly* classes. Since only *CEdit* is derived via the MFC hierarchy, member ambiguity is not a problem. Note that we put *CEdit* first in the list of derived classes. This is to satisfy a requirement of MFC, and it allows the MFC message maps to function properly. Another restriction (which is not a concern in this example) is that there must not be more than one base class which is derived from *CWnd*.

6. **Create the new floating number combo box class.** Create a subclass of *CComboBox* that the dialog will use later. Supply the following information to ClassWizard:

Class name:	CFloatCombo
Base class:	CComboBox
File:	FloatCombo.cpp

   Now, modify the class to also inherit from *CFloatOnly* by changing a few lines at the top of FloatCombo.h to look like this:

```
// FloatCombo.h file
#include "FloatOnly.h"
class CFloatCombo : public CComboBox, public CFloatOnly
...
```

7. **Use the WizardBar to handle WM_CHAR for CFloatEdit and CFloatCombo.** The controls receive a WM_CHAR message whenever the user presses a key. Handling this message allows you to evaluate the character

8.4
MAKE MULTIPLE INHERITANCE WORK IN MFC

and decide if you want to display the character. Add the following code to the *CFloatEdit* and *CFloatCombo* classes:

```
// FloatEdit.cpp file
void CFloatEdit::OnChar(UINT nChar, UINT nRepCnt, UINT nFlags)
{
    // get contents of edit control
    CString strText;
    GetWindowText(strText);

    // determine if new character is a floating number character
    if (IsFloatChar(nChar, strText))
        CEdit::OnChar(nChar, nRepCnt, nFlags);
}

// FloatCombo.cpp file
void CFloatCombo::OnChar(UINT nChar, UINT nRepCnt, UINT nFlags)
{
    // get contents of combobox edit window
    CString strText;
    GetWindowText(strText);

    // determine if new character is a floating number character
    if (IsFloatChar(nChar, strText))
        CComboBox::OnChar(nChar, nRepCnt, nFlags);
}
```

8. **Use ClassWizard to add member variables to CInheritDlg.** Add these member variables to attach dialog controls to *CFloatEdit* and *CFloatCombo* objects.

Control ID	Type	Member
IDC_FLTEDIT	CFloatEdit	m_wndEdit
IDC_FLTCOMBO	CFloatCombo	m_wndCombo

Since *CInheritDlg* references *CFloatEdit* and *CFloatCombo*, make sure you remember to add the class declaration files at the top of InheritDlg.cpp.

```
#include "FloatEdit.h"
#include "FloatCombo.h"

class CInheritDlg : public CDialog
{
...
```

9. **Edit the CInheritDlg::OnInitDialog function.** Handling the WM_CHAR message for the combo box is a little misleading—actually we are handling the WM_CHAR message for the edit window portion of the combo box (the combo box never receives WM_CHAR messages). This means we need to subclass the edit portion of the combo box. Add the following code to the

CInheritDlg::OnInitDialog function and make sure to add the code before the base class *OnInitDialog* function is called.

```
BOOL CInheritDlg::OnInitDialog()
{
    // subclass the edit portion of the combo box control
    HWND hWndEdit = GetDlgItem(IDC_FLTCOMBO)->GetWindow(GW_CHILD)->m_hWnd;
    m_wndCombo.SubclassWindow(hWndEdit);

    CDialog::OnInitDialog();
    CenterWindow();

    // Add "About..." menu item to system menu.
    // IDM_ABOUTBOX must be in the system command range.
    ASSERT((IDM_ABOUTBOX & 0xFFF0) == IDM_ABOUTBOX);
    ASSERT(IDM_ABOUTBOX < 0xF000);

    CMenu* pSysMenu = GetSystemMenu(FALSE);
    CString strAboutMenu;
    strAboutMenu.LoadString(IDS_ABOUTBOX);
    if (!strAboutMenu.IsEmpty())
    {
        pSysMenu->AppendMenu(MF_SEPARATOR);
        pSysMenu->AppendMenu(MF_STRING, IDM_ABOUTBOX, strAboutMenu);
    }

    return TRUE;
}
```

10. **Build and test the application.** Notice that you can enter any character into the top two controls, but you hear a beep when you enter invalid characters (anything but a period or a number) into the two bottom controls.

How It Works

In both the *CFloatEdit* and *CFloatCombo* classes, we have defined a message-handling member function for the WM_CHAR message. There's no real character validation code in the *OnChar* methods—they simply pass that task on to the *IsFloatChar* member function of the *CFloatOnly* class.

As we described above, *CFloatOnly* is a mix-in class, which is a type of pure abstract base class. We say this type of base class is "pure" because it is only suitable for deriving other classes. You would never want to instantiate an object of type *CFloatOnly*.

Comments

The floating-point validation routine is somewhat simplistic; it doesn't even support the negative sign. If you wanted to add support for the negative sign, you'd make changes in one place, *CFloatOnly::IsFloatChar*. If we had opted not to use multiple inheritance and instead copied the *IsFloatChar* code to every class that needed it, adding this new feature would be difficult since it exists in many places.

8.5 DETECT WHEN LAUNCHED APPLICATIONS TERMINATE UNDER WIN32

For more information on restrictions using multiple inheritance with MFC, consult MFC Technical Note 16.

COMPLEXITY: ADVANCED

8.5 How do I... Detect when launched applications terminate under Win32?

Problem

I launch other applications from my program, and I need to detect when they terminate. I used to install a notification callback function using the functions exported by the TOOLHELP.DLL library, but these are not supported under Win32. How do I detect when my launched applications terminate under Win32?

Technique

You are correct, Win32 does not support the TOOLHELP.DLL functions. However, some of them are easy to accomplish under Win32, especially using threads. To solve this problem, you simply create a thread using *AfxBeginThread*, launch the application by calling *CreateProcess*, then wait until the application terminates by calling *WaitForSingleObject*.

However, this How-To takes this a step further by creating a more dynamic example and demonstrates some thread synchronization techniques. MFC applications require you to use the *CWinThread* class to create secondary threads. This class is necessary to make the MFC library fully thread-safe. Plus, some type of thread synchronization is necessary to successfully free all the memory allocated by the *CWinThread* objects.

This How-To presents an application called Launch.exe that launches other programs and detects when they terminate. The path name of the launched application is added to a list box if the launch was successful. A separate thread is created for each launched application, and the thread waits for the application to terminate. After the launched program terminates, its name is removed from the list box.

Critical sections are used to synchronize access to the list so threads don't attempt to add strings to the list box simultaneously. An event object is used to terminate all the active secondary threads when the main program quits. This ensures that the application cooperates nicely with the instantiated *CWinThread* objects, by allowing the threads to terminate and deallocate the appropriate memory. Figure 8-20 shows the sample application in action.

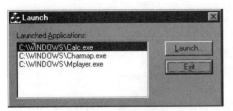

Figure 8-20 Launch program monitoring three launched applications

Steps

1. **Create a new project called Launch using the MFC AppWizard (exe).** Choose a Dialog-based application and press the Finish button.

   Classes to be created:
   Application: CLaunchApp in Launch.h and Launch.cpp
   Dialog: CLaunchDlg in LaunchDlg.h and LaunchDlg.cpp

   Features:
   + About box on system menu
   + 3D Controls
   + Uses shared DLL implementation (MFC40.DLL)

2. **Edit the IDD_LAUNCH_DIALOG dialog.** Add the following controls to the dialog box as shown in Figure 8-21. You launch applications by clicking the Launch... button, and the list box contains a list of them all.

Control	ID	Attributes
Launched Applications label	IDC_STATIC	Defaults
Applications list box	IDC_LIST	Defaults
Launch... button	IDC_LAUNCH	Default button
Exit button	IDCANCEL	Defaults

3. **Add a member variable to CLaunchDlg.** Add the following member variable to *CLaunchDlg* using the Member Variables tab in ClassWizard. The *m_wndList* will be used later to modify the contents of the list box control.

Control ID	Type	Member
IDC_LIST	CListBox	m_wndList

4. **Define a structure to hold thread information.** When a thread is created, the command line, event object, handle to the list box window, and critical

8.5
DETECT WHEN LAUNCHED APPLICATIONS TERMINATE UNDER WIN32

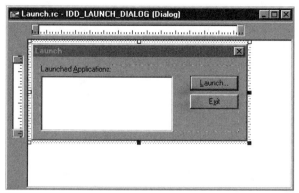

Figure 8-21 Creating the Launch example dialog box

section are passed to the thread function. Define a structure that contains these members in the file Launch.h.

```
// Launch.h : main header file for the LAUNCH application
//

#ifndef __AFXWIN_H__
    #error include 'stdafx.h' before including this file for PCH
#endif

#include "resource.h"        // main symbols

typedef struct
{
    CString strPathName;              // path to executable
    CEvent* pTermThreadEvent;         // terminate thread event
    HWND hWndList;                    // window handle to list box
    CCriticalSection* pcsList;        // critical section for list box
} THREADINFO, *FAR LPTHREADINFO;

...
```

5. **Include the MFC synchronization header file.** You must include afxmt.h since this example uses the new MFC synchronization classes. Add the following line to StdAfx.h:

```
#define VC_EXTRALEAN            // Exclude rarely-used stuff from Windows headers

#include <afxwin.h>             // MFC core and standard components
#include <afxext.h>             // MFC extensions
#ifndef _AFX_NO_AFXCMN_SUPPORT
#include <afxcmn.h>             // MFC support for Windows 95 Common Controls
#endif // _AFX_NO_AFXCMN_SUPPORT

#include <afxmt.h>              // MFC support for synchronization classes
```

CHAPTER 8
SYSTEM

6. **Add data members to the CLaunchDlg class.** An event object (a Win32 object, not C++ object) is created that allows the application to terminate all the monitoring threads. This event object is encapsulated in the *m_pTermThreadsEvent* data member. The critical section data member *m_csListBox* is used to synchronize access to the list box. Add the following two data members to the *CLaunchDlg* class in the file LaunchDlg.h:

```
public:
    CEvent*          m_pTermThreadsEvent;
    CCriticalSection m_csListBox;
```

7. **Edit CLaunchDlg::OnInitDialog.** An event object is created here that will be used later to terminate all the monitoring threads. Add the following code to the *OnInitDialog* member function for the *CLaunchDlg* class:

```
BOOL CLaunchDlg::OnInitDialog()
{
    CDialog::OnInitDialog();

    // Add "About..." menu item to system menu.

    // IDM_ABOUTBOX must be in the system command range.
    ASSERT((IDM_ABOUTBOX & 0xFFF0) == IDM_ABOUTBOX);
    ASSERT(IDM_ABOUTBOX < 0xF000);

    CMenu* pSysMenu = GetSystemMenu(FALSE);
    CString strAboutMenu;
    strAboutMenu.LoadString(IDS_ABOUTBOX);
    if (!strAboutMenu.IsEmpty())
    {
        pSysMenu->AppendMenu(MF_SEPARATOR);
        pSysMenu->AppendMenu(MF_STRING, IDM_ABOUTBOX, strAboutMenu);
    }

    // Set the icon for this dialog.  The framework does this automatically
    //  when the application's main window is not a dialog
    SetIcon(m_hIcon, TRUE);         // Set big icon
    SetIcon(m_hIcon, FALSE);        // Set small icon


    // Create event object. This event object can be used to terminate
    // all monitoring threads at any time. It is signaled when the main
    // application is about to terminate, thus preventing any memory
    // leaks with the allocated CWinThread objects.
    m_pTermThreadsEvent = new CEvent(FALSE, TRUE);
    ASSERT_VALID(m_pTermThreadsEvent);

    return TRUE;
}
```

8. **Use the WizardBar to handle BN_CLICKED for the Launch push button.** The BN_CLICKED notification message is sent to the dialog box window when the Launch push button is clicked. Use the WizardBar to handle the

8.5
DETECT WHEN LAUNCHED APPLICATIONS TERMINATE UNDER WIN32

BN_CLICKED message for the IDC_LAUNCH object ID for the *CLaunchDlg* class. Add the following code to the message handler:

```
void CLaunchDlg::OnLaunch()
{
    CFileDialog  dlgFile(TRUE, NULL, NULL,
         OFN_HIDEREADONLY, _T("Application (*.EXE)|*.EXE|"));

    // If select file, allocate memory to hold path name. This is very
    // important since the thread function will access this address
    // after this function has terminated. It is the responsibility of
    // the thread function to free the memory for the path name.
    if (dlgFile.DoModal() == IDOK)
    {
        // Allocate structure that will pass relevant information
        // to the thread function. The thread function is responsible
        // for freeing the structure.
        LPTHREADINFO pThreadInfo = new THREADINFO;
        if (pThreadInfo)
        {
            // fill in members of structure
            pThreadInfo->pTermThreadEvent = m_pTermThreadsEvent;
            pThreadInfo->hWndList = m_wndList.m_hWnd;
            pThreadInfo->pcsList = &m_csListBox;
            pThreadInfo->strPathName = dlgFile.GetPathName();

            // Create CWinThread object. The thread function will
            // retrieve and store the handle to this thread in the
            // list box. Then we can make sure the thread is
            // terminated before the main application is terminated.
            AfxBeginThread(LaunchAndWait, pThreadInfo);
        }
    }
}
```

9. **Use the WizardBar to handle WM_DESTROY for CLaunchDlg.** Before the dialog is destroyed, the monitoring threads need to be terminated. This allows the MFC class library to free the appropriate memory associated with all the monitoring threads. Add the following code to the message handler:

```
void CLaunchDlg::OnDestroy()
{
    // prevent other threads from accessing the list box
    m_csListBox.Lock();

    // get number of items in list box
    int nItems = m_wndList.GetCount();

    // process if there are items in list box
    if (nItems && nItems != LB_ERR)
    {
        // allocate an array of handles
        HANDLE* pHandles = new HANDLE[nItems];
```

continued on next page

continued from previous page

```
                // Retrieve each thread handle from list box. This is the
                // list of the currently active threads.
                int nIndex;
                for (nIndex=0; nIndex < nItems; nIndex++)
                    pHandles[nIndex] = (HANDLE)m_wndList.GetItemData(nIndex);

                // allow other threads to access the list box now
                m_csListBox.Unlock();

                // Terminate all the active threads. This causes the threads that
                // are still monitoring launched application to terminate because
                // they terminate when the launched application terminates OR
                // when this event becomes signaled.
                m_pTermThreadsEvent->SetEvent();

                // We signaled the event, which terminates all active monitoring
                // threads. Now sit back and wait for all of the threads to
                // terminate. This allows all of the allocated CWinThread objects
                // to terminate and clean up properly. Just deleting the
                // CWinThread objects will cause memory leaks.
                WaitForMultipleObjects(nItems, pHandles, TRUE, INFINITE);

                // free the memory used to store the list of thread handles
                delete pHandles;
        }

        // There were no items in list box, so
        // allow other threads to access the list box.
        else
                m_csListBox.Unlock();

        // delete the CEvent object that was allocated eariler
        delete m_pTermThreadsEvent;

        CDialog::OnDestroy();
}
```

10. Implement the thread function LaunchAndWait. The thread function *LaunchAndWait* launches an application (really a process) and waits for the process to terminate before returning. However, since this is a thread function, other threads in the same process continue to execute. Create the file Thread.cpp and add the following thread and helper functions to the file. After you finish, add Thread.cpp to the project.

```
#include "stdafx.h"
#include "LaunchDlg.h"
#include "Thread.h"

UINT LaunchAndWait(LPVOID pParam)
{
        // assign address of parameter
        LPTHREADINFO pThreadInfo = (LPTHREADINFO)pParam;

        // process structure that will receive info on the new process
        PROCESS_INFORMATION stProcessInfo;
```

8.5
DETECT WHEN LAUNCHED APPLICATIONS TERMINATE UNDER WIN32

```
    // launch application
    if (LaunchApplication(pThreadInfo->strPathName, &stProcessInfo))
    {
        // Need to store thread to list to prevent memory leaks with
        // CWinThread object. If our main app is requested to terminate
        // before this thread terminates, then we need to terminate
        // this thread first.

        // prevent other threads from accessing list box
        pThreadInfo->pcsList->Lock();

        AddToList(pThreadInfo->hWndList,                // list box
            pThreadInfo->strPathName,                   // app name
            (DWORD)AfxGetThread()->m_hThread);          // store thread

        // allow other threads to access list box
        pThreadInfo->pcsList->Unlock();

        // Wait for either the process to terminate or the event
        // to be signaled. If the event is signaled, then that
        // indicates the main application is terminating and all open
        // threads need to terminate also.
        HANDLE hThreads[2];
        hThreads[0] = pThreadInfo->pTermThreadEvent->m_hObject;
        hThreads[1] = stProcessInfo.hProcess;

        // wait for application to terminate or event to be signaled
        DWORD dwIndex = WaitForMultipleObjects(
                            2, hThreads, FALSE, INFINITE);

        // remove from list only if application terminated;
        // do not remove from list if event was signaled
        if (dwIndex)
        {
            // prevent other threads from accessing list box
            pThreadInfo->pcsList->Lock();

            RemoveFromList(pThreadInfo->hWndList,
                AfxGetThread()->m_hThread);

            // allow other threads to access list box
            pThreadInfo->pcsList->Unlock();
        }

        // close handles to process and its main thread
        CloseHandle(stProcessInfo.hThread);
        CloseHandle(stProcessInfo.hProcess);
    }

    // The main thread allocated the structure;
    // it is our responsibility to free it.
    if (pThreadInfo)
        delete pThreadInfo;

    return 0;
}
```

continued on next page

continued from previous page

```
BOOL LaunchApplication(LPCTSTR pCmdLine, PROCESS_INFORMATION* pProcessInfo)
{
    // startup structure for new process
    STARTUPINFO  stStartUpInfo;

    // since a lot of members are reserved or ignored, we can just set
    // all members to 0 and then reset the members we care about
    memset(&stStartUpInfo,0,sizeof(STARTUPINFO));

    stStartUpInfo.cb = sizeof(STARTUPINFO);          // size of structure
    stStartUpInfo.dwFlags = STARTF_USESHOWWINDOW;    // use wShowWindow member
    stStartUpInfo.wShowWindow = SW_SHOWDEFAULT;      // default value

    // create new process; process creates primary
    // thread and launches application
    return CreateProcess(NULL, (LPCTSTR)pCmdLine, NULL, NULL, FALSE,
            NORMAL_PRIORITY_CLASS, NULL,
            NULL, &stStartUpInfo, pProcessInfo);
}


void AddToList(HWND hWnd, LPCTSTR pCmdLine, DWORD hThread)
{
    // get pointer to window object
    CListBox* pList = (CListBox*)CWnd::FromHandle(hWnd);

    // add string to list box
    int nIndex = pList->AddString(pCmdLine);

    // associate monitoring thread with list box entry
    pList->SetItemData(nIndex, hThread);
}


void RemoveFromList(HWND hWnd, HANDLE hThread)
{
    // get pointer to window object
    CListBox* pList = (CListBox*)CWnd::FromHandle(hWnd);

    // find index that contains matching thread handle
    int   nItems = pList->GetCount();
    int   nIndex = 0;
    BOOL  bFound = FALSE;

    // loop until find match or reach end of list box
    while (!bFound && (nIndex < nItems))
    {
        // check if found matching thread handle
        if ((HANDLE)pList->GetItemData(nIndex) == hThread)
        {
            // remove string from list box
            pList->DeleteString(nIndex);
            bFound = TRUE;
        }
```

8.5 DETECT WHEN LAUNCHED APPLICATIONS TERMINATE UNDER WIN32

```
            nIndex++;
    }
}
```

11. **Create the header file.** Create the file Thread.h and add the following function prototypes to the file:

```
// monitor thread function
UINT LaunchAndWait(LPVOID pParam);

// helper functions
BOOL LaunchApplication(LPCTSTR pCmdLine, PROCESS_INFORMATION* pProcessInfo);
void AddToList(HWND hWnd, LPCTSTR pCmdLine, DWORD hThread);
void RemoveFromList(HWND hWnd, HANDLE hThread);
```

12. **Include the header file.** Include the Thread.h header file at the top of the file LaunchDlg.cpp like this:

```
#include "stdafx.h"
#include "Launch.h"
#include "LaunchDlg.h"
#include "Thread.h"
```

13. **Build and test the application.** Use the Launch button to start Notepad. Quit Notepad and you'll notice the path to Notepad.exe is removed from the list box. Launch and terminate other applications and watch how the applications are added and removed from the list box.

How It Works

CWinThread objects are used to represent all threads in MFC applications. Prior versions of MFC (before MFC 3.0) were not thread-safe and you could only use a very limited set of MFC classes in a secondary thread. However, MFC is now thread-safe as long as you create the threads by calling the *AfxBeginThread* function. There are two types of threads: user-interface threads and worker threads. User-interface threads usually handle user interaction, and worker threads usually perform some type of background processing or calculation.

The first parameter to the *AfxBeginThread* function points to the address of a function where the thread should start executing. The thread function accepts a single 32-bit argument and returns a 32-bit return code.

The *AfxBeginThread* function will pass the second parameter to your thread function. This allows you to pass a 32-bit number or a 32-bit pointer to the thread function. In step 8, we pass a pointer to the THREADINFO object. Think of it as a thread "care package"—it has all the information necessary for the thread to do its work.

You can launch an executable by calling the SDK function *CreateProcess*. Since it would take a lot of pages to describe each parameter, see the online documentation for details. Here is the condensed version: You can specify the name of the module to execute, the working directory, security of the process and primary thread, environment information, how the process is created, and the startup information, like this:

```
CreateProcess(NULL, (LPTSTR)pCmdLine, NULL, NULL, FALSE,
    NORMAL_PRIORITY_CLASS, NULL, NULL, &stStartUpInfo, &stProcessInfo);
```

Now you understand how to create a thread by calling the *AfxBeginThread* function and launch an application by calling the *CreateProcess* function, but how do you detect when the application terminates?

When a process object is executing, it is *nonsignaled*. The process object becomes *signaled* when it terminates. A thread can block its execution and wait for a synchronization object to become signaled by using the MFC *CSingleLock* class or calling the SDK function *WaitForSingleObject*. You specify how long you wish to wait by passing the time-out interval in milliseconds—a parameter of INFINITE indicates a very patient thread.

Event Objects

An event object is a synchronization object that has two states: signaled and nonsignaled. This example uses the MFC *CEvent* class in combination with the SDK function *WaitForMultipleObjects* to terminate all the active secondary threads. You create an event object by instantiating an *CEvent* object, and you set the state of the event to signaled by calling the *CEvent::SetEvent* function.

All the secondary threads call the *WaitForMultipleObjects* function to wait until the launched process becomes signaled or the event object becomes signaled. This allows the main thread to terminate all the active secondary threads by simply setting the event object to the signaled state, as in Figure 8-22.

Accessing Shared Resources

Have you ever thought about what would happen if there were no air traffic controllers, and airplanes used the runways whenever they wanted? Not a pretty thought, is it? Well, you will have the same situation in your multithreaded application if threads access shared resources, such as global variables, whenever they want. Just as an airline pilot requests permission for a runway, threads that access shared resources must request permission before continuing.

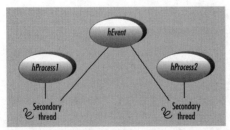

Figure 8-22 Both secondary threads will terminate if the event object is signaled

8.5
DETECT WHEN LAUNCHED APPLICATIONS TERMINATE UNDER WIN32

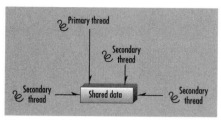

Figure 8-23 Access to shared data is not controlled

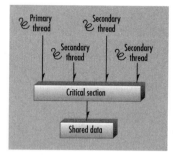

Figure 8-24 Access to shared data is controlled by the critical section

The designers of the operating system decided to implement many methods to control object synchronization: events, mutexes, semaphores, and critical sections. Synchronization objects coordinate the execution of multiple threads. This example uses a critical section object to coordinate access to the shared list box control.

Secondary threads add and delete strings from the list box, and the primary thread retrieves data from the list box. If access to the list box were not controlled, a thread could retrieve data from the list box and be interrupted by another thread that removes that data from the list box. Then, the first thread continues executing with invalid data. If this data happened to be a pointer, you would get a memory access violation if it was freed by the interrupting thread and the memory was accessed at a later time. Figure 8-23 shows separate threads accessing the same shared data. Figure 8-24 shows a critical section controlling access to the shared data—only one thread at a time can access the data.

Critical sections are very easy to use. Since they can be used only in single process applications, they are slightly faster and more efficient than other synchronization objects. Let's see how this example uses critical sections. First a *CCriticalSection* data member is declared in the *CLaunchDlg* class:

```
CCriticalSection   m_csListBox;
```

Now you just need to put wrappers around the code that accesses the shared resource. To request ownership of the critical section, call the *CCriticalSection::Lock* function. The call will immediately return if no other threads currently have ownership of the critical section. If another thread does have ownership of the critical section, your thread is blocked until the other thread releases ownership. When you are finished accessing the shared resource, you release ownership of the critical section by calling the *CCriticalSection::Unlock* function.

In conclusion, let's review the important elements of this project. A secondary thread is created by calling the *AfxBeginThread* function. This thread function launches an application by calling the *CreateProcess* function. It detects when the process terminates by calling the *WaitForMultipleObjects* function. The reason *WaitForMultipleObjects* is

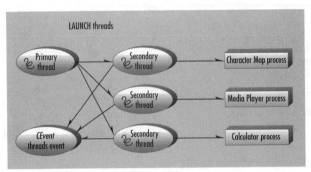

Figure 8-25 Process, threads, and event objects in the Launch application

called instead of *WaitForSingleObject* is to allow the thread to terminate if an event object is set to the signaled state. The main thread will set this event object to the signaled state to terminate all active secondary threads when the sample application itself is requested to terminate. This allows the *CWinThread* objects to be cleanly destroyed and frees up appropriate memory. Critical sections are used around the list box since multiple threads can access this control at any time. Figure 8-25 shows the objects that exist if the processes Calculator, Character Map, and Media Player are launched. The lines indicate the objects that the threads are waiting on to become signaled.

Comments

Visual C++ 4.0 includes several tools to help you develop multithreaded applications. You can obtain a list of all the processes and threads currently running in your system by running the Process Viewer application. It allows you to examine several characteristics of the processes and threads.

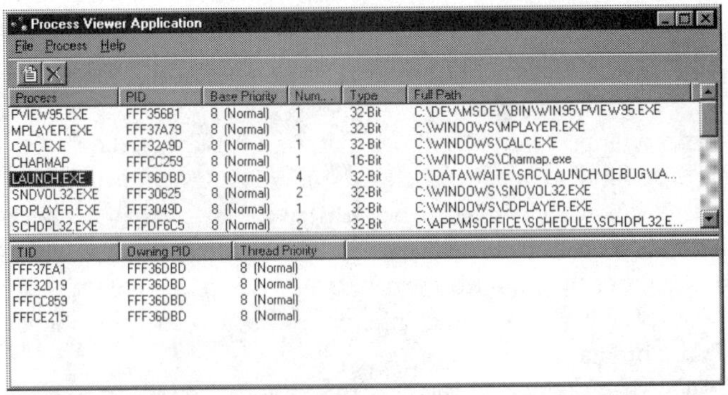

Figure 8-26 Using the Process Viewer application to look at process and thread information

8.5
DETECT WHEN LAUNCHED APPLICATIONS TERMINATE UNDER WIN32

The process view lists all the processes running in the system. It displays the name of the process, location of the process, priority, the process identifier, and number of threads. When you select a process from the process view, similar information is displayed for all its threads. Figure 8-26 shows information about the process LAUNCH. You can see it has four threads: Its primary thread and three secondary threads it created by calling the *AfxBeginThread* function.

The source code for a similar application is provided with Visual C++ (Samples\Sdk\Sdktools\Winnt\Pviewer), so you can see how to implement this type of functionality in your application by examining the source code.

The Spy++ tool allows you to examine process, thread, and window information. You can obtain a list of threads currently running on your system by opening the Threads or Processes windows. Process IDs, module names, and thread IDs are displayed. You can see that the LANCH process has four threads, as shown in Figure 8-27.

The source code for a spy-like application is also provided with Visual C++. The sample source is located in the Samples\Sdk\Sdktools\Spy directory.

Creating multithreaded applications can simplify the design of your application and improve its performance. It can also significantly complicate the design and actually decrease the performance. You should understand the benefits and tradeoffs of creating multithreaded applications, especially synchronization, and decide where you should, and should not, use threads in your application. The Visual C++ online documentation provides several good articles on creating multithreaded applications. Topics include multitasking, processes, threads, and synchronization.

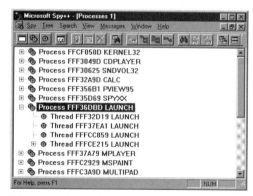

Figure 8-27 Using Spy++ to look at the processes and threads currently running in the system

485

CHAPTER 8
SYSTEM

COMPLEXITY
ADVANCED

8.6 How do I... Use system hooks under Win32?

Problem

I need a way to intercept messages sent to other applications, like mouse messages, using a system-wide hook. How do I install a hook under Win32?

Technique

A hook is a powerful mechanism that lets you install a procedure that intercepts messages before they reach their destination. You can intercept messages for a single application or all applications. Hooks are used in developer tools like Spy++ to show what messages are being sent to other windows. MFC uses hooks to intercept all WM_CREATE messages to subclass windows whenever you call the *Create* member function.

This How-To presents a sample program that applies an action to a target window (such as closing or minimizing) whenever you click the right-mouse button while pressing the [CTRL] key. The workload is distributed between two projects. One project creates the file Mousedll.dll and the other creates the program Mouse.exe that uses the mouse hook DLL.

Mousedll.dll is an Extension DLL that exports the class *CMouseHook*. It contains the implementation for the *CMouseHook* class, the code that installs and uninstalls a system-wide mouse hook, and the mouse hook procedure.

Mouse.exe has a much easier role. It simply instantiates a *CMouseHook* object and decides what action to apply to the target window. The target window is the first window up the parent window hierarchy that contains a system menu. If no window in the hierarchy contains a system menu, then the top-level window is used as the target window. The action is the type of message that will be sent to the target window whenever the user clicks the right-mouse button while pressing the [CTRL] key.

The user selects the type of action to apply to the target window from the Action combo box. The caption of the target window is displayed in the Target edit field to provide feedback to the user. Figure 8-28 shows the mouse application in action.

Figure 8-28 Sample application that installs a system-wide mouse hook

8.6 USE SYSTEM HOOKS UNDER WIN32

Steps to Create the Hook DLL

1. **Create a new project called Mousedll using the MFC AppWizard (dll).** Choose the MFC Extension DLL type and press the Finish button.

   Creating MFC Extension DLL (using a shared copy of MFC) Mousedll.dll targeting:
   Win32

   Main source code in: Mousedll.h and Mousedll.cpp

2. **Create a class declaration file.** Create a new file named Mousedll.h and save it in the project's directory. This file contains the declaration for the *CMouseHook* class that will be exported from the DLL. Add the following code to the file:

```
#ifndef _MOUSEDLL_H
#define _MOUSEDLL_H

class AFX_EXT_CLASS CMouseHook : public CObject
{
public:
        CMouseHook();
        ~CMouseHook();
        HHOOK   Start();
        BOOL    Stop();
        void    SetDisplayWindow(HWND hWnd);
        void    SetAction(UINT nAction);
};

#endif
```

Remember to include the header file in the main source file. Add the following to the Mousedll.cpp file:

```
#include "stdafx.h"
#include <afxdllx.h>
#include "Mousedll.h"
```

3. **Declare function prototypes.** Add the following prototypes to the top of the Mousedll.cpp file:

```
#include "stdafx.h"
#include <afxdllx.h>
#include "Mousedll.h"

#ifdef _DEBUG
#define new DEBUG_NEW
#undef THIS_FILE
static char THIS_FILE[] = __FILE__;
#endif

static AFX_EXTENSION_MODULE MousedllDLL = { NULL, NULL };
```

continued on next page

CHAPTER 8
SYSTEM

continued from previous page

```
// Function prototypes.
#define DLLEXPORT _declspec(dllexport)
extern "C" DLLEXPORT LRESULT WINAPI MouseHookProc(
        int nCode, WPARAM wParam, LPARAM lParam);
```

...

4. **Declare global shared data variables.** Each process gets its own instance copy of global variables in Win32 DLLs. The mouse hook procedure will need access to the global variables. Plus, the variables should be shared among all processes that load the DLL. This can be accomplished by specifying the #pragmadata_seg directive and specifying the section as shared in the SECTIONS part of the DEF file. Add the following global variables near the top of the Mousedll.cpp file:

```
// Shared data section.
#pragma data_seg(".sdata")
        HWND        glhWndPrevTarget = NULL;   // previous target window
        HWND        glhWndDisplay = NULL;      // window that message is sent to
        UINT        glnAction = NULL;          // message to send to target window
        HHOOK       glhHook = NULL;            // hook handle
        HINSTANCE   glhInstance = NULL;        // instance of DLL
#pragma data_seg()
```

Moving variables inside their own section is not enough to share those variables. The linker must know what sections to share. You can do this by adding entries to the SECTIONS section of the DEF file. Add the following code to the Mousedll.def file:

```
LIBRARY        "MOUSEDLL"
DESCRIPTION    'MOUSEDLL Windows Dynamic Link Library'

SECTIONS
    .sdata    READ WRITE SHARED

EXPORTS
    ; Explicit exports can go here
```

5. **Modify the DllMain function.** As mentioned before, the DLL will be attached to every process that receives a mouse message, but the DLL Extension functions only need to be called once. That is why they are invoked only if the DLL has not been attached yet. Make sure the *DllMain* function looks like this:

```
extern "C" int APIENTRY
DllMain(HINSTANCE hInstance, DWORD dwReason, LPVOID lpReserved)
{
    if (dwReason == DLL_PROCESS_ATTACH)
    {
        TRACE0("MOUSEDLL.DLL Initializing!\n");

        if (!MousedllDLL.bInitialized)
        {
```

8.6
USE SYSTEM HOOKS UNDER WIN32

```
            // Extension DLL one-time initialization
            AfxInitExtensionModule(MousedllDLL, hInstance);

            // Insert this DLL into the resource chain
            new CDynLinkLibrary(MousedllDLL);

            // save instance to global variable
            glhInstance = hInstance;
        }
    }

    else if (dwReason == DLL_PROCESS_DETACH)
    {
        TRACE0("MOUSEDLL.DLL Terminating!\n");
    }

    return 1;   // ok
}
```

6. **Add the code for the CMouseHook class.** Implement the constructor and destructor for the *CMouseHook* class. The constructor does not do anything in this sample application, but it may for your application. The destructor invokes the *Stop* member function to make sure the mouse hook is uninstalled. Add the following code to the Mousedll.cpp file:

```
// constructor
CMouseHook::CMouseHook()
{
}

// destructor
CMouseHook::~CMouseHook()
{
    Stop();   // uninstall mouse hook
}
```

The *Start* member function installs a system-wide mouse hook. Add the following code for this member function to the Mousedll.cpp file:

```
HHOOK CMouseHook::Start()
{
    // install systemwide mouse hook
    glhHook = SetWindowsHookEx(WH_MOUSE, MouseHookProc, glhInstance, 0);
    return glhHook;
}
```

The *Stop* member function uninstalls the mouse hook. As noted earlier, it is called in the destructor of the class so users of the class do not have to specifically invoke this function. Add the following code for this member function to the Mousedll.cpp file:

```
BOOL CMouseHook::Stop()
{
    BOOL bResult = FALSE;
```

continued on next page

continued from previous page

```
        // uninstall mouse hook if currently active
        if (glhHook)
        {
            // uninstall mouse hook
            bResult = UnhookWindowsHookEx(glhHook);
            if (bResult)
            {
                // initialize variables
                glhWndPrevTarget = NULL;
                glhWndDisplay = NULL;
                glnAction = NULL;
                glhHook = NULL;
            }
        }

        return bResult;
}
```

A *CMouseHook* object will set the text of a window with the caption of the target window. The target window is the window to which an action will be applied. The *SetDisplayWindow* function specifies what window will display this information. The *SetAction* function specifies the action to apply to the target window. Add the following code for these member functions to the Mousedll.cpp file:

```
// Store the window that will display the caption of the target window.
void CMouseHook::SetDisplayWindow(HWND hWnd)
{
        glhWndDisplay = hWnd;
}

// Store the action that will be sent to the target window.
void CMouseHook::SetAction(UINT nAction)
{
        glnAction = nAction;
}
```

7. **Implement the mouse hook procedure.** You install the mouse hook procedure in the *SetWindowsHookEx* function call. Since you created a system-wide hook, this function will be invoked by the system whenever any application (not just your application) retrieves a mouse message from its message queue. Pretty neat, huh? Add the following code to the Mousedll.cpp file:

```
extern "C" DLLEXPORT LRESULT WINAPI
MouseHookProc(int nCode, WPARAM wParam, LPARAM lParam)
{
        BOOL bStopMessage = FALSE;
        LPMOUSEHOOKSTRUCT pMouseEvent = (MOUSEHOOKSTRUCT FAR*)lParam;

        if (nCode >= 0)
        {
            // get the target window
            HWND hWndTarget = GetTargetWindow(pMouseEvent->hwnd);
```

8.6
USE SYSTEM HOOKS UNDER WIN32

```
            // process if over new target window
            if (hWndTarget != glhWndPrevTarget)
            {
                    // get caption of target window
                    char szCaption[100];
                    GetWindowText(hWndTarget, szCaption, 100);

                    // update display window
                    if (IsWindow(glhWndDisplay))
                            SendMessage(glhWndDisplay, WM_SETTEXT, 0,
                                    (LPARAM)(LPCTSTR)szCaption);

                    // save target window handle
                    glhWndPrevTarget = hWndTarget;
            }

            // see if right button is pressed
            if (wParam == WM_RBUTTONDOWN || wParam == WM_NCRBUTTONDOWN)
            {
                    // see if control key is pressed
                    SHORT nState = GetKeyState(VK_CONTROL);
                    if (nState & 0x8000)
                    {
                            // apply action to target window
                            PostMessage(hWndTarget,
                                    WM_SYSCOMMAND, glnAction, 0);

                            bStopMessage = TRUE;
                    }
            }
    }

    // return TRUE if applied action; otherwise call next hook function
    return (bStopMessage) ?
            TRUE : CallNextHookEx(glhHook, nCode, wParam, lParam);
}
```

8. **Implement helper function.** Whenever the mouse hook procedure is invoked, it determines the target window. The *GetTargetWindow* function performs this operation. Add the following code to the Mousedll.cpp file:

```
HWND GetTargetWindow(HWND hWnd)
{
        HWND hWndTarget=NULL;
        HWND hWndParent;

        // loop until find window with system menu or top-level window
        while (!hWndTarget)
        {
                // check if window has a system menu
                if (GetWindowLong(hWnd, GWL_STYLE) & WS_SYSMENU)
                        hWndTarget = hWnd;

                else
                {
```

continued on next page

```
            // get parent window
            hWndParent = GetParent(hWnd);

            // exit if not parent; otherwise check parent
            hWndParent ? hWnd = hWndParent : hWndTarget = hWnd;
        }
    }

    return hWndTarget;
}
```

9. Build the DLL project. Go ahead and build the DLL. The next project will link with the import library created in the build process. Now you are ready for the second half of this sample application—creating the executable.

Steps to Create the Hook Executable

10. Create a new project workspace with the MFC AppWizard (exe) called Mouse. Choose a dialog-based application and press the Finish button.

Classes to be created:
  Application: CMouseApp in Mouse.h and Mouse.cpp
  Dialog: CMouseDlg in MouseDlg.h and MouseDlg.cpp

Features:
  + About box on system menu
  + 3D Controls
  + Uses shared DLL implementation (MFC40.DLL)

11. Edit the IDD_MOUSE_DIALOG dialog. Add the following controls to the dialog box as shown in Figure 8-29. Notice that a minimize button was added to the dialog box. You add the minimize button by checking Minimize in the dialog's property box. The drop list combo box shows what action will be applied to the window. The target window's caption will be displayed in the edit control.

Control	ID	Attributes
Action label	IDC_STATIC	Defaults
Target label	IDC_STATIC	Defaults
Action combo box	IDC_ACTION	Drop List
Target edit	IDC_TARGET	Read-only
Exit button	IDCANCEL	Defaults

12. Add a member variable to CMouseDlg. Add the following member variables to *CMouseDlg* using the Member Variables tab in ClassWizard. The member variables will be used later to quickly access the combo box and edit controls.

8.6
USE SYSTEM HOOKS UNDER WIN32

Control ID	Type	Member
IDC_ACTION	CComboBox	m_WndAction
IDC_TARGET	CEdit	m_wndEdit

13. Add a mouse hook object as a data member. The *CMouseHook* class is exported from the file Mousedll.dll. Declare a data member of this type of class in the *CMouseDlg* class in the MouseDlg.h file as follows:

```
// Implementation
protected:
     HICON m_hIcon;
     CMouseHook m_hook;  // mouse hook (exported from dll)
```

You need the declaration of the *CMouseHook* class since you are declaring a data member of this type. Include the header file Mousedll.h at the top of Mousedlg.h.

```
#include "..\Mousedll\Mousedll.h"
```

14. Use the WizardBar to handle CBN_SELCHANGE for the combo box control. The CBN_SELCHANGE notification message is sent to the dialog box window when a new combo box item is selected. In our situation, this means the user is selecting a different action to perform to the target window, so you must pass this information along to the *CMouseHook* object. Use ClassWizard to handle the CBN_SELCHANGE message for the IDC_ACTION object ID for the *CMouseDlg* class. Add the following code to the message handler:

```
void CMouseDlg::OnSelchangeAction()
{
     // Get the current selection.
     int nIndex = m_wndAction.GetCurSel();

     // Tell hook to peform new action.
     m_hook.SetAction(m_wndAction.GetItemData(nIndex));
}
```

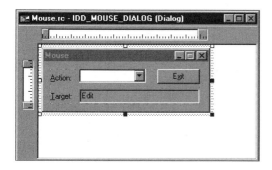

Figure 8-29 Creating the hook dialog box

CHAPTER 8
SYSTEM

15. Modify the CMouseDlg::OnInitDialog function. This example adds entries to the combo box when the dialog is initialized. Add the following code to the *OnInitDialog* member function of the *CMouseDlg* class:

```
BOOL CMouseDlg::OnInitDialog()
{
    CDialog::OnInitDialog();

    // Add "About..." menu item to system menu.

    // IDM_ABOUTBOX must be in the system command range.
    ASSERT((IDM_ABOUTBOX & 0xFFF0) == IDM_ABOUTBOX);
    ASSERT(IDM_ABOUTBOX < 0xF000);

    CMenu* pSysMenu = GetSystemMenu(FALSE);
    CString strAboutMenu;
    strAboutMenu.LoadString(IDS_ABOUTBOX);
    if (!strAboutMenu.IsEmpty())
    {
        pSysMenu->AppendMenu(MF_SEPARATOR);
        pSysMenu->AppendMenu(MF_STRING, IDM_ABOUTBOX, strAboutMenu);
    }

    // Set the icon for this dialog.  The framework does this automatically
    //  when the application's main window is not a dialog
    SetIcon(m_hIcon, TRUE);         // Set big icon
    SetIcon(m_hIcon, FALSE);        // Set small icon

    // Add entries to action combo box.
    int nIndex;
    nIndex = m_wndAction.AddString(_T("Close"));
    m_wndAction.SetItemData(nIndex, SC_CLOSE);

    nIndex = m_wndAction.AddString(_T("Minimize"));
    m_wndAction.SetItemData(nIndex, SC_MINIMIZE);

    nIndex = m_wndAction.AddString(_T("Maximize"));
    m_wndAction.SetItemData(nIndex, SC_MAXIMIZE);

    nIndex = m_wndAction.AddString(_T("Restore"));
    m_wndAction.SetItemData(nIndex, SC_RESTORE);

    // Initially select the minimize action.
    m_wndAction.SetCurSel(2);
    OnSelchangeAction();

    // Initialize hook class.
    m_hook.SetDisplayWindow(m_wndTarget.GetSafeHwnd());
    m_hook.Start();

    return TRUE;  // return TRUE  unless you set the focus to a control
}
```

8.6 USE SYSTEM HOOKS UNDER WIN32

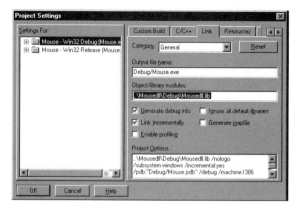

Figure 8-30 Link with the mouse hook DLL import library that was created earlier

16. **Link with the DLL import library.** You need to link with the import library that was created when the DLL was built. This import library resolves references to the DLL. Add ..\Mousedll\Debug\Mousedll.lib to the Project Settings Link tab as shown in Figure 8-30.

17. **Build the executable project.** Before you run the project, copy the Mousedll.dll file from the first project into the same directory as the executable (probably in Mouse\Debug directory). Run the project and notice that the edit control gets updated as you move the mouse over different windows. Minimize a window by pressing the [CTRL] key and clicking with the right-mouse button. Change the action to Close and right click on a window. Notice that the window is closed.

How It Works

You install a hook by calling the SDK *SetWindowsHookEx* function. The following is the function prototype for this function:

```
LRESULT SetWindowsHook(int idHook, HOOKPROC hkprc, HINSTANCE hMod, ⇒
DWORD dwThreadID)
```

The first parameter specifies what type of hook you want to install. Specifying WM_MOUSE for this argument tells Windows you want to install a mouse hook.

The second parameter specifies the address of the hook function. Windows will call this function to notify you of a particular event. The hook procedure can do three things with the message: pass the message along unchanged, change the message parameters, or discard the message and prevent it from going any further. As you can probably see, this technique is very powerful. It allows you to install hooks that change or prevent messages from going to an application or applications.

The third parameter specifies the module containing the hook procedure. Thread-specific hook procedures can be contained in an executable or DLL. System-wide hooks

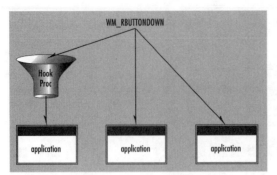

Figure 8-31 A thread-specific hook

must be contained in a DLL. For DLL hook procedures, you can simply save the value of the instance handle passed to your DLL's entry point function and pass it as this argument.

The fourth argument specifies the thread that your hook will be monitoring. If you specify a thread, this is referred to as a thread-specific hook. If you specify NULL, you are requesting to monitor all threads in the system, and this is referred to as a system-wide hook. Your hook will monitor existing applications and new applications as they are created. Figure 8-31 shows a thread-specific hook and Figure 8-32 shows a system-wide hook.

What happens if another application installs the same type of hook you installed? Windows does not replace your hook procedure, but instead it creates a chain of hook procedures. The most recently installed hook procedure is placed at the beginning of the chain, and the least recently installed hook procedure is at the end of the chain. Your hook procedure will still be invoked if the preceding hook procedure decides to pass the message to you by calling *CallNextHookEx* function. Figure 8-33 shows a hook chain consisting of two mouse hook procedures.

Note that it is not guaranteed that your hook procedure will receive the message with its original arguments or that it will receive the message at all. The preceding hook procedure can modify the message arguments before calling *CallNextHookEx*, or it can discard the message by returning TRUE.

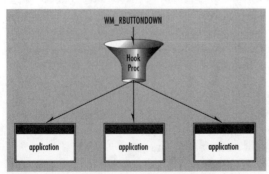

Figure 8-32 A system-wide hook

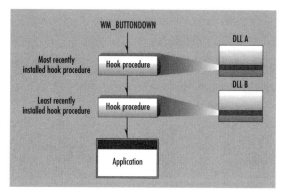

Figure 8-33 Hook procedure chain

Win32 DLLs

Win32 DLLs are different from Win16 DLLs. In both Win32 and Win16, the DLL's code is physically loaded into memory only once. Win32 does this by loading the DLL into global memory and mapping the DLL into the address space of each process that loads the DLL. The DLL is not necessarily mapped to the same address space for each process. The DLL becomes part of the process that loads it instead of part of the operating system, as in Win16.

In Win16, it was very easy to share data in a DLL. Each application that accesses the DLL has access to its global and static variables, as shown in Figure 8-34. In Win32, the DLL gets a unique copy of its global and static variables for each process that loads the DLL, as in Figure 8-35.

While this would normally be a good thing, in the present situation it is not. To see why, you need to understand how system-wide hooks work under Win32. You already know that system-wide hook procedures must reside in a DLL. You also know that a DLL is mapped into the address space of each process that loads the DLL. For the hook procedure to be invoked for all processes in the system, doesn't it sound like the hook DLL would need to be mapped into each process that triggers the hook procedure? That is exactly the case, which means you have quite a responsibility to implement your hook procedure correctly, or you could crash other applications!

The sample application stores five global variables. To provide feedback to the user, a window handle is stored in the variable *glhWndDisplay*. This variable stores the window handle that will display the caption of the target window. The previous target window

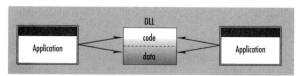

Figure 8-34 Win16 DLL's global and static variables are shared by all applications

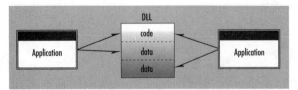

Figure 8-35 A unique copy of global and static variables exists for each process that loads a DLL in Win32

is saved to the variable *glhWndPrevTarget*. It is used so the hook procedure can determine when a new target window is encountered. The action that will be applied to the target window is saved in the variable *glnAction*. The handle to the hook is saved in the variable *glhHook* so the hook can be uninstalled later, and it is passed to the *CallNextHookEx* function. The instance of the DLL is also saved to the global variable *glhInstance,* since it is needed as an argument to the *SetWindowsHookEx* function.

You thought the DLL receives a unique copy of these global variables for each process that loads the DLL. So, how does the hook procedure know the value of the hook handle, what window to update, and what action to apply? You are right again, and now you can see the problem. Instance data is a great feature of Win32 DLLs, but in this situation you really want one set of global variables that the DLL accesses no matter what the context of the process.

A section of a DLL's data can be designated as shared memory. You do this by using the #pragma data_seg directive to set up a new named section. This tells the compiler to include particular variables in their own segment. However, this alone will not cause the data to be shared. You must also tell the linker that the variables in a particular section will be shared. You can do this from the linker's command line by specifying the SECTION flag as follows:

```
-SECTION:name, attribute
```

Another option is to specify the names under the SECTIONS section of your DEF file, as shown here:

```
SECTIONS
    name     attributes
```

The following example shows how you would share the two global variables *glhWnd* and *glnData*:

```
// in source file
#pragma data_seg(".sdata")
    HWND    glhWnd = 0;
    UINT    glnData = 0;
#pragma data_seg()

// in DEF file
SECTIONS
    .sdata READ WRITE SHARED
```

8.6 USE SYSTEM HOOKS UNDER WIN32

Notice that the variables are initialized. It is very important that you initialize the variables because the compiler will store all uninitialized data in the .bss section. This arrangement places the variables in a different section than you wanted, and they will not be shared (unless you specifically share the .bss section).

There is nothing special about the name .sdata (which stands for shared data). You can use a different name: MYDATA, .Fred, and Shared are all perfectly legitimate names.

Win32 DLLs have a single entry point that is used for loading and unloading the DLL. This replaces the *LibMain* and *WEP* (Windows Exit Procedure) functions in Win16. AppWizard automatically created the entry point function for you and named it DllMain. This function is invoked whenever a process or a thread loads or unloads your DLL. The reason is passed as the *dwReason* argument and can have the values of DLL_PROCESS_ATTACH, DLL_PROCESS_DETACH, DLL_THREAD_ATTACH, or DLL_THREAD_DETACH.

You already know that the hook DLL is being loaded by every process that triggers the hook. This will become more apparent if you place a *MessageBox* call in the PROCESS_ATTACH and PROCESS_DETACH statements. As an educational experiment, add the following code to the DLL_PROCESS_ATTACH reason in the *DllMain* function:

```
if (dwReason == DLL_PROCESS_ATTACH)
{
    MessageBox(NULL, _T("Hook DLL Process Attach"),
        _T("Mouse Hook"), MB_OK | MB_ICONINFORMATION);
```

To see how many times your DLL is unloaded, add the following code to the DLL_PROCESS_DETACH reason in the *DllMain* function:

```
else if (dwReason == DLL_PROCESS_DETACH)
{
    MessageBox(NULL, _T("Hook DLL Process Detach"),
        _T("Mouse Hook"), MB_OK | MB_ICONINFORMATION);
```

Remake Mousedll.dll, copy it back over to the executable's directory, and run the application. The EXE does not have to be rebuilt—one of the great advantages of DLLs. Notice that a debug message box is displayed whenever you move the cursor over a new process. This is because moving the cursor sends mouse messages to that process. Since you installed a mouse hook, your DLL containing the mouse hook procedure is loaded into that process, which invokes the DLL entry point function with the reason of DLL_PROCESS_ATTACH.

MFC Extension DLLs

AppWizard created the code for your DLL as an MFC Extension DLL. This is a DLL that implements reusable classes derived from existing MFC classes. Users of the Extension DLL can use the classes just as they use MFC classes. In our situation, the class *CMouseHook* is exported in the Mousedll.dll file and is used by the Mouse.exe application.

There is some limitation on Extension DLLs. Applications that use the DLL must also be MFC applications. If you are creating DLLs to be used by other applications created with a different language or class library, such as Visual Basic or Borland's OWL, then you will not want to create Extension DLLs. However, in this sample application and possibly in your application, it makes perfect sense. The hook DLL is not created with the intent of other applications using the exported *CMouseHook* class except for the one application that is designed to use the class. So creating an Extension DLL that exports classes to be used just by other MFC applications can be a very convenient way to dynamically reuse the code.

You can use the tool Dumpbin to display information about 32-bit executables and DLLs. Dump all the exported definitions of Mousedll.dll by executing this command:

```
dumpbin /exports mousedll.dll
```

You will notice that most of the exported function definitions appear strange or mangled. That is exactly what is happening. All of the *CMouseHook* class functions are exported as mangled names. The only function that is not mangled is the *MouseHookProc* function because it was declared with the extern "C" command. The following shows some of the function exported from Mousedll.dll:

```
??0CMouseHook@@QAE@XZ    (00001046)
??1CMouseHook@@UAE@XZ    (00001041)
??_7CMouseHook@@6B@      (00004058)
??_ECMouseHook@@UAEPAXI@Z (00001023)
??_GCMouseHook@@UAEPAXI@Z (00001032)
?SetAction@CMouseHook@@QAEXI@Z (00001028)
?SetDisplayWindow@CMouseHook@@QAEXPAUHWND__@@@Z (00001000)
?Start@CMouseHook@@QAEPAUHHOOK__@@XZ (00001014)
?Stop@CMouseHook@@QAEHXZ (00001019)
_MouseHookProc@12        (00001005)
```

You can discover a lot by using the Dumpbin tool. Look in the Visual C++ User's Guide for more information about using this tool.

Comments

When debugging DLLs, you can specify the executable that uses your DLL. You enter this information in the Executable For Debug Session edit field under the project's Debug section. Visual C++ will start the calling application that then loads your DLL. You can set breakpoints in the DLL's source code just as you can for any other project, and the debugger will break at the appropriate times.

Look at the Hooks and Spy sample applications to see additional applications that install task-specific and system-wide hooks. Check out the DllHusk sample application to learn more about creating MFC Extension DLLs.

For additional information about MFC and DLLs, see the Microsoft Foundation Class Library Technical Note 11, *Using MFC as Part of a DLL*, and Technical Note 33, *DLL Version of MFC*. There are several excellent articles on the Microsoft Development Library CD, including *DLLs in Win32* by Randy Kath, and *Win32 Hooks* by Kyle Marsh.

Hooks are very powerful, but with this power comes responsibility. As the developer of an application that installs a system-wide hook, remember that all messages may be funneling through your hook procedure. Make sure you don't cause a bottleneck in the system. Your DLL code will be mapped to all processes in the system, so be certain you don't do anything that will crash other processes.

8.7 How do I... Share data between 32-bit MFC applications?

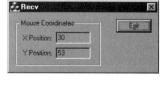

COMPLEXITY
ADVANCED

Problem

What's the best way to exchange information under Win32? Windows has always offered several ways to send information between applications, but I've found that none of these techniques works under Windows NT. Send/PostMessage doesn't cut it because two 32-bit values aren't enough, and passing a global memory handle around using the GMEM_SHARE flag doesn't work under Win32.

Technique

The preferred method to share memory under Win32 is to have two applications open their own view of the same memory-mapped file. You don't need a DLL to do this, and there are only a few APIs you need to learn.

Memory-mapped files are the only way for multiple processes to share a block of data simultaneously in Win32. "But wait," you say, "I don't have a file to share, just some block of memory!" Don't worry. The Win32 API call we'll be using, *CreateFileMapping*, lets you treat a region of memory as though it were a file. From then on, you can treat it just as you would any other pointer obtained with *malloc*.

We'll write two programs in this How-To: one to send the data (Send.exe) and one to receive the data (Recv.exe). The data we're sharing in this example is simple; it's just the current mouse coordinates. The Send application watches the mouse cursor and puts its current location into the memory-mapped file. Recv runs a thread that monitors the data in the memory-mapped file, and when it changes, it sends a message to the main thread with the new *x* and *y* values. Figure 8-36 shows the two programs communicating.

Figure 8-36 Send and Recv applications sharing data between processes

CHAPTER 8
SYSTEM

Steps to Create the Send Application

1. **Create a new project called Send using the MFC AppWizard (exe).** Select the Single-Document type and press the Finish button.

   Classes to be created:
   - Application: CSendApp in Send.h and Send.cpp
   - Frame: CMainFrame in MainFrm.h and MainFrm.cpp
   - Document: CSendDoc in SendDoc.h and SendDoc.cpp
   - View: CSendView in SendView.h and SendView.cpp

   Features:
   - + Initial toolbar in main frame
   - + Initial status bar in main frame
   - + Printing and Print Preview support in view
   - + 3D Controls
   - + Uses shared DLL implementation (MFC40.DLL)

2. **Add a member variable to CSendDoc.** Add the following two members to keep track of the memory-mapped file handle and pointer:

```
class CSendDoc : public CDocument
{
protected: // create from serialization only
       CSendDoc();
       DECLARE_DYNCREATE(CSendDoc)

// Attributes
public:
       HANDLE   m_hMapObject;
       LPLONG   m_pMapView;

...
```

3. **Edit CSendDoc::OnNewDocument.** Edit *OnNewDocument* to create the memory-mapped file and then map a view of the file into the process address space. If the creation of the memory-mapped file is successful, you'll get a pointer to where it starts in memory through *MapViewOfFile*. This pointer is saved in the document member variable *m_pMapView*.

```
BOOL CSendDoc::OnNewDocument()
{
       if (!CDocument::OnNewDocument())
              return FALSE;

       // Create memory mapped file.
       m_hMapObject = ::CreateFileMapping((HANDLE)-1, NULL,
              PAGE_READWRITE, 0, sizeof(DWORD), _T("shared_memory"));

       if (!m_hMapObject)
       {
```

8.7
SHARE DATA BETWEEN 32-BIT MFC APPLICATIONS

```
        AfxMessageBox(_T("Unable to create shared file"));
        return FALSE;
    }

    // Map view of file into our address space.
    m_pMapView = (LPLONG)::MapViewOfFile(
        m_hMapObject, FILE_MAP_WRITE, 0, 0, 0);

    if (!m_pMapView)
    {
        AfxMessageBox(_T("Unable to map shared file"));
        return FALSE;
    }

    return TRUE;
}
```

4. Use the WizardBar to add the CSendDoc::OnCloseDocument function. When the document is closing, we stick a -1 in the shared memory. Just for fun, we'll have Recv quit if it sees a -1 in the shared memory. Plus, you need to release your hold on the mapped file, hence the *CloseHandle* call. Add the following code to the *OnCloseDocument* function:

```
void CSendDoc::OnCloseDocument()
{
    // Store 'exit' code in shared memory.
    m_pMapView[0] = -1;

    // Close the shared memory file.
    ::CloseHandle (m_hMapObject);

    CDocument::OnCloseDocument();
}
```

5. Use the WizardBar to handle WM_MOUSEMOVE for CSendView. For this example, we store the position of the cursor in shared memory. Add the following code to the *OnMouseMove* function:

```
void CSendView::OnMouseMove(UINT nFlags, CPoint point)
{
    // Write position of mouse in shared memory.
    GetDocument()->m_pMapView[0] =
        MAKELONG((WORD)point.x, (WORD)point.y);

    CView::OnMouseMove(nFlags, point);
}
```

6. Compile the appliction. You could run it now, but it wouldn't do much. Wait until you've finished creating the Recv application.

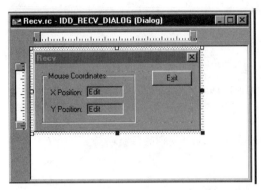

Figure 8-37 Creating the Recv dialog box

Steps to Create the Recv Application

7. Create a new project called Recv using the MFC AppWizard (exe). Choose a Dialog-based application and press the Finish button.

Classes to be created:
  Application: CRecvApp in Recv.h and Recv.cpp
  Dialog: CRecvDlg in RecvDlg.h and RecvDlg.cpp

Features:
  + About box on system menu
  + 3D Controls
  + Uses shared DLL implementation (MFC40.DLL)

8. Edit the IDD_RECV_DIALOG dialog. Add the following controls to the dialog box as shown in Figure 8-37. The edit controls will display the coordinates of the mouse in the Send application by accessing the shared memory between the two applications.

Control	ID	Attributes
Mouse Coordinates group box	IDC_STATIC	Defaults
X Position label	IDC_STATIC	Defaults
Y Position label	IDC_STATIC	Defaults
X Position edit	IDC_POSX	Read only
Y Position edit	IDC_POSY	Read only
Exit button	IDCANCEL	Defaults

9. Add a member variable to CRecvDlg. Add the following member variables to *CRecvDlg* using the Member Variables tab in ClassWizard. The two member variables store the cursor position of the Send application.

8.7
SHARE DATA BETWEEN 32-BIT MFC APPLICATIONS

Control ID	Type	Member
IDC_POSX	UINT	m_nPosX
IDC_POSY	UINT	m_nPosY

10. **Modify the CRecvDlg class header file.** Modify the *CRecvDlg* class declaration in RecvDlg.h to look like the following. This adds a destructor, data members, and a user defined message in the message map. The first two member variables keep track of the memory-mapped file. We use *m_pThread* to hold the pointer for the worker thread that monitors the state of the memory-mapped file. When the worker thread detects changes in the mouse coordinates, it sends the private message WM_SET_COORDINATES, which is handled by *CRecvDlg::OnSetCoordinates*.

```
class CRecvDlg : public CDialog
{
// Construction
public:
        CRecvDlg(CWnd* pParent = NULL);      // standard constructor
        ~CRecvDlg();                          // destructor

// Dialog Data
        //{{AFX_DATA(CRecvDlg)
        enum { IDD = IDD_RECV_DIALOG };
                // NOTE: the ClassWizard will add data members here
        //}}AFX_DATA

        // ClassWizard generated virtual function overrides
        //{{AFX_VIRTUAL(CRecvDlg)
        protected:
        virtual void DoDataExchange(CDataExchange* pDX);    // DDX/DDV support
        //}}AFX_VIRTUAL

// Implementation
protected:
        HANDLE m_hMapObject;       // memory mapped file
        LPLONG m_pMapView;         // pointer to data
        CWinThread* m_pThread;     // thread pointer

        HICON m_hIcon;

        // Generated message map functions
        //{{AFX_MSG(CRecvDlg)
        virtual BOOL OnInitDialog();
        afx_msg void OnSysCommand(UINT nID, LPARAM lParam);
        afx_msg void OnPaint();
        afx_msg HCURSOR OnQueryDragIcon();
        afx_msg LRESULT OnSetCoordinates(WPARAM wParam, LPARAM lParam);
        //}}AFX_MSG
        DECLARE_MESSAGE_MAP()
};
```

CHAPTER 8
SYSTEM

11. **Edit the CRecvDlg class implementation file.** Add the following code to the top of RecvDlg.cpp. The global *ThreadInfo* object stores the dialog *CWnd** and the pointer to the memory-mapped file area. Since you are allowed to pass only one parameter to a worker thread, we'll pass the address of *g_threadInfo*. *MyThreadProc* is a declaration for the worker thread procedure that will be passed to the thread creation routine *AfxBeginThread*.

```
#include "stdafx.h"
#include "Recv.h"
#include "RecvDlg.h"

#ifdef _DEBUG
#define new DEBUG_NEW
#undef THIS_FILE
static char THIS_FILE[] = __FILE__;
#endif

// Thread information structure (info passed to thread function).
class ThreadInfo
{
public:
        LPLONG  m_pMapView;
        CWnd*   m_pParent;
} g_threadInfo;

// User define message.
#define WM_SET_COORDINATES (WM_USER+100)

// Thread function declration.
UINT MyThreadProc(LPVOID pParam);
```

12. **Edit CRecvDlg::OnInitDialog.** We do three things in *OnInitDialog*. First, the memory-mapped file is opened using the name shared_memory; this works only if Send is currently running. If *OpenFileMapping* is successful, we get a pointer to the first byte of the memory-mapped file. Then we create the thread, passing it the address of the global *ThreadInfo* object.

```
BOOL CRecvDlg::OnInitDialog()
{
        CDialog::OnInitDialog();

        // Add "About..." menu item to system menu.

        // IDM_ABOUTBOX must be in the system command range.
        ASSERT((IDM_ABOUTBOX & 0xFFF0) == IDM_ABOUTBOX);
        ASSERT(IDM_ABOUTBOX < 0xF000);

        CMenu* pSysMenu = GetSystemMenu(FALSE);
        CString strAboutMenu;
        strAboutMenu.LoadString(IDS_ABOUTBOX);
        if (!strAboutMenu.IsEmpty())
        {
                pSysMenu->AppendMenu(MF_SEPARATOR);
                pSysMenu->AppendMenu(MF_STRING, IDM_ABOUTBOX, strAboutMenu);
        }
```

8.7
SHARE DATA BETWEEN 32-BIT MFC APPLICATIONS

```
    // Set the icon for this dialog.  The framework does this automatically
    //   when the application's main window is not a dialog
    SetIcon(m_hIcon, TRUE);         // Set big icon
    SetIcon(m_hIcon, FALSE);        // Set small icon

    // Open memory mapped file.
    m_hMapObject = OpenFileMapping(FILE_MAP_READ, FALSE, _T("shared_memory"));

    if (!m_hMapObject)
    {
        AfxMessageBox(_T("Can't open shared memory file"));
        return FALSE;
    }

    // Get pointer to shared data.
    m_pMapView = (LPLONG)MapViewOfFile
        (m_hMapObject, FILE_MAP_READ, 0, 0, 0);

    if (!m_pMapView)
    {
        AfxMessageBox(_T("Can't map view of shared memory file"));
        return FALSE;
    }

    // Fill in thread information.
    g_threadInfo.m_pMapView = m_pMapView;
    g_threadInfo.m_pParent = this;

    // Create worker thread.
    m_pThread = AfxBeginThread(MyThreadProc, &g_threadInfo);

    if (!m_pThread)
    {
        AfxMessageBox(_T("Can't create thread to monitor file"));
        return FALSE;
    }

    return TRUE;  // return TRUE  unless you set the focus to a control
}
```

13. **Implement the CRecvDlg::OnSetCoordinates function.** Add the following message handler to the bottom of RecvDlg.cpp. This function is called when the dialog box receives the WM_SET_COORDINATES user defined message and updates the values in the *x* and *y* edit controls.

```
LRESULT CRecvDlg::OnSetCoordinates(WPARAM wParam, LPARAM lParam)
{
    // Update edit controls with new coordinates.
    m_nPosX = HIWORD(lParam);
    m_nPosY = LOWORD(lParam);
    UpdateData(FALSE);

    return TRUE;
}
```

Remember to add the user defined message to the dialog's message map.

```
BEGIN_MESSAGE_MAP(CRecvDlg, CDialog)
    //{{AFX_MSG_MAP(CRecvDlg)
    ON_WM_SYSCOMMAND()
    ON_WM_PAINT()
    ON_WM_QUERYDRAGICON()
    ON_MESSAGE(WM_SET_COORDINATES, OnSetCoordinates)
    //}}AFX_MSG_MAP
END_MESSAGE_MAP()
```

14. **Implement the MyThreadProc thread function.** Add this code at the bottom of RecvDlg.cpp. This function is the worker thread function and is constantly running. It simply determines if the shared memory has changed and updates the GUI if it has.

```
UINT MyThreadProc(LPVOID pParam)
{
    // Get information from thread structure.
    LPLONG pMapView = ((ThreadInfo*)pParam)->m_pMapView;
    CWnd* pParent = ((ThreadInfo*)pParam)->m_pParent;

    long lPoint = 0;          // new position
    long lOldPoint = -1;      // remember old position

    Sleep(500);

    while (1)
    {
        lPoint = pMapView[0];

        // Check if shared memory contains the quit flag.
        if (lPoint == -1)
        {
            // Terminate application.
            pParent->PostMessage(WM_CLOSE);
            return 0;
        }

        // Check if cursor position has changed.
        if (lPoint != lOldPoint)
        {
            // Save new position and update GUI.
            lOldPoint = lPoint;
            pParent->PostMessage(WM_SET_COORDINATES, 0, lPoint);
        }

        Sleep(100);
    }

    return 0;
}
```

8.7
SHARE DATA BETWEEN 32-BIT MFC APPLICATIONS

15. **Implement the destructor.** Add the following code near the beginning of the RecvDlg.cpp. The *CRecvDlg* destructor terminates the worker thread if it is running.

```
CRecvDlg::~CRecvDlg()
{
    // Determine if thread is running.
    if (m_pThread)
    {
        // If so, terminate thread.
        if (TerminateThread(m_pThread->m_hThread, 0))
            delete m_pThread;
    }
}
```

16. **Build the Recv application.** After you've built Recv, run Send.exe first and then run Recv.exe. Arrange the two programs so both are visible at the same time. As you move the mouse cursor over the client area of Send, the mouse coordinates will be displayed in Recv.

How It Works

When Send starts, it attempts to create the memory-mapped file by calling *CreateFileMapping*. Since the first argument passed to *CreateFileMapping* is not a file name, we have to specify how big of a buffer we want. Since we're only storing two numbers (the *x* and *y* coordinates), the *sizeof(DWORD)* is enough memory.

CreateFileMapping creates a file-mapping object of the specified size backed by the operating system's paging file rather than by a named file in the file system. Both Send and Recv refer to this memory-mapped file by name (shared_memory).

When Recv starts up, it tries to get a pointer to the memory-mapped file. If it's successful (it will fail if Send isn't running), it fires off the worker thread using *AfxBeginThread*. The thread continues to monitor the memory-mapped file and sends messages back to the dialog if anything interesting happens. It also sends the WM_CLOSE to the dialog if it detects a −1 in the memory-mapped file.

Comments

While it's possible to set the value of the two edit controls from the worker thread, it's better to send a message to the dialog and let the dialog do it. The Visual C++ documentation discourages worker threads from using MFC objects not created by the thread.

CHAPTER 9
WINDOWS 95 SHELL

WINDOWS 95 SHELL

How do I...
- **9.1 Write a tray application to play CDs?**
- **9.2 Create a property sheet handler for a file or folder?**
- **9.3 Create an appbar to display the system palette?**
- **9.4 Extend the context menu for certain files?**

In Windows 95, applications can extend the shell in a number of ways. A *shell extension* enhances the shell by extra ways to manipulate files and folders. For example, a shell extension can add an extra property page to files and folders or add extra commands to the context menu. Windows 95 supports five types of shell extensions, two of which will be created in this chapter (property-sheet and context menu handlers).

The design of a shell extension is based on the Component Object Model in Object Linking and Embedding (OLE). The shell accesses an object through interfaces that have been registered with the system. Two of the How-Tos in this chapter implement the interfaces in a shell extension dynamic-link library (DLL), to support shell extensions.

An application desktop toolbar (also called an appbar) is a window that is similar to the Windows taskbar. It is anchored to an edge of the screen, and it typically contains buttons that give the user quick access to other applications and windows (like the Office 95 appbar). The system prevents other applications from using the desktop area occupied by an appbar. This chapter demonstrates how to write an appbar to display the current color palette.

The Windows taskbar includes a notification area or tray where an application can put an icon to indicate the status of an operation or to notify the user about an event.

CHAPTER 9
WINDOWS 95 SHELL

For example, an application might put a modem icon to indicate that a data transfer is in-progress. We'll create a mini-CD player whose entire interface runs through a tray icon.

9.1 Write a Tray Application to Play CDs

How about using the tray to house an entire application? This How-To creates a reusable AppWizard that gives you a framework for writing tray applications. You will write one that acts as a CD player. You can play and pause with the click of a button, display a track list, and popup a context menu to skip around to different tracks.

Additional Topics: Shell_NotifyIcon, Double- vs. Single-clicks, ColorWell OCX, OnActivate

9.2 Create a Property Sheet Handler for a File or Folder

This How-To creates a reusable framework for adding extra property pages in the Explorer. Your property page will display the subfolders of a given folder, along with the size of each one. It's great for hunting down directories that take up a lot of disk space.

Additional Topics: IShellExtInit, IShellPropSheetExt, IMPLEMENT_IUNKNOWN, custom registration, reference counting property pages, Cool.dll, ThreadProc

9.3 Create an Appbar to Display the System Palette

If you've ever worked on multimedia applications, you've probably been frustrated by palettes. This appbar makes it easy to monitor the current palette because the appbar is always visible. It automatically docks to the screen and stays on top. Tooltips displays the palette entry's RGB values.

Additional Topics: APPBARDATA, stay-on-top with SetWindowPos, FilterToolTipMessage

9.4 Extend the Context Menu for Certain Files

This context menu extension makes it easier to register and unregister OLE controls and In-Proc servers. You'll learn how to navigate the registry and use a special class to make OLE registration easier.

Additional Topics: DllUnregisterServer, CRegisterClass

9.1 How do I... Write a tray application to play CDs?

COMPLEXITY: INTERMEDIATE

Problem

I want to create a simple CD player that exists solely as a tray icon. It could use a menu to manipulate the CD and different icons to show the state (no CD, playing, paused). I'd also like to use tooltips to show the current track and the elapsed time.

Technique

Everything related to tray icons revolves around just one Windows function: *Shell_NotifyIcon*. This function controls the little bunch of icons in the Windows 95 task bar. The icons typically represent the state of currently running but hidden applications. In order to make one of these things, we need an application that manages the tray icon but doesn't have a visible main window.

First, you'll create a Dialog-based application and get rid of the dialog. Since this application's main window is hidden, it doesn't need the dialog. Next, we'll derive a new *CWnd* class to act as our main window. It also registers the icon with the tray and receives all mouse notifications. At this point, you'll wrap the whole thing up into a custom AppWizard in case you want to write new ones in the future.

The CD handling code comes from the multimedia chapter. You just need to hook up the menu options, like play and stop, to the appropriate *CCDAudio* methods. The application uses a timer to poll the CD player to determine if it's paused or playing (see Figure 9-1). Finally, we'll use the ColorWell OLE control from the OLE chapter to lay out a grid for selecting a track (see Figure 9-2).

Figure 9-1 QuickCD tray application

Figure 9-2 Choosing a CD track

CHAPTER 9
WINDOWS 95 SHELL

Microsoft distributes a free application called FlexCD, but without the source code. You can reverse-engineer FlexCD to create the version presented in this How-To, QuickCD.

Steps

1. **Create a new project called TrayApp using the MFC AppWizard (exe).** Choose the Dialog-based option in step 1 and the OLE controls option in step 2.

   Classes to be created:
   Application: CTrayApp in Tray.h and Tray.cpp
   Dialog: CTrayDlg in TrayDlg.h and TrayDlg.cpp

   Features:
   + About box on system menu
   + 3D Controls
   + Uses shared DLL implementation (MFC40.DLL)
   + OLE Controls support enabled

2. **Remove TrayDlg.cpp from the project.** Since the application doesn't have a visible main window, we can remove the *CTrayDlg* class from the project. Switch to FileView, select the TrayDlg.cpp file, and press the [DEL] key. Delete the TrayDlg.cpp and TrayDlg.h files from the Tray directory as well.

3. **Remove IDD_TRAY_DIALOG from the resource file.** Switch to ResourceView and delete the dialog IDD_TRAY_DIALOG.

4. **Fix the ClassWizard database.** When you remove a file created by App Studio or ClassWizard, you also need to remove it from the ClassWizard database. Simply bring up ClassWizard ([CTRL]+[W]) and press OK when the message about missing files appears. Another dialog is displayed, giving you the choice to remove *CTrayDlg* from the ClassWizard database. Press the Remove button.

   Repeat the same steps to remove *CAboutDlg* from the database.

5. **Create a new class called CAboutDlg.** I promise I'm not running you around in circles. The original *CAboutDlg* code was contained in the TrayDlg.cpp file, the one we just deleted in step 2. This step adds the class back to the project, but in its own file:

   Class name: CAboutDlg
   Base class: CDialog
   File: AboutDlg.cpp
   Dialog: IDD_ABOUTBOX

9.1
WRITE A TRAY APPLICATION TO PLAY CDS

6. **Create another new class called CTrayWnd.** This will be our new main window. It differs from a normal frame window because it's always invisible and never appears on the task bar. It exists only to manage the tray icon.

   Class name: CTrayWnd
   Base class: generic CWnd
   File: TrayWnd.cpp

7. **Use ClassWizard to add message handlers to CTrayWnd.** Add these new virtual functions and message handlers to *CTrayWnd*:

Object ID	Function	Message
CTrayWnd	OnTimer	WM_TIMER
CTrayWnd	OnLButtonUp	WM_LBUTTONUP
CTrayWnd	OnLButtonDblClk	WM_LBUTTONDBLCLK
CTrayWnd	OnRButtonUp	WM_RBUTTONUP
CTrayWnd	Create	
CTrayWnd	PostNcDestroy	

8. **Edit TrayWnd.h.** Remove all the arguments to *Create* and add the other methods as shown here:

```
class CTrayWnd : public CWnd
{
// Construction
public:
        CTrayWnd();

// Operations
public:

// Overrides
        // ClassWizard generated virtual function overrides
        //{{AFX_VIRTUAL(CTrayWnd)
        public:
        virtual BOOL Create();
        protected:
        virtual void PostNcDestroy();
        //}}AFX_VIRTUAL

// Implementation
public:
        virtual ~CTrayWnd();

        // Generated message map functions
protected:
        //{{AFX_MSG(CTrayWnd)
        afx_msg void OnLButtonDblClk(UINT nFlags, CPoint point);
        afx_msg void OnLButtonUp(UINT nFlags, CPoint point);
        afx_msg void OnRButtonUp(UINT nFlags, CPoint point);
        afx_msg void OnTimer(UINT nIDEvent);
```

continued on next page

continued from previous page

```
        //}}AFX_MSG
        DECLARE_MESSAGE_MAP()

        LONG OnTrayNotify(UINT wParam, LONG lParam);

        BOOL NotifyIcon(DWORD dwMessage, HICON hIcon, LPCSTR pszTip = NULL);
        BOOL NotifyIcon(DWORD dwMessage, HICON hIcon, UINT nStringResource);

        virtual void OnRightClick() { };
        virtual void OnLeftClick() { };
        virtual void OnLeftDoubleClick() { };

        BOOL m_bFireDoubleClick;
};
```

9. Edit TrayWnd.cpp. Make these modifications to the top of TrayWnd.cpp:

```
#include "stdafx.h"
#include "resource.h"
#include "TrayWnd.h"

...

#define TRAY_NOTIFYICON    (WM_USER+500)
#define CLICK_TIMER 4

...

BEGIN_MESSAGE_MAP(CTrayWnd, CWnd)
        //{{AFX_MSG_MAP(CTrayWnd)
        ON_WM_TIMER()
        ON_WM_LBUTTONDBLCLK()
        ON_WM_RBUTTONUP()
        ON_WM_LBUTTONUP()
        //}}AFX_MSG_MAP
        ON_MESSAGE(TRAY_NOTIFYICON, OnTrayNotify)
END_MESSAGE_MAP()

BOOL CTrayWnd::Create()
{
        return CreateEx(WS_EX_TOOLWINDOW, AfxRegisterWndClass(0), ⇒
"TrayIconHandler",
                WS_OVERLAPPED, 0, 0, 0, 0, NULL, NULL);
}
```

Since *CTrayWnd* is always invisible, there's no need to pass any arguments to *Create*. *CWnd::Create* doesn't allow the WS_OVERLAPPED style, so we have to use *CreateEx* instead. That's OK, because we're also using the new Windows 95 style WS_EX_TOOLWINDOW that prevents the TrayIconHandler from showing up on the task bar. Extended class styles like WS_EX_TOOLWINDOW can only be used with *CreateEx*.

9.1
WRITE A TRAY APPLICATION TO PLAY CDS

10. Edit CTrayWnd::PostNcDestroy. We'll use the same trick *CFrameWnd* uses to automatically delete itself. Add the following line of code:

```
void CTrayWnd::PostNcDestroy()
{
    CWnd::PostNcDestroy();
    delete this;
}
```

11. Code the mouse handlers. We never expect *CTrayWnd* to handle mouse events since it's always invisible. Instead, the mouse messages are posted from the tray notification handler.

```
void CTrayWnd::OnLButtonDblClk(UINT nFlags, CPoint point)
{
    OnLeftDoubleClick();
}

void CTrayWnd::OnLButtonUp(UINT nFlags, CPoint point)
{
    OnLeftClick();
}

void CTrayWnd::OnRButtonUp(UINT nFlags, CPoint point)
{
    OnRightClick();
}
```

12. Code the notify icon handlers. These two methods wrap the calls to *Shell_NotifyIcon*:

```
BOOL CTrayWnd::NotifyIcon(DWORD dwMessage, HICON hIcon, UINT nStringResource)
{
    CString msg;
    VERIFY(msg.LoadString(nStringResource));
    return NotifyIcon(dwMessage, hIcon, msg);
}

BOOL CTrayWnd::NotifyIcon(DWORD dwMessage, HICON hIcon, LPCSTR pszTip)
{
    ASSERT(dwMessage == NIM_ADD || dwMessage == NIM_DELETE || dwMessage ⇒
 == NIM_MODIFY);

    static HICON hCurrentIcon = NULL;

    // Either value can be NULL
    NOTIFYICONDATA tnid;
    tnid.cbSize = sizeof(NOTIFYICONDATA);
    tnid.hWnd = GetSafeHwnd();
    tnid.uID = 100;      // this function only supports one icon
    tnid.uCallbackMessage = TRAY_NOTIFYICON;
    tnid.uFlags = NIF_MESSAGE;
```

continued on next page

continued from previous page

```
        if (hIcon != NULL && hIcon != hCurrentIcon)
        {
            tnid.uFlags |= NIF_ICON;
            tnid.hIcon = hIcon;
            hCurrentIcon = hIcon;
        }

        if (pszTip != NULL)
        {
            tnid.uFlags |= NIF_TIP;
            lstrcpy(tnid.szTip, pszTip);
        }

        return Shell_NotifyIcon(dwMessage, &tnid);
}
```

13. **Code OnTrayNotify.** Windows forwards mouse events that occur over the icon to this function. We use the timer to distinguish between single- and double-clicks.

```
LONG CTrayWnd::OnTrayNotify(UINT wParam, LONG lParam)
{
        UINT uIconID = (UINT) wParam;
        UINT uMouseMsg = (UINT) lParam;

        if (uIconID != 100)
            return 0;

        // Why are we posting a fake message here?
        // We need to leave this notification function as soon as possible.
        // For example, if you want to create an OLE control in OnLButtonDown for some
        // reason, you'll get this cryptic message from MFC with
        // the error code RPC_E_CANTCALLOUT_ININPUTSYNCCALL.  From WinError.h:
        // "An outgoing call cannot be made since the application is dispatching
        // an input-synchronous call."

        switch (uMouseMsg)
        {
        case WM_LBUTTONDOWN:
                m_bFireDoubleClick = FALSE;
                SetTimer(CLICK_TIMER, GetDoubleClickTime(), NULL);
                break;

        case WM_LBUTTONUP:
                if (m_bFireDoubleClick)
                    PostMessage(WM_LBUTTONDBLCLK);
                break;

        case WM_LBUTTONDBLCLK:
                 m_bFireDoubleClick = TRUE;
                 KillTimer(CLICK_TIMER);
                 break;
```

9.1
WRITE A TRAY APPLICATION TO PLAY CDS

```
        case WM_RBUTTONUP:
                PostMessage(WM_RBUTTONUP);
                break;
        }

        return 0;
}
```

14. Code CTrayWnd::OnTimer. If the timer has fired, then we can safely assume that a single-click, not a double-click, has occurred.

```
void CTrayWnd::OnTimer(UINT nIDEvent)
{
        if (nIDEvent == CLICK_TIMER)
        {
                KillTimer(nIDEvent);
                PostMessage(WM_LBUTTONUP);
        }
}
```

15. Edit TrayWnd.cpp. Replace the line that includes TrayDlg.cpp as follows:

```
#include "stdafx.h"
#include "Tray.h"
#include "TrayWnd.h"
```

Change *InitInstance* to create a *CTrayWnd* instead of *CTrayDlg*:

```
BOOL CTrayApp::InitInstance()
{
        AfxEnableControlContainer();

        // Standard initialization
#ifdef _AFXDLL
        Enable3dControls();          // Call this when using MFC in a shared DLL
#else
        Enable3dControlsStatic();    // Call this when linking to MFC statically
#endif

        // Replace the next line of code to create a derived CTrayWnd
        CTrayWnd* pWnd = new CTrayWnd();
        VERIFY(pWnd->Create());

        m_pMainWnd = pWnd;

        return TRUE;
}
```

16. Compile the program. At this point, we need to compile Tray to make sure it's free of syntax errors in preparation for the next step. By the way, don't run the program; without a main window, it's not very interesting.

17. Create a new project called TrayWizard using the Custom AppWizard. We're going to promote our generic application to a custom AppWizard. Chose the option to create the new AppWizard based on an existing project,

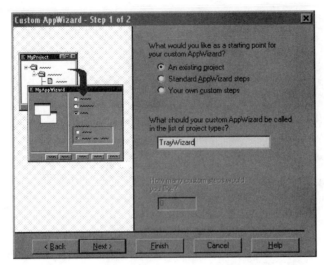

Figure 9-3 Creating a custom AppWizard based on an existing project

the one we just compiled in step 16. Call the new AppWizard, Tray Wizard, as shown in Figure 9-3.

In the second step, locate the Tray.mak file you created at the beginning of this How-To. Visual C++ tells you that the new AppWizard will create projects identical to Tray.mak, except with differently named, files, classes, and so on.

18. **Modify the IDI_TRAYWIZARD icon.** Depending on your artistic ability, you might want to customize the icon for this AppWizard. Your artwork will forever show up in the New Project dialog! My attempt is shown in Figure 9-4.

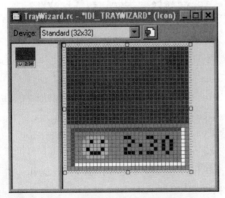

Figure 9-4 Icon for TrayWizard

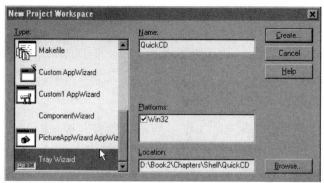

Figure 9-5 Creating a project with the Tray Wizard

19. **Edit TrayWizard\Template\confirm.inf.** TrayWizard displays this file in the final step to let the user know what is being generated. Modify the file to read the following:

```
An application with a hidden main window responsible for
registering the tray icon and handling the mouse events.

It is your responsibility to:

  - Derive a new class from CTrayWnd
  - Use CTrayWnd::NotifyIcon to register the icon
  - Create the new class in InitInstance
```

20. **Compile the TrayWizard.** Change the build target from Pseudo-Debug to Release, then compile. If all goes well, the makefile will copy the TrayWizard.awx file to the Visual C++ 4.0 Template directory (for example, \msdev\template).

21. **Create yet another project called QuickCD using the new Tray Wizard.** I admit, all these steps might seem like a lot of work, but now you have a reusable foundation to create any tray application. Select the Tray Wizard and call the new application QuickCD, as shown in Figure 9-5.

22. **Create three new icons.** Each new icon should only have the Small (16x16) device image. When you create a new icon in Visual C++ 4.0, it starts with only a 32x32 image. Add the new device image by pressing the (INSERT) key, then switch back to the Standard (32x32) image and choose Delete Device Image from the Image menu.

    The three new icons represent the three possible states for QuickCD: play, pause, and no CD present (see Figure 9-6). Call the icons IDI_PLAY, IDI_PAUSE, IDI_NOCD respectively.

CHAPTER 9
WINDOWS 95 SHELL

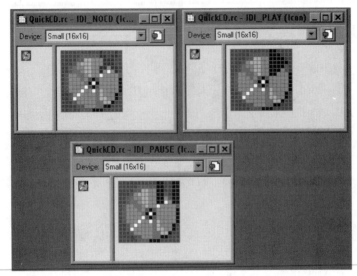

Figure 9-6 QuickCD state icons

23. **Add a new menu called IDR_MENU1.** This menu will be shown when the user clicks the right-mouse button on the tray icon (see Figure 9-7). The text and menu IDs are shown in the table below:

Item	ID
&Play from start	ID_PLAY_FROM_START
&Stop	ID_STOP
Pa&use	ID_PAUSE
&Next track	ID_NEXT_TRACK
Pre&vious track	ID_PREVIOUS_TRACK
&Eject CD	ID_EJECT_CD
Track &list...	ID_TRACK_LIST
&About QuickCD	ID_ABOUT
E&xit QuickCD	ID_EXIT

24. **Add three string resources.** QuickCD uses the strings in the following table for the tooltip text.

ID	Caption
IDS_TT_NOCD	No music CD in player
IDS_TT_PLAYING	Playing [%.2d] %.2d:%.2d
IDS_TT_PAUSED	Paused [%.2d] %.2d:%.2d

9.1
WRITE A TRAY APPLICATION TO PLAY CDS

Figure 9-7 The QuickCD menu IDR_MENU1

25. **Create an empty dialog called IDD_SETTINGS.** QuickCD populates this dialog at runtime with ColorWell controls (from Chapter 7), one for each CD track. The size isn't important since it changes depending on the number of CD tracks.

    Insert a new dialog and remove the OK and Cancel buttons. Rename the dialog to IDD_SETTINGS. Remove the Titlebar and System menu styles.

26. **Create a new class called CSettingsDlg.** Use ClassWizard to create a new class based on the new dialog IDD_SETTINGS using the following information:

Class name:	CSettingsDlg
Base class:	CDialog
File:	SettingsDlg.cpp
Dialog:	IDD_SETTINGS

    CTracksDlg might have been a better name for this dialog, but this was the original name.

27. **Copy CDAudio.cpp and CDAudio.h from the Multimedia chapter.** The Multimedia chapter introduced a new class called *CCDAudio*. Instead of typing the whole class in, simply copy the CDAudio.cpp and CCDAudio.h files from the *Visual C++ How-To* CD-ROM to the QuickCD directory. You'll find the files under Multimedia\DiscPlayer. Open the CDAudio.cpp file and insert it into the project (Hint: Use the context menu).

28. **Insert the ColorWell OLE Control from the OLE chapter.** One of the How-Tos in the OLE chapter demonstrated a ColorWell control. It happens to be the perfect control for selected a track (a coincidence?).

CHAPTER 9
WINDOWS 95 SHELL

Choose Component from the Insert menu and locate the ColorWell control in the OLE Controls tab. If you can't find it in the list, it's probably not registered. The Test Container provides an easy way to register controls. Start the Test Container (\msdev\bin\tstcon32.exe) and choose Register Controls from the File menu. Press the Register button and choose the OLE\ColorWell\ColorWell.ocx file from the *Visual C++ How-To* CD-ROM.

CColorWell and *COleFont* will be added to the project when you insert the ColorWell control.

29. **Create a new class called CPlayerWnd.** Use ClassWizard to create a new class using the following information:

Class name:	CPlayerWnd
Base class:	generic CWnd
File:	PlayerWnd.cpp

    Open PlayerWnd.h and PlayerWnd.cpp and replace every occurrence of *CWnd* with *CTrayWnd*.

30. **Add message handlers to CPlayerWnd and CSettingsDlg.** Add message-handling functions for these objects (you'll have to change the message filter for *CSettingsDlg* to Window):

Object ID	Function	Message
CSettingsDlg	OnInitDialog	WM_INITDIALOG
CSettingsDlg	OnActivate	WM_ACTIVATE
CSettingsDlg	OnDestroy	WM_DESTROY
CSettingsDlg	OnCmdMsg	
CPlayerWnd	OnCreate	WM_CREATE
CPlayerWnd	OnDestroy	WM_DESTROY
CPlayerWnd	OnTimer	WM_TIMER
ID_ABOUT	OnAbout	COMMAND
ID_EXIT	OnExit	COMMAND
ID_EJECT_CD	OnEjectCD	COMMAND
ID_NEXT_TRACK	OnNextTrack	COMMAND
ID_PAUSE	OnPause	COMMAND
ID_PLAY_FROM_START	OnPlayFromStart	COMMAND
ID_PREVIOUS_TRACK	OnPreviousTrack	COMMAND
ID_STOP	OnStop	COMMAND
ID_TRACK_LIST	OnTrackList	COMMAND

9.1
WRITE A TRAY APPLICATION TO PLAY CDS

31. Edit PlayerWnd.h. Add the following member variables to hold the three-state icons, the CD audio interface, and the current and total number of tracks.

```
#include "TrayWnd.h"
#include "CDAudio.h"

class CPlayerWnd : public CWnd
{
// Construction
public:
        CPlayerWnd();
        virtual ~CPlayerWnd();

...
        // Generated message map functions
protected:
        //{{AFX_MSG(CPlayerWnd)
        afx_msg void OnAbout();
        afx_msg void OnExit();
        afx_msg void OnEjectCd();
        afx_msg void OnNextTrack();
        afx_msg void OnPause();
        afx_msg void OnPlayFromStart();
        afx_msg void OnPreviousTrack();
        afx_msg void OnStop();
        afx_msg void OnTrackList();
        afx_msg int OnCreate(LPCREATESTRUCT lpCreateStruct);
        afx_msg void OnDestroy();
        afx_msg void OnTimer(UINT nIDEvent);
        //}}AFX_MSG
        DECLARE_MESSAGE_MAP()

        CCDAudio m_cd;
        BOOL m_bMediaPresent;
        int m_nCurTrack;
        int m_nTotalTracks;

        HICON m_hNoCDIcon;
        HICON m_hPauseIcon;
        HICON m_hPlayIcon;
};
```

32. Edit PlayerWnd.cpp. Modify the top of the file and the constructor to look like the following:

```
#include "stdafx.h"
#include "QuickCD.h"
#include "PlayerWnd.h"
#include "SettingsDlg.h"
#include "AboutDlg.h"

#define CD_TIMER_ID       5
#define CD_TIMER_VALUE    3000
```

continued on next page

continued from previous page
///
// CPlayerWnd

```
CPlayerWnd::CPlayerWnd()
{
    m_bMediaPresent = FALSE;
}
```

33. Code CPlayerWnd::OnCreate. This code loads the three-state icons and starts the timer that monitors the state of the CD player.

```
int CPlayerWnd::OnCreate(LPCREATESTRUCT lpCreateStruct)
{
    if (CTrayWnd::OnCreate(lpCreateStruct) == -1)
        return -1;

    // Load the icons
    m_hPlayIcon = AfxGetApp()->LoadIcon(IDI_PLAY);
    m_hPauseIcon = AfxGetApp()->LoadIcon(IDI_PAUSE);
    m_hNoCDIcon = AfxGetApp()->LoadIcon(IDI_NOCD);
    ASSERT(m_hPlayIcon && m_hPauseIcon && m_hNoCDIcon);

    // Start a timer to monitor the CD
    SetTimer(CD_TIMER_ID, CD_TIMER_VALUE, NULL);
    OnTimer(CD_TIMER_ID);       // force a timer message

    return 0;
}
```

34. Code CPlayerWnd::OnDestroy. Here, we remove any icon added to the tray. Without this line of code, the icon sticks around even after the application quits.

```
void CPlayerWnd::OnDestroy()
{
    CTrayWnd::OnDestroy();

    // remove the tray icon from the task bar
    NotifyIcon(NIM_DELETE, NULL);
}
```

35. Code CPlayerWnd::OnTimer. The CD player can be in one of three states each time the WM_TIMER message is fired:

- No CD is detected. Show the IDI_NOCD icon.
- A CD has just been inserted. Get the current track if it's already playing and the total number of tracks. Start the CD player and update the tray icon and tooltip text.
- The CD is playing or is paused. Get the current track and position; then update the tooltip text.

9.1
WRITE A TRAY APPLICATION TO PLAY CDS

```cpp
void CPlayerWnd::OnTimer(UINT nIDEvent)
{
    CTrayWnd::OnTimer(nIDEvent);
    static DWORD dwAction = NIM_ADD;

    if (nIDEvent != CD_TIMER_ID)
        return;

    if (m_cd.IsDeviceOpen() == FALSE)
        m_cd.Open(this);

    BOOL bMediaPresent = m_cd.IsMediaPresent();
    if (bMediaPresent)
    {
        if (!m_bMediaPresent)
        {
            // There wasn't a CD last time we checked.
            // Start it up if necessary and get the total number of tracks
            m_nTotalTracks = m_cd.GetNumberOfTracks();

            if (m_cd.IsPlaying() == FALSE)
            {
                m_nCurTrack = 1;
                m_cd.Play(1);
            }
        }

        // Update the tooltip text
        int track, min, sec;
        m_cd.GetPosition(track, min, sec);
        m_nCurTrack = track;

        CString msg;
        if (m_cd.IsPlaying())
        {
            msg.Format(IDS_TT_PLAYING, track, min, sec);
            NotifyIcon(dwAction, m_hPlayIcon, msg);
        } else {
            msg.Format(IDS_TT_PAUSED, track, min, sec);
            NotifyIcon(dwAction, m_hPauseIcon, msg);
        }

    } else {
        // Still no CD or it was ejected
        NotifyIcon(dwAction, m_hNoCDIcon, IDS_TT_NOCD);
    }

    // save media present info for next time
    m_bMediaPresent = bMediaPresent;
    dwAction = NIM_MODIFY;
}
```

36. Add the OnLeftClick helper function. Use the ClassView Add Function dialog to add the following virtual method. *CTrayWnd* calls *OnLeftClick* after processing its own notification message. This code simply toggles between playing or pausing.

```
void CPlayerWnd::OnLeftClick()
{
    // Only handle mouse clicks if there's a CD inserted
    if (m_cd.IsDeviceOpen() && m_cd.IsMediaPresent())
    {
        if (m_cd.IsPlaying())
            m_cd.Pause();
        else
            m_cd.ResumePlay();

        OnTimer(CD_TIMER_ID);    // this forces the icon to update right now
    }
}
```

37. Add the OnRightClick helper function. Use the ClassView Add Function dialog to add the following virtual method. We use *TrackPopupMenu* to display a menu of options. If no CD is found, most of the options are grayed out. Otherwise, the Track list option is made bold by using the new Windows 95 functions *GetMenuItemInfo* and *SetMenuItemInfo*.

```
void CPlayerWnd::OnRightClick()
{
    CPoint pt;
    GetCursorPos(&pt);

    CMenu menu;
    VERIFY(menu.LoadMenu(IDR_MENU1));
    CMenu* pPopup = menu.GetSubMenu(0);

    // If no CD is present, disable a few items
    if ( m_cd.IsDeviceOpen() == FALSE || !m_cd.IsMediaPresent())
    {
        pPopup->EnableMenuItem(ID_PLAY_FROM_START, MF_GRAYED);
        pPopup->EnableMenuItem(ID_STOP, MF_GRAYED);
        pPopup->EnableMenuItem(ID_PAUSE, MF_GRAYED);
        pPopup->EnableMenuItem(ID_NEXT_TRACK, MF_GRAYED);
        pPopup->EnableMenuItem(ID_PREVIOUS_TRACK, MF_GRAYED);
        pPopup->EnableMenuItem(ID_EJECT_CD, MF_GRAYED);
        pPopup->EnableMenuItem(ID_TRACK_LIST, MF_GRAYED);
    } else {
        // bold the Track List menu item to show that it's the default
        // option if you double-click the icon

        MENUITEMINFO info;
        info.cbSize = sizeof(MENUITEMINFO);
        info.fMask = MIIM_STATE;
```

9.1 WRITE A TRAY APPLICATION TO PLAY CDS

```
            GetMenuItemInfo(pPopup->m_hMenu, ID_TRACK_LIST, FALSE, &info);
            info.fState |= MFS_DEFAULT;
            SetMenuItemInfo(pPopup->m_hMenu, ID_TRACK_LIST, FALSE, &info);
        }

        // See Q135788: "Menus for Notification Icons
        // Don't Work Correctly" for an explanation of
        // why we need SetForegroundWindow and PostMessage

        SetForegroundWindow();
        pPopup->TrackPopupMenu(TPM_RIGHTBUTTON,
                pt.x, pt.y, this);
        PostMessage(WM_USER);
}
```

38. Add the OnLeftDoubleClick helper function. Use the ClassView Add Function dialog to add the following virtual method. If the user double-clicks the tray icon, *CPlayerWnd* shows the track list dialog by calling *OnTrackList*.

```
void CPlayerWnd::OnLeftDoubleClick()
{
    if (m_cd.IsDeviceOpen() && m_cd.IsMediaPresent())
    {
        SetForegroundWindow();
        OnTrackList();
    }
}
```

39. Code the menu handlers. The rest of the functions are straightforward. Most just make a single call to one of the *CCDAudio* methods. Any action that changes the state of the CD player (next track, stop, eject) is followed by an immediate call to *OnTimer*. That way, the icon and tooltip text is updated without waiting for the next timer tick (about 3 seconds).

```
void CPlayerWnd::OnAbout()
{
    CAboutDlg dlg;
    dlg.DoModal();
}

void CPlayerWnd::OnExit()
{
    // Don't call PostQuitMessage because PostNcDestroy won't be called
    PostMessage(WM_CLOSE);
}

void CPlayerWnd::OnEjectCd()
{
    m_cd.Eject();
    OnTimer(CD_TIMER_ID);
}

void CPlayerWnd::OnNextTrack()
{
```

continued on next page

continued from previous page

```
        if (m_nCurTrack == m_nTotalTracks)
            m_nCurTrack = 1;
        else
            m_nCurTrack++;

        m_cd.Play(m_nCurTrack);
        OnTimer(CD_TIMER_ID);
}

void CPlayerWnd::OnPause()
{
        m_cd.Pause();
        OnTimer(CD_TIMER_ID);
}

void CPlayerWnd::OnPlayFromStart()
{
        m_nCurTrack = 1;
        m_cd.Play(m_nCurTrack);
        OnTimer(CD_TIMER_ID);
}

void CPlayerWnd::OnPreviousTrack()
{
        if (m_nCurTrack == 1)
            m_nCurTrack = m_nTotalTracks;
        else
            m_nCurTrackñ;

        m_cd.Play(m_nCurTrack);
        OnTimer(CD_TIMER_ID);
}

void CPlayerWnd::OnStop()
{
        m_cd.Stop();
        OnTimer(CD_TIMER_ID);
}

void CPlayerWnd::OnTrackList()
{
        CSettingsDlg dlg;
        dlg.m_nCurTrack = m_nCurTrack;
        dlg.m_cTracks = m_cd.GetNumberOfTracks();

        if (dlg.DoModal() == IDOK)
            m_cd.Play(dlg.m_nSelectedTrack);
}
```

40. Edit SettingsDlg.h. Make these changes to SettingsDlg.h:

```
class CSettingsDlg : public CDialog
{
// Construction
public:
        CSettingsDlg(CWnd* pParent = NULL);   // standard constructor
```

9.1
WRITE A TRAY APPLICATION TO PLAY CDS

```
    UINT m_nSelectedTrack;
    UINT m_nCurTrack;
    UINT m_cTracks;

// Dialog Data
    //{{AFX_DATA(CSettingsDlg)
    enum { IDD = IDD_SETTINGS };
    //}}AFX_DATA

// Overrides
    // ClassWizard generated virtual function overrides
    //{{AFX_VIRTUAL(CSettingsDlg)
    public:
    virtual BOOL OnCmdMsg(UINT nID, int nCode, void* pExtra,
        AFX_CMDHANDLERINFO* pHandlerInfo);
    protected:
    virtual void DoDataExchange(CDataExchange* pDX);    // DDX/DDV support
    //}}AFX_VIRTUAL

// Implementation
protected:
    // Generated message map functions
    //{{AFX_MSG(CSettingsDlg)
    virtual BOOL OnInitDialog();
    afx_msg void OnDestroy();
    afx_msg void OnActivate(UINT nState, CWnd* pWndOther, BOOL bMinimized);
    //}}AFX_MSG
    DECLARE_MESSAGE_MAP()
    DECLARE_EVENTSINK_MAP()

    BOOL OnMyEvent(UINT idCtrl, AFX_EVENT* pEvent, AFX_CMDHANDLERINFO* ⇒
pHandlerInfo);
    BOOL OnClickColor(UINT nWellId);

    CPtrArray m_wells;
};
```

41. Edit SettingsDlg.cpp. Modify the top of the file like this:

```
#include "stdafx.h"
#include "QuickCD.h"
#include "SettingsDlg.h"
#include <afxpriv.h>
#include "ColorWell.h"

#define ID_WELL_FIRST 2000
#define ID_WELL_LAST 2100
#define NUM_WELLS_ACROSS 4

CSettingsDlg::CSettingsDlg(CWnd* pParent /*=NULL*/)
    : CDialog(CSettingsDlg::IDD, pParent)
{
    //{{AFX_DATA_INIT(CSettingsDlg)
    //}}AFX_DATA_INIT
    m_cTracks = 0;
    m_nCurTrack = 0;
}
```

CHAPTER 9
WINDOWS 95 SHELL

42. Edit CSettingsDlg::OnInitDialog. The client of *CSettingsDlg* must set *m_cTracks* before the dialog is shown through *DoModal*. That's because *OnInitDialog* tries to create a color well for each track, with the track number as the caption. The value of NUM_WELLS_ACROSS determines the number of wells in each row. After the controls have been created, the dialog is resized to fit the array of wells.

```
BOOL CSettingsDlg::OnInitDialog()
{
    CDialog::OnInitDialog();

    ASSERT(m_cTracks != 0);
    ASSERT(m_nCurTrack > 0 && m_nCurTrack <= m_cTracks);   // m_nCurTrack is 1 based
    ASSERT(m_cTracks < ID_WELL_LAST - ID_WELL_FIRST);      // sorry, that's the limit

    // Try to get NUM_WELLS_ACROSS controls in one row
    CSize size(22, 22);
    CPoint pos(0, 0);

    CColorWell* pWell;
    UINT nID = ID_WELL_FIRST;
    for (UINT i = 1; i <= m_cTracks; i++)
    {
        CString msg;
        msg.Format("%d", i);

        pWell = new CColorWell();
        if (pWell->Create(msg, WS_VISIBLE | WS_CHILD, CRect(pos, size),
            this, nID++) == FALSE)
        {
            delete pWell;
            break;
        }

        // COLORREF will automatically cast to OLE_COLOR
        // (see Q131101 "Converting between OLE_COLOR and COLORREF"
        if (i >= m_nCurTrack)
            pWell->SetBackColor(GetSysColor(COLOR_BTNHILIGHT));
        pWell->SetFlat(TRUE);

        if (i % NUM_WELLS_ACROSS == 0)
        {
            pos.y += size.cy;
            pos.x = 0;
        } else {
            pos.x += size.cx;
        }

        // Keep track of the well points so we can delete them in OnDestroy
        m_wells.Add(pWell);
    }

    // Resize the dialog so it's big enough to hold the controls plus a border
    // and position the window in the lower-right corner of the screen
```

9.1
WRITE A TRAY APPLICATION TO PLAY CDS

```
        CSize minSize(NUM_WELLS_ACROSS * size.cx + 8, pos.y + size.cy + 12);

        CRect rWorkArea;
        SystemParametersInfo(SPI_GETWORKAREA, 0, &rWorkArea, FALSE);

        MoveWindow(rWorkArea.right - minSize.cx - 10, rWorkArea.bottom - ⇒
minSize.cy - 10,
            minSize.cx, minSize.cy);

        return TRUE;
}
```

43. Code CSettingsDlg::OnDestroy. Clean up after yourself: Loop through the color well array and delete each one.

```
void CSettingsDlg::OnDestroy()
{
        CDialog::OnDestroy();

        for (int i=0; i < m_wells.GetSize(); i++)
        {
                CColorWell* pWell = (CColorWell*) m_wells.GetAt(i);
                pWell->DestroyWindow();
                delete pWell;
        }
}
```

44. Code CSettingsDlg::OnActivate. Here's a great trick: If the dialog loses focus for any reason, close it. This eliminates the need for a Cancel button.

```
void CSettingsDlg::OnActivate(UINT nState, CWnd* pWndOther, BOOL bMinimized)
{
        CDialog::OnActivate(nState, pWndOther, bMinimized);

        if (nState == WA_INACTIVE)
                PostMessage(WM_COMMAND, IDCANCEL);
}
```

45. Add the method CSettingsDlg::OnClickColor. When the user chooses a track, record the selection and close the dialog.

```
BEGIN_EVENTSINK_MAP(CSettingsDlg, CDialog)
    //{{AFX_EVENTSINK_MAP(CSettingsDlg)
    //}}AFX_EVENTSINK_MAP
    ON_EVENT_RANGE(CSettingsDlg, ID_WELL_FIRST, ID_WELL_LAST, DISPID_CLICK,
        OnClickColor, VTS_I4)
END_EVENTSINK_MAP()

BOOL CSettingsDlg::OnClickColor(UINT nId)
{
        m_nSelectedTrack = nId - ID_WELL_FIRST + 1;
        EndDialog(IDOK);
        return TRUE;
}
```

CHAPTER 9
WINDOWS 95 SHELL

46. Fix a bug in MFC 4.0. The ON_EVENT_RANGE macro is similar to ON_COMMAND_RANGE; it lets one method handle the same event fired by more than one control. There's only one problem: MFC 4.0 has a bug that causes the application to crash when the fired event doesn't pass any parameters. Since the *OnClickColor* event fired from the well doesn't pass any parameters, the application crashes.

At the time of this writing, I've been told the MFC 4.1 subscription release *might* have this bug fixed. The easiest way to check is to remove the call to *OnMyEvent* in *OnCmdMsg*. If it crashes in *memcpy*, the bug hasn't been fixed. Believe me, it took quite a while to figure this one out. The fix simply checks the number of event parameters before calling *memcpy*.

```
BOOL CSettingsDlg::OnCmdMsg(UINT nID, int nCode, void* pExtra,
    AFX_CMDHANDLERINFO* pHandlerInfo)
{
#ifndef _AFX_NO_OCC_SUPPORT
        if (nCode == CN_EVENT)
        {
                if (OnMyEvent(nID, (AFX_EVENT*) pExtra, pHandlerInfo))
                    return TRUE;
        }
#endif

        return CDialog::OnCmdMsg(nID, nCode, pExtra, pHandlerInfo);
}

BOOL CSettingsDlg::OnMyEvent(UINT idCtrl, AFX_EVENT* pEvent,
    AFX_CMDHANDLERINFO* pHandlerInfo)
{
        HRESULT hResult = S_OK;
        UINT uArgError = (UINT)-1; // no error yet
        const AFX_EVENTSINKMAP_ENTRY* pEntry = GetEventSinkEntry(idCtrl, pEvent);

        // no handler for this event
        if (pEntry == NULL)
            return FALSE;

        if (pHandlerInfo != NULL)
            return FALSE;

        BOOL bRange = (pEntry->nCtrlIDLast != (UINT)-1);
        BOOL bHandled = FALSE;

        if (pEvent->m_eventKind != AFX_EVENT::event)
            return FALSE;

        // make sure IsExpectingResult returns FALSE as appropriate
        BOOL bResultExpected = m_bResultExpected;
        m_bResultExpected = FALSE;
```

9.1
WRITE A TRAY APPLICATION TO PLAY CDS

```
        // do standard method call
        VARIANT var;
        AfxVariantInit(&var);

        DISPPARAMS dispparams;

        if (bRange)
        {
                memcpy(&dispparams, pEvent->m_pDispParams, sizeof(DISPPARAMS));
                dispparams.rgvarg = new VARIANT[++dispparams.cArgs];

                if (dispparams.cArgs-1 != 0) // <- my one line bug fix
                        memcpy(dispparams.rgvarg, pEvent->m_pDispParams->rgvarg,
                                sizeof(VARIANT) * dispparams.cArgs-1);

                VARIANT* pvarID = &dispparams.rgvarg[dispparams.cArgs-1];
                V_VT(pvarID) = VT_I4;
                V_I4(pvarID) = idCtrl;
        }

        hResult = CallMemberFunc(&pEntry->dispEntry, DISPATCH_METHOD, &var,
                (bRange ? &dispparams : pEvent->m_pDispParams), &uArgError);
        ASSERT(FAILED(hResult) || (V_VT(&var) == VT_BOOL));
        bHandled = V_BOOL(&var);

        if (bRange)
                delete [] dispparams.rgvarg;

        // restore original m_bResultExpected flag
        m_bResultExpected = bResultExpected;

        // fill error argument if one is available
        if (FAILED(hResult) && pEvent->m_puArgError != NULL && uArgError != -1)
                *pEvent->m_puArgError = uArgError;

        // fill result code
        pEvent->m_hResult = hResult;

        return bHandled;
}
```

47. Edit CQuickCDApp::InitInstance. Instruct the application to create an instance of *CPlayerWnd* instead of *CTrayWnd*.

```
BOOL CQuickCDApp::InitInstance()
{
        AfxEnableControlContainer();

#ifdef _AFXDLL
        Enable3dControls();         // Call this when using MFC in a shared DLL
#else
        Enable3dControlsStatic();   // Call this when linking to MFC statically
#endif
```

continued on next page

continued from previous page

```
        CPlayerWnd* pWnd = new CPlayerWnd();
        VERIFY(pWnd->Create());

        m_pMainWnd = pWnd;

        return TRUE;
}
```

You'll also need to add one more #include at the top:

```
#include "stdafx.h"
#include "QuickCD.h"
#include "PlayerWnd.h"
```

48. Modify the registry. If you want QuickCD.exe to launch whenever a CD is inserted, add the following to the registry using RegEdit.exe:

```
HKEY_CLASSES_ROOT\AudioCD\shell\play = "&Play"
HKEY_CLASSES_ROOT\AudioCD\shell\play\command = "[replace with path ⇒
to QuickCD.exe]"
```

49. Compile and test the program. If you run the program without a CD in the drive, the tray icon should show a little x. Insert an audio CD, and QuickCD will start playing the first track. If you single-click on the icon, the CD should pause; to play, click again. Double-clicking will display the track selection dialog. A single right-mouse click shows the context menu that lets you manipulate the CD.

How It Works

CTrayWnd was created as our application's main window instead of the normal *CFrameWnd* object. This custom *CWnd* class uses the WS_EX_TOOLWINDOW extend style to prevent it from showing up in the task bar. Also, since the window doesn't use the WS_VISIBLE style, it's never visible. Now that the window is safely hidden away, it can create the tray icon and service the mouse events generated by the icon.

CTrayWnd::NotifyIcon is a helper function that conveniently wraps the *Shell_NotifyIcon* function. *NotifyIcon* allows you to add or delete a tray icon or change its tooltip text. These feats are accomplished by filling in a NOTIFYICONDATA structure and passing it on to *Shell_NotifyIcon*.

The tray icon in turn communicates back to the *CTrayWnd* by posting mouse events using the message ID specified by *NotifyIcon* (TRAY_NOTIFYICON). By using the ON_MESSAGE macro, step 9 hooked up *OnTrayNotify* to respond to this message.

It's inside *OnTrayNotify* where we decode the messages as one of four possible mouse events: WM_LBUTTONDOWN, WM_LBUTTONUP, WM_LBUTTONDBLCLK, and WM_RBUTTONUP. Because it's impossible to distinguish a single-click from a double-click, we don't process the WM_LBUTTONDOWN message right away. Instead, you set a short timer of *GetDoubleClickTime* milliseconds long and wait. If the timer expires before you get a WM_LBUTTONDBLCLK, you should assume you are dealing with a single click and fire WM_LBUTTONUP. Otherwise note that you *should* treat the double-click as such and wait for the imminent WM_LBUTTONUP message. When it comes through, send post the WM_LBUTTONDBLCLK message.

Who are you posting these messages to? They're all sent to ourselves, the *CTrayWnd* object. Instead of doing something interesting with the tray notification events, we need to send a message so we can handle it a little bit later in the future. Basically, we need to leave the *OnTrayNotify* function as soon as possible. You'll discover this when you try to create an OLE control while processing the WM_LBUTTONDOWN message. A cryptic error message from MFC appears in the output window with the error code RPC_E_CANTCALLOUT_ININPUTSYNCCALL. According to WinError.h, this means "an outgoing call cannot be made since the application is dispatching an input-synchronous call."

You shouldn't do anything interesting on the receiving side of these posts except to make a call to an empty virtual function. For example WM_LBUTTONUP is handled by *CTrayWnd::OnLButtonUp* which in turn calls *OnLeftClick*. *CTrayWnd* is meant to be subclassed so the virtual methods like *OnLeftClick* can do something interesting like display a pop-up menu, or pause the CD player.

Custom AppWizard

By the time step 16 is reached, we have a nice generic framework for registering tray icons. Step 17 takes a snapshot of the project by turning it into a Custom AppWizard. The next few steps use this AppWizard to generate a real tray application, QuickCD.

CPlayerWnd

In order to do something useful, you can derive a new class called *CPlayerWnd* from *CTrayWnd* in step 29. This new class knows what to do with the mouse messages:

- Pause or play the CD when the left button is pressed
- Display the tracks dialog on a double-click
- Show a popup menu on a right-mouse click

CPlayerWnd::OnLeftClick is simple. It pauses the CD if it's currently playing, or plays the CD if it's currently paused. Either way, it simulates a timer message so the icon state and tooltip can be updated.

A right-mouse click displays a menu of options. If there's no CD in the drive, most of the entries are grayed out. Otherwise, one of the menu items is made the default, indicating that a double-click will always run that option. The MFS_DEFAULT menu state turns one of the menu items bold, in this case the Track List option is made the default.

Finally, the *OnLeftDoubleClick* message displays the track dialog, *CSettingsDlg*. This dialog uses the ColorWell OLE Control from the OLE chapter. *CSettingsDlg::OnInitDialog* dynamically creates an array of *CColorWell* windows in a grid. Since the controls are created at runtime, you'll have to handle their click events differently. If there was only one control, ON_EVENT would map that control's event to a method. Another macro called ON_EVENT_RANGE handles the same event but from more than one control. However, you'll find that if that event doesn't pass any parameters, MFC crashes in *memcpy*. Step 46 fixes the bug, but versions after MFC 4.0 might include the fix.

COMPLEXITY
ADVANCED

9.2 How do I... Create a property sheet handler for a file or folder?

Problem

I'd like to add my own property page to the sheet displayed when a user chooses the Properties menu in the Explorer. For example, if you right-click on a folder and choose Properties, I'd like a page to display all the subfolders and the disk space occupied by each one.

There's a little bit of documentation about property sheet handlers in Books Online and on the Microsoft Development Network CD-ROMs, but neither shows how to approach the problem with MFC and *CPropertyPages*. How do I do this?

Technique

The Windows 95 user interface supports seven types of user interface extensions (known as *handlers*). One of these, the *property sheet handler*, adds pages to the standard property sheet displayed for a file or folder object. A property sheet extension registers itself as a handler for a particular file name extension or for all folders. In this How-To, you'll learn how to write a property sheet handler for folders, using the *CPropertySheet* class and a good dose of OLE COM interfaces.

To initialize an instance of a property sheet handler, the system uses the *IShellExtInit* interface. Like all COM interfaces, *IShellExtInit* supports the three standard *IUnknown* methods. We'll use a helper file to implement the *IUnknown* methods since the supporting code rarely changes. The only other function *IShellExtInit* requires us to code is *Initialize*. It's through this method that Windows 95 and the Explorer pass the selected folder to your class.

The other interface we'll need to support is the *IShellPropSheetExt* interface. In addition to the *IUnknown* functions, the interface includes *AddPages* and *ReplacePages*. We'll create an instance of a class derived from *CPropertyPage* and add it to the property sheet. As it turns out, it's tricky using MFC-based property pages in conjunction with the DLL version of MFC, but we have code to fix those problems.

The first steps create a DLL to host the class that supports *IShellPropSheetExt* and *IShellExtInit*. Next, we add an awful lot of code to support self-registration since a few special registry entries need to be made. Besides implementing the two OLE interfaces, we have to write the code that handles the property page. As a developer, you might

9.2
CREATE A PROPERTY SHEET HANDLER FOR A FILE OR FOLDER

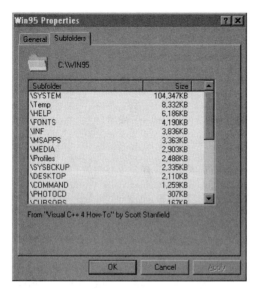

Figure 9-8 An MFC-based property sheet extension

find this handler particularly useful. When you're finished with the steps below, you'll be able to see the size taken up by all the subfolders of a particular folder (see Figure 9-8). It's great for reclaiming hard disk space, given that those pre-compiled header files are quite large.

Steps

1. Create a new project called Subfolders with the MFC AppWizard (dll).
Make sure you chose the DLL AppWizard instead of the EXE AppWizard.
Choose the shared MFC DLL option and turn on the option for OLE automation.

```
Creating Regular DLL (using a shared copy of MFC) Subfolder.dll
Main source code in: Subfolder.h and Subfolder.cpp
Features:
   + OLE Automation support enabled
   + Using a shared copy of MFC
```

2. Edit StdAfx.h. Add these lines to the bottom of StdAfx.h:

```
#include <afxmt.h>      // MFC support for thread synchronization objects

// We always want to include <Afxctl.h> for the DECLARE_OLECREATE_EX definition.
// However, if we're static linking to MFC, we have to fake out Afxctl.h by
// temporarily defining _AFXDLL.

#ifndef _AFXDLL
#define _AFXDLL
#include <afxctl.h>
```

continued on next page

continued from previous page

```
#undef _AFXDLL
#else
#include <afxctl.h>
#endif

// We only include WinNetwk.h because, without it, shlobj.h complains
// about NETRESOURCE!
#include <winnetwk.h>
#include <shlobj.h>          // Shell extension interfaces

#include "COMHelp.h"
```

3. Add a global function called DllUnregisterServer to Subfolder.cpp (MFC 4.0 only). AppWizard added three entry points necessary to support OLE Automation: *DllCanUnloadNow, DllGetClassObject,* and *DllRegisterServer.* The first two are used by COM and Windows to retrieve objects and to determine whether or not the Subfolder DLL can be unloaded from memory. The third DLL entry point, *DllRegisterServer,* adds or updates registry information for all the classes implemented by the DLL.

There is another function AppWizard didn't provide but requires for the DLL to be self-registering, called *DllUnregisterServer.* It removes the registry information added by *DllRegisterServer.*

How do these two entry points get called? Visual Basic uses them to register files identified by the user. Regsvr32.exe, a small OLE utility in \MSDEV\BIN, uses these two methods to register or unregister OLE controls and inproc servers with the system. MFC takes care of the registration; we have to add code to undo those actions. Add the following code to the bottom of Subfolder.cpp:

```
STDAPI DllUnregisterServer(void)
{
    // The documentation for UpdateRegistryAll doesn't mention
    // that the function takes one argument.

    AFX_MANAGE_STATE(AfxGetStaticModuleState());
    COleObjectFactory::UpdateRegistryAll(FALSE);
    return S_OK;
}
```

4. Edit Subfolder.def (MFC 4.0 only). Edit the DEF file so the linker knows what functions should be exported:

```
; Subfolder.def : Declares the module parameters for the DLL.

LIBRARY          "SUBFOLDER"
DESCRIPTION      'SUBFOLDER Windows Dynamic Link Library'

EXPORTS
        DllCanUnloadNow PRIVATE
        DllGetClassObject PRIVATE
        DllRegisterServer PRIVATE
        DllUnregisterServer PRIVATE
```

9.2
CREATE A PROPERTY SHEET HANDLER FOR A FILE OR FOLDER

5. Edit Subfolder.rc. One last step is needed to make this DLL truly self-registering. If you read the MFC Encyclopedia article called *Self-Registering DLLs*, it describes a way for applications to identify a DLL that supports self-registration by actually loading it and scanning for these entry points. To accomplish this, we have to add a new string to the version resource. The version editor in App Studio doesn't support this feature, so you have to open the Subfolder.rc file as a Text file instead of Auto using CTRL+O. Add the following line:

```
BEGIN
    BLOCK "StringFileInfo"
    BEGIN
        BLOCK "040904B0"
        BEGIN
            VALUE "CompanyName",      "\0"
            VALUE "FileDescription",  "SUBFOLDER DLL\0"
            VALUE "FileVersion",      "1, 0, 0, 1\0"
            VALUE "InternalName",     "SUBFOLDER\0"
            VALUE "LegalCopyright",   "Copyright \251 1996\0"
            VALUE "LegalTrademarks",  "\0"
            VALUE "OriginalFilename", "SUBFOLDER.DLL\0"
            VALUE "ProductName",      "SUBFOLDER Dynamic Link Library\0"
            VALUE "ProductVersion",   "1, 0, 0, 1\0"
            VALUE "OLESelfRegister",  "\0"
        END
    END
    BLOCK "VarFileInfo"
    BEGIN
        VALUE "Translation", 0x409, 1200
    END
END
```

6. Create a new file called RegisterClass.h. If you are creating simple OLE controls or inproc servers, MFC will more than likely take care of all the registration details for you. In fact, it's not that easy to override the built-in registration features of a ControlWizard-generated DLL. However, since we need to add some special entries to the registry, the next few steps will create a reusable class to make the registration/unregistration task a lot easier. A couple of methods in this class are used later in the RegServer How-To.

Create a new file called RegisterClass.h and add this code to it:

```
#ifndef _REGISTERCLASS_
#define _REGISTERCLASS_

#include <winreg.h>         // for HKEY_CLASSES_ROOT

class CRegisterClass
{
public:
    CRegisterClass(REFCLSID clsid, LPCTSTR pszTypeName, HKEY hkeyRoot =
HKEY_CLASSES_ROOT);
```

continued on next page

CHAPTER 9
WINDOWS 95 SHELL

continued from previous page

```
        void AddEntry(LPCTSTR key, LPCTSTR value, LPCTSTR valueName = NULL);
        int  AddSymbol(LPCTSTR symbol);
        int  AddSymbolAlias(LPCTSTR symbol, LPCTSTR alias);

        BOOL Register(BOOL bRegister = TRUE);
        BOOL SetRegKey(LPCTSTR lpszKey, LPCTSTR lpszValue, LPCTSTR ⇒
lpszValueName = NULL);
        BOOL DelRegKey(LPCTSTR lpszKey, LPCTSTR lpszValueName = NULL);

        BOOL RemoveKey(LPCTSTR key);    // recursively remove key

protected:
        BOOL Helper(BOOL bUnregister, LPCTSTR const* ppSymbols, int nSymbols);

        HKEY m_hkeyRoot;
        CStringArray m_keys;
        CStringArray m_values;
        CStringArray m_valueNames;
        CStringArray m_symbols;
};
#endif
```

7. Create a new file called RegisterClass.cpp. The implementation of *CRegisterClass* is a bit long. Most of the code manipulates the registry. If following the steps and typing in the code, you might want to just copy the files off the CD-ROM. When you've finished, insert RegisterClass.cpp into the project.

```
#include "stdafx.h"
#include "RegisterClass.h"

#define GUID_CCH 39  // Characters in string form of guid, including '\0'

CRegisterClass::CRegisterClass(REFCLSID clsid, LPCTSTR pszTypeName, ⇒
HKEY hkeyRoot)
        : m_hkeyRoot(hkeyRoot)
{
        // The constructor calculates three predefined symbols:
        // ClassID   %1 = "{4d3450049-1e19-..."
        // TypeName  %2 = "MyComponent.Object"
        // FullPath  %3 = "c:\mycode\debug\myobject.dll"

        // Format class ID as a string
        OLECHAR szClassID[GUID_CCH];
        int cchGuid = ::StringFromGUID2(clsid, szClassID, GUID_CCH);

        // Convert to multibyte from unicode
        CString strClassID(szClassID);

        ASSERT(cchGuid == GUID_CCH);   // Did StringFromGUID2 work?
        if (cchGuid != GUID_CCH)
        {
                TRACE("StringFromGUID2 failed\n");
                return;
        }
```

9.2
CREATE A PROPERTY SHEET HANDLER FOR A FILE OR FOLDER

```
        CString strPathName;
        TCHAR szLongPathName[_MAX_PATH];
        ::GetModuleFileName(AfxGetResourceHandle(), szLongPathName, _MAX_PATH);
        ::GetShortPathName(szLongPathName,
                strPathName.GetBuffer(_MAX_PATH), _MAX_PATH);
        strPathName.ReleaseBuffer();

        CString strTypeName(pszTypeName);

        m_symbols.Add(strClassID);
        m_symbols.Add(strTypeName);
        m_symbols.Add(strPathName);
}

LONG AFXAPI _RecursiveRegDeleteKey(HKEY hParentKey, LPCTSTR szKeyName);

BOOL CRegisterClass::RemoveKey(LPCTSTR key)
{
        CString strKey;

        // Build an array of pointers to the symbols
        int nSymbols = m_symbols.GetSize();
        CString* pStrings = m_symbols.GetData();

        LPCTSTR* ppSymbols = new LPCTSTR[nSymbols];
        for (int i=0; i < nSymbols; i++)
                ppSymbols[i] = (LPCTSTR) pStrings[i];

        AfxFormatStrings(strKey, key, ppSymbols, nSymbols);
        BOOL bRet = _RecursiveRegDeleteKey(m_hkeyRoot, strKey) == ERROR_SUCCESS;

        delete [] ppSymbols;
        return bRet;
}

void CRegisterClass::AddEntry(LPCTSTR key, LPCTSTR value, LPCTSTR valueName)
{
        ASSERT(AfxIsValidString(key));
        ASSERT(AfxIsValidString(value));
        ASSERT(valueName == NULL || AfxIsValidString(valueName));

        m_keys.Add(key);
        m_values.Add(value);
        m_valueNames.Add(valueName);
}

int CRegisterClass::AddSymbol(LPCTSTR pSymbol)
{
        return m_symbols.Add(pSymbol);
}

int CRegisterClass::AddSymbolAlias(LPCTSTR pSymbol, LPCTSTR pAlias)
{
        TCHAR szValue[MAX_PATH];
        LONG lSize = sizeof(szValue);
```

continued on next page

continued from previous page

```
        // Don't replace pSymbol's existing value
        if (RegQueryValue(HKEY_CLASSES_ROOT, pSymbol, szValue, &lSize) ⇒
== ERROR_SUCCESS)
        {
            // If alias already exists for symbol, use it
            // instead of requested alias (pAlias)
            if (lSize > 1)
                return AddSymbol(szValue);
        }

        // SetRegKey will add pSymbol if it doesn't exist with pAlias as its value
        SetRegKey(pSymbol, pAlias);
        return AddSymbol(pAlias);
}

BOOL CRegisterClass::Register(BOOL bRegister)
{
        // Build an array of pointers to the symbols
        int nSymbols = m_symbols.GetSize();
        CString* pStrings = m_symbols.GetData();

        LPCTSTR* ppSymbols = new LPCTSTR[nSymbols];
        for (int i=0; i < nSymbols; i++)
                ppSymbols[i] = (LPCTSTR) pStrings[i];

        BOOL bRet = Helper(bRegister, ppSymbols, nSymbols);
        delete ppSymbols;        // not delete [] ppSymbols!
        return bRet;
}

BOOL CRegisterClass::Helper(BOOL bRegister, LPCTSTR const* ppSymbols, ⇒
int nSymbols)
{
        ASSERT(nSymbols != 0);

        CString strKey;
        CString strValue;
        CString strValueName;    // (can be NULL)

        BOOL bResult = TRUE;
        int nItems = m_keys.GetSize();

        for (int i = 0; i < nItems; i++)
        {
                AfxFormatStrings(strKey, m_keys[i], ppSymbols, nSymbols);
                AfxFormatStrings(strValue, m_values[i], ppSymbols, nSymbols);
                AfxFormatStrings(strValueName, m_valueNames[i], ppSymbols, nSymbols);

                if (strKey.IsEmpty())
                        continue;

                if (bRegister)
                {
                        if (!SetRegKey(strKey, strValue, strValueName))
                        {
```

9.2
CREATE A PROPERTY SHEET HANDLER FOR A FILE OR FOLDER

```
                    TRACE("Error: failed to set key '%s' to value '%s'.\n",
                        (LPCTSTR) strKey, (LPCTSTR) strValue);
                    bResult = FALSE;
                    break;
                }
            } else {
                if (!DelRegKey(strKey, strValueName))
                {
                    TRACE("Failed to delete key %s\n", (LPCTSTR) strKey);
                    bResult = FALSE;
                    break;
                }
            }
        }

        return bResult;
}

BOOL CRegisterClass::DelRegKey(LPCTSTR lpszKey, LPCTSTR lpszValueName)
{
        if (lpszValueName == NULL || lstrlen(lpszValueName) == 0)
        {
            ASSERT(AfxIsValidString(lpszKey));
            return (::RegDeleteKey(m_hkeyRoot, lpszKey) == ERROR_SUCCESS);
        } else {
            HKEY hKey;
            if (::RegOpenKey(m_hkeyRoot, lpszKey, &hKey) == ERROR_SUCCESS)
            {
                LONG lResult = ::RegDeleteValue(hKey, lpszValueName);
                if(::RegCloseKey(hKey) == ERROR_SUCCESS && lResult == ⇒
ERROR_SUCCESS)
                    return TRUE;
            }
            return FALSE;
        }
}

BOOL CRegisterClass::SetRegKey(LPCTSTR lpszKey, LPCTSTR lpszValue, ⇒
LPCTSTR lpszValueName)
{
        if (lpszValueName == NULL || lstrlen(lpszValueName) == 0)
        {
            if (::RegSetValue(m_hkeyRoot, lpszKey, REG_SZ,
                    lpszValue, lstrlen(lpszValue)) != ERROR_SUCCESS)
            {
                TRACE1("Warning: registration database update failed for ⇒
key '%s'.\n",
                    lpszKey);
                return FALSE;
            }
            return TRUE;
        }
        else
        {
            HKEY hKey;
```

continued on next page

continued from previous page

```
            if(::RegCreateKey(m_hkeyRoot, lpszKey, &hKey) == ERROR_SUCCESS)
            {
                LONG lResult = ::RegSetValueEx(hKey, lpszValueName, 0, REG_SZ,
                    (CONST BYTE*)lpszValue, lstrlen(lpszValue) + sizeof(TCHAR) );

                if(::RegCloseKey(hKey) == ERROR_SUCCESS && lResult == ERROR_SUCCESS)
                    return TRUE;
            }
            TRACE1("Warning: registration database update failed for key '%s'.\n",
                lpszKey);
            return FALSE;
        }
}

// Under Win32, a reg key may not be deleted unless it is empty.
// Thus, to delete a tree, one must recursively enumerate and
// delete all of the sub-keys.

LONG AFXAPI _RecursiveRegDeleteKey(HKEY hParentKey, LPCTSTR szKeyName)
{
        DWORD   dwIndex = 0L;
        TCHAR   szSubKeyName[256];
        HKEY    hCurrentKey;
        DWORD   dwResult;

        if ((dwResult = RegOpenKey(hParentKey, szKeyName, &hCurrentKey)) ==
            ERROR_SUCCESS)
        {
            // Remove all subkeys of the key to delete
            while ((dwResult = RegEnumKey(hCurrentKey, 0, szSubKeyName, 255)) ==
                ERROR_SUCCESS)
            {
                if ((dwResult = _RecursiveRegDeleteKey(hCurrentKey,
                    szSubKeyName)) != ERROR_SUCCESS)
                    break;
            }

            // If all went well, we should now be able to delete the requested key
            if ((dwResult == ERROR_NO_MORE_ITEMS) || (dwResult == ERROR_BADKEY))
            {
                dwResult = RegDeleteKey(hParentKey, szKeyName);
            }
        }

        RegCloseKey(hCurrentKey);
        return dwResult;
}
```

By the way, a lot of this code is buried deep within MFC. I wanted to bring it to the surface in a nicely wrapped class.

8. Create a file called COMHelp.h. This next bit of code will save you tons of time. It condenses the *IUnknown* implementation down to a single line of

9.2
CREATE A PROPERTY SHEET HANDLER FOR A FILE OR FOLDER

code. You'll find it useful in any project where you have to implement an OLE interface in MFC.

```
// IUnknown macros for implementing redirection to parent
//    IUnknown implementation

// Use this macro once in your CPP file like this:
// IMPLMENT_IUNKNOWN(CInterface, Interface)


#ifndef IMPLEMENT_IUNKNOWN

#define IMPLEMENT_IUNKNOWN_ADDREF(ObjectClass, InterfaceClass) \
     STDMETHODIMP_(ULONG) ObjectClass::X##InterfaceClass::AddRef(void) \
     { \
          METHOD_PROLOGUE(ObjectClass, InterfaceClass); \
          return pThis->ExternalAddRef(); \
     }

#define IMPLEMENT_IUNKNOWN_RELEASE(ObjectClass, InterfaceClass) \
     STDMETHODIMP_(ULONG) ObjectClass::X##InterfaceClass::Release(void) \
     { \
          METHOD_PROLOGUE(ObjectClass, InterfaceClass); \
          return pThis->ExternalRelease(); \
     }

#define IMPLEMENT_IUNKNOWN_QUERYINTERFACE(ObjectClass, InterfaceClass) \
     STDMETHODIMP ObjectClass::X##InterfaceClass::QueryInterface(REFIID ⇒
riid, LPVOID *ppVoid) \
     { \
          METHOD_PROLOGUE(ObjectClass, InterfaceClass); \
          return (HRESULT)pThis->ExternalQueryInterface(&riid, ppVoid); \
     }

#define IMPLEMENT_IUNKNOWN(ObjectClass, InterfaceClass) \
     IMPLEMENT_IUNKNOWN_ADDREF(ObjectClass, InterfaceClass) \
     IMPLEMENT_IUNKNOWN_RELEASE(ObjectClass, InterfaceClass) \
     IMPLEMENT_IUNKNOWN_QUERYINTERFACE(ObjectClass, InterfaceClass)

#endif
```

9. **Create a new file called InitGuids.cpp.** This file simply provides a single place for the definition of all the OLE interfaces we'll be using in this project. Insert the file into the project after you add the code.

```
#include "stdafx.h"

// Initialize GUIDs (should be done only once per DLL/EXE)
//
#pragma data_seg(".text")
#define INITGUID
#include <initguid.h>
#include <shlguid.h>
#pragma data_seg()
```

Now, we're ready to start adding code specific to shell extension property pages.

10. Create a new class called CProperties. Later steps will implement the two OLE interfaces necessary to support shell extensions and property pages. *CCmdTarget* includes most of the COM framework we'll need to support these interfaces. Bring up ClassWizard and derive a class from *CCmdTarget* called *CProperties*. Select the option to make the class createable by the type ID SUBFOLDER.PROPERTIES.

Class name:	CProperties
Base class:	CCmdTarget
File:	Properties.cpp

11. Edit Properties.h. In order to hook the registration process, we have to change the DECLARE_OLECREATE macro to DECLARE_OLECREATE_EX. The new macro derives a new class from *COleObjectFactory* and nests it within *CProperties*. It supports the *IClassFactory* interface through the MFC implementation, but more importantly lets us do our own registration. The standard DECLARE_OLECREATE doesn't do that.

```
class CProperties : public CCmdTarget
{
        DECLARE_DYNCREATE(CProperties)
        CProperties();

// Attributes
public:
        TCHAR m_szPath[MAX_PATH];       // path to file or folder in question

// Operations
public:

// Overrides
        // ClassWizard generated virtual function overrides
        //{{AFX_VIRTUAL(CProperties)
        public:
        virtual void OnFinalRelease();
        //}}AFX_VIRTUAL

// Implementation
protected:
        virtual ~CProperties();

        // Generated message map functions
        //{{AFX_MSG(CProperties)
        //}}AFX_MSG

        DECLARE_MESSAGE_MAP()
        DECLARE_OLECREATE(CProperties)
```

9.2
CREATE A PROPERTY SHEET HANDLER FOR A FILE OR FOLDER

```
    // Generated OLE dispatch map functions
    //{{AFX_DISPATCH(CProperties)
    //}}AFX_DISPATCH
    DECLARE_DISPATCH_MAP()
    DECLARE_INTERFACE_MAP()

    BEGIN_INTERFACE_PART(ShellExtInit, IShellExtInit)
        INIT_INTERFACE_PART(CProperties, ShellExtInit)
        STDMETHOD(Initialize)(LPCITEMIDLIST pidlFolder, LPDATAOBJECT lpdobj,
            HKEY hKeyProgID);
    END_INTERFACE_PART(ShellExtInit)

    BEGIN_INTERFACE_PART(ShellPropExt, IShellPropSheetExt)
        INIT_INTERFACE_PART(CProperties, ShellPropExt)
        STDMETHOD(ReplacePage)(UINT uPageID, LPFNADDPROPSHEETPAGE ⇒
lpfnReplaceWith,
            LPARAM lParam);
        STDMETHOD(AddPages)(LPFNADDPROPSHEETPAGE lpfnAddPage, LPARAM lParam);
    END_INTERFACE_PART(ShellPropExt)
};
```

12. Edit Properties.cpp. Add a few #include lines to the top and two INTER-FACE_MAP entries further down in the file:

```
#include "stdafx.h"
#include "Subfolder.h"
#include "Properties.h"

#include "RegisterClass.h"
#include "SubfolderPage.h"

...

BEGIN_INTERFACE_MAP(CProperties, CCmdTarget)
    INTERFACE_PART(CProperties, IID_IProperties, Dispatch)
    INTERFACE_PART(CProperties, IID_IShellExtInit, ShellExtInit)
    INTERFACE_PART(CProperties, IID_IShellPropSheetExt, ShellPropExt)
END_INTERFACE_MAP()
```

13. Add the UpdateRegistry method. Earlier we added the DECLARE_OLECREATE_EX macro. This allows us to override the *UpdateRegistry* method in the embedded *CPropertiesFactory* object. Our implementation lets *COleObjectFactory* make most of the registry changes before we add (or remove) two other entries using the *CRegisterClass*. Property sheet extensions must have an extra registry value called ThreadingModel. The other registry entry attaches the Subfolder.Properties object to the PropertySheetHandlers for all folders in the system. If you wanted to create a property sheet handler for bitmap files, you would just replace Folder below with ".bmp". Add this code to the bottom of Properties.cpp:

```
// Note: IMPLEMENT_OLECREATE was changed to IMPLEMENT_OLECREATE_EX
//
IMPLEMENT_OLECREATE_EX(CProperties, "SUBFOLDER.PROPERTIES", 0x9d88e7a2,
0x5c83, 0x11cf, 0x81, 0x31, 0x0, 0x20, 0xaf, 0xd0, 0x39, 0x5e)
```

continued on next page

continued from previous page

```
BOOL CProperties::CPropertiesFactory::UpdateRegistry(BOOL bRegister)
{
        CRegisterClass reg(m_clsid, "Subfolder.Properties");
        VERIFY(reg.AddSymbol("Folder") == 3);    // zero based...it's really %4
        reg.AddEntry("CLSID\\%1\\InProcServer32", "Apartment", "ThreadingModel");
        reg.AddEntry("%4\\shellex\\PropertySheetHandlers\\%2", "%1");

        if (bRegister)
        {
                COleObjectFactory::UpdateRegistry(TRUE);
                return reg.Register();
        } else {
                reg.Register(FALSE);
#ifdef _AFXDLL
                return AfxOleUnregisterClass(m_clsid, NULL);
#else
                reg.RemoveKey("CLSID\\%1");
                reg.RemoveKey("%2");
                return TRUE;
#endif
        }
}
```

14. **Implement the IShellExtInit interface.** Add the following code to the bottom of Properties.cpp:

```
///////////////////////////////////
// IShellExtInit implementation

IMPLEMENT_IUNKNOWN(CProperties, ShellExtInit)

STDMETHODIMP CProperties::XShellExtInit::Initialize (LPCITEMIDLIST
        pidlFolder, LPDATAOBJECT lpdobj, HKEY hKeyProgID)
{
        METHOD_PROLOGUE(CProperties, ShellExtInit)

        STGMEDIUM medium;
        FORMATETC fe = { CF_HDROP, NULL, DVASPECT_CONTENT, -1, TYMED_HGLOBAL };

        // Fail the call if lpdobj is NULL.
        //
        if (lpdobj == NULL)
                return E_FAIL;

        // Render the data referenced by the IDataObject pointer to an HGLOBAL
        // storage medium in CF_HDROP format.
        //
        HRESULT hr = lpdobj->GetData (&fe, &medium);
        if (FAILED (hr))
                return E_FAIL;

        // If only one file is selected, retrieve the filename and store it in
        // m_szPath. Otherwise fail the call.
        //
        if (DragQueryFile ((HDROP) medium.hGlobal, 0xFFFFFFFF, NULL, 0) == 1)
```

9.2
CREATE A PROPERTY SHEET HANDLER FOR A FILE OR FOLDER

```
    {
        DragQueryFile ((HDROP) medium.hGlobal, 0, pThis->m_szPath,
            sizeof (pThis->m_szPath));
        hr = NOERROR;
    }
    else
        hr = E_FAIL;

    ReleaseStgMedium (&medium);
    return hr;
}
```

15. **Implement the IShellPropExt interface.** Add the following code to the bottom of Properties.cpp:

```
///////////////////////////////////
// IShellPropExt implementation

IMPLEMENT_IUNKNOWN(CProperties, ShellPropExt)

STDMETHODIMP CProperties::XShellPropExt::AddPages (LPFNADDPROPSHEETPAGE
    lpfnAddPage, LPARAM lParam)
{
    METHOD_PROLOGUE(CProperties, ShellPropExt)

    CSubfolderPage* pPage = new CSubfolderPage();
    pPage->m_strPath = pThis->m_szPath;

    HPROPSHEETPAGE hPSP = CreatePropertySheetPage (&pPage->m_psp);
    if (hPSP == NULL)
    {
        AfxMessageBox("CreatePropertySheetPage failed!");
        AfxThrowMemoryException();
    } else
        if (!lpfnAddPage (hPSP, lParam))
            DestroyPropertySheetPage (hPSP);

    return NOERROR;
}

STDMETHODIMP CProperties::XShellPropExt::ReplacePage (UINT uPageID,
    LPFNADDPROPSHEETPAGE lpfnReplaceWith, LPARAM lParam)
{
    METHOD_PROLOGUE(CProperties, ShellPropExt)
    return E_FAIL;
}
```

16. **Create a new class called CShellPropPage.** Use ClassWizard to create a new class using the following information:

Class name:	CShellPropPage
Base class:	CPropertyPage
File:	ShellPropPage.cpp

Ignore the Developer Studio warning about creating the class with an invalid ID. We'll fix that problem later.

17. Edit ShellPropPage.h. Add a default argument to the constructor and remove the *enum*:

```
///////////////////////////////////////////////////////////////
// CShellPropPage dialog

// This class has three features for property pages used in shell
// extensions:
// 1. Adds the PSP_USEREFPARENT flag so the shell maintains the ⇒
//      reference count
// 2. Hooks the prop page creation stream in order to set the correct
//      module state (The Win95 shell is creating the prop page instead
//      of an MFC app)
// 3. Deletes "this" when the property page receives WM_NCDESTROY
//      since the interface that created it is long gone.

class CShellPropPage : public CPropertyPage
{
        DECLARE_DYNCREATE(CShellPropPage)

// Construction
public:
        CShellPropPage(UINT nID = 0);
        virtual ~CShellPropPage();

// Dialog Data
        //{{AFX_DATA(CShellPropPage)
        //}}AFX_DATA

// Overrides
        // ClassWizard generates virtual function overrides
        //{{AFX_VIRTUAL(CShellPropPage)
        protected:
        virtual void DoDataExchange(CDataExchange* pDX);    // DDX/DDV support
        //}}AFX_VIRTUAL

// Implementation
protected:
        // Generated message map functions
        //{{AFX_MSG(CShellPropPage)
        //}}AFX_MSG
        DECLARE_MESSAGE_MAP()
};
```

Make sure you add the virtual keyword in front of the destructor since we'll be deriving a class from this one later.

18. Use the WizardBar to add CShellPropPage::OnNcDestroy. Add the following code:

```
void CShellPropPage::PostNcDestroy()
{
```

9.2
CREATE A PROPERTY SHEET HANDLER FOR A FILE OR FOLDER

```
        CPropertyPage::PostNcDestroy();
        delete this;
}
```

19. Edit the CShellPropPage constructor. Add a default argument and the following lines of code:

```
// forward declaration for the WM_CREATE callback
UINT CALLBACK PropPageCallback(HWND, UINT message, LPPROPSHEETPAGE ⇒
pPropPage);

CShellPropPage::CShellPropPage(UINT nID) : CPropertyPage(nID)
{
        // Do not put a call to AfxOleLockApp() in here because it's
        // possible for the shell to construct this object, but never
        // actually display it, meaning it won't be destroyed. Therefore, the
        // dtor wouldn't be called and the AfxOleUnlockApp would never be called.
        // The DLL would never be allowed to unload (through DllCanUnloadNow).

        // set up our own callback
        m_psp.pfnCallback = PropPageCallback;
        m_psp.dwFlags |= PSP_USECALLBACK | PSP_USEREFPARENT;

        // let the shell maintain the reference count
        m_psp.pcRefParent = (UINT*) &(AfxGetModuleState()->m_nObjectCount);
}
```

20. Add the PropPageCallback helper. Add the following code to the bottom of ShellPropPage.cpp:

```
UINT CALLBACK
PropPageCallback(HWND, UINT message, LPPROPSHEETPAGE pPropPage)
{
        // This next line forces the module state to "stick".
        // If we had used AFX_MANAGE_STATE(AfxGetStaticModuleState) instead,
        // the thread's module state would have reset back to NULL when
        // this function returned. Then, when the hook proc eventually executes,
        // the module state will still be NULL causing the hook proc to
        // attach the window to the wrong AfxWndProc (AfxWndProcBase
        // instead of AfxWndProcDllStatic).

#ifdef _AFXDLL
        AfxGetThreadState()->m_pModuleState = AfxGetStaticModuleState();
#endif

        // The rest of the code is from AfxPropPageCallback in DLGPROP.CPP.

        switch (message)
        {
        case PSPCB_CREATE:
                {
                        ASSERT(AfxIsValidAddress(pPropPage, sizeof(PROPSHEETPAGE)));
                        CPropertyPage* pPage = (CPropertyPage *) pPropPage->lParam;
                        ASSERT_VALID(pPage);
```

continued on next page

continued from previous page

```
                TRY
                {
                        AfxHookWindowCreate(pPage);
                }
                CATCH_ALL(e)
                {
                        // Note: DELETE_EXCEPTION(e) not necessary
                        return FALSE;
                }
                END_CATCH_ALL
        }
        return TRUE;

    case PSPCB_RELEASE:
        AfxUnhookWindowCreate();
        break;
    }

    return 0;
}
```

Before you close the file, add this #include to the top:

```
#include "stdafx.h"
#include "Subfolder.h"
#include "ShellPropPage.h"
#include <afxpriv.h> // for AfxHookWindowCreate
```

21. **Create a property page dialog called IDD_SUBFOLDER_PAGE.** Press CTRL+R to insert a new dialog resource based on IDD_PROPPAGE_MEDIUM. Change the name to IDD_SUBFOLDER_PAGE and the caption to Subfolders. For now, place a single static control called IDC_DIRECTORY_NAME. We'll come back later and embellish this dialog.

22. **Create a new class called CSubfolderPage.** Use ClassWizard to create a new class based on the IDD_SUBFOLDER_PAGE dialog using the following information:

Class name:	CSubfolderPage
Base class:	CPropertyPage
File:	SubfolderPage.cpp
Dialog:	IDD_SUBFOLDER_PAGE

    Now replace every occurrence of *CPropertyPage* with *CShellPropPage* in SubfolderPage.cpp and SubfolderPage.h. Add this line to the top of SubfolderPage.h:

```
#include "ShellPropPage.h"
```

9.2
CREATE A PROPERTY SHEET HANDLER FOR A FILE OR FOLDER

23. Add a member variable to CSubfolderPage. Add this variable to *CSubfolderPage* using the Member Variables tab in ClassWizard:

Control ID	Type	Member
IDC_DIRECTORY_NAME	CString	m_strPath

24. Build and register the DLL. If the compile was successful, select the Register Control item from the Tools menu. To see the fruits of your labor, bring up Explorer and show the Properties for the Win95 folder. Mine looks like the one shown in Figure 9-9.

25. Make a copy of the Win95 System file Cool.dll. You must think I'm crazy. As it turns out, there's a file called Cool.dll in the Win95\System directory that is loaded with great-looking icons. We want to extract one of them for use in the property page. Since it's constantly in use by the system, you can only open a copy of the file. Select the file in the Explorer, then press (CTRL)+(C), then (CTRL)+(V). Now you have a file called Copy of Cool.dll that you can drag into Developer Studio.

Select the icon called 19. Next, hold down the (CTRL) key and drag the icon to the Subfolder resource area. Now, you can close Copy of Cool.dll and rename 19 to something more meaningful like IDI_FOLDER.

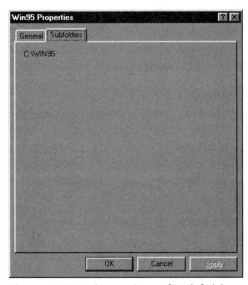

Figure 9-9 Early version of Subfolder property page

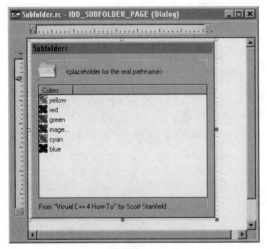

Figure 9-10 Subfolder dialog with icon and list control

26. **Modify the IDD_SUBFOLDER_PAGE dialog.** Add a list control and the icon from the previous step to the dialog so it looks like the one shown in Figure 9-10.

Control	ID	Attributes
Static text	IDC_DIRECTORY_NAME	Default
List control	IDC_FOLDER_LIST	Report view; single selection
Icon	IDC_STATIC	Icon type; IDI_FOLDER image

27. **Add a member variable to CSubfolderPage.** Add this variable to *CSubfolderPage* using the Member Variables tab in ClassWizard:

Control ID	Type	Member
IDC_FOLDER_LIST	CListCtrl	m_list

28. **Add some methods to CSubfolderPage with ClassWizard.** While still in ClassWizard, use the Message Maps tab to add the following methods:

Object	Function	Message
CSubfolderPage	OnInitDialog	WM_INITDIALOG
CSubfolderPage	OnDestroy	WM_DESTROY
IDC_FOLDER_LIST	OnColumnClick	LVN_COLUMNCLICK

9.2
CREATE A PROPERTY SHEET HANDLER FOR A FILE OR FOLDER

29. Edit SubfolderPage.h. Make the following modifications to SubfolderPage.h:

```
class CSubfolderPage : public CShellPropPage
{
        DECLARE_DYNCREATE(CSubfolderPage)

// Construction
public:
        CSubfolderPage();
        ~CSubfolderPage();

        void SetFolderSize(int index, DWORD dwSize);
        CEvent m_event;

// Dialog Data
        //{{AFX_DATA(CSubfolderPage)
        enum { IDD = IDD_SUBFOLDER_PAGE };
        CListCtrl    m_list;
        CString      m_strPath;
        //}}AFX_DATA

// Overrides
        // ClassWizard generate virtual function overrides
        //{{AFX_VIRTUAL(CSubfolderPage)
        protected:
        virtual void DoDataExchange(CDataExchange* pDX);    // DDX/DDV support
        //}}AFX_VIRTUAL

// Implementation
protected:
        // Generated message map functions
        //{{AFX_MSG(CSubfolderPage)
        afx_msg void OnColumnClick(NMHDR* pNMHDR, LRESULT* pResult);
        afx_msg void OnDestroy();
        virtual BOOL OnInitDialog();
        //}}AFX_MSG
        DECLARE_MESSAGE_MAP()

        CString AsString(DWORD dwNumber);
        CWinThread* m_pThread;
};
```

30. Edit SubfolderPage.cpp. I'll explain how the *CSubfolderPage* works in the next section. For now, warm up your fingers and start typing:

```
/////////////////////////////////////
// Local helpers used in this file

// Callback for sorting columns in the list control
static int CALLBACK CompareFunc(LPARAM lParam1, LPARAM lParam2, LPARAM ⇒
lParamSort);

// Thread entry point for calculating the subfolder sizes
static UINT ThreadProc(LPVOID pParam);
```

continued on next page

CHAPTER 9
WINDOWS 95 SHELL

continued from previous page

```cpp
// Recursive functions to calculate folder size
BOOL GetFolderSize(CEvent* pEvent, LPCSTR pszPath, DWORD& dwSize);
int GetSubfolders(LPCSTR pszPath, CStringArray& folders);

/////////////////////////////////////////////////////////////////////////
// CSubfolderPage property page

IMPLEMENT_DYNCREATE(CSubfolderPage, CShellPropPage)

CSubfolderPage::CSubfolderPage() : CShellPropPage(CSubfolderPage::IDD)
{
        //{{AFX_DATA_INIT(CSubfolderPage)
        m_strPath = _T("");
        //}}AFX_DATA_INIT
        m_pThread = NULL;
        m_event.ResetEvent();
}


CSubfolderPage::~CSubfolderPage()
{
}


void CSubfolderPage::DoDataExchange(CDataExchange* pDX)
{
        CShellPropPage::DoDataExchange(pDX);
        //{{AFX_DATA_MAP(CSubfolderPage)
        DDX_Control(pDX, IDC_FOLDER_LIST, m_list);
        DDX_Text(pDX, IDC_DIRECTORY_NAME, m_strPath);
        //}}AFX_DATA_MAP
}


BEGIN_MESSAGE_MAP(CSubfolderPage, CShellPropPage)
        //{{AFX_MSG_MAP(CSubfolderPage)
        ON_NOTIFY(LVN_COLUMNCLICK, IDC_FOLDER_LIST, OnColumnClick)
        ON_WM_DESTROY()
        //}}AFX_MSG_MAP
END_MESSAGE_MAP()

/////////////////////////////////////////////////////////////////////////
// CSubfolderPage message handlers

void CSubfolderPage::OnColumnClick(NMHDR* pNMHDR, LRESULT* pResult)
{
        NM_LISTVIEW* pNMListView = (NM_LISTVIEW*)pNMHDR;

        if (pNMListView->iSubItem == 1)
                m_list.SortItems ((PFNLVCOMPARE) CompareFunc, 1);
        *pResult = 0;
}

void CSubfolderPage::OnDestroy()
{
        // The event must be in manual mode because the thread might
        // trip on it *twice*, once to stop it in the middle of a calculation,
        // and another time right before it exits
```

9.2
CREATE A PROPERTY SHEET HANDLER FOR A FILE OR FOLDER

```
        m_event.SetEvent();
        WaitForSingleObject(m_pThread->m_hThread, INFINITE);

        CShellPropPage::OnDestroy();
}

BOOL CSubfolderPage::OnInitDialog()
{
        CShellPropPage::OnInitDialog();

        // Add two columns to the list view
        m_list.InsertColumn(0, "Subfolder", LVCFMT_LEFT, 180, 0);
        m_list.InsertColumn(1, "Size", LVCFMT_RIGHT, 75, 1);

        // Start the thread
        m_pThread = AfxBeginThread (ThreadProc, this);

        return TRUE;
}

#include <math.h>   // for ceil()

void CSubfolderPage::SetFolderSize(int index, DWORD dwSize)
{
        CString number;

        // round the size to the nearest 1K
        double dlSize = (double) dwSize / 1024;
        dlSize = ceil(dlSize);
        number = AsString((DWORD) dlSize);
        number += "KB";
        m_list.SetItemText(index, 1, (LPCSTR) number);
        m_list.SetItemData(index, dwSize);
}

///////////////////////////////////
// CSubfolderPage helpers

CString CSubfolderPage::AsString(DWORD dwNumber)
{
        CString sNumber;
        _ltoa( (long) dwNumber, sNumber.GetBuffer(20), 10);
        sNumber.ReleaseBuffer();

        int nLen = sNumber.GetLength();
        if (nLen <= 3)
                return sNumber;

        CString sDest;
        int nNumCommas = (sNumber.GetLength()-1) / 3;
        char *pStart = sDest.GetBuffer( nNumCommas + nLen);
        char *pEnd = pStart + nNumCommas + nLen -1;

        int nSrcIndex = nLen - 1;   // index of the last character
        int nCount = 1;
        while (nSrcIndex != -1)
        {
```

continued on next page

continued from previous page

```
            if ((nCount++ % 4) == 0)
                *pEnd-- = ',';

            *pEnd-- = sNumber[nSrcIndexñ];
    }

    sDest.ReleaseBuffer();
    return sDest;
}

int CALLBACK CompareFunc(LPARAM lParam1, LPARAM lParam2, LPARAM lParamSort)
{
    if (lParam1 < lParam2)
        return 1;
    else if (lParam1 > lParam2)
        return -1;
    else
        return 0;
}

////////////////////////////////////////
// Thread functions

UINT ThreadProc(LPVOID pParam)
{
    ASSERT(pParam != NULL);

    CSubfolderPage* pPage = (CSubfolderPage*) pParam;
    CEvent* pEvent = &pPage->m_event;

    // Get the subfolders
    CStringArray folders;
    GetSubfolders(pPage->m_strPath, folders);

    // Add the subfolders to the list view
    int index=0;
    for (int i=0; i < folders.GetSize(); i++)
    {
        // Extract the last part of the path and add it to the list
        CString name;
        name = folders[i].Mid(folders[i].ReverseFind('\\'));
        pPage->m_list.InsertItem(index++, name);
    }

    // Calculate the size of each subfolder
    DWORD dwSize = 0;
    for (i = 0; i < folders.GetSize(); i++)
    {
        if (GetFolderSize(pEvent, folders[i], dwSize))
            pPage->SetFolderSize(i, dwSize);
        else
            break;

        dwSize = 0;
    }
```

9.2 CREATE A PROPERTY SHEET HANDLER FOR A FILE OR FOLDER

```
        // Block here until the caller thread gives us permission
        WaitForSingleObject(pEvent->m_hObject, INFINITE);
        return 0;
}

BOOL GetFolderSize(CEvent* pEvent, LPCSTR pszPath, DWORD& dwSize)
{
        CStringArray folders;

        // Before we start, check to see if the property page is closing down
        if (WaitForSingleObject(pEvent->m_hObject, 0) == WAIT_OBJECT_0)
            return FALSE;

        int nCount = GetSubfolders(pszPath, folders);

        for (int i = 0; i < nCount; i++)
        {
            if (GetFolderSize(pEvent, folders[i], dwSize) == FALSE)
                return FALSE;
        }

        // figure out how big the files are in this directory
        DWORD dwAttrib = FILE_ATTRIBUTE_NORMAL | FILE_ATTRIBUTE_READONLY |
            FILE_ATTRIBUTE_ARCHIVE;

        // Get all the files
        WIN32_FIND_DATA FindData;
        BOOL bGotFile;

        CString path(pszPath);
        path += "\\*.*";

        HANDLE hFindFile = FindFirstFile (path, &FindData);
        bGotFile = (hFindFile != INVALID_HANDLE_VALUE);
        while (bGotFile)
        {
            if (FindData.dwFileAttributes & dwAttrib)
                dwSize += FindData.nFileSizeLow;

            bGotFile = FindNextFile (hFindFile, &FindData);
        }
        FindClose(hFindFile);

        return TRUE;
}

int GetSubfolders(LPCSTR pszPath, CStringArray& folders)
{
        CString search(pszPath);
        search += "\\*.*";

        int nCount = 0;
        DWORD dwAttrib = FILE_ATTRIBUTE_DIRECTORY;
```

continued on next page

continued from previous page

```
        // Get all the subdirectories (excluding "." and "..") of path
        WIN32_FIND_DATA FindData;
        BOOL bGotFile;

        HANDLE hFindFile = FindFirstFile (search, &FindData);
        bGotFile = (hFindFile != INVALID_HANDLE_VALUE);
        while (bGotFile)
        {
            if (FindData.dwFileAttributes & dwAttrib)
            {
                if (strcmp(FindData.cFileName, ".") &&
                    strcmp(FindData.cFileName, ".."))
                {
                    CString temp;
                    temp.Format("%s\\%s", pszPath, FindData.cFileName);
                    nCount++;
                    folders.Add((LPCSTR) temp);
                }
            }
            bGotFile = FindNextFile (hFindFile, &FindData);
        }
        FindClose(hFindFile);

        return nCount;
}
```

31. **Compile the DLL.** You don't need to register the DLL again if you did that in step 24. Now, display the property sheet for the Win95 directory and you should see something similar to Figure 9-8.

How It Works

The original version of Subfolders was about half as long, but it didn't support self-registration. I thought it would be a fairly easy feature to add, but was I ever wrong. I'll outline the problems I ran into below.

Registering the Class

First, I need to explain the registry entries required to install the Subfolder.dll. If the DLL wasn't self-registering, the following REG file would be required:

```
REGEDIT4

; Subfolder.Properties entries
[HKEY_CLASSES_ROOT\Subfolder.Properties]
@="Subfolder.Properties"

[HKEY_CLASSES_ROOT\Subfolder.Properties\CLSID]
@="{9D88E7A2-5C83-11CF-8131-0020AFD0395E}"

; Folder entries
[HKEY_CLASSES_ROOT\Folder\shellex\PropertySheetHandlers\Subfolder.Properties]
@="{9D88E7A2-5C83-11CF-8131-0020AFD0395E}"
```

9.2
CREATE A PROPERTY SHEET HANDLER FOR A FILE OR FOLDER

```
; CLSID entries
[HKEY_CLASSES_ROOT\CLSID\{9D88E7A2-5C83-11CF-8131-0020AFD0395E}]
@="Subfolder.Properties"

[HKEY_CLASSES_ROOT\CLSID\{9D88E7A2-5C83-11CF-8131-0020AFD0395E}\ProgID]
@="Subfolder.Properties"

[HKEY_CLASSES_ROOT\CLSID\{9D88E7A2-5C83-11CF-8131-0020AFD0395E}\InProcServer32]
@="D:\\BOOK2\\CHAPTERS\\SHELL\\SUBFOL~1.DLL"
"ThreadingModel"="Apartment"
```

There are three sections to this registry file. The first two keys, Subfolder.Properties, are never used but MFC adds them to the registry anyway. MFC simply associates the human-readable name Subfolder.Properites with the 128-bit GUID. However, as you can see by the next section, the GUID, not Subfolder.Properties is associated directly with the Folder entry. If this were a handler for a bitmap file, Folder would be replaced by ".bmp".

The last section registers the CLSID in the appropriate section. InProcServer32 tells Windows where to find the file that supports this interface. Unfortunately, MFC registers the short filename, so it's a little difficult to read.

If an OLE DLL is self-registering, it needs to support two callbacks: *DllRegisterServer* and *DllUnregisterServer*. The AppWizard generated version only adds *DllRegisterServer*, but between it and other MFC code, it's enough to register OLE Controls. In our case, we have to add the ThreadingModel entry and the shellex\PropertySheetHandlers.

All MFC objects that use DECLARE_OLECREATE are really adding a variable of type *COleObjectFactory* to their *CCmdTarget* class. Then, when ClassWizard adds the IMPLEMENT_OLECREATE code to your file, it is setting up your class for *DllRegisterServer* to do its magic.

DECLARE_OLECREATE_EX

I did some research into the MFC code and found that if you replace the DECLARE_OLECREATE macro with DECLARE_OLECREATE_EX, the *COleObjectFactory* variable is not placed in *CProperties*. Instead, a derived version called *CPropertiesFactory* is created, giving you the ability to override one of its virtual methods: *UpdateRegistry*. Of course, none of this is really documented. Anyway, now we have a bit of code that is called when you select Register Control from the Tools menu:

```
BOOL CProperties::CPropertiesFactory::UpdateRegistry(BOOL bRegister)
{
    CRegisterClass reg(m_clsid, "Subfolder.Properties");
    VERIFY(reg.AddSymbol("Folder") == 3);  // zero based...it's really %4
    reg.AddEntry("CLSID\\%1\\InProcServer32", "Apartment", "ThreadingModel");
    reg.AddEntry("%4\\shellex\\PropertySheetHandlers\\%2", "%1");

    if (bRegister)
    {
        COleObjectFactory::UpdateRegistry(TRUE);
        return reg.Register();
    } else {
```

continued on next page

CHAPTER 9
WINDOWS 95 SHELL

continued from previous page

```
        reg.Register(FALSE);
        return AfxOleUnregisterClass(m_clsid, NULL);
    }
}
```

We're using a helper class called *CRegisterClass* to make it easier to register and unregister the object with the system. I won't go into details about *CRegisterClass* except to tell you that it was inspired by some internal MFC code that deals with the registry. It's a very powerful class in that you can use just one method, *Register*, to add or remove your entries from the registry. And, as you know by now, your applications must have an uninstall feature to earn the Windows 95 compatible logo.

DLL vs. Static Version of MFC

I thought tracking down DECLARE_OLECREATE_EX was pretty cool until I found out the compiler couldn't find its definition! DECLARE_OLECREATE is defined in AfxDisp.h, the file holding all the MFC OLE automation classes. But DECLARE_OLECREATE_EX is in a completely different file, AfxCtl.h, even though it only differs by a couple of characters. As it turns out, only OLE Controls use the _EX version, but since we didn't use the OLE Control AppWizard, AfxCtl.h wasn't included.

No problem, I thought. I'll just include AfxCtl.h in StdAfx.h. Bzzt. The first line of this file stops the compiler and spews out this warning:

```
error Please define _AFXDLL when including afxctl.h
```

It took me a while to realize the ramifications of this message. It was telling me that the only way I could include this file was if I used the DLL version of MFC, not the static version I was currently linking against. Fine. I'll just change to the DLL version

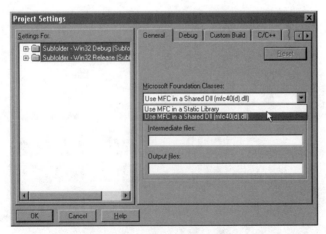

Figure 9-11 Switching from the static to the DLL version of MFC

9.2
CREATE A PROPERTY SHEET HANDLER FOR A FILE OR FOLDER

of MFC, I thought again. Figure 9-11 shows how I did this. By the way, you chose the DLL version in step 1; I'm now explaining why we did that.

The 12-hour Bug

Now, the project was compiling and my DECLARE_OLECREATE_EX trick seemed to be working. However, as soon as I tried to use the property page from the Explorer, an assertion was thrown in the depths of WM_INITDIALOG. It took a long time for me to realize that my instance of *CShellPropPage* couldn't find its HWND. In other words, the association MFC makes between an HWND and its corresponding *CWnd** couldn't be found in the global handle map.

Something about the word global reminded me about a serious looking Technote I read when Visual C++ 4.0 first came it: Technote #58, MFC Module State Implementation. The first paragraph reads: *This technical note describes the implementation of MFC "module state" constructs. An understanding of the module state implementation is critical for using the MFC shared DLLs from a DLL (or OLE inprocess server).* One of the side-effects of not setting the module state would affect global data like the handle map.

After poring over every line about module states, both in the online documentation and the MFC source code, I learned an interesting fact. Every entry point in an MFC app that uses the DLL version of MFC is responsible for correctly switching between module states. An *entry point* is any place where the flow of execution can enter the module's code including:

- Member functions of OLE/COM interfaces
- Exported functions in a DLL
- Window procedures

All the METHOD_PROLOGUE lines satisfy the first requirement; they handle the state switching for OLE/COM interfaces. *DllRegisterServer* is an exported function, but it correctly sets the module state by calling AFX_MANAGE_STATE. MFC handles the third requirement because all Windows messages are routed through *AfxWndProc*. Where could the "leak" be? There had to be another entry point in Subfolder.dll that wasn't switching module states upon entry.

The Property Page Callback

All my sleuthing led me to a peculiar looking function called *AfxPropPageCallback*. The structure passed to *CreatePropertySheetPage* allows you to pass a pointer to an application-defined callback function that is called when the page is created. Did you just say callback function? MFC sets this callback function to *AfxPropPageCallback*. If you examine its source code at the top of DlgProp.cpp, you'll see it doesn't have any code to set the module state. Here's the same code with the bug fix:

```
UINT CALLBACK
PropPageCallback(HWND, UINT message, LPPROPSHEETPAGE pPropPage)
{
```

continued on next page

```
// This next line forces the module state to "stick".
// If we had used AFX_MANAGE_STATE(AfxGetStaticModuleState) instead,
// the thread's module state would have reset back to NULL when
// this function returned. Then, when the hook proc eventually executes,
// the module state will still be NULL causing the hook proc to
// attach the window to the wrong AfxWndProc (AfxWndProcBase
// instead of AfxWndProcDllStatic).

AfxGetThreadState()->m_pModuleState = AfxGetStaticModuleState();

// The rest of the code is from AfxPropPageCallback in DLGPROP.CPP.

switch (message)
{
case PSPCB_CREATE:
    {
        ASSERT(AfxIsValidAddress(pPropPage, sizeof(PROPSHEETPAGE)));
        CPropertyPage* pPage = (CPropertyPage *) pPropPage->lParam;
        ASSERT_VALID(pPage);
        TRY
        {
            AfxHookWindowCreate(pPage);
        }
        CATCH_ALL(e)
        {
            // Note: DELETE_EXCEPTION(e) not necessary
            return FALSE;
        }
        END_CATCH_ALL
    }
    return TRUE;

case PSPCB_RELEASE:
    AfxUnhookWindowCreate();
    break;
}

return 0;
}
```

By overriding the MFC-supplied callback and using my own in *CShellPropPage*, the module state is correctly set and everything works fine. If I hadn't switched to the DLL version of MFC, I would have never noticed this problem because module-state switching doesn't apply to static linked applications. And the whole reason I switched to the DLL version was to get the support of DECLARE_OLECREATE_EX. And I needed that stuff to support custom self-registration. And I needed self-registration, well, because I just wanted it.

Whew! That's why this How-To is marked Advanced. This bug might be fixed in future versions of Visual C++ 4.0, but now you know a bit more about module-state switching.

9.2
CREATE A PROPERTY SHEET HANDLER FOR A FILE OR FOLDER

IShellExtInit and IShellPropSheetExt

Back to business. Windows 95 says that if we support these two OLE/COM interfaces and we're properly registered, we will have a property sheet handler. The registration part is easy (right!), so how do we add support for these two interfaces? First let me say that if you've never implemented OLE interfaces with MFC, you've got to read Technote #38, MFC/OLE IUnknown Implementation. It explains all these macros and weird, nested classes. I have to admit, I didn't really understand it either until I wrote this program.

COMHelp.h really helps us implement the *IUnknown* portions of these two interfaces. All that's left is two more functions (really it's three, but *RemovePages* is never called).

IShellExtInit::Initialize prepares the handler by passing it the name of the file or folder in question. Well, it's not that straightforward. Since the information is passed through *IDataObject*, you have to use *QueryDragFile* to pull the filename out of the data object. If more than one file was selected, we bail out because I didn't know how to handle more than one file. The path is stored in *m_szPath* so we can pass it to the *CSubfolderPage* later.

The shell calls the *IShellPropExt::AddPages* method when it is about to display the property sheet. Here's our chance to add our *CSubfolderPage* to the list. We simply create an instance of *CSubfolderPage*, pass the path to the selected folder, and call *::CreatePropertySheetPage*. The return value is passed to the shell through a function pointer passed to *AddPages*.

CSubFolderPage

By the time *CSubFolderPage::OnInitDialog* has been reached, all the OLE and module-state switching stuff doesn't matter; we're back on familiar turf. *OnInitDialog* inserts two columns called Subfolder and Size, then starts a thread. That's it. All the interesting bit of code happens in *ThreadProc*.

ThreadProc first makes a list of all the subfolders. For example, if you we're looking at C:\Win95, the subfolders would be C:\Win95\System, C:\Win95\Media, C:\Win95\Fonts, and so on. Each folder is added to the list view so you see something happen right away. Then, through the power of recursion, each subfolder is asked to return its size in bytes. If that subfolder has subfolders, they in turn are asked to report their size. Eventually, you find a folder with no children, and its size is simply the sum of all its files. The sum is bubbled back to the top where it's added to the list view.

Stopping the Thread

Since it's possible to close the property page before the thread has finished, how does the property page kill the thread? It could simply *delete* the thread pointer, but that results in a lot of memory leaks. The method I finally settled on was to communicate the intention to the thread and let it gracefully shutdown.

Here's how it works. When the WM_DESTROY message reaches *CSubfolderPage*, it immediately sets or triggers an event (an operating system synchronization object, not an OLE Control event) with this code:

```
void CSubfolderPage::OnDestroy()
{
    // The event must be in manual mode because the thread might
    // trip on it *twice*, once to stop it in the middle of a calculation,
    // and another time right before it exits

    m_event.SetEvent();
    WaitForSingleObject(m_pThread->m_hThread, INFINITE);

    CShellPropPage::OnDestroy();
}
```

Next it goes to sleep, waiting indefinitely for the thread to terminate. Now, how does the thread terminate? The thread is paranoid about the event being set. Each time it starts to get a subfolder size, it checks the state of the event. If it has been signaled, the thread unravels the recursion and returns.

Right before the thread returns, however, there's a line of code instructing it to wait indefinitely for the event to be set. That's because if the thread completes its task without being interrupted, it needs to park itself before it's given permission to quit.

```
UINT ThreadProc(...)
{
...
    // Block here until the caller thread gives us permission
    WaitForSingleObject(pEvent->m_hObject, INFINITE);
    return 0;
}
```

The thread really is necessary because the user might want to dismiss the property page before it finishes calculating the subfolder sizes. It may take more than 30 seconds on some very large directories.

How Do You Debug this Thing?

If you venture off to develop your own shell extension, what do you do if it doesn't work? In most applications, you can simply set a breakpoint, run the program, and start debugging. But you need a way to debug the Explorer, since it's the application using your DLL. Here's how to do it:

1. Choose Settings from the Project menu. Click the Debug tab, and type the full path to Explore.exe (c:\win95\explore.exe) in the Executable for Debug Session edit box.

2. Close all other running applications.

3. Press the Start button, then choose Shutdown.

4. Hold down the [CTRL]+[ALT]+[SHIFT] keys and press the No button.

9.2
CREATE A PROPERTY SHEET HANDLER FOR A FILE OR FOLDER

5. The explorer is no longer running, and along with it, the taskbar and the desktop. You can still launch applications by using [CTRL]+[ESC] to show the Task Manager. Or, simply press [ALT]-[TAB] to get back to Visual C++ 4.0.

Windows takes its time unloading DLLs that are no longer in use. You can force the system to unload DLLs very quickly by changing a value in the registry. Run Regedit.exe and locate the key HKEY_LOCAL_MACHINE\Software\Microsoft\Windows\CurrentVersion\explorer. Add a new key called AlwaysUnloadDll and set its value to 1. Now, all extension DLLs will be unloaded so the compiler won't complain when it tries to write to a DLL file already in use.

Comments

If I hadn't tried to make this control self-registrable, it would have been a lot shorter. But it would have required an extra *.reg file. Plus, we both learned a lot about the inner workings of module-state switching and self-registration. However, I later discovered that you could temporary fool the precompiler with the following code in StdAfx.h:

```
// We always want to include <Afxctl.h> for the DECLARE_OLECREATE_EX definition.
// However, if we're static linking to MFC, we have to fake out Afxctl.h by
// temporarily defining _AFXDLL.

#ifndef _AFXDLL
#define _AFXDLL
#include <afxctl.h>
#undef _AFXDLL
#else
#include <afxctl.h>
#endif
```

Remember, if we are *not* linking to the DLL version of MFC, then _AFXDLL won't be set by the compiler. If you switch from the DLL version of MFC to the static one, as shown in Figure 9-11, then the Settings dialog automatically removes the _AFXDLL definition. I learned that you could still include AfxCtl.h, as long as you temporarily defined _AFXDLL. If I had thought of this trick first, I wouldn't have found all the fun problems with module state switching. With this fix, and similar code in a few other places, you can now switch between the static and DLL version of MFC without problems.

If you want to find more information about shell extensions, the Microsoft Development Library has several good articles on them. Be warned: They all take a decidedly C & SDK approach.

CHAPTER 9
WINDOWS 95 SHELL

9.3 How do I... Create an appbar to display the system palette?

COMPLEXITY
INTERMEDIATE

Problem

I want to create an application to display the current palette, but show it in an appbar. That way, it doesn't interfere with other applications. How do I create a window that can be docked to any edge of the screen, like the taskbar?

Technique

An *appbar* is a window that is similar to the taskbar. Anchored to one edge of the screen, it gives the user quick access to commands or information. It sounds like a toolbar, but it differs in one key area: The system prevents other applications from occupying the area reserved by the appbar.

You can program the appbar to "stay on top," preventing other applications from hiding portions of it. This trick will come in handy when we implement a simple palette viewer (see Figure 9-12). If you've ever done any multimedia programming, you know how important it is to keep your eye on the palette. We'll also use tooltips to display the current palette index and color if the mouse hovers over one of the indices.

All communication with the system goes through a new SDK function called *SHAppBarMessage*. Its first parameter is a structure of type APPBARDATA. It's a good

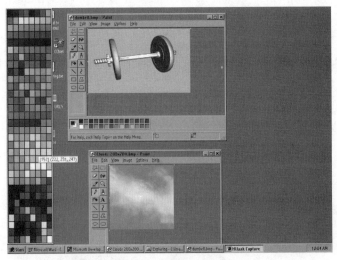

Figure 9-12 The palette viewer AppBar

9.3
CREATE AN APPBAR TO DISPLAY THE SYSTEM PALETTE

candidate for a wrapper class, one that provides type-safe checking and easier to read code. We'll create a class called *CAppBarData* to manage the structure and make the calls to *SHAppBarMessage*.

After we've derived a generic *CWnd* class for our main window (*CAppBarWnd*), we'll derive another class from it to display the system palette. It will also handle the tooltip notification messages to show the selected color.

Steps

1. Create a new project called AppBar using the MFC AppWizard (exe). Choose the Dialog-based option in step 1.

Classes to be created:
    Application: CTrayApp in Tray.h and Tray.cpp
    Dialog: CTrayDlg in TrayDlg.h and TrayDlg.cpp

Features:
+ About box on system menu
+ 3D Controls
+ Uses shared DLL implementation (MFC40.DLL)

2. Remove AppBarDlg.cpp from the project. Since the application doesn't really use a dialog as its main window, we can remove the *CAppBarDlg* class from the project. Switch to FileView, select the AppBarDlg.cpp file and press the [DEL] key. Delete the AppBarDlg.cpp and AppBarDlg.h files from the AppBar directory as well. This step and the next three are the same ones used in the QuickCD How-To in this chapter.

3. Remove IDD_APPBAR_DIALOG from the resource file. Switch to ResourceView and delete the dialog IDD_APPBAR_DIALOG.

4. Fix the ClassWizard database. When you remove a file created by App Studio or ClassWizard, you also need to remove it from the ClassWizard database. Simply bring up ClassWizard ([CTRL]+[W]) and press OK when the message about missing files appears. Another dialog is displayed, giving you the choice to remove *CAppBarDlg* from the ClassWizard database. Press the Remove button.

Repeat the same steps to remove *CAboutDlg* from the database.

5. Create a new class called CAboutDlg. The original *CAboutDlg* code was contained in the AppBarDlg.cpp file, the one we just deleted. This step adds the class back to the project, but in its own file:

    Class name: CAboutDlg
    Base class: CDialog
    File: AboutDlg.cpp
    Dialog: IDD_ABOUTBOX

6. Create a new file called AppBarData.h. Now, we're going to write a fairly long but simple class to wrap the APPBARDATA struct in an easy-to-use class called *CAppBarData*. Add this code to the file and save it:

```cpp
// CAppBarData is a wrapper for the APPBARDATA struct.
// It adds member functions for all the possible
// SHAppBarMessage permutations

#define APPBAR_CALLBACK (WM_USER + 502)

class CAppBarData
{
public:
        CAppBarData();
        CAppBarData(CWnd* pWnd, UINT uEdge, const CRect& rc,
            LPARAM lParam = NULL, UINT uCallbackMsg = APPBAR_CALLBACK);
        CAppBarData(const CAppBarData& source);

        void Initialize(CWnd* pWnd, UINT uEdge, const CRect& rc,
            LPARAM lParam = NULL, UINT uCallbackMsg = APPBAR_CALLBACK);

        const CAppBarData& operator=(const CAppBarData& that);
        operator LPRECT();

// Attributes
        void SetRect(LPCRECT lprc)   { m_data.rc = *lprc; }
        void SetEdge(UINT uEdge)     { m_data.uEdge = uEdge; }
        UINT GetEdge() const         { return m_data.uEdge; }
        BOOL IsRegistered()          { return m_bIsRegistered; }

// Operators
        void Activate();
        HWND GetAutoHideBar();
        void GetState(BOOL& bAlwaysOnTop, BOOL& bAutoHide);
        CRect GetTaskBarPos();
        BOOL New();
        void QueryPos();
        void Remove();

        BOOL SetAutoHideBar(BOOL bHide = TRUE);
        BOOL IsAutoHideEnabled();

        void SetPos();
        void WindowPosChanged();

protected:
        BOOL m_bAutoHide;
        APPBARDATA m_data;
        BOOL m_bIsRegistered;
};
```

7. Create a new file called AppBarData.cpp. Add this code to the file and insert it into the project:

```cpp
#include "StdAfx.h"
#include "AppBarData.h"
```

9.3
CREATE AN APPBAR TO DISPLAY THE SYSTEM PALETTE

```cpp
CAppBarData::CAppBarData()
{
    m_bAutoHide = FALSE;
}

CAppBarData::CAppBarData(CWnd* pWnd, UINT uEdge, const CRect& rc,
        LPARAM lParam, UINT uCallbackMsg)
{
    Initialize(pWnd, uEdge, rc, lParam, uCallbackMsg);
}

void CAppBarData::Initialize(CWnd* pWnd, UINT uEdge, const CRect& rc,
        LPARAM lParam, UINT uCallbackMsg)
{
    m_data.cbSize = sizeof(APPBARDATA);
    m_data.hWnd = pWnd->GetSafeHwnd();
    m_data.uEdge = uEdge;
    m_data.rc = rc;
    m_data.lParam = lParam;
    m_data.uCallbackMessage = uCallbackMsg;
}


CAppBarData::CAppBarData(const CAppBarData& source)
{
    memcpy(&m_data, &(source.m_data), source.m_data.cbSize);
    m_bIsRegistered = source.m_bIsRegistered;
}

const CAppBarData& CAppBarData::operator=(const CAppBarData& that)
{
    memcpy(&m_data, &(that.m_data), that.m_data.cbSize);
    m_bIsRegistered = that.m_bIsRegistered;
    return *this;
}

CAppBarData::operator LPRECT()
{
    return &(m_data.rc);
}

void CAppBarData::Activate()
{
    SHAppBarMessage(ABM_ACTIVATE, &m_data);
}

HWND CAppBarData::GetAutoHideBar()
{
    return (HWND) SHAppBarMessage(ABM_GETAUTOHIDEBAR, &m_data);
}

BOOL CAppBarData::IsAutoHideEnabled()
{
    return m_bAutoHide;
}
```

continued on next page

continued from previous page

```
CRect CAppBarData::GetTaskBarPos()
{
    SHAppBarMessage(ABM_GETTASKBARPOS, &m_data);
    return m_data.rc;
}

BOOL CAppBarData::New()
{
    m_bIsRegistered = SHAppBarMessage(ABM_NEW, &m_data);
    return m_bIsRegistered;
}

void CAppBarData::QueryPos()
{
    SHAppBarMessage(ABM_QUERYPOS, &m_data);
}

void CAppBarData::Remove()
{
    SHAppBarMessage(ABM_REMOVE, &m_data);
}

BOOL CAppBarData::SetAutoHideBar(BOOL bHide)
{
    m_data.lParam = bHide;
    if (SHAppBarMessage(ABM_SETAUTOHIDEBAR, &m_data))
    {
        m_bAutoHide = bHide;
        return TRUE;
    } else
        return FALSE;
}

void CAppBarData::SetPos()
{
    SHAppBarMessage(ABM_SETPOS, &m_data);
}

void CAppBarData::WindowPosChanged()
{
    SHAppBarMessage(ABM_WINDOWPOSCHANGED, &m_data);
}
```

8. Create a new class called CAppBarWnd. Use ClassWizard to create a new class using the following information:

Class name:	CAppBarWnd
Base class:	generic CWnd
File:	AppBarWnd.cpp

9.3
CREATE AN APPBAR TO DISPLAY THE SYSTEM PALETTE

9. Add some methods with ClassWizard. While still in ClassWizard, use the Message Maps tab to add the following methods:

Object	Function	Message
CAppBarWnd	OnCreate	WM_CREATE
CAppBarWnd	OnDestroy	WM_DESTROY
CAppBarWnd	OnActivate	WM_ACTIVATE
CAppBarWnd	OnSize	WM_SIZE
CAppBarWnd	OnMove	WM_MOVE
CAppBarWnd	OnWindowPosChanged	WM_WINDOWPOSCHANGED
CAppBarWnd	OnNcHitTest	WM_NCHITTEST
CAppBarWnd	Create	
CAppBarWnd	PostNcDestroy	

10. Edit AppBarWnd.h. Make the following changes to AppBarWnd.h. Make sure you modify the parameters to *Create*.

```
#include "AppBarData.h"

class CAppBarWnd : public CWnd
{
// Construction
public:
        CAppBarWnd();
        virtual ~CAppBarWnd();

// Operations
public:
        void SetAlwaysOnTop(BOOL bOnTop);
        BOOL SetSide(UINT uSide);

// Overrides
        // ClassWizard generated virtual function overrides
        //{{AFX_VIRTUAL(CAppBarWnd)
        public:
        virtual BOOL Create(LPCTSTR lpszWindowName, DWORD dwStyle, const RECT& rect);
        protected:
        virtual void PostNcDestroy();
        //}}AFX_VIRTUAL

        // Generated message map functions
protected:
        //{{AFX_MSG(CAppBarWnd)
        afx_msg void OnActivate(UINT nState, CWnd* pWndOther, BOOL bMinimized);
        afx_msg int OnCreate(LPCREATESTRUCT lpCreateStruct);
        afx_msg void OnDestroy();
        afx_msg void OnSize(UINT nType, int cx, int cy);
        afx_msg void OnMove(int x, int y);
        afx_msg void OnWindowPosChanged(WINDOWPOS FAR* lpwndpos);
        afx_msg UINT OnNcHitTest(CPoint point);
```

continued on next page

CHAPTER 9
WINDOWS 95 SHELL

continued from previous page

```
    //}}AFX_MSG
    LONG OnAppBarNotify(UINT wParam, LONG lParam);
    LONG OnDisplayChange(UINT wParam, LONG lParam);
    DECLARE_MESSAGE_MAP()

    void ModifyRect(LPRECT lpRect, const CSize& size);
    void QuerySetPos(const CRect& rc, BOOL bMove = TRUE);

    CAppBarData m_abd;
    CSize m_sizeScreen;
    CSize m_sizeCurrent;
    BOOL m_bOnTop;
};
```

11. Code the CAppBarWnd constructor and modify the message map. Add the following code:

```
CAppBarWnd::CAppBarWnd()
{
        m_bOnTop = TRUE;

        m_sizeScreen.cx = GetSystemMetrics(SM_CXSCREEN);
        m_sizeScreen.cy = GetSystemMetrics(SM_CYSCREEN);
}
...
BEGIN_MESSAGE_MAP(CAppBarWnd, CWnd)
        //{{AFX_MSG_MAP(CAppBarWnd)
        ON_WM_CREATE()
        ON_WM_DESTROY()
        ON_WM_SIZE()
        ON_WM_MOVE()
        ON_WM_NCHITTEST()
        ON_WM_WINDOWPOSCHANGED()
        ON_WM_ACTIVATE()
        //}}AFX_MSG_MAP
        ON_MESSAGE(WM_DISPLAYCHANGE, OnDisplayChange)
        ON_MESSAGE(APPBAR_CALLBACK, OnAppBarNotify)
END_MESSAGE_MAP()
```

12. Edit CAppBarWnd::Create. *Create* registers a custom window class so the cursor changes to a cross when it moves over the window. WS_EX_TOOLWINDOW prevents the window from appearing in the task list.

```
BOOL CAppBarWnd::Create(LPCTSTR lpszWindowName, DWORD dwStyle, const RECT& rect)
{
        CString className = AfxRegisterWndClass(CS_DBLCLKS | CS_VREDRAW | ⇒
            CS_HREDRAW,
                ::LoadCursor(NULL, IDC_CROSS), ::GetSysColorBrush(COLOR_WINDOW));

        return CWnd::CreateEx(WS_EX_CLIENTEDGE | WS_EX_TOOLWINDOW,
            className, lpszWindowName, dwStyle | WS_VISIBLE, rect.left, rect.right,
            rect.right - rect.left, rect.bottom - rect.top, NULL, NULL);
}
```

9.3
CREATE AN APPBAR TO DISPLAY THE SYSTEM PALETTE

13. Edit **CAppBarWnd::PostNcDestroy**. Since our main window is acting as the frame for the application, it should delete itself when it is destroyed. *CFrameWnd* does the same thing.

```
void CAppBarWnd::PostNcDestroy()
{
    CWnd::PostNcDestroy();
    delete this;
}
```

14. Code **CAppBarWnd::OnCreate**. *CAppBarWnd* records the initial size and registers the window with the system through *CAppBarData::Initialize*.

```
int CAppBarWnd::OnCreate(LPCREATESTRUCT lpCreateStruct)
{
    if (CWnd::OnCreate(lpCreateStruct) == -1)
        return -1;

    m_sizeCurrent.cx = lpCreateStruct->cx;
    m_sizeCurrent.cy = lpCreateStruct->cy;

    m_abd.Initialize(this, 0, CRect(0,0,0,0));

    return 0;
}
```

15. Edit **CAppBarWnd::OnDestroy**. Remove the appbar from the system so Windows can shuffle the windows around it to take up the empty space. If you don't call *Remove*, the appbar area becomes unusable because the system thinks it is still in occupied.

```
void CAppBarWnd::OnDestroy()
{
    m_abd.Remove();
    CWnd::OnDestroy();
}
```

16. Code **CAppBarWnd::OnActivate**. Again, we're just passing these messages onto Windows through *CAppBarData*.

```
void CAppBarWnd::OnActivate(UINT nState, CWnd* pWndOther, BOOL bMinimized)
{
    m_abd.Activate();
}
```

17. Code **CAppBarWnd::OnSize**. We need to negotiate the new window size with the system. The desired rectangle is passed to *QuerySetPos*, which returns the final, acceptable rectangle. *m_sizeCurrent* keeps track of the last used width and height, since only one of them is valid at any time. For example, Windows sets the appbar width if it's attached to the top of the screen.

CHAPTER 9
WINDOWS 95 SHELL

We have to record the height in case the user switches it to the left or right side, then later puts it back on top.

```
void CAppBarWnd::OnSize(UINT nType, int cx, int cy)
{
    CWnd::OnSize(nType, cx, cy);

    // Bail if the client width or height is zero
    if ((cx == 0) || (cy == 0))
        return;

    // Let the system know the appbar size has changed
    CRect rc;
    GetWindowRect(&rc);
    QuerySetPos(rc);

    GetWindowRect(&rc);

    if (m_abd.GetEdge() == ABE_TOP || m_abd.GetEdge() == ABE_BOTTOM)
        m_sizeCurrent.cy = rc.Height();
    else
        m_sizeCurrent.cx = rc.Width();
}
```

18. **Edit CAppBarWnd::OnMove.** Forward this message to the system:

```
void CAppBarWnd::OnMove(int x, int y)
{
    CRect rc;
    GetWindowRect(&rc);
    QuerySetPos(rc);
}
```

19. **Code CAppBarWnd::OnWindowPosChanged.** Let the system know the window position has changed.

```
void CAppBarWnd::OnWindowPosChanged(WINDOWPOS FAR* lpwndpos)
{
    m_abd.WindowPosChanged();
    Default();
}
```

20. **Edit CAppBarWnd::OnNcHitTest.** We want to disable sizing in all directions except the inside edge.

```
UINT CAppBarWnd::OnNcHitTest(CPoint point)
{
    LRESULT lHitTest = CWnd::OnNcHitTest(point);

    UINT uSide = m_abd.GetEdge();
    if ((uSide == ABE_TOP) && (lHitTest == HTBOTTOM))
        return HTBOTTOM;

    if ((uSide == ABE_BOTTOM) && (lHitTest == HTTOP))
        return HTTOP;
```

9.3
CREATE AN APPBAR TO DISPLAY THE SYSTEM PALETTE

```
    if ((uSide == ABE_LEFT) && (lHitTest == HTRIGHT))
        return HTRIGHT;

    if ((uSide == ABE_RIGHT) && (lHitTest == HTLEFT))
        return HTLEFT;

    return HTCLIENT;
}
```

21. Add OnDisplayChange. Add this method at the bottom of the file to record the size of the screen if the resolution changes.

```
LONG CAppBarWnd::OnDisplayChange(UINT wParam, LONG lParam)
{
    m_sizeScreen.cx = LOWORD(lParam);
    m_sizeScreen.cy = HIWORD(lParam);
    return 0;
}
```

22. Add OnAppBarNotify. The system posts a notification event to our window when it wants to tells us about three events: Other taskbars have changed state, a full-screen application is starting, or our size needs recalculation. Add this code to the bottom of AppBarWnd.cpp:

```
LONG CAppBarWnd::OnAppBarNotify(UINT wParam, LONG lParam)
{
    static CWnd* pwndZOrder = NULL;

    switch (wParam)
    {
    // Notifies the appbar that the taskbar's autohide or always-on-top
    // state has changed.  The appbar can use this to conform to the
    // settings of the system taskbar.
    case ABN_STATECHANGE:
        break;

    // Notifies the appbar when a full screen application is opening or
    // closing.  When a full screen app is opening, the appbar must
    // drop to the bottom of the Z-Order.  When the app is closing, we
    // should restore our Z-order position.
    case ABN_FULLSCREENAPP:
        if (lParam)
        {
            // A full screen app is opening. Move us to the bottom
            // of the Z-Order.

            // First get the window that we're underneath so we can
            // correctly restore our position
            pwndZOrder = GetWindow(GW_HWNDPREV);

            // Now move ourselves to the bottom of the Z-Order
            SetWindowPos(&CWnd::wndBottom, 0, 0, 0, 0,
                        SWP_NOMOVE | SWP_NOSIZE | SWP_NOACTIVATE);
        }
        else
```

continued on next page

continued from previous page

```
        {
            // The app is closing.  Restore the Z-order
            SetWindowPos(m_bOnTop ? &CWnd::wndTopMost : pwndZOrder, ⇒
                0, 0, 0, 0,
                        SWP_NOMOVE | SWP_NOSIZE | SWP_NOACTIVATE);

            pwndZOrder = NULL;
        }
        break;

        // An event has occurred that might affect our size and
        // position like a screen resolution change.
    case ABN_POSCHANGED:
        CRect rc(CPoint(0, 0), m_sizeScreen);
        CRect rcWindow;

        // Reposition based using our current size to the new screen dimensions
        GetWindowRect(&rcWindow);
        ModifyRect(&rc, rcWindow.Size());
        QuerySetPos(rc);
        break;
    }

    return 0;
}
```

23. Add the other helper methods to AppBarWnd.cpp. Insert this code at the bottom of the file:

```
///////////////////////////////////////////////////////////////////
CAppBarWnd operations and helper methods

BOOL CAppBarWnd::SetSide(UINT uSide)
{
    CRect rc(CPoint(0, 0), m_sizeScreen);
    BOOL fAutoHide = FALSE;

    m_abd.SetEdge(uSide);

    // Adjust the rectangle to set our height or width depending on the
    // side we want.
    ModifyRect(&rc, m_sizeCurrent);

    // Move the appbar to the new screen space.
    QuerySetPos(rc);

    return TRUE;
}


void CAppBarWnd::QuerySetPos(const CRect& rc, BOOL fMove)
{
    // skot
    m_abd.SetRect(rc);
```

9.3
CREATE AN APPBAR TO DISPLAY THE SYSTEM PALETTE

```
    // skot
    int iWidth = 0;
    int iHeight = 0;

    // Calculate the part we want to occupy.  We only figure out the top
    // and bottom coordinates if we're on the top or bottom of the screen.
    // Likewise for the left and right.  We will always try to occupy the
    // full height or width of the screen edge.
    if ((ABE_LEFT == m_abd.GetEdge()) || (ABE_RIGHT == m_abd.GetEdge()))
    {
        LPRECT pRect = (LPRECT) m_abd;

        iWidth = pRect->right - pRect->left;
        pRect->top = 0;
        pRect->bottom = m_sizeScreen.cy;
    }
    else
    {
        LPRECT pRect = (LPRECT) m_abd;

        iHeight = pRect->bottom - pRect->top;
        pRect->left = 0;
        pRect->right = m_sizeScreen.cx;
    }

    // Propose this new rectangle
    m_abd.QueryPos();

    // Analyaze what the system approved

    // The system will return an approved position along the edge we're asking
    // for. However, if we can't get the exact position requested, the system
    // only updates the edge that's incorrect. For example, if we want to
    // attach to the bottom of the screen and the taskbar is already there,
    // we'll pass in a rect like 0, 964, 1280, 1024 and the system will return
    // 0, 964, 1280, 996. Since the appbar has to be above the taskbar, the
    // bottom of the rect was adjusted to 996. We need to adjust the opposite
    // edge of the rectangle to preserve the height we want.

    LPRECT pRect = (LPRECT) m_abd;
    ModifyRect(pRect, CSize(iWidth, iHeight));

    // Tell the system we're moving to this new approved position.
    m_abd.SetPos();

    if (fMove)
        MoveWindow((LPRECT) m_abd, TRUE);
}


void CAppBarWnd::SetAlwaysOnTop(BOOL bOnTop)
{
    // Update the window position to HWND_TOPMOST if we're to be always
    // on top, or HWND_NOTOPMOST if we're not.
```

continued on next page

continued from previous page

```
        SetWindowPos((bOnTop) ? &CWnd::wndTopMost : &CWnd::wndNoTopMost,
            0, 0, 0, 0, SWP_NOMOVE | SWP_NOSIZE | SWP_NOACTIVATE);

        // Store the setting in the appbar OPTIONS struct.
        m_bOnTop = bOnTop;
}


void CAppBarWnd::ModifyRect(LPRECT lpRect, const CSize& size)
{
        switch (m_abd.GetEdge())
        {
        case ABE_TOP:
            lpRect->bottom = lpRect->top + size.cy;
            break;

        case ABE_BOTTOM:
            lpRect->top = lpRect->bottom - size.cy;
            break;

        case ABE_LEFT:
            lpRect->right = lpRect->left + size.cx;
            break;

        case ABE_RIGHT:
            lpRect->left = lpRect->right - size.cx;
            break;
        }
}
```

24. Create a menu called IDM_MENU. Create a new menu like the one shown in Figure 9-13 using the table below:

Menu ID	Caption
ID_LEFT	&Left
ID_RIGHT	&Right
ID_TOP	&Top
ID_BOTTOM	&Bottom
ID_ALWAYSONTOP	Al&ways on top
ID_ABOUT	&About
ID_EXIT	E&xit

25. **Create a new class called CPaletteWnd.** Now that we have a nice reusable class for creating AppBars, we'll derive a new class and add some interesting functionality. Use ClassWizard to create a new class using the following information:

Class name: CPaletteWnd
Base class: generic CWnd
File: PaletteWnd.cpp

9.3
CREATE AN APPBAR TO DISPLAY THE SYSTEM PALETTE

Figure 9-13 AppBar menu

Replace every occurrence of *CWnd* with *CAppBarWnd* in PaletteWnd.cpp and PaletteWnd.h.

26. **Add message handlers to CPaletteWnd.** Use ClassWizard to add message-handling functions for these messages:

Object ID	Function	Message
CPaletteWnd	OnCreate	WM_CREATE
CPaletteWnd	OnPaint	WM_PAINT
CPaletteWnd	OnContextMenu	WM_CONTEXTMENU
CPaletteWnd	OnCommand	
CPaletteWnd	PreTranslateMessage	

27. **Edit PaletteWnd.h.** Add a few helper methods and variables to *CPaletteWnd* using the following code:

```
#include "AppBarWnd.h"

/////////////////////////////////////////////////////////////////////
// CPaletteWnd window

class CPaletteWnd : public CAppBarWnd
{
// Construction
public:
        CPaletteWnd();
        virtual ~CPaletteWnd();

// Overrides
        // ClassWizard generated virtual function overrides
        //{{AFX_VIRTUAL(CPaletteWnd)
        public:
        virtual BOOL OnCommand(WPARAM wParam, LPARAM lParam);
        virtual BOOL PreTranslateMessage(MSG* pMsg);
        //}}AFX_VIRTUAL
```

continued on next page

continued from previous page

```
        // Generated message map functions
protected:
        //{{AFX_MSG(CPaletteWnd)
        afx_msg void OnPaint();
        afx_msg void OnContextMenu(CWnd* pWnd, CPoint point);
        afx_msg int OnCreate(LPCREATESTRUCT lpCreateStruct);
        //}}AFX_MSG
        DECLARE_MESSAGE_MAP()

        virtual int OnToolHitTest(CPoint point, TOOLINFO* pTI) const;

        CSize GetExtent() const;
        void HitTest(const CPoint& point, CRect& r, int& index, COLORREF& ⇒
cr) const;

        CToolTipCtrl m_tip;
        CPalette m_pal;
        BOOL m_bCaptured;
};
```

28. Edit PaletteWnd.cpp. Add this #include to the top of the file:

```
#include "stdafx.h"
#include "AppBar.h"
#include "PaletteWnd.h"
#include "AboutDlg.h"
```

29. Edit CPaletteWnd::OnCreate. The following code creates a special logical palette where every entry is an index into the current system palette. The *peFlags* value PC_EXPLICIT specifies that the low-order word of the logical palette entry designates a hardware palette index. This flag allows us to show the contents of the display device palette. We also start the appbar docked on the left side of the screen.

```
int CPaletteWnd::OnCreate(LPCREATESTRUCT lpCreateStruct)
{
        if (CAppBarWnd::OnCreate(lpCreateStruct) == -1)
            return -1;

        // Create the tooltip control
        EnableToolTips(TRUE);

        // Create the palette
        LOGPALETTE* pPal = (LOGPALETTE*) malloc(sizeof(LOGPALETTE) +
            256 * sizeof(PALETTEENTRY));

        if (pPal)
        {
            pPal->palVersion = 0x300;
            pPal->palNumEntries = 256;
            for (int i=0; i < 256; i++)
            {
                pPal->palPalEntry[i].peRed = i;
                pPal->palPalEntry[i].peGreen = 0;
```

9.3
CREATE AN APPBAR TO DISPLAY THE SYSTEM PALETTE

```
            pPal->palPalEntry[i].peBlue = 0;
            pPal->palPalEntry[i].peFlags = PC_EXPLICIT;
        }
        m_pal.CreatePalette(pPal);
        free (pPal);
    }
    m_bCaptured = FALSE;

    m_abd.New();
    SetSide(ABE_LEFT);

    return 0;
}
```

30. Code CPaletteWnd::OnPaint. The first part sets the mapping mode to a logical *xCells* by *yCells* grid. It makes the painting code easier if we can assume the client area is an 8x32 array of pixels. Everything is scaled by 10 to avoid rounding errors in the mapping mode conversion.

```
void CPaletteWnd::OnPaint()
{
    CPaintDC dc(this); // device context for painting

    CRect rc;
    GetClientRect(rc);
    CSize sz = GetExtent();

    dc.SelectPalette(&m_pal, FALSE);
    dc.RealizePalette();

    // Set mapping mode to a logical xCells x yCells area
    dc.SetMapMode(MM_ANISOTROPIC);
    dc.SetWindowExt(sz.cx * 10, sz.cy * 10);
    dc.SetViewportExt(rc.Size());
    dc.SetViewportOrg(rc.left, rc.top);

    for (int y = 0; y < sz.cy; y++)
    {
        for (int x = 0; x < sz.cx; x++)
        {
            CBrush br (PALETTEINDEX((y*sz.cx) + x));
            CBrush* pOld = dc.SelectObject(&br);

            dc.Rectangle(x*10, y*10, (x*10)+10, (y*10)+10);
            dc.SelectObject(pOld);
        }
    }
}
```

31. Code CPaletteWnd::OnContextMenu. When the user presses the right-mouse button over the window, we catch the WM_CONTEXTMENU message and display a pop-up menu.

```
void CPaletteWnd::OnContextMenu(CAppBarWnd* pWnd, CPoint point)
{
```

continued on next page

continued from previous page

```
        CMenu topMenu;
        topMenu.LoadMenu(IDM_MENU);
        CMenu* pMenu = topMenu.GetSubMenu(0);

        pMenu->TrackPopupMenu(TPM_RIGHTBUTTON, point.x, point.y, this);
}
```

32. **Code CPaletteWnd::OnCommand.** It's easier to handle all the menu commands in one method like *OnCommand* instead of writing seven one-line methods:

```
BOOL CPaletteWnd::OnCommand(WPARAM wParam, LPARAM lParam)
{
        if (CWnd::OnCommand(wParam, lParam))
            return TRUE;

        // crack message parameters
        UINT nID = LOWORD(wParam);
        HWND hWndCtrl = (HWND)lParam;
        int nCode = HIWORD(wParam);

        switch (nID)
        {
        case ID_BOTTOM:
            SetSide(ABE_BOTTOM); break;
        case ID_TOP:
            SetSide(ABE_TOP); break;
        case ID_LEFT:
            SetSide(ABE_LEFT); break;
        case ID_RIGHT:
            SetSide(ABE_RIGHT); break;
        case ID_EXIT:
            PostMessage(WM_CLOSE); break;
        case ID_ALWAYSONTOP:
            SetAlwaysOnTop(TRUE); break;
        case ID_ABOUT:
            {
                CAboutDlg dlg;
                dlg.DoModal();
            }
            break;

        default:
            return FALSE;
        }

        return TRUE;
}
```

33. **Code CPaletteWnd::PreTranslateMessage.** We have to add one line of code here to hook the tooltip into the message stream:

```
BOOL CPaletteWnd::PreTranslateMessage(MSG* pMsg)
{
        FilterToolTipMessage(pMsg);
        return CAppBarWnd::PreTranslateMessage(pMsg);
}
```

9.3
CREATE AN APPBAR TO DISPLAY THE SYSTEM PALETTE

34. Add CPaletteWnd::OnToolHitTest. The tooltip wants to know where the mouse is parked. We have to respond by setting the tooltip text and the bounding rect for the color cell the mouse sits over. Add this code to the bottom of the file:

```
int CPaletteWnd::OnToolHitTest(CPoint point, TOOLINFO* pTI) const
{
    CRect r;
    int index;
    COLORREF cr;
    HitTest(point, r, index, cr);

    pTI->hwnd = m_hWnd;
    pTI->uId = index;
    pTI->rect = r;
    pTI->uFlags = TTF_NOTBUTTON | TTF_ALWAYSTIP;// | TTF_CENTERTIP;

    char* pMsg = new char[50];
    wsprintf(pMsg, "[%d] (%d, %d, %d)", index, GetRValue(cr), GetGValue(cr),
        GetBValue(cr));
    pTI->lpszText = pMsg;

    return index;
}
```

35. Add two helper methods. Add these functions to the bottom of PaletteWnd.cpp:

```
///////////////////////////////
// CPaletteWnd helper methods

void CPaletteWnd::HitTest(const CPoint& pt, CRect& r, int& index, ⇒
COLORREF& cr) const
{
    CClientDC dc((CWnd *) this);
    CSize sz = GetExtent();
    CRect rc;
    GetClientRect(rc);

    CPoint point(pt);       // construct a point we can modify

    // Set mapping mode to a logical xCells x yCells area
    dc.SetMapMode(MM_ANISOTROPIC);
    dc.SetWindowExt(sz.cx * 10, sz.cy * 10);
    dc.SetViewportExt(rc.Size());
    dc.SetViewportOrg(rc.left, rc.top);

    dc.DPtoLP(&point);

    index = (point.y/10 * sz.cx) + point.x/10;

    // calculate the bounding rect for the color we're over in logical coordinates
    r.SetRect(0, 0, 10, 10);
    point.x = (index % sz.cx) * 10;
```

continued on next page

continued from previous page

```
            point.y = (index / sz.cx) * 10;
            r.OffsetRect(point);

            // Find the color in the middle of the bounding rect
            CPoint ptHalf = r.BottomRight() - r.TopLeft();
            ptHalf.x /= 2;
            ptHalf.y /= 2;
            CPoint ptCenter = r.TopLeft() + ptHalf;
            cr = dc.GetPixel(ptCenter);

            dc.LPtoDP(r);
    }

CSize CPaletteWnd::GetExtent() const
{
        UINT nEdge = m_abd.GetEdge();
        if (nEdge == ABE_LEFT || nEdge == ABE_RIGHT)
                return CSize(8, 32);
        else
                return CSize(32, 8);
}
```

36. Edit AppBar.cpp. Now we can create the *CPaletteWnd* in *InitInstance*. Make the following modifications to *CAppBar::InitInstance*:

```
#include "stdafx.h"
#include "AppBar.h"
#include "PaletteWnd.h"

...

BOOL CAppBarApp::InitInstance()
{
        // Standard initialization

#ifdef _AFXDLL
        Enable3dControls();             // Call this when using MFC in a shared DLL
#else
        Enable3dControlsStatic();       // Call this when linking to MFC statically
#endif

        CRect r(0, 0, 150, 80);
        CPaletteWnd* pWnd = new CPaletteWnd();

        VERIFY(pWnd->Create("AppBar Test", WS_POPUP | WS_THICKFRAME | ⇒
WS_CLIPCHILDREN, r));

        m_pMainWnd = pWnd;

        return TRUE;
}
```

37. Build and test the application. While you can run the program in any color mode, you'll get the best results if you change your display to 256 colors. Test the tooltips by parking the mouse over one of the color cells. Also try the context menu features by docking the window to different sides and testing the stay on top feature.

How It Works

Most of the code is accounting. It's your responsibility to inform the system every time the app gets focus, moves, or changes size. The shell can only manage the size and position of the other applications if you dutifully pass these messages on to *SHAppBarMessage*.

All shell communication goes through a single function, *SHAppBarMessage*. Its first parameter is a structure of type APPBARDATA. Since you can use *SHAppBarMessage* frequently to manage the size and state of the appbar, a few steps were added to create a wrapper class called *CAppBarData*. A single instance of the class is used by *CAppBarWnd* to handle the appbar.

Comments

Since most of the code in *CAppBarWnd* exists just to notify the system when the window has changed position, it seems like the shell could somehow "hook" these messages. That way we wouldn't have to write all this code just to forward the events.

COMPLEXITY
ADVANCED

9.4 How do I... Extend the context menu for certain files?

Problem

Now that I've been developing OLE Controls, I'm always registering or unregistering them with either RegSvr32.exe or using the Tools Register Control menu in Developer Studio. I'd like to simply click on the *.OCX with mouse button 2, and choose Register or Unregister from the context menu. How do I write such a context menu handler? Since OLE inproc servers use the same techniques for registering, I'd like the same technique applied to the DLL files too.

Technique

There are two problems to solve here: writing a context menu handler and registering an OLE object. A context menu handler is a shell extension that adds menu items to any of the shell's context menus. There are two types of context menus: *drag-and-drop handlers* and *context menu extensions*. We're going to implement the second type, since I doubt you'll want the option to register the control while dragging it to a new location.

When you click on a file within the shell's namespace (Explorer, the desktop, from the Open dialog), it creates the default context menu for the file and then loads its registered context menu extensions so they can add extra menu items. The extensions are typically written as a DLL (or inproc server if you want to use the fancy OLE terminology). This How-To will write a handler that adds two menu items, Register and Unregister, to the context menu displayed for DLLs and OLE Controls. The internal code behaves just like RegSvr32.exe; it will locate and call the object's *DllRegisterServer* or *DllUnregisterServer* function.

The DLL implements the context menu interface, *IContextMenu*, to add menu items to the context menu. The menu items can be either class-specific (applicable to all files of a particular type) or instance-specific (applicable to a single file). In our example, our menu extensions operate on single files only, so they won't appear if more than one DLL or OCX file was selected.

In addition to the *IUnknown* member functions, the handler must implement the other *IContextMenu* functions: *QueryContextMenu*, *InvokeCommand*, and *GetCommandString*. The combination of these three supports the addition and handling of the new menu items. Our specific implementation will be explained in the How It Works section.

Note: A large part of this code is very similar to the Subfolder How-To in section 9.2.

Steps

1. **Create a new project called RegServer with the MFC AppWizard (dll).**
   Make sure you chose the DLL AppWizard instead of the EXE AppWizard. Choose the statically linked MFC option and turn on the option for OLE automation.

```
Creating Regular DLL (using MFC statically linked) RegServer.dll
Main source code in: RegServer.h and RegServer.cpp
Features:
   + OLE Automation support enabled
```

2. **Edit StdAfx.h.** Modify StdAfx.h to look like the code below (some unused headers have been deleted):

```
#define VC_EXTRALEAN        // Exclude rarely-used stuff from Windows headers

#include <afxwin.h>         // MFC core and standard components
#include <afxext.h>         // MFC extensions

#ifndef _AFX_NO_OLE_SUPPORT
#include <afxole.h>         // MFC OLE classes
#include <afxodlgs.h>       // MFC OLE dialog classes
#include <afxdisp.h>        // MFC OLE automation classes
#endif // _AFX_NO_OLE_SUPPORT
```

9.4
EXTEND THE CONTEXT MENU FOR CERTAIN FILES

```
// We always want to include <Afxctl.h> for the DECLARE_OLECREATE_EX definition.
// However, if we're static linking to MFC, we have to fake out Afxctl.h by
// temporarily defining _AFXDLL.

#ifndef _AFXDLL
#define _AFXDLL
#include <afxctl.h>
#undef _AFXDLL
#else
#include <afxctl.h>
#endif

// We only include WinNetwk.h because, without it, shlobj.h complains
// about NETRESOURCE!
#include <winnetwk.h>
#include <shlobj.h>           // Shell extension interfaces

#include "COMHelp.h"
```

3. Add a global function called DllUnregisterServer to RegServer.cpp (MFC 4.0 only). For an explanation of *DllUnregisterServer* and why we have to add it, please see step 3 in How-To 9.2. Add the following code to the bottom of RegServer.cpp:

```
STDAPI DllUnregisterServer(void)
{
    // The documentation for UpdateRegistryAll doesn't mention
    // that the function takes one argument.

    AFX_MANAGE_STATE(AfxGetStaticModuleState());
    COleObjectFactory::UpdateRegistryAll(FALSE);
    return S_OK;
}
```

4. Edit RegServer.def (MFC 4.0 only). Add a line to the DEF file so the linker knows to export *DllUnregisterServer*:

```
; RegServer.def : Declares the module parameters for the DLL.

LIBRARY          "REGSERVER"
DESCRIPTION      'REGSERVER Windows Dynamic Link Library'

EXPORTS
    DllCanUnloadNow PRIVATE
    DllGetClassObject PRIVATE
    DllRegisterServer PRIVATE
    DllUnregisterServer PRIVATE
```

5. Copy four files from How-To 9.2. Copy the following files from the Shell\Subfolder directory on the CD-ROM accompanying this book to the RegServer project: RegisterClass.cpp, RegisterClass.h, InitGuids.cpp, and COMHelp.h. Refer to steps 6 through 9 in How-To 9.2 for the source code and an explanation of each file. Open InitGuids.cpp and RegisterClass.cpp and insert them into the project.

6. **Create a new class called CRegisterMenu.** Later steps will implement the two OLE interfaces necessary to support shell context menus. *CCmdTarget* includes most of the COM framework we'll need to support these interfaces. Use ClassWizard to derive a new class from *CCmdTarget* called *CRegisterMenu*. Select the option to make the class createable by the type ID REGSERVER.REGISTERMENU.

   Class name: CRegisterMenu
   Base class: CCmdTarget
   File: RegisterMenu.cpp

7. **Edit RegisterMenu.h.** In order to hook the registration process, we have to change the DECLARE_OLECREATE macro to DECLARE_OLECREATE_EX. The macro derives a new class from *COleObjectFactory* and nests it within *CRegisterMenu*. It supports the *IClassFactory* interface through the MFC implementation, but more importantly lets us do our own registration. The standard DECLARE_OLECREATE doesn't do that.

```
class CRegisterMenu : public CCmdTarget
{
        DECLARE_DYNCREATE(CRegisterMenu)

        CRegisterMenu();            // protected constructor used by dynamic creation

// Attributes
public:
        TCHAR m_szPath[MAX_PATH];   // path to file or folder in question

// Operations
public:

// Overrides
        // ClassWizard generated virtual function overrides
        //{{AFX_VIRTUAL(CRegisterMenu)
        public:
        virtual void OnFinalRelease();
        //}}AFX_VIRTUAL

// Implementation
protected:
        virtual ~CRegisterMenu();

        // Generated message map functions
        //{{AFX_MSG(CRegisterMenu)
        //}}AFX_MSG

        DECLARE_MESSAGE_MAP()
        DECLARE_OLECREATE_EX(CRegisterMenu)
```

9.4
EXTEND THE CONTEXT MENU FOR CERTAIN FILES

```
    // Generated OLE dispatch map functions
    //{{AFX_DISPATCH(CRegisterMenu)
    //}}AFX_DISPATCH
    DECLARE_DISPATCH_MAP()
    DECLARE_INTERFACE_MAP()

    BEGIN_INTERFACE_PART(ShellExtInit, IShellExtInit)
        INIT_INTERFACE_PART(CRegisterMenu, ShellExtInit)
        STDMETHOD(Initialize)(LPCITEMIDLIST pidlFolder, LPDATAOBJECT lpdobj,
            HKEY hKeyProgID);
    END_INTERFACE_PART(ShellExtInit)

    BEGIN_INTERFACE_PART(ContextMenu, IContextMenu)
        INIT_INTERFACE_PART(CRegisterMenu, ContextMenu)
        STDMETHOD(QueryContextMenu)(HMENU hMenu, UINT indexMenu,
            UINT idCmdFirst, UINT idCmdLast, UINT uFlags);
        STDMETHOD(InvokeCommand)(LPCMINVOKECOMMANDINFO lpici);
        STDMETHOD(GetCommandString)(UINT idCmd, UINT uType,
            UINT* pwReserved, LPSTR pszName, UINT cchMax);
    END_INTERFACE_PART(ContextMenu)

    void DoMenu(UINT nCmd, LPCMINVOKECOMMANDINFO lpcmi);
};
```

8. Edit RegisterMenu.cpp. Add a couple of #include lines to the top and two INTERFACE_MAP entries further down in the file:

```
#include "stdafx.h"
#include "RegServer.h"
#include "RegisterMenu.h"

#include "RegisterClass.h"

...

BEGIN_INTERFACE_MAP(CRegisterMenu, CCmdTarget)
    INTERFACE_PART(CRegisterMenu, IID_IRegisterMenu, Dispatch)
    INTERFACE_PART(CRegisterMenu, IID_IShellExtInit, ShellExtInit)
    INTERFACE_PART(CRegisterMenu, IID_IContextMenu, ContextMenu)
END_INTERFACE_MAP()

BEGIN_INTERFACE_MAP(CProperties, CCmdTarget)
    INTERFACE_PART(CProperties, IID_IProperties, Dispatch)
    INTERFACE_PART(CProperties, IID_IShellExtInit, ShellExtInit)
    INTERFACE_PART(CProperties, IID_IShellPropSheetExt, ShellPropExt)
END_INTERFACE_MAP()
```

9. Add the UpdateRegistry method. Earlier we added the DECLARE_OLECREATE_EX macro. This allows us to override the *UpdateRegistry* method in the embedded *CRegistryMenuFactory* object. Our implementation lets *COleObjectFactory* make most of the registry changes before we add (or remove) two other entries using the *CRegisterClass*. Property sheet extensions must have an extra registry value called ThreadingModel. The other registry entry attaches the RegServer.RegisterMenu object to the

ContextMenuHandlers key for all files with the DLL or OCX extension. Add this code to the bottom of RegisterMenu.cpp:

```
// Note: IMPLEMENT_OLECREATE was changed to IMPLEMENT_OLECREATE_EX
//
IMPLEMENT_OLECREATE_EX(CRegisterMenu, "REGSERVER.REGISTERMENU", 0x917cf125,
0x67c0, 0x11cf, 0x9d, 0xff, 0x68, 0x7, 0x2, 0xc1, 0x7c, 0xa)

/////////////////////////////////////////////////////////////////////////////
// CRegisterMenu message handlers

BOOL CRegisterMenu::CRegisterMenuFactory::UpdateRegistry(BOOL bRegister)
{
    CRegisterClass reg(m_clsid, "RegServer.RegisterMenu");

    VERIFY(reg.AddSymbolAlias(".dll", "dllfile") == 3);  // zero based ⇒
...it's really %4
    VERIFY(reg.AddSymbolAlias(".ocx", "ocxfile") == 4);  // %5

    reg.AddEntry("CLSID\\%1\\InProcServer32", "Apartment",  ⇒
"ThreadingModel");
    reg.AddEntry("%4\\shellex\\ContextMenuHandlers\\%2", "%1");
    reg.AddEntry("%5\\shellex\\ContextMenuHandlers\\%2", "%1");

    if (bRegister)
    {
        COleObjectFactory::UpdateRegistry(TRUE);
        return reg.Register();
    } else {
        reg.Register(FALSE);
#ifdef _AFXDLL
        return AfxOleUnregisterClass(m_clsid, NULL);
#else
        reg.RemoveKey("CLSID\\%1");
        reg.RemoveKey("%2");
        return TRUE;
#endif
    }
}
```

10. **Implement the IShellExtInit interface.** The following implementation of *IShellExtInit::Initialize* is identical to the one shown in the property page shell extension. That's because both extensions require an implementation of the *IShellExtInit* interface. The code below stores the selected filename in the *m_szPath* member variable.

```
IMPLEMENT_IUNKNOWN(CRegisterMenu, ShellExtInit)

STDMETHODIMP CRegisterMenu::XShellExtInit::Initialize (LPCITEMIDLIST pidlFolder,
    LPDATAOBJECT lpdobj, HKEY hKeyProgID)
{
    METHOD_PROLOGUE(CRegisterMenu, ShellExtInit)

    STGMEDIUM medium;
    FORMATETC fe = { CF_HDROP, NULL, DVASPECT_CONTENT, -1, TYMED_HGLOBAL };
```

9.4
EXTEND THE CONTEXT MENU FOR CERTAIN FILES

```
    // Fail the call if lpdobj is NULL.
    //
    if (lpdobj == NULL)
        return E_FAIL;

    // Render the data referenced by the IDataObject pointer to an HGLOBAL
    // storage medium in CF_HDROP format.
    //
    HRESULT hr = lpdobj->GetData (&fe, &medium);
    if (FAILED (hr))
        return E_FAIL;

    // If only one file is selected, retrieve the file name and store it in
    // m_szFile. Otherwise fail the call.
    //
    if (DragQueryFile ((HDROP) medium.hGlobal, 0xFFFFFFFF, NULL, 0) == 1)
    {
        DragQueryFile ((HDROP) medium.hGlobal, 0, pThis->m_szPath,
            sizeof (pThis->m_szPath));
        hr = NOERROR;
    }
    else
        hr = E_FAIL;

    ReleaseStgMedium (&medium);
    return hr;
}
```

11. **Implement the IContextMenu interface.** The three functions are described in the How It Works section.

```
///////////////////////////////////
// IContextMenu implementation

IMPLEMENT_IUNKNOWN(CRegisterMenu, ContextMenu)

STDMETHODIMP CRegisterMenu::XContextMenu::QueryContextMenu (HMENU hMenu, ⇒
UINT indexMenu,
    UINT idCmdFirst, UINT idCmdLast, UINT uFlags)
{
    METHOD_PROLOGUE(CRegisterMenu, ContextMenu);

    UINT idCmd = idCmdFirst;

    InsertMenu(hMenu, indexMenu++, MF_STRING | MF_BYPOSITION, idCmd++, ⇒
"&Register");
    InsertMenu(hMenu, indexMenu++, MF_STRING | MF_BYPOSITION, idCmd++, ⇒
"&Unregister");

    // return the number of menus added
    return MAKE_HRESULT(SEVERITY_SUCCESS, FACILITY_NULL, idCmd-idCmdFirst);
}

STDMETHODIMP CRegisterMenu::XContextMenu::InvokeCommand ⇒
(LPCMINVOKECOMMANDINFO lpcmi)
{
```

continued on next page

continued from previous page

```
        METHOD_PROLOGUE(CRegisterMenu, ContextMenu);

        // If the high-order word of lpcmi->lpVerb is not NULL, this
        // function was called by an application and lpVerb is a command
        // that should be activated. Otherwise, the shell has called this
        // function, and the low-order word of lpcmi->lpVerb is the
        // identifier of the menu item that the user selected.
        if (!HIWORD(lpcmi->lpVerb))
        {
            UINT idCmd = LOWORD(lpcmi->lpVerb);
            pThis->DoMenu(idCmd, lpcmi);
            return NOERROR;
        }

        return E_INVALIDARG;
}

STDMETHODIMP CRegisterMenu::XContextMenu::GetCommandString (UINT idCmd, ⇒
UINT uType,
        UINT* pwReserved, LPSTR pszName, UINT cchMax)
{
        METHOD_PROLOGUE(CRegisterMenu, ContextMenu);

        switch (idCmd)
        {
        case 0:
            lstrcpy(pszName, "Register inproc server or control");
            break;

        case 1:
            lstrcpy(pszName, "Unregister inproc server or control");
            break;

        default:
            return E_INVALIDARG;
        }

        return NOERROR;
}
```

12. **Add the DoMenu helper.** This method will be called when the Register or Unregister item is selected.

```
////////////////////////////
// Helper method

typedef HRESULT (*REGISTERFCN)(void);

void CRegisterMenu::DoMenu(UINT nCmd, LPCMINVOKECOMMANDINFO lpcmi)
{
        ASSERT(nCmd == 0 || nCmd == 1);     // only two menus should have been added

        CString msg;
        UINT nStringID;
```

9.4
EXTEND THE CONTEXT MENU FOR CERTAIN FILES

```
    HINSTANCE hLib = LoadLibrary(m_szPath);
    if (hLib == (HINSTANCE) NULL)
    {
        AfxFormatString1(msg, IDS_LOAD_FAILED, m_szPath);
        AfxMessageBox(msg, MB_OK | MB_ICONEXCLAMATION);
        return;
    }

    REGISTERFCN lpRegister;
    if (nCmd == 0)
        lpRegister = (REGISTERFCN) GetProcAddress(hLib, "DllRegisterServer");
    else
        lpRegister = (REGISTERFCN) GetProcAddress(hLib, "DllUnregisterServer");

    HRESULT hr;
    if (lpRegister != NULL)
        hr = (*lpRegister)();

    if (hr == S_OK)
        nStringID = (nCmd == 0) ? IDS_OK_REGISTER : IDS_OK_UNREGISTER;
    else
        nStringID = (nCmd == 0) ? IDS_ERROR_REGISTER : IDS_ERROR_UNREGISTER;

    AfxFormatString1(msg, nStringID, m_szPath);
    AfxMessageBox(msg, MB_OK | (hr == S_OK) ? MB_ICONINFORMATION
        : MB_ICONEXCLAMATION);

    FreeLibrary(hLib);
    return;
}
```

13. Add string resources. Switch to the ResourceView and insert a string table since the DLL won't have one. Add the following strings:

String ID	Caption
IDS_LOAD_FAILED	Unable to load %1.
IDS_OK_REGISTER	DllRegisterServer in %1 succeeded.
IDS_OK_UNREGISTER	DllUnregisterServer in %1 succeeded.
IDS_ERROR_REGISTER	DllRegisterServer in %1 failed.
IDS_ERROR_UNREGISTER	DllUnregisterServer in %1 failed.

14. Build the DLL. After you compile the project, click the Register Control item from the Tools menu. Now that RegServer has been properly registered, you can use the RegServer context menus to register other OLE Controls or inproc servers.

Let's see it work. Use the Explorer to display the Shell\Subfolder\Release directory. Right-click on the Subfolder.dll file and you should see a context menu similar to the one shown in Figure 9-14. Choose the Register option. If Subfolder.dll was registered properly, you'll see a dialog box that says DllRegisterServer succeeded.

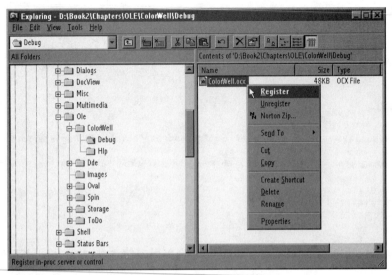

Figure 9-14 The RegServer context menu handler

Just to be sure, display the property page for some directory. You should now see an extra tab next to General called Subfolders. Next, to remove Subfolder.dll from the registry, bring up the context menu for the file and choose Unregister. Now you will only see the General tab.

How It Works

Before RegServer can register other controls, it must be registered itself. Just like all OLE controls and inproc servers, RegServer implements two special functions, *DllRegisterServer* and *DllUnregisterServer*. There is a detailed explanation of these two functions in the Subfolder How-To 9.2. For now, it is enough to say that after you choose Register Control from the Tools menu, RegServer adds a few entries to the registry.

The first entry creates an alias for files with the DLL or OCX extension. Since the shell ignores keys under a file extension in the registry, we have to associate our context menus with a file extension alias, in this case dllfile and ocxfile. Under each of these keys, we add the following:

HKEY_CLASSES_ROOT\dllfile\shellex\ContextMenuHandlers\RegServer.RegisterMenu = ⇒ {our CLSID}

When the user wants to display the context menu for a DLL, the shell locates its alias (dllfile) and sees if a context menu handler is registered. It then uses *CoCreateInstance* to get an interface pointer to *IContextMenu* for the CLSID.

IContextMenu

When the system is about to display the context menu for a file, it calls *QueryContextMenu* on its *IContextMenu* interface pointer. Our code used the *InsertMenu* SDK function to

9.4
EXTEND THE CONTEXT MENU FOR CERTAIN FILES

add two menu items directly into the context menu. The only trick to this implementation is remembering to return the number of menu items you just added (see step 11).

While the menu is displayed, the system shows help text in the Explorer status bar as the mouse travels over each item. *IContextMenu::GetCommandString* returns the status bar text for each menu item.

The system calls *InvokeCommand* when the user selects a context menu item. After assuring the Shell "invoked" us by examining the high-order word of one of the parameters for NULL, we simply pass the arguments on to a helper function called *DoMenu*.

DoMenu first attempts to load the DLL or OCX using the *LoadLibrary* SDK call. If it fails, a friendly message box warns the user and the function returns. Otherwise, it attempts to locate the address of either *DllRegisterServer* or *DllUnregisterServer*, depending on which menu item was chosen. *DoMenu* examines the return value after it executes one of these two functions (they have identical function signatures) and displays the appropriate message box. The Register Control item in the Tools menu calls RegSvr32.exe to do the same thing *DoMenu* does.

Comments

There's actually an easier way to register and unregister controls without writing a single line of code. First you need to copy RegSvr32.exe from the \msdev\bin directory to the Windows directory. Next, add the following items to the registry:

```
HKEY_CLASSES_ROOT\dllfile\shell\Register = "Register"
HKEY_CLASSES_ROOT\dllfile\shell\Unregister = "Unregister"
HKEY_CLASSES_ROOT\dllfile\shell\Register\command = "regsvr32.exe %1"
HKEY_CLASSES_ROOT\dllfile\shell\Unregister\command = "regsvr32.exe /u %1"
```

That's it! Of course, you can do more complicated things in a context menu handler.

One more thing: You can use RegServer to unregister itself. Just right-mouse click on RegServer.dll and choose Unregister. Ironic, isn't it?

APPENDIX

COMMON QUESTIONS, ANSWERS, AND TIPS

Many problems that you encounter in Visual C++ can easily be solved with just a few lines of code. This section contains answers to common questions about Visual C++ 4.0 and MFC. The questions range from beginning to advanced and will help you become more productive using Visual C++. Topics are divided into the following categories: Developer Studio, debugging, applications, views and frames, toolbars and status bars, dialogs, controls, graphics device interface (GDI), fonts and text, menus, and system.

Developer Studio

Q. *How can I quickly open a header file?*

While in the source code editor, press button 2 over the header file and select Open "header file" from the context menu. For ClassWizard generated code, you can also press CTRL+SHIFT+H or press the ".h" button on the editor window toolbar as shown in Figure A-1.

Q. *How do I assign shortcut keys?*

You can assign new shortcut keys, or modify current ones, in the Keyboard tab of the Customize dialog. To display this dialog, select the Customize... item from the Tools menu. The Editor section specifies the type of editor the shortcut keys will be assigned to. For example, Main means the shortcut is valid all the time, InfoViewer means it's only valid while you're in the InfoViewer, and so on. Figure A-2 shows the Customize dialog.

APPENDIX
COMMON QUESTIONS, ANSWERS, AND TIPS

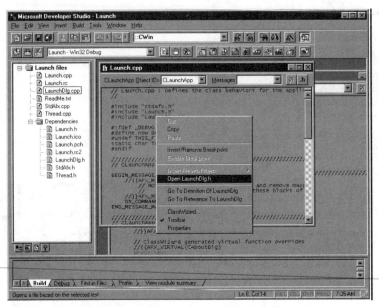

Figure A-1 Quickly opening source header file using context menu

Here are the shortcuts we find useful (note "." and "," are really for the < and > keys indicating direction).

Editor	Categories	Command	Shortcut
InfoViewer	Help	InfoViewerTopicNext	.
InfoViewer	Help	InfoViewerTopicPrev	,
Main	Help	InfoViewerSearch	CTRL+ALT+S
Main	Help	InfoViewerHistoryList	CTRL+ALT+H
Main	Help	InfoViewerResults	CTRL+ALT+R
Main	File	FileFindInFiles	CTRL+ALT+F

Q. How do I select a rectangular block of text?

Hold down the ALT key before and while you drag the mouse.

Q. How can I find matching parentheses and #if statements in my source code?

You can find matching parentheses, brackets, and angle brackets by adding a GoToMatchBrace shortcut. You can find matching #if statements by adding keyboard shortcuts to Edit ConditionalUp and ConditionalDown.

APPENDIX
DEVELOPER STUDIO

Figure A-2 Customizing Developer Studio's keyboard assignments

Q. Are there any recording and playback functions in the editor?

You can start recording by selecting Record Keystrokes from the Tools menu ([CTRL]+[Q]) and stop recording by selecting the Stop Recording from the Tools menu ([CTRL]+[Q]). Select Playback Recording from the Tools menu ([CTRL]+[SHIFT]+[Q]) to playback the recording.

Q. Is there a quick way to change the indention level of a block of code?

You can change the indention level of a block of code by highlighting the code and pressing the [TAB] key to indent and [SHIFT]+[TAB] to unindent.

Q. What is a good non-proportional font to use?

Lucida Console 8-point is a good font, and it was designed specifically for use on screens. It is still quite readable at the smaller size, and you get more information on the screen. You specify font information in the Format tab in the Options dialog. To display this dialog, select the Options... item under the Tools menu.

For more information about typefaces for the screen and Chuck Bigelow, the co-designer of Lucida Console, read the article by Daniel Will-Harris at http://www.will-harris.com/typoscrn.htm.

Q. How do I modify Developer Studio's toolbars?

You can rearrange toolbar buttons by pressing the [ALT] key and dragging the button to a new location. Furthermore, the Customize dialog allows you to select what toolbars are visible as well as rearrange and resize toolbar components such as buttons and drop-down combo boxes. You can display this

APPENDIX
COMMON QUESTIONS, ANSWERS, AND TIPS

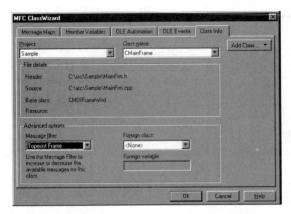

Figure A-3 Modifying the message filter for a class

dialog by selecting the Toolbars item from the View menu or by right-clicking on the toolbar. Press the New button to create a new toolbar with your own custom buttons.

Q. How do I display the current time in Developer Studio's status bar?

You can configure a lot of options for your Developer Studio environment by bringing up the Option dialog from the Tools menu. To display a clock, select the Workspace tab and set the Display clock on status bar check box.

Q. Why doesn't ClassWizard show all of the Windows messages for my class?

ClassWizard lists the most appropriate messages for your class depending on its primary Window type (dialog, top-most frame window, generic window, and so on). For example, Windows sends palette messages like WM_QUERYNEWPALETTE only to an application's topmost frame window. Therefore, ClassWizard doesn't show this message in the Message Maps for regular windows.

You can change the messages displayed by selecting a different message filter in the Class Info tab of ClassWizard. Available filters are categorized by the type of window or dialog box they pertain to. Figure A-3 shows the Class Info tab dialog.

Q. How do I add resource identifiers to my project?

Resource identifiers are stored in the file Resource.h. You can modify this file directly, but it is easier and safer to add new identifiers through the Resource Symbols dialog. Select the menu item Resource Symbols... from the View menu to display this dialog. Figure A-4 shows the Resource Symbols dialog.

APPENDIX
DEVELOPER STUDIO

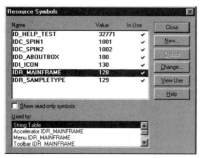

Figure A-4 Viewing the resource symbols for a project

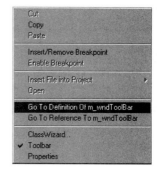

Figure A-5 Quickly jumping to symbol definitions via context menu

Q. *How do I undock dockable windows?*

You can either click on the window's border and drag it to a new location or just double click on the border. You can redock the window by dragging it to the docking site or double clicking the window's caption. Hold down the (CTRL) key while dragging to prevent the window from docking to a new site.

Q. *How do I jump to a symbols definition?*

You can press (F12) while the cursor is over the symbol, or you can click on the symbol with button 2 and select the Go To Definition <symbol> item from the context menu as shown in Figure A-5.

Q. *How do I resize a drop-down or drop-list combo box in the resource editor?*

You can resize the height of the combo box by clicking on the drop-down arrow portion of the combo box. Windows uses this height to resize the list box when the user presses the arrow button.

Q. *Can I add strings to a combo box when I am in the resource editor?*

As a matter of fact, you can! Bring up the properties dialog for the combo box and select the General tab as shown in Figure A-6. The ASCII codes for the strings are saved in the resource file and dynamically loaded into your combo box at run-time. If you want the strings to appear in the same order they were typed, make sure the Sort option is unchecked.

Q. *How do I insert an OLE custom control in my dialog?*

Press button 2 on the dialog and select Insert OLE Control... from the context menu. A dialog will appear showing you all the OLE controls that have been

APPENDIX
COMMON QUESTIONS, ANSWERS, AND TIPS

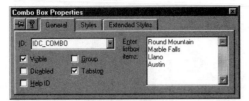

Figure A-6 Adding default entries to combo box

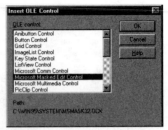

Figure A-7 Inserting an OLE control into dialog box

registered in your system. Select the desired control and press OK. The Insert OLE Control dialog is shown in Figure A-7.

Q. How do I unregister my OLE custom control?

You can run the utility REGSRV32.EXE with the /u (unregister) argument. To add this to your tools menu, select the Customize... item from the Tools menu and add the entries as shown in Figure A-8.

Debugging

Q. How can I quickly evaluate a variable?

You can highlight the variable and press [SHIFT]+[F9] to bring up the QuickWatch debug dialog. Or, you can simply rest the cursor over the variable and a Data Tip will display the value of the variable.

Figure A-8 Adding an unregister control command to the Tools menu

APPENDIX
DEBUGGING

Q. Is there a quick way to add variables to the Watch debug window?

You can add variables to the Watch and Memory debug windows by simply highlighting the variables and dragging them into the Watch window.

Q. Is there a way to automatically adjust the column width of the Watch debug window?

Since Watch and Variable windows use list view controls, you can automatically adjust the width of any column by double clicking the column divider bar. The column will be resized to the width of the widest item in that column.

Q. How do I display Unicode data types in the debug Watch window?

You can specify the "su" format for Unicode strings and the "mu" format for Unicode characters. Figure A-9 uses the "su" format to view the UNICODE string *szExeName*.

Q. How can I modify the instruction pointer when debugging?

Modifying the instruction pointer is a common and useful debugging technique. You can manually modify the instruction pointer in the Registers debug window by typing in the new address (usually retrieved from the Disassembly window). Or, you can simply select the next line you want to execute in your source code, click button 2 to display the debug context menu and select the Set Next Statement menu item. This technique is useful for skipping over code without recompiling the application.

Q. How can I view information about my executable?

You can use the utility dumpbin.exe to view information about executables, DLLs, libraries, and object files. You can view exported and import definitions, symbols, and even disassemble instructions. The dumpbin utility is located in the msdev\bin directory. You can run it from the command line, or you can add it to your Tools menu. Figure A-10 shows you how to add a new item to the Tools menu that displays a summary about your project file. Notice that the Redirect to Output Window option is selected.

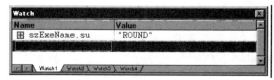

Figure A-9 Viewing Unicode strings in the debug window

APPENDIX
COMMON QUESTIONS, ANSWERS, AND TIPS

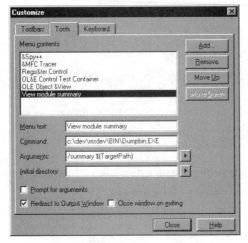

Figure A-10 Adding dumpbin utility to the Tools menu

Applications

Q. *How do I get my application's instance handle?*

Your application's instance handle is stored in *CWinAppIm_hInstance,* and you can call *AfxGetInstanceHandle* to retrieve its value.

```
// Get application's instance handle.
HANDLE hInstance = AfxGetInstanceHandle();
```

Q. *How do I get a pointer to my application's main window from anywhere in my code?*

A pointer to your main frame window is stored in *CWinThread:: m_pMainWnd,* and you can call *AfxGetMainWnd* to retrieve its value. The following example minimizes the application:

```
// Minimize application.
AfxGetMainWnd()->ShowWindow(SW_SHOWMINIMIZED);
```

Q. *How do I get an icon from another application at runtime?*

An icon is a resource in an application's executable or DLL. You can call the new SDK function *SHGetFileInfo* or the old *ExtractIcon* function to retrieve a handle to icon resources. You can use the *SHGetFileInfo* function to retrieve other information about a file such as small and large icons, file attributes, and

APPENDIX
APPLICATIONS

file type. The following example uses both functions to display notepad's icon in the upper-left corner of a view:

```
// Example using new SHGetFileInfo function.
void CSampleView::OnDraw(CDC* pDC)
{
    // Retrieve handle to icon.
    if (::SHGetFileInfo(_T("c:\\windows\\notepad.exe"),
            0, &stFileInfo, sizeof(stFileInfo), SHGFI_ICON))
    {
        // Draw icon.
        pDC->DrawIcon(10, 10, stFileInfo.hIcon);
    }
}


// Example using old ExtractIcon function.
void CSampleView::OnDraw(CDC* pDC)
{
    // Retrieve handle to icon.
    HICON hIcon = ::ExtractIcon(
            AfxGetInstanceHandle(), _T("notepad.exe"), 0);

    // Draw icon.
    if (hIcon && hIcon!=(HICON)-1)
        pDC->DrawIcon(10, 10, hIcon);
}
```

Q. How do I programmatically terminate my application?

The cleanest way to terminate your application is to post a WM_CLOSE message to your main window. Your *CWnd::OnClose* member function will be called, which allows you to prompt the user to save any modified data. Furthermore, you can tell a window to close (instead of asking) by posting a WM_DESTROY message to the window. The following example shows you how to terminate your own application and demonstrates a generic TerminateWindow function:

```
// Terminate our application.
AfxGetMainWnd()->PostMessage(WM_CLOSE);


// Generic function to terminate other windows.
void TerminateWindow(LPCTSTR pCaption)
{
    // Find window with matching caption.
    CWnd* pWnd = CWnd::FindWindow(NULL, pCaption);

    // If found window, ask it to close.
    if (pWnd)
        pWnd->PostMessage(WM_CLOSE);
}
```

APPENDIX
COMMON QUESTIONS, ANSWERS, AND TIPS

Q. *How do I launch another application?*

Call the SDK function *WinExec*, *ShellExecute*, or *CreateProcess*. The *WinExec* function is the easiest to use and takes two arguments: the program command line and the show state. The *ShellExecute* function is more flexible and allows you to open a file using Windows associations as well as specify a working directory. The *CreateProcess* function is the recommended technique for launching applications, and it is the most complicated. You can specify process and thread security attributes, inheritance information, and priority class information. The following example demonstrates how to launch an application using all three functions:

```
// Launch the calculator application.
::WinExec(_T("calc.exe"), SW_SHOW);


// Open file.txt with its associated application. Launch the application
// minimized and set the working directory to c:\data.
::ShellExecute(NULL, NULL, _T("file.txt"),
    NULL, _T("c:\\data"), SW_SHOWMINIMIZED);


// Launch Media Player using CreateProcess.
// Allocate and initialize startup and process structures.
STARTUPINFO infoStart;
PROCESS_INFORMATION infoProcess;

memset(&infoStart, 0, sizeof(infoStart));
infoStart.cb = sizeof(STARTUPINFO);

// Create the new process with default values.
CreateProcess(NULL, _T("mplayer.exe"), NULL, NULL, FALSE,
    NORMAL_PRIORITY_CLASS, NULL, NULL, &infoStart, &infoProcess);
```

Q. *How do I determine what directory my application was launched from?*

Call the SDK function *GetModuleFileName* to retrieve your application's full path and then strip off the executable's name component. The following example is a function you can call to determine what directory your application was launched from. Note that the framework calls *GetModuleFileName* during initialization and stores the path to your help file in *CWinApp::m_pszHelpFilePath*. If you don't specify a new path for your help file, you can use *m_pszHelpFilePath* instead of calling *GetModuleFileName*.

```
void GetLaunchedDir(CString& strLaunched)
{
    TCHAR szFullPath[MAX_PATH];
    TCHAR szDir[_MAX_DIR];
    TCHAR szDrive[_MAX_DRIVE];
```

APPENDIX
APPLICATIONS

```
    // Get application's full path.
    ::GetModuleFileName(NULL, szFullPath, MAX_PATH);

    // Break full path into separate components.
    _splitpath(szFullPath, szDrive, szDir, NULL, NULL);

    // Store application's drive and path.
    strLaunched.Format(_T("%s%s"), szDrive, szDir);
}
```

Notice that this function returns a long path name. Some functions in the framework, such as *AfxOleRegisterControlClass* and *CDocManager::RegisterShellFileTypes*, use a semi-documented function called *AfxGetModuleShortFileName* instead of *GetModuleFileName*. This function returns a module's short path name instead of a long path and is declared in AFXPRIV.H and implemented in FILECORE.CPP. The following is the implementation of this function (with the MAC defines removed):

```
void AFXAPI AfxGetModuleShortFileName(HINSTANCE hInst, CString& ⇒
strShortName)
{
    TCHAR szLongPathName[_MAX_PATH];
    ::GetModuleFileName(hInst, szLongPathName, _MAX_PATH);
    ::GetShortPathName(szLongPathName,
        strShortName.GetBuffer(_MAX_PATH), _MAX_PATH);
    strShortName.ReleaseBuffer();
}
```

Q. *How do I determine the current working directory of my application?*

Call the SDK function *GetCurrentDirectory* to get the path of the current working directory. The following example creates a function that returns the current working directory in a *CString* object:

```
CString GetCurrentWorkingDir()
{
    CString strDir;
    ::GetCurrentDirectory(MAX_PATH, strDir.GetBuffer (MAX_PATH));
    strDir.ReleaseBuffer();
    return strDir;
}
```

Q. *How do I handle my own user-defined messages?*

Since Windows is an event-driven environment, you often need to add you own user-defined messages. ClassWizard does not allow you to add user-defined messages, so you must enter them manually. But once they're entered, you can use ClassWizard to browse them like any other message. The following steps demonstrate how to add a user defined message:

APPENDIX
COMMON QUESTIONS, ANSWERS, AND TIPS

First, define your message. Microsoft recommends you add at least 100 to WM_USER for user defined messages when developing Windows 95 applications, since a lot of the new controls also use WM_USER messages.

```
#define WM_MY_MESSAGE   (WM_USER + 100)
```

Next, implement the handler for this function. The function takes a WPARAM and LPARAM argument and returns a LRESULT.

```
LRESULT CMainFrame::OnMyMessage(WPARAM wParam, LPARAM lParam)
{
        // TODO: handle user defined message

        return 0;
}
```

Now, you need to declare your message handler function in the AFX_MSG block in your class header file.

```
class CMainFrame : public CMDIFrameWnd
{
        ...

// Generated message map functions
protected:
        //{{AFX_MSG(CMainFrame)
        afx_msg int OnCreate(LPCREATESTRUCT lpCreateStruct);
        afx_msg void OnTimer(UINT nIDEvent);
        afx_msg LRESULT OnMyMessage(WPARAM wParam, LPARAM lParam);
        //}}AFX_MSG
        DECLARE_MESSAGE_MAP()
};
```

Finally, you need to map your message to your message handler function by using the ON_MESSAGE macro in the message map block of your class.

```
BEGIN_MESSAGE_MAP(CMainFrame, CMDIFrameWnd)
        //{{AFX_MSG_MAP(CMainFrame)
        ON_WM_CREATE()
        ON_WM_TIMER()
        ON_MESSAGE(WM_MY_MESSAGE, OnMyMessage)
        //}}AFX_MSG_MAP
END_MESSAGE_MAP()
```

If you need a message that is guaranteed to be unique throughout the entire system, you can call the SDK function *RegisterWindowMessage* and use the ON_REGISTERED_MESSAGE macro instead of the ON_MESSAGE macro. The rest of the steps are the same as adding a user-defined message.

APPENDIX
VIEWS AND FRAMES

Figure A-11 Modifying the default windows styles created by AppWizard

Views and Frames

Q. How do I change the icon for my window?

You need to send the new WM_SETICON message to your window. The following example sets the icon for the application's main window:

```
// Load icon resource.
HICON hIcon = AfxGetApp()->LoadIcon(IDI_ICON);
ASSERT(hIcon);

// Specify new icon for window.
AfxGetMainWnd()->SendMessage(WM_SETICON, TRUE, (LPARAM)hIcon);
```

Q. How do I change the default style of a window created by AppWizard?

Step 4 of AppWizard has an Advanced button that allows you to specify attributes about SDI and MDI frame windows. Figure A-11 shows the Window Styles portion of the Advanced Options dialog:

As you can see, this does not allow you to modify everything about a window. You can override *CWnd::PreCreateWindow* and modify the CREATESTRUCT structure to specify different window styles, as well as other creation information. The following example removes the maximize button from the window and sets its initial position and size

```
BOOL CMainFrame::PreCreateWindow(CREATESTRUCT& cs)
{
    // Remove the maximize button style from the window.
    cs.style &= ~WS_MAXIMIZEBOX;
```

continued on next page

615

continued from previous page

```
    // Set the position of the window to the upper-left corner.
    cs.x = cs.y = 0;

    // Set the width and height of the window.
    cs.cx = GetSystemMetrics(SM_CXSCREEN);
    cs.cy = GetSystemMetrics(SM_CYSCREEN) / 2;

    return CMDIFrameWnd::PreCreateWindow(cs);
}
```

Q. How do I center a window?

You can call *CWnd::CenterWindow* to center a window. Don't pass any arguments to center the window relative to its parent; otherwise, you'll have to pass a *CWnd** as the first argument. This function has always been part of MFC, but has only been documented since MFC 3.0.

```
// Center window relative to its parent.
CenterWindow();

// Center window relative to the screen.
CenterWindow(CWnd::GetDesktopWindow());

// Center the application's main window.
AfxGetMainWnd()->CenterWindow();
```

Q. How do I create an application that is initially minimized or maximized?

If you are creating a new application, you can select the Advanced button in step 4 of AppWizard and check either the minimized or maximized check box in the main frame styles group. Otherwise set *CWinApp::m_nCmdShow* to either SW_SHOWMINIMIZED or SW_SHOWMAXIMIZED in your application's *InitInstance* function. Note that you can minimize or maximize a window anywhere in your code by calling *CWnd::ShowWindow*.

```
BOOL CSampleApp::InitInstance()
{
    ...

    m_nCmdShow = SW_SHOWMINIMIZED;

    // Initially minimize application.
    pMainFrame->ShowWindow(m_nCmdShow);

    ...
}
```

APPENDIX
VIEWS AND FRAMES

Q. How do I create MDI child frames that are initially minimized or maximized?

If you are creating a new application, you can select the Advanced button in step 4 of AppWizard and check either the minimized or maximize check box in the MDI child frame styles group. If you have an existing application, override the *PreCreateWindow* function of your MDI child frame class and set the WS_MAXIMIZE or WS_MINIMIZE style bits.

```
BOOL CChildFrame::PreCreateWindow(CREATESTRUCT& cs)
{
    // Cause MDI child frame to be displayed as an icon.
    cs.style |= WS_MINIMIZE;
    return CMDIChildWnd::PreCreateWindow(cs);
}
```

If you did not derive a class from *CMDIChildWnd*, you can specify how the MDI child frame should be displayed by calling *CWnd::ShowWindow* in your view's *OnInitialUpdate* function. Pass SW_SHOWMAXIMIZED to maximize the window and SW_SHOWMINIMIZED to minimize the window.

```
void CSampleView::OnInitialUpdate()
{
    // Maximize the MDI child frame.
    GetParentFrame()->ShowWindow(SW_SHOWMAXIMIZED);
    CView::OnInitialUpdate();
}
```

Q. How do I force my application to stay minimized?

Windows sends a WM_QUERYOPEN message to your application when it should be restored to its original size. Use ClassWizard to handle this message and return FALSE to prevent your application from being restored.

```
BOOL CMainFrame::OnQueryOpen()
{
    // No, I want to stay minimized!
    return FALSE;
}
```

Q. How do I limit the resizing of my window to a particular size?

Windows sends a WM_GETMAXMININFO message to determine the position, size, and tracking size of a window. Use ClassWizard to handle this message to limit the tracking size of your window. The following example limits the tracking size to one quarter of the screen:

```
void CMainFrame::OnGetMinMaxInfo(MINMAXINFO FAR* lpMMI)
{
    lpMMI->ptMaxTrackSize.x = GetSystemMetrics(SM_CXSCREEN) / 2;
    lpMMI->ptMaxTrackSize.y = GetSystemMetrics(SM_CYSCREEN) / 2;
    CMDIFrameWnd::OnGetMinMaxInfo(lpMMI);
}
```

APPENDIX
COMMON QUESTIONS, ANSWERS, AND TIPS

Q. *How do I make a window invisible?*

You can make a window invisible by calling *CWnd::ShowWindow* with SW_HIDE as the show state. To determine if a window is visible, you can call *CWnd::IsWindowVisible*. The following example creates a function that toggles the visible state of a window by calling *CWnd::FindWindow* to locate the window and *ShowWindow* to hide or show the window.

```
void ToggleWindow(LPCTSTR pCaption)
{
    // Find window with matching caption.
    CWnd* pWnd = CWnd::FindWindow(NULL, pCaption);

    // If found window, toggle its visible state.
    if (pWnd)
        pWnd->ShowWindow(pWnd->IsWindowVisible() ? SW_HIDE : SW_SHOW);
}
```

Q. *How do I make my window stay on top of other windows?*

Windows 3.1 introduced the concept of a topmost window. A topmost window stays on top of all other non-topmost windows even when it is not the active window. Specify the WS_EX_TOPMOST extended window style when you create the window to make it a topmost window. The topmost style can be added and removed at runtime by calling *CWnd::SetWindowPos*. To determine if the topmost style is set, call *CWnd::GetExStyle*. The following example creates a function that toggles the topmost style of a specified window:

```
void ToggleTopMost(CWnd* pWnd)
{
    ASSERT_VALID(pWnd);
    pWnd->SetWindowPos((pWnd->GetExStyle() & WS_EX_TOPMOST) ?
        &wndNoTopMost : &wndTopMost, 0, 0, 0, 0,
        SSP_NOSIZE | WSP_NOMOVE);
}
```

Q. *How do I create a CEditView that supports word wrap?*

You need to turn off the ES_AUTOHSCROLL and WS_HSCROLL style bits of your *CEditView* object by overriding *CWnd::PreCreateWindow* and modifying the CREATESTRUCT structure. Since *CEditView::PreCreateWindow* explicitly sets *cs.style*, make sure you modify *cs.style* after you call the base class function.

```
BOOL CSampleEditView::PreCreateWindow(CREATESTRUCT& cs)
{
    // First call base class function.
    BOOL bResult = CEditView::PreCreateWindow(cs);

    // Now specify the new window style.
    cs.style &= ~(ES_AUTOHSCROLL | WS_HSCROLL);
    return bResult;
}
```

APPENDIX
VIEWS AND FRAMES

Q. Are there any views based on common controls?

MFC provides several view classes derived from *CView* that encapsulate the functionality of common control but still work with the frameworks document view architecture. The *CEditView* encapsulates the edit control, *CTreeView* holds the tree list control, *CListView* encapsulates the list view control, and *CRichEditView* handles the rich edit control.

Q. How do I move a window to a new position?

Call *CWnd::SetWindowPos* and specify the SWP_NOSIZE flag. The new position is relative to the window's parent (top-level windows are relative to the screen). You can call *CWnd::MoveWindow*, but you must also specify the size of the window.

```
// Move window to position 100, 100 of its parent window.
SetWindowPos(NULL, 100, 100, 0, 0, SWP_NOSIZE | SWP_NOZORDER);
```

Q. How do I resize a window?

Call *CWnd::SetWindowPos* and specify the SWP_NOMOVE flag. You can call *CWnd::MoveWindow*, but you must also specify the position of the window.

```
// Get the size of the window.
CRect rcWindow;
GetWindowRect(rcWindow);

// Make the window twice as wide and twice as tall.
SetWindowPos(NULL, 0, 0, rcWindow.Width()*2, rcWindow.Height()*2,
    SWP_NOMOVE | SWP_NOZORDER);
```

Q. How do I let the user move my window by clicking anywhere on the window—not just the caption bar?

Windows sends a WM_NCHITTEST message to a window when it needs to determine the location of the mouse relative to the window. You can handle this message and fool Windows into thinking the mouse is actually over your window's caption when it really isn't. For dialog boxes and dialog-based applications, use ClassWizard to handle the WM_NCHITTEST message and call the base class function. If the function indicates that the mouse is over the client area by returning HTCLIENT, return a value of HTCAPTION to make Windows think the mouse is over the caption.

```
UINT CSampleDialog::OnNcHitTest(CPoint point)
{
    UINT nHitTest = CDialog::OnNcHitTest(point);
    return (nHitTest == HTCLIENT) ? HTCAPTION : nHitTest;
}
```

This technique has two disadvantages: The window will be maximized when someone double-clicks in its client area, and it does not work with frame

APPENDIX
COMMON QUESTIONS, ANSWERS, AND TIPS

windows that contain views. An alternate technique detects when the user presses the left-mouse button and fools the frame window into thinking someone clicked its caption bar. Use ClassWizard to handle the WM_LBUTTONDOWN message in your view and post a WM_NCLBUTTONDOWN message with a hit test of HTCAPTION to its frame window.

```
void CSampleView::OnLButtonDown(UINT nFlags, CPoint point)
{
    CView::OnLButtonDown(nFlags, point);

    // Fool frame window into thinking someone clicked on its caption bar.
    GetParentFrame()->PostMessage(
        WM_NCLBUTTONDOWN, HTCAPTION, MAKELPARAM(point.x, point.y));
}
```

You can also use this technique for dialog boxes and dialog-based applications. The call to *CWnd::GetParentFrame* is not necessary though.

```
void CSampleDialog::OnLButtonDown(UINT nFlags, CPoint point)
{
    CDialog::OnLButtonDown(nFlags, point);

    // Fool dialog into thinking someone clicked on its caption bar.
    PostMessage(WM_NCLBUTTONDOWN, HTCAPTION, MAKELPARAM(point.x, point.y));
}
```

Q. *How do I change the background color of my view?*

Windows sends a WM_ERASEBKGND message to a window to tell it that its background needs to be erased. Use ClassWizard to override the default processing of this message, erase (actually paint) the background yourself, and return TRUE to prevent Windows from erasing the window.

```
// Paint area that needs to be erased.
BOOL CSampleView::OnEraseBkgnd (CDC* pDC)
{
    // Create a purple brush.
    CBrush brush(RGB(128,0,128));

    // Select the brush into the device context.
    CBrush* pOldBrush = pDC->SelectObject(&brush);

    // Get the area that needs to be erased.
    CRect rcClip;
    pDC->GetClipBox(&rcClip);

    // Paint the area.
    pDC->PatBlt(rcClip.left, rcClip.top,
        rcClip.Width(), rcClip.Height(), PATCOPY);

    // Unselect brush out of device context.
    pDC->SelectObject(pOldBrush);

    // Return nonzero to halt further processing.
    return TRUE;
}
```

APPENDIX
VIEWS AND FRAMES

Q. *How do I change the title of my window?*

You can change the title of any window (including controls) by calling *CWnd::SetWindowText*.

```
// Set title for application's main frame window.
AfxGetMainWnd()->SetWindowText(_T("Application title"));

// Set title for View's MDI child frame window.
GetParentFrame()->SetWindowText("_T("MDI Child Frame new title"));

// Set title for dialog's push button control.
GetDlgItem(IDC_BUTTON)->SetWindowText(_T("Button new title"));
```

If you are constantly updating a window's title (remember controls are window also), you should consider using the semi-documented *AfxSetWindowText* function. This function is declared in AFXPRIV.H and implemented in WINUTIL.CPP. You won't find it in the on-line help, but it is semi-documented in AFXPRIV.H and will probably be officially documented in a future release of MFC. The following is the implementation of *AfxSetWindowText*:

```
void AFXAPI AfxSetWindowText(HWND hWndCtrl, LPCTSTR lpszNew)
{
    int nNewLen = lstrlen(lpszNew);
    TCHAR szOld[256];
    // fast check to see if text really changes (reduces flash in controls)
    if (nNewLen > _countof(szOld) ||
        ::GetWindowText(hWndCtrl, szOld, _countof(szOld)) != nNewLen ||
        lstrcmp(szOld, lpszNew) != 0)
    {
        // change it
        ::SetWindowText(hWndCtrl, lpszNew);
    }
}
```

Q. *How do I prevent the main frame window from displaying the name of the active document in its caption?*

Main frame windows and MDI child frame windows are normally created with the FWS_ADDTOTITLE style bit set. You need to disable this style bit if you don't want the document name to be automatically appended to the caption. Use ClassWizard to override *CWnd::PreCreateWindow* and turn off the FWS_ADDTOTITLE style.

```
BOOL CMainFrame::PreCreateWindow(CREATESTRUCT& cs)
{
    // Turn off FWS_ADDTOTITLE in main frame.
    cs.style &= ~FWS_ADDTOTITLE;
    return CMDIFrameWnd::PreCreateWindow(cs);
}
```

Turning off FWS_ADDTOTITLE for an MDI child window will create a window with an empty title. You can set the title by calling

APPENDIX
COMMON QUESTIONS, ANSWERS, AND TIPS

CWnd::SetWindowText—remember to follow the user interface style guidelines when you set the title yourself.

Q. How can I retrieve information about the current message a window is processing?

You can call *CWnd::GetCurrentMessage* to retrieve a MSG pointer. For example, you could use ClassWizard to map several menu item handlers to one common function and then call *GetCurrentMessage* to determine what menu item was selected.

```
void CMainFrame::OnCommonMenuHandler()
{
    // Display selected menu item in debug window.
    TRACE("Menu item %u was selected.\n", GetCurrentMessage()->wParam);
}
```

Q. How do I create an irregularly shaped window?

You can use the new SDK function *SetWindowRgn*. This function limits the drawing and mouse messages to a specified region within a window—truly making the window any irregular shape you specify. Figure A-12 demonstrates how to create an application that uses an ellipse for its main window. The spheres you see in the following figure are actual windows.

Use AppWizard to create a Dialog-based application and use the resource editor to remove all the default controls, captions, and borders, from the main dialog resource as shown in Figure A-13.

Figure A-12 Example of irregular-shaped windows

APPENDIX
VIEWS AND FRAMES

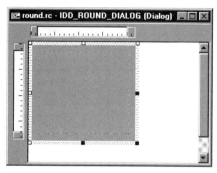

Figure A-13 Dialog resource specifies the size of the window

Add a *CRgn* data member to the dialog class. This data member will be used later to create the region for the window.

```
class CRoundDlg : public CDialog
{
    ...
private:
    CRgn m_rgn;   // window region

    ...
};
```

Modify the *OnInitDialog* function to create an ellipse region and assign that region to the window by calling *SetWindowRgn*.

```
BOOL CRoundDlg::OnInitDialog()
{
    CDialog::OnInitDialog();

    // Get size of dialog.
    CRect rcDialog;
    GetClientRect(rcDialog);

    // Create region and assign to window.
    m_rgn.CreateEllipticRgn(0, 0, rcDialog.Width(), rcDialog.Height());
    SetWindowRgn(GetSafeHwnd(), (HRGN)m_rgn, TRUE);

    return TRUE;
}
```

That's it—just by creating a region and calling *SetWindowRgn* you now have an irregularly shaped window! However, I went ahead and modified the *OnPaint* function like the following to make the window look like a sphere:

```
void CRoundDlg::OnPaint()
{
    CPaintDC dc(this);   // device context for painting
```

continued on next page

APPENDIX
COMMON QUESTIONS, ANSWERS, AND TIPS

continued from previous page

```
    // draw ellipse with out any border
    dc.SelectStockObject(NULL_PEN);

    // get the RGB color components of the sphere color
    COLORREF color = RGB(0,0,255);
    BYTE byRed = GetRValue(color);
    BYTE byGreen = GetGValue(color);
    BYTE byBlue = GetBValue(color);

    // get the size of the view window
    CRect rect;
    GetClientRect(rect);

    // get minimum number of units
    int nUnits = min(rect.right, rect.bottom);

    // calculate the horizontal and vertical step size
    float fltStepHorz = (float)rect.right / nUnits;
    float fltStepVert = (float)rect.bottom / nUnits;

    int nEllipse = nUnits / 3;   // calculate how many to draw
    int nIndex;                  // current ellipse that is being drawn

    CBrush  brush;       // brush used for ellipse fill color
    CBrush* pBrushOld;   // previous brush that was selected into dc

    // draw ellipse, gradually moving towards upper-right corner
    for (nIndex=0; nIndex <= nEllipse; nIndex++)
    {
        // create solid brush
        brush.CreateSolidBrush(RGB(((nIndex*byRed)/nEllipse),
            ((nIndex*byGreen)/nEllipse), ((nIndex*byBlue)/nEllipse)));

        // select brush into dc
        pBrushOld = dc.SelectObject(&brush);

        // draw ellipse
        dc.Ellipse((int)fltStepHorz*nIndex*2, (int)fltStepVert*nIndex,
            rect.right-((int)fltStepHorz*nIndex)+1,
            rect.bottom-((int)fltStepVert*(nIndex*2))+1);

        // deselect brush form dc so we can delete the brush
        dc.SelectObject(pBrushOld);

        // delete the brush
        brush.DeleteObject();
    }
}
```

Finally, I also handled the WM_NCHITTEST message so the window could be moved when clicked anywhere on the window.

```
UINT CRoundDlg::OnNcHitTest(CPoint point)
{
    // Let user move window by clicking anywhere on the window.
    UINT nHitTest = CDialog::OnNcHitTest(point);
    return (nHitTest == HTCLIENT) ? HTCAPTION : nHitTest;
}
```

APPENDIX
TOOLBARS AND STATUS BARS

Toolbars and Status Bars

Q. *How can I get a pointer to the status bar and toolbar from anywhere in my code?*

By default, the framework creates the status bar and toolbar as children of the main frame window. The status bar has an identifier of AFX_IDW_STATUS_BAR, and the toolbar has an identifier of AFX_IDW_TOOLBAR. The following example shows you how to get a pointer to these child windows by calling *CWnd::GetDescendantWindow* along with *AfxGetMainWnd*:

```
// Get pointer to status bar.
CStatusBar* pStatusBar =
    (CStatusBar*)AfxGetMainWnd()->GetDescendantWindow(AFX_IDW_STATUS_BAR);

// Get pointer to toolbar.
CToolBar* pToolBar =
    (CToolBar*)AfxGetMainWnd()->GetDescendantWindow(AFX_IDW_TOOLBAR);
```

Q. *How can I disable and enable ToolTips for a toolbar?*

The toolbar will display ToolTips if the CBRS_TOOLTIPS style bit is set. To enable and disable ToolTips, you need to set and clear this style bit. The following example creates a member function that does this by calling *CControlBar::GetBarStyle* and *CControlBar::SetBarStyle*:

```
void CMainFrame::EnableToolTips(BOOL bDisplayTips)
{
    ASSERT_VALID(m_wndToolBar);

    DWORD dwStyle = m_wndToolBar.GetBarStyle();

    if (bDisplayTips)
        dwStyle |= CBRS_TOOLTIPS;
    else
        dwStyle &= ~CBRS_TOOLTIPS;

    m_wndToolBar.SetBarStyle(dwStyle);
}
```

Q. *How can I set the caption of a toolbar?*

A toolbar is just a window, so you can call *CWnd::SetWindowText* to set its caption. It is a good idea to set the caption of dockable toolbars as demonstrated in the following example:

```
int CMainFrame::OnCreate(LPCREATESTRUCT lpCreateStruct)
{
    ...
```

continued on next page

continued from previous page

```
        // Set the caption of the toolbar.
        m_wndToolBar.SetWindowText(_T"Standard");

        ...
}
```

Dialogs

Q. *How do I create and use modeless dialog box?*

MFC encapsulates modal and modeless dialogs in the same class, but using a modeless dialog requires a few extra steps.

First, create your dialog resource using the resource editor and use ClassWizard to create a new class derived from *CDialog*. Modal and modeless dialogs are terminated differently: Modal dialogs are terminated by calling *CDialog::EndDialog*, whereas modeless dialogs are terminated by calling *CWnd::DestroyWindow*. The functions *CDialog::OnOK* and *CDialog::OnCancel* call *EndDialog*, so you need to call *DestroyWindow* and override these functions for modeless dialogs.

```
void CSampleDialog::OnOK()
{
        // Retrieve and validate dialog data.
        if (!UpdateData(TRUE))
        {
                // the UpdateData routine will set focus to correct item
                TRACE0("UpdateData failed during dialog termination.\n");
                return;
        }

        // Call DestroyWindow instead of EndDialog.
        DestroyWindow();
}


void CSampleDialog::OnCancel()
{
        // Call DestroyWindow instead of EndDialog.
        DestroyWindow();
}
```

Next, you need to delete the C++ object that represents the dialog correctly. This is easy to do with modal dialogs, since you just delete the C++ object after the creation function returns. Modeless dialogs are not synchronous though; the creation function return immediately, and you don't know when to delete the C++ object. The framework calls *CWnd::PostNcDestroy* when a window has been destroyed. You can override this function and perform cleanup operations—such as deleting the *this* pointer.

APPENDIX
DIALOGS

```
void CSampleDialog::PostNcDestroy()
{
    // Delete the C++ object that represents this dialog.
    delete this;
}
```

Finally, the only thing left to do is to create the modeless dialog. You call *CDialog::DoModal* to create a modal dialog, but you call *CDialog::Create* to create a modeless dialog. The following example shows an application creating a modeless dialog:

```
Void CMainFrame::OnSampleDialog()
{
    // Allocate a modeless dialog object.
    CSampleDialog* pDialog = new CSampleDialog;
    ASSERT_VALID(pDialog);

    // Create the modeless dialog.
    BOOL bResult = pDialog->Create(IDD_DIALOG);
    ASSERT(bResult);
}
```

Q. How do I display a bitmap in my dialog?

Thanks to the new Win32 advanced static controls and Microsoft's resource editor, it is very easy to display bitmaps in your dialog. Just drag the picture control to your dialog and select the appropriate properties. You can easily display icons, bitmaps, and enhanced metafiles. Figure A-14 shows the picture control properties dialog:

Q. How do I change the background color of a dialog or form view?

To change the background color for all your application's dialogs you can call *CWinApp::SetDialogBkColor*. The first argument specifies the background

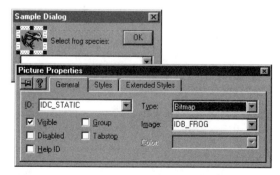

Figure A-14 Using static control to display bitmap images

color, and the second argument specifies the text color. The following example sets all the application's dialogs to display a blue background and yellow text.

```
BOOL CSampleApp::InitInstance()
{
    ...
    // Use blue dialogs with yellow text.
    SetDialogBkColor(RGB(0,0,255), RGB(255,255,0));
    ...
}
```

Windows sends the WM_CTLCOLOR message to a dialog whenever the dialog (or one of its child controls) needs to be drawn. Usually, you let Windows decide what brush to use when it paints your background, but you can override this message and specify your own brush. The following example demonstrates the steps to create a dialog with a red background.

First, add a CBrush member variable to your dialog based class:

```
class CMyFormView : public CFormView
{
    ...
    private:
        CBrush m_brush;   // background brush
    ...
};
```

Next, initialize the brush to the desired background color in your class constructor.

```
CMyFormView::CMyFormView()
{
    // Initialize background brush.
    m_brush.CreateSolidBrush(RGB(0,0,255));
}
```

Finally, use ClassWizard to handle the WM_CTLCOLOR message and return a handle to the brush you want to use to draw the background of your dialog. Notice that you have to check the *nCtlColor* argument, since this function is also called when dialog controls need to be drawn.

```
HBRUSH CMyFormView::OnCtlColor(CDC* pDC, CWnd* pWnd, UINT nCtlColor)
{
    // Determine if drawing a dialog box. If we are, return handle to
    // our own background brush. Otherwise let Windows handle it.
    if (nCtlColor == CTLCOLOR_DLG)
        return (HBRUSH) m_brush.GetSafeHandle();

    return CFormView::OnCtlColor(pDC, pWnd, nCtlColor);
}
```

APPENDIX
CONTROLS

Q. How do I get a pointer to a dialog control?

You have two options. You can call *CWnd::GetDlgItem* with a control's identifier and get a *CWnd** pointer to it that must be cast in order to invoke member functions. For instance, the following example calls *GetDlgItem,* but it must cast the return value to a *CSpinButtonCtrl** so it can invoke the *CSpinButtonCtrl::SetPos* function.

```
BOOL CSampleDialog::OnInitDialog()
{
    CDialog::OnInitDialog();

    // Get pointer to spin button.
    CSpinButtonCtrl* pSpin = (CSpinButtonCtrl*)GetDlgItem(IDC_SPIN);
    ASSERT_VALID(pSpin);

    // Set spin button's default position.
    pSpin->SetPos(10);

    return TRUE;
}
```

As an alternative, you can use ClassWizard to associate controls to member variables. Simply select the Member Variables tab in ClassWizard and select the Add Variable... button. If you are in the dialog resource editor, you can double-click the control while pressing the [CTRL] key to bring up the Add Member Variable dialog.

Controls

Q. How do I enable and disable controls?

Controls are windows, so you can call *CWnd::EnableWindow* to enable and disable controls.

```
// Disable button controls.
m_wndOK.EnableWindow(FALSE);
m_wndApply.EnableWindow(FALSE);
```

Q. How do I change a control's font?

Since controls are windows, you can use call *CWnd::SetFont* to specify a new font. This function takes a *CFont* pointer as its only argument. Make sure that the font object is not destroyed before the control is destroyed (allocating a *CFont* object on the stack will not work). The following example changes the font of a push button to an 8-point Arial font:

```
// Declare font object in class declaration (.H file).
private:
    CFont m_font;
```

continued on next page

APPENDIX
COMMON QUESTIONS, ANSWERS, AND TIPS

```
// Set font in class implementation (.CPP file). Note m_wndButton is a
// member variable added by ClassWizard. DDX routines hook the member
// variable to a dialog button control.

BOOL CSampleDialog::OnInitDialog()
{
    ...

    // Create an 8-point Arial font.
    m_font.CreateFont(MulDiv(8, -pDC->GetDeviceCaps(LOGPIXELSY), 72),
        0, 0, 0, FW_NORMAL, 0, 0, 0, ANSI_CHARSET, OUT_STROKE_PRECIS,
        CLIP_STROKE_PRECIS, DRAFT_QUALITY,
        VARIABLE_PITCH | FF_SWISS, _T("Arial"));

    // Set font for push button.
    m_wndButton.SetFont(&m_font);

    ...
}
```

Q. How do I use OLE_COLOR data types in my OLE control?

Functions like *COleControl::GetForeColor* and *COleControl::GetBackColor* return colors as a OLE_COLOR data type, but GDI objects such as pens and brushes require the COLORREF data type. You can easily convert an OLE_COLOR type to a COLORREF type by calling *COleControl::TranslateColor*. The following example creates a brush of the current background color:

```
void CSampleControl::OnDraw(CDC* pdc,
    const CRect& rcBounds, const CRect& rcInvalid)
{
    // Create a brush of the current background color.
    CBrush brushBack(TranslateColor(GetBackColor()));

    // Paint the background using the current background color.
    pdc->FillRect(rcBounds, &brushBack);

    // Other drawing commands.
    ...
}
```

Q. How can I display a list of files without using the common file open dialog?

Windows will automatically fill in a list box or combo box with available drives or files in a specified directory by calling *CWnd::DlgDirList* or *CWnd::DlgDirListComboBox*. The following example fills in a combo box with the files in the Windows directory:

```
BOOL CSampleDlg::OnInitDialog()
{
    CDialog::OnInitDialog();
```

APPENDIX
CONTROLS

```
    TCHAR szPath[MAX_PATH] = {"c:\\windows"};
    int nResult = DlgDirListComboBox(szPath, IDC_COMBO, IDC_CURDIR,
        DDL_READWRITE | DDL_READONLY | DDL_HIDDEN |
        DDL_SYSTEM | DDL_ARCHIVE);

    return TRUE;
}
```

The example combo box is shown in Figure A-15.

Q. Why do my spin button controls look backwards?

You need to set the range of a spin button control by calling *CSpinCtrl::SetRange*. A spin button has a default upper limit of 0 and lower limit of 100. That means the value will move from 100 to 0 when the value is increased. The following sample sets the range of the spin button from 0 to 100:

```
BOOL CAboutDlg::OnInitDialog()
{
    CDialog::OnInitDialog();

    // set the lower and upper limit of the spin button
    m_wndSpin.SetRange(0, 100);

    return TRUE;
}
```

Don't feel bad. At the time of this writing, the Copies spin button control in the Print dialog for Visual C++ 4.0 had this same problem: The number of copies decreases when you press the up button and increases when you press the down button.

Q. Why doesn't my spin button control automatically update the edit control next to it?

If you are using the auto buddy feature of a spin button, you need to make sure the buddy window precedes the spin button control in the dialog's tab

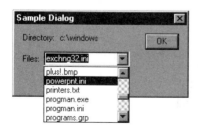

Figure A-15 Using DlgDirListComboBox to display contents of a directory

APPENDIX
COMMON QUESTIONS, ANSWERS, AND TIPS

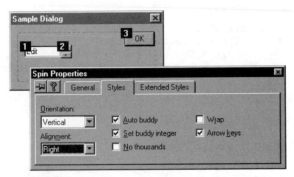

Figure A-16 Make sure you specify the correct tab order for auto buddy spin controls

order. You set the tab order of a dialog by selecting the Tab Order item from the Layout menu (or press CTRL+D). Figure A-16 shows a dialog with the correct tab order:

Q. How do I display push buttons with bitmaps?

There are several great new creation styles for Windows 95 buttons—in particular, BS_BITMAP and BS_ICON. To have bitmap buttons, you need to specify the BS_BITMAP or BS_ICON style when you create the button and call *CButton::SetBitamp* or *CButton::SetIcon*. Figure A-17 creates a dialog that contains three icon image push buttons.

First, set the icon property for the buttons as shown in Figure A-17.

Then, call *CButton::SetIcon* when the dialog is initialed. Notice that the following example uses icons instead of bitmaps. You have to be careful when you

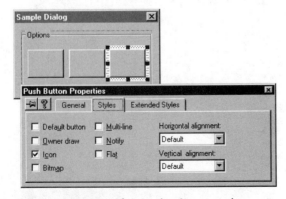

Figure A-17 Specifying the icon push buttons

632

APPENDIX
CONTROLS

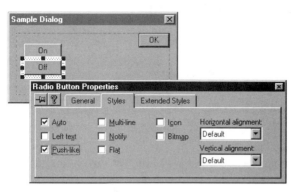

Figure A-18 Specifying three-state push button properties

use bitmaps, because you don't know what color to use as the background—not everyone uses light gray. An icon has the advantage of transparent bits.

```
BOOL CSampleDlg::OnInitDialog()
{
    CDialog::OnInitDialog();

    // Set the images for the push buttons.
    m_wndButton1.SetIcon(AfxGetApp()->LoadIcon(IDI_OPTION1));
    m_wndButton2.SetIcon(AfxGetApp()->LoadIcon(IDI_OPTION2));
    m_wndButton3.SetIcon(AfxGetApp()->LoadIcon(IDI_OPTION3));

    return TRUE;
}
```

Q. How can I have three-state push buttons?

You can use the new BS_PUSHBUTTON style bit with check boxes and radio buttons to create three-state push buttons. This is very easy! Just drag the check boxes and radio buttons to your dialog and specify the Push-like property as shown in Figure A-18. The buttons will behave and look like three-state push buttons without any additional programming.

Q. How do I dynamically create controls?

Allocate an instance of the control object and call its *Create* member function. Two of the most common mistakes developers make are forgetting to specify the WS_VISIBLE flag and allocating a control object on the stack. The following example dynamically creates a push button control:

```
// In class declaration (.H file).
private:
    CButton* m_pButton;
```

continued on next page

APPENDIX
COMMON QUESTIONS, ANSWERS, AND TIPS

continued from previous page

```
// In class implementation (.CPP file).
m_pButton = new CButton;
ASSERT_VALID(m_pButton);

m_pButton->Create(_T("Button Title"), WS_CHILD | WS_VISIBLE | BS_PUSHBUTTON,
    CRect(0, 0, 100, 24), this,IDC_MYBUTTON);
```

Q. *How do I limit the allowable characters in an edit control?*

If you want to only allow numbers in your edit control, you can use a standard edit control and specify the new ES_NUMBERS creation flag. This is a new flag for Windows 95 that limits an edit control to just numeric characters. If you need more flexibility, you should check out the Microsoft masked edit control. This is a very useful OLE custom control that ships with Visual C++ 4.0. Figure A-19 shows the properties dialog for a masked edit control that accepts phone numbers.

If you want to process the characters yourself rather than use an OLE custom control, the following text is just for you. You can derive a class from *CEdit*, process the WM_CHAR message, and filter out certain characters from an edit control. First, use ClassWizard to create a class derived from *CEdit*. Next, subclass the edit control by defining a member variable in your dialog's class and calling *CWnd::SubclassDlgItem* in *OnInitDialog*.

```
// In your dialog class declaration (.H file).
private:
    CMyEdit m_wndEdit;  // Instance of your new edit control.

// In your dialog class implementation (.CPP file).
BOOL CSampleDialog::OnInitDialog()
{
    ...

    // Subclass the edit control.
    m_wndEdit.SubclassDlgItem(IDC_EDIT, this);

    ...
}
```

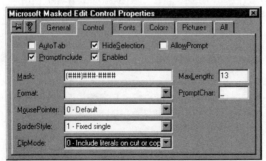

Figure A-19 Using the masked edit control to only accept phone numbers

APPENDIX
CONTROLS

Now, use ClassWizard to handle the WM_CHAR message and evaluate the *nChar* argument and decide what action to perform. You can prevent the character from being displayed, pass the character along unmodified, or modify the character. The following example demonstrates how you can display alphabetic characters. If a character is alphabetic, call *CWnd::OnChar;* for all other characters, don't call *OnChar*.

```
// Only display alphabetic characters.
void CMyEdit::OnChar(UINT nChar, UINT nRepCnt, UINT nFlags)
{
    // Determine if nChar is an alphabetic character.
    if (::IsCharAlpha((TCHAR)nChar))
        CEdit::OnChar(nChar, nRepCnt, nFlags);
}
```

To modify a character, you cannot simply call *CEdit::OnChar* with the modified *nChar* argument. *CEdit::OnChar* calls *CWnd::Default*, which retrieves the original values for *wParam* and *lParam*. To modify a character, you need to modify *nChar* and call *CWnd::DefWindowProc*. The following example makes all characters uppercase:

```
// Make all characters uppercase
void CMyEdit::OnChar(UINT nChar, UINT nRepCnt, UINT nFlags)
{
    // Make sure character is uppercase.
    if (::IsCharAlpha((TCHAR)nChar))
        nChar = ::CharUpper(nChar);

    // Bypass default OnChar processing and directly call
    // default window proc.
    DefWindowProc(WM_CHAR, nChar, MAKELPARAM(nRepCnt, nFlags));
}
```

Q. *How do I change the color of controls?*

You have two options: You can specify the control's color in its parent class, or you can take advantage of the new *message reflections* capabilities of MFC 4.0 and specify the color in the control's class (where it belongs).

The framework calls *CWnd::OnCtlColor* for a control's parent window (usually a dialog box) when a control needs to be painted. You can override this function and specify new drawing attributes for a control in your parent window class. For example, the following changes all the edit controls contained in the dialog to use red text:

```
HBRUSH CAboutDlg::OnCtlColor(CDC* pDC, CWnd* pWnd, UINT nCtlColor)
{
    HBRUSH hbr = CDialog::OnCtlColor(pDC, pWnd, nCtlColor);

    // Draw red text for all edit controls.
    if (nCtlColor == CTLCOLOR_EDIT)
        pDC->SetTextColor(RGB(255, 0, 0));

    return hbr;
}
```

APPENDIX
COMMON QUESTIONS, ANSWERS, AND TIPS

However, this is not very object-oriented since every parent has to process the notification message and specify the drawing attributes for each control. It makes more sense for the control to process this message and decide how to draw it.

Message reflection allows you to do precisely that. Notification messages are first sent to the parent window, but if they are not processed by the parent they are passed to the control. The following are the steps you need to follow to create a custom-colored list box control.

First, use ClassWizard to create a class that is derived from *CListBox* and add the following data members to this class:

```
class CMyListBox : public CListBox
{
...

private:
        COLORREF m_clrFore;     // foreground color
        COLORREF m_clrBack;     // background color
        CBrush   m_brush;       // background brush

...
};
```

Next, you need to initialize the data members in the class constructor.

```
CMyListBox::CMyListBox()
{
        // Initialize data members.
        m_clrFore = RGB(255, 255, 0);       // yellow text
        m_clrBack = RGB(0, 0, 255);         // blue background
        m_brush.CreateSolidBrush(m_clrBack);
}
```

Finally, use ClassWizard to handle the reflected WM_CTLCOLOR message (=WM_CTLCOLOR) and specify the new drawing attributes.

```
HBRUSH CMyListBox::CtlColor(CDC* pDC, UINT nCtlColor)
{
        pDC->SetTextColor(m_clrFore);
        pDC->SetBkColor(m_clrBack);
        return (HBRUSH)m_brush.GetSafeHandle();
}
```

Now, the control is deciding how it should be drawn. It will be drawn to resemble, yet be independent of, its parent.

Q. How do I prevent a list box from flashing when I add a lot of items to it?

You can prevent a *CListBox* control (or any window) from redrawing by calling *CWnd::SetRedraw* to clear its redraw flag. When adding several items to a list box you can clear the redraw flag, add the items, and then reset the redraw flag. To make sure the list box is redrawn with the new items, call *CWnd::Invalidate* after calling *SetRedraw(TRUE)*.

```
// Disable redrawing.
pListBox->SetRedraw(FALSE);

// Fill in the list box here

// Enable drawing and make sure list box is redrawn.
pListBox->SetRedraw(TRUE);
pListBox->Invalidate();
```

Q. *How do I append text to an edit control?*

You have to do it yourself since there is not a *CEdit::AppendText* function. You can move the selection to the end of the edit control by calling *CEdit::SetSel*, then append the text by calling *CEdit::ReplaceSel*. The following example implements an *AppendText* method:

```
void CMyEdit::AppendText(LPCSTR pText)
{
    int nLen = GetWindowTextLength();
    SetFocus();
    SetSel(nLen, nLen);

    ReplaceSel(pText);
}
```

GDI

Q. *How do I access predefined GDI objects?*

Windows has several predefined brushes, pens, and fonts you can use by calling *CDC::SelectStockObject*. The following example draws an ellipse in a view using a predefined Windows pen and brush GDI object:

```
// Draw ellipse using stock black pen and gray brush.
void CSampleView::OnDraw(CDC* pDC)
{
    // Determine size of view.
    CRect rcView;
    GetClientRect(rcView);

    // Use stock black pen and stock gray brush to draw ellipse.
    pDC->SelectStockObject(BLACK_PEN);
    pDC->SelectStockObject(GRAY_BRUSH);

    // Draw the ellipse.
    pDC->Ellipse(rcView);
}
```

APPENDIX
COMMON QUESTIONS, ANSWERS, AND TIPS

You can also call the new *GetSysColorBrush* SDK function to get one of the system color brushes. The following example draws an ellipse in a view using the background color for tooltips system brush:

```
void CSampleView::OnDraw(CDC* pDC)
{
    // Determine size of view.
    CRect rcView;
    GetClientRect(rcView);

    // Use background color for tooltips brush.
    CBrush* pOrgBrush = pDC->SelectObject(
        CBrush::FromHandle(::GetSysColorBrush(COLOR_INFOBK)));

    // Draw the ellipse.
    pDC->Ellipse(rcView);

    // Restore original brush.
    pDC->SelectObject(pOrgBrush);
}
```

Q. *How do I get the attributes of a GDI object?*

You can call *GDIObject::GetObject*. This function fills in a buffer with information specific to the GDI object. The following example creates some useful helper functions:

```
// Determine if font is bold.
BOOL IsFontBold(const CFont& font)
{
    LOGFONT stFont;
    font.GetObject(sizeof(LOGFONT), &stFont);
    return (stFont.lfBold) ? TRUE : FALSE;
}


// Return the size of a bitmap.
CSize GetBitmapSize(const CBitmap& bitmap)
{
    BITMAP stBitmap;
    bitmap.GetObject(sizeof(BITMAP), &stBitmap);
    return CSize(stBitmap.bmWidth, stBitmap.bmHeight);
}


// Create a pen with the same color as a brush.
BOOL CreatePenFromBrush(CPen& pen, cost CBrush& brush)
{
    LOGBRUSH stBrush;
    brush.GetObject(sizeof(LOGBRUSH), &stBrush);
    return pen.CreatePen(PS_SOLID, 0, stBrush.lbColor);
}
```

APPENDIX
GDI

Q. How do I implement a rubber band rectangle?

CRectTracker is a very flexible and useful class. You can create a rubber band rectangle by calling *CRectTracker::TrackRubberBand* in response to the WM_LBUTTONDOWN message. The following example demonstrates how easy it is to use *CRectTracker* by moving and resizing a blue ellipse in a view.

First, declare a *CRectTracker* data member in your document class:

```
class CSampleView : public CView
{
    ...

    public:
        CRectTracker   m_tracker;

    ...
};
```

Next, initialize the *CRectTracker* object in the constructor of your document class.

```
CSampleDoc::CSampleDoc()
{
    // Initialize tracker position, size and style.
    m_tracker.m_rect.SetRect(0, 0, 10, 10);
    m_tracker.m_nStyle = CRectTracker::resizeInside |
        CRectTracker::dottedLine;
}
```

Now, draw the ellipse and the tracker rectangle in your view's *OnDraw* function:

```
void CSampleView::OnDraw(CDC* pDC)
{
    CSampleDoc* pDoc = GetDocument();
    ASSERT_VALID(pDoc);

    // Select blue brush into device context.
    CBrush brush(RGB(0,0,255));
    CBrush* pOldBrush = pDC->SelectObject(&brush);

    // Draw ellipse in tracking rectangle.
    CRect rcEllipse;
    pDoc->m_tracker.GetTrueRect(rcEllipse);
    pDC->Ellipse(rcEllipse);

    // Draw tracking rectangle.
    pDoc->m_tracker.Draw(pDC);

    // Select blue brush out of device context.
    pDC->SelectObject(pOldBrush);
}
```

APPENDIX
COMMON QUESTIONS, ANSWERS, AND TIPS

Finally, use ClassWizard to handle the WM_LBUTTONDOWN message for your view and add the following code that resizes, drags, or moves the ellipse depending where the user clicks.

```
void CSampleView::OnLButtonDown(UINT nFlags, CPoint point)
{
    // Get pointer to document.
    CSampleDoc* pDoc = GetDocument();
    ASSERT_VALID(pDoc);

    // If clicked on ellipse, drag or resize it. Otherwise create a
    // rubber-band rectangle and create a new ellipse.
    BOOL bResult = pDoc->m_tracker.HitTest(point) !=
        CRectTracker::hitNothing;

    // Tracker rectangle changed so update views.
    if (bResult)
    {
        pDoc->m_tracker.Track(this, point, TRUE);
        pDoc->SetModifiedFlag();
        pDoc->UpdateAllViews(NULL);
    }

    else
        pDoc->m_tracker.TrackRubberBand(this, point, TRUE);

    CView::OnLButtonDown(nFlags, point);
}
```

Q. *How do I draw text that preserves the background color?*

You can set the background mode by calling *CDC::SetBkMode* and passing OPAQUE to fill in the background with the current background color or TRANSPARENT to leave the background unmodified. The following example draws some text in red with a black shadow by setting the background mode to TRANSPARENT and drawing the string twice. The black string is slightly offset and behind the red string, but still visible because of the background mode.

```
void CSampleView::OnDraw(CDC* pDC)
{
    // Determine size of view.
    CRect rcView;
    GetClientRect(rcView);

    // Create sample string to display.
    CString str(_T("Awesome Shadow Text ..."));

    // Set the background mode to transparent.
    pDC->SetBkMode(TRANSPARENT);

    // Draw black shadow text.
    rcView.OffsetRect(1, 1);
```

APPENDIX
FONTS AND TEXT

```
    pDC->SetTextColor(RGB(0,0,0));
    pDC->DrawText(str, str.GetLength(), rcView,
        DT_SINGLELINE | DT_CENTER | DT_VCENTER);

    // Draw red text.
    rcView.OffsetRect(-1, -1);
    pDC->SetTextColor(RGB(255,0,0));
    pDC->DrawText(str, str.GetLength(), rcView,
        DT_SINGLELINE | DT_CENTER | DT_VCENTER);
}
```

Fonts and Text

Q. How do I create a font of a certain point size?

You specify font size in logical units, but sometimes it might be more convenient to specify its size in points. You can use the following calculation to convert point size to a font height.

```
int nHeight = MulDiv(nPointSize, -dc.GetDeviceCaps(LOGPIXELSY), 72);
```

The following example creates an 8-point Arial font:

```
...

CClientDC dc(AfxGetMainWnd());

m_font.CreateFont(MulDiv(8, -dc.GetDeviceCaps(LOGPIXELSY),
    72), 0, 0, 0, FW_NORMAL, 0, 0, 0, ANSI_CHARSET,
    OUT_STROKE_PRECIS, CLIP_STROKE_PRECIS, DRAFT_QUALITY,
    VARIABLE_PITCH | FF_SWISS, _T("Arial")));

...
```

Q. How do I calculate the size (in pixels) of a string?

The function *CDC::GetTextExtent* computes the height and width of a string based on the currently selected font. If you are using a font other than the system font, it is important to select that font into the device context before calling *GetTextExtent*. If you do not, you will get incorrect results because the calculation will be based on the system font. The following sample dynamically adjusts the size of a push button whenever its title changes. The size of the push button is based on the button's font and the size of its title. *OnSetText* is called in response to WM_SETTEXT messages by using the ON_MESSAGE macro to define a user-defined message.

```
LRESULT CMyButton::OnSetText(WPARAM wParam, LPARAM lParam)
{
    // Pass message to window procedure.
    LRESULT bResult = CallWindowProc(*GetSuperWndProcAddr(),
        m_hWnd, GetCurrentMessage()->message, wParam, lParam);
```

continued on next page

```
        // Get title of push button.
        CString strTitle;
        GetWindowText(strTitle);

        // Select current font into device context.
        CDC* pDC = GetDC();
        CFont* pFont = GetFont();
        CFont* pOldFont = pDC->SelectObject(pFont);

        // Calculate size of title.
        CSize size = pDC->GetTextExtent(strTitle, strTitle.GetLength());

        // Adjust the button's size based on its title.
        // Add a 5-pixel border around the button.
        SetWindowPos(NULL, 0, 0, size.cx + 10, size.cy + 10,
             SWP_NOMOVE | SWP_NOZORDER | SWP_NOACTIVATE);

        // Clean up.
        pDC->SelectFont(pOldFont);
        ReleaseDC(pDC);

        return bResult;
}
```

Q. How do I display rotated text?

You can display rotated text as long as you use a TrueType or GDI stroke font (some hardware devices also support rotating raster fonts). The *lfEscapement* member of the LOGFONT structure determines the angle between the base line of the text and the *X* axis. The angle is specified in tenths of degrees—not degrees. For example, set *lfEscapement* to 450 to create a font that is rotated by 45 degrees.

To ensure that all fonts rotate in the same direction based on the coordinate system in which they are used, make sure you set the CLIP_LH_ANGLES bit of the *lfClipPrecision* member. If you do not, some fonts may rotate in the opposite direction. The following example uses a 14-point Arial font to draw a string at 15-degree intervals. The output of this program is shown in Figure A-20.

```
void CSampleView::OnDraw(CDC* pDC)
{
        // Determine the size of the window.
        CRect rcClient;
        GetClientRect(rcClient);

        // Create sample string.
        CString str(_T("Wheeee... I am rotating!"));

        // Draw transparent, red text.
        pDC->SetBkMode(TRANSPARENT);
        pDC->SetTextColor(RGB(255,0,0));

        CFont   font;          // font object
        LOGFONT stFont;        // font definition
```

APPENDIX
FONTS AND TEXT

```
// Set font attributes that will not change.
memset(&stFont, 0, sizeof(LOGFONT));
stFont.lfHeight = MulDiv(14, -pDC->GetDeviceCaps(LOGPIXELSY), 72);
stFont.lfWeight = FW_NORMAL;
stFont.lfClipPrecision = CLIP_LH_ANGLES;
strcpy(stFont.lfFaceName, "Arial");

// Draw text at 15degree intervals.
for (int nAngle=0; nAngle < 3600; nAngle += 150)
{
    // Specify new angle.
    stFont.lfEscapement = nAngle;

    // Create and select font into dc.
    font.CreateFontIndirect(&stFont);
    CFont* pOldFont = pDC->SelectObject(&font);

    // Draw the text.
    pDC->TextOut(rcClient.right/2, rcClient.bottom/2, str);

    // Select font out of dc and destroy font GDI object.
    pDC->SelectObject(pOldFont);
    font.DeleteObject();
}
}
```

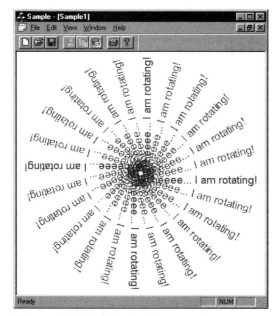

Figure A-20 Displaying rotated text

APPENDIX
COMMON QUESTIONS, ANSWERS, AND TIPS

Q. *How do I correctly display strings that contain tab characters?*

Tab characters need to be expanded when calling the GDI text drawing functions. You can do this by calling *CDC::TabbedTextOut* or *CDC::DrawText* and specifying the DT_EXPANDTABS flag. The *TabbedTextOut* function is pretty flexible and allows you to specify an array of tab positions. The following example specifies a tab expansion of 20 device units:

```
void CSampleView::OnDraw(CDC* pDC)
{
    CTestDoc* pDoc = GetDocument();
    ASSERT_VALID(pDoc);

    CString str;
    str.Format(_T("Cathy\tNorman\tOliver"));

    int nTabStop = 20;   // tabs are every 20 pixels
    pDC->TabbedTextOut(10, 10, str, 1, &nTabStop, 10);
}
```

Q. *How do I display an ellipsis at the end of my string when it is too long?*

Call *CDC::DrawText* and specify the DT_END_ELLIPSIS flag. This replaces characters at the end of the string with ellipses to ensure that it fits within the specified bounding rectangle. If you are displaying path information, specify the DT_PATH_ELLIPSIS flag to replace characters in the middle of the string with the ellipses.

```
void CSampleView::OnDraw(CDC* pDC)
{
    CTestDoc* pDoc = GetDocument();
    ASSERT_VALID(pDoc);

    // Add ellipsis to end of string if it does not fit.
    pDC->DrawText(CString("This is a long string"),
        CRect(10,10,80,30), DT_LEFT | DT_END_ELLIPSIS);

    // Add ellipsis to middle of string if it does not fit.
    pDC->DrawText(AfxGetApp()->m_pszHelpFilePath,
        CRect(10, 40, 200, 60), DT_LEFT | DT_PATH_ELLIPSIS);
}
```

Q. *What is the quickest way to format a CString object?*

You can call *CString::Format,* which has the same format arguments as the *printf* function. The following example demonstrates how to use the Format function.

```
// Get size of window.
CRect rcWindow;
GetWindowRect(rcWindow);
```

APPENDIX
MENUS

```
// Format message string.
CString strMessage;
strMessage.Format(_T("Window Size (%d, %d)"),
    rcWindow.Width(), rcWindow.Height());

// Display the message.
MessageBox(strMessage);
```

Menus

Q. *Why does my menu item stay disabled even when I call EnableMenuItem?*

You need to set *CFrameWnd::m_bAutoMenuEnable* to FALSE. If this data member is TRUE (the default value), the framework automatically disables any menu items that do not have an ON_UPDATE_COMMAND_UI or ON_COMMAND handler.

```
// Disable MFC from automatically disabling menu items.
m_bAutoMenuEnable = FALSE;

// Now enable the menu item.
CMenu* pMenu = GetMenu();
ASSERT_VALID(pMenu);

pMenu->EnableMenuItem(ID_MENU_ITEM, MF_BYCOMMAND | MF_ENABLED);
```

Q. *How do I add a menu item to the system menu?*

Adding a menu item to the system menu requires three steps.

First, define your menu item identifier using the Resource Symbols dialog (to display this dialog, select Resource Symbols... from the View menu). This identifier should be greater then 0x0F and less then 0xF000.

Next, call *CWnd::GetSystemMenu* to get a pointer to the system menu and call *CMenu::AppendMenu* to add items to the menu. The following example adds a two new menu items to the system menu:

```
int CMainFrame::OnCreate(LPCREATESTRUCT lpCreateStruct)
{
    ...

    // Make sure system menu item is in the right range.
    ASSERT((IDM_MYSYSITEM & 0xFFF0) == IDM_MYSYSITEM);
    ASSERT(IDM_MYSYSITEM < 0xF000);

    // Get pointer to system menu.
    CMenu* pSysMenu = GetSystemMenu(FALSE);
    ASSERT_VALID(pSysMenu);
```

continued on next page

APPENDIX
COMMON QUESTIONS, ANSWERS, AND TIPS

continued from previous page

```
        // Add a separator and our menu item to system menu.
        CString strMenuItem(_T("New menu item"));
        pSysMenu->AppendMenu(MF_SEPARATOR);
        pSysMenu->AppendMenu(MF_STRING, IDM_MYSYSITEM, strMenuItem);

        ...
}
```

Now, you need to detect when your system menu item is selected. Use ClassWizard to handle the WM_SYSCOMMAND message and check the *nID* argument for your identifier.

```
void CMainFrame::OnSysCommand(UINT nID, LPARAM lParam)
{
        // Determine if our system menu item was selected.
        if ((nID & 0xFFF0) == IDM_MYSYSITEM)
        {
                // TODO - process system menu item
        }
        else
                CMDIFrameWnd::OnSysCommand(nID, lParam);
}
```

Finally, a good UI application should display a help message in the status bar when the system menu item is highlighted. You can implement this by simply adding an entry to the string table containing the system menu item identifier. The string table is shown in Figure A-21.

The previous technique illustrates how AppWizard adds the About... item to dialog-based applications.

Q. How do I determine the number of menu rows my top-level menu occupies?

You can do this by using some simple subtraction and division. First, you need to calculate the height of your main frame window and its client area. Next, subtract the height of the client area, frame borders, and caption from the height of the window frame. Finally, divide by the height of the menu bar.

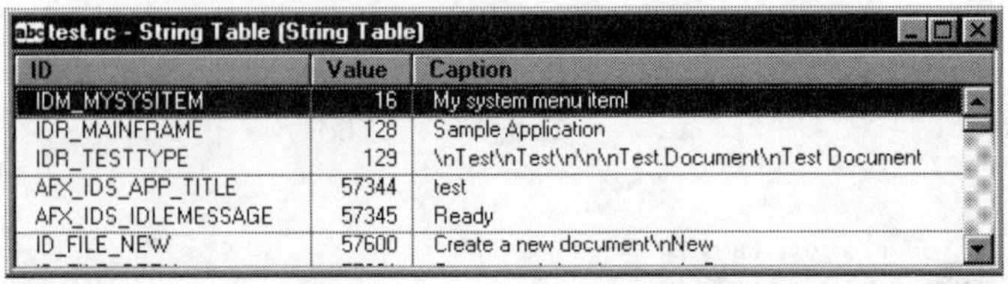

ID	Value	Caption
IDM_MYSYSITEM	16	My system menu item!
IDR_MAINFRAME	128	Sample Application
IDR_TESTTYPE	129	\nTest\nTest\n\n\nTest.Document\nTest Document
AFX_IDS_APP_TITLE	57344	test
AFX_IDS_IDLEMESSAGE	57345	Ready
ID_FILE_NEW	57600	Create a new document\nNew

Figure A-21 Adding system menu status text to string table

APPENDIX
SYSTEM

The following example implements a member function to calculate the number of rows the main frame menu occupies:

```
int CMainFrame::GetMenuRows()
{
    CRect rcFrame, rcClient;

    GetWindowRect(rcFrame);
    GetClientRect(rcClient);

    return (rcFrame.Height() - rcClient.Height() -
        ::GetSystemMetrics(SM_CYCAPTION) -
        (::GetSystemMetrics(SM_CYFRAME)*2)) /
        ::GetSystemMetrics(SM_CYMENU);
}
```

System

Q. How do I determine what system colors are specified in the 60users' environment?

You can call the SDK function *GetSysColor* to get the color of a specific display element. The following example shows how this function is used in the MFC *CMiniFrameWnd::OnNcPaint* function to set the color of the window's caption:

```
void CMiniFrameWnd::OnNcPaint()
{
    ...

    dc.SetTextColor(::GetSysColor(m_bActive ?
        COLOR_CAPTIONTEXT : COLOR_INACTIVECAPTIONTEXT));

    ...
}
```

Q. How do I retrieve and set system-wide parameters?

The SDK function *SystemParametersInfo* was introduced in the Windows 3.1 SDK. You can call this function to retrieve and set system settings, such as keyboard repeat rate, mouse double-click delay, icon font, and wallpaper settings.

```
// Create a font that is used for icon titles.
LOGFONT stFont;
::SystemParametersInfo(SPI_GETICONTITLELOGFONT,
    sizeof(LOGFONT), &stFont, SPIF_SENDWININICHANGE);

m_font.CreateFontIndirect(&stFont);


// Change the wallpaper to leaves.bmp.
::SystemParametersInfo(SPI_SETDESKWALLPAPER, 0, _T("forest.bmp"),
    SPIF_UPDATEINIFILE);
```

APPENDIX
COMMON QUESTIONS, ANSWERS, AND TIPS

Q. *How do I use a predefined Windows cursor?*

Call *CWinApp::LoadStandardCursor* and pass the cursor identifier as the argument.

```
BOOL CSampleDialog::OnSetCursor(CWnd* pWnd, UINT nHitTest, UINT message)
{
    // Display wait cursor if busy.
    if (m_bBusy)
    {
        SetCursor (AfxGetApp()->LoadStandardCursor(IDC_WAIT));
        return TRUE;
    }

    return CDialog::OnSetCursor(pWnd, nHitTest, message);
}
```

Q. *How do I determine the current screen resolution?*

Call the SDK function *GetSystemMetrics*. This function retrieves information about other elements of the Window display, such as caption size, border size, and scroll bar size.

```
// Initialize CSize object with screen size.
CSize sizeScreen (GetSystemMetrics(SM_CXSCREEN),
    GetSystemMetrics(SM_CYSCREEN));
```

Q. *How do I retrieve the same task list used by the old Task Manager application?*

The old Task Manager application displays a list of top-level windows. To make the list, a window must be visible, contain a title, and not be owned by another window. Call *CWnd::GetWindow* to retrieve the list of top-level windows and call the *CWnd* methods *IsWindowVisible*, *GetWindowTextLength*, and *GetOwner* to determine whether the window should be on the list. The following example fills in a list box with captions of Task Manager windows:

```
void GetTaskList(CListBox& list)
{
    CString strCaption;        // Caption of window.

    list.ResetContent();       // Clear list box.

    // Get first window in window list.
    ASSERT_VALID(AfxGetMainWnd());
    CWnd* pWnd = AfxGetMainWnd()->GetWindow(GW_HWNDFIRST);

    // Walk window list.
    while (pWnd)
    {
        // I window visible, has a caption, and does not have an owner?
        if (pWnd->IsWindowVisible() &&
            pWnd->GetWindowTextLength() && !pWnd->GetOwner())
        {
```

APPENDIX
SYSTEM

```
            // Add caption of window to list box.
            pWnd->GetWindowText(strCaption);
            list.AddString(strCaption);
        }

        // Get next window in window list.
        pWnd = pWnd->GetWindow(GW_HWNDNEXT);
    }
}
```

Q. *How do I determine the Windows and Windows system directories?*

There are two SDK functions exactly for this purpose: *GetWindowsDirectory* and *GetSystemDirectory*. The following example shows how to use these two functions:

```
TCHAR szDir[MAX_PATH];

// Get the full path of the Windows directory.
::GetWindowsDirectory(szDir, MAX_PATH);
TRACE("Windows directory %s\n", szDir);

// Get the full path of the Windows system directory.
::GetSystemDirectory(szDir, MAX_PATH);
TRACE("Windows system directory %s\n", szDir);
```

Q. *Where should I create temporary files?*

Call the SDK function *GetTempPath* to determine the directory designated for temporary files. This function first checks the TMP environment variable for the temporary path. If TMP is not specified, it checks the TEMP environment variable. Finally, it returns to the current directory if TEMP is not specified. The following example demonstrates how to create a temporary file.

```
...
        // Get unique temporary file.
        CString strFile;
        GetUniqueTempName(strFile);

        TRY
        {
            // Create file and write data. Note that file is closed
            // in the destructor of the CFile object.
            CFile file(strFile, CFile::modeCreate | CFile::modeWrite);

            // write data
        }

        CATCH(CFileException, e)
        {
            // error opening file
        }

        END_CATCH
```

continued on next page

APPENDIX
COMMON QUESTIONS, ANSWERS, AND TIPS

continued from previous page

...

```
void GetUniqueTempName(CString& strTempName)
{
    // Get the temporary files directory.
    TCHAR szTempPath[MAX_PATH];
    DWORD dwResult = ::GetTempPath(MAX_PATH, szTempPath);
    ASSERT(dwResult);

    // Create a unique temporary file.
    TCHAR szTempFile[MAX_PATH];
    UINT nResult = GetTempFileName(szTempPath, _T("~ex"), 0, szTempFile);
    ASSERT(nResult);

    strTempName = szTempFile;
}
```

Q. *How do I access the desktop window?*

The static *CWnd::GetDesktopWindow* function returns a pointer to the desktop window. The following example shows how the MFC function *CFrameWnd::BeginModalState* uses this function to walk the internal window list.

```
void CFrameWnd::BeginModalState()
{
    ...

    // first count all windows that need to be disabled
    UINT nCount = 0;
    HWND hWnd = ::GetWindow(::GetDesktopWindow(), GW_CHILD);
    while (hWnd != NULL)
    {
        if (::IsWindowEnabled(hWnd) &&
            CWnd::FromHandlePermanent(hWnd) != NULL &&
            AfxIsDescendant(pParent->m_hWnd, hWnd) &&
            ::SendMessage(hWnd, WM_DISABLEMODAL, 0, 0) == 0)
        {
            ++nCount;
        }
        hWnd = ::GetWindow(hWnd, GW_HWNDNEXT);
    }

    ...
}
```

INDEX

3D graphics, 154, 250–260
3D style of pane, 78–81

A

About, 78, 315, 404, 406
Action, 498
ActivateFrame, 59–61
Add Function, 38, 109, 118, 138, 186, 223, 273, 288, 317, 328–329, 334
Add Member Variable, 631
Add Method, 364
add status bar, 84
Add Variable, 23, 39, 41, 118, 149, 180, 278, 344, 347, 631
AddDocTemplate, 20
AddItem, 186, 188
AddPages, 540, 569
AddPoint, 42
AddString, 132, 135, 188
Advanced Options, 617
AfxBeginThread, 473, 481–483, 485, 506, 509
AfxCtl, 566, 571
_AFXDLL, 456, 571
AfxExtractSubString, 111
AfxFormatString, 328
AfxGetInstanceHandle, 612
AfxGetMainWnd, 612, 627
AfxGetModuleShortFileName, 615
AFX_IDS_IDLEMESSAGE, 318
AFX_IDS_STATUS_BAR, 318
AFX_IDW_STATUS_BAR, 119, 627
AFX_IDW_TOOLBAR, 627
AfxLoadLibrary, 450
AfxLoadString, 111
AFX_MANAGE_STATE, 567
AFX_MSG, 31, 99, 616

AFX_MSG_MAP, 321
AfxOleInit, 376, 383
AfxOleLockApp, 362
AfxOleRegisterControlClass, 615
AfxPriv, 86, 111, 615, 623
AfxPropPageCallback, 567
AfxRegisterWndClass, 131
_AfxRelease, 383
AfxSetResourceHandle, 448, 457
AfxSetWindowText, 623
Afxwin, 268
AfxWndProc, 567
ambiguous class methods, 466
AM/PM indicator, 78
animation, 250–260
  bitmaps, 290–309
  icons, 270–275
annotating bitmap with text, 276–281
appbar displaying system palette, 572–591
APPBARDATA, 572, 574, 591
AppendFilterSuffix, 31, 34, 321–322, 324
AppendMenu, 153, 647
AppendText, 639
application tips, 612–616
Apply push button, 48
associating data with list box item, 131–136
associating multiple file extensions with document, 16–21
AsString, 9
asynchronous playback, 225–226
autocaptions, changing, 44
auto-cleanup, 343
AutoLoad, 235
automation server in OLE, 357–369
AutoScroll, 23, 25, 27
average character width, 172–173

651

B

BackColor, 429
background in client area, 264–270
Barcore, 68
BEGIN_MESSAGE_MAP, 30, 321
BEING_PROPPAGEIDS, 422
biBitCount, 210
biClrUsed, 210
biSize, 210
BitBlt, 268, 276, 280
bitmaps (BMPs)
    adding to dialog box, 281–290
    in a list box, 182–193
    size, 15
    viewer, 10–11, 16, 29
BN_CLICKED, 140, 178, 222–223, 288, 333, 346, 375, 464, 476–477
Books Online, 34, 55, 97, 129, 148, 227, 268, 325–326
BS_BITMAP, 634
BS_ICON, 634
BS_PUSHBUTTON, 635
buffer size, 28

C

CAboutDlg, 316–317, 516, 573–574
CacheData, 377
CacheGlobalData, 374, 376–377
CAddName, 393, 395
CalcFixedLayout, 119–120
CalcInsideRect, 113
CalcWindowRect, 15, 210
CallNextHookEx, 496, 498
CAppBar, 590
Caption, 429
caption updating, 115
CArchive, 292, 380–381
card games, 290–309
CARDS.DLL, 290–292, 294, 305–309
caret position and direction, 98, 102
CArray, 35
CAutoScrollView, 22–25, 27–28, 221
CAviFileDialog, 200–202
CBackDlg, 291, 308
CBarDialogDlg, 108–109
CBigWaveDlg, 222–224
CBitmap, 264–270

CBitmapButton, 235–236, 238, 241
CBitmapClient, 266–268, 270
CBmpBarCtrl, 92–94
CBmpListCtrl, 182–186, 188, 191–193
CBmpPaneView, 93–96
CBN_SELCHANGE, 244, 493
CBRS_TOOLTIPS, 627
CBrush, 145, 630
CButton, 174, 634
CCaptionBarView, 118–119
CCDAudio, 227–234, 238, 246, 248
CChildFrame, 11–14, 35, 38, 41–44, 82, 85–86, 94–95, 117, 119
CClockFormatDlg, 70–72, 76
CCmdTarget, 550, 565, 594
CCmdUI, 119
CColorDialog, 142, 144, 360–361
CColorView, 49–51, 54
CColorWell, 525–526, 539
CControlBar, 82, 111–113, 119, 627
CCriticalSection, 483
CCtlColorDlg, 143–145
CCursorDlg, 128, 130
CCustomOpenApp, 330
CD player, 227–250, 515–540
CDataExchange, 351–352
CDC (device context) text drawing methods, 276–281
CDDEObj, 397–398, 401–402
CDebugView, 38, 41–42, 44
CDialog, 337, 342, 628–629
CDibView, 204, 207, 209–210
CDiscPlayerDlg, 237–238, 245–246
CDK (OLE Custom Control Development Kit), 403
CDN_INITDONE, 331
CDocExtApp, 18–20
CDocManager, 17, 615
CDocTemplate, 18, 21
CDocument, 16, 292, 307
CDragList, 372–375, 377
cdtDraw, 290
cdtInit, 306
cdtTerm, 306
CDWordArray, 39
CDynamicMenuDlg, 149–152
CEdit, 97–98, 100, 136, 379, 470, 636, 639
CEditView, 620–621

INDEX

CenterWindow, 618
CEvent, 482
CFileDialog, 28–29, 32–33, 199–200, 202, 319, 323–331
CFloatCombo, 467, 469–472
CFloatEdit, 137–140, 467, 469–472
CFloatOnly, 467–470, 472
CFont, 81, 631
CFormView, 10, 16, 47–48, 382, 393
CFrameWnd, 6, 10, 86, 538, 647
CF_TEXT, 377–378
CGdiObject, 145, 268
CGLView, 252–259
CHILD, 446
ChoosePixelFormat, 259
CImageList, 92, 96–97, 282, 289
CImageWell, 282–286
CInheritDlg, 471
Class Info, 63, 209, 608
Class Name, 63
ClassView, 79, 109, 118, 138
ClassWizard information file, 344–345
client area, 11, 15
CLinePosition, 97, 99
CLines, 35, 37–40, 42
clipboard support with OLE, 362
CLIP_LH_ANGLES, 644
clipping regions, 91–92
CList, 36, 131, 134, 162, 173, 188
CListBox, 377, 379, 638
CListView, 161, 621
clock display, adding to status bar, 65–78
CLockSplitter, 47, 51, 53
CloseDevice, 219, 226
CloseHandle, 503
CMapStringToString, 395–396
CMDIBarView, 82
CMDIChildFrame, 86
CMDIChildWnd, 11, 82
CMDIFrameWnd, 268–269
CMenu, 647
CMenuButton, 174–176, 180–181
CMeterBar, 87–88, 91
CMeterCtrl, 154–161
CMFileDialog, 324
CMiniFrameWnd, 649
CMultiDocTemplate, 16, 38, 43

CMultiFileDialog, 29, 32–34, 319–320, 323–324
CMultiOpenApp, 29–33
CMyToolBar, 103, 105, 109–110
CNewTypeDlg, 17–18
CoGetMalloc, 383
COleControl, 404–405, 425–426, 632
COleDataObject, 379
COleDataSource, 376–377
COleDoc, 380–381, 383–386, 395
COleDropTarget, 372, 378–379
COleFont, 526
COleIPFrameWnd, 369
COleObjectFactory, 551, 565, 594–595
COleServerItem, 368–369
COleStreamFile, 396
color cell control with OLE, 426–435
colored cursors, 125–131
COLORREF, 632
colors of controls and list boxes, changing, 141–148
ColorWell OCX, 525–526
CombineRgn, 307
combo box resizing, 609
COMHelp, 569
COMMDLG, 326
Commit, 396
common file dialog, 28, 31, 34
component-based development, 355
compound files, 380
ConditionalUp/Down, 606
CONNECT, 401–402
context menu extension, 591–601
control bars, 9
Control Method, 424
control tips, 631–639
controlling access to shared resources, 473–485
controlling view size, 10–16
ControlWizard, 403
Cool.dll, 557
CopyToClipboard, 362
CPaletteWnd, 584–590
CPicture, 14, 20, 82–86
CPoint object, 39
CProgressCtrl, 87
CProperties, 550–551, 565
CPropertyPage, 540, 556
CPropertySheet, 540

653

Create, 96–97, 157, 289, 517–518, 577–578, 629
Create versus DoModal, 337, 339, 342–343
CreateClient, 269
CreateEx, 518
CreateFileMapping, 501, 509
CreateFontIndirect, 281
CreateMutex, 445
CreatePopupMenu, 152
CreateProcess, 473, 481–483, 614
CreatePropertySheetPage, 567, 569
CreateRectRgnIndirect, 307
CreateStatic, 54
CreateStorage, 395
CREATESTRUCT, 259, 617, 620
CreateView, 54
CreateWindowEx, 270
creating storages, 380–396
CRectTracker, 641
CRecvDlg, 504–509
CRegisterClass, 544, 551, 566, 595
CRegisterMenu, 594
CRegKey, 458–459, 461, 464–465
CRgn, 290–309, 625
CRichEditView, 621
CRuntimeClass, 43
CScrollBar, 308
CScrollView, 10–11, 16, 22–23, 28
CSettingsDlg, 534, 539
CShellPropPage, 553–556, 567–568
CSingleLock, 482
CSizeView, 12, 15
CSLID, 564–565
CSliderCtrl, 308
CS_OWNDC, 253
CSphereView, 46, 50–53, 55
CSpinButtonCtrl, 631
CSpinCtrl, 633
CSpinPropPage, 422
CSplitterWnd, 45–46, 51, 53–55
cs.style, 620
CStaticBar, 111–120
CStaticCmdUI, 115–116, 119
CStatusBar, 59–61, 73–75, 78, 81, 85, 87, 91–92, 98, 111
CStorageDoc, 389
CStorageView, 382, 392–393
CString, 344–345, 448, 465, 615, 646

CTabList, 162–166
CTabStopDlg, 163–165
CTestApp, 213
CTestDoc, 383, 388
CTestView, 393, 395
CTLCOLOR_LISTBOX, 145
CToggleBar, 73–75
CToolBar, 59–61, 103, 110
CTreeView, 621
custom background erasing, 161
custom character handling, 136–137
custom control, 174, 182
  with OLE, 403–426
custom registration, 564–565
customizing, 605, 607, 610
  automatic text captions, 35–44
  DDX/DDV routines, 344–352
  File Open common dialog, 325–331
CVideoPlayApp, 213
CVideoPreviewApp, 201
CVideoView, 213–214
CView, 23, 55, 251, 291, 621
CWave, 218, 225–227
CWinApp, 29–30, 33, 77, 130, 458, 612, 614, 618, 629, 650
CWinThread, 473, 481, 484, 612
CWnd, 343, 351, 379, 470, 613–652

D

Data Tip, 610
date and time for specific locale, 76–77
DateFmtEnumProc, 76
DDE (Dynamic Data Exchange), 355–356
DDE Management Library (DDEML), 397–402
DdeCallback, 402
DDX/DDV routines, customizing, 344–352
&Debug Window, 37
debugging tips, 35, 610–612
DECLARE_OLECREATE_EX, 550–551, 565–568, 594
#defines, 318
definitions, 609
DefWindowProc, 637
DelayRate, 409, 426
Delete Device Image, 127
DeleteItem, 188–191
DeleteString, 377
DestroyWindow, 337, 343, 628

INDEX

detecting when launched applications terminate, 473–485
Developer Studio tips, 605–610
device context (DC), 258, 424
device-independent bitmaps (DIBs), 16–21, 202–211
DFVIEW, 381, 395
dialog
  boxes, expanding and contracting, 331–336
  tips, 628–631
  toolbar, 103–111
Dialog Data Exchange (DDX), 344
Dialog Data Validation (DDV), 344
dialog unit (DLU) measurements, 171
display help for dialog boxes, 314–318
DisplayErrorMsg, 220
DisplayMenu, 176–177
DispTest, 368
dithered *versus* solid colors, 146–147, 210
DlgDirList, 632–633
DlgProp, 567
DllCanUnloadNow, 542
DllClassObject, 542
DllMain, 488, 499
DLL_PROCESS_ATTACH, 499
DllRegisterServer, 542, 565, 567, 592, 599–601
DllUnregisterServer, 542, 565, 592–593, 600–601
dockable windows, 609
DOCMGR, 17
document template string segments, 20–21
documents of same type with different extensions, 16–21
DoMenu, 598, 601
DoModal, 32–33, 200, 202, 323, 326, 330, 534, 629
DoModal *versus* Create, 336–337, 342–343
DoPaint, 91
DoPropExchange, 412, 426, 430
double- *versus* single-clicks, 538–539
DownEnabled, 410
drag-and-drop in OLE, 370–379
dragging an object off-screen, 22–28
Draw, 92, 97, 289, 307–308
Draw Metafile, 424
DrawDib, 209–211
DrawEdge, 181, 434
DrawFocusRect, 181

drawing sphere, 52–53
drawing text onto bitmap, 276–281
DrawItem, 174, 178, 181, 188, 191
DrawScene, 256, 259
DrawText, 111, 119, 161, 181, 192, 280, 434, 646
DrawTriangle, 179–180
drop down menus, 174–181
DROPEFFECT_MOVE, 377
Dump, 466
dumpbin, 611–612
dwCallback, 225, 249
dwKeyState, 379
DWORD, 39–40, 97, 465
dwReason, 499
dwView, 42
dynamic shortcut menus, 148–154

E

editor window toolbar, 605
Eject, 249
elliptical regions, 22, 24, 646
EnableMenuItem, 647
EnableVisibleChildren, 334–336
EnableWindow, 335–336, 631
EN_CHANGE, 222, 280
EndDialog, 337, 628
EnumDateFormats/EnumTimeFormats, 66, 69, 76
ES_AUTOHSCROLL, 620
ES_HSCROLL, 620
ES_NUMBERS, 636
Event Log, 423
events, 405
Excel macros, 366–368
ExitInstance, 305–306, 450
ExpandDialog, 331–336
Explorer, 19, 21, 127, 570, 599
exporting classes from extension DLL, 499–500
extension DLL, 499–500
ExtTextOut, 270

F

FaceColor, 424
FAQ (Frequently Asked Questions)
  applications, 612–616
  controls, 631–639

655

debugging, 610–612
Developer Studio, 605–610
dialogs, 628–631
fonts and text, 643–647
graphics device interface (GDI), 639–643
menus, 647–649
system, 649–652
toolbars and status bars, 627–628
views and frames, 617–626
file extensions, 16–21
File information through _stat, 325–326
File New, 17, 19, 37, 44
File Open, 16, 19–20, 29, 32, 323, 326
File Save All, 127
File Save As, 20
FILECORE, 615
FileIconDlg, 329
fileNewName, 18
Files into Project, 452, 455
Filled Ellipse, 271
FillRect, 269–270, 434
filtering
  keystrokes, 466–473
  menu commands in OnCommand, 153
FindWindow, 445, 447, 620
FireClickColor, 429
Flat, 429
FloatControlDlg, 140
floating-point numbers, 136–141, 349
fluency in more than one language, 447–458
focus rectangles, 191
Font, 429
font and text tips, 643–647
fonts, 78–81
  non-proportional, 607
ForeColor, 429
foreign language versions of resource DLLs, 447–458
Format, 646
frame tips, 617–626
FreeLibrary, 306
FromString, 9
FWS_ADDTOTITLE, 623

G

GDI (graphics device interface) tips, 639–643
GDI-based TransparentBlt function, 189
GDIObject, 640
GetActiveView, 11
GetBackColor, 632
GetBarStyle, 627
GetBits, 210
GetCaretPosition, 98
GetClassLong, 275
GetClipBox, 308
GetClipRect, 307
GetClipRgn, 308
GetCommandString, 592, 601
GetCurrentDirectory, 615
GetCurrentMessage, 624
GetDateFormat, 76
GetDescendantWindow, 318, 627
GetDesktopWindow, 446, 652
GetDialogBaseUnits, 172
GetDlgCtrlID, 130, 147, 318
GetDlgItem, 631
GetEmbeddedItem, 361
GetExStyle, 620
GetFolderPath, 331
GetForeColor, 632
GetGlobalData, 379
GetItemData, 131–132, 135–136
GetItemRect, 75
GetLastActivePopup, 447
GetLength, 249
GetMenuItemInfo, 530
GetMessageBar, 86
GetMinMaxInfo, 11–15
GetModuleFileName, 614–615
GetNextPathName, 33–34, 324–325
GetNumberOfTracks, 249
GetObject, 268, 640
GetOpenFileNamePreview, 199–201
GetOwner, 650
GetPaneInfo, 81
GetParent, 330
GetParentFrame, 86, 622
GetParts, 91
GetPosition, 249
GetProfileBinary, 458
GetProp, 446
GetRect, 91
GetSafeHandle, 145
Get/Set Methods, 404
GetStartPosition, 33, 324
GetSuperWndProcAddr, 268

INDEX

GetSysColor, 649
GetSysColorBrush, 181, 640
GetSystemDirectory, 651
GetSystemMenu, 647
GetSystemMetrics, 650
GetTargetWindow, 491
GetTempPath, 651
GetTextExtent, 173, 643
GetTimeFormat, 76
GetTotalSize, 11, 15, 54
GetTrackLength, 249
GetWindow, 153, 335, 446, 650
GetWindowPlacement, 8–9
GetWindowsDirectory, 651
GetWindowText, 351, 650
GetXValue, 55
GMEM_SHARE, 374
g_months, 351–352
Go To Definition, 609
GoToMatchBrace, 606
graphics, 250–260
g_threadInfo, 506

H

HANDLE, 145
handling menu messages, 65
HBRUSH, 145
HCURSOR, 130
header files, 605–606
HitTest, 417
hkey, 465
HKEY_CURRENT_USER, 126
Hook, 498
HTCAPTION, 621–622
HTCLIENT, 621
HWND, 153, 567
HWNDNEXT, 446

I

IClassFactory, 550
icons, 270–275
IContextMenu, 592, 597, 600–601
IDataObject, 569
IDC_ACTION, 493
IDC_ADD, 375
IDC_ANY_MONTH, 346
IDC_APPLY, 464

IDC_DIVIDER, 334
IDC_EDITFILE, 222
IDC_FILE, 222
IDC_MORE, 333
IDC_PATH, 328–330
IDC_PLACEHOLDER, 161
IDC_PLAY, 223
IDC_1Q_MONTH, 346–347
IDC_START_TIMER, 155
IDC_STAYDOWN, 180
IDC_STOP, 223
IDC_SUM, 140
IDC_TYPE, 338
IDD_ABOUTBOX, 316
IDD_ABOUTBOX_SPIN, 422
IDD_CLOCK_FORMAT, 69
IDD_COLOR, 48
IDD_FORMVIEW, 47
IDD_PROPPAGE_SPIN, 421
IDD_SETTINGS, 525
ID_EDIT_CHANGECOLOR, 360
ID_FILE_OPEN, 29–30, 33, 320–321
idFrom, 111
IDI_FOLDER, 557
ID_INDICATOR_BYTES, 84
ID_INDICATOR_CARET, 98–99
ID_INDICATOR_CLOCK, 67
ID_INDICATOR_PIXELS, 83
IDI_NOCD, 523, 528
IDI_PAUSE, 523
IDI_PLAY, 523
idle states, 74–75
IDM_MENU, 584
IDR_DEBUGTYPE, 36–37
IDR_DIBTYPE, 17–18, 20
IDR-LINESTYPE, 36–37
IDR_MAINFRAME, 72, 83, 89, 104, 275, 452, 455
IDR_PICTURETYPE, 17–18, 20–21
IDR_TOOLBAR, 93, 97
IDS_COUNTDOWN, 342
IEnum, 396
#if, 606
IfClipPrecision, 644
#ifdef_WIN32, 308
IfEscapement, 644
illegal characters, 136–141, 349
ILockBytes, 380

IMalloc, 383, 396
IMPLEMENT_IUNKNOWN, 548–549
IMPLEMENT_OLECREATE, 565
IMPLIB, 308
#include, 556, 586
incremental saves in OLE, 380–396
indentation level, 607
indicator
  array, 99
  lights, adding to status bars, 91–97
InflateRect, 434
InfoViewer, 91, 111–112, 605
Initialize, 306, 540, 569, 579, 596
InitInstance, 12, 18, 20, 38, 201, 213, 274,
    305–306, 330, 376, 383, 395, 442–447, 450,
    521, 537, 590, 618
inproc server, 592
Insert Dialog, 48
Insert File into Project, 221
Insert Icon, 271
Insert OLE Control, 609–610
Insert Resource Cursor, 127
Insert Toolbar, 93
InsertMenu, 600
Instance, 498
INTERFACE_MAP, 551, 595
Invalidate, 639
InvalidateControl, 425
InvalidateRgn, 307
invisible windows, 620
Invoke Methods, 424
InvokeCommand, 592, 601
IPropShellExt, 569
IsDataAvailable, 378–379
IsFloatChar, 469–470, 472
IShellExtInit, 540, 552, 569, 596
IShellPropExt, 553
IShellPropSheetExt, 540, 569
IsIconic, 446
IsMediaPresent/Playing, 249
IStorage, 383–385, 395–396
IsWindowVisible, 620, 650
IUnknown, 540, 548, 569

K

KillTimer, 238
Knowledge Base, 127

L

language-specific resources, localizing, 447–458
LB_ADDSTRING, 379
LBN_SELCHANGE, 132
LB_SETITEMDATA, 134
LB_SETTABSTOPS, 172
LBS_MULTICOLUMN, 161
LBS_USETABSTOPS, 162
lengthy operations, posting percent completed,
    154–161
<<Less, 332
Lightfv, 259
line and column positions in status bar, 97–102
&Lines Window, 37
Linked Text, 134
list box
  associating data with, 131–136
  changing colors of, 141–148
list control, 44
LoadBarState, 6
LoadCursor, 130
LoadFromStorage, 383, 386, 396
LoadIcon, 270–275
LoadLibrary, 306, 601
LoadNewIcon, 271–275
LoadStandardCursor, 650
LoadString, 448, 457–458
LoadToolBar, 110–111
LoadWindowPlacement, 6–10
local message processing, 27
locale-specific date and time, 76
localizing applications, 447–458
Lock, 483
Lock Bar check box, 50
locking splitter window containing different
    views, 44–55
LOGFONT, 81, 281, 644
LPARAM, 111, 153, 616, 637
LPDRAWITEMSTRUCT parameters, 188
LPENUMSTATSTG, 396
lpstrElementName, 225
LRESULT, 616

M

Main, 605
MAINFRM, 51, 78, 80, 86
malloc, 501

INDEX

MapViewOfFile, 502
masked edit control, 636
matching parentheses, 606
maximizing first pane while displaying menu help, 61–65
_MAX_PATH, 28, 319
m_bar, 85, 119
m_bAutoDelete, 385
m_bAutoMenuEnable, 647
m_bAutoScroll, 27
m_bFlat, 434
m_bIsScrolling, 27
m_bLocked, 47
m_bMediaPresent, 238
m_bModeless, 339, 343
m_bPaneOn, 75
m_brush, 145
m_bSaveAndValidate, 351–352
m_bSelected, 429, 431
m_bStayDown, 180
MCI_CLOSE, 226, 248
MCI_FROM, 249
mciGetErrorString, 250
MCI_NOTIFY, 223, 225, 245, 247
MCI_OPEN, 225, 248
MCI_PAUSE, 249
MCI_PLAY, 249
mciSendCommand, 225, 246–247, 249–250
MCI_SET, 249
MCI_STATUS_PARAMS, 249
MCI_TO, 249
MCI_WAIT, 225, 247
MCIWnd (Media Control Interface Window), 211, 213–215
m_color, 46, 53, 283
m_csListBox, 476
m_cTracks, 534
m_cxAvailable, 119
m_cxPaneWidth, 65
m_dataSource, 374
MDI child frame, 11, 15–16
MeasureItem, 188, 191–192
Member Variables, 49, 184, 347, 504, 631
memcpy, 536, 540
Memory debug, 611
memory device contexts, 276–281
memory-mapped files, 501–509
menu help, including, 61–65

menu tips, 647–649
MenuButtonCtrl, 176–179
message filter, 608
Message Maps, 36, 558, 577, 608
message queue, 27, 74–75
message reflection, 174
MessageBox, 499
Meter Test command, 90
METHOD_PROLOGUE, 567
MFC class library, rebuilding, 10
MFC Encyclopedia, 543
MFC source code, 31
m_font, 278
MFS_DEFAULT, 539
m_hAVI, 214
m_hLib, 306
m_hPrevInstance, 442, 445
m_hWndMDIClient, 268–269
Microsoft Development Library, 46, 500
Microsoft Foundation Class Library, 500
Microsoft Knowledge Base, 270, 343
Microsoft Technical Note, 86, 91
MIDI (musical instrument digital interface), 216
minimized icons, animating, 270–275
mix-in classes, 467
MK_CONTROL, 379
m_lastPoint, 118
m_lf, 81
m_list, 96, 307
m_lpRootStg, 383–384
MM_ANISOTROPIC mapping mode, 363
m_menu, 153
m_meter, 161
MM_MCNOTIFY, 219, 223–225, 245–247
m_nCmdShow, 618
m_nDirection, 408
mnemonic keys, 336
m_nMenuItems, 153
m_nPanelID, 75
m_nSeconds, 340
modal *versus* modeless dialogs, 336–343
ModifyStyleEx, 114
m_ofn, 202, 323
monitoring state of memory-mapped files, 501–509
More>>, 331–332
mouse clicks, detecting in status bar, 75

mouse messages, routing to application, 486–500
MoveWindow, 621
movie file playback, 211–215
m_pDlg, 340
m_pDlgWnd, 351
m_pDropTarget, 379
m_pMainWnd, 612
m_pMapView, 502
m_points array, 41, 44
m_posBitmap, 278
m_pOther, 119
m_pszExeName, 445
m_pszFileName, 33, 324
m_pszHelpFilePath, 614
m_pTermThreadsEvent, 476
m_pThread, 505
m_size, 306
m_sizeBitmap, 278
m_sizeCurrent, 579
m_strOwner, 460
m_szPath, 569, 596
Multi File Open Dialog, 320
multicolumn list box, 173
multilevel commits in OLE, 380–396
Multimedia\DiscPlayer directory, 234
multiple file selection, 28
multiple inheritance, 466–473
multiple instances of running application, preventing, 441–447
multiple view selection, 28–34
Multiple-Document, 454
multithreaded applications, 473–485
mutex, 445
m_wndList, 474
m_wndNewClient, 268
m_wndSplitter, 51
m_wndStatusBar, 73–74
m_wState, 408
MyThreadProc, 506, 508

N

National Language Support API (NLSAPI), 72, 76
nChar, 141
nCtlColor, 145, 630
nEnd, 101–102
New Device Image, 271

New Key, 126
New String Value, 126
New Window, 305
Next Statement, 611
nID, 130, 648
nMapFactor, 28
/NOENTRY, 452, 456
non-rectangular shapes, 281–290
nonsignaled, 482
NotifyChanged, 366
NOTIFYICONDATA, 538
nStart, 101–102
NUM_WELLS_ACROSS, 534
nWidth, 179

O

Object IDs combo-box, 83
object server in OLE, 357–369
OFN_ALLOWMULTISELECT, 32, 323
OLE Controls Inside Out by Adam Denning, 426
OLE (Object Linking and Embedding), 13, 355–356
  automation server, 357–369
  Automation tab, 364–365
  clipboard support, 362
  color cell control, 426–435
  custom control, 403–426
  drag-and-drop, 370–379
  incremental saves, 380–396
  multilevel commits, 380–396
  object server, 357–369
  spin control, 403–426
  structured storage, 380–396
OLE_COLOR, 422, 632
OnActivate, 535
OnActivateView, 208–210
OnAdd, 134, 144, 164
OnAppAbout, 318
OnAppBarNotify, 581
OnApply, 50, 465
OnAutoScroll, 27–28
OnBackColor, 144–145
OnCancel, 337, 628
OnCancelMode, 418
OnChangeEdit, 222, 280
OnChar, 141, 470, 472, 637
OnClick, 288
OnClickColor, 535–536

INDEX

OnClose, 6–8, 613
OnCloseDocument, 385, 503
OnCmdMsg, 536
OnCommand, 151, 153, 588
ON_COMMAND, 647
ON_COMMAND_RANGE, 536
OnContextMenu, 150, 153, 587
OnCreate, 6–8, 80, 85–86, 119, 240, 253, 258–259, 267–268, 273, 528
OnCtlColor, 141–142, 145–147, 637
OnDelete, 165
OnDestroy, 134–135, 246, 255, 258, 274, 528, 535, 579
OnDisableColorChange, 409
OnDisplayChange, 581
OnDragEnter, 378–379
OnDragOver, 378–379
OnDraw, 22, 24–25, 40, 52, 55, 118, 254, 307, 362–363, 413, 424, 430, 451, 641
OnDrop, 378–379
OnEditChangeColor, 360, 366
OnEditCopy, 362
OnEject, 244
OnEnableColorChange, 410
OnEraseBkgnd, 158, 266, 268–269, 289–290, 418
ON_EVENT, 539
ON_EVENT_RANGE, 536, 540
OnFileNameChange, 329, 331
OnFileNew, 13
OnFileOpen, 29, 31, 33–34, 319, 322
OnFolderChange, 329, 331
OnFormatClockPane, 72–73, 77
OnGetMinMaxInfo, 11–15, 94
OnHScroll, 304, 308
OnIdle, 77
OnInitDialog, 108, 144, 152, 159, 180, 192, 241, 278, 288, 335, 375, 463, 472, 476, 494, 506, 534, 539, 569, 625, 636
OnInitDone, 328, 330–331
OnInitialUpdate, 15, 22, 24, 40–41, 44, 49, 95–96, 208, 210, 214–215, 254, 259, 394
OnInitInstance, 8
OnInitMenuPopUp, 62
OnLBSelChangeNotify, 330–331
OnLButtonDown, 40, 75, 419, 425
OnLButtonUp, 420, 539
OnLeftClick, 530, 539

OnLeftDoubleClick, 531, 539
OnLoadDocument, 383, 396
OnLockBar, 50
OnMCINotify, 224
ON_MESSAGE, 115, 616, 643
OnMouseMove, 47, 307, 318, 420, 434
OnMove, 580
OnNcCalcSize, 434
OnNcDestroy, 554
OnNcHitTest, 580
OnNcPaint, 434, 649
OnNeedText, 111
OnNewCD, 238
OnNewDocument, 207, 384, 391, 395, 502
OnNext, 243
ON_NOTIFY, 110
OnNotifySize, 214
OnOK, 337, 372, 628
OnOpenDocument, 207, 386
ON_OWNDC, 259
OnPaint, 158, 278–279, 289, 304, 587, 625
OnPause, 243
OnPlay, 242
OnPrev, 243
OnQueryNewPalette, 208
ON_REGISTERED_MESSAGE, 616
OnReset, 165
OnResetState, 430
OnSaveDocument, 383, 385, 395
OnSelChangeList, 134, 165
OnSelChangeNameList, 394
OnSelChangeTrack, 244
OnSetCoordinates, 505, 507
OnSetCursor, 47, 125, 129–130, 151, 256, 315, 318
OnSetExtent, 411, 426
OnSetMessageString, 86
OnSetText, 643
OnSize, 87, 90, 255, 268
OnSizeParent, 115
OnStartTimer, 160
OnStatusBarChangeFont, 80
OnTestMeterBar, 89–90
OnTextColor, 144–145
OnTimer, 160, 244, 255, 273, 419, 521, 528, 531
OnToolHitTest, 589
OnTrackList, 531

661

OnUpdate, 41–42
OnUpdateCaretPos, 98–101
OnUpdateClock, 69, 74, 77
ON_UPDATE_COMMAND_UI, 65–66, 83, 85, 119, 647
OnUpdateFrameTitle, 43–44
OnUpdateIndicatorBytes, 84–85
OnUpdateIndicatorPixels, 84–85
OnUpdateStaticBar, 118–119
OnVerticalChanged, 408
OnViewChangeFont, 80
OnViewDebugWindow, 37
OnViewLinesWindow, 37
OnWindowPosChanged, 580
OPAQUE background mode, 280, 642
Open, 465
OpenDevice, 218, 225
OpenDocumentFile, 29, 34, 319, 324–325
OpenFileMapping, 506
OPENFILENAME, 199, 202
OpenGL, 250–260
opening multiple
  documents, 28–34
  files, 319–325
optimized paint handling through regions, 290–309

P

painting
  background bitmaps, 264–270
  custom buttons, 174–181
Palette tab, 127
palettes, monitoring, 572–591
pane styles and rectangles, 87, 91
parent/child relationship, 54
parsing the toolbar resource, 109–110
Pause, 249
PC_EXPLICIT, 586
pcFlags, 586
pCmdUI, 85
percentage of task completed, monitoring, 86–91
Persistent Window Position, 6
PIXELFORMATDESCRIPTOR, 259
Play, 219, 225, 249
playing
  audio CD, 227–250
  AVI files in a CView, 211–215

large WAV files, 216–227
pObject, 42
POINT, 40, 417
point sizing type, 643
polar coordinates, 258–259
Polyline, 35, 40, 413
popup menus, 62–65, 150–153, 177–181, 302
PostMessage, 377
PostNcDestroy, 343, 519, 579, 628
pragma, 201
#pragma data_seg, 488
PreCreateWindow, 12, 253, 259, 445, 617, 619–620, 623
PrepareEditCtrl, 352
PreTranslateMessage, 588
preview window, 199–202
printf, 646
Process Viewer, 484
PROCESS_ATTACH/DETACH, 499
progress information, in minimalized application, 270–275
projects
  AnimateIcon, 270–275
  AppBar, 572–591
  AutoScroll, 22–28
  Background, 264–270
  BarDialog, 103–111
  BigWave, 216–227
  BmpList, 182–193
  BmpPane, 91–97
  CaptionBar, 111–120
  ColorWell, 426–435
  CtlColor, 141–148
  Cursor, 125–131
  CustomDDX, 344–352
  CustomOpen, 325–331
  DDE (Dynamic Data Exchange), 397–402
  DialogHelp, 314–318
  DiscPlayer, 227–250
  DocExt, 16–21
  DrawDib, 202–211
  DynamicMenu, 148–154
  Expand, 331–336
  FloatControl, 136–141
  Inherit, 466–473
  Language, 447–458
  Launch, 473–485
  LinePosition, 97–102

INDEX

Lines, 35–44
ListData, 131–136
MDIBar, 81–86
MenuButton, 174–181
Meter, 154–161
Modeless, 336–343
Mousedll, 486–500
MultiOpen, 28–34, 319–325
OpenGL, 250–260
Oval, 357–369
PaneWidth, 61–65
Poker, 290–309
ProgressMeter, 86–91
Registry, 458–465
RegServer, 591–601
Remember, 5–10
Send, 501–509
Single, 441–447
SizeView, 10–16
Sphere, 44–55
Spin, 403–426
StatusBarFont, 78–81
Storage, 380–396
Subfolders, 540–571
TabStop, 161–173
TextOnBitmap, 276–281
TimePane, 65–78
ToDo, 370–379
TransBitmap, 281–290
TrayApp, 515–540
VideoPlay, 211–215
VideoPreview, 199–202
property pages, 404
property sheet handler for file or folder, 540–571
proportionally spaced fonts, 171–173
PropPageCallback, 554
PROPPAGEIDS, 422
PtInRect, 75
ptMaxTrackSize, 15

Q

quadric shapes, 259
QueryContextMenu, 592, 600
QueryDragFile, 569
QuerySetPos, 579
QuickWatch debug, 610

R

raster operations, 281–290
rcLarge, 334, 336
rcSmall, 334
RDW_FRAME flag, 434
Read, 465
ReadName, 396
RealizePalette, 209
reBounds, 413
RecalcLayout, 81
Record Keystrokes, 607
Redirect to Output Window, 611
RedrawWindow, 268, 434
reference counting property pages, 565–568
RefreshWindow, 365
RegCreateKeyEx, 465
RegEdit, 126, 538
Regional Settings control panel, 76, 78
Register, 375, 378, 566
  Control, 565, 600–601
  debug, 611
RegisterShellFileTypes, 615
RegisterWindowMessage, 616
registration database, 458–465, 591–601
RegServer, 599–601
Release, 305–306, 523
ReleaseCapture, 431
Remove, 579
RemoveMenu, 152
RemovePages, 569
rendering context (RC), 258–259
RepeatRate, 409, 426
ReplacePages, 540
ReplaceSel, 639
ResizeParentToFit, 15
resizing columns in multicolumn list box, 161–173
Resource Symbols, 608, 647
resource-only DLLs, 447
ResourceView, 47, 93, 104, 127, 327, 516, 599
RestoreDC, 290
restricting view size, 10–16
ResumePlay, 249
RIFF (resource interchange file format), 216
rotated text, 644–645
row and column positions, displaying in status bar, 97–102

RPC_E_CANTCALLOUT_ININPUTSYNCCALL, 539
runtime loading of a DLL, 290–309

S

SaveBarState, 6
SaveDC, 290
SaveToStorage, 383, 385–386, 395
SaveWindowPlacement, 6–9
saving position and state information, 5–10
SBT_OWNERDRAW, 92
scroll
  bars, 14
  during mouse drags, 22–28
  speed, 27
ScrollToPosition, 27–28
SECTION, 498
Select Playback Recording, 607
selecting multiple
  files, 319–325
  views, 28–34
SelectStockObject, 639
self-draw, 182
  buttons, 174
  list boxes, 182–193
Send, 501, 504, 509
Serialize, 292, 362, 396
serializing methods, 290–309
SetAction, 490
SetBarStyle, 627
SetBitmap, 634
SetBkColor, 146–147, 270
SetBkMode, 642
SetButtons, 110
SetCapture, 431
SetClassLong, 275
SetColumnHeight, 192
SetColumnInfo, 54
SetColumnSpace, 162
SetColumnWidth, 192
SetCursor, 130
SetDialogBkColor, 629
SetDisplayWindow, 490
SetEvent, 482
SetFont, 78, 631
SetForegroundWindow, 446
SetIcon, 634
SetImageList, 96

SetItemData, 131–132, 135–136
SetListStyle, 42
SetMenuItemInfo, 530
SetModifiedFlag, 307, 366
SetPaneInfo, 64, 81
SetPaneText, 317–318
SetParts, 90
SetPoint, 417
SetPos, 91, 307, 631
SetProp, 445
SetRange, 633
SetRedraw, 638–639
SetRegistryKey, 6, 8, 458
SetRGB, 366–368
SetRowInfo, 54
SetSel, 639
SetTabStops, 162, 172
SetText, 92, 97, 115, 119–120
SetThePixelFormat, 253, 256
SetTimer, 77–78, 238, 275, 419
Settings, 452
SetToSystemColors, 404, 406, 411
SetWindowPlacement, 6, 8
SetWindowPos, 620–621
SetWindowRgn, 624–625
SetWindowsHookEx, 490, 495, 498
SetWindowText, 623–624, 627
SHAppBarMessage, 572–573, 591
shared memory in Win32 DLLs, 497
sharing data among applications, 501–509
  with DDE, 397–402
ShellExecute, 565, 614
Shell_NotifyIcon, 515, 519
SHGetFileInfo, 331, 612
shortcut
  keys, 605
  menus, 148–154
showing different views of a single document, 35–44
ShowWindow, 366, 446, 618, 620
signaled, 482
sizeof(DWORD), 509
sizing a CView, 210
sndPlaySound, 216
Sort, 609
speed penalty, 173
SphereDoc, 46
spin control, 48–49

INDEX

with OLE, 403–426
splitter bars, 10, 14, 44
splitter window, 45, 53
Spy++ tool, 54
Start, 489
Start Timer button, 154–155
static
  member callbacks, 402
  splitters, 45
  variables, 91
status bar
  attached to CView, 82
  displaying dialog box help, 314–318
  displaying row and column positions, 97–102
  indicator lighting, 91–97
  monitoring percentage of task completed, 86–91
  pane styles, 78–81
  showing current time in, 65–78
  tips, 627–628
StdAfx, 72, 201, 204, 212, 217, 371, 395, 475, 541, 566, 571
StepIt, 91
StgCreateDocfile, 384–385
StgOpenStorage, 386
Stop, 220, 249, 489, 607
storing application information and user preferences, 458–465
StretchDIBits, 211
stretching bitmaps by resizing window, 202–211
string resources, 31–32, 447
strtod, 141
strtok, 33
structured storage in OLE, 380–396
SubclassDlgItem, 636
subclassing
  combo box edit window, 467
  list boxes, 371
  MDI client window, 264–270
SW_HIDE, 620
SwitchToView, 39, 43–44
SWP_NOSIZE, 621
SW_SHOWMAXIMIZED/SHOWMINIMIZED, 618–619
system
  hooks, 486–500
  tips, 649–652

SystemParametersInfo, 114, 281, 649
szExeName, 611

T

TabbedTextOut, 646
tabstops for creating multicolumn list box, 161–173
Task Manager, 650
TEMP, 651
TerminateWindow, 613
TEST, 321
Test Container, 423–425
text
  blocks, 606
  captions, 35–44
  clipboard format, 370–371
  superimposed on bitmap, 276–281
  tips, 643–647
theApp (global variable), 37–38
ThreadInfo, 481, 506
ThreadingModel, 551, 565, 595
ThreadProc, 569
three-state push buttons, 635
time style, 78
TimeFmtEnumProc, 76
TimeProc, 77–78
timers, 68–69
TODO, 278, 442
toolbar
  for all views, 81–86
  for a dialog, 103–111
  tips, 627–628
tooltip text notification messages, 109–110
tracking cursor movement between controls, 125–131
TrackPopupMenu, 150, 153, 177, 181, 308, 530
TrackRubberBand, 641
TranslateColor, 632
TRANSPARENT background mode, 280, 642
transparent bitmaps, 281–290
TransparentBlt function, 189, 192
tray application to play CDs, 515–540
TTN_NEEDTEXT, 110

U

undocking, 609
Unicode, 611

Unlock, 483
UpdateAllViews, 42, 44, 50, 53, 307, 366
UpdateCaretPos, 99
UPDATE_COMMAND_UI, 84
UpdateData, 465
UpdateInfo, 238–239
UpdatePosition, 238, 240
UpdateRegistry, 551, 565
UpdateTrackInfo, 238–239
UpEnabled, 410–411
Use Split Window, 45
user-defined messages, 615–616
users, keeping posted, 154–161

V

video preview window, 199–202
View, 35
view and frame tips, 617–626
View Debug, 43
Visual Basic control (VBX), 403

W

WaitForMultipleObjects, 482–483
WaitForSingleObject, 473, 482, 484
Watch debug, 611
WAV (waveform audio) file player, 216–227
wDeviceID, 225
wglCreateContext, 258
wglDeleteContext, 258
Win32 DLLs, 497–499
Win32 registry, 458–465
WINCORE, 110
window
　class variables, 270–275
　placement, 6–8
　properties, 446–447
　scrolling during mouse drags, 22–28
　style, 617
Windows Interface Guidelines, 427, 434
WinError, 539
WinExec, 614
Winfrm, 86
WINUTIL, 623
WM_CANCELMODE, 425
WM_CHAR, 138, 141, 470–472, 636–637
WM_CLOSE, 9, 509, 613
WM_COMMAND, 148, 151, 153–154
WM_CONTEXTMENU, 153, 587
WM_CREATE, 85, 88, 95, 113, 117, 267, 375, 378, 487
WM_CTLCOLOR, 141, 145, 630, 638
WM_DESTROY, 317, 442, 477, 570, 613
WM_DRAWITEM, 92
WM_DROPFILES, 224
WM_ERASEBKGND, 114, 154, 161, 268, 284, 419, 425, 622
WM_GETITEMDATA, 132
WM_GETMINMAXINFO, 11
WM_HSCROLL, 308
WM_IDLEUPDATECMDUI, 318
WM_INITDIALOG, 71, 103, 159, 567
WM_INITMENUPOPUP, 62, 64–65
WM_LBUTTONDBLCLK, 425, 538–539
WM_LBUTTONDOWN, 47, 53, 96, 118, 371, 374, 377, 419, 425, 538–539, 622, 641–642
WM_LBUTTONUP, 25, 27, 377, 420, 426, 538–539
WM_MENUSELECT, 62, 64
WM_MOUSE, 494
WM_MOUSEMOVE, 318, 420, 425, 431, 434
WM_NCCALCSIZE, 433–434
WM_NCHITTEST, 621, 626
WM_NCLBUTTONDOWN, 622
WM_NCPAINT, 429, 431, 434
WM_NOTIFY, 110–111
WM_PAINT, 25, 114, 154, 285, 289
WM_PALETTECHANGED, 208–210
WM_QUERYNEWPALETTE, 208, 210
WM_QUERYOPEN, 619
WM_RBUTTONDOWN, 153
WM_RBUTTONUP, 538
WM_SET_COORDINATES, 505, 507
WM_SETCURSOR, 53, 125, 128–130, 315–316, 318
WM_SETFONT, 78
WM_SETICON, 617
WM_SETITEMDATA, 131
WM_SETMESSAGESTRING, 85–86, 318
WM_SETTEXT, 643
WM_SIZE, 36, 88, 91, 95, 119–120, 258, 268
WM_SIZEPARENT, 115, 119
WM_SYSCOMMAND, 648
WM_TIMER, 68, 74, 77, 90, 240, 244, 418, 426, 528
WM_USER, 616

INDEX

WM_WININICHANGED, 405–406
WndDisplay, 497
WndPrevTarget, 498
word wrap, 620
wParam, 153, 616, 637
Write, 465
WriteProfileBinary, 458
WriteProfileString, 6, 8
WS_CHILD, 326, 330
WS_CLIPCHILDREN, 253, 259
WS_CLIPSIBLINGS, 253, 259
WS_EX_CLIENTEDGE, 114, 154
WS_EX_STATICEDGE, 154
WS_EX_TOOLWINDOW, 518, 538, 578
WS_EX_TOPMOST, 620
WS_MAXIMIZE/MINIMIZE, 619
WS_POPUP, 330
WS_THICKFRAME, 16
WS_VISIBLE, 538, 635

NOTES

NOTES

NOTES

ENVIRONMENTAL AWARENESS

Books have a substantial influence on the destruction of the forests of the Earth. For example, it takes 17 trees to produce one ton of paper. A first printing of 30,000 copies of a typical 480-page book consumes 108,000 pounds of paper, which will require 918 trees!

Waite Group Press™ is against the clear-cutting of forests and supports reforestation of the Pacific Northwest of the United States and Canada, where most of this paper comes from. As a publisher with several hundred thousand books sold each year, we feel an obligation to give back to the planet. We will therefore support organizations which seek to preserve the forests of planet Earth.

WAITE GROUP PRESS™

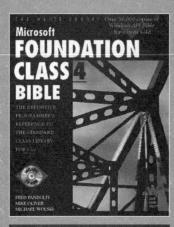

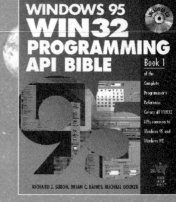

MICROSOFT FOUNDATION CLASS 4 BIBLE
Fred Pandolfi, Mike Oliver, Michael Wolski

Microsoft Foundation Class 4 Bible is the most complete and easy-to-use reference available on MFC, the industry standard for C++ Windows 95 development. It covers all aspects of Windows programming organized by function and with thorough indexing and jumptables to make it easy to find exactly what you need.

The CD includes the entire text of the book in WinHelp format, source code, hundreds of practical examples, and sample programs.

Available Now • 1000 pages
ISBN: 1-57169-021-2
U.S. $59.99 Can. $81.99
1—CD-ROM

OPENGL SUPERBIBLE
Richard S. Wright Jr. and Michael R. Sweet

The most comprehensive, definitive guide to OpenGL programming for Windows NT and Windows 95 available. This new addition to the popular SuperBible series offers hundreds of tricks and techniques for mastering OpenGL—the powerful 3D graphics API that is the undisputed king in the special effects and entertainment industry. The CD includes all the source code and binaries for the examples in the book, as well as executable files for Intel, MIPS, APLHA, and PowerPC-based systems., a free OCX control and OpenGL VRML Viewer.

Available August 1996
900 pages
ISBN: 1-57169-073-5
U.S. $59.99 Can. $81.99
1—CD-ROM

WINDOWS 95 WIN32 PROGRAMMING API BIBLE
Richard J. Simon

Following the proven format of its best-selling predecessors, *Windows API Bible* and *Windows API New Testament*, *Windows 95 Win32 Programming API Bible* covers all Win32 APIs common to both Windows 95 and Windows NT and provides an overview of new Windows 95 programming style and techniques, as well as Windows API. This is a vital Windows 95 programming resource.

Available Now • 1,300 pages
ISBN: 1-57169-009-3
U.S. $54.95 Can. $74.95
1—CD-ROM

Send for our unique catalog to get more information about these books as well as our outstanding and award-winning titles.

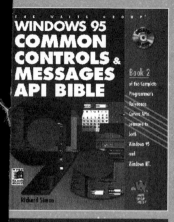
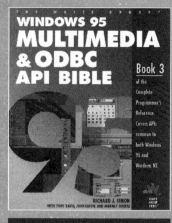
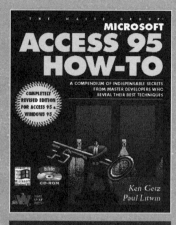

WAITE GROUP PRESS™

WINDOWS 95 COMMON CONTROLS & MESSAGES API BIBLE
Richard J. Simon

To get Microsoft's Windows 95 seal of compatibility for your application, you'll want *Windows 95 Database & Controls API Bible*, the only reference book that covers inter-applications for both Windows 95 and Windows NT. Using the acclaimed Waite Group Bible format, the book is designed for both C and C++ programmers of all levels and contains hundreds of examples.

Available Now • 1,000 pages
ISBN: 1-57169-010-7
U.S. $54.99 Can. $74.99
1–CD-ROM

WINDOWS 95 MULTIMEDIA & ODBC API BIBLE
Richard J. Simon

This exhaustive reference on communication programming calls covers Open Database Connectivity 2.5, Telephony, Common Messaging Calls, and Multimedia APIs. Thorough coverage on every function includes concise descriptions and hundreds of examples, detailed instructions, code, usage syntax, parameters, professional tips, and possible pitfalls. The bundled CD-ROM contains all the example programs and source code developed in the book.

Available Now • 1,100 pages
ISBN: 1-57169-011-5
U.S. $54.99 Can. $74.99
1–CD-ROM

MICROSOFT ACCESS 95 HOW-TO
Ken Getz, Paul Litwin

Microsoft Access 95 How-To shows beginners, power users, and database professionals the best tips, tricks, and techniques for mastering this flexible 32-bit database. These user-friendly How-Tos offer step-by-step solutions to real-life Access development problems. The CD contains all the examples, sample databases, code resources, utilities, OLE controls, demos, and more.

Available Now • 700 pages
ISBN: 1-57169-052-2
U.S. $44.99 Can. $59.99
1–CD-ROM

TO ORDER TOLL FREE, CALL 1-800-428-5331
• FAX 1-800-882-8583 •

Source Code: MCBP

OR SEND ORDER FORM TO: MACMILLAN COMPUTER PUBLISHING, ATTENTION: ORDER DEPT., 201 W. 103rd ST., INDIANAPOLIS, IN 46290

Qty	Book	US Price	Total
___	Microsoft Foundation Class 4 Bible	$59.99	___
___	OpenGL SuperBible	$59.99	___
___	Win95 Win32 Programming API Bible	$54.95	___
___	Win95 Com. Con. & Messages API Bible	$54.97	___
___	Win95 Multimedia & ODBC API Bible	$54.97	___
___	Microsoft Access 95 How-To	$44.99	___

Calif. residents add 7.25% Sales Tax ___

Shipping
$2.50/title
Please add appropriate sales tax for your state
Canada ($10/$4) ___
TOTAL ___

Ship to:
Name _____
Company _____
Address _____
City, State, Zip _____
Phone _____

Payment Method (Please make checks payable to Macmillan Computer Publishing USA)
☐ Check Enclosed   ☐ Visa   ☐ MasterCard   ☐ AmericanExpress

Card#_____ Exp. Date _____
Signature _____

SHIPPING: All shipments are handled F.O.B., Indianapolis. Products are shipped UPS, unless you request otherwise. Please provide a street address and include proper shipping and handling charges.

SATISFACTION GUARANTEED OR YOUR MONEY BACK.

This is a legal agreement between you, the end user and purchaser, and The Waite Group®, Inc., and the authors of the programs contained in the disk. By opening the sealed disk package, you are agreeing to be bound by the terms of this Agreement. If you do not agree with the terms of this Agreement, promptly return the unopened disk package and the accompanying items (including the related book and other written material) to the place you obtained them for a refund.

SOFTWARE LICENSE

1. The Waite Group, Inc. grants you the right to use one copy of the enclosed software programs (the programs) on a single computer system (whether a single CPU, part of a licensed network, or a terminal connected to a single CPU). Each concurrent user of the program must have exclusive use of the related Waite Group, Inc. written materials.

2. The program, including the copyrights in each program, is owned by the respective author and the copyright in the entire work is owned by The Waite Group, Inc. and they are therefore protected under the copyright laws of the United States and other nations, under international treaties. You may make only one copy of the disk containing the programs exclusively for backup or archival purposes, or you may transfer the programs to one hard disk drive, using the original for backup or archival purposes. You may make no other copies of the programs, and you may make no copies of all or any part of the related Waite Group, Inc. written materials.

3. You may not rent or lease the programs, but you may transfer ownership of the programs and related written materials (including any and all updates and earlier versions) if you keep no copies of either, and if you make sure the transferee agrees to the terms of this license.

4. You may not decompile, reverse engineer, disassemble, copy, create a derivative work, or otherwise use the programs except as stated in this Agreement.

GOVERNING LAW

This Agreement is governed by the laws of the State of California.

LIMITED WARRANTY

The following warranties shall be effective for 90 days from the date of purchase: (i) The Waite Group, Inc. warrants the enclosed disk to be free of defects in materials and workmanship under normal use; and (ii) The Waite Group, Inc. warrants that the programs, unless modified by the purchaser, will substantially perform the functions described in the documentation provided by The Waite Group, Inc. when operated on the designated hardware and operating system. The Waite Group, Inc. does not warrant that the programs will meet purchaser's requirements or that operation of a program will be uninterrupted or error-free. The program warranty does not cover any program that has been altered or changed in any way by anyone other than The Waite Group, Inc. The Waite Group, Inc. is not responsible for problems caused by changes in the operating characteristics of computer hardware or computer operating systems that are made after the release of the programs, nor for problems in the interaction of the programs with each other or other software.

THESE WARRANTIES ARE EXCLUSIVE AND IN LIEU OF ALL OTHER WARRANTIES OF MERCHANTABILITY OR FITNESS FOR A PARTICULAR PURPOSE OR OF ANY OTHER WARRANTY, WHETHER EXPRESS OR IMPLIED.

EXCLUSIVE REMEDY

The Waite Group, Inc. will replace any defective disk without charge if the defective disk is returned to The Waite Group, Inc. within 90 days from date of purchase.

This is Purchaser's sole and exclusive remedy for any breach of warranty or claim for contract, tort, or damages.

LIMITATION OF LIABILITY

THE WAITE GROUP, INC. AND THE AUTHORS OF THE PROGRAMS SHALL NOT IN ANY CASE BE LIABLE FOR SPECIAL, INCIDENTAL, CONSEQUENTIAL, INDIRECT, OR OTHER SIMILAR DAMAGES ARISING FROM ANY BREACH OF THESE WARRANTIES EVEN IF THE WAITE GROUP, INC. OR ITS AGENT HAS BEEN ADVISED OF THE POSSIBILITY OF SUCH DAMAGES.

THE LIABILITY FOR DAMAGES OF THE WAITE GROUP, INC. AND THE AUTHORS OF THE PROGRAMS UNDER THIS AGREEMENT SHALL IN NO EVENT EXCEED THE PURCHASE PRICE PAID.

COMPLETE AGREEMENT

This Agreement constitutes the complete agreement between The Waite Group, Inc. and the authors of the programs, and you, the purchaser.

Some states do not allow the exclusion or limitation of implied warranties or liability for incidental or consequential damages, so the above exclusions or limitations may not apply to you. This limited warranty gives you specific legal rights; you may have others, which vary from state to state.

SATISFACTION REPORT CARD

Please fill out this card if you wish to know of future updates to
Visual C++ 4 How-To, or to receive our catalog.

Name: _____ Last Name: _____

Address: _____

_____ State: _____ Zip: _____

Address: _____

Telephone: (_____) _____

Product was acquired: Month _____ Day _____ Year _____ Your Occupation: _____

How would you rate *Visual C++ 4 How-To*?

☐ Excellent ☐ Very Good ☐ Good
☐ Below Average ☐ Poor

What did you like MOST about this book? _____
_____
_____

What did you like LEAST about this book? _____
_____
_____

Please describe any problems you may have encountered with installing or using the disk: _____
_____

How did you use this book (problem-solver, tutorial, reference...)?
_____

What is your level of computer expertise?

☐ New User ☐ Dabbler ☐ Hacker
☐ Power User ☐ Programmer ☐ Experienced Professional

What computer languages are you familiar with? _____
_____

Please describe your computer hardware:

Computer _____ Hard disk _____
5.25" drives _____ 3.5" disk drives _____
Video card _____ Monitor _____
Sound card _____ Peripherals _____
Modem _____ CD ROM _____

Where did you buy this book?

☐ Bookstore (name): _____
☐ Discount store (name): _____
☐ Computer store (name): _____
☐ Catalog (name): _____
☐ Direct from WGP   ☐ Other _____

What price did you pay for this book? _____

What influenced your purchase of this book?

☐ Recommendation   ☐ Advertisement
☐ Magazine review   ☐ Store display
☐ Mailing   ☐ Book's format
☐ Reputation of Waite Group Press   ☐ Other

How many computer books do you buy each year? _____

How many other Waite Group books do you own? _____

What is your favorite Waite Group book? _____
_____

Is there any program or subject you would like to see Waite Group Press cover in a similar approach? _____
_____

Additional comments? _____
_____
_____

Please send to: Waite Group Press
                  200 Tamal Plaza
                  Corte Madera, CA 94925

☐ Check here for a free Waite Group catalog

BEFORE YOU OPEN THE DISK OR CD-ROM PACKAGE ON THE FACING PAGE, CAREFULLY READ THE LICENSE AGREEMENT.

Opening this package indicates that you agree to abide by the license agreement found in the back of this book. If you do not agree with it, promptly return the unopened disk package (including the related book) to the place you obtained them for a refund.